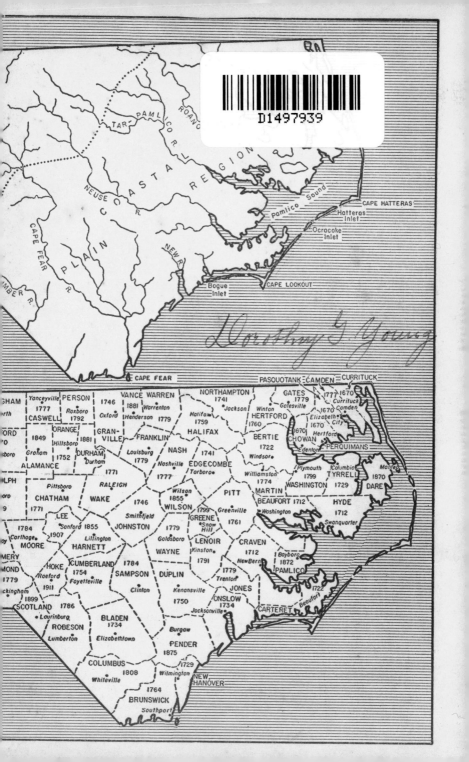

Dorothy G. Young

CAPE HATTERAS

Hatteras Inlet

Ocracoke Inlet

Pamlico Sound

Bogue Inlet

CAPE LOOKOUT

CAPE FEAR

CAPE FEAR

PASQUOTANK CAMDEN CURRITUCK

GHAM Yanceyville PERSON 1746	VANCE WARREN	NORTHAMPTON 1741 Jackson	GATES 1779	1777 1670 Currituck	

Yanceyville PERSON 1777 Roxboro 1792
CASWELL
orth

1746 1881 Warrenton
Oxford Henderson 1779

NORTHAMPTON 1741
Jackson
Halifax
1759

Winton Galesville
HERTFORD 1760
Elizabeth City

GATES 1779

1777 1670
Currituck
1670 Camden

ORD ro sboro
1849
Graham 1752
ORANGE Hillsboro
DURHAM 1771
Durham

GRAN-VILLE 1881
FRANKLIN Louisburg 1779

HALIFAX
1722
Windsor

BERTIE
1670 Hertford
CHOWAN Edenton

1670
Elizabeth City

PERQUIMANS

ALAMANCE
LPH

NASH 1741
Nashville
EDGECOMBE Tarboro
1777

Williamston

Plymouth 1799
WASHINGTON 1729

Columbia TYRRELL 1872

Manteo
1870
DARE

oro 9

Pittsboro
CHATHAM RALEIGH
1771 WAKE 1746

Wilson 1855
WILSON 1799
PITT Greenville

MARTIN 1774
BEAUFORT 1712
Washington

HYDE
1712

LEE
1784 Sanford 1855
Carthage 1907
MOORE

Smithfield
JOHNSTON 1779

GREENE Snow Hill 1761

Swanquarter

LENOIR
Kinston 1791

CRAVEN 1712
Bayboro
NewBern PAMLICO 1872

MERY MOND 1779 ckingham

HOKE Raeford 1911
CUMBERLAND 1754 Fayetteville

HARNETT Lillington

WAYNE Goldsboro

1784
SAMPSON DUPLIN
Clinton

JONES 1779 Trenton

1722
Beaufort

1899
SCOTLAND 1786
Laurinburg
ROBESON Lumberton

BLADEN 1734
Elizabethtown

Kenansville 1750

ONSLOW 1734
Jacksonville

CARTERET

COLUMBUS 1808
Whiteville

Burgaw

PENDER 1875

1729

1764
BRUNSWICK Southport

Wilmington
NEW HANOVER

THE NORTH CAROLINA GUIDE

Advisory Editors

THE
NORTH
CAROLINA
GUIDE

Edited by

BLACKWELL P.
ROBINSON

Chapel Hill

THE UNIVERSITY OF NORTH CAROLINA PRESS

PREFACE

IN THE PAST decade and a half, the picture of North Carolina has changed significantly—since the publication of the original edition of *North Carolina: A Guide to the Old North State,* one of the *American Guide Series.* This series, undertaken primarily as a relief project during the depression, has stood the test of time as a permanently important contribution to the understanding of our country. Nearly all of the state guides are still in demand. The original edition of this book was considered one of the outstanding volumes in the series. In fact, the editor feels a sense of deep appreciation to the late Edwin Bjorkman, North Carolina Director of the Federal Writers' Project, to his colleagues, and to the hundreds of men and women who contributed the material for the original edition. The correction of errors has been a very minor part of the editorial work. Moreover, the original format and arrangement of material was so soundly conceived and so carefully worked out that no important changes in the scheme of presentation have been necessary for this new edition.

Nevertheless the task has been a formidable one, such as would convince even the most skeptical of the tremendous changes that have been wrought in North Carolina since the 1930's. There has been a real need, not only to bring up to date such obvious factual data as new population figures, new and relocated highways, new college enrollment figures, and corrected altitudes, but also to point up the strides that have been made in the industrial field, in increased recreational development, and in the cultural and historical area. Older industries have expanded; new ones have been founded; modern functional buildings and factories have sprung up; new residential and business areas, new power projects, and new hospitals have been developed. The vast increase in recreational facilities—from the continued development of the Great Smoky Mountains National Park and the Blue Ridge Parkway, through the various new State Parks and the winter facilities in the Sandhills to the Cape Hatteras National Seashore Recreation

Area—have given to the State the slogan "Variety Vacationland." And no longer are North Carolinians limited to one outdoor drama, *The Lost Colony*—as they were in 1939.

A renewed interest in the preservation of the historical sites of the State has been evidenced by innumerable local projects and by the creation of the State Historical Sites Commission. The restoration of Old Salem and of Tryon's Palace in New Bern, now in progress, are highlighting this movement. New writers, new architects, new musicians, new historians, new political leaders have all pointed the way to increased intellectual and cultural vigor.

Acknowledgments of appreciation for making the present project possible would be legion. Unfortunately, only a few can here be cited. The North Carolina Department of Conservation and Development, which sponsored the original edition of this work, made the revised edition possible by a grant for basic editorial expenses. To George R. Ross, former Director of the Department, who gave great encouragement to the project in its initial state; to Ben Douglas, the present Director, under whom the project was formally begun; to Charles Parker, Director of the State News Bureau, whose knowledge and interest have been unflagging; to Thomas Morse, Director of State Parks, whose cooperation has been most helpful—deep appreciation is extended.

To the editorial advisory board of the *Guide,* chosen to represent various sections and interests of the State, the editor is greatly indebted for invaluable suggestions and advice and—in some instances—for long hours of detailed corrections of manuscript: Donald P. Anderson of North Carolina State College, Christopher Crittenden of the State Department of Archives and History, John Harden of Burlington Mills, Hugh T. Lefler of the University of North Carolina, Hugh Morton of Wilmington and Grandfather Mountain, and George M. Stephens of the Stephens Press.

The editor is also grateful to the various staff members of the State Department of Archives and History and the State Highway and Public Works Commission, to the Chambers of Commerce throughout the State; to Miss Mary Lindsay Thornton and William Powell of the Carolina Room of the University of North Carolina and to the entire staff of the Southern Historical Collection at Chapel Hill; and to Miss Georgia Faison of the Reference Department of the Library. Special acknowledgments are also made to Mrs. Lyman Cotten, Virgil Mann, John Allcott, Benjamin Swalin, Walter Spearman, Phillips Russell, all of Chapel Hill, and to Mr. James Stenhouse, Charlotte architect and chairman of the Historic Sites Commission, for constructive advice in their specialized fields. And special appreciation is due to Bill Sharpe of *The State Magazine,* who has made many valuable contributions, not only through his magazine but through his practical and detailed knowledge of the State.

COUNTY REPRESENTATIVES

The difficulties in correcting and bringing up to date the detailed factual material on the individual towns and cities and the hundred counties of North Carolina could not have been surmounted without the patriotic contributions of the following county representatives who gave generously and unselfishly of their time and superior knowledge:

Alamance	Mr. Walter Whitaker	University, Alabama
Alexander	Mrs. R. S. Ferguson	Taylorsville
	Rev. Henry Ridenhour	Taylorsville
Alleghany	Miss Clyde Fields	Sparta
Anson	Miss Virginia Horne	Wadesboro
Ashe	Mrs. Ed M. Anderson	Jefferson
Avery	Mr. Robert Woodside	Crossnore
Beaufort	Mrs. Pauline Worthy	Washington
Bertie	Mr. Holley Mackie Bell	Windsor
	Dr. William Jacocks	Chapel Hill
	Mr. John E. Tyler	Roxobel
Bladen	Mrs. E. F. McCulloch	Elizabethtown
Brunswick	Mr. E. Lawrence Lee	Chapel Hill
	Mr. Cornelius D. Thomas	Clarendon Plantation
Buncombe	Mr. George M. Stephens	Asheville
Burke	Dr. Charles Vernon	Chapel Hill
Cabarrus	Mr. Luther Barnhardt	N. C. State College
	Mrs. Charles Cannon	Concord
Caldwell	Mr. C. M. Abernethy	Lenoir
Camden	Mr. J. H. Pugh	Camden
Carteret	Miss Dorothy Avery	Beaufort
Caswell	Miss Annie Yancey Gwyn	"Stamps Quarter"
	Mrs. Yancey Kerr	Yanceyville
	Mrs. L. B. Satterfield	Milton
Catawba	Dr. J. E. Hodges	Maiden
Chatham	Mr. Lawrence F. London	Chapel Hill
	Mr. William B. Morgan	Pittsboro
Cherokee	Mr. Percy Ferebee	Andrews
Chowan	Miss Elizabeth V. Moore	Edenton

Clay	Mr. Thomas Gray	Hayesville
Cleveland	Mrs. O. Max Gardner	Shelby
Columbus	Mrs. Seth L. Smith	Whiteville
Craven	Mr. George P. Arrington	New Bern
Cumberland	Mrs. Hector McKethan	Fayetteville
Currituck	Mrs. Faytie H. Cox	Moyock
Dare	Mr. Aycock Brown	Manteo
	Mr. David Stick	Kill Devil Hills
Davidson	Miss Jewell Sink	Thomasville
Davie	Miss Mary Heitman	Mocksville
	Mr. Gordon Tomlinson	Mocksville
Duplin	Mrs. John D. Robinson	Wallace
Durham	Mr. R. O. Everett	Durham
Edgecombe	Mr. Marshall Staton	Tarboro
	Mrs. Elias Carr	"Bracebridge Hall"
Forsyth	Mrs. Z. T. Bynum, Jr.	Winston-Salem
	Miss Lila Fisher	Winston-Salem
	Dr. Douglas Rights	Winston-Salem
Franklin	Mrs. May Davis Hill	Chapel Hill
Gaston	Miss Alma Goode	Gastonia
Gates	Mr. W. T. Cross	Gatesville
Graham	Dr. Edward D. Ingram	Robbinsville
Granville	Mr. William A. Mitchiner	Oxford
Greene	Mr. B. L. Davis	Snow Hill
Guilford	Mr. James G. W. MacClamroch	Greensboro
	Mr. S. C. Clark	High Point
Halifax	Mrs. Sterling Gary	Halifax
	Miss Nannie Gary	Halifax
	Dr. Claiborne Smith	Scotland Neck
Harnett	Mr. Leon McDonald	Olivia
	Mr. Malcolm Fowler	Lillington
Haywood	Mr. H. C. Wilburn	Waynesville
Henderson	Mrs. Sadie Smathers Patton	Hendersonville
Hertford	Mrs. W. D. Boone	Winton
Hoke	Senator J. B. Thomas	Raeford
	Mr. Arnold A. McKay	Raeford
Hyde	Mr. N. W. Shelton	Swanquarter
Iredell	Mr. Louis Brown	Statesville

Jackson	Dean W. E. Bird	Cullowhee
Johnston	Mr. William S. Powell	Chapel Hill
	Mrs. Dewey H. Huggins	Clayton
Jones	Senator John T. Larkins	Trenton
Lee	Mr. John Monger	Sanford
Lenoir	Mr. Charles L. McCullers	Kinston
Lincoln	Mrs. Joseph Graham	"Forest Home"
McDowell	Miss Mary M. Greenlee	Mooresville
Macon	Mr. Neville Sloan	Franklin
Madison	Mr. John A. McLeod	Mars Hill
Martin	Mr. Warren Biggs	Williamston
	Mr. Ed L. Grady	Williamston
Mecklenburg	Mr. Chalmers Davidson	Davidson
Mitchell	Mr. Jason Deyton	Bakersville
Montgomery	Col. Jeffrey Stanback	Mt. Gilead
Moore	Mr. R. E. Wicker	Pinehurst
	Mr. Edwin McKeithen	Aberdeen
	Mr. James W. Tufts	Pinehurst
Nash	Mr. L. S. Inscoe	Nashville
New Hanover	Mr. Louis Moore	Wilmington
Northampton	Mrs. Louis A. Froelich	Jackson
	Mr. Henry W. Lewis	Chapel Hill
Onslow	Mr. J. Parsons Brown	Jacksonville
Orange	Mr. L. J. Phipps	Chapel Hill
Pamlico	Mr. Richard Noble	Bayboro
Pasquotank	Mr. Jerome Flora	Elizabeth City
	Mr. J. H. Moore	Elizabeth City
Pender	Miss Mattie Bloodworth	Burgaw
Perquimans	Gen. John E. Wood	Elizabeth City
Person	Mr. William Merritt	Roxboro
Pitt	Mr. J. L. Jackson	Raleigh
Polk	Mrs. Sadie Smathers Patton	Hendersonville
Randolph	Mrs. Hal Worth	Asheboro
Richmond	Mr. Isaac S. London	Rockingham
Robeson	Mrs. F. K. Biggs, Sr.	Lumberton
Rockingham	Mr. Hugh Frank Rankin	Chapel Hill

Rowan	Mr. James S. Brawley	Salisbury
	Miss Mary Henderson	Chapel Hill
Rutherford	Mr. Clarence Griffin	Forest City
Sampson	Mrs. Taft Bass	Clinton
Scotland	Mr. Arnold A. McKay	Raeford
Stanly	Mrs. G. D. B. Reynolds	Albemarle
Stokes	Mr. Charles D. Rodenbough	Walnut Cove
Surry	Mrs. Robert Jackson	Chapel Hill
Swain	Mrs. Lucile K. Boyden	Fontana Village
Transylvania	Mr. Oliver Orr	Brevard
Tyrrell	Mr. W. S. Tarlton	Raleigh
Union	Mr. Roland F. Beasley	Monroe
Vance	Mrs. R. G. S. Davis, Sr.	Henderson
	Mr. S. T. Peace	Henderson
Wake	Mr. Edwin A. Miles	Raleigh
Warren	Miss Amma Graham	Warrenton
Washington	Mrs. Addie Brinkley	Plymouth
Watauga	Mr. D. J. Whitener	Boone
Wayne	Miss Gertrude Weil	Goldsboro
	Mrs. C. E. Wilkins	Goldsboro
Wilkes	Miss Ruth Linney	Roaring River
Wilson	Mr. Hugh Johnson, Jr.	Wilson
Yadkin	Mr. William Rutledge	Yadkinville
Yancey	Mr. Rush Wray	Burnsville

CONTENTS

PART I
GENERAL BACKGROUND

PART II
CITIES AND TOWNS

PART III

TOURS

PART IV

NATIONAL PARK AND FORESTS

Photographs not otherwise credited have been furnished by the North Carolina News Bureau of the Department of Conservation and Development

GENERAL INFORMATION

Transportation: The State Highway System in 1954 embraced 68,190 miles, of which approximately 31,000 miles were paved (information concerning road conditions, detours, and ferries may be obtained from the State Highway and Public Works Commission). Bus and truck lines serve virtually all places on this highway network, and important interstate motor carrier operations are based in North Carolina. Thirty railroads operate 4,531 miles of track. Of these, three trunk-lines, the Southern, Seaboard Air Line, and the Atlantic Coast Line, with subsidiary lines, traverse North Carolina in a general north-south direction; the Southern Railway and the Norfolk Southern Railroad, with subsidiaries, cross the State in an east-west direction. Six commercial airlines, including Eastern, Capital, and Piedmont, serve the State, and there are approximately 140 airports. Ocean shipping terminals at Wilmington and Morehead City are operated by the State Ports Authority. The U. S. Intracoastal Waterway affords sheltered passage for commercial and pleasure traffic throughout the 330-miles length of the State's coast. By a series of canals connecting rivers, sounds, bays, and creeks, the route traverses Currituck, Albemarle, Pamlico, and Bogue sounds; Albemarle and Chesapeake and Dismal Swamp canals; Alligator, Pungo, Newport, Bay rivers; and Pamlico, Neuse, and Cape Fear estuaries (see *Intracoastal Waterway,* Part I, Atlantic Section, issued by the U.S. Government Printing Office, 1951, or write the U.S. Engineer Office Wilmington, N.C.). Major navigable rivers include the Cape Fear, Chowan, Neuse, Pamlico, Pasquotank, Pungo, and Roanoke.

Motor Vehicle Laws: A detailed list of speed and weight regulations is posted at the State line on all main routes. Briefly, the limit is 55 miles an hour on the open highway, 35 miles in residential districts, and 20 miles in business districts, unless otherwise noted.

National uniform code applies for operation of motorcars on State highways. Comity rule prevails for operation of cars carrying licenses obtained outside of North Carolina, every holder of an out-of-state license receiving the same courtesy that the State issuing the license grants to the holder of a North Carolina license. Drivers' licenses are required. A person who engages in any gainful employment or who establishes a residence in North Carolina must procure license for all vehicles registered in his or her name at the time employment is accepted or residence established. Minimum age 16 yrs. if application is signed by parent or guardian, otherwise 18. Hand signals must be used; spotlights are permitted; accidents must be reported to some civil authority. *Prohibited:* Coasting in neutral, parking on highways, passing school bus when loading or unloading.

Liquor Regulations: Some counties have package liquor stores under county option. One gallon only of tax-paid liquor may be brought into dry counties, but the seal on bottles must be unbroken while it is being transported.

Climate and Traveling Equipment: Light, informal clothing is worn throughout most of the year, but even in summer travelers in the mountains should have medium-weight topcoats or sweaters, as evenings are generally cool. Sun glasses are needed for trips along the coast. North Carolina has four distinct seasons, but severe cold is rare and golf and outdoor sports are enjoyed the year around. Pinehurst, Southern Pines, Sedgefield, and Tryon are well known winter resorts.

Poisonous Plants and Venomous Snakes: Poison-ivy grows in wooded areas, along fences and streams; poison sumac occurs in wet swampy lands. Rattlesnakes and copperheads occur in remote sections. Cottonmouth moccasins and coral snakes are found only in eastern and southeastern sections.

Recreational Areas: Coast—North Carolina has a coast line of 330 miles with many beaches and resorts offering facilities for salt water fishing and water sports.

Sandhills—Resort facilities available at Southern Pines and Pinehurst.

Piedmont—Artificial lakes along the Yadkin and Catawba rivers; State Parks.

Mountain—Highways and hiking and bridle trails lead to mountain peaks, many of which are more than a mile high; camping grounds, trout streams, artificial lakes, wild game.

Parks: There are 28 State and National parks (*see* INDEX), forests (*see* NATIONAL FORESTS), and historical sites. These include 17 State Parks, The Great Smoky Mountains National Park (*see* GREAT SMOKY MOUNTAINS NATIONAL PARK), and the Blue Ridge Parkway (*see* TOUR 20)— most visited national parks in the United States—and the Cape Hatteras

National Seashore Recreation Area (*see* Tour 1a *and* Drive Along the Banks)—the first national seashore park in America. Additional information on all these may be obtained from the Department of Conservation and Development, Raleigh, N.C.

Appalachian Trail (roughly following the North Carolina-Tennessee boundary between Unaka Mountain and Davenport Gap, thence in a southeasterly direction to the Georgia line): For a complete log and description of this trail, which extends from Mount Katahdin, Maine, to Mount Oglethorpe, Ga., see *A Guide to the Southern Appalachians,* published by The Appalachian Trail Conference, Inc., Washington, D.C., 1951. Maps, booklets, and folders may be obtained from the following sources: Regional Forester, Southern (Eighth) Region, of the Forest Service of the U.S. Department of Agriculture, Atlanta, Ga.; North Carolina National Forests, U.S. Forest Service, Asheville; and Great Smoky Mountains National Park, Gatlinburg, Tenn.

State Wildlife Management Areas: There are 26 wildlife areas in the State.

State owned—Angola, Holly Shelter, Northwest River Marsh, Sandhills, and Little Grandfather Mountain.

Cooperative U.S. Forest Service lands—Santeetlah, Fires Creek, Standing Indian, Wayah, Pisgah National Game Preserve, Sherwood Forest, Mt. Mitchell, Daniel Boone, Rich-laurel, Flattop Mountain, Uharrie, and Croatan.

U.S. Soil Conservation Service—Caswell Land Use.

Private lands—South Mountains, Camp Charles, Gaddy's Pond, Lake Tillery, Orton Plantation, Iredell Lake, High Rock, and Richlands Dam Lake Watershed.

On all but the private lands, permit hunting and fishing is allowed in season. Arrangements for hunting or fishing on State-administered wildlife areas may be made through the North Carolina Wildlife Resources Commission, Raleigh.

Federal Wildlife Refuges: Swanquarter, Lake Mattamuskeet, and Pea Island are administered by the U.S. Fish and Wildlife Service. On Lake Mattamuskeet the State administers the hunting of waterfowl in two compartments on south side of lake. Fishing is allowed by permit only.

Fish and Game: There are 345 species of identified fish in the inland and commercial fishing waters of the State, including trout, warm water game fish, migratory fish, and salt water species. North Carolina ranks fourth in the nation in the quantity of fishing waters. There are 60 game species (including waterfowl) to be found in the State, including bear, deer, boar, wild turkey, grouse, quail, squirrels, rabbits, fur bearers, and waterfowl. Over $100,000,000 is spent each year in the pursuit of hunting, fishing, and trapping in the State.

Fishing Licenses: Issued by authorized license agents located throughout each county. Nonresident, $6.10; State resident, $3.10, County resident, $1.10; One-day resident, $.60; combination hunting and fishing state resident $4.10. All residents over 16 years of age and a nonresident over 12 years of age must obtain a special trout license ($1.10) before fishing by any method in designated trout waters. All residents over 16 years of age who fish by hook and line or rod and reel outside of their county of residence must have in their possession a statewide fishing license or a daily permit. Statewide or county resident license is required before fishing in one's county of residence if artificial bait is used. All nonresidents over 12 years of age must obtain a nonresident state fishing license to fish in public waters. Any landowner and member of his family under 21 years of age may fish on his own property without regard to any license requirements. Licenses are not required to fish in the Atlantic Ocean or commercial fishing waters. For size and creel limits see State hunting and fishing laws.

Hunting Licenses: Issued by authorized license agents located throughout each county. Nonresident, $15.75; State resident, $3.10; combination hunting and fishing, $4.10; county, $1.10; hunting guide, $5.25; nonresident trappers, $25.25; state trappers, $3.25; county trapper, $2.25.

Persons who have lived in the State for 6 months preceding application for license are regarded as residents. A nonresident who owns land in the State consisting of 100 acres or more may hunt thereon without license. No license is required of a resident owner of land, or a dependent minor member of his family, to hunt upon such land. The lessee of a farm for cultivation may hunt thereon without license. A member of the family of a resident, under 16 years of age, may hunt under the license of his parent or guardian. A nonresident minor child of a resident may secure and use a resident license when visiting a resident parent. For size and bag limits see State hunting and fishing laws.

General Service Bureaus for Tourists: State Tourist Bureau, Dept. of Conservation and Development, Raleigh; North Carolina National Forests, Asheville; Great Smoky Mountains National Park, Gatlinburg, Tenn.; Blue Ridge Parkway Office, Asheville.

A "Calendar of Events," published quarterly, may be secured from the State News Bureau, Raleigh.

A complete Chronology of the State may be found in Lefler and New-some, *North Carolina: The History of a Southern State* (Chapel Hill: University of North Carolina Press, 1954).

More detailed information on the industrial picture and on recreational facilities (such as parks, hunting and fishing areas, etc.), may be obtained from the State Department of Conservation and Development, Raleigh.

An index map to the standard topographic maps of North Carolina and the quadrangle maps themselves may be obtained (small fee) from the Supt. of Public Documents, Washington, D.C.; or from the Brown Book Corp., 12-14 College St., Asheville; or from Mr. S. Peyton Cason, Raleigh Blue Printers, 107 W. Martin St., Raleigh.

Part I

GENERAL BACKGROUND

Folkways and Folklore

WHAT MANNER OF MAN is a North Carolinian? How can you tell a Tar Heel? What ingredients went into his making? Is he different, and if so, how and why?

There is no slide-rule answer to these questions, but it may be interesting to explore them. The Tar Heel is not a distinct species, but he may have some distinguishing marks.

North Carolinians are what they are largely because of racial heritage. This is mainly Anglo-Saxon with a strong infusion of Scotch and a weaker one of German blood; about a third of the population is Negro. The Anglo-Saxons account for the law-making, law-abiding, commercial-minded, self-reliant, practical and determined strain; the Scotch are the proud, stoical, imaginative, high-tempered, democratic folk, their heroes being the parson, the teacher and the statesman; the Germans are the shrewd, the economical, the hard-working and the good-humored, placing much stress on church, school and business, but not much on politics; the Negro is the one who works most and loafs most, suffers most and rejoices most, is the most violent and the most patient, the one who enjoys and endures most and absorbs the shocks of life as a rubber tire absorbs the shocks of the road.

The environment plays its part too. The State was not settled from the sea as Virginia and South Carolina were; its Outer Banks fended off immigration from Britain and Europe; North Carolina was settled at second hand from its neighbor states to the north and south, with some Scots and Germans from Pennsylvania sliding down the Appalachians and rolling off into Tarheelia. So it came about that North Carolina did not develop either urban life or the big plantation system—for better for worse—to anything like the extent that Virginia and South Carolina did. There was more of isolation and homogeneity, less of caste and culture in North Carolina. So Tar Heels adopted the somewhat invidious motto *"Esse Quam Videri,"* and took perhaps excessive pride in referring to their state as "a vale of humility between

3

two mountains of conceit." We were mighty proud of not being proud.

We did, however, in such a historical setting, become independent, courageous, resourceful, democratic, gregarious and individualistic, although we would use plainer words than these Latin terms to describe ourselves.

The people developed differently in the eastern and the western parts of the State. The coastal plain was the level land of slavepower and the plantation, whereas the piedmont was the rolling land of waterpower and industry. So the east, as Jonathan Daniels put it, became "expansive, leisurely ... conversational, concerned with good living, devoted to pleasure, politically fixed, but politically philosophical ... the easterner's gregariousness is little short of Gargantuan ... he finds it a trifle to go a hundred miles to a dance ... his social set is a whole population."

The piedmont is more serious, hard-working, and practical, with its Calvinistic, Quaker and Moravian influences.

Before the Civil War the easterners were the rich relatives and the westerners the poor ones; but these roles have become increasingly reversed. There was a time when the people of the two halves pulled against each other; now they work well together and usually consider that what is best for the whole state is best for its parts.

What is a Tar Heel? It is not easy to describe him, but when we glance back over the history of his state we may catch a glimpse of his veritable face and hear his voice unmistakably, here and there, now and then.

His voice was heard when one of the Regulators said before the Revolution, with more sense than grammar, "Though there is a few men who have the gift or art of reasoning, yet every man has a feeling and knows when he has justice done him as well as the most learned."

Plain and democratic? Yes, there was Nat Macon who followed Jefferson in so far as he followed anybody. Macon's voice had a Tar Heel touch to it when he argued that five dollars a day was ample pay for a congressman and when he explained that his rule in Congress was that "if a measure did not arouse great enthusiasm in any one section of the nation," he would consider voting for it, but not otherwise. Tar Heel democratic overtones could be heard in Hinton Rowan Helper's *The Impending Crisis,* which held that slavery was evil because of its effects on those whites who owned no slaves.

Courage and fortitude? The voice is that of Isaac Erwin Avery on whose body after the Battle of Gettysburg was found a blood-stained envelope with the words, "Tell my father I died with my face to the enemy," of which Ambassador Bryce said, "It is the message of our race to the world." And the voice is that of Jonathan Worth (later Governor Worth): "I think the South is committing suicide, but my lot is cast with the South, and being unable to manage the ship I intend to face the breakers and go down with my companions."

There is a progressive strain in this Tar Heel, a realistic and resourceful determination to get ahead with the work for a better way of life for himself and his fellows. It comes out in a speech of Gov. Charles B. Aycock: "It undoubtedly appears cheaper to neglect the aged, the feeble, the infirm, the defective, to forget the children of this generation; but the man who does it is cursed of God and the state that permits it is certain of destruction." This was not a solitary voice, but rather a chorus joined in by Walter Hines Page, Edwin A. Alderman, Clarence Poe, Josephus Daniels, Cornelia Phillips Spencer, Charles D. McIver, J. Y. Joyner, Edward K. Graham and many others to this day who conceive of "education and democracy" as twin levers by which a people can lift themselves.

There is often a kindness in the voice which covers a lot of humanity in its acceptance of all sorts and conditions of men. It is heard in O. Henry's Brickdust Row hero who sees "no longer a rabble but his brothers seeking the ideal," and it is a newspaperman of a past generation musing on the man next door: "His amusements are limited. He is apt to do the same thing day after day and he is not apt to make a great deal of money, but he learns to know a great many people and to love and be loved by a few. . . . He sees people, not as they seem to be but as they are. If he is happy there are those who will rejoice with him. If he suffers, men reach out their hands to touch him understandingly. If he does anything that is good and praiseworthy, his community knows it and applauds, and he climbs not very high on the ladder of fame before his State sees it and nods approval."

But there is no pouring Tar Heels into a mold. The point is that we are by preference and habit individualists, or what we call "characters."

So much for our good side. Generally we are liable to be pretty good folks, but we have a bad side too, and the truth is that we can be, when we take a notion or for no reason at all, as violent, ornery, cantankerous, stubborn, narrow and lazy as any people anywhere on earth, civilized or uncivilized.

We cut and shoot one another at a rate not even equaled in the centers of urban civilization. True, we consider our violence too valuable to waste on outsiders and so confine it to ourselves; the Frenchman who said he was amazed at Americans "because they shoot people they haven't even met" may have been right about New York or Chicago, but he wasn't talking about North Carolina; Tar Heels hardly ever kill or maim anybody unless he is either an old friend or a close relative. It's true that this violence is light-hearted and is mostly confined to Negroes fighting Negroes and Anglo-Saxons or Scots reverting to type, especially those who in other states would be called the "lower classes," but the fact is that most of us are too quick-tempered.

Furthermore we sometimes have fits of laziness and indifference which set our reformers wild.

And we are not always averse to mediocrity. Emerson said that the South's besetting sin was pride—"lordliness" was his word for it. North Carolinians rarely fell into that trap—perhaps their motto on their state seal and their sense of humor helped them. So they did not have the trouble some of their neighboring states did with what the analytical historian Arnold J. Toynbee calls a "nemesis of creativity—the idolization of a once glorious past." In going to the other extreme we have run into another kind of danger and have been too often and too easily satisfied with much less than perfection, so that one of our individualists, Judge Robert W. Winston, once described the State as a "militant mediocracy."

But we are not happy in our mediocrity. It suits neither our Episcopalianism in the east nor our Calvinism in the west. No sooner are we comfortably settled in the sty of mediocrity than the gadfly of ambition, duty and idealism gets us on the glory road, and so we issue declarations of independence, fight battles, write books, speak speeches, found universities, organize great businesses, and raise cain in general. University, that's the word which explains our progress, many people think. The University of North Carolina at Chapel Hill has set standards of excellence in many fields, so that wise men from other states and countries often say that they feel as if they should take off their shoes in that "holy ground" (not a bad idea either on a hot summer evening around the Old Well). Other institutions of higher education also hold the standard high, notably Duke University, State College, Woman's College, Wake Forest, Davidson, and others. Yes, we Tar Heels have our ups and downs. Ordinarily we are willing enough to sip the weak tea of mediocrity, but ever so often there comes a time when we go off on a root-tooting binge inspired by our incurable thirst for "Old Excellence Guaranteed 200-proof," even though we know it won't last.

Our folkways change, and with them our amusements, as we move from a personal and rural to an urban and mechanical age. Thus the ice cream suppers with Japanese lanterns on the lawn to raise money for the church and the baseball team has given way to the community chest campaign. The romantic couple who used to take a buggy ride down a honeysuckle-bordered lane now park their convertible in a drive-in theater. The taffy pull has lost out to the candy box at the drug store. The drug store is no longer the loafing and gossip-exchange emporium it used to be; the filling station is trying to take its place but has not yet succeeded. The old dime novel (*Nick Carter, Young Wild West, The Liberty Boys of '76,* blessed be their memory) has been supplanted by the comic book and the Spillane paper-backed duet of sex and sadism. The town that used to have a baseball team now has a golf club. The old swimming hole (for boys only) is now a tiled country club pool (strictly coeducational).

Yes, North Carolina folkways have changed a lot in the past two or three decades. But there are areas, mostly isolated ones on the coast or in the mountains, where the old order has not yielded much to the new, and where the older people—the younger ones have moved away to make more money—cling to the older ways of speaking, singing, dancing, thinking and acting.

In Rodanthe on the Outer Banks, for instance, the people celebrate Old Christmas on January 5 with singing, square dancing, an oyster roast and the annual appearance of "Old Buck," legendary monster of the Hatteras woods, fashioned of slats and cowhide and wearing the horns and skull of a steer, and a scary sight for children who have been bad during the year.

Today a lot of farmers who used to farm by the moon now farm by Dr. Clarence Poe's *Progressive Farmer,* but not all of them do. Some still think it best to plant crops which fruit underground, such as potatoes and peanuts, in the dark of the moon. There is still a split of authority on whether it is safe to kill hogs when the moon is full. It is well established that the safest way to keep from being superstitious is to carry in your pants pocket at all times the left hind foot of a graveyard rabbit, either silver-mounted or *au naturel.* Few Tar Heels care to tempt fate by walking under a ladder on Friday the 13th. Whiffledust is sometimes placed on the threshold of the courthouse by friends of the defendant where the judge and lawyers must walk over it; it seems to be effective in 50 per cent of the cases, thus roughly equaling the record of the bar. Occasionally some nocturnal and mysterious animal terrifies a rural community or small town; often the "varmint" is built up, half fearfully and half facetiously, to the proportions of a "vampire" or a "whangdoodle," but should never be confused with "Raw Head and Bloody Bones," who is not animal but human, or at least used to be before he became a "hant."

Children as always play ball games, hiding games, hopping games, battle games, courting games, guessing games and kissing games, indeed all sorts of games in which very ancient rhymes are relied on, beginning with such verses as "Chick-o-my, chick-o-my, craney crow," "Bum, bum, bum, where you come from?" "Here comes three dukes a-ridin'," "Round the house, skip to my Lou," and "King William Was King George's Son."

The most beautiful and moving expressions of folklore are the ballads, old and new, the love songs and devil ditties which come to us mostly from the mountains but which are liable to take root and flourish anywhere. Yet and still, "the most fertile ground" for them, as Cecil Sharp found, was "on either side of the big mountain range (known as The Great Divide) which separates the states of North Carolina and Tennessee." Some of the ballads, such as *Lady Isabel and the Elf Knight, Young Beichan* and *The Cruel Mother,* go 'way back to the England and Scotland of a hundred or a thousand years ago, whereas the devil ditty may be as young and rowdy as the "careless love" of last night. But they all have the blood and fury, the simplicity and sweetness, the weeping and laughter, the horror and beauty of life itself in them, sometimes on the surface and at other times very deep down indeed. They tell of love and hate, faith and perfidy, pride and humility, heroism and cowardice; they always catch Life in her dramatic moments, and in them Life comes as close to speaking to us honestly, freely and directly as she ever does in any art.

FOOD AND DRINK

"NORTH CAROLINA FOOD," says an authority, "is substantial, but does not soar." That is true, by and large, but Tar Heel cuisine covers quite a wide range from chitterlings to syllabub, from the broiled bluefish of Kitty Hawk to the corn-beans-and-acorn bread of the Cherokee Reservation, from a Halifax rockfish muddle to a Moravian cookie, and from immature but precociously vigorous corn liquor in a half-gallon fruit jar to "Mrs. Durham's Pink Rose Petal Wine."

The plainest food is the poor man's meal of fatback and cornbread, with sorghum poured in the plate for dessert and sopped up with what is left of the pone.

Chitterlings and 'possum (but not at the same time) are esteemed by many plain food eaters as delicacies but it is not hard to get up an argument about that. Chitterlings (called "chit'lins") are the intestines of a hog and are eaten boiled or fried with lots of red pepper and vinegar. Either you like chit'lins or you give them a wide berth.

'Possums are nocturnal animals with a fondness for graveyards, wherefore some people whose imaginations are stronger than their stomachs think they are not fit to eat. Others are convinced that roast 'possum basted with barbecue sauce and nestling, like a miniature roast pig, in a sweet potato ambuscade is a perfectly delectable meal. However, Br'er 'Possum is usually so fat that it takes quite a lot of red pepper to make him digestible and a lot of strong drink to wash him down properly.

North Carolina cooking is affected by the geography of the State from the Outer Banks through the coastal plain and the piedmont to the mountains.

At Rodanthe on the Outer Banks they eat roast oysters on Twelfth Night. There is plenty of good seafood at the North Carolina beaches, with emphasis on the bluefish of Kitty Hawk and the shrimp of Wrightsville and Morehead. Fish muddles are popular in the coastal plain particularly when the rock are running in the Roanoke. A muddle is a stew made of various kinds of fish seasoned with fried fat meat, onions, potatoes, and pepper; at least it starts off that way. Salt herring with hot biscuits or buckwheat cakes is a favorite breakfast dish in the east; salt mullet, mackerel, and baked fresh shad with roe stuffing are popular over much of the State.

Distinctive foods in the western half of the State include the Moravian old-fashioned Christmas cookies, sugarcakes, buns and citron pies of Winston-Salem; the bread (and formerly the wine) made by the Waldensians at Valdese; the deer and bear meat cured around Mt. Mitchell; sourwood honey and the Cherokee Indian bread.

Tar Heels have always been great pork eaters, and in some parts of the coastal plain they have developed its preparation—barbecue, sausages, hams—into something closely resembling a fine art. John Lawson, one of the earliest explorers, dubbed the Carolina pork "some of the sweetest meat that the world affords." The best barbecue—roast pig basted with a sauce made of vinegar, salt and pepper—which should be eaten while the fat is still crisp, is made in the area around Edgecombe and Nash counties.

The eastern North Carolina ham, when properly cured and aged for two or three years, is accounted by Tar Heel connoisseurs to be the best meat in the country, if not in the world. These hams were cured over hickory smoke, *con amore,* then coated with salt and pepper and hung up to age. The curing could not be forced, the aging took a lot of time and shrank a lot of ham, but the result was frequently a masterpiece. It is almost impossible to find a great vintage ham nowadays; the art is becoming a lost one in a too-hurried age. Nevertheless, reasonably good hams can be found in Johnston, Onslow, Wake and Jones counties, among others; they may not "soar," but they make very pleasant eating.

Tar Heels have never been much at cooking beef, but they do very well with game and poultry. The preparation of ducks, geese, rabbits, quail, and chickens is an old story to them. Few things taste better to a North Carolinian on a frosty morning than a brace of quail (which he calls "birds" or "partridges") browned in butter with a rasher of bacon across their breasts like a decoration of nobility.

Chicken, of course, is the mainstay of the menu all over the State—chicken prepared in almost all conceivable ways, baked with cornbread stuffing and giblet gravy, smothered, stewed, creamed, curried, hashed, croquetted, shortcaked, or fried until the outer covering is golden-crisp. Tar Heels agree with the Negro preacher who, when asked what part of the chicken he preferred, answered truthfully, "I likes the breas' and all the res'."

Outside of baker's bread, Tar Heels like (in an ascending scale from plain to fancy) cornbread, ashcakes, hoecakes, johnny cakes, cracklin' bread, potato bread, soda biscuits, buttermilk biscuits, rolls, muffins, popovers that pop, buckwheat cakes, eggbread or batterbread (called "spoonbread" in Virginia), bland Sally Lunn and flaky beaten biscuits; the last two are company bread.

In North Carolina, as in most of the South, good cooking was a matter of hospitality, not commerce, and was more likely to be found in the home than in the restaurant. Under the impetus of the tourist business things are changing some; good cooking can often be found in the big hotels, especially the resort ones, though it is not often distinctively North Carolinian or even Southern.*

The best Tar Heel cuisine is still amateur—the outdoor barbecue (not to be confused with the roadside Bar-B-Q), brunswick stew, fish fry and Sunday School picnic. Excellent cooking can be found in homes —if you can get an invitation to dinner—where fine food is a traditional art, with recipes and family cooks handed down from mother to daughter; that is to say, it is an art not written down in books but transmitted by word of mouth from generation to generation; and it is unfortunately becoming a lost art.

The State is well supplied with such adjuncts of a meal as melons, fruits, pickles, nuts, drinks and smokes. Watermelons abound and the Ridgeway cantaloupes grown in Warren County are among the best in the world. Mt. Olive is an important pickle-processing center. Peaches are raised commercially on a large scale in the Sandhills section, apples in the mountains and peanuts in the sandy northeastern part of the coastal plain. Various sorts of berries and nuts—*e.g.* cranberries, blueberries, blackberries, hickory nuts, pecans, walnuts and peanuts— are cultivated or grow wild.

* Visitors do well to enlist the experience of competent local judges to aid them in selecting a restaurant if they are seeking distinctive food.

North Carolina drinks range in time, variety and potency from the hickory nut milk which the Indians taught the pioneer mothers to give their children before there were any cows and the Indian yaupon tea which is still drunk on the Outer Banks, through the sweet and rather bland scuppernong wine, blackberry wine, dandelion wine, apple cider, locust beer and persimmon beer—not to mention the old Nash County apple brandy of treasured memory which was as smooth as magnolias in cream—to the illicit corn liquor of modern times which stings like an armor-piercing projectile and slugs with brass knucks, but which is prized by some drinkers who crave sudden and direct action.

The cigarette, pipe or cigar with which most people finish their meals is not unlikely to have some North Carolina tobacco (known abroad as "Virginia tobacco") in it. This state is the prime raiser of that "holy herb" of the Indians which was supposed to cause intoxication, raise spirits, ward off hunger and thirst, and cure all known diseases. We still use it to put a thin film of smoke between us and the realities of a harsh world, especially after a meal.

SPEECH

NORTH CAROLINIANS' speech is as varied as the topography of their state. The pronunciation of the people on the Outer Banks and the easternmost part of the coastal plain is said to have come from Devonshire or Western England with the first colonists and ship-wrecked sailors. Its most distinctive feature is the use of an "oi" sound for "i" or "y." Thus a "banker" will say "hoigh toide in Hoyde County" or "you just roide over to the Sound soide"—or used to before book learning corrupted his native tongue which he came by honestly, since the most ancient maps of Roanoke Island spell it "Oisland."

In the coastal plain the accent is mainly English, with overtones which are doubtless English also from Virginia and South Carolina.

In the piedmont there is some German and Scotch influence; unlike the English-speaking folks of the coastal plain, the piedmonters roll their "r's," retain their final "g's," and pronounce *house* to rhyme with the German *"aus."*

In the mountains the people have retained many early Scotch and English ways of speech.

The more isolated and less educated people are, the more they tend to abide by the linguistic landmarks their fathers have set, rather than follow after newfangled and fashionable modes of speech. So it comes about that what we consider Negro or hillbilly talk is quite likely to be the speech and enunciation of fashionable London or Edinborough of a century or so ago, indeed the talk of Elizabeth I and Sir Walter Raleigh, Shakespeare and Marlowe, Dryden and Pope, Addison and Swift, no matter how wrong it may sound today.

Thus, as Prof. George P. Wilson tells us in *The Frank C. Brown Collection of North Carolina Folklore,* Shakespeare used "blowed" for blown, Bacon "mought" for might, and Elizabeth "hit" for it. Other usages in North Carolina which smack of illiteracy but have high authority in antiquity are:

Arter for after (which is the only way to make the nursery rhyme of Jack and Jill come out properly);

Ast for asked;

Fitten for fitting;

Cowcumber for cucumber;

Ingern for onion;

Git for get;

Chainy for china;

Obleege for oblige;

Jine for join; *bile* for boil; *pizen* for poison;

Learn for teach;

Mushmillion for muskmelon.

But North Carolina dialect is more than "fossilized language." It is full of the beauty, humor, pathos, vulgarity, joy, color and virility of life; it has some "sparkles of liberty, spirit and edge" to it.

Its beauty is indicated by these samples collected by Professor Wilson: "Jane has pensy eyes . . . So fur back in them coves you had to keep wipin' at the shadows . . . morn gloam (the first light of day) . . . rain seed (mottled clouds) . . . sun-ball . . . element (the sky) . . . and quietus (the calm that comes to some living thing after death, used in pity by an old woman about a wild animal killed by the dogs)."

Our dialect is often funny and always expressive:

Giggle-soup is liquor;

Slipper-slide is a shoe horn;

A *claphat* woman is a hasty one;

Journey-proud applies to one who won't stop telling you about a trip;

Briar-patch children are not quite legitimate;

A *smidgen* is a little, but a *slue* is a lot, and it might be a *lavish* or in some cases *a God's plenty.*

From *kin-see to kain't see* is a full day's work. A man lives *down the road a piece* or perhaps only *a whoop and a holler.* Sometimes we feel, with Sir Walter Scott, that a thing is *ill-convenient,* or, with Shakespeare, that a girl is right *peart.* We have *plunder* rooms where we keep worn-out *play-pretties* or toys. Like Wycliffe, we *reckon* and we sometimes put things in a *poke.* The *widow-woman* goes to the *tooth-den-*

tist, as she used to do in England. And a girl may apologize for not speaking to you as she passed you in an automobile, by saying "If I'd a-knowed it was you I'd a-flang out my arm and wove to you." Sounds like Chaucer.

Yes, our speech, especially at its worst, has aristocratic antecedents on the dialectal family tree.

LITERATURE

NORTH CAROLINA literature got its start in a nice blend of fiction and nonfiction when Phillip Amadas and Arthur Barlow in 1584 described Roanoke Island as "the goodliest land under the cope of heaven." This promising piece of real estate which they were trying to promote, and which later turned out to be not an island but a continent, made them lyrical. The soil, to hear them tell it, was "sweete, fruitfull and wholesome," the timber trees were "sweet smelling," the cedars were the "highest and reddest in the world," the vines bowed down with grapes, the woods abounded with game, the waters with fish ("the goodliest and best fish") and even the savage Indians were "mannerly and civill."

In 1709 John Lawson, surveyor, explorer and promoter, followed suit with his *History of Carolina* and affirmed the following facts:

"The Inhabitants of Carolina, through the richness of the soil, live an easy and pleasant life . . . The Beef of Carolina equalizes the best that our neighboring colonies afford . . . The Veal is very good and white, so is the milk very pleasant and rich . . . The sheep thrive very well . . . The horses are well shaped and swift . . . The Pork exceeds any in Europe . . . As for Goats, they have been found to thrive and increase very well . . . The Women are the most industrious Sex . . . The Women are very fruitful, most houses being full of little ones. It has been observed that Women long married and without children in other places, have removed to Carolina and become joyful Mothers."

In 1737 Dr. John Brickell kept the literary strain aloft by writing "glorified propaganda for Lord Granville's princely domain," in a book which he called *The Natural History of North Carolina.*

After that for about a century North Carolina literature was somewhat scarce. The people were more interested in raising families, crops, liberty poles and hell than they were in writing books. Whoever is interested in the literature of that time, which may have some antiquarian and historical importance, can find out about it in Dr. Archibald Henderson's *North Carolina, the Old North State and the New.*

Two examples should be mentioned. In 1838 the first genuine North

Carolina novel appeared; it was *Eoneguski,* a story of the Cherokee Indians by Robert Strange of Fayetteville. In 1850 Calvin H. Wiley wrote the first novel of contemporary North Carolina, called *Nags Head or Two Years Among 'The Bankers'.*

In 1857 a book on slavery by a Tar Heel hit North Carolina and the South like a blockbuster. It was Hinton R. Helper's *The Impending Crisis,* a fiery plea for the abolition of slavery, not because of its effects on the poor Negroes but because of its effects on the poor whites who did not own any slaves. It was dedicated to the non-slaveholding whites and it denounced slaveowners as "lords of the lash," and "knights of the bowie knife." In their turn, Helper's fellow countrymen referred to him in their milder moments as "that vile wretch Helper." He became a hated Helper indeed. His book had an immense circulation for that time, estimated at 1,000,000 copies, and it influenced Lincoln's speeches in his first campaign. The North Carolina legislature dubbed it "incendiary literature" and made it a felony to circulate it; the first offense was punishable by a public whipping or at least a year in prison, the second by death.

After the Civil War literature in North Carolina picked up a bit. Judge Albion W. Tourgée, a Union officer and lawyer who moved from the North to Greensboro shortly after Appomattox, wrote a book about Reconstruction entitled *A Fool's Errand, by One of the Fools* (1879) which sold 135,000 copies in its first year. It was not a bad book either.

Frances Fisher Tiernan of Salisbury began writing novels in 1870 under the pen name of Christian Reid and wrote half a hundred which were quite popular; one of them, *The Land of the Sky* (1876), gave a name to the mountains which helped start the tourist trade.

In the early 1900's Thomas Dixon of Shelby wrote nearly a score of novels and other works many of which painted in the most lurid colors the melodramatic plight of the South and the tragedy of Reconstruction. Two of them, *The Leopard's Spots* and *The Klansman,* formed the basis for D. W. Griffith's motion picture, *The Birth of a Nation.*

A more analytical piece of fiction was Walter Hines Page's autobiographical and sociological novel, *The Southerner* (1909).

Not long before that two North Carolina novels appeared which are among the finest examples of unconscious humor anywhere. One was *Myrtle Lawn* (1880) by Robert E. Ballard of Franklin County, a romance written in the most absurdly high-flown phraseology, bearing on its frontispiece a foreword ending as follows: "This is a panoramic painting in words such a work as Shakespeare or Macauley might have dashed off in a happy hour of literary excitement . . . (Signed) CRITIC." The other was *The Balsam Groves of Grandfather Moun-*

tain by Shepherd M. Dugger, a son of the Appalachians; it may well be the funniest book in existence; it is the only book that is not like any other book; no author before or since has thought of combining a fervid romance of the Victorian era with advertisements of boarding houses in the mountains.

But it was only after 1900 that North Carolina really struck its stride in literature; it has been increasing the pace ever since.

The Novel

In the field of the novel Thomas Wolfe towers like his mountains above the rest with his magnificent series of autobiographical novels which make vivid "the legend of man's hunger in his youth"; all of them were written in the brief span between 1928 and 1938.

Quite a few other Tar Heels have in the last few decades written what now amounts to a sizable body of successful fiction. Among them are the novelists Burke Davis (*Yorktown*), Bernice Kelly Harris (*Purslane*), LeGette Blythe (*Bold Galilean*), Ovid Pierce (*The Plantation*), Fred Ross (*Jackson Mahaffey*), Tom Wicker (*The Kingpin*), Worth Tuttle Hedden (*Love Is a Wound*), Robert Marshall (*Julia Gwynn*), Edythe Latham (*The Sounding Brass*), May Davies Martinet (*Taw Jameson*), Sam Byrd (*Small Town South*), Lettie Rogers (*The Storm Cloud*), Chalmers Davidson (*Cloud Over Catawba*), Pierson Ricks (*The Hunter's Horn*), Laurette MacDuffie (*The Stone in the Rain*), Tim Pridgen (*Tory Oath*), Marion Hargrove (*See Here, Private Hargrove*), and Frances Gray Patton (*Good Morning, Miss Dove*).

At the same time North Carolina attracted a considerable number of novelists to take up residence in her borders, among whom were Olive Tilford Dargan, Elizabeth Boatwright Coker and Carl Sandburg in the mountains; Inglis Fletcher on the coast; Marian Sims in Charlotte; James Boyd, Struthers Burt and Katharine Newlin Burt in Southern Pines; Hiram Haydn, Robie Macauley and Peter Taylor in Greensboro; and James Street, Betty Smith, Josephina Niggli, Noel Houston, Foster FitzSimons, Max Steele, Daphne Athas and others in Chapel Hill.

Short Story

Two of America's greatest short story writers were born in Greensboro—William Sydney Porter (O. Henry) and Wilbur Daniel Steele. But they are by no means the only writers in that difficult medium to whom North Carolina can point with pride. Charles W. Chestnutt, a Negro, wrote perceptive and moving stories about his race. Frances Gray Patton's collection of stories, *The Finer Things of Life,* is first-rate, and so is James Boyd's collection published posthumously, entitled *Old Pines and Other Stories.* Other short story writers identified with North Carolina who have done good work are Joe Mitchell, Joe Knox, Peter Taylor, Hoke Norris, and Crichton Thorne.

Poetry

While North Carolina has had no great poets to boast of, she has produced a number of minor poets of distinction. Probably the two closest to the Tar Heel scene are John Charles McNeill (*Lyrics from Cotton Land*) and James Larkin Pearson (*Fifty Acres*), the present poet laureate. Their poetry constitutes the "wine of the country" and needs no bush.

Early poets include William Gaston, author of *The Old North State,* Edwin W. Fuller (*The Angel in the Cloud*), Theophilus Hunter (whose *Hesper* was the first book released under the copyright of the Confederate States of America), John Henry Boner, Henry Jerome Stockard and Benjamin Sledd.

Frank Borden Hanes of Winston-Salem has written two successful novels in verse, *Abel Anders* and *The Bat Brothers.* Helen Bevington of Durham (*Nineteen Million Elephants*) writes charming and sophisticated light verse, and Randall Jarrell of Greensboro is accounted one of the country's best modern poets. Carl Sandburg, now living at Flat Rock, won a Pulitzer prize with his *Collected Poems.* Other Tar Heel poets of ability are Olive Tilford Dargan, Anne Blackwell Payne, Charles Edward Eaton, Thad Stem, Jr., Edwin McNeill Poteat, Lucy Cherry Crisp, Zoe Kincaid Brockman, Rebecca Cushman, Mary Louise Medley, and Stewart Atkins.

Richard Walser's anthologies of North Carolina short stories and poetry include many of these.

Other Forms of Literature

The State has had quite a sizable number of able biographers, including A. L. Brooks, C. Alfonso Smith, William E. Dodd, Gerald W. Johnson, Phillips Russell, LeGette Blythe, Robert W. Winston, Lodwick Hartley, Newman Ivey White, and the great biographer of Lincoln, Carl Sandburg.

Not a small part of the literature of the South has taken the form of oratory, and North Carolina is no exception. The collected addresses of Charles B. Aycock, Edwin A. Alderman, and Edward Kidder Graham, for example, are worth reading even now for the light they throw on the modern South and the power and beauty of their style. So also are the letters of Walter Hines Page, Cornelia Phillips Spencer and Walter Clark.

But it has been in the field of regional analysis that North Carolina scholars have done work unequalled in the nation for insight and illumination. This work has been centered mainly at Chapel Hill and Duke University, and it includes such outstanding books as Howard W. Odum's *Southern Regions,* Rupert B. Vance's *Human Geography of the South,* Jonathan Daniels' *A Southerner Discovers the South,* Josephus Daniels' autobiographical series, Alex Heard's *A Two-Party South,* S. H. Hobbs' *North Carolina: Economic and Social,* W. J. Cash's *The Mind of the South,* Calvin B. Hoover's and B. U. Ratchford's *Economic Resources and Policies of the South,* W. T. Couch's creative editing of such books as *Culture in the South* and *What The Negro Wants,* and J. Saunders Redding's *No Day of Triumph.*

To these should be added certain charming and enlightening views of the Tar Heel scene, such as Robert B. House's *Miss Sue and the Sheriff,* John Harden's *Tar Heel Ghosts,* William Meade Prince's *The Southern Part of Heaven,* Hope S. Chamberlain's *This Was Home,* Phillips Russell's *The Woman Who Rang the Bell,* Muriel Earley Sheppard's *Cabin in the Laurels,* Horace Kephart's *Our Southern Highlanders,* and David Stick's *Graveyard of the Atlantic.* We like to write about ourselves, and we don't do it badly.

North Carolina has some cause to feel proud of the writers she has "borned," developed, attracted, and, alas, evicted.

THE THEATER

THE HISTORY of the drama in North Carolina goes back to 1759 when Thomas Godfrey, Jr., then living in Wilmington, completed what is said to be the first tragedy written by an American and produced on the American stage. It was *The Prince of Parthia,* a five-act drama in blank verse, and it was produced in Philadelphia in 1767, but it was not until 80 years later, 1847, that Wilmington got around to producing it in its theater.

A comedy, *Nolens Volens* or *The Biter Bit* was written by Edward Hall and published in New Bern in 1809; and another Tar Heel, Lemuel Sawyer, wrote a comedy, *Blackbeard,* in 1824, which was performed in the Bowery Theater in New York in 1833.

There was a good deal of activity in the drama in this state in the early 1800's. Thalian or Thespian societies in New Bern, Wilmington, Warrenton, Edenton, Fayetteville, Halifax, Raleigh, Salisbury and other towns put on various plays and dramatic entertainments.

But from the end of the Civil War to about 1920 there was not much going on in the drama; now and then a road show would make the rounds but that was certainly not much. North Carolina's only gifts to the American theater were Augustin Daly (1838-1899), a successful producer, and the De Mille family, several of whose members became celebrated on stage and screen.

It was not until 1919, or 160 years after the authorship of *The Prince of Parthia,* that North Carolinians went in for writing drama as a continuous and serious enterprise.

Professor Frederick H. Koch, coming from North Dakota, where he had pioneered in teaching his students to write folk plays, settled down in Chapel Hill and inaugurated the Carolina Playmakers, a group of students who wrote, produced and acted dramas of the life about them. "Proff" Koch struck pay dirt in Tarheelia's hills and plains; among his distinguished "alumni" were Paul Green, Betty Smith, Thomas Wolfe. Koch succeeded brilliantly because he limited his students to writing plays about the life which they knew by experience, whereas, if left to their own devices and desires, they would of course have written inspired and insipid tragedies of Italian princesses dying by the battalion with such speeches on their lips as "Bury me in the sea so that the stars may move over my bosom!"

As it was, "Proff" Koch made them understand, as Tom Wolfe put it, that "The dramatic is not the unusual. It is happening daily in our lives." So he and his fellow students wrote of what they knew—of tenant farmers, landlords, mill hands, mill owners, Negroes, the life of the farm, the village, the town. Their work, amateurish as it was, frequently had more freshness, vitality and realism about it than was or is found on Broadway or in Hollywood.

The outstanding playwright to come from Koch's classes was Paul Green, who is indeed one of the most distinguished dramatists of our time. In 1927 he won the Pulitzer Prize for Drama with his first full-length play, *In Abraham's Bosom,* a serious and sympathetic study of Negro life. Other plays of his dealing with his people and their problems are *The House of Connelly,* a drama of the changing South; *The Enchanted Maze,* a satire on higher education; *Tread the Green Grass, Roll, Sweet Chariot,* and *Johnny Johnson.* He has also written short stories, essays and a novel, *This Body the Earth,* all bearing the hallmark of a conscientious, sympathetic, thoughtful and expert artist.

His best and most moving drama, many think, is *The Lost Colony,* which was first performed on Roanoke Island in 1937 and is still running in the summer. This symphonic drama, which combines historic setting, action, music and the dance, is the story of the heroic attempt to found Sir Walter Raleigh's ill-fated colony on that island nearly 400 years ago. This dramatization of the aspirations, struggles, perils and final mysterious disappearance of the colonists from the face of the earth in the vast American wilderness has stirred the spirits and lifted the hearts of many thousands. To witness the drama is a powerfully moving experience for Americans, from the time when the lights are lowered in the open-air amphitheater on the edge of the water and the play begins with the Minister saying, "Friends we are gathered here this evening to honor the spiritual birthplace of our nation and to memorialize those heroic men and women who made it so," to the end, tragic but uplifting, when the colonists march out into the darkness of the unknown land with flags flying, chanting:

"O God, our Father, Lord above,
O bright Immortal, Holy One,
Secure within thy boundless love,
We walk this way of death alone."

Paul Green's *The Lost Colony* was the first example of a new form of outdoor drama which recreated dramatic phases of our nation's history in their original settings. Other dramas by Green in this form are *The Common Glory* at Williamsburg, Virginia, *Faith of Our Fathers* at Washington, D. C., and *The Seventeenth Star* in Ohio.

Kermit Hunter, another Carolina Playmaker, has adopted and successfully used this form in *Unto These Hills,* the dramatization of the tribulations of the Cherokee Indians of Western North Carolina, which is playing in the summers at the Cherokee Reservation; *Horn in the*

West, which is produced at Boone, and *Forever This Land* which re-enacted the early life of Abraham Lincoln in Springfield, Ill.

Since the death of Professor Koch, the work of the Carolina Play-makers has been ably carried on by his former student, Professor Samuel Selden.

In theatrical fare of a commercial nature, North Carolina, like the rest of the country, gets what nourishment it can from the thin pigeon soup it imports from Hollywood and, on rare occasions, Broadway. But the State does quite well in supplementing this menu with ama-teur productions, notable among which are those of the Playlikers at Woman's College, and the little theater offerings at Charlotte, Raleigh and Asheville.

ART

FROM 1585, WHEN John White executed his painting of the Indians and the life they lived on Roanoke Island, to about 1925 North Caro-linians showed no great interest in the art of painting and little more in that of sculpture.

It is true that there were family portraits and paintings in the homes of wealthy families in this State before 1860, a number of them executed by such reputable painters as Benjamin West, Henry Inman, the paint-ing Peale family and the ubiquitous Thomas Sully. St. James Church of Wilmington has a painting of Christ by an unknown artist which was taken from a pirate ship in 1748. Portraits of famous men, mostly North Carolinians, are displayed in the public buildings in Raleigh, Chapel Hill and other places. There are small collections of paintings in the Wachovia Museum at Winston-Salem, Flora MacDonald Col-lege at Red Springs, and the Biltmore House of George W. Vanderbilt near Asheville.

This State had greater interest in sculpture, as a more durable me-dium for memorializing its great men. After the Civil War statues of Confederate soldiers sprang up on the courthouse squares, and even the street intersections, of almost every county seat. The Capitol Square in Raleigh was, and is, adorned by some good sculpture, including statues of the Women of the Confederacy by Augustus Lukman, George Washington by Houdon, Lawson Wyatt by Gutzon Borglum, Charles D. McIver by F. Wellington Ruckstall, and Charles B. Aycock by Borglum, while busts of John M. Morehead, William A. Graham, and Matt W. Ransom repose in the capitol rotunda. To the statuary on the grounds has been added in recent years a triple monument by Charles Keck to the "Three Presidents" from North Carolina, Jackson, Polk and Johnson.

But the truth is that, in the 340 years intervening between White's drawings and the formation of the North Carolina Art Society in the 1920's, the Old North State was not vitally interested in art.

Perhaps the outstanding painter residing in this State in all that time was Elliot Daingerfield (1859-1932), a native of Virginia, who headed the Permanent Art School at Blowing Rock and who painted a large number of landscapes and religious subjects which would doubtless offend the modern taste as too "pretty."

It was not until the middle '20's that an art movement, made possible by the growing wealth and culture of the State, got under way; it has been increasing in effectiveness ever since.

The mainspring of this movement was the North Carolina Art Society, which was started by Mrs. Katherine Pendleton Arrington and a few other far-seeing citizens who were determined to make their fellow Tar Heels art-conscious.

This society was organized for the purpose of promoting art appreciation and education, and eventually of establishing a worthy state museum of art. With Mrs. Arrington as its leading spirit, it carried forward the first two objectives by placing original paintings and reproductions of masterpieces in the public schools, by encouraging young artists and by holding in Raleigh annual exhibitions of works of art from out-of-state galleries.

In 1929 the Legislature placed the Art Society under the patronage and control of the State, incorporating it and giving it legal power to receive donations. Since then it has received support from the State and collections of art from various sources. In 1943 the State Art Gallery was opened in Raleigh and it has consistently broadened its activities. In addition to traveling exhibits it displays the Phifer collection of paintings, ancient glass, Coptic textiles and contemporary works by North Carolina artists. It publishes a gallery bulletin and makes annual awards to artists in the State.

In 1947 the Legislature, at the exhortation of Robert Lee Humber, an attorney of Greenville and former Rhodes scholar, appropriated $1,000,000 for the purchase of paintings for a proposed State Art Museum. This appropriation was contingent on its being matched by another million dollars, something which seemed at the time most unlikely. However, the Samuel H. Kress Foundation, at Humber's urging, did match it with paintings mainly of the Renaissance period, valued at a million dollars or more.

In 1951 a State Art Commission was appointed and it purchased with the million appropriated for that purpose 200 paintings by various old masters, including Rubens, Reynolds, Rembrandt, Memling, Romney, Van Dyck, Canaletto, Guardi, Sully, Copley, Gainsborough, and others. These two collections are housed in the Old State Highway Building, now remodeled as the State Art Museum. It may well be the outstanding art collection south of Washington.

North Carolina artists who have made their reputations and earned their living in other states include Francis Speight and Hobson Pittman, Charles Baskerville and Donald Mattison.

Those who have done or are doing good work in North Carolina include Clement Strudwick of Hillsboro; Duncan Stuart, Katherine Morris, Isabel Bowen Henderson, Mabel Pugh, Mary Tillery, and Primrose McPherson of Raleigh; Kenneth Ness of Chapel Hill; Henry Rood and Gregory D. Ivey of Greensboro; Claude Howell of Wilmington; and Pulitzer Award Winner Philip Moose of Newton.

Notable camera studies of the mountains have been made by George Masa, and of other parts of the State by Mrs. Bayard Wootten and Charles Farrell.

Among the art galleries in the State are the State Art Museum, Raleigh; the Mint Museum, Charlotte; the Person Hall and Morehead galleries at Chapel Hill; the Weatherspoon Art Gallery in Greensboro; the Duke University gallery in Durham; others are located in Asheville, Hickory, Greenville, Fayetteville; various colleges have some art collections.

HANDICRAFTS

HANDICRAFTS FLOURISHED mainly in the mountains where people had to make the things they needed or do without them. So they made clothes, blankets, curtains, bedspreads with such names as *Saint Anne's Robe, Whig Rose,* and *Bony Part's March;* hooked rugs of rags dyed many colors; baskets of lithe woods including willow, honeysuckle and hickory; brooms of the ubiquitous broomstraw; chairs, stools and benches of oak, maple and hickory; the green wood frames tightening on the dry wooden seats and slats so that nails and pegs were not necessary to hold them together.

Pottery has long been made in several parts of the State. In the 1700's a group of potters from Staffordshire, England, settled in the Sandhills section, and their descendants still fashion churns, crocks, bowls, jugs, plates, pitchers, cups and saucers in beautiful forms and colors. Notable potteries in this area are Jugtown, near Steeds, which Mr. and Mrs. Jacques Busbee fostered, and Cole's Pottery near Seagrove. Others are Hilton's Pottery in Catawba County, Pisgah Forest Pottery near Asheville, and the Omar Khayyam Pottery near Chandler.

Metal handiwork is done at Banner Elk and fine silverware, some with dogwood design, is made by Stuart Nye not far from Asheville.

The Southern Highland Handicraft Guild stimulates work in the mountains and operates its own salesroom in Asheville. Schools teaching handicraft are located at Penland, Higgins, Crossnore, Hot Springs, Asheville and Cherokee.

Folks who once made things for neighbors in the next cove now make them for tourists from the next state or the next nation; the neighborhood has expanded.

MUSIC

NORTH CAROLINA got her first music with her first settlers. The folks, whether they came to the mountains by way of Pennsylvania or to Hatteras by way of shipwreck, brought their songs with them.

Our folk music ranges from the careless ribaldry of *Careless Love* to the deep spiritual insight of *Deep River;* from the violent action of Lord Thomas in the ballad of *Lord Thomas and Fair Ellen,* who with his sword "chopped off" the brown girl's head "and throwed it against the wall," to the lyric wonder of *One Morning in May* with its concluding line, "to see slanting waters, hear nightingales sing."

Our folk songs, like the poor, we have with us always, and they serve us on all conceivable occasions. There are courting songs (*Madam, I Have Gold and Silver*), lullabies (*The Poor Little Lamb Cried Mammy,* which is surely the most fearsome lullaby ever sung), drinking songs (*Show Me the Way to Go Home, Babe*), play-party and dance songs (*Buffalo Gals, Won't You Come Out Tonight*), animal songs (*The Old Gray Mare Came Tearing Through The Wilderness*), work songs (*I Wish my Capt'n Would Go Blind*), folk lyrics (*Down in the Valley*), war songs (*Colonel Harvey, He Was Scared*) and religious songs (*I Wonder as I Wander*).

These songs are good and evil, sweet and mean, solemn and funny, beautiful and ugly; there are spirituals and there are devil ditties; they are all that people are; they are ourselves.

To the folk music something new was added in the early life of the State. This was the music which the Moravians brought with them when they settled in what is now Winston-Salem. It began with the hymn which accompanied the felling of the first tree for the first house in 1753; it burst forth in the *Psalm of Joy* celebrating the victorious peace following the American Revolution in 1783, and after 200 years of continuous development it is still heard in the annual Easter sunrise service in Old Salem.

There is a good deal going on in music in North Carolina today. The foundations for this widespread and vigorous movement were laid by a number of Tar Heels including Mrs. Crosby Adams in the mountains, Paul John Weaver at Chapel Hill, Dr. Wade R. Brown and H. Hugh Altvater at Greensboro, and Hattie Parrott and the Pfohl family in Winston-Salem, much of it with the co-operation of the North Carolina Federation of Music Clubs.

Out of this interest has come music in many forms—symphony orchestras, choruses, opera, folk song festivals and jazz bands.

One of the most important developments in recent years is the North Carolina Symphony Orchestra. Organized, directed and conducted by Dr. Benjamin Swalin of Chapel Hill, and supported partly by the State and partly by private subscription, this fine orchestra carries good music to all the people of the State, by bus, boat, and any other means of transportation that happens to be handy, from Hatteras to the Cherokee Reservation in the Great Smokies.* In 1953 it traveled 10,000 miles to give 123 concerts. It devotes a good deal of its time and energy to bringing the appreciation of music to school children; this work is under the inspiring direction of Adeline McCall of Chapel Hill. In 1953, 140,000 school children heard concerts in which they had been given background information about the programs beforehand; to watch them responding to various kinds of music, from Beethoven and Mozart to *Sourwood Mountain* and *Gum Tree Canoe,* is a heart-warming experience.

Other symphony orchestras in the State are located in Greensboro, Charlotte and Winston-Salem.

The Grass Roots Opera Company, organized by Mr. and Mrs. A. J. Fletcher of Raleigh, takes both grand and light opera in English translation to North Carolinians in town and countryside, without benefit of any scenery or much costuming, for a guarantee of $60 for a small opera like Mozart's *Cosi fan Tutti* to $110 for a full-sized one like Bizet's *Carmen.*

The Transylvania Music Camp, which was started in 1936 by James Christian Pfohl, is primarily a summer school for musicians; each year, however, it puts on a music festival which attracts some of the best lecturers and performers in the county, such as Olin Downs, Joseph Szigeti and Eileen Farrell.

"About sundown the first week in August," Bascom Lamar Lunsford of South Turkey Creek not far from Asheville, who is known as "the Minstrel of the Appalachians," conducts a Mountain Dance and Folk Festival at Asheville. He also puts on a Carolina Folk Festival at Chapel Hill some time during the summer. Mr. Lunsford knows as

---

* The Orchestra has also toured in various states of the South and has had national recognition from publications such as TIME MAGAZINE, NEWSWEEK, COLLIER'S and others, as well as having national listening audiences by way of MBS, CBS, and NBC

much as the next one about folk songs and dances; he is a fiddle, mouth harp, banjo and guitar player from way back, in addition to being a Grade-A square-dance caller. When he was supported by such performers as the Soco Gap Folk Dancers, Singers and Players, together with Buck-and-Wing Dancer Lily Lee Baker, Banjo Picker Aunt Samantha Bumgardner, and Square Dance Caller Sam Queen, a good time was likely to be had by all, especially when the fiddler started up with Lunsford's *Old Mountain Dew,* or Sam called for the dancers to do the *Ocean Wave,* the *Georgey Rang-Tang,* the *Grapevine Twist* or the *Bird in the Cage.*

North Carolina composers of ability include Lamar Stringfield who won a Pulitzer prize in 1928 with his suite *From the Southern Mountains,* Charles G. Vardell of Salem College who composed *Carolina Symphony,* Hunter Johnson who won the *Prix de Rome* in 1938, Lily Strickland of Hendersonville, Wilton Mason of Chapel Hill, William Klenz of Duke University, Rob Roy Peery of Salisbury, and Hermine W. Eichorn, Elliott Weisgarber, R. Nathaniel Dett and Herbert Hazelman of Greensboro.

Among University of North Carolina graduates who made good on the national musical scene are Thor Johnson, symphony orchestra conductor, and Norman Cordon, Metropolitan opera singer.

Tar Heel dance band leaders who acquired large followings among those who like modern jazz are John Scott Trotter, James Kern, "Kay" Kyser, Hal Kemp, Skinnay Ennis, Johnny Long, "Jelly" Leftwich, Tal Henry, Les Brown, and James Garber.

WILLIAM T. POLK,
Associate Editor, *Greensboro Daily News.*

Natural Setting

NORTH CAROLINA, one of the Thirteen Colonies that formed the original United States of America, is bounded on the north by Virginia, on the east by the Atlantic Ocean, on the south by South Carolina and Georgia, and on the west by Tennessee. Except for the North Carolina-Virginia boundary, which, with but slight variations, runs due east and west, the State's boundaries are irregular. Situated between latitudes 33° 27′ 37″ N. and 36° 34′ 25″ N., and longitudes 75° 27′ W. and 84° 20′ W., the State lies entirely within the warmer part of the north temperate zone.

The extreme length of the State from east to west is 503 miles, and from north to south 187 miles. The average length from east to west is approximately 410 miles, and from north to south, approximately 115 miles. The State's total area is 52,286 square miles, with 48,666 square miles of land and 3,620 square miles of water.

The population in 1950 (U. S. Census) was 4,061,929. North Carolina ranked tenth in population among the states. Of its inhabitants 2,693,-828 were classified as rural and 1,368,101 as urban. The population of the largest city (Charlotte) was 134,042.

North Carolina is popularly known as the Old North State to distinguish it from its southern neighbor, and as the Tar Heel State from a designation attributed to Cornwallis' soldiers, who, after crossing a river into which tar had been poured, emerged with the substance adhering to their heels.

Sloping down from the crest of the Appalachian system to the Atlantic seaboard, North Carolina lies wholly within the Atlantic border region, with its three great natural divisions: the mountain region, the piedmont plateau, and the coastal plain.

Nearly half of the State's area lies in the coastal plain, the broad almost level, forested or agricultural "low country" extending from the seacoast inland to the fall line. Its extreme eastern boundary is a long chain of islands known as "banks," a narrow barrier against the Atlantic. The banks are constantly shifting sand dunes, which in places are only one or two feet above tide level, but which at Kill Devil Hill in Dare County reach a height of 100 feet. From the banks three famous capes project into the Atlantic: treacherous Hatteras, "graveyard of the Atlantic," and Lookout and Fear, guarding the entrances to the State's chief port towns, Morehead City–Beaufort and Wilmington. Between the banks and the shore a chain of sounds, including Pamlico and Albemarle, stretches along the State's entire 320 miles of sea front. Notable among the numerous islands lying within the sounds are Roanoke and Harkers.

Bordering the sounds on the mainland is the tidewater area, a belt from 30 to 80 miles wide, where the land is level and sometimes swampy. To the north a part of the Great Dismal Swamp spreads across the border of Virginia into North Carolina; and farther south, swamps in Hyde, Tyrrell, and Dare counties cover some 300 square miles. These swamplands, locally known as "dismals" and "pocosins," occur on the divides or watersheds between the rivers and sounds. In this region are 15 natural lakes, largest of which is Lake Mattamuskeet, near the coast in Hyde County. Characteristic of the southeast is the savanna, a treeless prairie-land with a thick growth of grass and wild flowers. The savannas, the largest of which covers some 3,000 acres, have been created by a lack of drainage and a close impervious soil.

Many of the largest rivers of the coastal plain rise in the western piedmont and join the sounds as broad estuaries. To the north are the Roanoke, rising in piedmont Virginia, and the Chowan, formed by two rivers which rise in eastern Virginia. Draining the central portion of the plain are the Tar-Pamlico and the Neuse; to the south is the Cape Fear. The larger rivers are navigable almost to the border of the piedmont. In a series of terraces, the coastal plain rises gradually from sea level to a height of about 500 feet at its western margin.

The fall line, at the head of river navigation, marks the western edge of the coastal plain. Running from Northampton and Halifax counties on the Virginia border, the line extends in a southwesterly direction through Anson County on the South Carolina border.

The piedmont plateau, extending from the fall line west to the Blue Ridge, consists of rolling hill country, with stiff clay soils and numerous swift streams capable of producing great power for industrial and urban development. In this region, the most densely populated in the State, the Broad, the Catawba, and the Yadkin rivers, which have their sources on the southeastern slopes of the Blue Ridge, pursue easterly courses until they turn southward and flow into South Carolina, where the Catawba becomes the Wateree. At its western edge the piedmont plateau rises from 1,200 to 1,500 feet above sea level. Spurs from the

Blue Ridge reach out eastward and southward, and a few straggling irregular ranges cross the breadth of the plateau.

The Blue Ridge, or eastern Appalachian chain, is a steep, ragged escarpment rising suddenly above the piedmont. It is bordered on the west by a lower plateau of more than 6,000 square miles, with an elevation of 2,000 to 3,000 feet. This plateau is bordered on the north and west by the Iron, Stone, Unaka, Bald, Great Smoky, and Unicoi mountains, all of which are part of the western Appalachian chain. Several cross chains, higher and more massive than the principal ranges, cut the great plateau into a checkerboard of small mountain-framed areas with independent drainage systems.

Both the Blue Ridge and the Great Smoky ranges reach their culminating heights in western North Carolina, and together they constitute the greatest mass of mountains in the eastern half of the United States. More than 40 peaks rise 6,000 feet or more above sea level. Among these, Mount Mitchell, on the Black Mountain spur of the Blue Ridge, attains a height of 6,684 feet, the highest elevation east of the Mississippi. Some 80 peaks are from 5,000 to 6,000 feet high, and hundreds are from 4,000 to 5,000 feet.

The Blue Ridge, a straggling irregular mountain chain, crosses the State in a northeast-southwest direction. Near the South Carolina border it turns westward and for a considerable distance forms the boundary between the two Carolinas. By a southwestern projection into Georgia, the range unites again with the western Appalachian chain.

The Great Smoky Mountains border the plateau sharply on the west, the main chain forming the boundary between North Carolina and Tennessee. The mean altitude of the range is higher than that of the Blue Ridge, and some of its peaks rise higher above their bases than any others in eastern America.

The crest of the Blue Ridge is the principal watershed within the State. Rainfall on the eastern slope flows into the Atlantic; from the western slope it reaches the Gulf of Mexico by way of the Mississippi River. Fed by many tributaries, the Hiwassee, the Little Tennessee, and the French Broad rivers flow westerly and northwesterly from the Blue Ridge into Tennessee. Farther north the New River flows through Virginia and into the Ohio River. Within Tennessee, the Nolichucky and Pigeon rivers empty into the French Broad. The Elk and the Watauga are important tributaries of the Holston River in Tennessee.

Most of the valleys formed by the streams of the mountain region are deep and narrow. The gorge of the Little Tennessee at the foot of the Great Smoky Mountains is from 200 to 500 feet deep. Large and small streams have many waterfalls.

The North Carolina streams have made possible the building of over one hundred hydroelectric plants. Steady operation is maintained by the relatively high and well distributed rainfall of the mountain and piedmont areas. In addition to these valley storage basins, thousands of farm ponds made in recent years add immeasurably to water conservation.

CLIMATE

ONE MAY not speak of the "the climate" of North Carolina, for the great contrasts in altitude force the recognition of "climates." Mid-winter temperatures on the mountain tops are frequently as low as 25° or 30° below zero, while on Smith Island, below Southport, a minimum temperature variation of 50° or 60° is to be noted. The recorded mean annual temperatures range from 48° at Linville to 64° at Southport. In the mountains, North Carolina has the most pronounced isothermal belts of any Eastern state. These are zones with moderate winter night temperatures caused by air drainage effects.

The rainfall is abundant, but, more important, it is well distributed throughout the year with an average for the coastal plain of 48 inches. The greatest rainfall is of course on the high mountain slopes where more than 80 inches has been recorded. The frequent summer afternoon mountain showers help develop these extremes. In the valleys between the ranges the rainfall is no greater and often not as great as in the adjoining piedmont province. At Highlands the average annual rainfall is 84 inches; at Marshall, 50 miles distant, it is only 39 inches.

Snowfall diminishes eastward; only sporadic and brief storms sweep over the piedmont and upper coastal plain. On Baldhead Island, off the southeastern coast, snow and freezing temperatures are extremely rare. On the ocean shore, however, the moderation of the temperature is due more to the contiguous water masses than any influence of the Gulf Stream.

Contrasting with the winter cloudiness of the northern states bordering the Great Lakes, North Carolinians enjoy an average of 61% sunshine with more than that in the eastern half of the State.

GEOLOGY

Mountains and Piedmont. The great diversity of terrain in North Carolina is related to the eons of geological time. The geologic story involves the entire Eastern United States. As a result of the last pulsation, North Carolina possesses not only a great number of high elevations, but near the sea, a great expanse of lowland or sea terraces, known as the Pamlico (land lying less than 20 feet above sea level). Related to these terraces are the two great sounds, Albemarle and Pamlico, which give North Carolina one of the longest continuous shore lines of any state. This includes both sides of the 320-mile long Outer Banks.

On the site of the present mountains there once was a great arm of the sea. Lying to the east of this gulf, a great land mass called Appalachia towered to great heights. Gradually Appalachia wore away, and the area once covered by the sea was buckled into the ancestors of the present day mountain ranges of North Carolina. Excessive heat and pressure altered the rocks to metamorphic types; accompanying the earth movement, volcanoes covered the surface with both lava and ash.

At first, erosion was rapid, for no upland forest plants had evolved to protect the weathered slopes. Today the gently sloping piedmont with its low elevation of 350-1800 feet is all that is left of this ancient mountain mass of Old Appalachia. Since Jurassic time, or for some 200 million years, the piedmont has remained much as it is today.

A new uplift took place farther west when the hard rocks of the old eroded mass pressed from the southeast against the sediments formed in the inland sea. Not only the western margin of old rocks was elevated, but the softer sediments were pushed into vast folds, which attained great heights. The Blue Ridge, consisting of resistant rocks, instead of being a mere ridge as in Virginia, was a much broader mass in North Carolina. It extended from near the Mt. Mitchell range on the east to the boundary of the Smoky Mountains National Park. Erosion reduced these mountains to their present condition. A geologically recent uplift of the region created the Asheville plateau from which the present high, hard rock peaks arise. The Blue Ridge Parkway follows the southeastern side of the broad, complex hard rock mountain system to the junction of Haywood, Transylvania, and Jackson counties. From this point it turns northwest along the ridge of the Balsam Mountains to the Smoky Mountains National Park.

In the piedmont, local down-faults occurred in Triassic time giving rise to large basins of deposition. These troughs became filled with stratified sediments. In the eastern one, which extends nearly across the State, a 40-inch coal seam known as the Cumnock bed was mined for many years. The operation has recently been abandoned.

Coastal Plain. The evolution of the mountains and piedmont involved some 500 million years. In contrast, the record of the stream and ocean activity, on the coastal plain, involved but the last 60 million years. Crustal movement must have been in part responsible for the ocean's greatest landward advance during the last half-million years. An important factor in changing the ocean levels is believed to have been the formation and melting of the great glacial ice masses. Some geologists believe that during the last Wisconsin glacial advance, 10,000 years ago, the ocean was 300 feet below its present level. During warmer interglacial periods the ocean level was higher than at present and responsible for wave-cut terraces and barrier beaches.

LAKES OF NORTH CAROLINA

EROSION destroyed all natural lakes that might have existed in the piedmont and mountain areas. The present lakes and ponds there are the result of dam building. In contrast, the early explorers found a great many coastal plain lakes, all partly or completely surrounded by peat. These lakes are believed to occupy depressions made through the local destruction of the peat by fires set by the Indians many millennia ago.

Carolina Bays. The Carolina Bays are one of the most remarkable physiographic features in the world. Their origin is still much debated among scientists. Scattered in the southern half of the North Carolina plain and spreading over the entire coastal plain of South Carolina are thousands of shallow depressions. All have almost mathematically perfect elliptical shapes, with all their long axes parallel. They are oriented in a northwest-southeast direction and vary from a tenth of a mile to 7 miles in length. The rims are slightly elevated and consist of coarse white sand which in aerial photographs stands in strong contrast to the dark aspect of the evergreen shrub cover growing on the peat. Because the elliptical depressions, almost invariably shrub bogs, have marginal bay trees (sweet, red, and loblolly), the name "Carolina bays" has been given to these unique physiographic structures.

Roads which traverse regions where the bays are abundant tend to be built on the rims. The motorist in such a region will be impressed by the long regular curves in the road when it picks up a bay rim. Such may be frequently encountered in the Bladen Lake region. These lakes contain only a remnant of the former peat bog left in the northwest ends of the depression.

One theory suggests that these bays were formerly filled with peat which at some time of extremely low water became destroyed by fire. When the water returned, these small lakes were enlarged by wave and current action on the peat border. This process is going on at present in all of the bay lakes.

Very different theories have been offered as to their origin, ranging from the fish-nest hypothesis to what this writer believes is the correct one—the meteorite concept. Some have thought they represent blowouts, others ancient lagoons. One leading physiographer, learning of the artesian source in the bottom of White Lake, believed all the bay areas formerly had such upward moving water under them. He suggested that the water dissolved away soluble materials, resulting in a shallow sink hole which filled with water.

Dr. W. F. Prouty, former head of the Department of Geology at the University of North Carolina, was one of the chief protagonists for the meteorite theory. His monograph has gone far toward establishing that sometime in late Pleistocene time a "comet-head" of meteorites, traveling at astronomical speed, fell on the Carolinas' coastal plain and in one great catastrophe, measured in minutes, produced these estimated half million shallow craters. At a strategically located bay near Wilmington, the present writer found evidence that the basin originated about a quarter of a million years ago.

Among these lakes is a popular resort, White Lake, in Bladen County. In contrast to all the others, which are dark water lakes and undesirable for recreation purposes, White Lake has water as clear as that of an indoor swimming pool. This lake is a huge spring, fed by artesian water rising from an unknown depth. Water slowly moves into the banks and keeps the lake clear of dark material that tends to be washed in by wave action. It is one of the most beautiful small lakes in the southeast.

Lake Waccamaw, the largest of the Carolina Bay lakes, is located in Columbus County and is 5.3 miles long with but a small portion of uneroded bog in its northwest end. Despite its area, it has a maximum depth of only 10.8 feet. The north shore, enjoying the prevailing summer south and southwest winds, has become a well known resort center. The south shore is undeveloped due to its inaccessibility by roads. It occupies one of the largest Carolina Bay depressions, but its water is not as hard as some of the Bladen Lakes.

Lower Coastal Plain Lakes. On the broad flat sea terraces of the lower coastal plain, which were formerly covered by extensive sheets of peat, a number of lakes of varying size have been initiated by fire. Notable among this type are Phelps and Pungo in Washington County, Alligator and Mattamuskeet in Hyde, Catfish in Jones and Ellis, Long, and Great Lakes in Carteret. These are all dark water lakes, which has prevented them from becoming important as recreation areas. The one exception is Mattamuskeet. An unsuccessful attempt, with a loss of $17,000,000, was made to drain it for farming. It has now reverted to Federal Wildlife control. A hotel for duck and geese hunters is maintained on the south side of the lake.

MINERAL RESOURCES

NEARLY EVERY MINERAL recognized in the United States has been found in North Carolina. Whereas the State has a wide variety of minerals, only a few of the metallic and nonmetallic types have been found in sufficient quantities to be of commercial value.

Metallic Minerals. Metallic minerals which were easy to mold and carve were used by the Indians. Early white explorers noted that the natives had tobacco pipes "tipt with silver," as well as ornaments made of gold and copper. Exploitation for these and other minerals began with the early history of the State and is still continuing today.

Gold and silver have been mined in more than 400 separate localities in the State. Until 1849, North Carolina was one of the major gold producing states in the Union. Noteworthy in the annals of early mining is the record of a 17-pound nugget found in 1799 at the Reed mine in Cabarrus County. Recently, however, exploration and exploitation for gold and silver have been small scale ventures.

Although copper ores have been mined in at least 15 different counties, only those in Ashe, Swain, and Jackson have produced notable quantities of the metal.

Of the ferrous group, iron, molybdenum, nickel, chromium, titanium, tungsten, and manganese ores have been mined in North Carolina. Iron deposits in the State are generally low grade, and the producing localities are widely scattered. Hundreds of small deposits have been worked for both export and for local furnaces, but only two districts have produced sizable quantities of ore. The Cranberry mine in Avery County was closed in 1938 after having yielded two million tons of magnetite ore. Cherokee County has been examined numerous times for large quantities of low grade ores, with only moderate success. Many unsuccessful prospects for nickel and chromium have been established in the mountains of the State. During recent years, exploration has centered around Webster and Addie in Jackson County. Molybdenum occurs in the granite belts of North Carolina. Titanium ores have been mined in Caldwell and Clay counties for paint pigments, and new uses for the metal have made the titanium sands north of Albemarle Sound an attractive prospect. Manganese oxides found in small deposits in the mountains must depend upon advances in technology to become important ores. One of the largest single operations for tungsten minerals in the United States is located near Townsville, in Vance County.

Of the non-ferrous metals, lead, zinc, lithium, and tin have been mined profitably in North Carolina. Lead and zinc sulfides have been produced at Silver Hill in Davidson County, and prospects for these minerals have been established in Haywood, McDowell, and Montgomery counties. Near Kings Mountain is one of the few areas in the United States where tin ore was once mined. In the same district, spodumene is produced for its lithium content.

Non-Metallic Minerals. Both industrial and gem quality non-metallics have been mined in the State. This group, which includes feldspars, micas, clays, crushed and building stone, olivene, sand and gravel, quartz, talc, pyrophyllite, and gem stones, constitutes the major source of income for the mineral industries of North Carolina. Since 1917, North Carolina has been the leading state in feldspar production, with 90% coming from the Spruce Pine district in Mitchell, Yancey, and Avery counties. This area is also a major producer of muscovite; other districts around Kings Mountain, Shelby, and Franklin contribute substantial quantities of this strategic mineral. Vermiculite, a hydrated mica used for thermal insulation, has been mined from several small deposits in the western counties. The olivene in Jackson County has been mined for both chemical and refractory industries. Sand and gravel deposits, nearly always associated with river beds, are widely scattered throughout the State. Quartz has been quarried from veins in both the piedmont and Blue Ridge provinces. The extremely high grade deposit from the Chestnut Flats mine in Mitchell County supplied the raw material for the Hale telescope at Mount Palomar. Granite, gneiss, limestone, slate, and marble are used extensively for crushed and dimension stone. North Carolina ranks among the leading states producing crushed stone. Important deposits of talc are being worked in Cherokee County, and pyrophyllite, a talc-like mineral, has been mined for many years in Moore and Chatham counties and more recently in Granville County.

Clays for important pottery, porcelain, and brick industries are supplied from mines in the State. Kaolin and halloysite are mined in Avery, Yancey, Mitchell, and Macon counties, and significant deposits of brick clays occur in the Durham-Sanford basin. A low grade bituminous coal, found near Sanford, has been mined as a source of energy for local industries.

The list of gem stones found in North Carolina is imposing. A few small diamonds have been found in the piedmont area. In Transylvania and Macon counties both sapphire and ruby have been recovered. Emeralds have been found in the Spruce Pine district, and zircon crystals have been recognized at numerous localities in the mountains. Hiddenite, a mineral first identified in Alexander County, is prized for its deep green color. The semi-precious gems, aquamarine, kyanite, garnet, and amethyst have been found in both the piedmont and in the mountains.

Further exploration will undoubtedly reveal new deposits of both metallic and non-metallic minerals. With these expected new finds the North Carolina mineral industries will continue to expand.

FLORA

NORTH CAROLINA leads as the State with the greatest diversity of natural conditions in the eastern United States. This concept was expressed in *The Natural Gardens of North Carolina* as follows: "North Carolina is unique among the eastern states for possessing within her borders the best examples of the most diverse vegetations as these two criteria are judged in combination. Whoever the men were who designed the geographical biscuit cutter which sliced out the Old North State, they succeeded so well botanically that one might think of them as possessed with less political sense than vegetational acumen. In one east-west state unit they succeeded in including the very finest examples of the southern Appalachian high mountain plant communities, which constitute the southern extension of the Canadian balsam fir forest, along with very extensive developments of typical southern low country plant associations, savannas, pocosins, and swamps which range northward from the Gulf. In a very real sense North Carolina, though lying at right angles to the north-south longitudinal lines, unites Canada and Florida within a little over two-thirds of her length. On the same winter days when sub-zero weather and deep snows are holding the Christmas tree forest of balsams and spruces in a death-like silence, the palmetto trees of Smith Island are softly vocal with the summer-like whisperings of warm breezes fresh from the Gulf Stream. John Brickell, early North Carolina naturalist, was correct when he wrote in 1737, 'Of the Plants growing in this Country, I have given an Account of not the hundredth Part of what remains; a Catalog of which would be a Work of many years, and more than the Age of one Man to perfect, or bring into regular classes, this Country being so very large and different in its situation and its Soil.' "

The best way to interpret the flora of a State is to deal with it on a community basis, as the more prominent and stabilized community types are correlated with diverse habitats. Because of the great diversity of climate and soils in North Carolina, the number of these major community types is twice that of a state like Ohio, without mountains or coastal plain, and three times that of one like Iowa, with its still more uniform climatic and soil conditions. North Carolina has a minimum of 17 major distinctive types of plant communities with gradations in space and time existing between them. Some of these are very important economically. Some are distributed widely in the State; others are strictly regional.

Forest communities are found on 18 million acres or 59 per cent of the State area. Of these forest stands, one-half are to be found included in farms. One-third of the forests are of hardwoods, the remainder being in second-growth pine, much of which has come up in abandoned fields which formerly produced cotton.

Rock Community of Lichens and Mosses. These plants, found everywhere on rock exposures, initiate soil-building and give the soft colors to rocks.

Old Field Community of Herbaceous Weeds. These include crabgrass, tall weeds, and the broomsedge grasses. The latter represent a multimillion dollar value, for by their presence erosion is almost completely checked. The thick stands, yellow to reddish in color, add much to the beauty of the North Carolina landscapes everywhere.

Dry Woodland. This community, made up largely of pines (exclusive of longleaf) inevitably follows the broomsedge in the old field succession. Especially is this true in the piedmont and coastal plain. In the former, all even-aged stands of pine, no matter how tall, indicate a former field. Many thousands of acres formerly in cotton are now in pine, chiefly loblolly and short leaf.

These young pine stands are becoming increasingly valuable as the demand for pulpwood grows. The loblolly pine type occupies 26% of all the forest land. Chiefly confined to the coastal plain, it also includes about 640,000 acres in the eastern part of the piedmont.

J. W. Cruikshank, in his survey of forest resources, states: "Shortleaf pine is the major forest type in the piedmont. About half of its 2.3 million acres in the piedmont is stocked chiefly with shortleaf pine, generally of old-field origin. On the remaining half the pine is mixed with white, black, southern red, and scarlet oaks, yellow poplar, and other hardwoods. Eastern red cedar often forms a thin understory in these mixed stands. On the eastern margin of the type, loblolly pine merges with the shortleaf, and on the western border there is an infiltration of Virginia pine. In the mountains shortleaf pine is associated chiefly with Virginia pine, red oaks, white oaks, and chestnut. The relatively few scattered stands of this type in the Coastal Plain resemble in composition those in the piedmont."

This valuable community type is well represented in the 600-acre Duke Forest adjoining the campus of Duke University. It is under intensive study by the Graduate Forestry School of that institution.

Deciduous Forest. Ranging from high mountain slopes to the leeward side of the high dunes, on the coast, this community in the central and eastern regions exists only in second-growth remnants and as cut-over lands in the mountains. Its number of tree species, about 175, exceeds that of all Europe. This was the great climax community type of the eastern United States and is still the largest plant community in North Carolina. It was formerly abundantly represented on the finer sands of the coastal plain.

In North Carolina a number of trees such as the beech, tulip poplar, and white and black oaks range widely from east to west. Others tend to be regional in distribution. The more important mountain species are sweet and yellow birch, buckeye, hemlock, northern red oak, chestnut oak, and chestnut.

The chestnut, a distinctively mountain tree, has undergone mass destruction by a fungous parasite from China. This organism came into the country at New York in 1903 on imported nursery stock. It could not be controlled since it grows just beneath the bark. By 1920 it reached North Carolina where the chestnut on many mountain slopes constituted half of the trees. The dead old trees and the dying shoots which sprouted from their bases are still to be seen everywhere in the mountains.

The piedmont was originally dominated by oak and hickories with an admixture in openings of Virginia pine and shortleaf pine, the former in the upper and the latter in the lower piedmont where the loblolly pine, spilling over from the northern coastal plain, is also prominent. There are no hardwoods which are strictly confined to this physiographic area. The piedmont forest species may be found eastward on the finer drained soils of the coastal plain, especially on the upper terraces. In both the piedmont and coastal plain bottomlands, which are temporarily inundated during the winter and spring, the following large trees are to be seen: river birch, sweet gum, swamp red maple, green ash, elm, sycamore, and hackberry.

In the deciduous forest throughout the State grows the small tree which a few years ago was made the "State Flower"—the dogwood. In an earlier day this plant served as an indicator of fertile soil since it is dependent on a high calcium supply. The pioneers chose their farm sites by the presence of this valuable indicator plant.

Aquatic Community. Submerged plants and those with floating leaves are included here. The greatest development of this community is in the innumerable branches of the great sound estuaries which are of fresh water. In addition to water lilies, the arrow-leaved spatterdock, a yellow water lily, is often to be seen. The beautifully developed Greenfield Lake in the suburbs of Wilmington (*see* WILMINGTON) is especially rich in aquatic plants.

A narrow-leaved species of pond weed which bears nutritious tubers and seeds has made Currituck Sound famous for duck hunting. The birds come here by thousands to feed on this aquatic plant. Occasionally seen is the smallest flowering plant in the world, wolffia, less than a pinhead in size.

Fresh Water Marshes. All shallow water areas along shore lines of fresh water bodies are favorable for the tall cattails and sedges together with many broadleaved plants like the arrowheads and pickerel weed. Large acreages of this type dominate the shallow shore waters of the sound estuaries. This community has taken over all the old areas formerly in rice production in the vicinity of Wilmington.

Wet Woodlands. This community consists of willow and alder, which border water bodies, and river birch, ash, maple, sycamore, and other trees found on the river flood plains. The ash trees are especially in demand.

Swamp Forests. These consist of swamp gum and cypress chiefly, with occasional stands of white cedar. These trees are established only in drouth seasons when the water table drops below the soil surface. Seeds germinate only in contact with air. On the lower sea terraces or eastern half of the coastal plain vast areas were formerly dominated by this community growing on peat. Indian fires, followed by the cutting, drainage, and fires of the white man, have greatly reduced them. Correlated with the high humidity of the swamp air is the frequent presence of the Spanish moss which enhances the eerie aspect of the shadowy forests standing in dark water. One woman, newcomer to the South, upon first encountering the moss-laden trees by moonlight, exclaimed, "Oh! How ghastly!" Before the days of drainage ditches the swamp forests were much more extensive, covering large areas of the flat uplands of the lower coastal plain terraces.

Shrub Bogs. The Indian called these extensive, flat, elevated, peat-soil areas, covered with evergreen shrubs, "pocosins" which interpreted means "upland swamp." The early settlers called them "bays" from the bay trees (3 kinds) common on their borders. The waterlogging in rainy seasons is due to the flat terrain and their non-draining subsoils. In drouth seasons the upland site makes possible a drop of the water table to many feet below, exposing the dry peat to destruction by fire.

The predominant condition, however, is the high soil water, making possible peat accumulation. The organic layer may range from a few inches to many feet thick. Three physiographic types may be recognized: (1) Estuary bays, occupying large former estuaries when the ocean stood at higher levels than at present. Angola and Holly Shelter Bays in Pender County are examples. (2) Branch bays on broad flat uplands at the head of stream branches. The Green Swamp is an example. (3) Carolina Bays, the elliptical depressions scattered by thousands over the coastal plain of North and South Carolina. About 20 species of shrubs have survived fire and become adapted to the extreme changes in soil water content. Cyrilla, Zenobia cane or reed (Arundinaria) and the fetterbush are most common. The loblolly bay with its large thick leaves and large flowers is the showiest of all the bog species. It is a small tree readily regenerating after fire. It stands above the general shrub level and does much to break the general monotony of the lower shrub mass. Climbing far and spreading yards over the dense vegetation is the famous blaspheme-vine (Smilax laurifolia), the nemesis of hunters. Without a machete, a man cannot break through it, where it is abundant.

This community type makes up a large part of the Dismal Swamp, great areas in Tyrell, Dare, and Hyde counties, the Open Grounds of Carteret County, White Oak pocosin in Jones and Onslow counties, Angola and Holly Shelter Bays in Duplin, Pender and New Hanover counties, and the Great Green "Swamp" in Brunswick County.

It is believed that most of these larger areas were formerly in swamp forests dominated by the swamp gum tree (Nyssa biflora). With the coming of the Indian and his carelessness with fire, followed by the white man and his frequent "accidental" fires, they have lost many feet of peat, and the vegetation has changed to the shrub-bog type.

Savannas. In this classification are the perennial herbaceous plants which grow in upland non-draining mineral soil. They are developed on the lower terraces. Toothache grass dominates the savannas on fine sand soils, while wire-grass (same species of the sandhills) dominates the coarse sand areas. Associated with the former are an unusual number of beautiful wild flowers, including orchids. Also present are numerous insectivorous plants, trumpets, pitcher plants, sundews, and the remarkable Venus's Fly-trap.

The Venus's Fly-trap. Darwin's reaction to this plant was to call it "the most wonderful plant in the world." And Linnaeus earlier wrote, "Though I have seen and examined no small number of plants, I must confess I never met with so wonderful a phenomenon." Each half of the round leaf blade is equipped with three trigger hairs. Upon being touched by an insect or spider, an impulse is carried to the cells of the leaf which, by a sudden change in the relative internal osmotic pressures of the upper and under sides, brings about a quick closing of the leaf on the small animal victim. Digestion follows through the secretion of enzymes. The fly-traps are found only in North and South Carolina, being confined in numbers to an area designated by a 75-mile radius of Wilmington. The largest number of the plants are in North Carolina. They are to be looked for in the transition zones from shrub-bog to savanna or in the open savannas, especially those dominated by wire grass (Aristida stricta). The best time to find them is in late May when the cluster of white flowers on a foot-high stalk may be easily observed.

The savannas are fire made. Most of them, especially the larger ones, were once covered by swamp forest growing on peat. Indian fires in dry periods reduced them first to shrub-bogs. Under continuing and frequent fire these were in turn reduced to savannas. Perennial herbs, with their underground stems protected by the mineral soil, may persist indefinitely or as long as the fires persist.

Salt Marshes. In this category are narrow-leaved grasses, rushes, and other herbs with roots adapted to living in the 3 per cent salt concentration of ocean water. The commonest grass is the salt or cord grass which dominates the deeper water areas; in contrast, a tall, dark-gray rush forms solid stands in the shallower water. The boundary between them is always a sharp one. A great salt marsh lies on the south side of Roanoke Island. The salt marsh vegetation builds peat as fast as the ocean rises. Such peat has been found to reach a depth of 40 feet on the North River shore of Currituck County, indicating a continuous rise of the sea in recent millennia.

Sandhill Community. One has but to mention two winter resort centers, Pinehurst and Southern Pines, to locate the most extensive appearance of this community. The pine included in the names of the towns referred to, is the longleaf pine, a species which in beauty and the practical consideration of fire resistance, surpasses all the eastern United States pines. Associated with it and occurring in pure stand where the pines have been removed is the fork-leaved black-jack and turkey oak. Associated with both of these trees and widely spread throughout the sandhills are the tussocks of the narrow-leaved wiregrass, one of the poverty grasses.

The key to the sandhills is the simple fact that these rolling uplands carry a soil made of loose, porous, coarse sand. As a continuous area the sandhills involve parts of Lee, Harnett, Moore, Cumberland, Richmond, Hoke, and Scotland counties. There are many local areas to the southeast of the main sandhill region, one of the largest being on the ancient elevated shoals extending both north and south of Wilmington.

The interest in the sandhills as a resort area is in part related to the porosity of the soil. Rain is so quickly absorbed that minutes after a heavy precipitation one may go afield without concern about wet feet. The second-growth longleaf pines present such a unique and green-in-winter landscape that the northern visitor finds the sandhills a land of enchantment.

Agriculturally the great feature of this area are the extensive peach orchards which are grown on this normally sterile soil with the aid of fertilizers. So numerous are these orchards that the western side of the sandhills becomes a show place at peach blossom time.

The middle and eastern sandhills of coarse sandy non-agricultural lands is the location of the large military reservation, Fort Bragg.

Seaside or Salt-spray Community. No one who has been down to the sea can have failed to have seen the streamlined asymmetric form the shrubs and trees have assumed where they are close to the strand. Their compact upsloping surfaces make them appear to be trimmed or trained by the sea winds. But this concept has recently been proved erroneous. These shrubs have been pruned by the salt spray carried in the dry higher winds. New upward-growing branches appear as though scorched, due to the chlorine toxicity. Only certain species of shrubs can tolerate this peculiar habitat. The ones most frequently seen are wax myrtle, yaupon, and waterbush. Beyond them, in the slightly weaker spray zone, the live oak tree is the only one that can survive the recurrent salt treatment. None of the woody plants mentioned can stand the high salt spray intensity of the dunes immediately next to the sea. Here the sea oats, one of our most beautiful grasses, takes over. This species has evolved a remarkable assemblage of adaptive structures which keeps the salt out of the internal tissues, even though these plants are literally bathed in salt water whenever ordinary winds blow from the sea. The grass is recognized by its large panicle of showy pale yellow spikelets.

Balsam-Spruce Community. This cold-adapted forest, dominated by Frazer's balsam and red spruce—trees closely related to the boreal forest trees of Canada—is strictly confined to the low temperature areas of the higher mountain tops and upper slopes. These areas are also ones of high precipitation, making them cold and wet, a combination which results in an acid bog type of soil, especially where the hylocomium moss has developed a thick soft mat between the trees. The high trails through the balsam-spruce woods are the most enjoyable to ride or hike over. Always the air is cool and humid. Everywhere the dark recesses and the trees contrast most amazingly with glimpses of sky above. The mossy forest floor in midsummer may be decorated with innumerable flowers of the purple wood sorrel and a delicate white violet. And a most subtle fragrance is noticeable if there is not too much wind. Days spent on the high trails are not soon forgotten.

Fire Cherry and Red Elder. On the high mountain tops and the contiguous high altitude slopes, where lumbering and fire have removed the balsam-spruce community or the high-altitude deciduous forest, the fire or pin cherry trees appear as though from nowhere from the still viable long-buried seeds. Both are frequently seen along the Blue Ridge Parkway.

High Mountain Shrub Bald. Perhaps the most gorgeous natural scene which the tourist may encounter in eastern North America is a rhododendron bald in bloom in early June. The bushes are almost hidden by the masses of large rose-colored flowers. These balds are not infrequent along the Parkway and make an unforgettable impression. Other less showy shrubs such as laurel and hazelnut may dominate a bald, and blueberries are of frequent occurrence. The rhododendrons are commonly in such dense stand that the mountain people call such balds "slicks." They are notable communities for having under them the most acid of all soils in the eastern United States. It is not clear how this community type came to replace the original forest.

High Mountain Grass Balds. When the first white men ascended the higher ridges, they were amazed to emerge suddenly from the dense forest into what appeared as local pastures. Found in widely scattered places, these pastures were covered with a luscious growth of mountain oat grass, under which was a deep loam sod entirely different from the nearby forest soil. From them excellent views of neighboring ranges may be had. In midsummer the stately turkcap lily enlivens them with color. Andrew's bald near Clingman's Dome in the Smoky Mountain National Park is one of these. Most of them are on gentle slopes and have springs at their bases. Trails leading to them will also be covered with oat grass. It thus appears that these original grassy areas are expanded trails or summer Indian village sites of the early hunter Indian. He profoundly upset the ordinary succession of pin cherry trees, and when he finally abandoned the country, the mountain oat grass took over and held the area against the forest.

CAPE HATTERAS LIGHTHOUSE, OUTER BANKS   JOCKEY'S RIDGE, NAGS HEAD

VILLAGE OF RODANTHE, OUTER BANKS

AERIAL VIEW OF FORT MACON, NEAR MOREHEAD CITY AND BEAUFORT (DAN W. WADE)

PONY PENNING, SHACKLEFORD BANKS

INTRACOASTAL WATERWAY

BIG PINNACLE, PILOT MOUNTAIN

LONG-LEAF PINE AND DOGWOOD, NEAR PINEHURST

LAKE LURE FROM CHIMNEY ROCK (ASHEVILLE CHAMBER OF COMMERCE)

MOUNTAIN FARM, HAYWOOD COUNTY

MOUNT MITCHELL FRAMED IN RHODODENDRON

GRANDFATHER MOUNTAIN FROM LINVILLE

MILE-HIGH SWINGING BRIDGE ATOP GRANDFATHER MOUNTAIN (HUGH MORTON)

WHITEWATER FALLS, NEAR BREVARD

FOREST RESOURCES

ALTHOUGH NORTH CAROLINA has been an important agricultural state since early colonial time, more than half of the land area of the State is now in timber. Forty-one of North Carolina's 100 counties have more than 60 per cent of their land area covered with trees and only 9 counties have less than 40 per cent of their area in wooded land. Forests, therefore, are widely distributed and the amount of land in trees is one of the features of the State that impresses visitors from other parts of the country.

Almost two-thirds of the timber in these forest lands is softwood, largely pine, but there is also some cypress and cedar. The deciduous hardwoods were the predominant trees in the original forests which covered the State in pre-colonial days. These forests were destroyed by the early settlers as they prepared the land for farming. Much of the land now in pine was at one time under cultivation, and the pines represent an early stage in a natural regeneration of the original forest types.

The forests of North Carolina cover more than 18 million acres, only about 6 per cent of which is owned by the federal government. More than half of the non-federal forest land is attached to farms. The value of all the timber suitable for lumber is estimated to be 875 million dollars. The timber cut in 1952 alone was valued at 64 million dollars.

In 1952 the value of the plants and equipment devoted to forest product industries in North Carolina was 178 million dollars. These industries employed 18 per cent of all the people engaged in manufacturing in the State and payrolls totalled 255 million dollars. The value of the output of the forest product industries in this same year was 773 million dollars, a production figure exceeded only by the value of the products of the textile and tobacco industries of the State. North Carolina now ranks sixth among the states in lumber production and first in the manufacture of wooden furniture and first in the production of hardwood veneers and plywood.

The forests of western North Carolina contain a much higher percentage of the deciduous hardwoods than the timber lands of the east. In the early years of the twentieth century there were many magnificent chestnut trees in the forests on the mountain slopes. These are now completely eliminated as a forest resource by a fungous disease introduced from Asia. The gaunt skeletons of these great trees are still conspicuous in the mountain forests. The dead chestnut trees are used as a source of tannin and pulpwood. When cut and polished, the worm-eaten wood of these dead chestnuts makes very attractive panelling which is prized for its decorative features.

The paper industry is rapidly becoming a major consumer of forest products of North Carolina. In 1952 the value of the paper products manufactured in this State was 244 million dollars. The soil and the climate of eastern and central North Carolina are exceptionally favorable for the growth of loblolly pine. This tree reaches pulpwood size in 15-20 years and provides the chief source of pulpwood for the growing kraft paper industry.

There are three large national forests in North Carolina in each of which facilities are provided for visitors who wish to hunt, fish, hike, or merely to enjoy the scenery.

Croatan National Forest consists of 146,831 acres located only a few miles from the Atlantic Ocean. It contains 5 large lakes and has two improved forest camps and picnic grounds. Deer, bear, turkey, quail, and migratory bird hunting are permitted at proper seasons of the year.

Nantahala National Forest in the western mountains contains 386,161 acres, 7 lakes and the famous Fontana Dam. Some 80 miles of the Appalachian Trail fall within the forest boundaries. Lake and stream fishing, hiking, boating, and swimming are all available. There are 8 improved forest camps and picnic grounds. The azaleas and rhododendrons provide spectacular color in the late spring.

Pisgah National Forest is also in the mountains and is the largest of the three national forests of the State. Hunting in season and fishing, hiking, and swimming are all possible. There are 18 improved forest camps and picnic sites for visitors. The display of color when the rhododendrons of Pisgah Forest are in flower is famous for its beauty.

WILD ANIMALS

THE EARLY mammalian wildlife of North Carolina was as abundant and diversified as anywhere in the eastern United States. Even the woods bison and elk were encountered as far east as the lower coastal plain. The extensive fresh-water estuaries made North Carolina notable for untold numbers of waterfowl and whaling was an important industry for many years. The abundance of animal life in the "Old North State" is illustrated by the following estimates: mammals 89, birds 364, insects 11,094, arthropods other than insects 816, mollusks 422, fish 418, and reptiles 72.

A recent publication by the North Carolina Wildlife Resources Commission entitled "Tarheel Wildlife" (1953) summarizes the present status of most of the game animals. The more important of these will be dealt with briefly.

Whitetail Deer. Due to restocking activities and increased protection, the deer population is growing, but it is still far short of reaching the number which could be maintained on the non-agricultural areas. Some 50,000—60,000 deer are in the State with but a fifth of them in the mountain region. The piedmont Uharie Refuge in Montgomery and Stanly counties has about 1000 and the rest are in the sandhills and the isolated swamps and shrub-bogs of the coastal plain.

Black Bear. This game animal has a distribution very similar to that of the deer. The total population is estimated at close to 4,000, the big majority of them again in the east.

The Wild Boar. An introduced species (1912) from Europe, some 150 of these game animals are now wild in Graham County together with a number of small herds in Polk and Clay counties.

Beaver. Formerly widespread over the State as indicated by the number of "Beaver Creeks," this animal was extirpated shortly after 1900. As a result of recent introductions from Pennsylvania there are now about 500 individuals present. They may be seen in the Sandhills Wildlife Management Area in Richmond County.

Wildcat. Formerly ubiquitous, this predator has steadily diminished in numbers. It is now found primarily in the more inaccessible areas of the mountains and coastal plain. As many as 8 to 10 wildcats are trapped each year on the Holly Shelter Refuge in Pender County.

Mink and Otter. Though greatly reduced in numbers the mink may still be trapped throughout the State. The otter, however, is now confined to the coastal plain, being more common along the borders of the estuaries.

Muskrat. To be found throughout the State, this valuable fur bearer is found in greatest concentration in the marshes of Currituck Sound. Here the animal catch is over 30,000, which is one-third of the State's total.

Skunk. The spotted skunk is strictly confined to the mountains, but the striped one is to be found in the mountains, the southern piedmont, and the coastal plain. They are scarce throughout most of the State.

Raccoon and Opossum. Both of these animals range throughout the State but the distribution is spotty. Restocking has been practiced in the case of the raccoon with numbers of animals being brought in from other states.

Foxes. The gray fox is to be found throughout the State. The red fox, a non-native, has been introduced into mountain and piedmont counties and into two in the coastal plain. Fox hunting is a well organized sport.

Rabbits and Squirrels. These small game animals are still abundant in all parts of the State. The spectacular fox squirrel is most common in the sandhills and adjoining coastal plain counties. The garrulous red squirrel or "boomer" is restricted to the mountain counties.

Waterfowl. One of the greatest over-wintering grounds for waterfowl on the continent is found in the broad fresh water estuaries of the sounds. In Currituck Sound one of the pondweeds called sago, which produces highly nutritious seeds and tubers, grows from a depth of 9 feet and in such luxuriance as to support an amazing number of ducks and geese. This sound has always been noted among hunters for its variety and number of birds. However, in days of the colonists, the records indicate millions of fowl kept the daytime sky heavily traced with their flock movements from one feeding ground to another. Before bag limit laws were passed two men were reported as having killed 4 Canada geese, 5 swan, 75 canvasbacks, and 892 ruddy ducks in one day on Currituck Sound.

In addition to the estuaries a number of lakes on the low lying Pamlico sea terrace attract large numbers of birds. The largest and best known is Lake Mattamuskeet in Hyde County (*see* TOUR *14*). For a period between 1909 and 1933 an unfortunate attempt was made to farm the lake bottom after the water was pumped at great expense over a "dike" into the ocean. Some 17 million dollars were lost in the venture. Today, with the aid of the new owner, the Federal government, the ducks and geese are back, and the old pumping plant has been remodeled into a hunter's lodge with a look-out platform on the chimney from which one may get an excellent view over the 50,000 acres of water.

One of the most interesting bodies of water in the world in relation to wildfowl is the Gaddy Pond in Anson County, a mere 4 acres (*see* TOUR *10*). Here 10,000 Canadian geese visit each year with most of them remaining through the winter. With infinite patience and a few pecks of corn, Mr. Lockhart Gaddy, in 1938, so gained the confidence of 9 of these geese that they would come near him. Others came and still others acquired the same confidence until at the present time, in the winter, hundreds of visitors can feed these wild geese as one feeds door-yard chickens on a farm. Mrs. Gaddy, who is continuing the project, charges a small fee to help defray the cost of the tons of corn necessary to carry the geese through the winter until their migration to Canada in March.

In addition to the open water feeders are the rails, gallinules, and soras which inhabit the vast eastern shore marshes. The clapper rail or marsh hen is the most common, being extensively hunted in the salt marshes of the southeast. Soras and marsh hens live in the fresh water marshes and are the two most hunted marsh species. Widely distributed along river courses is the wood duck which is reported as increasing in numbers. It is now probably present in every county.

The following waterfowl have been reported within the State:

Whistling Swan	American Golden-eye
Canada Goose	Buffle-head
Snow Goose	Ruddy Duck
Blue Goose	Baldpate
American Brant	Green-winged Teal
Mallard	Blue-winged Teal
Black Duck	Shoveler
Redhead	Pintail
Greater Scaup	Wood Duck
Lesser Scaup	Canvasback
Ring-necked Duck	Old Squaw
White-winged Scoter	Hooded Merganser
Surf Scoter	Red-breasted Merganser
American Scoter	American Merganser

Upland Game Birds. Quail occurs throughout the State but is more abundant east of the mountains. The wild turkey in greatly reduced numbers is to be found largely in the eastern half of the State. So few are there that county by county estimates are made with only a few reporting as many as 300. The latest total for the State is about 8,000. The ruffed grouse, a cyclic species, formerly ranged as far east as Person County but is now totally confined to the mountain region where it is abundant. The mourning dove is found in greatest numbers in the piedmont.

No less than 364 kinds of birds have been recorded for North Carolina. Because of the State's geographic location the number of migrants crossing in spring and fall is large, especially warblers and shorebirds. A few of the more interesting species, in addition to the waterfowl already mentioned, are the bald eagle, great blue heron, oyster-catcher, laughing gull, common tern, black skimmer, hummingbird, pileated woodpecker, purple martin, raven, prothonotary warbler, bobolink, and painted bunting. The mockingbird is common everywhere, and other beautiful singers are the veery in the mountains and the wood thrush at the lower elevations. All sections of the State are rich in bird life at all seasons of the year. The Carolina Bird Club is composed of 1400 members, publishes a quarterly magazine, *The Chat,* and can be reached through the State Museum in Raleigh.

Fishes. In addition to over 300 miles of ocean along the banks, the State has unusually extensive fisheries in the sounds and their estuaries, the long river courses, the natural lakes of the coastal plain, and the rapidly growing number of farm ponds.

Non-food Fish. Of greatest importance commercially are the non-food fish, especially the menhaden. These account for one-half of the fisherman's income. The menhaden is a plankton feeder and migrates in great schools along the coast in the spring and fall. The fishermen in two small power boats throw a long net around the school, followed by a concentration of the fish when the nets are taken in. On the large boat which now comes alongside is a huge dip net which scoops the fish a ton at a time. It is not infrequent to capture 400,000 fish from a single school. It is estimated that over 200 million menhaden are processed annually from which not only the valuable oil is extracted but other concentrates like Vitamin D.

Food and Game Fish. The principal food fish are: trout, flounder, croaker, spot, white perch, mullet, mackerel, bluefish, white shad, herring or alewives, butterfish, pompano, striped and channel bass. To be mentioned in addition are the game fish: dolphin, amberjack, sailfish, and red drum. Following the fish schools and frequently entering the sounds and river mouths is the mammalian porpoise.

Shellfish. Among the invertebrate sea animals which are erroneously classified as shellfish, the shrimp easily leads in financial yield. This crustacean is caught by small trawlers dragging nets along the offshore bottoms. One species is a night feeder which necessitates all-night fishing. Oysters have been increasing in recent years, the North Carolina sound waters having been found to be very favorable for their development. Large numbers of clams and crabs also contribute to the income of the approximately 7,000 fishermen active on the State's coast.

Reptiles. Though of little economic importance, mention should be made of the huge loggerhead sea turtles which regularly visit the unoccupied beaches chiefly south of Cape Lookout for the purpose of laying their complement of some 200 soft shelled, golf-ball-like eggs just beyond the strand. These are deposited in a cylindrically shaped hole and carefully covered with sand after which the turtle returns to the sea. Once having begun the egg laying, the animal is not disturbed by the presence of men. These turtles range from 250-500 pounds when mature. Their prominent tracks up the strand at night are easily noted and the female turtle located. A favorite nesting ground is the east-facing Bald Head Island beach. In the fresh water estuaries in the Wilmington region alligators are still to be found. Regarding poisonous snakes it may be stated that the coastal plain has four (rattlesnake, copperhead, water moccasin, and coral snake), the piedmont one (copperhead), and the mountains two (rattlesnake and copperhead). The incidence of death by snake bite is very low, yet the tourist in going into rough country east or west should still be snake conscious.

B. W. WELLS
Professor of Botany
N. C. State College

EXPLORATIONS AND ATTEMPTS
AT SETTLEMENT

THE FIRST European who is known to have explored the coast of what is now North Carolina was Giovanni da Verrazzano, a Florentine navigator in the service of France. In 1524 he explored the Cape Fear coast and on July 8 of that year sent to King Francis I the "earliest description known to exist of the Atlantic coast north of Cape Fear." Verrazzano described the country, with its "faire fields and plains," its temperate climate and "good and wholesome aire," its trees which were "greater and better than any in Europe," and its "sweet and odoriferous flowers," its great bounty of game and fowl of every kind, and its natives who were "charmed by their first sight of white men." He concluded that the country was "as pleasant and delectable to behold, as is possible to imagine."

Despite this glowing report of North Carolina's first press agent, France was too busily engaged in European politics, diplomacy, and war to colonize the region.

Spanish Exploration. In July, 1526, Lucas Vásquez de Ayllón, Spanish official, slave trader, and explorer, led an expedition from Santo Domingo to the Carolina coastal area. His party, which consisted of over 500 men and women, a few Negro slaves, and 89 horses, entered the "Río Jordan" (most likely the Cape Fear) and attempted to plant a colony. But the large number of deaths from fever and starvation caused Ayllón to move the colony southward to a place called San Miguel, in present South Carolina. But disease and starvation continued to take their toll, and after Ayllón's death on Oct. 18 the colony, now reduced to about 150 persons, returned to the West Indies.

In 1540 an expedition led by Hernando de Soto, marching from Florida in quest of "gold-bearing mountains" which the Indians told him were to be found to the north, penetrated the mountains of southwestern North Carolina in present Jackson, Macon, Clay, and Cherokee counties, and on his trip westward crossed the Little Tennessee River, the first Mississippi tributary discovered by Europeans. In 1561 Angel de Villafañe led a Spanish expedition from Vera Cruz as far north as Cape Hatteras, but this expedition was "driven in distress" to Santo Domingo. In 1566-67 an expedition led by Juan Pardo and Hernán Boyano marched from the Gulf region to the mountains of North Carolina.

Neither the French nor Spanish planted a permanent colony, and so the Carolina country was left to the Indians and to eventual colonization by the English.

The First English Colony in the New World. The first English colony planted in the New World was sent out by Walter Raleigh, soldier, courtier, historian, poet, and recipient of lands and other favors from Queen Elizabeth. Although his efforts to "plant the English nation" in America were doomed to failure, "the idea remained," and Raleigh has been justly called the "Father of English America," and Roanoke Island "the birthplace of English America." On March 25, 1584, Raleigh obtained a patent from Queen Elizabeth conveying to him, his heirs, and assigns the title to any lands that he might discover "not actually possessed of any Christian prince, nor inhabited by Christian people." Raleigh was authorized to plant colonies and to establish a government, in which the settlers were to have "all the priviledges of free Denizens, and persons native of England," but no laws could be passed "repugnant to the laws of England."

On April 27, 1584, Raleigh sent out an expedition under Capt. Philip Amadas and Arthur Barlowe to explore the country and to select a site for settlement. Early in July, after a voyage of 67 days, the expedition reached the North Carolina coast, and a few days later came to an island "which the Indians called Roanoke." After two months, spent in exploring and trading with the natives, the expedition returned to England, taking with them two "lusty men, whose names were Wanchese and Manteo." Soon after their arrival in England, Barlowe wrote a glowing report to Raleigh, describing the soil as "the most plentifull, sweete, fruitful and wholsome of all the world," containing the "highest and reddest Cedars of the world," and inhabited by "the most gentle, very handsome and goodly people," who were "loving and faithful, voide of all guile and treason, and such as live after the manner of the golden age."

Barlowe's report was received enthusiastically by Raleigh, Queen Elizabeth, and others interested in "planting the English nation" in the

New World. Raleigh was knighted and the new land christened "Virginia," in honor of the unmarried Queen.

The Ralph Lane Colony, 1585-1586. In 1585 Raleigh sent out his first colony, with Ralph Lane as "lieutenant governor" and Richard Grenville in command of the squadron of "seven ships well stocked and manned." Among the 108 men were John White, a "skilful painter"; Thomas Hariot, a learned mathematician and scientist; Thomas Cavendish, who later circumnavigated the globe, as well as apothecaries, a physician, and a clergyman. The rank and file of the "Roanoke Hundred" had probably served in the army.

On Aug. 17, 1585, the expedition arrived at Roanoke Island, where Lane soon built "Fort Raleigh." The colony was beset with problems from the start. It suffered from friction among the leaders, Indian hostility, and scarcity of food, tools, and articles necessary to establish settlement on a sound basis. Too much time was spent in looking for gold and too little in building houses and growing crops. By the spring of 1586 "supplies" were perilously low, and the colony was faced with famine. At this critical juncture, Francis Drake's fleet appeared and took the whole group back to England.

Within a month after the colony's departure, three English ships, outfitted by Raleigh and commanded by Grenville, arrived with supplies and additional men. Grenville searched in vain for the settlers and then set sail for England, leaving behind 15 men "furnished plentifully with all manner of provisions for two years," in order to hold England's claim to the country.

Though this colony had failed, it was not without historical significance. Besides being the first English colony in the New World, it resulted in Hariot's informative book about "Virginia" and in 75 famous paintings of Indian life by John White.

The "Lost Colony." In April, 1587, Raleigh, "intending to persevere in the planting of his Country of Virginia," sent out another colony headed by John White as governor. This group, which consisted of over 100 settlers, including 17 women and 9 children, was instructed to go by Roanoke Island, pick up the 15 men left there by Grenville, and proceed to Chesapeake Bay to establish a fort and settlement.

When White reached Roanoke Island he found the houses built by Lane still standing, the fort in ruins, but no signs of the 15 men left by Grenville. According to White's narrative—our only source of information—Fernández, the commander of the fleet, refused to transport the colony to the Chesapeake. Whereupon Gov. White put his men to work rebuilding the fort and "repayring houses and building new ones."

By August of that year supplies had begun to run low, and White was "constrayned to returne into England." After being detained in England by the war then raging with Spain, White returned to Roanoke Island in 1590 to find his colony gone. There was no trace except a few broken pieces of armor, the word CROATOAN carved on a tree, and the letters CRO on another tree.

The two best-known incidents in the life of the "Lost Colony" were the baptism of Manteo—the first recorded Protestant baptismal service in the New World, and the birth, on Aug. 18, 1587, of White's granddaughter, Virginia Dare, the first child born in America of English parents.

The Fate of the "Lost Colony." What happened to the "Lost Colony" is an intriguing and apparently unanswerable question. Some writers have contended that the settlers—or a majority of them—were killed by the Indians; others that they mingled with the natives and that the so-called Croatans of present-day Robeson County are their descendants. Still others have maintained that the Spaniards from Florida destroyed the colony, and there is ample documentary evidence to indicate that Spanish officials at St. Augustine, Fla., planned to do just that. One of the most plausible theories—though seldom advanced—is that the colonists, finally despairing of relief, sailed for England in a boat which had been left with them by White in 1587 and were lost at sea.

Exploration and Settlement of the Albemarle Sound Region. Soon after the failure of the Roanoke Island ventures, the first permanent English colony was planted at Jamestown, Va., in 1607. Within a few years most of the good land close to navigable streams was taken up. The desire for "fertile bottom lands" and fresh hunting grounds caused explorers, hunters, traders, and farmers to follow the streams of southeastern Virginia into the Chowan River–Albemarle Sound area. This movement was a gradual process, and the exact date of its beginning is obscure.

The first recorded expedition was made by John Pory, speaker of the historic Virginia legislature of 1619 and secretary of that colony, who, in 1622, traveled overland as far south as the Chowan River through a "very fruitful and pleasant Country, yielding two harvests in a yeere." This region was already attracting some attention in England, for on Oct. 30, 1629, Sir Robert Heath, the Attorney General of Charles I, was granted "A certaine Region or Territory" between 31 and 36 degrees north latitude, and from sea to sea, which was to be incorporated into the "Province of Carolina" (Land of Charles). Heath failed to settle his grant, but traders meanwhile continued to come into Carolina from Virginia. In 1653 Roger Green of Nansemond County,

Va., obtained from the legislature of that colony a grant of 10,000 acres for the first 100 persons who "should first seat on the Roanoke and on the lands of the south side of the Chowan." Green was to get 1,000 acres "as a reward." Documentary evidence fails to show that this project materialized, though some writers have said that it did and have dated the permanent settlement of North Carolina from 1653.

The oldest recorded land grant in North Carolina was made to George Durant, March 1, 1662, by King Kilcocanen, King of the Yeopim Indians, for a tract of land in present Perquimans County. There had been some grants before this date, for this deed refers to previous land sales.

A PROPRIETARY COLONY, 1663-1729

IN 1660, CHARLES II was "restored" to the English throne, largely through the efforts of a few loyal friends, who held high positions in the Government and in the army. In 1663, 8 of these men applied to the King for a grant of all the land claimed by England south of Virginia. On April 3, 1663, Charles II granted them the territory of Carolina, with the same boundaries as those in the Heath grant mentioned above.

The 8 grantees of Carolina were distinguished men. Edward Hyde, Earl of Clarendon, was Lord High Chancellor and the King's first minister; George Monck, newly created Duke of Albemarle, was master of the King's Horse and Captain General of all his forces; and Anthony Ashley-Cooper was Chancellor of the Exchequer. William, Earl of Craven, Sir George Carteret, Sir John Colleton, Sir William Berkeley, and John, Lord Berkeley, also held important positions. The Proprietors were given control of the land, paying only a nominal rent of "twenty marks of lawful money of England" annually. They were also granted authority to establish a government, but laws were to be enacted only with the "advice, assent and approbation of the freemen, or the greater part of them, and of their delegates."

When the Proprietors learned that their charter did not include settlements already made in the Albemarle Sound region, they asked for and procured a new charter, in 1665. This extended the boundaries of Carolina 30 minutes northward and two degrees southward—far into Spanish Florida, thus making the new boundaries 36° 30′ to 29° and west to the Pacific Ocean.

Proprietary Plans for Three "Counties." The Proprietors planned to develop three counties: Albemarle, Clarendon (in the Cape Fear region), and Craven (in the present South Carolina area). These counties were to have governors, legislatures, and courts. Their subdivisions were to be "precincts," which would be comparable to our present "counties." Albemarle was the first of the three counties to be settled and the first to have a governor, William Drummond, and a legislature. Clarendon County lasted only a few years (1664-67), and Craven County was beyond the bounds of present North Carolina. From 1667 to 1689, the only organized government in what is now North Carolina was the County of Albemarle.

The Troubled History of Albemarle County. To encourage settlement of their "fair and spacious Province," the Proprietors offered land grants of 100 acres to freemen and lesser amounts to servants at the expiration of their indentures, the right of the people to participate in law making, and many other inducements; and the Albemarle Assembly of 1669 passed laws designed to stimulate immigration and otherwise promote the colony's welfare. Tax exemption was granted to all "newcomers" for one year's stay of all suits "on any debt or other cause of action" which had arisen outside the colony.

The history of Albemarle County is a story of unrest, confusion, slow growth, and even armed rebellion. The Proprietors were unhappy because the colony grew slowly and was unprofitable, while the settlers felt that the Proprietors neglected the colony. Land titles were not clear. The British Navigation Acts interfered with trade and were a factor in causing the Culpeper Rebellion, in which the people deposed the governor and put in office men of their own choosing. The failure of the Proprietors to establish a strong, stable, and efficient government was a great handicap to the growth and progress of Albemarle. Some of its governors were weak and ineffective, some were unscrupulous, most were unsatisfactory. Hence the governors failed to preserve order, promote the welfare of the people, or defend the colony against Indians and pirates. No less than 5 Albemarle governors were deposed, in one way or another, and Seth Sothel, a Proprietor and the last governor of Albemarle County, was accused by the Assembly of numerous crimes, was tried, convicted, and banished in 1689. His successor, Philip Ludwell, was appointed governor of Carolina "north and east of Cape feare."

From 1689 to 1712 the government of the North Carolina region was administered by a deputy appointed by the "Governor of Carolina," Edward Tynte, who resided in Charleston. Each region had its separate legislature, and gradually the terms "North Carolina" and "South Carolina" came into use. In 1712 Edward Hyde became the first governor of "North Carolina separate from Carolina."

The Indians. There were perhaps 30,000 to 35,000 Indians in North Carolina at the time white settlement began, and John Lawson listed 29 tribes in 1709. Of the various tribes, only 5 have been of particular significance in North Carolina history: the Hatteras, with whom the whites had their first contact; the Chowanoc, with whom the settlers had their first war, though a minor one; the Tuscarora, the largest and most warlike tribe of eastern North Carolina, numbering some 6,000 to 8,000 people, with whom the whites had the most deadly Indian war in North Carolina history; the Catawba; and the Cherokee. The latter tribe, or confederacy, numbered perhaps 20,000 in early years and as late as 1735 had "sixty-four towns and villages, populous and full of children."

How the Indians Lived. The unit of Indian society was the tribe or "nation," apparently based on blood relationships. Each tribe had a chief or head man, sometimes called a king. The Indians usually lived in "villages" or "towns." In some tribes, they had houses or huts; in others, they lived in tents made of animal skins tied or woven together and usually round. Cooking was crude and primitive. Meat was placed upon sharp sticks and broiled over the fire, and roasting food in hot ashes was a prevalent practice.

In many of the tribes the women did most of the planting, cultivating, and harvesting of crops. They also cooked, made clothes, wove mats and baskets from grass, reeds, and rushes, and cared for the children. Farm implements were crude affairs usually formed from wood or bone. The Indians grew corn, potatoes, beans, peas, and many other vegetables.

The primary pursuits of Indian men were hunting, fishing, and fighting. They hunted with bows and arrows, tomahawks, spears, knives, and clubs, and later with guns procured from white traders. Boats were made of trees, hollowed out by burning and referred to by whites as "dugouts."

At first relations between Indians and whites were relatively peaceful. But the aggressive attitude of the whites and the resentment of the natives made hostilities inevitable. The whites taught the natives the use of "firewater" (whiskey), introduced among them smallpox and other "white men's diseases," enslaved many of their children, and "debauced their women."

Indian Contributions. The Indians made many contributions to white civilization. They taught the whites the methods of clearing land, hill cultivation, and fertilization, and contributed such crops as corn, tobacco, potatoes, various vegetables, and many varieties of fruits. Cultural contributions were made by the natives in the form of Indian words, myths, legends, and traditions. A permanent influence has been the preservation of hundreds of beautiful Indian place names—rivers, towns, and counties (20 of the present 100). Except for the Cherokee, the Indians have disappeared from North Carolina, but "their name is on your waters—ye may not wash it out."

Growth and Expansion of the Colony. After 1700 settlers began to move into the colony at a more rapid rate. On March 8, 1705 (old style calendar), the Assembly incorporated the town of Bath, the first town in North Carolina. In 1710 New Bern was founded by a group of several hundred German Palatines, along with some Swiss and English, under the leadership of Christoph Von Graffenried (or De Graffenried), head of a Swiss land company, and John Lawson, surveyor-general of the colony. Edenton and Beaufort were begun about the same time, but were not incorporated until 1722. Brunswick, near the mouth of the Cape Fear, was founded about 1727, and Wilmington a few years later.

Just as the colony began to expand and prosper, 4 serious problems arose to retard its growth: the fight over the Established Church, which culminated in the Cary Rebellion; the Tuscarora War of 1711-13; the great increase of piracy along the coast; and the boundary controversy with Virginia.

The immediate cause of the Tuscarora War may be traced to the settlement of New Bern. The dissension and internal weakness of the colony resulting from the Cary Rebellion provided an opportune moment for the Indians to launch an all-out attack. On Sept. 22, 1711, the Tuscaroras attacked white settlements from the Neuse to the Pamlico. Hundreds of whites were killed, and the whole area was "totally wasted and ruined." Gov. Hyde called on Virginia and South Carolina for aid. The latter colony voted money and men. With over 500 men, largely Indians, Col. John ("Tuscarora Jack") Barnwell marched 300 miles through the wilderness and defeated the Tuscaroras in two battles near New Bern, in Jan., 1712. A "truce was patched up," but within less than a year the Indians rose again. This time, a large expedition from South Carolina, headed by Col. James Moore, won a "glorious victory" at Fort Nohoroco on Contentnea Creek, March 25, 1713. The power of the Tuscarora in North Carolina was broken by this decisive defeat. King Tom Blunt and the "friendly Tuscaroras" were rewarded for their neutrality by being given a large tract of land, later known as "Indian Woods," located in present Bertie County.

North Carolina Pirates. North Carolina commerce also suffered from piratical raids, particularly from 1713 (the close of Queen Anne's War) to 1718. The most notorious pirates in North Carolina history were

Edward Teach, better known as "Blackbeard," and Stede Bonnet. The former was killed by Lieut. Robert Maynard of the Royal Navy, in a battle near Ocracoke Inlet, Nov. 22, 1718; the latter was captured by an expedition from South Carolina and was taken to Charleston, tried, convicted, and hanged on Dec. 10, 1718, along with 29 other pirates.

The "Dividing Line Betwixt Virginia and North Carolina." North Carolina and Virginia had a prolonged and bitter dispute about the boundary between the two colonies, the former insisting that the 1663 charter provision of 36° was the proper one, the latter contending that the 1665 charter provision of 36° 30′ was the effective one. In 1728 commissioners representing the two colonies ran the line westward as far as present Stokes County. North Carolina gained virtually all of the region in dispute, and its commissioners reported that "there was taken by the line into Carolina a very great quantity of Lands and Number of Families that before had been under Virginia." An incidental result of the survey was the unusually charming specimen of literature by William Byrd (one of the Virginia commissioners), *History of the Dividing Line Betwixt Virginia and North Carolina.*

About this time (July 25, 1729), North Carolina became a royal colony, when 7 of the 8 Proprietors—at their own request—sold their shares in "Carolina" to George II for £17,500 (£2,500 each), plus a lump sum of £5,000 to satisfy their claims for acreages in quit rents due them. The Carteret share was not sold and later became the Granville District.

A ROYAL COLONY, 1729-1775

An Era of Progress. The history of the royal colony of North Carolina from 1729 to 1775 was characterized by a steady and rapid growth of population; the settlement of the Cape Fear Valley and the piedmont; the expansion of agriculture, industry, and trade; some improvement in transportation and the beginnings of a crude postal system; a higher standard of living, reflected in better homes, finer furniture, more and better tools and implements, and more comfortable living conditions; the rapid growth of dissenting religious sects; the founding of many churches, a few schools, and some libraries; and the publication of the first books and newspapers in the colony.

Royal government was characterized by greater stability, stronger administration, and better enforcement of law and order than had prevailed under the proprietary regime. Most of the 5 governors during the royal period were of higher caliber, better character, and more experience than the proprietary governors, and they compared favorably with the governors of other colonies.

Population Growth. In 1729 there were only about 30,000 whites and fewer than 6,000 Negroes in North Carolina. Most of the settlers were of English stock and lived largely in the Tidewater area. By 1765 the population had increased to 120,000 and by 1775 to an estimated 345,000, of whom 80,000 were Negroes. North Carolina had become the fourth most populous English continental colony, exceeded only by Virginia, Pennsylvania, and Massachusetts. This ninefold increase in population in about half a century was partially due to a high birth rate, but it was due largely to a great influx of "foreigners."

During the royal era, Scotch-Irish, Germans, Scottish Highlanders, Welsh, English, and a few other national stocks poured into the Upper Cape Fear Valley and into the back country. Settlements reached the "foot of the mountains" by 1760 and soon pushed across the mountains. A vast area, hitherto almost unbroken wilderness, was turned into farms and homes. Roads, bridges, and ferries were built; sawmills and gristmills were established; lumber, naval stores, and other industries were developed. Old towns such as Edenton and New Bern took on new life. Many new towns were begun, most significant of which were Wilmington, Halifax, Hillsboro, Salisbury, Salem, Charlotte, and what is now Fayetteville. The creation of 26 new counties is ample evidence of the growth and expansion of population.

The earliest, largest, and most numerous settlement of Highlanders in America was the one in North Carolina in the years between 1729 and 1775. The Highlanders came into the Cape Fear Valley in large numbers, particularly after their defeat by the British at the Battle of Culloden in 1746. At the head of navigation on the Cape Fear a town was begun, which was incorporated as Campbelltown in 1762 and later joined with Cross Creek. It was renamed Fayetteville in 1783, in honor of Gen. Lafayette.

At the same time that the Highland Scots were settling the Cape Fear Valley, thousands of Scotch-Irish (racially Scotch and geographically Irish) and Germans were moving into backcountry North Carolina, chiefly from Pennsylvania. In 1766 Gov. Arthur Dobbs wrote that "this province is settling faster than any on the continent, last autumn and winter, upwards of one thousand wagons passed thro' Salisbury with families from the northward, to settle in this province chiefly," and a South Carolina newspaper of 1768 said, "There is scarce any history either ancient or modern, which affords an account of such a rapid and sudden increase of inhabitants in a back frontier country, as that of North Carolina."

The Scotch-Irish made a great contribution to the growth, expansion, and development of North Carolina. They established Presbyterian churches throughout a wide area. Within a short time they established schools. They developed agriculture and a variety of industries. They had a flair for politics, and they had fighting qualities acquired in their rough, hardy, outdoor life, which stood them in good stead on the frontier.

The Germans who came to the colony belonged to three religious sects—Moravian, Lutheran, and Reformed—and settled mainly in Rowan County which was created in 1753. Salisbury was founded in the same year and incorporated two years later, and St. John's Lutheran Church in that town was organized in 1768.

In 1753 the Moravians began the settlement of the "Wachovia" tract of about 100,000 acres which had been purchased from Lord Granville. Bethabara ("Oldtown") was founded in that year; Bethania ("New Town"), in 1759; and Salem in 1766. The Moravians tended to segregate themselves from other settlements. They preserved their religious, social, and economic customs. They emphasized community cooperation and common ownership of property. It was not until 1849 that the congregation abandoned its supervision of business and not until 1856 that the lease system was dropped. By the outbreak of the Revolution in 1775, Salem had at least 30 dwelling houses, a "congregation house," a "single brethren's house," a community store, and an excellent tavern. A visitor in 1786 reported that "every house in Salem is supplied with water brought in conduits a mile and a half." They also had water-works and a fire department.

Agriculture. At least 95 per cent of North Carolinians in the colonial era were engaged in agriculture or related industries. This was a natural development favored by the abundance, fertility, and cheapness of land; by the imperative need of the people for self-sufficiency; by the desire, if not necessity, for articles of export; and by the application of British mercantilist principles, which insisted on "returns" from the colonies of goods that did not compete with British manufacturers.

Land was so plentiful and the desire so great to get the colony settled that some very large tracts were granted to individuals and to companies. Roger Moore, Thomas Pollock, Cullen Pollock, Edward Moseley, and several other planters owned over 10,000 acres each. But large grants were the exception rather than the rule, and North Carolina came to be a "colony of small landowners" who lived on and cultivated their own soil.

The major crops of the colony were corn, tobacco, peas, beans, wheat, and rice. Tobacco became the leading "money crop"; its culture—seedbeds, transplanting, worming, pruning, suckering—was much the same as it is today, but the "weed" was of the burley type and not the "bright leaf," and it was air-cured or sun-cured—a process which took from 5 to 6 weeks.

Next to naval stores (tar, pitch, rosin, and turpentine), "provisions" —corn, wheat, beans, and peas—constituted the largest item of export. Corn was grown in all parts of the province. Some rice was grown in the Lower Cape Fear Valley, but it was not a crop of major importance. North Carolina farmers also produced hemp, flax, indigo, and a small amount of cotton. Honey, wine, sorghum, hops, timothy grass, white potatoes, sweet potatoes, and a great variety of fruits and vegetables were also grown, chiefly for home consumption.

Methods of farming were generally backward and unscientific. There was little or no crop rotation. Manures and fertilizers were not used. Land was abundant and cheap, and the exhaustive system of cultivation soon resulted in "soil exhaustion." Farm tools and implements were scarce. Bishop Spangenberg, in a 140 mile journey in the summer of 1752, reported that he saw "not one wagon or plough, nor any sign of one."

Crop Pests and Other Farm Problems. The colonial farmer suffered from droughts, floods, hailstorms, and other vagaries of the weather. He faced the perennial problem of crop pests: the smaller variety consisting of worms, bugs, and weevils, and the larger variety, usually called "vermin," which included most of the wild animals and fowls of the forest. One of the most serious problems was that of overproduction and falling prices, especially tobacco.

Livestock and Cattle. The principal draft animals were oxen, but the horse was "the indispensable animal." There were no mules. The farmers had milch cows, beef cattle, hogs, chickens, geese, and other kinds of fowl. Horses, cattle, and hogs were branded or marked and were allowed to run at large on the almost unlimited range. Hogs, usually of the "razor-back" or "wind-splitter" species, were produced in vast quantities, and large droves of them—sometimes as many as 500—were marched on foot to Virginia, or even Pennsylvania. "Black cattle" became famous in the backcountry, and by 1775 North Carolina had the highest rank in beef cattle production it has ever held. An estimated 50,000 were exported annually.

Industry. The North Carolina farmer was a self-sufficient and versatile jack-of-all-trades. He was a combination farmer, engineer, hunter and trapper, carpenter, mechanic, and businessman. Many articles were processed in the home for local consumption. Among the leading household industries were: foodstuffs, "intoxicating beverages," cloth making, leather tanning, furniture, and candle and soap making.

The leading commercial industry in early North Carolina was naval stores—tar, pitch, rosin, and turpentine. Blessed with vast long-leafed pine forests and aided by British subsidies, North Carolina became the leading colonial producer of these stores. In fact, it led the world in their production from 1720 to 1870, and it was this industry which gave to North Carolina its nickname, "Tar Heel State." In the eighteenth century, seven-tenths of the tar, more than half the turpentine, and one-fifth of the pitch exported from all the colonies to England came from North Carolina. The annual value of naval stores exported from the colony in the late colonial period was about £50,000, in addition to the British bounties paid.

Lumbering was also an industry of large proportions, and lumber was exported in many forms, chiefly barrel staves, headings, hoops of oak, shingles, and boards. About two-fifths of the shingles, one-seventh of the barrel staves, and one-eleventh of the pine boards exported from the continental colonies were from North Carolina.

There was some shipbuilding in the colony from the beginning, but it never became a major industry. Some potash, hemp, flour, and several other articles were also produced in the colony.

Transportation, Trade, and Communication. The first roads in North Carolina were Indian trails or "trading paths," usually well located along the shortest and best routes. As population grew and expanded, these narrow trails were widened by constant usage, and some of them were made into "roads" by order of provincial or local authorities. According to contemporary writers these roads were "poor," "wretched," "exceeding bad," and "miserable." They were not graded, surfaced, drained, or adequately marked. There were few bridges, and ferries were inadequate, inconvenient, and expensive.

Many road laws were passed, but they were not rigidly enforced. As late as 1778 it was reported that the main post road running through the State "has become so bad, through the neglect of the Overseers of it, as greatly to delay the Post Riders and Travellers in general. Trees have fallen across it, and are not removed; the Roots are not cut up; a number of the Causeways are Swampy and full of Holes; and many of the Bridges are almost impassible." Efforts at road building in the coastal plain were hampered by the numerous rivers, creeks, and swamps. Yet many roads were built after 1760. There were several north-south roads leading from Virginia to South Carolina, such as the one running through Edenton, Bath, Wilmington, and Brunswick; the one from

Halifax to Tarboro; and the one from Cross Creek (now Fayetteville) to the north. North Carolina did not establish a stage line until 1789—long after most of the other states. The Northeast Branch of the Cape Fear was crossed by a bridge which, according to Janet Schaw, "opens at the middle to both sides and rises by pullies, so as to suffer Ships to pass under it." This was one of the first drawbridges in this country.

Vehicles. Travel and transport over the roads were slow, difficult, unpleasant, and at times dangerous. Two-wheel carts which could transport about 1,000 pounds, and four-wheel wagons, which could haul about twice that amount, averaged about 20 miles a day. Such "pleasure vehicles" as gigs, chairs, chariots, and coaches could travel 30 to 40 miles a day. Riders on horseback frequently made as much as 50 miles a day. The horse was indispensable for land travel and transport, and people rode horseback for long distances. Travel on foot was the slowest but surest and safest mode of travel, and people walked great distances. A group of Moravians walked from Bethlehem, Penn., to Wachovia, a distance of some 400 miles, in 30 days.

Lodgings and other accommodations along the routes of travel were few and were usually of a poor quality. Travelers fortunate enough to obtain lodging in the home of a planter fared well; those who stopped at the homes of small farmers usually found "miserable conditions"; and those who stayed at the "ordinaries" (inns or taverns) faced a real experience. Despite the law that required tavern keepers to provide "good and sufficient Houses, Lodgings, and entertainment for Travellers, their servants and Horses," most of these places were "wretched." There were a few excellent taverns, such as the one at Bute Courthouse run by Jethro Sumner, the Horniblow Tavern at Edenton, and the one at Salem (still standing) where the landlord was instructed to treat his guests with "kindness and cordiality, but not to encourage them to be intemperate," and to behave so that the guests could tell "that we are an honest and a Christian people, such as they have never before found in a tavern."

Travel by Water. Though North Carolina had few good outlets for ocean commerce, it had an excellent system of inland waterways. Most of the large plantations and many of the small farms were located on or near navigable waters; all of the important towns in the coastal plain were situated on watercourses; and along some of the rivers, especially the Roanoke and Cape Fear, there were "many warehouses and stores."

The most prevalent types of craft used on inland waters were canoes, periaugers, scows, and flatboats. Most household inventories listed one or more canoes. John Brickell wrote that some canoes were so large that they "will carry two or three Horses over these large Rivers, and others so small that they will carry only two or three men."

Ocean Trade. Colonial North Carolina had 5 official "ports of entry"— Bath, Currituck, Beaufort, Roanoke (Edenton), and Brunswick. The last three were the most important, and the "Port of Brunswick" included the town of Wilmington. The chief exports of the colony were: (1) naval stores, largely to England; (2) provisions, chiefly to the West Indies; (3) lumber products also largely to the West Indies; and (4) tobacco, chiefly to England.

Postal System. Mail service in the colony was irregular, slow, and unsatisfactory. As late as 1773 it took two weeks for a New Bern letter to reach Salem, and the next year, post riders were averaging only 16 miles a day.

The Social Order. North Carolina society was rather distinctly stratified. The white population of the colony consisted of three elements: (1) gentry or planter aristocracy; (2) small farmer and artisans; (3) the indentured "Christian servants." The gentry, the smallest, most wealthy, best educated, and most influential of these groups, was composed mainly of large landholders, but it also included public officials, wealthy merchants, Anglican ministers, and the leading lawyers, doctors, and other professional men. The planters occupied the best sites along the Roanoke, Tar, Neuse, Cape Fear, and other eastern rivers.

The planter's home and its furnishings, and even his personal appearance, all reflected his influence and superior social status. The average planter probably lived in a plain, unpainted, wooden house, lacking architectural grace and sacrificing beauty to comfort and convenience. But North Carolina had some large and imposing houses—Orton, the home of "King Roger" Moore, which has been called "the finest colonial residence in North Carolina"; Kendall, the home of George Moore; Lilliput, the residence of Eleazer Allen; Castle Hayne, the home of Hugh Waddell; the Cupola House at Edenton; and the John Wright Stanly House at New Bern.

Hospitality. Stories of North Carolina hospitality were early carried to distant regions. John Lawson, writing in 1709, observed: "As the land is very fruitful, so are the planters hospitable to all that come to visit them; there being very few Housekeepers, but what live very nobly; and give away more provisions to Coasters and Guests who come to see them, than they expend amongst their own families." John Brickell, writing two decades later, said that "the better sort, or those of good Economy," kept "plenty of wine, Rum and other Liquors at their own Houses, which they generously make use of among their Friends and

Acquaintances, after a most decent and discreet Manner." And Elkanah Watson, in 1786, wrote: "Travellers with any pretensions to respectability seldom stop at the wretched taverns; but custom sanctions their freely calling at the planter's residence, and he seems to consider himself the party obliged by this freedom."

The Small Farmers. Small farmers and artisans constituted by far the largest element of the colony's white population. The small "farmer"—also called "husbandman" and "yeoman"—seldom owned more than 200 acres of land; perhaps the majority held 50 acres or less. The typical farm was a small clearing in the forest, which provided the owner with food, fuel, and materials for shelter and clothing. R. D. W. Connor has aptly described these people as "a strong, fearless, independent race, simple in taste, crude in manners, provincial in outlook, democratic in social relations, tenacious of their rights, sensitive to encroachments on their personal liberties, and, when interested in religion at all, earnest, narrow, and dogmatic."

The lowest social stratum among the whites consisted of several classes of non-free workers—voluntary servants ("redemptioners"), involuntary servants, and apprentices. North Carolina never had as many "Christian servants" as did Virginia, Maryland, and Pennsylvania. This was due to the colony's limited contacts with the outside world, its indirect settlement from other colonies, and to the introduction of Negro slavery at an early date.

Free Negroes and Slaves. At the bottom of the social pyramid were the Negroes—free and slave. There were some free Negroes in the colony as early as 1701. In 1790, the free Negro population was over 5,000, largely in the eastern counties.

Slavery was encouraged by the Lords Proprietors, who offered 50 acres of land for each slave above 14 years of age brought into the colony. As early as 1694 a few white planters claimed "headrights" for the importation of slaves. But Negro slavery grew slowly at first. In 1712 the estimated number was only 800. There was a rapid increase after 1729, and after 1763 slave population increased at a more rapid rate than that of whites. The Census of 1790 reported the State's white population at 288,204 and the slave population at 100,572 or a little more than one-third of the total.

Religion. The Anglican Church was established by law early in the eighteenth century, but as late as 1739 the governor reported that only at Bath and Edenton were church services regularly held, and that the state of religion was "really scandalous." The situation improved in the latter part of the colonial era, but the Anglican Church was never strong or popular in North Carolina. The colony had a smaller number of Anglican clergymen than any other colony of comparable population —only 46 clergymen during the whole colonial era, and 33 of these were missionaries of the Society for the Propagation of the Gospel.

The most significant development in the religious life of colonial North Carolina after 1730 was the growth and spread of "dissenting sects," notably Presbyterians, Baptists, Quakers, Lutherans, Moravians, German Reformed, and Methodists. Organized congregations of Presbyterians originated with the Scottish Highlanders in the Cape Fear Valley. They were further increased with the large Scotch-Irish influx into the piedmont region. Hugh McAden, the "father of Presbyterianism in North Carolina," made a missionary tour of the colony in 1755 and 1756. In 1757 the Philadelphia Synod sent the Reverend James Campbell, who became the first regular Presbyterian pastor in North Carolina, serving three churches in the Cape Fear Valley. Alexander Craighead, in 1758, became pastor of the Sugaw Creek Church in Mecklenburg County. In May, 1770, the Orange Presbytery was organized, consisting of 8 congregations in North Carolina and 4 in South Carolina. The first meeting of this Presbytery was at Hawfields Church, in present Alamance County.

There were a few Baptists among the early settlers of the Albemarle region. But there was no organized Baptist congregation until 1727, when the Chowan Church near present Cisco in Chowan County, was founded by the Reverend Paul Palmer, the earliest recorded Baptist preacher in North Carolina. Two years later Shiloh Church, in present Camden County, was begun by Palmer. The most significant Baptist Church in the eastern portion of the colony was that at Kehukee, Halifax County, organized in 1742 by the Reverend William Sojourner. In 1765 the Kehukee Association was organized "out of churches which had been reformed to an orthodox standard," and by 1775 it had 61 churches and an estimated 5,000 members.

The most important landmark in Baptist history, however, was the founding of Sandy Creek Church, in present Randolph County,' in 1755 by the Reverend Shubal Stearns. This church, "the mother of all Separate Baptists," increased from 16 to 606 members within a few years. Within 17 years, 42 churches and 125 ministers had "sprung from the parent church." In 1758 the Sandy Creek Association was organized, and for the next 12 years all Separate Baptist churches in Virginia and the Carolinas were affiliated with this association, which had yearly meetings. By 1775 the Baptists of one variety or another were the most numerous sect in North Carolina.

The Lutherans and German Reformed settled largely in the present counties of Rowan, Davidson, Cabarrus, and Stanly. The three oldest

Reformed churches in the State—Grace (in Rowan) and Leonard's and Beck's (in Davidson), were "union Churches," where the two sects worshipped on alternate Sundays. Reverend Samuel Suther was the first Reformed preacher in charge of a particular church (Grace) in the colony. Zion (Organ) church in present Cabarrus County, St. John's in Salisbury, and St. John's in Cabarrus were the earliest Lutheran congregations. In 1773 the first Lutheran minister, Adolph Nussman, came to the colony and for the next 21 years "labored faithfully in poverty and privations," serving congregations in Rowan, Cabarrus, Iredell, Catawba, Lincoln, Davidson, Guilford, and Stokes counties.

The Methodists were the last Protestant sect to appear in the colony. The first "Methodist sermon" in North Carolina was preached at Currituck Courthouse, Sept. 12, 1772, by the Reverend Joseph Pilmore (or Pilmoor). The first North Carolina circuit was organized in 1776. The formal organization of the Methodist Church in the United States took place at Baltimore in 1784, and the first annual conference of the North Carolina church was held at Green Hill's home near Louisburg, N. C., April 20, 1785, with Superintendents Francis Asbury and Thomas Coke present.

Education. Education in early North Carolina, as in other colonies, was closely associated with the church. Nearly all teachers were clergymen, lay readers, or candidates for the ministry. The first professional teacher of whom there is record was Charles Griffin, a "reader" in the Anglican Church, who opened a school in Pasquotank County in 1705.

The lack of a public school system did not mean that the people in general were illiterate. Children of the planters, and perhaps of some of the farmers, were taught at home by their parents or by a tutor. The sons of some wealthy planters were sent to colleges in other colonies or to English and Scottish universities. The education of the poor and of orphans was provided for through the apprenticeship system and by the legal requirement that guardians give their wards the "rudiments of learning" and teach them a "useful trade."

In 1754 an act was passed which appropriated £6,000 "for founding and endowing a Public School" in the colony, but shortly thereafter this money was "borrowed and employed" for military purposes. No public schools were established in North Carolina prior to 1840, but scores of academies were established prior to 1800, among which were Tate's Academy at Wilmington (1760), Crowfield Academy in Mecklenburg County (1765), and the famous "log college" begun by the Reverend David Caldwell at what is now Greensboro (1767). New Bern had 5 academies in 1800; Warrenton had several famous ones, especially the Warrenton Academy, headed by Marcus George, and the well-known "Mordecai Female Seminary." Other famous academies were Hall's Clio's Nursery at Statesville and the Salem Female Academy, which was the forerunner of Salem College.

North Carolina's First College. The only college in North Carolina prior to the founding of the State University was Queen's College at Charlotte, which operated for a few years between 1771 and 1780. This "college" was authorized to grant degrees, and it was to be financed by a "duty of six pence per gallon on all rum brought into and disposed of in Mecklenburg County for ten years following the passage of the act."

The printing press did not appear in North Carolina until 1749, when the Assembly appointed James Davis as "Public Printer." Davis set up his press at New Bern in June of that year, and the earliest known imprint from it was a 14-page *Journal of the House of Burgesses of the Province of North-Carolina.* In 1751, he published *A Collection of all the Public Acts of Assembly, of the Province of North Carolina: Now in Force and Use,* sometimes called "Swann's Revisal," and also known as "The Yellow Jacket," because of the color of its binding. Davis also founded the first newspaper in the colony, *The North Carolina Gazette,* a weekly paper begun in 1751.

REVOLUTION AND INDEPENDENCE

AS A BRITISH colony, North Carolina was drawn into the various Anglo-French wars for supremacy in North America. North Carolinians did not take an active part in the first two of these conflicts, but hundreds of men in the colony fought for the British in the War of Jenkins' Ear against Spain (1739-44) and in King George's War against France (1744-48). An even larger number participated in the Great War for Empire, commonly known as the French and Indian War (1754-63). Hugh Waddell of Wilmington was one of the heroes of this war. At Fort Dobbs, near the present town of Statesville, he defeated the Cherokee Indians, who had turned against their former English allies and had gone on the warpath in the backcountry.

North Carolina Resistance to British Taxation. At the close of the Great War for Empire, England was complete master of North America east of the Mississippi, but the mother country, faced with a national debt which had doubled as a result of the war, inaugurated a "New Colonial Policy," designed to tighten up on colonial administration and to raise additional revenues from the colonies by means of taxation. Parliament passed a number of laws to this end, the most objectionable of which was the Stamp Act of 1765, which levied taxes on legal documents, newspapers, dice, playing cards, and many other articles. The people of North Carolina, led by the Sons of Liberty, maintained that England had no right to levy a direct tax on the colony, and they resisted enforcement of this law. At Wilmington there were demonstrations, and at Brunswick there was an armed uprising, with the results that officials designated to handle the stamps resigned. Not a single stamp was sold in North Carolina.

When Parliament in 1767 passed the Townshend Acts taxing glass, lead, tea, and a few other articles, non-importation associations in various parts of the colony made effective use of an economic boycott. Countermanded orders and refusal of the colonies to pay debts to British creditors led Parliament in 1770 to repeal all of these taxes, except that on tea. The tea tax was retained at the insistence of George III, in order to "retain the principle" of taxation of the colonies.

The Regulator Movement. Meanwhile, the farmers of Orange, Anson, Rowan, and other backcountry counties were struggling against local governments which to them seemed inefficient, dishonest, and intolerable. Sheriffs, justices of the peace, clerks, and other county officials were all appointed by the royal governor and constituted the "courthouse ring," which seemed to ignore the wishes of the masses of small farmers. These aggrieved farmers, led by Herman Husband, Rednap Howell, and others, complained bitterly about dishonest sheriffs, corrupt lawyers and court officials, extortionate fees, and excessive taxes. Nor were they happy about the large sums of public money being spent to erect the handsome "Governor's Palace" at New Bern. When the legislature, called by Gov. William Tryon and dominated by the eastern planter aristocracy, failed to solve their problems, they organized in 1768 as the "Regulators," pledged "to regulate" the evils of local government. Later they resorted to violence and rioted in the "court town" of Hillsboro, dragging the judge from the bench, breaking up court, conducting a mock court of their own, and doing damage to the property of Edmund Fanning and other officials. Finally Gov. Tryon led an expedition of over 1,000 militia, most of whom were from the east, to Hillsboro, and at the Battle of Alamance Creek on May 16, 1771, the Regulators were defeated Six Regulators were hanged at Hillsboro; within a short time more than 6,000 accepted the governor's pardon proclamation. Many of the Regulators were still disaffected, however, and hundreds migrated to the Tennessee Country. The grievances of which the Regulators complained were not redressed until the revision of the State constitution in 1835. Some writers have claimed that Alamance was the "first battle of the American Revolution," though the facts are obvious that the Regulators were not fighting to overthrow British rule and that there was not a British redcoat in the colony at that time. It has been asserted that most of the Regulators became Tories, but scholarly investigation has revealed that there were more Whigs than Tories among the known Regulators.

The End of Royal Rule. As the American Revolution approached in 1774, the elected representatives of the people, led by John Harvey, and in open defiance of Gov. Josiah Martin, held a provincial congress at New Bern to formulate plans for resistance and to elect delegates to the Continental Congress at Philadelphia.

On Oct. 25 of the same year, 51 Edenton ladies held a meeting and pledged themselves not to buy tea or any other British goods until the rights of the colonists were respected.

The shooting war started at Lexington and Concord, Mass., April 19, 1775. North Carolina's last royal governor, Josiah Martin, fled, and royal authority broke down. A provisional government was set up. There was a provincial council which, in a sense, replaced the governor. The provincial congress was the law-making body, while safety committees were chosen in counties and towns to take charge of local government and raise troops and military supplies.

According to tradition, the Mecklenburg County Safety Committee met at Charlotte, May 20, 1775, and drew up a declaration of independence from the mother country. Historians have long questioned the authenticity of this "declaration," since no contemporary account of it has ever been discovered, but many years ago the State legislature authorized the placing of the date May 20, 1775, on the State seal and the State flag. It is certain, however, that the Mecklenburg Committee, on May 31, 1775, drew up a strong set of "Resolves," declaring that "all commissions civil and military heretofore granted by the Crown to be exercised in these colonies are null and void and the constitution of each particular colony wholly suspended." Adam Boyd's *Cape Fear Mercury* published these resolutions and for this act was arraigned by the governor as "a most infamous publication."

The Battle of Moore's Creek Bridge. Many North Carolinians were loath to go to war with England. These Tories, or Loyalists, included many of the official class, some large planters and producers of naval stores (which were subsidized by Parliament), some of the Anglican clergymen, large numbers of the Scottish Highlanders, some of the Regulators, and some who were naturally conservative and dreaded a break with empire. Organizing into an army, the Tories met the North Carolina Whigs at Moore's Creek Bridge, 18 miles above Wilmington, Feb. 27, 1776, and suffered a crushing defeat. Aptly called the "Lexington and Concord of the South," this victory crushed the Loyalists, prevented a large scale British invasion, which had been planned by Gov. Martin and approved by the British leaders, awakened and unified the Whigs of North Carolina, and hastened the movement for independence.

The Halifax Resolves, First Official State Action for Independence. On April 12, 1776, the Fourth Provincial Congress, meeting at Halifax, drew up a resolution authorizing the North Carolina delegates in the Continental Congress "to concur with the delegates of the other colonies in declaring Independency." This was the "first authoritative, explicit declaration, by more than a month, by any colony in favor of full, final separation from Britain." In the latter part of that year the Fifth Provincial Congress framed the first State Constitution, the salient features of which were a bill of rights; provision for legislative, executive, and judicial branches of government, with the legislative branch given virtual control over the other two divisions; property and religious qualifications for voting and officeholding; representation of 6 borough towns in the legislature, along with county representation, one for each county in the Senate, and two for each county in the House of Commons; suffrage for free Negroes, though not specifically stated; separation of church and state; and a general provision for public schools and "one or more universities." This constitution went into effect in January, 1777, without being submitted to popular vote. Richard Caswell was the first governor of the independent State and New Bern was the capital.

Problems of the New State. The new State government faced many critical problems. Troops had to be raised, organized, trained, and equipped. Additional revenues had to be raised to prosecute the war and to operate the new government. Tories had to be watched, though their ardor had been cooled by the defeat at Moore's Creek. The Cherokee Indians, who were keeping the frontier settlements in a state of constant alarm, had to be subdued. There were also the acute problems of taxes, paper currency, and inflation. Perhaps the greatest problems were those of unifying the State politically and of making a constitution work. In a situation which necessitated centralization of power in the prosecution of the war, this latter problem was even more difficult, since the constitution emphasized decentralization of power.

North Carolina's Military Contributions. There was little fighting in the State until the last year of the Revolution, but North Carolina soldiers were active elsewhere. During the course of the conflict, the State furnished approximately 7,000 soldiers to the Continental Line, and perhaps 10,000 State militiamen saw limited service during the war. North Carolina soldiers helped drive Lord Dunmore from Virginia in the winter of 1775-76 and assisted in the defense of South Carolina and Georgia. The State militia, led by Griffith Rutherford, crushed the Cherokees in the summer of 1776 and drove these Indians deeper into the mountain recesses. Many North Carolina soldiers and officers fought under Gen. George Washington at Brandywine, Germantown, and Monmouth, and more than a thousand of these men suffered at Valley Forge in the winter of 1777-78. Hundreds of men from backcountry North Carolina rendered valiant service in the complete defeat of Patrick Ferguson's army at King's Mountain on Oct. 7, 1780, and against Lord Charles Cornwallis' at Guilford Courthouse, March 15, 1781. Cornwallis' surrender at Yorktown, Oct. 19, 1781, can be traced in part to the disastrous defeat at King's Mountain, to Cornwallis' heavy losses, especially of his officers at Guilford Courthouse, and to his failure to recruit many Tories in the State, reverses which caused his historic retreat through the State to Wilmington and then overland to Virginia, culminating in the Yorktown surrender.

THE CRITICAL YEARS FOLLOWING THE REVOLUTION

THE YEARS FROM 1781 to 1789 were extremely critical for the 350,000 people in the State's 47 counties. Archibald D. Murphey some years later said: "When the war ended, the people were in poverty, society in disorder, morals and manners almost prostrate." There were many grave problems: a weak and inefficient state government, unsatisfactory local government, political strife and bitterness between Conservatives and Radicals, economic depression, and general social demoralization. Problems which demanded immediate action were demobilization of soldiers; release of prisoners of war; State policy regarding confiscated Tory property (under the laws of 1777 and 1779 vast tracts of Tory lands had been confiscated and sold by the State); and the location of a permanent capital. Other post-war problems were: the disposition of the State's western lands (present Tennessee), the relation of North Carolina to the Union, and the role of the State government in education and in internal improvements.

The "Lost State" of Franklin. Just before and during the Revolution intrepid pioneers like Daniel Boone and James Robertson and land speculators like Richard Henderson had made their way into the transmontane country of present Kentucky and Tennessee. The settlement of what later became the State of Tennessee (1796) began with the founding of Watauga just prior to the Revolution. By 1783 there were thousands of people beyond the mountains, and by 1789 the North Carolina legislature had created 7 counties in the Tennessee country, Washington (1777), Sullivan (1779), Greene (1783), Davidson (1783), Sumner (1787), Hawkins (1787), and Tennessee (1788).

The North Carolina legislature first ceded the State's western lands to the United States in 1784, though it revoked this cession later that year. Nevertheless, the settlers in the Tennessee country, led by John Sevier, organized the State of Franklin, with a constitution, a separate legislature, and Sevier as governor. The "Lost State" of Franklin collapsed, however, because it failed to secure the approval of the Continental Congress or the legislatures of North Carolina and Virginia. Finally, in 1789, North Carolina ceded its western lands to the United States government, and in 1796 the region was admitted to the Union as the State of Tennessee.

Settlement of the Mountain Region. Meanwhile white settlements were being made in the mountain area of North Carolina. By treaties with the Cherokee Indians in 1777, all lands east of the Blue Ridge were ceded to the State; and, by Indian treaties with the United States in 1785, 1791, and 1795, nearly all lands in North Carolina east of the Alleghenies became State property. Settlers now poured into the region, among them being the Davidsons, Pattons, McDowells, Vances, Bairds, and Lowries. Buncombe County was created in 1791, and the town of Asheville was incorporated in 1797.

North Carolina and the Union. Perhaps the most urgent postwar problem confronting North Carolina was the State's relation to the Federal Union. The legislature unanimously ratified the Articles of Confederation in 1778, but the State's reaction to the United States Constitution was a different story. The people of North Carolina were from the beginning inclined toward individualism and democracy; they seemed to feel that "that government is best which governs least." Their fear of a strong central government and of a constitution which had no bill of rights led them to reject the Constitution at the Hillsboro Convention in 1788 by a vote of 185 to 84. At the same time, this convention suggested a large number of amendments, some of which were incorporated in a Federal bill of rights (the first 10 amendments).

The Constitution was ratified, however, by 11 of the states, all but North Carolina and Rhode Island, and went into effect in the spring of 1789. As a result of this action, and after an "intensive campaign of education" on the part of William R. Davie, James Iredell, Hugh Williamson, and other Federalist leaders, North Carolina ratified the Constitution at the Fayetteville Convention, Nov. 21, 1789, by a vote of 195 to 77. The State was now under the "Federal Roof," but it entered the Union too late to vote for Washington in 1789 (it left the Union too late to vote for Confederate President Jefferson Davis in 1861). It was next to the last original state to enter the Union and the next to the last to leave it in 1861.

North Carolina Politics, 1789-1815. Though predominantly a state of small farmers, most of the State's congressional delegation from 1789 to 1793 were Federalist in politics. But they never gave hearty support to the national bank, tariff, and other Hamiltonian policies, of the Federalist party. Most of the governors after 1789 were Jeffersonian Republicans, and the legislature was overwhelmingly Republican after 1792. Pres. Washington visited Halifax, Tarboro, Greenville, Salisbury, Charlotte, Salem, and other places in the State on his "Southern tour" of 1791, and the State's electors voted for "the general" in 1792, but North Carolinians were not enthusiastic about the domestic or foreign policy of Washington's administration, such as the assumption of state debts, the neutrality proclamation, and Jay's Treaty.

Nathaniel Macon, Exemplar of North Carolina. Under the leadership of Willie Jones of Halifax and later of Nathaniel Macon of Warren County, North Carolina became a bulwark of Republicanism. The *Raleigh Register,* founded in 1799 by Joseph Gales, at the instigation of Macon, was the major Republican organ and the State's most powerful newspaper for the next half century.

Nathaniel Macon was the perfect exemplar of North Carolina Republicanism and the high priest of the status quo. For 37 years this Warren County tobacco planter sat in Congress, and for more than a quarter century he dominated North Carolina politics. He believed that government should be a policeman for the protection of life and property and nothing more. Government should be cheap, simple, and democratic. He thought conditions in North Carolina were almost ideal. It was "a meek state and just people" with no "grand notions or magnificent opinions." Therefore he opposed the "grand notions" of public schools, internal improvements, and constitutional reform.

North Carolina in the Second War with Great Britain. The second war with Great Britain, 1812-15, was not popular in North Carolina, a State which had little commerce, and less interest in the seizure of Canada, so eagerly desired by the War Hawks in Congress. The State, however, met its quota of troops, raised some 14,000 militiamen, and spent over $100,000 of its own funds to equip them. North Carolina's most notable contribution to the war was the exploits of three individuals—Lt. Col. Benjamin Forsythe of the army, Capt. Johnston Blakeley of the navy, and Otway Burns, captain of a privateer.

The defenseless condition of the North Carolina coast was the cause of many complaints, particularly after a British fleet landed at Ocracoke and Portsmouth in July, 1813. In 1815, the State legislature, which had previously criticized the national administration for the conduct of the war, praised Pres. James Madison for "firmness, energy and wisdom" in prosecuting the war and for an honorable peace.

There was rejoicing in the State, especially after news of Andrew Jackson's overwhelming victory over the British at New Orleans in January, 1815. North Carolina and the United States were now "free from Europe" and could turn to the solution of their domestic problems, such as education, internal improvements, and constitutional reform.

The University of North Carolina Founded. There were no public schools or colleges in North Carolina for many years after the Revolution, and a growing need was felt for better educational facilities. The Constitution of 1776 had provided "that a school or schools shall be established by the Legislature for the convenient Instruction of Youth" and provided for "one or more Universities." But the political leaders of the State did not interpret this to mean that the State should establish schools and colleges supported by public funds. They felt that the private academies, which were chartered by the legislature, fulfilled this constitutional provision. More than 40 academies were established prior to 1800, and more than 400 prior to 1860.

Thirteen years elapsed before the legislature did anything about establishing "one or more Universities." Prominent Federalists, led by William R. Davie, often called "the Father of the University," finally succeeded in getting a bill passed in 1789, chartering the University of North Carolina. New Hope Chapel, now Chapel Hill, was the site selected. The cornerstone of "Old East" building was laid in 1793, and in 1795 the University opened its doors to students, the first state university to do so. The University was the recipient of land grants from Gerrard, Smith, and others, whose names are perpetuated in buildings on the campus. The legislature granted the infant University a loan of $10,000 which was later converted into a gift, but made no appropriations for its support, and the trustees had to depend chiefly on gifts and tuition fees to operate the institution. For several years the University had a "Presiding Professor," a system which never proved very satisfactory, and finally Joseph Caldwell became the first president of the University of North Carolina.

A Permanent Capital Located. As has been indicated, there was no fixed seat of government in the colony, prior to the selection of New Bern as capital in the 1760's. During the Revolution the legislature met at Hillsboro, Halifax, Smithfield, Wake Court House, New Bern, Fayetteville, and Tarboro. This "itinerant form of government" had many obvious drawbacks, and the Hillsboro Convention of 1788 authorized a permanent capital to be located within 10 miles of Isaac Hunter's plantation in Wake County, the exact site to be chosen by the State legislature. After considerable investigation of possible sites, a legislative committee in 1792 bought 1,000 acres of land from Joel Lane near Wake Court House, and the city of Raleigh was laid out. The first capitol, which was completed in 1794, was burned in 1831. The present capitol was begun in 1833 and completed in 1840.

THE RIP VAN WINKLE STATE
(1815-1835)

FROM 1815 TO 1835, North Carolina was so undeveloped, backward, and indifferent to its condition that it was often called the "Ireland of America" and the "Rip Van Winkle" state. In 1830 a legislative committee reported that North Carolina was "a State without foreign commerce, for want of seaports or a staple; without internal communication by rivers, roads, or canals; without a cash market for any article of agricultural product; without manufactures; in short without any object to which native industry and active enterprise could be directed." In addition to all of these handicaps, there was general political apathy under a one-party system, which resulted in indifference to all economic, social, and cultural improvements.

Manufacturing on a factory basis did not develop in North Carolina until long after 1815. In that year the State had only one cotton mill, three paper mills, and 23 small iron works. There were some small corn and flour mills, whiskey and turpentine distilleries, and establishments for making hats, guns, and a few other products. In thousands of homes throughout the State thread was spun and woven into cloth on hand-operated wheels and looms.

Agriculture was the predominant occupation of the people of North Carolina. In a total population of 638,829, as revealed by the Census of 1820, only 6,800 whites and 6,700 Negroes lived in the 6 towns of more than 1,000 population each. New Bern, the largest city, had only 3,663 people. In 1816 only 1⅓ million dollars worth of produce, chiefly naval stores. lumber, tobacco, rice, corn, and other agricultural products, were shipped through all North Carolina ports, more than a million dollars worth of this through Wilmington.

Emigration from North Carolina. North Carolina dropped in population from fourth place among the states in 1790 to seventh place in 1840, though it had about the highest birth rate in the nation. Soil exhaustion, the lure of fertile and cheap lands in the west, lack of internal improvements and educational facilities, and unhappy conditions generally led many people to leave the State. Among the thousands who migrated from North Carolina were the families of three presidents of the United States, Andrew Jackson, James K. Polk, and Andrew Johnson; two vice-presidents, Johnson and William R. D. King; three cabinet members, Jacob Thompson, John H. Eaton, and Hoke Smith; two speakers of the House of Representatives, Polk and Joseph G. Cannon; more than a score of Congressmen, including Thomas Hart Benton; governors of 7 other states including 5 of Tennessee, three of Alabama, two of Arkansas, one of Oregon Territory, a vice-president of the Republic of Texas, and the first governor of the State of Texas. Among other prominent Americans born in North Carolina were: Dolly Madison, famous "first lady"; William S. Porter ("O. Henry"), famous short-story writer; Richard J. Gatling, inventor of the Gatling gun; James Long, who led the first expedition into Texas; Nathaniel Rochester, founder of Rochester, N. Y.; and Hiram R. Revels, the first Negro to serve in the United States Congress.

Archibald DeBow Murphey and a few other leaders in the State urged as a remedy the building of transportation facilities, the stimulation of manufacturing, the promotion of education, and the development of the State's vast resources. But the government, dominated by the landed aristocracy of the east, was unwilling to launch such a program of internal improvements.

Constitutional Changes of 1835. By 1830 more than half the State's population lived west of Raleigh. Yet most of the governors, councillors of state, judges, and the majority of the legislature came from the east. Whenever a new county was created in the west, to take care of the expanding population in that area, one would also be formed in the east, so that the east continued to dominate the government. The west could not obtain equitable representation in the legislature under the provisions of the 1776 Constitution, and since this document contained no provision for amendment, the only way to change the Constitution was by a convention called by the legislature. For more than a decade, western leaders tried in vain to get a convention called. From 1831 to 1835, North Carolina appeared to be on the verge of a revolution over this issue. Finally, at a convention held in Raleigh in 1835, significant changes were made in the Constitution. Provisions were adopted, and later ratified by popular vote, for the reapportionment of representation in the legislature; popular election of the governor for a two-year term; abolition of borough representation in the legislature; disfranchisement of the free Negro; and the partial removal of religious qualifications for voting and office holding. The 50-acre requirement to vote for state senator was retained, but all adult white male taxpayers were eligible to vote for governor and for members of the lower house of the legislature.

THE STATE'S FIRST "AGE OF PROGRESS," 1835-1860

THE CONVENTION of 1835 was a turning point in North Carolina history. The constitutional reforms of 1835, which increased the political power of the people and of the west, paved the way for a quarter-century of remarkable development in North Carolina, the first real age of progress in the history of the State. This development was carried on for 15 years under Whig and then for 10 years under Democratic leadership. The State government erected a magnificent capitol, gave financial aid to the building of a state system of railroads and plank roads, provided the major support for a statewide system of public schools, established institutions for the care of the blind and deaf and insane, reformed the tax system, and began a liberalization of criminal law and the legal status of women. The University grew rapidly, and many colleges and academies were established by private and religious agencies. There was a great increase in the number and circulation of newspapers and the beginnings of an indigenous authorship and literature. Agricultural conditions were improved, factories were established, wealth and trade increased. The State government itself took the lead in this development.

North Carolina's First Public Schools. A genuine educational revival began about 1835. The constitutional reforms of that year paved the way for public schools, and the distribution of the surplus Federal revenue in 1837 (North Carolina's share was $1,433,757) provided the means. The first public school law was passed in 1839, and the first public schools were opened in 1840. By 1846 every county had one or more public schools, and the state education fund exceeded $2,000,000. By 1850 more than 100,000 children were attending 2,657 "common

schools." Under Calvin H. Wiley, who in 1853 became the first State
Superintendent of Common Schools, a unified school program was
inaugurated. The North Carolina school system was the best in the
South in 1860.

Many Colleges Established. At the same time many denominational
colleges were being established. Wake Forest College (Baptist) had
its beginning as the Wake Forest Institute, opened in 1834. Davidson
College (Presbyterian) opened for students in 1837. Trinity College
(Methodist), now Duke University, had its beginning about 1838 at
Trinity in Randolph County. New Garden Boarding School (Quaker),
now Guilford College, was opened to students in 1837. Other colleges
for men chartered before 1860 were Floral (Presbyterian) at Maxton
in 1841, Catawba (German Reformed) at Newton in 1851, and North
Carolina College at Mount Pleasant (Lutheran) in 1859. Salem Female
Academy (later Salem College) was founded by the Moravians in
1802. Between 1842 and 1858 other colleges established for girls were:
Greensboro Female College (Methodist) in 1838, Davenport Female
College (Methodist) at Lenoir in 1858, Saint Mary's School at Raleigh
(Episcopal) in 1842, Chowan Baptist Female Institute (Baptist) in
Murfreesboro in 1848, Oxford Female College (Baptist) in 1851, States-
ville Female College (Presbyterian) in 1856, and Peace Female Institute
(Presbyterian) at Raleigh in 1857. The Census of 1860 reported 16
colleges in North Carolina with 94 teachers and 1,540 students.

North Carolina also began to respond to the growing humanitarian
sentiment that the State owed an obligation to its dependent, defective,
and delinquent citizens. A school for the deaf was opened in Raleigh
in 1845, and a "department for the blind" was added in 1851. In 1856 a
State Hospital for the Insane was opened in Raleigh on a beautiful tree-
covered hill, now appropriately called "Dix Hill," in honor of Miss
Dorothea L. Dix of Massachusetts, nationally famous for her activity
in behalf of the insane.

North Carolina's First Railroads. The Whigs adopted the policy of state
aid to railroad construction and inaugurated an era of railroad construction which revolutionized the life of the State. Two railroad lines were
completed in 1840: the Wilmington and Raleigh (later named the Wilmington and Weldon), which ran from Wilmington to Weldon, on
the Roanoke River, 161 miles; and the Raleigh and Gaston, 86 miles
long. In 1856 the 223-mile North Carolina Railroad was completed
from Goldsboro to Charlotte. The Wilmington, Charlotte and Rutherfordton Railroad was completed in 1854. The 96-mile Atlantic and
North Carolina Railroad from Goldsboro to Beaufort was completed

in 1858, and the western North Carolina Railroad from Salisbury to Morganton in 1860. In 1860 North Carolina's railroad system comprised 891 miles, built at a cost of almost $17,000,000.

Plank Roads—the "Farmers' Railroads." The State also purchased $180,000 worth of stock in private plank road companies. Between 1849 and 1860 no less than 84 of these companies were organized, but only about a dozen of these roads were built with a total mileage of about 500 miles at a cost of about $1,000,000. Fayetteville was the chief terminus of the plank roads. The Fayetteville and Western, the "Appian Way of North Carolina," which ran 129 miles from that town through High Point and Salem to Bethania in Forsyth County, was the longest plank road ever built anywhere.

Plank roads, which were called "farmers' railroads" provided all-weather and easy transportation to markets. Most of these roads were 8 feet wide and built of parallel rows of heavy timber, usually pine, covered crosswise with thick planks laid close together. Tolls were collected at tollgates and houses along the road. There were 15 toll houses between Fayetteville and Bethania. For a few years the plank roads prospered; but the planks settled and wore out quickly, and the roads were never rebuilt. The first "good roads movement" in North Carolina had virtually ended by 1860.

Agricultural Progress. Agriculture continued as the chief economic pursuit of North Carolinians. Rising crop prices and cheaper and better transportation greatly increased the volume of crop production, sales, and profits of farmers, especially those living within reach of plank roads, railroads, and navigable waters. The total value of North Carolina crops increased from $22,900,000 in 1850 to $33,400,000 in 1860, and land values more than doubled during the "prosperous fifties."

Tobacco production jumped from 12,000,000 in 1850 to 33,000,000 pounds in 1860, an increase partially due to the development of bright-leaf tobacco on the Slade plantation near Yanceyville. Cotton production rose from about 35,000 bales in 1840 to 74,000 in 1850, and over 145,000 bales in 1860. The State also produced 8,000,000 pounds of rice in 1860, nearly all of it in Brunswick County, and almost 5,000,000 bushels of wheat, 30,000,000 bushels of corn, and a large variety of other farm crops.

Interest in agricultural reform was reflected in the organization of the State Agricultural Society at Raleigh in 1852, the formation of many county societies, and the publication of several agricultural journals. The State Agricultural Society began the following year to hold an annual fair in the capital city.

Industrial Growth. Between 1853 and 1860 there was an increase in the number of manufacturing establishments of all kinds in the State from 2,663 to 3,689; in the invested capital, from $7,500,000 to more than $9,700,000; and in the total value of manufactured products from $9,700,000 to $16,700,000.

Turpentine, the leading industry, which was concentrated in the area between Fayetteville and Wilmington, was produced by 1,526 establishments, having a total product of $5,300,000, one-third of the State's total in manufactures. Flour and meal, worth $4,350,000, ranked second in value; tobacco products were third ($1,117,000); lumber was fourth ($1,074,000); and cotton textiles fifth ($1,046,000).

Gold Mining. Prior to the discovery of gold in California in 1848, North Carolina was the leading gold producing state. At least 350 localities in the State have been worked for gold at one time or another. In 1848 Gold Hill, in Rowan County, had 5 stores, one tavern, 4 doctors, and 1,000 laborers in the near-by mines. One of the largest nuggets of gold, 28 pounds, was found near present Concord, and the *Mining Magazine* of October, 1853, estimated that the Reed mine had yielded $10,000,000, probably an overestimate. The total gold production before 1860 has been estimated at sums ranging from $50,000,000 to $65,000,000. At times gold mining employed about 30,000 men and ranked next to agriculture in importance. A branch of the United States Mint was opened at Charlotte in 1837 and coined $5,059,188 prior to 1861. About $9,000,000 of North Carolina gold was also coined at the Philadelphia mint. A private mint in Rutherford County, operated by Christopher and Augustus Bechtler, minted $3,625,840 into gold coins and manufactured considerable quantities of jewelry.

Despite the economic progress of North Carolina in the two decades after 1840, North Carolina in 1860 ranked twelfth in the Union, with a total population of 992,622 (968,068 rural and only 24,554 urban), which included 331,059 Negro slaves, 30,463 free Negroes, and 1,168 Indians.

Social Classes in Ante-Bellum North Carolina. The highest social class, the gentry, or planter aristocracy, comprised the owners of large plantations and more than 20 slaves, as well as the most prominent public officials, professional men, and business leaders. It numbered about 6 per cent of the total white population. Much larger was the middle class, small slaveholding farmers, small merchants and manufacturers, and lesser public officials and professional men, numbering about 20 to 25 per cent of the white population. Still larger was the third class of yeomen and mechanics, independent, small, non-slaveholding farmers, naval stores workers, miners, mechanics, tradesmen, overseers, and some of the farm tenants—numbering 60 to 65 per cent of the total white population. At the bottom of the social pyramid were the "poor whites," a class numbering over 5 per cent of the white people, consisting of landless tenants and laborers who had failed in the struggle of life because of incapacity, laziness, improvidence, or disease.

Slavery and Slaveholding. The majority of North Carolinians never held slaves at any time. The percentage of slaveholding families in the State was 31 per cent in 1790, 26.8 per cent in 1850, and about 28 per cent in 1860. The total number of slaveholding families in 1860 was 34,677, divided as follows:

Number of Slaves	Families
1 to 4	16,071
5 to 19	14,522
20 to 49	3,321
50 to 99	611
100 to 199	133
200 to 300	15
over 300 and less than 500	4

Free Negroes. North Carolina had more free Negroes than any Southern state, except Virginia and Maryland. Between 1790 and 1860 they had increased from 4,975 to 30,463. The chief source of the free Negro population was manumission, or the granting of freedom to individual slaves by the masters and the legislature. Other sources were purchases of freedom by the slave themselves, births by free Negro and white mothers, and immigration, though both race-mixing and free Negro immigration were prohibited by law. A few free Negroes owned slaves; in 1830, 190 owned 629 slaves. In 1830 Gooden Bowen of Bladen County and John Walker of New Hanover owned 44 slaves each. In 1860 there were only 8 free Negro slaveholders with a total of 25 slaves.

A few free Negroes rose to positions of eminence and influence, notably Ralph Freeman, a Baptist preacher; John Chavis, a Presbyterian minister and teacher of Negroes and whites, in separate schools; and Henry Evans, a Methodist preacher at Fayetteville.

From 1816 to 1830 the movement for emancipation of slaves in North Carolina was stronger than in any other Southern state. At least 40 abolition societies were operating in 1826. In the 1850's some of the nation's major anti-slavery leaders were North Carolinians, notably Benjamin Hedrick, D. R. Goodloe, and Hinton Rowan Helper.

A STATE IN THE CONFEDERACY

NORTH CAROLINA was one of the original thirteen states which created the Union, and it believed firmly in the preservation of that Union. It was bound closely to the United States by the ties of commerce and two generations of experience in founding, operating, and developing the nation. Its location in the upper South made it less extremely Southern in its social and economic system than the states of the lower South. Like other Southern states—and most Northern states prior to 1860—North Carolinians believed in state rights, but the State refused to join Virginia in a protest against the Alien and Sedition Acts of 1798, and it refused to endorse South Carolina's nullification of Federal tariff laws in 1832-33, though North Carolina was the only state in the Union prior to 1860 which voted consistently against all protective tariffs.

But for the most part, North Carolina aligned itself with the South in all disputes with the North. It resented economic vassalage to the industrial and commercial Northeast and believed firmly in slavery as a necessary police system by which the whites might control the slaves and maintain the peace, safety, and prosperity of the State. Apologetic for slavery at first, but fearful and resentful of the abolition movement, the State gradually shifted after 1830 to a strong defense of slavery and enacted stringent laws for the control of Negro slaves and free Negroes. However, violent attacks on slavery were made by a few individuals in the State, among whom were Levi and Vestal Coffin, reputed founders of the Underground Railroad, and Hinton Rowan Helper, author of the *Impending Crisis of the South,* published in 1857.

Opposition to Secession. Union sentiment was strong in North Carolina, even among many slaveholders. In the presidential election of 1860, John C. Breckinridge, candidate of the "Southern Democrats," barely carried the State over John Bell, candidate of the "Constitutional Union" party. North Carolina was not a party to the organization of the Confederate States of America in February, 1861. The State sent commissioners to Montgomery, the first Confederate capital (later transferred to Richmond), to work for an amicable adjustment of sectional issues, but they were ignored by Confederate officials. Delegates were also sent to a national Peace Conference at Washington, D. C., in an effort to avert hostilities. Meanwhile, the State voted 47,323 to 46,672 against holding a convention to consider secession.

The events of April, 1861, forced North Carolina into war. Confederate troops fired on Fort Sumter, in Charleston harbor, April 12, and captured it two days later. On April 15, Pres. Abraham Lincoln asked the states in the union to furnish 75,000 men to suppress the Southern "insurrection." To the request for two regiments from North Carolina, Gov. John W. Ellis replied: "I can be no party to this wicked violation of the laws of the country, and to this war upon the liberties of a free people. You can get no troops from North Carolina."

North Carolina Forced to Secede. The outbreak of hostilities and Lincoln's call for troops, followed by his proclamation blocking Southern ports, unified North Carolina. All of the 14 Unionist newspapers in the State went over to the Secessionist Party. Zebulon Vance, colorful "war governor" from 1862 to 1865, later wrote that he "was pleading for the Union with hand upraised when news came of Fort Sumter and Lincoln's call for troops. When my hand came down from that impassioned gesticulation, it fell slowly and sadly by the side of a Secessionist." A convention of 120 delegates, meeting at Raleigh on May 20, 1861, adopted a secession ordinance, introduced by Burton Craige, declaring "that the union now subsisting between the state of North Carolina and the other states, under the title of 'The United States of America,' is hereby dissolved, and that the state of North Carolina is in full possession and exercise of all those rights of sovereignty which belong and appertain to a free and independent state." On the same day, the convention ratified the Constitution of the Confederate States of America.

As bands played martial music, guns fired salutes, church bells pealed, and people paraded and shouted for joy, some sober and thoughtful people, like George E. Badger, former United States Secretary of the Navy, believed that they were celebrating a tragedy, "the death knell of slavery," and eventual defeat. But the die was cast, and there was general enthusiasm in the State for the cause of "Southern Independence."

North Carolina's Military Contribution to the Confederacy. North Carolinians have liked to boast that its men were "First at Bethel, fartherest at Gettysburg and Chickamauga, and last at Appomattox," and that "North Carolina heroism hallowed and marked every important battlefield." The State's greatest contribution to the Confederate cause was man power. With one-ninth of the population of the Confederacy, North Carolina furnished between one-sixth and one-seventh of all Confederate soldiers. Altogether it contributed 125,000 men—a larger number than its voting population. In the entire war 19,673 North Carolinians were killed in battle—more than one-fourth of the Confederate battle deaths, and 20,602 died of disease. The North Carolina losses of 40,275 were greater than that of any other Confederate state.

North Carolina was a secondary though important battlefield of the war. Eleven battles and 73 skirmishes were fought on its soil. Early in the war Federal forces captured Hatteras Inlet (Aug. 29, 1861), Roanoke Island (Feb. 8, 1862), New Bern (March 14), Washington (March 21), Fort Macon (April 26), and Plymouth (Dec. 13). The Federal forces occupied the entire Sound region and held much of it throughout the war. The largest battle in the State and the "bloodiest battle ever fought on North Carolina soil" occurred at Bentonville, March 20 and 21, 1865. Gen. William T. Sherman's army defeated Gen. Joseph E. Johnston's Confederate forces; Confederate casualties were reported at 2,606 and Federal at 1,646.

Gen. Robert E. Lee had already surrendered the Army of Northern Virginia to Gen. U. S. Grant at Appomattox Courthouse, Virginia. The Confederacy was defeated, and on April 26, Johnston surrendered to Sherman at the Bennett House, three miles west of Durham on the Hillsboro Road.

Blockade-Running. The port of Wilmington held out almost to the very end as the chief Confederate center of blockade-running. It was defended by powerful Fort Fisher at the mouth of the Cape Fear. This fort, called "the Gibraltar of America," had withstood Federal attacks in 1862 and 1864, but it was forced to surrender on Jan. 15, 1865. Wilmington was occupied about a week later, and, in February, 1865, Federal forces took over the Wilmington and Weldon Railroad, which Robert E. Lee had called "The life line of the Confederacy." During the course of the war, North Carolina blockade-runners had made 365 successful trips to Nassau and 65 to other ports, and Gov. Vance estimated that $65,000,000 worth of goods, at gold prices, had been brought into Wilmington. Whereas near the end of the war Confederate soldiers from other states were ragged and cold, those from North Carolina were well clothed. In 1865 there were 92,000 surplus uniforms, ready-made and in cloth, in the State's warehouses, though the State had sold some of its supplies to the Confederate government.

North Carolina and State Rights. While contributing heavily to the Confederate cause, no state was more jealous of its rights than North Carolina. Gov. Zebulon B. Vance protested against many policies of the Confederate government, particularly the conscription law, the impressment of property, the suspension of the writ of *habeas corpus,* and the use of Virginia officers in North Carolina. On one occasion he threatened to "take North Carolina out of the Confederacy," if Confederate Pres. Jefferson Davis did not alter his policies regarding North Carolina. Vance thought the conscription law was "harsh and odious" and, in a letter to Pres. Davis, said it was "a rich man's war and a poor man's fight." Unless the "illegal seizures of property and other depredations" by Confederate Cavalry ceased, Vance said he would "be compelled in some sections to call out my militia and levy actual war against them."

One of the State's greatest problems on the home front was inflation. Prices rose to dizzy heights. In 1865 bacon was selling for $7.50 a pound, wheat at $50 a bushel, coffee at $100 a pound, and flour at $500 a barrel.

THE TRAGIC ERA OF
RECONSTRUCTION

THE WAR for Southern Independence destroyed much of the State's wealth, took the lives of 40,000 of its young men, left a heritage of defeat, and blighted almost every phase of the State's life. Railroads, factories, public buildings, bridges, roads, schoolhouses, private homes, and barns were destroyed or in need of repair. A capital investment of over $200,000,000 was wiped out by the abolition of slavery. Confederate bonds were worthless, and State bonds had depreciated greatly in value and might be repudiated. With Confederate and State currency worthless, few people had any cash or credit facilities. Many stores, factories, banks, newspapers, academies, and colleges had closed.

Tired, maimed, hungry, penniless soldiers straggled home to find cattle and stock gone, barns and cribs and smokehouses empty, clothes worn out, farms run down, and buildings, fences, and tools in bad repair. With little but their land, labor, and memory of defeat, these soldiers and their families courageously went to work to wrest a meager living from the soil and to rebuild their fortunes and the State.

The Freedmen and the Freedmen's Bureau. One of the greatest problems confronting North Carolina after the war was the freedmen. Could 350,000 Negroes and 650,000 whites, many of whom had owned slaves, live side by side in peace and for the good of each other? The natural reaction of the freedmen was to test their new freedom by moving about from place to place and doing those things which they had not been permitted to do under slavery. As R. D. W. Connor wrote: "To abandon his plow in the middle of the row, to stride defiantly by his former master, out of the yard and down the dusty road

—that, indeed, was a test of freedom that even the most ignorant Negro could understand."

The United States government attempted to solve this problem by establishing the Freedmen's Bureau with a network of local units and officials in each Southern state to assist the freedmen to find employment, to establish schools, buy or rent land, make fair labor contracts, combat disease and poverty, and settle other problems. During its three and a half years of existence in North Carolina, the Freedmen's Bureau distributed $1,500,000 worth of food and large quantities of clothing, established hospitals and cared for more than 40,000 patients, and organized 431 schools with 439 teachers and over 20,000 pupils. Some destitute whites also shared in these benefits. There was never any serious danger of "40 acres and a mule" being distributed to the freedmen, though some might have expected this gift.

Presidential Reconstruction. The government of North Carolina collapsed early in 1865 under military pressure, and on April 29, Gen. John Schofield took command of the State. Immediately he issued proclamations declaring a cessation of hostilities and the emancipation of slaves, and he made plans for the organization of a police force of each county. In May, Pres. Andrew Johnson appointed William W. Holden as "provisional governor of the State of North Carolina." He also issued an Amnesty Proclamation, offering pardon to all who would take an oath of allegiance to the United States Constitution and promise to obey the law of Congress. Fourteen classes, including civilian officeholders and men worth as much as $20,000, were excluded. Later in the year Jonathan Worth was elected governor over Holden and assumed the governorship on Dec. 28, 1865, thus putting the president's plan of reconstruction into full operation.

The Congress of the United States, however, refused to seat Southern senators and representatives. The adoption of the so-called Black Code by the legislature of 1866 played into the hands of the Radicals in Congress, who were determined to block the president's plan of reconstruction. This code, defining the rights of Negroes, was more liberal than those of other states, but it did not give the Negroes the right to vote, nor did it give them equal rights with the whites in all respects. Among other provisions, it validated the marriages of former slaves; declared Negroes entitled to the same rights and privileges as whites in suits at law and equity; made the criminal law applicable to the two races alike, except in the punishment for an assault with intent to rape; provided for the admission of the testimony of Negroes in the courts; and made provision for the protection of Negroes from fraud and ignorance in making contracts with white persons.

Congressional or Military Reconstruction. As a result of the "Black Code" and the reported "Southern Outrages" against Negroes and Union soldiers—many of which were partially or wholly untrue—the Radicals in Congress nullified the presidential plan of reconstruction by the passage of the Reconstruction Act of March 2, 1867. Under this law, the South was divided into 5 military districts, each in complete charge of a United States general and military forces. North Carolina and South Carolina became Military District Number Two under the command of Gen. Daniel E. Sickles, and later of Gen. E. R. S. Canby, with headquarters in South Carolina. This law also required that a convention in each state draft a new constitution which would grant Negro suffrage. In the election of delegates to the convention, Negroes could register and vote, but many prominent whites—perhaps 10 per cent in North Carolina—were not allowed to vote, since their "political disabilities" had not been removed. When the new constitution was approved by the voters of the State and by Congress and when the new legislature chosen under the provisions of the new constitution ratified the Fourteenth Amendment to the Federal Constitution, the State would be permitted to return to the Union.

The total registration of voters in 1868 was 179,653—whites 106,721 and Negroes 72,932. In the Constitutional Convention (Jan. 14–March 17, 1868), at Raleigh, there were 107 Republicans, of whom 18 were carpetbaggers, 15 Negroes, and 74 native whites. Only 13 Conservatives (Democrats) were present.

The State Constitution of 1868. The Constitution of 1868, often erroneously called the Canby Constitution and frequently condemned as a radical break with North Carolina traditions made by outsiders, contained a liberal Bill of Rights. Many of the changes in the Constitution proper were modern, progressive, liberal, and democratic. Some of the most significant were: the abolition of slavery; provision for universal manhood suffrage, white and Negro; the elimination of all property and religious qualifications for voting and officeholding, except the disbarment of atheists from public office; popular election of state and county officials; abolition of the county court system and the adoption of the township-county commission form of local government; provision for a Board of Charities and Public Welfare; and for "a general and uniform system of Public Schools" to be open "for at least four months in every year." The University of North Carolina was declared to have "an inseparable connection with the Free Public School system of the state," and as soon as practicable, the legislature should "establish and maintain in connection with the University, a Department of Agriculture, of Mechanics, of Mining, and of Normal

Instruction." Four new elective state offices were created; lieutenant-governor, auditor, superintendent of public works, and superintendent of public instruction. The elective Council of State was replaced by an *ex officio* one, the two-year term of office for the governor was changed to 4 years, and the name House of Commons was changed to House of Representatives. The number of capital offenses was reduced to 4—murder, burglary, arson, and rape—and it was stated that the purpose of punishment should be "not only to satisfy justice, but also to reform the offender, and thus prevent crime."

The Constitution was adopted by a popular vote of 93,084 to 74,015, and when the next legislature met, it promptly ratified the Fourteenth Amendment. Congress approved the new constitution and admitted North Carolina representatives and senators on July 20, 1868. North Carolina was back in the Union at last. But the State was in control of the Republican party whose radical policies and Negro-carpetbag-scalawag membership was distasteful to the native white majority.

The Ku Klux Klan and the Restoration of Home Rule. For several years North Carolina had bad government, though it never suffered as much from carpetbaggers and Negro politicians as some of the other Southern states. There was a great increase in crime and violence. The Union League, a Northern and Republican secret organization, was active among the Negroes. The native whites countered with the Ku Klux Klan (first appeared in North Carolina in 1867) and other secret societies, designed to combat the influence of the Union League, to "protect Southern womanhood," to "eliminate bad government," to "put the Negro in his place," and to "restore white supremacy." The reports of a congressional committee revealed at least 260 Klan "visitations" in 20 North Carolina counties, 174 of which were directed against Negroes. It is noteworthy that the chief Ku Klux activity was not in the East where Negroes were most numerous but in such piedmont counties as Alamance, Caswell, Chatham, and Orange.

Matters came to a head in 1870. Maintaining that there was disorder in Caswell and Alamance counties because of Ku Klux activities, Gov. Holden, acting under the Shoffner Act of 1868, proclaimed these counties in a state of insurrection. Military arrests were made and a number of leading citizens were imprisoned without jury trial. In the election of 1870 the Conservatives (Democrats) gained control of the legislature. This body impeached Gov. Holden for "high crimes and misdemeanors," and after a trial which lasted from Feb. 2 to March 23, 1871, he was found guilty and removed from office—the only governor in North Carolina history to be removed from office by this method. Thereafter the Democrats gradually gained control of all phases of state government, though they did not win the governorship until the election of Zebulon B. Vance over Thomas Settle in the famous "battle of the giants" in 1876.

Thirty amendments were added to the 1868 constitution in 1875, most of which were the results of the experiences of Reconstruction. Secret political societies were declared illegal; schools for whites and Negroes were to be kept separate; marriages between whites and Negroes were forbidden; residence rquirements for voting were raised; the legislature was authorized to appoint justices of the peace and was given virtual control of county government. The most significant change was the replacement of popular vote by legislative control of county government—to insure white and Democratic control, especially in the eastern counties with large Negro populations.

RECOVERY AND PROGRESS
(1865-1900)

AGRICULTURAL recovery and expansion were handicapped by the destruction of farm property and livestock during the war; by the lack of capital and credit for repairs, replacements, operation, and expansion; by the inadequacies and high costs of transportation; and by the revolution in the farm labor system produced by the sudden and uncompensated emancipation of approximately 350,000 slaves.

Despite these handicaps, agriculture quickly reached its prewar volume of production—cotton and oats by 1870; corn, hogs, milch cows, and beef cattle by 1880, and tobacco in the 1880's. North Carolina was the only state to become a large producer of both cotton and tobacco.

The Spread of Farm Tenancy. One of the most significant results of the war was the break-up of large plantations into smaller farms and the rapid rise of farm tenancy. The number of farms in the State increased from 75,203 in 1860 to 93,565 in 1870, to 157,609 in 1880, and to 225,000 in 1900. The corresponding decreases in average acreage per farm were from 316 to 212 to 142 and to 101 acres. North Carolina became a state of small farms and has remained so to the present.

The share-cropping tenant system developed as the natural readjustment in a region inhabited by landowners who lacked capital and labor and by Negroes who were experienced in farm labor but lacking in land and capital. Under the share-cropping system the landowner furnished the tenant with team, tools, seed, and perhaps fertilizer, and received from the tenant one-half to two-thirds of the staple crop after harvest. He generally furnished provisions for the tenant family and received payment in either cash or crops. Although some farm leaders opposed this system, circumstances forced it on North Carolina, and it is still the prevalent system of farming. The *Reconstructed Farmer*, published at Tarboro, declared:

> What demoralizes the labor of our country more than anything else is *farming on shares*— The manner in which share laborers are managed is a curse to the country, for in many instances they are put off on land ... that will not support them for the first year, no matter how good the cultivation of the crop may be ...

By 1880 one-third of the State's farms were operated by tenants; by 1900 the percentage was 41.4. Contrary to a rather general belief, tenancy was not a racial institution. White tenants outnumbered Negro tenants at all times, though a higher percentage of Negro farmers were tenants than was true of the whites. Farm tenancy was most closely associated with the regions of cotton and tobacco production.

The Plight of the Farmers. There was expansion and prosperity in postwar manufacturing, transportation, and banking, but agriculture, despite its quick recovery in volume of production, experienced a generation of chronic economic depression and growing grievances. North Carolina agriculture was definitely a part of the national picture of over-production, falling prices for farm commodities, less rapidly-shrinking expenses and burdens, high taxes on land, exorbitant credit costs, and waning political and social prestige. The farmer was "gradually but steadily becoming poorer and poorer every year." Prices of things he sold were low and getting lower. Prices of articles he bought, such as fertilizer and cotton bagging, were high and, in some instances, getting higher.

The Progressive Farmer (Raleigh), April 28, 1887, expressed the farmer's plight:

> There is something radically wrong in our industrial system. There is a screw loose. The wheels have dropped out of balance.
>
> The railroads have never been so prosperous, and yet agriculture languishes. The banks have never done a more profitable business, and yet agriculture languishes. Manufacturing enterprises never made more money or were in more flourishing condition, and yet agriculture languishes.... Towns and cities flourish and "boom" and grow and "boom," and yet agriculture languishes.

Demands of the "Embattled Farmers." North Carolina farmers, like those in the rest of the nation, finally began to organize in an effort to solve their problems. The Grange, which began nationally in 1869, first appeared in North Carolina in 1875. Within a short time there were 501 granges in the State with a total membership of 15,000. In 1887 the Farmers' Alliance was organized in the State under the leadership of Leonidas L. Polk, founder of the *Progressive Farmer* and State Commissioner of Agriculture. In 1890 the State had 2,147 local units of the Alliance and a total membership of 90,000.

North Carolina farm leaders demanded of the Federal government a reduction in protective tariffs, regulation of railroads and trusts, and expansion of the currency. They demanded of the state government tax reform, legal limitations of interest rates, railroad regulation, and educational reform. Many farmers came to realize that the Democratic party had become the guardian of the railroads, manufacturers, and other "special interests," and that agriculture, the state's major economic pursuit, was not one of these interests. As farm prices continued to drop in the late 1880's and early 1890's, the "embattled farmers," organized the Peoples' Party (Populist). The Populists fused with the Republicans in 1896 and swept the State. Daniel L. Russell, a Republican, was elected governor, and the legislature was controlled by "fusionists."

The Industrial Revolution in North Carolina. The development of factory industry was the most significant postwar development in North Carolina. By 1870, 33 cotton mills were making products in excess of the 39 establishments in 1860. By 1870 tobacco manufacturing had recovered about two-thirds of its prewar production. The State was also producing more turpentine than ever before and led the nation in this respect. By 1880 North Carolina industry had surpassed its prewar volume and prosperity. The following decade was marked by rapid industrialization. The "gospel of salvation through manufacturing" was preached throughout the State, and profits made the gospel real.

The Cotton Textile Industry. During the 20 years after 1880, an average of 6 new cotton mills were built each year. In 1900 there were 177 cotton mills, capitalized at $33,000,000, employing 30,273 workers, and producing goods valued at $28,000,000.

The North Carolina textile industry was based largely on local enterprise, management, capital, and labor. In the 1890's there was a notable movement of Northern capital into the State's textile industry and a small beginning of the exodus of Northern mills to the South. In 1895, Ceasar and Moses Cone opened textile mills in the Greensboro area.

Rapid Growth of Tobacco Manufacturing. In contrast with the cotton textile industry, which had favorable publicity in the press and even from the pulpit, the phenomenal development of tobacco manufacturing in the State was almost wholly the result of private initiative and ruthless competitive power. The story of young James Buchanan ("Buck") Duke's going with his father at the close of the war to peddle his "Pro Bono Publico" tobacco from a wagon in order to gain supplies to last through the winter, and of this same Buck Duke's becoming, within 30 years, a multimillionaire and the head of one of American's most powerful trusts, sounds as if it might have come from a "success story" of Horatio Alger.

In 1868 Durham had only one tobacco factory; in 1872 it had 12 (Duke's first factory in Durham was not until 1874). Winston, like Durham, witnessed a rapid development in the tobacco industry. Reidsville developed as a tobacco manufacturing center, as did a number of other towns. By 1900 there were 96 tobacco factories in the State, making products worth $14,000,000.

The Furniture Industry. The furniture industry in North Carolina followed a pattern somewhat similar to that of tobacco manufacturing. It began in small shops, with little capital, producing chiefly for local markets. It prospered because of an increasing demand, proximity to raw materials, and low labor costs.

In 1882 David A. and William E. White opened a plant at Mebane for the manufacture of spindles, and from this a furniture factory later evolved. The High Point Furniture Company, started in 1888, is said to have been the first furniture factory in the State. By 1900 there were 44 furniture factories in North Carolina, employing 2,000 workers, and producing furniture valued at $1,500,000. High Point had 24 of these factories; Thomasville, 8; Lexington and Winston-Salem, 6 each; Mount Airy, Statesville, Hickory, Greensboro, Sanford, and Dunn also had furniture factories.

The expansion of industry was reflected in the growth of towns. From 1870 to 1900, the number of towns in excess of 10,000 population, increased from one (Wilmington) to 6 (Wilmington, Charlotte, Asheville, Winston-Salem, Raleigh, and Greensboro). But the State was still predominantly rural, as only 187,000 of the State's 1,707,000 people lived in census-sized towns in 1900.

Development in Transportation and Communication. The western North Carolina Railroad was extended from Salisbury to Old Fort in 1869 and a few years later to Asheville. This, together with the Carolina Central from Charlotte to Shelby and the Raleigh and Augusta from Raleigh to Hamlet—a total of less than 600 miles—was the extent of railroad construction in North Carolina from 1865 to 1880. In 1871 the State government abandoned the policy of State aid to railroads.

In 1895 it leased the North Carolina Railroad to the recently organized Southern Railway Company for 99 years. In 1904 the Atlantic and North Carolina Railroad was leased to the Howland Improvement Company for 91 years. Three major railway systems emerged in North Carolina: the Southern (1894), the Atlantic Coast Line (1900), and the Seaboard Air Line (1900). By 1900 the State had a network of 3,800 miles of railroad consolidated into these three systems and controlled by private capital chiefly from outside the State.

Little effort was made to improve highways or waterways. The antiquated, ineffective system of county control of highways, dating from the colonial era, prevailed until after 1900. Roads were built and kept in repair by the men of each township, who were required by law to work on the roads a few days each year—a system that never operated satisfactorily. After 1885 some counties began to supplement the "labor tax" with special roads taxes and improved methods of road building. Mecklenburg, Buncombe, and Guilford were the first counties to establish county road systems. These roads were built by convict labor at a cost of from $2,700 to $4,000 per mile. The day when North Carolina would be known as the "good roads state" was far in the future. A few of the towns improved their streets and sidewalks, and in 1889 the first electric street railway began operating in Asheville. The first telephone exchanges in the State were opened at Raleigh and Wilmington in 1879. The first rural free delivery mail route in North Carolina—and one of the earliest in the United States—was established in the China Grove community of Rowan County in 1896.

The Slow Revival of Education. Many of the colleges, academies, and "old field" schools of the State closed during the war for lack of teachers or pupils. The University survived as a mere shadow of the robust institution of the previous decade. Lack of public confidence, loss of financial support, and dearth of students closed the University in 1870. A student expressed it vividly when he wrote on a classroom black-board: "Today this University busted and went to hell." A new Board of Trustees, aided by Mrs. Cornelia Phillips Spencer and other friends of the University, was successful in reopening the University in 1875 under the administration of Pres. Kemp P. Battle and a new faculty, but it was not until 6 years later that the legislature made its first appropriation for the University—$10,000.

The state system of "common schools" collapsed in the three years after the war. The Constitution of 1868 required a 4 months' school term, and the legislature of 1869 passed a forward-looking school law, designed to carry out this constitutional mandate, and also appropriated $100,000 for public schools. This law might have established an excellent school system had the act been rigidly enforced and the revenues been ample. But such was not the case. The State's resources were limited; schoolhouses were few and in bad repair; the collection of taxes was poor; and many townships failed to provide schools in accordance with the law. In 1870 there were 1,398 schools operating in 74 counties at a cost of $43,000 and with an enrollment of 49,999—a total of only one-fifth to one-seventh of the children of school age. In 1900, the public schools were open only about 70 days in the year, and teachers were paid only about $24 a month. There were no compulsory school laws, and only about half of the children of school age attended. In that year the State's public school system was worse than it had been in 1860 and was perhaps the poorest in the United States.

Toward the close of the century several institutions of higher learning were opened. Among these were: the Fayetteville Colored Normal (1877); the North Carolina College of Agriculture and Mechanic Arts, at Raleigh (chartered 1887 and opened 1889); the State Normal and Industrial School for white girls, at Greensboro (1891); the North Carolina Agricultural and Mechanical College for the Colored Race, Greensboro (1891); and the Elizabeth City Colored Normal (1892). Trinity College, now Duke University, was transferred from Randolph County to Durham in 1892.

THE DAWN OF A NEW ERA

THE ACCESSION of Gov. Charles B. Aycock in 1901 and the ratification of the suffrage amendment coincided with the beginning of a period of material expansion and economic prosperity in the nation and marked the dawn of a new era in North Carolina. There was a marked decline in political bitterness and racial antagonism. Under a new leadership, more youthful, progressive, democratic, and sensitive to the needs of the people, the dominant Democratic party sought to promote educational and social progress long overdue. Profiting by the blunder of resistance to change which drove the party from power in the 1890's, the rejuvenated Democratic party sought popular favor by rendering public service. Its leaders were dominated by the idea that the State government is not a necessary evil but the beneficent servant or agent of the whole people. The old political commonwealth of North Carolina was gradually transformed into the modern progressive social commonwealth, in which the government is alive to the social and economic needs of its citizens.

Private industry and government cooperated to solve the transportation needs by means of the railroad, improved highways, the automobile and motor truck, and the airplane. Phenomenal expansion of industry made North Carolina an important manufacturing state and provided the wealth which made social and educational progress possible. Higher farm prices, improved methods of farming, and better transportation brought greater prosperity and happiness to the rural population.

Railroad Transportation. Railroad construction and consolidation continued after 1900, but at a slower pace than before. In 1906 the Norfolk and Southern Railway Company was organized. This made the fourth large system in the State. The most important new railroads were the Winston-Salem Southbound, completed from Wadesboro to Winston-Salem in 1911, and the Carolina, Clinchfield and Ohio, connecting North Carolina with the middle west, completed about 1914. The state railway mileage in the 1950's was approximately 4,500 miles.

Better roadbeds and bridges, steel coaches, improved heating and lighting, stronger and faster locomotives, double-tracked main lines, streamlined and air-conditioned trains, and other physical improvements made rail travel safer and more comfortable as the years passed.

The "embattled farmers" of the 1890's led a crusade against the "evil practices" of railroads, and the "farmer's legislature" of 1891 prohibited rate discriminations and created a regulatory railroad commission. In 1899 this was replaced by a Corporation Commission empowered to supervise railroads, banks, telephones, telegraphs, street railways, and express companies. In 1923 the Corporation Commission was authorized to require the adjustment of train schedules, to order the provision of adequate warehousing facilities, and to promote the more expeditious handling of less than carload lots. In 1925 supervision was extended to motor vehicles. In 1933 the North Carolina Corporation Commission was replaced by an elective Utilities Commissioner, and in 1941 a three-member Utility Commission, appointed by the governor, was established; in 1949 the number was increased to 5.

North Carolina has suffered from freight rate differentials, because it has been in a higher "rate zone" than Virginia and the Northeast. In recent years, some readjustments have been made favorable to North Carolina freight rates.

Development of Ports. Since 1900 numerous improvements have been made in the State's water transportation facilities. The Federal government has provided by dredging and locks a 30-foot channel from the ocean to Wilmington and a channel with a minimum depth of 8 feet from Wilmington to Fayetteville. The Inland or Intracoastal Waterway, 8 to 12 feet deep, traversed the entire eastern part of the State in 1936. The State has two ports of entry for ocean-going vessels—Wilmington and Morehead City. In 1949 the legislature authorized $7,500,000 in bonds for the construction and improvement of these ports. In 1952 terminal facilities at these ports were completed.

The First Airplane Flight. On Dec. 17, 1903, at Kill Devil Hill, Orville and Wilbur Wright made the first flight in a power-driven airplane. An impressive monument erected by the United States government marks the site of this epoch-making achievement. By 1954, 6 commercial airlines served the State, and there were 155 airports.

The "Good Roads State." Far more important to the economic and social progress of the State of North Carolina was the development by the State and local governments of a vast network of improved highways. In 1915 the legislature established the State Highway Commission to cooperate and advise with counties in road building. The next year Congress passed the Federal Highway Act and began to give money to the states on a matching basis to improve major interstate roads.

Under the administration of Cameron Morrison, the "Good Roads Governor," the Highway Act of 1921 increased the powers of the Highway Commission, directed the building and maintenance of a state system of almost 6,000 miles of good roads connecting all county seats, state institutions and leading towns, and authorizing a bond issue of $50,000,000. Under the direction of Frank Page, chairman of the Highway Commission, an era of unprecedented construction of concrete, asphalt, sand-clay, and gravel roads began which soon brought fame to North Carolina as a "Good Roads State." The rapid increase in the number of motor vehicles in the State to about half a million in 1935 and to 1,289,548 registered motor vehicles, including 919,586 passenger cars in 1953, provided adequate revenue for road construction, maintenance, and debt service.

In 1949 Gov. Kerr Scott urged rural road improvements as the chief feature of his "Go Forward" program, and the State voted a $200,000,000 bond issue to be allocated to the counties for secondary roads. In Scott's 4 years as governor, the State paved approximately 12,000 miles of secondary roads and stabilized for all-weather travel more than 15,000 miles more. At this date the State Highway system embraces 66,547 miles of roads of which 26,864 miles are paved and most of the remainder stabilized for all-weather travel.

The value of good roads was reflected in many ways. By 1941 North Carolina had 50 per cent more truck-tractors than any other state of the Southeast, and by 1948 the wholesale trade of the State was $800 per capita compared to Virginia's $680. In that year, the wholesale trade of Charlotte exceeded that of Richmond by 55 per cent and was gain-ing rapidly on Atlanta, the only southeastern city which surpassed it. At last North Carolina products were being shipped from the State's cities and towns "by a means of transport that required no intermediate port," and the State was released from the economic bondage to cities of other states. At last landlocked North Carolina was freed from the drastic handicaps of inadequate water transportation and relative economic isolation.

The Industrialization of North Carolina. Improved transportation facilities and the development of electric power combined with mild climate, abundant labor, and proximity to the raw materials of cotton, tobacco, and lumber to speed up the industrialization of North Carolina after 1900.

The generation and distribution of electric power has been a major factor in this phenomenal industrial progress. The Duke Power Company, organized as the Southern Power Company in 1904 and developed by James B. Duke, and the Carolina Power and Light Company have been the largest of numerous power companies in the State. In 1954 over 60 municipalities owned and operated their own electric plants, but only a few of these owned their generating plants.

Between 1900 and 1951 the value of North Carolina manufactures increased from $95,000,000 to $6,181,000,000, the number of industrial laborers from 70,570 to 402,631, and total wages from $14,000,000 to $788,812,000. North Carolina became the leading industrial state of the Southeast and the nation's largest producer of cotton textiles, tobacco products, and wooden furniture. Industry surpassed agriculture as the State's chief source of wealth. But the leading industries were all associated with the local abundance of raw materials produced on the farm.

"Tobacco Land." The value of tobacco manufactures, consisting chiefly of cigarettes and pipe tobacco, increased from $16,000,000 in 1900 to $1,284,000,000 in 1951. Tobacco manufacturing is concentrated in Winston-Salem, Durham, Reidsville, and Greensboro. Camels, Chesterfields, Lucky Strikes, and Old Golds are produced in these 4 cities, respectively. Growing about two-fifths of the nation's crop and manufacturing more than half of the nation's tobacco products, North Carolina is truly "Tobacco Land."

Phenomenal Textile Development. Because of its decentralization, its extensive employment of labor, and the value added by manufactures, textile manufacturing has been the major industry in North Carolina except for a few years in the 1920's and 1930's. The total value of textile manufactures increased from $30,000,000 in 1900 to $2,688,000,000 in

1951, and the number of workers from 32,000 to more than 210,000. In 1951 there were 939 textile mills in the State, and Gaston County had more mills than any county in the United States.

North Carolina took the lead in the nation in cotton goods and nylon hosiery, and it led the South in the production of all knit goods and rayon. The State boasts of the largest towel mill in the world at Kannapolis, the largest hosiery mill at Durham, the largest denim mill at Greensboro, the largest damask mill at Roanoke Rapids, the largest men's underwear factory at Winston-Salem, and the world's "combed yarn capital," Gastonia. In 1950 the State produced over 780,000,000 pairs of all types of hosiery, including 40 per cent of the nation's nylon hose.

One of the most significant developments in North Carolina textiles after 1930 was the purchase of many smaller mills by larger companies, such as Burlington Mills. Founded in 1923 and working only 200 employees in 1924, this company in 1950 had 76 plants in 50 communities in 7 states and 5 foreign countries with about 28,000 employees and an annual product of about $300,000,000.

Another noteworthy trend in North Carolina textiles has been the "passing of the mill village," that is, the sale of "company-houses" to the employees. By 1950, more mills in the State, both in actual numbers—83—and percentagewise—21.8—had sold their dwellings than in all other Southern states combined.

In contrast with many mill towns of some states, the highways leading to many of North Carolina's industrial towns are lined with houses of mill workers and have been called "stringtowns," a development closely related to the building of good roads which enabled mill owners to draw labor "from the countryside for miles around."

Other Industries. The forest products industry, chiefly lumber, paper, and furniture, ranked third among the State's manufactures and in 1951 produced over $100,000,000 worth of goods.

Other industries which grew rapidly were food products—largely flour, bread, and other foodstuffs—and chemicals, especially fertilizers and cottonseed oil.

The most spectacular growth of all, though hardly to be considered a manufacture, has been the tourist industry, which since 1950 has risen to an estimated value of over $300,000,000 a year.

Mineral Production. In recent years, North Carolina has usually ranked thirty-seventh among the states in mineral production, but it produces almost 100 per cent of the nation's supply of primary kaolin, 70 per cent of its mica, 35 per cent of its feldspar and granite, limestone, gravel, and sand in commercial quantities. The largest tungsten mine in the

United States is near Henderson, and Mount Airy has the largest open-faced granite quarry in the world.

The State's 1950 population of 4,061,929 was an increase of 13.7 per cent over 1940. Urban population increased from 27.3 per cent in 1940 to 33.7 per cent in 1950. At that date Charlotte had 134,000 people; Winston-Salem, 87,811; Greensboro, 74,389; Durham, 71,311; Raleigh, 65,679; Asheville, 53,000; Wilmington, 45,043; High Point, 39,973; Kannapolis (unincorporated), 28,448; and Rocky Mount, 27,679. The State had 523 towns of 1,000 inhabitants or more. In short, North Carolina is "a State of small farms and small towns."

Agricultural Program. Though agriculture developed more slowly than industry, it expanded greatly and continued as the primary occupation of North Carolinians. From 1900 to 1952 there was an increase in the number of farms—from 224,637 in 1900 to 288,508—and a decrease in the average size of farms—from 101.3 to 67 acres. In 1952, North Carolina had the largest rural population in the nation, 1,376,664, and only Texas had a larger number of farms.

Until surpassed by tobacco in the 1920's, cotton was the State's major crop, with a record production of 1,250,000 bales in 1926. In 1951, it was only 550,000 bales.

Tobacco production increased at a phenomenal rate—from 128 million pounds in 1900 to 979 million pounds in 1951. The farmer's cash income of $522,982,000 in 1951 was greater than from all other crops combined. The North Carolina tobacco crop was worth more than "all the wheat in Kansas, or all the pigs in Iowa, or all the cotton in Mississippi."

Other major crops in 1951 were corn (68,000,000 bushels), worth $112,000,000, hay valued at $37,000,000, and peanuts at $35,000,000. The State ranked high as a producer of soy beans, Irish potatoes, sweet potatoes, strawberries, and a variety of vegetables and fruits.

Low prices for staple crops in the depression years after 1929 compelled an increase in diversified, live-at-home, and livestock farming. In 1951 the North Carolina farmers' cash income from cattle was $110,000,000; hogs, $36,000,000; and poultry, $20,000,000.

Under stimulus of the Federal government, the State created the North Carolina Rural Electrification Authority in 1935 to stimulate the construction of rural power lines. As of July 1, 1951, NCREA reported 261,440 farms with electric power, and the State ranked second in the nation in the number of farms electrified—85 per cent.

An Educational Crusade. In 1902 Gov. Charles B. Aycock and other leaders launched the most remarkable educational campaign in the history of North Carolina. Within two years a far-reaching educational revolution was under way. During the first decade of the century, nearly 3,000 schoolhouses were built—an average of about one a day. The total value of public schools rose from $1,000,000 in 1900 to $110,000,000 in 1930, and to $350,000,000 in 1952. During the same period, the total cost of schools rose from $1,000,000 to $33,000,000, and to over $125,000,000. The minimum constitutional school term was increased from 4 to 6 months in 1918, to 8 months in 1933, and to 9 months in 1943.

Universities and Colleges. The state government, educational foundations, and philanthropic individuals revolutionized the facilities of higher education after 1900. The State increased its annual appropriations for maintenance of its colleges and universities from $155,000 in 1901 to $3,282,000 in 1927 and to $18,318,058 in 1952. The result was a remarkable expansion in physical plants, teaching staffs, and breadth and quality of educational programs. There was marked increase and growth of graduate and professional schools. In the 1920's the University of North Carolina achieved leadership in the South and distinction in the nation in the field of higher education. By 1950, 11 of its departments received national ranking, with Johns Hopkins being the only Southern institution exceeding it in this respect.

The general assembly of 1931, at the request of Gov. O. Max Gardner, consolidated the State College of Agriculture and Engineering at Raleigh, the State College for Women in Greensboro, and the University of North Carolina at Chapel Hill into the University of North Carolina. At the beginning of 1953 the three units of the University of North Carolina had 12,000 students, 1,200 faculty members, and physical plants valued at about $100,000,000. The State was also maintaining 12 standard colleges for whites, Negroes, and Indians. There were also 41 private and denominational colleges for whites and Negroes in the State.

In 1924 James B. Duke created the Duke Endowment of about $40,000,000 and at Duke's death in 1925, the endowment was more than doubled, and a large portion of the more than $80,000,000 was assigned to Trinity College, which changed its name to Duke University. Davidson College and Johnson C. Smith University for Negroes at Charlotte also received smaller portions of income from the Duke Endowment.

Wake Forest College was also the beneficiary of several large bequests in the 1940's and 1950's. The first of these gifts led to the building of the Bowman Gray Medical School at Winston-Salem in 1941. In 1946 the Zachary Smith Reynolds Foundation offered the income from $10,000,000 to Wake Forest, contingent upon transferring the college to Winston-Salem. Charles Babcock offered a site of 350 acres and an anonymous donor promised $2,000,000 if the Baptists would raise an additional $3,000,000 by the end of 1953. This amount was raised, and the college authorities predicted that the New Wake Forest College would be in operation at Winston-Salem by 1956.

Libraries and Publications. In 1897 Durham established the first tax supported library in the State. By 1951 the total number of volumes in county and city libraries had risen to 2,386,154 and total circulation to 10,505,353. The largest libraries in the State in 1954 were those at Duke University with over 1,130,000 volumes and the University of North Carolina at Chapel Hill with about 675,000 volumes. These two libraries achieved high rank among the general and research libraries in the South and nation. Each became well known for its great collection of documents relating to Southern history, and the combined resources of the two libraries made Chapel Hill-Durham one of the great research centers of the nation in the field of history and other social studies.

There was a decrease in the number and an increase in the quality, size, and circulation of newspapers. In 1954 the State had about 200 newspapers, including 46 dailies, with a circulation of almost 2,000,000. By publishing many feature articles as well as news, the newspapers helped stimulate popular interest in history, literature, and state development.

The University of North Carolina Press at Chapel Hill and Duke University Press in Durham achieved national and international distinction for the quality and quantity of their scholarly books and journals. *The State,* now a bi-weekly magazine published in Raleigh, is devoted exclusively to articles and stories of a popular nature about North Carolina and reaches a wide audience.

Writing and Preserving the State's History. In the twentieth century, for the first time, the literary production of North Carolina—by birth and by adoption—achieved national distinction in quantity and quality. Until about 1930 chief interest and activity were in the fields of history and biography. Among the State's outstanding writers in these fields in the first quarter of the twentieth century were John Spencer Bassett, Holland Thompson, William E. Dodd, Stephen B. Weeks, Charles L. Raper, H. M. Wagstaff, R. D. W. Connor, J. G. de Roulhac Hamilton, William K. Boyd, Archibald Henderson, M. deL. Haywood, Edgar W. Knight, Charles L. Coon, and Robert W. Winston. General histories of the State were written by S. A. Ashe; by Connor, Boyd, and Hamilton (1919); by Connor (1929); and by Henderson (1939). The *Colonial Records of North Carolina,* edited by W. L. Saunders, and the *State Records of North Carolina,* edited by Walter Clark, are among the best printed records of any state in the nation, and *The Moravian Records,* edited by Adelaide L. Fries, has been called "the greatest corpus of historical material" for any Southern colony.

The North Carolina Historical Commission (now the State Department of Archives and History), has been active for over half a century in collecting, preserving, and publishing the State's historical records. It has published scores of valuable books, and its quarterly *North Carolina Historical Review* has been acclaimed as one of the best state historical periodicals in the nation.

Non-Fiction Writers. After 1930 hundreds of volumes of history, biography, autobiography, sociology, science, literature, religion, folklore, architecture, music, and other areas of knowledge rolled from the presses. Among the significant writers in these fields were: W. L. Blythe, A. L. Brooks, W. J. Cash, C. C. Crittenden, Jonathan Daniels, Josephus Daniels, Chalmers Davidson, Adelaide L. Fries, L. L. Gobbel, Fletcher M. Green, Gerald Johnson, Guion G. Johnson, John Tate Lanning, A. R. Newsome, G. W. Paschal, William Meade Prince, Phillips Russell, J. C. Sitterson, M. L. Skaggs, David Stick, Charles S. Sydnor, Nannie M. Tilley, Manly Wade Wellman, D. J. Whitener, and Robert Woody. Among the State's distinguished writers were Howard W. Odum and Rupert Vance in sociology, Robert E. Coker and B. W. Wells in science, Newman I. White and Lodwick Hartley in English literature, Edgar W. Knight in the history of education, Edwin McNeill Poteat in religion, and Louis R. Wilson in library science.

Increase in Church Membership. While North Carolina was witnessing an intellectual revolution, church membership was increasing at a rapid rate. In 1951 the North Carolina Council of Churches reported a total church membership in the State of 2,300,000: Baptists, 1,000,000; Methodists, 575,000; Presbyterians, 135,000; Lutherans, 50,000; Episcopalians, 35,000; Disciples of Christ, 35,000; Congregational Christian, 25,000; Evangelical and Reformed, 15,000; Friends, 15,000; Moravians, 15,000; all others, 400,000.

North Carolina in World War I. In April, 1917, the United States entered World War I on the side of England, France, and the other "Allies" against Germany, Austria, and the other "Central Powers." North Carolina turned its attention from local politics and problems to do its part in the war. The State sent 86,457 men into the service of the United States, of whom nearly 2,400 lost their lives and another 4,000 were wounded.

There were no military units composed entirely of North Carolinians; but two army divisions containing many Tar Heels became famous—the Thirtieth or Old Hickory Division, which helped to break the strong German "Hindenburg Line," and the Eighty-first or Wildcat Division, which took part in the Meuse-Argonne offensive near the close of the war.

Army cantonments were established at Camp Polk, near Raleigh; Camp Greene, near Charlotte; Camp Bragg (later Fort Bragg), near Fayetteville; and elsewhere, where thousands of troops were trained. During the war, which ended on Nov. 11, 1918, North Carolinians contributed over $3,000,000 to the Red Cross and other service organizations and bought $60,000,000 worth of bonds to help finance the war.

North Carolina in World War II. The national defense program and American participation in World War II (1941-45) had important effects on North Carolina. Fort Bragg was greatly enlarged, so that with its 122,000 acres and 3,135 buildings and a "maximum load of nearly 100,000 men," it was "the most comprehensive of Army installations, performing more different functions than any other camp." More than 100 army, navy, marine, and coast-guard stations were established in the State. Camp Lejeune was the second largest Marine base in the country, Cherry Point one of the largest Marine Air bases. Camp Butner and Camp Davis were among the largest Infantry camps, and Camp Mackall was the second largest Airborne training center in the nation. There were large air installations at Greensboro and Goldsboro, Marine and Navy installations at Elizabeth City and Edenton, and a Navy receiving station and center at Wilmington. In these various installations, more than 2,000,000 fighting men were trained for combat.

From the State's total population of three and a half million, 370,324 North Carolinians entered the various armed services and served around the world in every important battle zone. More than 7,000 of these lost their lives, and many thousands were wounded. North Carolinians purchased over $1,800,000,000 of United States bonds.

Eighty-three of North Carolina's major industrial plants manufactured and sold direct to various defense agencies $1,358,000,000 worth of war materials. North Carolina delivered to the Quartermaster Corps more textile goods than did any other state—sheets, blankets, clothing, tents, bandages, parachutes, tire cords and fabrics, and other materials. At Kure Beach, the Ethyl-Dow plant manufactured all the tetra-ethyl lead used in the war, and the State supplied more than 50 per cent of all mica. North Carolina ranked fourth in the production of lumber for the Armed Forces. Twenty-eight of the industrial plants of the State received a total of 72 Army-Navy "E" awards for outstanding war production records.

State Political Trends. North Carolina has been a strong Democratic state since 1900. An unbroken succession of Democratic governors, Charles B. Aycock, Robert B. Glenn, William W. Kitchin, Locke Craig, Thomas W. Bickett, Cameron Morrison, Angus W. McLean, O. Max Gardner, J. C. B. Ehringhaus, Clyde R. Hoey, J. Melville Broughton, R. Gregg Cherry, W. Kerr Scott, and William B. Umstead, won easy victories in every election from 1900 through 1952.

Though the Republican vote was substantial in both total and percentage, that party succeeded in electing no governor, no state officer, no United States senator, and only 8 representatives in Congress from 1900 to 1953. In the presidential contest of 1928, Republican Herbert Hoover carried the State, and in 1952 Republican Dwight D. Eisenhower polled 558,107 votes, the largest vote ever received by a Republican in North Carolina, though not as large as the 652,803 votes received by Democratic Adlai E. Stevenson.

The Role of North Carolina in National Politics. In national politics North Carolina had little influence from 1860 to 1913. But during the Democratic administration of Woodrow Wilson (1913-21), North Carolina played a significant role in national affairs. Josephus Daniels was Secretary of the Navy for the whole 8 years; F. M. Simmons, Lee S. Overman, Claude Kitchin, E. W. Pou, and E. Y. Webb headed important committees in Congress, and Walter Hines Page was Ambassador to England.

Under the New Deal and Fair Deal administrations of Franklin D. Roosevelt and Harry S. Truman (1933-53), more North Carolinians held important positions in the national administration than at any time in history. Among these were: Josephus Daniels, Ambassador to Mexico; Lindsay Warren, Comptroller General of the United States; R. D. W. Connor, National Archivist; Kenneth Royall, Secretary of War and then Secretary of the Army, after the creation of the Department of Defense; Gordon Gray, Secretary of the Army; James Webb, Director of the Budget; J. Crawford Biggs, Solicitor General; Frank McNinch, Chairman of the Federal Communications Commission; Garland Ferguson, Chairman of the Federal Trade Commission; S. Clay Williams, Chairman of the National Recovery Administration; George Allen, Ambassador to Iran (1946-50), to Yugoslavia (1950-53), and to India after 1953; Capus Waynick, Ambassador to Nicaragua (1948-50) and to Colombia (1950-53). *The Official Register of the United States* for 1952 listed some 300 North Carolinians holding top Federal jobs. Jonathan Daniels was an administrative assistant to Pres. Roosevelt, 1942-45, and served for a time as press secretary to Pres. Truman. Daniels' *The Man of Independence* was perhaps the most intimate and valuable biography of Truman published prior to 1955.

Development of Natural Resources. To coordinate and expand its services in conserving, utilizing, and developing its natural resources, the State created the Department of Conservation and Development in 1925. This department enforced the fish and game laws, issued hunting and fishing licenses, operated fish hatcheries, maintained game and wild life preserves and sanctuaries, and sought to protect and develop the fish and game resources of the State. It supervised state parks and the work of forest wardens and operated forest nurseries for reforestation. It maintained stream-gauging stations and carried on studies of water resources, power development, beach erosion, stream pollution, flood control, and other conservation projects. Under the direction of the state geologist, it collected data on mineral deposits and mining operations and worked toward the development of a wider use of mineral resources. Since 1937, in particular, it has publicized the scenic, commercial, and industrial attractions of North Carolina to draw tourists and industry. By 1954 the "tourist industry" in North Carolina amounted to over $300,000,000 a year.

State and National Parks. Climate, scenery, flora and fauna, topography, historic places, good roads, modern hotels, and advertising combined to make North Carolina attractive for recreation, sports, and health. Summer resorts along the coast and the inland sounds and in the mountains and winter resorts in the Sandhills developed extensively with the aid of individuals and corporations. But the State itself contributed to recreational development by its program of good roads, advertising, and state parks. By 1952 the State had acquired and developed 15 state parks and recreational areas, among which are Mount Mitchell atop the highest mountain in the eastern United States, Rendezvous Mountain in Wilkes County, Hanging Rock in Stokes County, Morrow Mountain in Stanly County, Town Creek Indian Mound in Montgomery County, and Fort Macon near Beaufort. The United States government also contributed greatly to recreational development by the creation of 4 large national forests—Pisgah and Nantahala in the mountains, Uharie in the piedmont, and Croatan in the coastal plain. The United States government also established the Great Smoky Mountains National Park containing about a half-million acres in North Carolina and Tennessee.

America's most magnificent highway, the Blue Ridge Parkway, connects the Great Smoky Mountains and the Shenandoah National Parks. When completed it will extend for a distance of about 480 miles.

HUGH T. LEFLER
Professor of History
University of North Carolina

GLIDER FLIGHT BY WRIGHT BROTHERS, KILL DEVIL HILL

WRIGHT BROTHERS' NATIONAL MEMORIAL, NAGS HEAD

CUPOLA HOUSE, EDENTON

JOHN WRIGHT STANLY HOUSE, NEW BERN (HIGHTON)

ARTIST'S CONCEPTION OF TRYON'S PALACE AT NEW BERN

ELIZABETHAN GARDENS, ROANOKE ISLAND

OCONALUFTEE INDIAN VILLAGE, CHEROKEE (JOHN PARRIS)

CHEROKEE BALL GAME

EAGLE DANCE FROM "UNTO THESE HILLS," CHEROKEE

SCENE FROM "THE LOST COLONY," MANTEO

MEDICINE DANCE FROM "HORN IN THE WEST," BOONE

RECONSTRUCTION OF RALPH LANE'S FORT ON ROANOKE ISLAND

BIRTHPLACE OF ANDREW JOHNSON, RALEIGH

OLD MARKET HOUSE, FAYETTEVILLE

Architecture

THE STORY OF architecture from Roanoke Island west to the Smokies is the story all over Anglo-America, with adaptations to suit the people, their local problems and resources, their contacts, and what an old man called "the times we is in at." *

During the years of struggle for subsistence—whether along the rivers in the 17th century, or down the Shenandoah Valley into the piedmont in the 18th, or up the mountain coves in the 19th—settlers built as their fathers had built, or as materials within reach dictated. Whenever the pressure eased, new sets of circumstances fostered new departures in space-planning; and the development either of structural innovations or of stylistic pretensions often occurred in direct ratio with the degree of prosperity inside—and of acquaintanceship outside—any given area. The time-lag in acceptance of each phase of architectural expression after its evolution elsewhere has varied for different parts of North Carolina from less than a decade to upwards of a century. In this broad State, therefore, the dating of undocumented buildings by their characteristics can be rated a more than usually hazardous sport.

At Fort Raleigh National Historic Site on Roanoke Island, both documentary and archeological evidence sufficed by 1950 to permit reconstruction by the National Park Service of Gov. Ralph Lane's "new Fort" of 1585, a brave little star-shaped earthwork with surrounding ditch. Conjectural today is the exact aspect of Lane's "decent dwelling houses" in the nearby "Citie," or village, and of the "newe Cottages" added in 1587 by Gov. John White's ill-fated colony. But

---

* Books on the subject, generously illustrated, have come out since publication of the first edition of this *Guide*, e.g.: B. Wootten & A. Henderson, *Old Homes and Gardens of North Carolina* (Chapel Hill, 1939); and F. B. Johnston & T. T. Waterman, *The Early Architecture of North Carolina* (Chapel Hill, 1941).

Over 225 North Carolina buildings are represented by photographs or measured drawings in the collection of the Historic American Buildings Survey at the Library of Congress, Washington, D. C.; and above 600 have been listed for reference by the North Carolina Chapter of The American Institute of Architects.

building habits were strong amongst English artificers. The typical one-room frame house will have had its joints mortised-and-tenoned and pegged by a carpenter, as for generations past; the walls filled in between framing-pieces with wattle (woven saplings) and daub (clay); the thatched roofs low-eaved and steep-gabled for headroom in the loft, reached by a ladder within; the single end-chimneys of timber and clay, until brick could be made and oyster-shells burned for lime mortar; the floor simply of earth, if not bricked over; the window or windows small, shuttered but unglazed; and the door secure in two crossed thicknesses of plank.

A century later, with more time and artificers and imported nails, English settlers along the rivers of Albemarle Sound may have nogged such frame walls with brick, certainly sided them with weatherboard-ing, and covered them with roofs of long cypress shingles. Almost two centuries after Fort Raleigh, moreover, new piedmont arrivals from Europe briefly continued the Medieval tradition of exposed-frame con-struction in the first Moravian settlements and in Salem, the central town, where buildings erected near the Square by skilled artificers of the General Economy are now being preserved, repaired, restored, and reconstructed. In 1768 the Rev. Frederic William Marshall adjudged weatherboarding "the most expensive method" for protecting the ex-posed frame of the Brothers' house on the Square, to which a brick extension toward the south was added in 1785-86; and its north end was not until 1800 plastered over with lime mortar, nor sided with beaded-edge weatherboarding until 1825. By that time, building customs peculiar to all non-English settlers and their descendants had almost en-tirely merged into the American scene.

Within the first century after Fort Raleigh, security of a different sort characterized the earliest recorded construction work here on a technical principle alien to artificers from the British Isles, and intro-duced possibly by a certain Maryland "Sweed" who migrated south about that time: "ye Logg house" prison, which was put up in January, 1678, purposely to confine an unpopular official. Nobody knows whether this little 10-or-11-foot bird-cage, which afforded only one-fourth the liberty of the 20-foot Maryland loghouse jail of 1669, had its logs left round and saddle-notched at the ends, or hewn square and dovetailed for a snug fit. Variations on both methods are found later. By 1728 William Byrd II, one of the Virginia-Carolina boundary commissioners, could report in that area a preponderance of "Log-houses...finisht without Nails or other Iron-Work," and the technique went on to be exploited by Scottish, Scotch-Irish, German, and some English settlers who built one- or two-room dwellings in the piedmont and beyond.

An example of the "dog-run" or "possum-trot" plan, with covered breezeway connecting two separate rooms, may be seen at Green River Plantation, Polk County.

In a sense that plan was not unlike the basic two-room-and-central-passage frame house—so admirably adapted to the climate—which is believed to have become well established here alongside the one-room type in the later 1600's. Unhappily evidence is scanty, and the tourist who grew up in, or around the corner from, a 17th-century house elsewhere should be braced to find no more of those in North Carolina than houses of 1682 in Philadelphia. Here, whatever such buildings escaped the "savages' ravages" in the early 18th century have since succumbed to fire, termites, or neglect.

Some of those 17th-century houses will have had their two rooms—"hall" and "parlor"—separated by a passage, which was both entered and air-conditioned by stout doors fore and aft, and which led by a stair at the back to the half-story under the steep-gable roof, sometimes framed for "Dormant Windoes." Such a house, flanked by brick chimneys laid up in a pattern, probably had its rooms floored with wide boards; plastered, or else lined with vertical wainscot; lighted by small-paned casement windows; and, one hopes, provided at an early date with the "good Closets" mentioned by Dr. John Brickell of Edenton in 1731. By this time, also, 12-to-24-pane sliding "Sash Winders" had become fairly common along the coast, although a dated example before 1723 is wanting. A frame house only slightly at variance with the type described—having its stair less advantageously cut out of one of the rooms—is the Thomas White house, which has stood since the early 18th century on Harvey's Neck (across the Perquimans River from Durant's Neck) near the larger contemporary White–Newbold house, a continuant of the plan-type all in brick with its Flemish-bond walls formed in part by the backs of the enclosed chimneys.

This basic two-room-and-central-passage type has been subject to endless variations on the theme which compass practically the entire story of architecture in the State. The theme has been varied by combination of weatherboarded frame walls front and back with brick chimney-walls at the ends, or by introduction of partitions to set off additional rooms; both variations appear in the Old Brick house on Pasquotank River of the early 18th century (from which the mid-century interior shown in Johnston-Waterman is the altered installation, after 1934, in a private home, Greenville, Del.). Other variations were achieved by changing the pitch of the gable roof to form a gambrel for more headroom aloft, or by projecting a lean-to roof over added rooms at the back (both in the Joel Lane house, Raleigh, 1760); by construction in piedmont stone, increase in height to two full stories, or inclusion of the passage in a larger room omitting one partition (all in the Hezekiah Alexander house near Charlotte, 1774, restored); by elimination of one whole end, leaving a tandem-room-and-side-passage plan (in the Eubank house, New Bern, 1774, and others along the coast and inland); or by extension of shed roofs over breezy "Balconies or Piazzas in front and sometimes back . . . found convenient on account of the great Summer Heats" experienced by perspiring travelers like the Philadelphia merchant, William Attmore, who wrote in 1787 of New Bern but might as well have been writing of Beaufort or Wilmington.

The present-day traveler will not want to miss two atypical houses which nevertheless bespeak interesting contacts before the Province became a State. The first of these is the Cupola house, Edenton, built in Chowan Precinct for Currituck-born Col. Richard Sanderson, Jr., of Perquimans, between 1724 and 1726 (despite the "1758" visible on the gable finial). A four-room-and-central-passage house, it exhibits the only surviving instance anywhere in the South of the bracketed "jetty" or second-story overhang, usual in Medieval Europe and 17th-century New England. Specification of this element of the frame as "a fashionable oversett," in the contemporary contract for a now-vanished courthouse eastward in Currituck, suggests recent though belated introduction of the element about that time by some nostalgic New Englander settling along the coast; in those days many vessels every year put in to Port Roanoke (Edenton) from New England ports, especially from Boston. The cupola is less easily traced, if of the original date; that element was already common in England, newly imported to Williamsburg, Va., and known in Boston. Today's prospective visitor who may pass near The Brooklyn Museum on the way south would do well to see there—for comparison with woodwork still in place at the Cupola house—the handsome drawing-room and library interiors executed for a later owner, Francis Corbin, Esq., by Robert Kirshaw, carpenter, between 1756 and 1758 (accounting for the finial date).

The second of the two houses is the Royal Governor's house—Tryon's Palace—designed by John Hawks from Lincolnshire, "surveyor of the works" or pre-professional architect. The two-story house, connected by curved colonnades with two outlying wings, was built of brick with white trim in 1767-70; burned, except for the west wing, in 1798; and is a reconstruction project. William Attmore, merchant-son of a Philadelphia joiner, viewing the Palace in 1787 when it had already been turned to other uses than those of the Royal Governor and Assembly, remarked that "The King of G. Britain's Arms, are still suffered to appear in a pediment at the front of the Building; which considering the independent spirit of the people averse to every vestige of Royalty appears Something strange." He noticed at once, also, the "very elegant" interior feature around which all the rooms were disposed, "The grand Staircase lighted from the Sky by a low Dome, which being glazed kept out the Weather." Although he neglected to mention it, the service stair balanced the "grand Staircase" across the central passage in the plan. Hawks's design reflected the English Palladian forms popular in the time of his elderly master, Stiff Leadbetter of Eton in Buckinghamshire and London, a carpenter-builder for Lord Foley, Lord Harcourt, and other patrons, and surveyor to St. Paul's Cathedral, London, from 1756 until his death 10 years later. The Palace design felt scarcely if at all the influence of the current ornamental fashion, excitedly described by a young Philadelphia carpenter—homecoming from London study—as the "new, bold, light and elegant taste, which has lately been introduced by the great architect [Robert Adam] of the Adelphi Buildings . . . and which is now universally practised all over Britain." After the War for Independence the Adam "taste" was to have its vogue in North Carolina, as will be seen.

Of the once-predominant weatherboarded frame meetinghouses in the Province, Pasquotank Monthly Meeting of Friends (Quakers) agreed to build the first in 1703, immediately after commencement of the first frame Anglican "Chappel" for Chowan Parish in 1702. Many others for the several denominations are a matter of record, but the buildings themselves have gone the way of those 20,000 U.S. country churches abandoned to decay within the past 25 years alone, according to estimates of the National Council of Churches. The best view now obtainable of an 18th-century frame house of worship is to be had in the Anglican chapel of St. John's, Williamsboro, which was moved from its 1757 site in 1771-73, signed in the mortar of the new foundation by John Lynch from over the line in Mecklenburg County, Va., and is now restored.

All three of the first Anglican churches in brick possess, or once possessed, special architectural features. The earliest and smallest is St. Thomas', Bath, of 1734, which is thought to have had originally a hipped roof like many Virginia churches. It may have been built under the supervision of Justice Robert Peyton, who had stopped off on the way south from Kingston Parish, now Mathews County, Va., to see after construction of the courthouse already mentioned in Currituck, where his brother Benjamin was a justice in 1723.

The next completed and largest of the brick churches was St. Philip's, Brunswick, of 1740-67. Once the Chapel Royal, with elevated pew for the Royal Governor, it is now a picturesque ruin dignified by a great

Palladian window over the departed altar. Such a chancel window—composed of a round-arched opening flanked by lower and narrower square-top openings—had been used by Sir Christopher Wren in some of his London churches, and was currently being modeled abroad in several engraved plates of James Gibbs's *Book of Architecture* (London, 1728). Not at all common over here, the Palladian window was soon to appear again in drawings for the King's Chapel, Boston, by Capt. Peter Harrison of Newport, R.I., mariner-merchant and avocational designer who frequently sailed in and out of Port Brunswick after 1739 with London cargoes for the gifted public servant of this Province, Col. Edward Moseley. Each of these cultivated gentlemen possessed a fine library, including books of architecture, and one man or the other—or both together—may have had something to do with the ambitious design for St. Philip's. Even a contemporary joiner owned "11 books of architecture" by the time he died in Craven County about 1755.

The best preserved of the brick churches is St. Paul's, Edenton, begun in 1736 just after Col. Moseley left the Edenton area for his estates nearer St. Philip's. Formerly surveyor-general and an excellent draftsman, Col. Moseley may have suggested for St. Paul's the apsidal sanctuary enframing the altar. Such an apse, unusual for the time this side of the Atlantic, was a lineal descendant of those in the earliest Christian churches of ancient Rome. From that apse at the east end of the church to the square entrance tower with octagonal spire (restored, like the interior woodwork originally finished in 1774), St. Paul's abides in its graveyard as a notable example of the small, 3-aisled, provincial English parish church of its day, evolved in the course of centuries to meet definite liturgical needs which it frankly displays, outside and in.

Not far from St. Paul's, at the head of the long vista down Edenton Green and across the Bay, stands the Chowan County Courthouse, one of the most distinguished 18th-century public buildings in the South—or in the United States, for that matter. The Courthouse was built in 1767 by (traditionally) Gilbert Leigh, under supervision of 5 "Trustees & Directors" who were bonded to Gov. Tryon for the purpose by Act of the Assembly. Gilbert Leigh is believed to have come from Virginia, where he or some of the Trustees may have known the old Isle of Wight County Courthouse of about 1750, somewhat similar in plan only. Whoever determined the Chowan design broke with two established public-building types in this Province. One of those types resembled an enlarged version of the two-room-and-central-passage frame house, with the courtroom weighting down one end of the plan; such had been "ye Gran Court House" in Perquimans Precinct, built between 1694 and 1701 and soon destroyed. The other followed the

English market house type, open below with a room or rooms above; this type had been seen in the "fashionable oversett fram'd work standing upon Sedar Blocks" specified for Currituck in 1723, and in the second Craven County Courthouse elevated upon brick piers and groin-vaults, a building long under construction but completed under the superintendence of John Hawks in 1766. Several early examples of the second type are known, but none is extant; a late survival of the type at the center of Fayetteville, built in the days of Romantic stylism, associated the round arches of "Roman" and a turret of "Greek" derivation with the pointed arches of "Gothic."

The two-story Chowan County Courthouse which embodies the significant break with both the older types is admirable not alone for the proportions of its façade, its fine brick work with white trim, its graceful cupola, and the remarkable paneling of its large second-floor room. The observant eye will see at once that this building, like nearby St. Paul's, reveals both outside and inside exactly which universal need of mankind it was designed to satisfy architecturally. The courtroom, instead of weighting down one end of the plan or taking second place above a market, occupies the important central space as befits the dignity of the Law and terminates in an apse for the judge's chair. The apse recalls those in ancient Roman courts of law (basilicas), of which the Chowan County Courthouse is a secular—as St. Paul's is an ecclesiastical—descendant. Related as the Courthouse is with the vista down the Green and across the Bay, no more telling example need be sought anywhere of the provincial English Baroque public building.

After the War for Independence from England, there ensued a not unpredictable phase of self-conscious nationalism in which the Thirteen Colonies gradually came of age in terms of design as well as government. No longer could it be thought decorous for the Assembly here to meet in the Royal Governor's house at New Bern, nor to wander from one courthouse to another amongst the borough towns. Prime needs for the new State were a capital town and a capitol. It was not the first time the need for a town had called forth a preconceived plan here. Bath-Town—laid out by Surveyor-General John Lawson before its incorporation in 1706—had been followed by New Bern (1710), "The Town on Queen Anne's Creek" (1712, soon Edenton), Beaufort (by 1722), and Brunswick (by 1727). Succeeding decades saw their chessboard street-pattern carried up-river, eventually to meet itself being brought down the Shenandoah Valley by new settlers familiar with the Philadelphia plan established in 1682. There, the cross-streets of the chessboard had been intended to focus on a central square, with subsidiary squares in the quadrants; but the magnetic attraction of trade along the navigable Delaware River so far exceeded the intellectual charms of a plan on paper that the central square long awaited company.

Inevitably the pattern came to be imposed in North Carolina not only upon flat coastal sites, which it suited fairly well, but upon hillier piedmont terrain with which its capacity for cooperation was limited by its inflexible regularity. Sometimes the cross-street-and-chessboard alone appeared, as at Salisbury (1753) and Hillsboro (1754); sometimes the streets led to a square, as at Salem (1766). So it was that the Hon. William Christmas—surveyor who platted Warrenton in 1779, and state senator from Franklin County in 1792—in the latter year perpetuated the 110-year-old Philadelphia plan in "the unalterable seat of government" for the new State of North Carolina: the new City of Raleigh, constant reminder of Sir Walter and his Roanoke Island settlement for Elizabeth I. Only a few months earlier, the new nation's capital city had been laid out by L'Enfant, its chessboard traversed diagonally by French Baroque avenues after the manner of Louis XIV's Versailles. The new capital city of Raleigh—like Philadelphia—carried on the 17th-century English Palladian squares, which themselves had been formed upon the precepts of the ancient Roman theorist, Vitruvius. Designers at a later day were to study the terrain and the people more assiduously than precedent, in their search for direct solutions to actual problems.

Only slight precedent existed for a great deal that the new State had to get done quickly in order to satisfy needs not included in the universal old trio of dwelling, worship, and government. Nevertheless government must first be taken care of, and education for participation in government. In the middle of Union (later Capitol) Square in the new government town, as yet unpopulated, Rhody Atkins put up in 1792-94 the simplest possible brick box for a State House; and in 1793-95 James Patterson did the same on lonely Chapel Hill with Old East building, the first State University building opened to students in any one of the United States. Both buildings were to be enriched somewhat later after the pressure eased, but fire would claim in 1831 the State House together with its seated statue of George Washington by Canova, a remarkable purchase which had recently made the last lap of its long journey from Italy by ox-drawn transport from Fayetteville.

Meanwhile, hard to imagine today is the magnitude of the difficulties surmounted by Atkins and Patterson, who contracted to make something out of nothing at a distance of almost 200 miles from the nearest seaport-town, Wilmington. Even 40-odd years later at the river-town of Fayetteville, in direct communication with Wilmington, an experienced captain of ordnance, sent to establish single-handed the Arsenal ordered by Congress to be the "great place of [military] construction and deposit in the South," had no choice but to report to his colonel commanding in 1836: "Of bricks there are none in the country. . . . The few that have been used here, have been fabricated of clay manipulated by the trampling of cattle. Such an apparatus as a clay-mill or brick-press is unknown in this region. . . . Almost every gentleman here who has had occasion to use Bricks in any quantity has been compelled to manufacture them with his own force, after the peculiar fashion of the country."

Comparable problems in logistics had been less acute nearer the coastal towns. In the 1790's, well-known builders from several states had not hesitated to submit proposals for construction of the old frame lighthouse at Baldhead below Wilmington, begun by this State and completed by the U.S. Treasury Department (then in charge of aids to navigation); nor for erection of the latter's 90-foot sandstone lighthouse tower at Cape Hatteras, replaced in 1870 by the 193-foot brick tower still standing on that treacherous sandy bank. Indeed, competence quite out of the ordinary for 1826-34 in the United States is apparent in the masonry construction of the ramps, stairs, and brick-vaulted "bomb-proofs" of Fort Macon, built off Beaufort as part of a national system of maritime defenses but now part of the N.C. State Park System.

From the very beginning of Statehood, there had been no lack of praiseworthy theory and intent, as evidenced by the handsome paper-plan for the capital town, the reasoned vision essential to establishment of the State University, and the foresighted protection of Cape Fear trade by a lighthouse. Moreover, the Assembly in 1795-96 enacted a sound law requiring each county court to appoint and bond a treasurer of public buildings to "superintend" construction of courthouses and jails and to "recommend alterations, repairs or improvements." True, nobody had been ready by 1787 for the schemes of English-born Col. William Tatham, assemblyman that year from the new Robeson County; hence by 1801 he became superintendent of construction for the complicated London Docks at Wapping on the Thames. But the War of 1812 was hardly over before North Carolina awakened in spectacular fashion to the need for better design of trade-communications —"internal improvements," as then called everywhere—which were forthwith projected under the enlightened leadership of Archibald D. Murphey, state senator from piedmont Orange County.

Under the Murphey program, this State led many of the rest by retaining the professional services of designers trained as architect-engineers. Though the two professions were still one in this country at that time, and not destined to suffer their temporary cleavage until after mid-century, nevertheless their practitioners were honored with distinct titles in North Carolina by 1819—almost as early as in Paris, where

Napoleon I's *Ecole des Beaux-Arts* and *Ecole Polytechnique* encouraged the distinction—namely: Capt. William Nichols, state architect, who supervised the "Classicizing" of the box-like State House with east and west porticoes, a dome, and a plaster jacket; and Hamilton Fulton, Esq., state engineer, straight from London with the last word on canal and lock construction for inland navigation.

Some of the dual practitioners who preceded and followed these separate dignitaries here call up unexpected associations. Thus B. F. Baldwin, the first to submit his report on *Inland Navigation* to the Assembly's commissioners in 1816, had come from near Boston in place of his brother Loammi, Jr., who shortly became Virginia's principal engineer and, a decade later, the designer of America's first dry docks at Norfolk, Va., and Charlestown, Mass. Extensive professional counsel was given in 1818 to one of the Assembly's commissioners by English-born B. Henry Latrobe, dean of the double profession over here, whose varied practice ranged from the Virginia Penitentiary of 1797 to the New Orleans Waterworks which claimed his life in 1820, besides his many years in Washington as the nation's first surveyor of the public buildings, appointed in 1803 by avocational-designer Pres. Thomas Jefferson; by coincidence, Latrobe's Moravian grandfather Henry Antes, millwright and Philadelphia County justice, had been one of the Brethren responsible for surveying the Wachovia Tract here in 1753.

Even Ithiel Town, of Connecticut and elsewhere—usually thought of in another connection soon to be mentioned—was recorded by the U.S. Patent Office in 1820 as a Fayetteville resident, busy with his Clarendon Bridge for the through-highway over the Cape Fear River when he patented his internationally famous light-weight bridge design. He may not even have known that up the future route of North Carolina's "Appian Way"—the Plank Road of 1849 from Fayetteville to Salem—stood the heavy timber frame of the Moravian Brothers' house, not weatherboarded until 1825. It might have served as a reminder to anyone who happened to think about it that the genuine link between the Middle Ages and the 19th century lay not in the Romantic resuscitation of "Gothic" ornament but in the transmutation of that timber frame into Town's more economical sawn-plank "lattice" truss, soon to be tried out in iron for railroad bridges which would forecast not only the doom of canals but the promise of construction in steel. At Fayetteville, Ithiel Town must have known Robert Leckie the Scot, equally busy at the time with a canal there, and in 1829 the Washington City patentee of his own hydraulic-cement, a forerunner of plastic concrete. Few Americans today would care to abandon entirely the combined results to date of 125-year-old patented inventions such as Town's and Leckie's, which—when skillfully related to a site and to people, in delicately developed space-enclosures of ferro-concrete, for example—transcend mere materials and technics with a gallant lift of the spirit.

Realization of this basic inseparability of architecture and engineering, despite their 19th-century cleavage, became fairly general among professionals and non-professionals alike by the second quarter of the 20th century. Otherwise it might be necessary to spell out today how much more fundamental for the ultimate advancement of the State of North Carolina were the architect-engineers' perfectly timed contributions to satisfaction of human needs in the Early Republic than were all the belatedly "Adam-esque" ornamental urns, rosettes, festoons, colonnettes, and kindred surface trivia—lovely in themselves, of course —in fine houses from the coast up through the piedmont. That obvious fact accepted, the intriguing examples of Romantic stylism in any part of the Western world can be viewed dispassionately without danger of reviving the precarious social insecurity which inspired them.

Seen in retrospect, Romantic stylism had followed from its rise to its decline a predictable course, which is best reviewed before examination of the tangible results. In the lifetime of Robert Adam (who died the year William Christmas laid out Raleigh and Rhody Atkins began the State House), the European nations, expanding their colonial empires and world trade, were nevertheless thoroughly upset by wars and by revolutions—political, industrial, and social. Men who could afford the luxury of doing so sought escape from the least pleasant realities in Romantic daydreaming: about faraway places in the austere Classical past of Greece and Rome, or in the exotic Oriental present seen through the China trade; and likewise about long-ago times in the Middle Ages when knighthood had bloomed nearer home in Europe. The same kinds of daydreaming affected all of the arts—literature, painting, music, and so on.

In architecture, those daydreams—materializing first as playful garden temples for the nobility, in carefully manicured "natural" woodland settings—soon rubbed off as ornamental frosting on more serious buildings, often leaving relatively untouched their space-composition and structural form. Then, as the guillotine in France rhythmically dispatched the heads of the ruling class during the Revolution, so in England machinery of the industrial revolution played roulette with wealth and power. The new little men of money who began to rise to the top had long been accustomed to having their minds made up for them in matters artistic—by the Royal Academies for France and her satellites, and by the cultivated gentry for England and her colonies, meaning us. These new men-at-the-top everywhere, untrained and inexperienced in the arts, were on their own for the first time when it came to making artistic judgments, and cautiously sought refuge in conservative imitation of the Romantic stylism which happened to be fashionable when they took over. The same attitude would have obtained had the fashionable thing at the time involved horizontal logs topped by bulbous domes, as in Russia. In the West it happened to be Romantic stylism, a product of its time.

At the very moment, therefore, when bolder initiative and the direct approach to problems might have stepped out to meet new needs for unprecedented types of buildings with freshly invented materials and know-how, almost everybody ran for cover to the pages of historical pattern-books on how to be safe though banal. In the United States, the 7 pattern-books issued by one man alone—Asher Benjamin—between 1797 and the Civil War went into 44 known editions and possibly two more, while the architectural stand-bys published in London during Robert Adam's lifetime continued to be reverently handed down from grandfather to grandson over here as Biblical authority for building. Authority became the secure substitute for facing an architectural problem and thinking it through on its own terms. Yet no other peoples had allowed themselves to be thus enslaved, unless possibly the ancient, other-worldly Egyptians. Men in every age before had prided themselves on being "modern." But wasteful decades of the 19th and 20th centuries were required to diminish the roster of men emotionally conditioned to follow in the arts rather than lead.

North Carolina proved no exception to the Western world. After the War for Independence many intrinsically charming or even handsome buildings went up, and whether or not they marked an advance toward the 21st century, they tell a fascinating story of the 19th and 20th, and deserve to be judged by the standards of inventive copyism which prevailed in their day. In the design of houses, the familiar plan-types persisted, primarily the basic two-room-and-central-passage type together with its many possible variations already described. Occasionally a room broke into a curve or even a full "Adam-esque" oval, as in the ballroom with coupled Ionic pilasters which was added in 1830 to the Halliday-Williams house in Fayetteville; or the stair swept up in a self-supporting spiral, as in the lamented Montmorenci near Warrenton, of 1825.

One special variant developed out of an 18th-century plan by Robert Morris in *Rural Architecture* (London, 1750). For this the central passage gave way to two rooms in tandem, directly entered, and flanked by two projecting wings either enclosed or left open to the breeze. The stair, relegated to a back corner of the main block, led up to a second story which was covered by a gable roof headed fore and aft like a temple front instead of sidewise as before. The lower roofs of the one-story wings received varied treatment, those of the Hazel–Nash house in

Hillsboro repeating the head-on gable either side at smaller scale. There also, a one-story porch or piazza of "Greek" Ionic columns across the main block was designed to accompany three pointed "Gothic" windows, one in each of the gables; if the traditional date about 1818 be accurate, it was early for that kind of mixture.

Could one house only be seen, it might well be the one said to have been begun in 1789 and completed by hands unknown in 1801 for a trustee of the University, former Gov. Samuel Johnston of Edenton, and by him romantically named Hayes after the seat of Sir Walter Raleigh, which it in no way resembles, of course. The four-room-and-passage plan and square monitor do resemble, in principle only, the plan and cupola of the Cupola house; and the curved colonnades with outlying wings and the hipped roof generally perpetuate similar elements in Tryon's Palace, itself a descendant of 16th-century Palladian Mannerist villas by way of early 18th-century England, as has been seen. At that point the pedigree of Hayes gallops off in all directions. Up the long driveway approach from the town side, a short flight of steps lined with delicate wrought-iron balustrades leads to a wonderfully slender semicircular portico sheltering a door accented by sidelights and segmental fanlight. This is all very "Adam-esque" indeed, as is the scale of the interior trim. But the trim displays the "Greek" fret, and the bay side of the house dazzles the unsuspecting eye with a monumental porch or piazza of full two-story height on a brick basement, with 6 columns of an order which might be described loosely as "Roman." The "Gothic" interior of the west or library wing, said to have been a later redecoration, combines small and brutally large scale with the delightful naïveté of 18th-century Rococo "Gothic" garden temples. Amongst all these contradictory components, there is hardly any consistency at all, yet an enviable verve compared with the stereotyped pseudo-"Colonial" copyism of timid real-estate developers at a later day.

Practically the whole gamut of plan- or elevation-variants is run in the examples cited, and many of the detail-variants as well. Upon those it is next to impossible to generalize, the situation as regards ornament being so completely every man—his skill, his tools, and his pattern-books, not to mention his client—for himself. If it were to be said that finer-scale "Adam-esque" detail tended to appear near the coast—as in the brick tandem-room-and-side-passage Smallwood–Ward house in New Bern, 1812-16—then immediately it must be pointed out that exceedingly fine scale is likewise to be found inland in Burnside, near Williamsboro, about 1810; in its companion interior with elaborate ceiling ornament in Ingleside, Lincoln County, about 1817; in Jacob Stigerwalt's Mill Hill, near Concord, 1821; and so on. And moreover that the most robust "Greek" orders—aside from the Corinthian at the Belo house, Winston-Salem, 1849—are paradoxically to be seen in two coastal examples: the Doric temple portico added in 1840 to Orton, near old Brunswick; and the Corinthian colonnade around three sides of the Bellamy house across the Cape Fear River in Wilmington, 1859.

At the latter, Italianate "Renaissance" detail is already intermingled, as also in Cooleemee, Davie County, 1853, which displays a splendid stair at the center of a radial-wing plan comparable in principle to those formal curiosities—inspired in many states in the 1850's by publication of Orson S. Fowler's *A Home for All*—the octagonal houses: the Hill-Jones house in Carteret County, and the Murray-Sanderson house near Lake Mattamuskeet. A lighter-weight polygonal structure, designed a century later as a "geodesic" dome by R. Buckminster Fuller and James W. Fitzgibbon, AIA, would take to the air from the N.C. State College campus in Raleigh, cable-hooked to a helicopter of the sagacious U.S. Marine Corps.

The climax of Romantic stylism in domestic architecture was anything but a home for all: Biltmore house, near Asheville, 1890-95, some 780 feet long and covering four of the surrounding 12,000 acres landscaped by Frederic Law Olmsted, Sr. Half a century before, in 1846, its architect Richard Morris Hunt had been the first American to enter the *Ecole des Beaux-Arts* for rigorous training by the French method; and 40 years before, in 1854, he had served under M. Lefuel as *inspecteur* for construction of part of Napoleon III's augmentation of the Louvre. Nevertheless he conveyed to the Smokies not the Napoleon III "Baroque" of the Louvre additions but the much earlier transitional Francis I "Renaissance" of the Loire Valley *châteaux*. A master of mass and of ornament, Hunt—had he been so minded—could have done wonders as freely as his contemporary Louis Sullivan; for by the time Biltmore was finished Sullivan's erstwhile lieutenant, Frank Lloyd Wright, had already designed and completed, for example, a low-cost housing group in Chicago prophetic of that American's reverse influence on Europe even before World War I. Few European-trained Americans such as Hunt, however, succeeded in concentrating on the fundamental principles they had learned, fascinated as they were by the valises-full of European stylistic motifs they had brought back in their architectural luggage.

By coincidence today's traveler may see in the Dr. S. Weizenblatt house, Asheville, 1941, a representative design by Marcel Breuer, former student and staff member of the renowned Bauhaus—located first in Weimar and then in Dessau, Germany—and likewise former staff member with Walter Gropius at Harvard. From 1919 on, the Bauhaus comprised a group of creative artists in many fields working with

Walter Gropius to train young designers and had as its objects the deeper perception of space, planes, and textures, specifically by the inter-relation of art, industry, and daily life through the medium of archi-tecture. When closed by Hitler, the Bauhaus proved no less influential than it had been before, inasmuch as leading educational institutions, especially in the United States, immediately sought out and engaged the gifted staff members thus dispersed. North Carolina profited by the stimulating presence at Black Mountain College of Josef Albers, until his departure for Yale.

Gradual abandonment of American architectural dependence on Europe had become more than ever apparent after World War I, and the majority of practitioners today have naturally been attuned to the architecture of tomorrow for more years than have their prospective clients. Indeed, citation of contemporary examples of their work paral-lel with developments elsewhere—so difficult when the first edition of this *Guide* went to press—is now equally difficult by reason of abundance. Of the many contemporary houses now being completed annually, it may be well to cite some of the architects' own homes, theoretically the embodiment—within chronic financial limitations—of their own best judgment untrammeled by the desires of clients whose interests it is their pleasure and duty to serve on other occasions. A random geographical selection, with apologies to architects whose homes happen not to be mentioned, might include those of: Arthur Gould Odell, Jr., AIA, Charlotte; John Erwin Ramsay, AIA, Salisbury; Edward Loewenstein, AIA, Greensboro; Henry L. Kamphoefner, AIA, and G. Milton Small, AIA, both in Raleigh; and John J. Rowland, AIA, Kinston.

The happy situation with respect to rising standards of flexibility has been in part the result of a swift change in architectural climate felt hereabout especially since organization in 1946 of the Department of City and Regional Planning at the University of North Carolina, Chapel Hill; and the reorganization in 1948 of the School of Design—comprising the Departments of Architecture and Landscape Architec-ture—at North Carolina State College, Raleigh. Distinguished practi-tioners from all over the world make stops of longer or shorter duration at these institutions, and students have won the highest awards in national competition. Organization of the profession in the State had come slowly, measured by formation in 1857 of The American Institute of Architects. The North Carolina Chapter, AIA, preceded by one or two local organizations of members scattered from Wilmington to Asheville, received its charter in 1913, and in 1915 this State became the 10th in line by establishing its North Carolina Board of Architectural Examination and Registration. One is reminded of the State's early move toward recognition of the infant profession by appointment soon after the War of 1812 of a state architect.

The story of other human needs satisfied in the time of the first state architect has yet to be told, and the satisfaction of religious needs is always likely to be the most ultraconservative architecturally. Shortly after the War for Independence the series of Anglican churches already discussed was followed by a series of Moravian churches, the first in stone with parsonage attached, the other two of brick, and all with turrets: the church at Bethabara, near Winston-Salem, 1788; the Home Moravian Church at the corner of the Square in Salem, 1800; and the church at nearby Bethania, 1807. The Lutherans also built not dissimilar churches in stone, as for example Grace Church near China Grove, Rowan County, of uncertain date. Whatever German flavor remained in any of these was fast giving way to general American characteristics, although there is no danger of their being mistaken for New England meetinghouses. That possibility does exist, however, in the case of the First Presbyterian Church, New Bern, built in 1819-22 by (traditionally) Uriah Sandy, whose name has been sought elsewhere in vain. Of weatherboarded frame painted white, the church presents to the visitor an Ionic portico in place of the closed vestibule ornamented with pilasters which is sometimes found in the colder clime. As there, so in New Bern, the square tower rises in diminishing stages to an octagonal cupola. Essentially this is a descendant of the English Baroque churches of Wren, decked out with Romantic touches of "Greek" as was its exact contemporary in London, St. Pancras.

The churches of special consequence in the next several decades were Anglican and "Gothic"—more uniformly the former than the latter. Liturgical requirements, as fully predetermined as the rules of Classical proportion, had always made cooperation between the two difficult, whereas the Age of Faith itself had given rise to forms responsive to the needs of the liturgy, and the Age of Romanticism had only to reinterpret them freely, so it was believed. Two apparently related brick churches are St. Matthew's, Hillsboro, 1825-26, and St. Luke's, Salisbury, 1828; both have been repaired and altered from time to time. The name of John Berry of Hillsboro, brickmason, is associated with both; so is that of John Hawks's grandson, the Rev. Francis L. Hawks, in 1825 only a vestryman of St. Matthew's. There the matter rests, with informal collaboration a probability.

An architectural grandson of B. Henry Latrobe—through William Strickland, shortly to be mentioned—was Thomas U. Walter of Philadelphia, designer of St. James's, Wilmington, 1839, and the Chapel of the Cross, Chapel Hill, 1842-45. It is unlikely that he spent much—if any—time at the sites, any more than he did in 1840 at Hibernian Hall,

Charleston, S.C., for which he had won the design competition yet lost a place on the cornerstone to the actual builders. Not that he never deigned to leave Philadelphia. In 1839 he was just back from a European study trip, and by 1843 he was off to Venezuela to design and build the harbor works at La Guaira before adding the wings and iron dome to the national Capitol at Washington in subsequent decades. Eventually he succeeded as president of The American Institute of Architects the founder and first president, English-born Richard Upjohn, architect of Christ Church, Raleigh, 1848-54, whose design is—of all those cited—the most clearly indicative of a birthright knowledge of the English parish church of the Middle Ages, even though he employed 14th-century diagonal buttresses to support walls pierced with 13th-century lancet windows. The Galilee porch connecting the church with its detached tower is a noteworthy feature, and its graceful broach spire of stone (completed 1861) is particularly admirable both in itself and for the part it plays in pinning the composition down to the corner of Capitol Square. Today a number of church buildings have been projected in this State comparable to those already beloved elsewhere by worshipers young in spirit; but at this writing congregations on the whole fear to meet their God unless safely garbed, as it were, in Early Christian togas or Medieval armor.

Easily the most monumental building in the State is—as it should be symbolically—the Capitol, which rose in 1833-40 on the site of the brick box burned in 1831. Ithiel Town of Connecticut, early a member of the Associated Housewright Society in Boston and already met with above at the Clarendon Bridge, was by now of New York, in partnership on and off with Alexander Jackson Davis—soon to be heard of again. One or the other or both determined the basic design and produced a few drawings which combined "Greek" Doric proportions and detail with a "Roman" dome in a way which had become acceptable through Romantic use. Superintendent in Raleigh was the Scot David Paton, who had spent nearly a year in Sir John Soane's office in London. His exertions were praised by many, including Latrobe's pupil Robert Mills of Charleston, S.C., and Washington City, who seems never to have designed a building in this State through which he passed back and forth so many times. Paton's 229 drawings for the building, executed after hours to keep up with the stonemasons whose work he superintended by day, should alone be enough to entitle him to more consideration as a lively participant in the design than he has sometimes received. After a visit home to Edinburgh, he settled in Brooklyn, N.Y., where he practiced architecture and taught drawing throughout his life. Beyond reproach in the Capitol are the clean lines and uninterrupted surfaces outside and in, which serve as a foil for the rich ornament so tellingly placed. Alteration would snatch from the people something fine which is by right their heritage.

Among public buildings in the State of smaller size, there stands out the U.S. Branch Mint, Charlotte (reconstructed as the Mint Museum, 1933-36). It was first built in 1835-40 while the Capitol was going up in Raleigh, and by the Raleigh firm of Perry & Ligon from the design of Latrobe's pupil William Strickland, master of T. U. Walter. Burned in 1844, it was reconstructed by 1846 approximately as before, though the façade varied in some respects from Strickland's drawing. Despite its official character as the mint for the gold center of the United States before the '49 rush to California, the building is nearly domestic in scale for all its "Greek" dignity, and particularly happy in the unifying effect of its exterior wall paneling.

Two courthouses of special interest survive: the old Orange County Courthouse, Hillsboro, by John Berry, 1845-46; and the old Rowan County Courthouse, Salisbury, 1855. Proportions of the "Greek" Doric order governed both, and the temple form was adhered to at Salisbury. At Hillsboro, however, Berry the brickmason not only used brick with white trim in the 18th-century way but added a square clock-tower with octagonal cupola, the result being a homelike sort of courthouse with somewhat the air of a village church. Fortunately both buildings have been preserved with a minimum of alteration, and necessary expansion managed on other sites.

Two early semi-public buildings which provided incidentally for popular gatherings clarify the approach to contemporary buildings for similar purposes. One is the Masons' Hall for St. John's Lodge No. 3, New Bern, by John Dewey, 1801-9, wherein suitable quarters for the Theatrical Association were completed in 1805. On the exterior Dewey forestalled possible monotony of the end wall by variations in plane, which he marked by quoins and rounded off with an "Adam-esque" recessed semi-ellipse in the pediment; internally the building partook of the character of New Bern houses.

The other building will be remembered by senior residents of Raleigh as the "best ventilated" gathering place in town, with the "handsomest gas fixtures" and a "complete set of eleven scenes and 26 wings, —all done in the best style" by a "scenic artist" from Philadelphia's "Chesnut Street Theatre": the Tucker Building, by B. F. Warner of New York, 1867. Tucker Hall upstairs was ceremoniously dedicated that year with an address by former Gov. David L. Swain, still president of the University, and the Raleigh *Daily Sentinel* left its readers in no doubt about any part of "this superb building." Those responsible for its perfection were severally credited, except for the one firm vital to this paragraph, namely the firm that shipped to Raleigh these highly significant articles: "eight iron columns of the Corinthian order, to support the center of the hall floor," and "the front, which is of iron in the composite order, presenting a most imposing appearance, and the immense plate glass of the main windows." Chances are that the iron castings had been fetched down from the Richmond Architectural Iron Works and Stove Company, which advertised in the newspapers hereabout; but Wilmington had Hart & Bailey's Iron and Copper Works and Machine Shop also, and within two years Thomas H. Briggs was advertising right in Raleigh itself "Iron Fronts, Verandas, Fences, and all kinds of Ornamental Works."

So it was that the industrial revolution forecast in the 1820's by the inventions of Town and Leckie and the rest began to revolve in the State capital, courtesy of that "public-spirited firm" Messrs. W. H. & R. S. Tucker, who turned "Quick Sales and Small Profits" in their dry goods establishment on the street floor. Were it not for the "immense plate glass" of the "Iron-Front Building," which maintained visibility of dust-free merchandise, the columniated sales floor with meeting hall above would be recognizable at first glance as lineal descendant of the market house type, later even than Fayetteville. Division of the twin purposes of the building came inevitably and soon, and its structural iron—though not "fireproof" as so many fondly believed—was destined to save many a square foot for additional machinery in early textile mills and tobacco factories. Nevertheless there remained long years before structural steel was as easily come by, and still more before hidden rods of that tensile material would be trusted to carry the "pull" stresses while the "push" went to collaborating concrete.

In the division of the market house type into buildings for industry, commerce, and popular gatherings, many instances will be noticeable to the traveler without individual citation. Almost the entire architectural history of the tobacco industry, for example, may be followed through the various parts of the Liggett & Myers Tobacco Company plant in Durham, from the former W. Duke Sons & Company building, by W. H. Linthicum "Architect & Builder" of Durham, 1884, to the new cigarette factory, by Lockwood Greene, Engineers, Inc., of New York, 1948. Greensboro has guaranteed further survival of the market house type perched on stilts with an ordinance requiring provision by every new commercial building of its own necessary parking space. Anticipating a similar ordinance in Charlotte, J. N. Pease & Company have provided underground parking for the Jefferson Standard Life Insurance Company building, with ground level parking beneath the elevated offices of the Home Finance Group, Inc.

As for popular gatherings, Raleigh has become known throughout the Western hemisphere and Western Europe for the North Carolina State Fair Pavilion, intended particularly for judging livestock in an agricultural State, and dedicated in 1953 as officially as was Tucker Hall

86 years earlier. Carried out with some modifications of the original scheme by William Henley Deitrick, AIA, and his staff, in consultation with Severud–Elstad–Krueger, Engineers, the structure makes tangible the late Matthew Nowicki's breath-taking conception of two oblique parabolic arches buttressing each other in compression at their crossing like the frame of a camp stool, of which the canvas seat is simulated by the catenary roof suspended by tension cables over the vast uninterrupted arena. The far-sighted Civic Center of Charlotte, under construction from the design by A. G. Odell, Jr. and Associates, is located some three miles from the business district to obviate traffic problems, and now includes the circular shallow-domed Coliseum, for athletic and related events, and the blocked masses of the Auditorium, or theater and concert hall, the two to be connected at a future day by a building for exhibits and meeting rooms.

The upswing in large-scale enterprises is matched by the small, and the tourist will notice here and there near a perhaps unlikely looking stretch of highway some small clinic of contemporary design with facilities for serving two or three counties hitherto totally without any health unit; this despite early humanitarian ventures such as the State Hospital for the Insane, Raleigh, 1849-56, from the design of Alexander Jackson Davis of New York, Ithiel Town's sometime partner. Although North Carolina is no state of cities, it has not escaped its share of slums, and low-cost housing groups for each race may be found in any of the larger centers of population, as well as peripheral villages disposed around shopping centers for a higher income bracket.

Probably no single human need has been subject to more concentrated effort toward architectural fulfillment within recent years than the need for public schools. College and academy buildings had early been given a degree of architectural attention in the 19th century, especially between the depressions of 1819 and 1837, and during the idealistic 1840's. In particular a "Greek" flavor was imparted by Alexander Jackson Davis to the University campus at Chapel Hill, and also to Davidson College for which he designed Eumanean Hall, 1849, and Philanthropic Hall, 1850. At his visit to Chapel Hill in the 1840's the group of buildings consisted of James Patterson's Old East of 1793 with the south end of 1824; a chapel said to have been designed by Samuel Hopkins and also built by Patterson, 1795, later incorporated in Person Hall; South building by John Close, 1814; and Gerrard Hall of 1824 by William Nichols, the state architect, who began Old West in 1828.

By the time Davis was through sending drawings down from New York, Old East and Old West both possessed new north ends; Gerrard Hall, a portico; and there had been built from Davis' design by John Berry the present Playmakers Theater, then Smith building for the

Library, notable particularly for its four "American" column-capitals of corn, tobacco, and wheat motifs imported bodily from New York. An internationally-known architectural critic, writing of these buildings in 1943, has dared to put into words what many dare not: "Collegiate education then sought architectural expression in the most 'modern' vein, as it stood (or tried to stand) in intellectual matters for the most advanced thinking of the time." The logical continuation of this thought will reveal a deplorable applicability to almost all collegiate buildings in the State, even the newest anachronisms, save for the skillful remodeling and extension of North Carolina State College's obsolete library building as quarters for the School of Design by F. Carter Williams, AIA, in collaboration with George Matsumoto, AIA.

Whatever melancholy lack of perspective has, so to say, activated architectural passivity among institutions to which others should be able to look for responsible leadership has been somewhat compensated for by the awareness of life in this third quarter of the 20th century made manifest in the accomplishments of the North Carolina State Department of Public Instruction. No longer has the biennial report to deprecate, as was the case half a century ago, any "111 white and 195 colored log houses and many old frame houses unfit for use." Today dozens of light, airy, economical, and efficient school buildings might be cited, such as the Double Oaks Elementary School, Charlotte, by A. G. Odell, Jr. and Associates, the first school in this State and the only Negro school in the United States to receive an award in the "School Executive" competition, 1954, as well as an award of merit conferred by The American Institute of Architects. For older youth are such, for example, as the New Bern high school, by Burett H. Stephens–Robert H. Stephens, AIA; and so all the way across the State to the West Buncombe high school near Asheville, by Six Associates, Inc., in this case primarily Anthony Lord, AIA.

Despite a continuing shortage of classrooms with the current influx of "war babies," $50 million from State appropriation, together with an estimated $120 million in local bond issues voted, have—as pointed out by the Division of School Planning—"presented to the architects and building contractors a massive opportunity to serve almost all of the people of the state." Seldom has one common problem so caught hold on the cooperative imagination of all persons potentially concerned. The generation now growing up to take for granted their happy and convenient surroundings will possess the strength to face and solve the new architectural problems bound to rise in the 21st century.

LOUISE HALL, AIA
Associate Professor of Architecture
Duke University

The Big Change*

RECENTLY I decided to see if I could support, through documentation, my own conviction that our system of universal education has been an indispensable factor in the astounding development of this country, which Frederick Lewis Allen describes in his best seller, "The Big Change."

For this purpose, I selected the State of North Carolina which, at the turn of the century, was a poor state, and today ranks as one of the leaders, not only of the South, but of the nation, in statecraft, in industry, and in education.

In the last 50 years, while the population of the South was increasing by 88 per cent and the population of the nation as a whole by 98 per cent, the population of North Carolina increased by 113 per cent. In the past twelve years, a total of 5,047 new businesses have poured into the state. Long the national leader in the manufacture of tobacco products (North Carolina now produces more than half of the nation's cigarettes —55 per cent), the state now also leads the nation in the manufacture of textile products and wooden furniture.

North Carolina's current prosperity, then, was one of the reasons why I became interested in tracing its development.

How poor was North Carolina at the turn of the century? Although its population was close to two million, there were only 70,570 North Carolinians employed in industry at the time, and they were receiving an annual salary of $196.52, which was about *half* the annual average salary of workers the country over. In value added by manufacture of all kinds in the year 1899, North Carolina ranked 22nd among the states, with a total figure of $40 million. In value of farm property it also ranked 22nd.

In the North Carolina of 1900 there were 20 white illiterates for every

* Excerpts from Address of Roy E. Larsen to the American Association of School Administrators, Atlantic City, New Jersey, February 17, 1953; reproduced by permission of author and publisher.

one hundred of the white population over ten years of age. If the number of Negro illiterates were averaged into this figure, the illiteracy rate would, of course, be even higher.

There were exactly nine public libraries to serve North Carolina's reading public in 1900, and although there were 27 daily newspapers, the circulation of the most popular one, the *Raleigh News and Observer,* was only 5,800. The *combined* circulation of the five most popular periodicals published in North Carolina in 1900 was 37,000.

As we might expect, the public school system was deplorable, R. D. W. Connor and Clarence Poe, in their excellent book, *The Life and Speeches of Charles B. Aycock,* have described the situation when Aycock became Governor in January, 1901, as follows:

"At that time ... 'North Carolina did not believe in public education.' Only 30 districts in the state, all urban, considered education of sufficient importance to levy a school tax for the support of the schools. The average salary paid to county superintendents annually was less than one dollar a day, to public school teachers, $91.25 for the term.... There were no professional teachers in the public school. Practically no interest was manifested in the building or equipment of schoolhouses. The children of more than 950 public school districts were altogether without schoolhouses, while those in 1,132 districts sat on rough pine boards in log houses chinked with clay. Perhaps under all these circumstances," concluded Connor and Poe, "it was well enough that the schools were kept open only 73 days in the year and that less than *one-third* of the children of school age attended them."

The change in the educational picture, and hence in the illiteracy rate, in the next generation and a half was, as you know, staggering. By 1924, 64 per cent instead of 30 per cent of the North Carolina school population was attending the schools, and by 1950 attendance was up to 73 per cent.

Most of the increase came at the high school level. There were 735 high schools in 1924, instead of 30, and the number of high school graduates was 35 *times* what it had been in 1900, despite the fact that the state's total population had increased by only a little over a third.

But in North Carolina, as elsewhere, the enrollment flood had only begun. In 1950, there were six times as many high school graduates as there had been in 1924 and 155 times as many as in 1900: Total average daily attendance in elementary and secondary schools was now 798,000, instead of the 207,000 of 1900.

And while all of this was going on, the length of the school term had increased also. By 1924, it was almost exactly twice what it had been in 1900, and by 1950, it was 24 per cent longer than it had been in 1924.

The expansion of public school education in North Carolina had of course made possible the growth of many other less formal agencies of general education. By 1950 there were 13 times as many public libraries in North Carolina as there had been in 1900. The circulation of the *Raleigh News and Observer* was 20 times what it had been in 1900 while the state's population had only a little more than doubled. As to literacy—in 1947, only 2.7 per cent of the *total* population—white and colored—14 years of age or older was unable to read.

The time for mass circulations and syndicated columnists had arrived. The combined North Carolina circulation of the nation's five largest magazines jumped from 80,000 in 1916 to 130,000 in 1925 to 323,000 in 1950.

Consider the effect that this general cultural and educational growth had on the material prosperity of North Carolina in the course of 50 years.

By 1925, the number of North Carolinians in industry had more than doubled, and their annual salary had more than tripled. In the next quarter of a century, the number employed in industry more than doubled again, and salaries again tripled.

Production of electric energy—a good measure of overall growth—multiplied fantastically in North Carolina in the same period. In 1902 production was 8,000,000 kilowatt hours. In 1920, it was 733,000,000 kilowatt hours. In 1928, it was 2,245,000,000 kilowatt hours. By 1950, production was an outstanding 9,108,000,000 kilowatt hours and was still rising fast!

While the value of farm property the nation over a little less than quadrupled, the value of farm property in North Carolina increased eleven times! While the value added by manufacture for the entire nation increased some 14 times, the value added by manufacture in North Carolina increased 40 times; North Carolina had moved from 22nd to 12th in value of farm property and from 22nd to 14th in value added by manufacture.

ROY E. LARSEN
President, *Time,* Incorporated

Part II

CITIES AND TOWNS

NOTES ON THE USE OF PART II

A departure has been made in certain instances from the type of material included in the former *Guide*. Such changes and omissions were believed valid because of the increased development of the State and because of the ephemeral nature of some of the information.

1. Adequate accommodations in various places may be assumed unless stated to the contrary. *Collins Travelbook of North Carolina,* published annually (obtainable annually without cost from the State Tourist Bureau, Raleigh), furnishes complete information on hotels, motels, inns, and restaurants.

2. Listings of motion picture houses have been deleted as well as taxi cab fares, greens fees, and other rates.

3. Population figures are those of the U.S. Census (1950) where available; for unincorporated towns and towns of less than 1,000, the *Rand-McNally Commercial Atlas and Marketing Guide* (1954) was used.

4. All cities with a population of over 30,000 were automatically treated separately. Others, such as Edenton, Chapel Hill, and New Bern, are considered sufficiently important historically to be treated in this manner.

Asheville

Information Services: Chamber of Commerce, City Hall; Carolina Motor Club, 16 S. Pack Sq.; Jaycee Information Booth, Pack Sq.

Railroad Stations: Depot St. (Asheville) and Biltmore Village (**2 m.** S.), for Southern Ry.

Bus Station: Union Bus Terminal, 33 Coxe Ave., for Greyhound, Smoky Mountain Trailways, Queen City Trailways, Carolina Scenic Trailways, Mars Hill-Weaverville Lines.

Suburban Buses: Leave from Pack Sq. and the head of Ashland Ave. near Union Bus Station.

City Buses: Meet at Pack Sq. and Pritchard Park.

Sightseeing Buses: Operated by private concerns to Great Smoky Mountains National Park, Mount Pisgah, and other scenic points; inquire Chamber of Commerce.

Airport: Asheville-Hendersonville, **6 m.** S. on US 25A and **6 m.** L. on Airport Rd., for Delta, Piedmont, and Capital Air Lines.

Radio and Television Stations: WWNC (570), WSKY (1230), WISE (1310), WISE-TV (channel 62), WLOS (1380), WLOS-FM (104.3), WLOS-TV (channel 13).

Newspapers: Asheville Citizen (morn.), *Asheville Times* (eve.), *Sunday Citizen-Times* (Sun.).

Swimming: Recreation Park, **5 m.** E. on Swannanoa Rd.; Malvern Hills Park, Haywood Rd., West Asheville.

Golf: Country Club of Asheville, off Kimberly Ave., 18 holes; Biltmore Forest Country Club, 18 holes; Beaver Lake Golf Course, 18 holes; Municipal Golf Course, **3 m.** E. on Swannanoa Rd., 18 holes.

Tennis: Free courts: Aston Park, Montford Park, Malvern Hills; membership or fee at YMCA and 2 country clubs; inquire City Hall.

Baseball: McCormick Field, Biltmore Ave. at Valley St., leased to Asheville Tourists.

Football: Memorial Stadium, off Biltmore Ave. near McCormick Field.

Riding: Grove Park Riding Academy, off Macon Ave.

Camping: Free camping sites in National Forests; inquire U. S. Forest Service, Federal Bldg. or Chamber of Commerce.

Hunting and Fishing: Inquire Chamber of Commerce.

Annual Events: Land of the Sky Open Golf Tournament, late March or early April; Sunrise Service, Easter Sunday; Women's Spring Golf Tournament, 3rd week April; Mountain Youth Jamboree, April; N. C. Open Tennis Tournament, 2nd week July; Craftsman's Fair, 3rd week July; Women's Invitation Golf Tournament, 4th week July; Mountain Folk and Dance Festival, Aug.; Men's Invitation Golf Tournament, 2nd and 3rd week Aug.; Parade of Barber Shop Quartets, Aug.; Kennel Club Show, Oct.; October Fair; Big Game Hunts in Pisgah Forest, Nov. and Dec.

ASHEVILLE (2,216 alt., 53,000 pop.) is situated on a plateau ringed by the Blue Ridge, Pisgah, and Newfound mountains. It is the economic and cultural center of 18 mountain counties in western North Carolina and combines the features of a tourist and health resort with those of an industrial and agricultural-wholesale center.

Near the eastern entrance of the Great Smoky Mountains National Park and bordered by national forest lands, the city is in the midst of recreational areas containing more than a million acres. Some of the finest primeval forests in the United States are accessible by motor roads and hiking trails.

Asheville's streets follow natural contours. The business section presents an uneven mixture of old and new buildings, with Pack Square in the center at the junction of the principal highways and dominated on the east by the civic center. The French Broad River, whose gorge provides the only railroad outlet to the north, borders the western section known as West Asheville. Along the river's banks, as well as those of its tributary, the Swannanoa, are railroad yards and numerous industrial plants.

The city's population, coming from all parts of the country, is cosmopolitan rather than typically southern. The finer homes are in such sections as Lake View Park, Grove Park, suburban Biltmore Forest, and on some of the older streets. On the west slope of Beaucatcher Mountain, surrounding the modern high school for Negro children and a few churches, are numerous houses occupied by Negroes. The 12,435 Negroes in Asheville, 23 per cent of the total population, maintain a business center on Eagle and Valley Sts. and another on Southside Ave.

The site of Asheville was a part of the Cherokee Indian hunting ground. In 1673 James Needham and Gabriel Arthur came into Cherokee territory to establish trade with the Indians, who, by 1700, were bartering skins for guns. Long before the Revolution white hunters explored what is now Buncombe County.

There were no settlements before the Revolution because the English had fixed the boundary of white domain at the foot of the Blue Ridge and guaranteed the territorial integrity of the Indians. This assurance made the Cherokee allies of the British during the Revolution and inspired their raids upon colonial settlements. To end Indian aggression, Gen. Griffith Rutherford led his colonial force through the region in 1776, marching down the Swannanoa River as far as present Asheville, then proceeding westward to crush the Cherokee and destroy their villages.

In 1792 Buncombe County was formed from Rutherford and Burke counties, its territory extending to the western boundary of the State. It was named for Col. Edward Buncombe, a Revolutionary figure.

The definition of "buncombe" (spelled also bunkum and contracted to bunk), as meaning anything said, written, or done for mere show, had its origin in a speech made in the Sixteenth Congress by Felix Walker, Representative from the district of which Buncombe County was a part. The address was a masterpiece of fence-sitting, and when a colleague asked the purpose of it, Walker replied: "I was just talking for Buncombe."

In 1794 John Burton laid out a town tract of 21 acres for the county seat near the heart of the present business district and named it Morristown in honor of Robert Morris who helped finance the American Revolution and who once had large land holdings in this section. Three years later when the settlement was incorporated it was renamed in honor of Gov. Samuel Ashe (1795-98).

With the construction of the Buncombe Turnpike in 1824 the region became more accessible from South Carolina, Georgia, and other Southern states. Visitors and health seekers came in increasing numbers to escape the summer heat of the southern coastal plains and many remained to build homes. A fashionable resort grew up at Sulphur Springs, west of the town, when Asheville was little more than a stage stop "between the two Greenvilles" (S. C. and Tenn.).

To the Confederate Army the county contributed 7 of the 10 companies composing the 60th N. C. Regiment, including the Buncombe Riflemen. Battery Park Hill took its name from an artillery unit stationed on that eminence. Federal troops occupied the city during the final months of the conflict, after a minor skirmish a few miles north of town, and burned an armory on Valley St.

Tobacco became a profitable crop during the Reconstruction period and several warehouses were built. Falling prices led to abandonment of the industry until 1931, when, because of the successful cultivation of burley tobacco in the region, the city again became a tobacco market center.

From 1880, with completion of the first railroad, Asheville experienced a slow but steady growth as industrial plants increased in number and size and new residents built homes. Textile mills were established and plants were set up for the manufacture of wood and mica products, foodstuffs, and other commodities.

The coming of George Vanderbilt, New York capitalist, in 1889, and of E. W. Grove, St. Louis manufacturer, in 1900, and the improvement projects they conducted, served to attract wider attention to the city and to accelerate its growth. Vanderbilt founded Biltmore Village, south of the city, purchased 130,000 acres of mountain lands, and developed Biltmore Estate with its great chateau. Grove established the residential section bearing his name, built Grove Park Inn, and cut the top off Battery Park Hill, using the mass of earth and stone to fill a ravine south of Patton Ave., now the Coxe Ave. section. The first streetcar was operated in 1889; the last was replaced by buses in 1934.

In the middle 1920's the Florida real estate boom spread to Asheville. Wild speculation and unwholesome overexpansion, both public and private, caused bank failures and a distressing public debt. In 1936 a debt settlement, based on a long-time amortization plan, was effected with the creditors of the city and county.

Among well-known writers who have made their homes in Asheville are: Edwin Bjorkman, author, critic, and translator; Ruth and Latrobe Carroll, illustrator-authors of children's books; Olive Dargan (Fielding Burke), poet and author of *Highland Annals* and *Call Home the Heart;* Helen Topping Miller, novelist and short-story writer; William Sydney Porter (O. Henry), short-story writer; Lula Vollmer, author of *Sun-Up;* and Thomas Wolfe, author of *Look Homeward, Angel; Of Time and the River,* and others.

Asheville offers a variety of opportunities for those interested in music (both classic and folk), drama, and art. During the winter the Civic Music Association engages outstanding artists and groups, while the Chamber Music Series sponsors instrumental groups. The first week in August the Asheville Mountain Dance and Folk Festival brings together ballad singers, musicians, and square dance teams under the direction of the famous Bascom Lamar Lunsford of nearby South Turkey Creek, who founded the festival in 1927.

The Asheville Community Theatre maintains a paid director to produce plays during the winter with actors from the membership. The Children's Theatre also brings a winter series of professional shows.

The Asheville Artists' Guild holds 4 annual exhibits in the Asheville Art Museum on Charlotte St., where it has a small permanent collection of paintings and a library of art books. The Asheville Photographic Society presents an annual exhibit by its members and usually a salon by photographers from other cities. In July mountain craftsmen from several states gather for a week at the City Auditorium for the Craftsman's Fair to show an extensive collection of their finest pieces. While there they carry on their work, perform folk dancing and music, and tell folk tales for the public. The sponsor is their own marketing organization, the Southern Highland Handicraft Guild.

The Civic Arts Center was incorporated in 1953 to combine the efforts of the cultural organizations and to establish a center with auditorium, exhibition hall, and work room.

The Carolina Mountain Club and the Wilderness Hikers lead weekly trips open to visitors. Inquire at Chamber of Commerce.

Private educational institutions include the College of St. Genevieve-of-the-Pines, Victoria Rd., with affiliated Catholic secondary and elementary schools; Asheville School on US 19-23 (**5 m.** W.), offering college preparation; Christ School near US 25 (**10 m.** S.), offering college preparation; Allen School, Woodfin St., offering high school, vocational and arts training for Negro girls; the elementary-through-college Plonk School of Creative Arts; and Asheville Country Day School, Merrimon Ave., offering elementary and high school training to boys and girls.

POINTS OF INTEREST

1. PACK SQUARE, at intersection of Biltmore Ave., Broadway, and Patton Ave., named for George Willis Pack, philanthropist, a native of N. Y. State, was formerly the courthouse square. The first courthouse, of logs, erected in 1793, was succeeded in turn by 4 other buildings. The fifth, a three-story brick structure, was torn down in 1903 after Mr. Pack had given land on East College St. for a new building.

The VANCE MONUMENT, on the west side of the square, is a 75-foot hewn-granite obelisk erected in 1897 to honor Zebulon Baird Vance (1830-94). A native of Buncombe County, Vance was in succession a U. S. Congressman, Colonel of Confederate troops, twice Governor of the State, and at the time of his death, U. S. Senator. It is said that he loved every foot of North Carolina soil from the Dismal Swamp to Cherokee, and that he gave $5 to every baby named for him until they became too numerous. The monument was financed through popular subscription aided by a gift from Mr. Pack.

2. The PACK MEMORIAL PUBLIC LIBRARY (*open 9-6 week days*), S. Pack Sq., is the outgrowth of a private library association started in 1879. In 1954 the entire public library system had a bookstock in excess of 95,000. The three-story marble structure, named for George Willis Pack (1831-1906), donor of the present site and previous building, was erected in 1925. It operates as a departmentalized library with 60,430 volumes. In the reference department is the notable Thomas Wolfe collection, in which virtually every known published item by or about him, including foreign editions, has been assembled.

The SONDLEY REFERENCE LIBRARY, 2nd floor, is largely composed of the original Sondley collection of 35,000 books and pamphlets, a bequest to the city by Forester Alexander Sondley (1857-1931), lawyer, scholar, and book collector, whose personal library resulted from a lifetime of search and scholarship. The Sondley collection is notable for its many rare volumes. The oldest imprint is the St. Jerome's *Epistles,* published in Parma, Italy, in 1480. The earliest imprint in the fine collection of Caroliniana is Harriot's *Briefe and true report of the new found land of Virginia,* published by DeBry in Frankfort, Germany, in 1590. The library has the second printing of the first edition in Latin and a reprint of the English. Among important special collections are those dealing with North Carolina and the Southeastern states, the American Indian with emphasis on the Cherokee, American History, Folklore, Genealogy, Botany, and Minerals. A specialized bibliography, *Leaves from the Sondley,* includes in volumes 1 and 2 the following titles: Books ... published before 1700, American imprints, 1752-

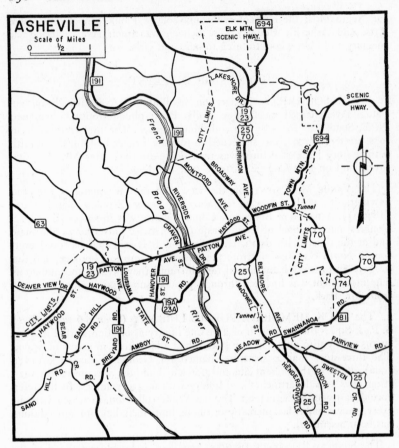

1820, Southeastern imprints, 1821-1859, Confederate imprints, 1860-1865, Southeastern imprints (Reconstruction period), 1866-77, American newspapers, American Indians, Folkways, Botany, Conchology, Mineralogy, Ornithology, and Zoology. The unique items in this collection have drawn scholars and specialists from all parts of the country.

The LIBRARY EXHIBITION ROOM, ground floor, offers a continuous schedule of exhibits on classical and modern art, literature, science, and history. Weekly programs of recorded classical and modern music are heard over a high fidelity sound system. Other programs include scheduled chamber music concerts, story hours, lectures, and moving pictures of educational and artistic value. Outstanding exhibits have included paintings from the National Gallery of Art, the Thomas Wolfe collection, and an assembled exhibit honoring Carl Sandburg.

3. The CITY-COUNTY PLAZA, E. of Pack Sq., is terraced and landscaped with streets and walks. Behind it rise the city hall and the county courthouse.

The CITY HALL (R) is built of brick, marble, and terra cotta in shades harmonizing with the natural colors of the clay soil. Designed by Douglas Ellington and built in 1927, the 9-story building is surmounted by a tower covered with varicolored tiling. A feather-motif, recalling early Indian history, is the prevailing feature of the decorations. The trim and wainscot of the entrance loggia are of Georgia pink marble; the vaulted ceiling is of dull gold tile, bordered in pink, black, and orange. Symbolic murals in the council chamber on the second floor, the work of Clifford Addams of New York, depict the story of the Indians and white settlers. The carillon in the tower was presented to the city by the Buncombe County War Mothers as a memorial to the World War I dead.

The BUNCOMBE COUNTY COURTHOUSE (L), 15 stories in height, was designed by Milburn and Heister of Washington, D. C., and built during the boom period (1925-27). The structure is of cream-colored brick with classic details of Indiana limestone and granite. The upper 5 stories serve as a county jail.

4. The THOMAS WOLFE MEMORIAL (*open daily except Mon., small entrance fee*), 48 Spruce St., was the famous novelist's home, described as "Dixieland," in *Look Homeward, Angel*. Maintained by the Thomas Wolfe Memorial Assoc., it has been furnished mainly with the original family possessions.

5. The FIRST BAPTIST CHURCH, SE. corner Oak and Woodfin Sts., is constructed of buff brick, wood, and metal with tall brick columns fronting the façade. Designed by Douglas Ellington and completed in 1927, it has an octagonal dome of varicolored tile, surmounted with a copper lantern.

6. ASHEVILLE-BILTMORE COLLEGE, S. end of Sunset Mountain, a group of stone buildings overlooking the city, is a two-year community college founded in 1927. It is supported by city and county funds and draws from Asheville and the surrounding counties. Liberal arts and sub-professional courses are offered to the day students, and night classes in downtown Asheville and on the campus give vocational and liberal arts training.

7. SUNSET MOUNTAIN, E. end of College St. (NC 694), presents an extensive view of Asheville and the surrounding mountain ranges. The mountain was named because of the impressive sunsets seen from its summit (3,100 alt.). It may be reached by a hiking trail starting near the end of Macon Ave. or by a paved road beginning at the west end of College St.

8. The TOBACCO MARKET (*open in season*), operating 11 warehouses for the sale of burley tobacco, usually opens the 2nd week in Dec. and closes about Jan. 15. Mountain farmers bring in their tobacco to be sold by

auctioneers who use the rapid-fire jargon peculiar to the trade. In the 1953-54 season, sales on the local market aggregated 9,370,653 pounds.

9. The McDOWELL HOUSE (*private*), 283 Victoria Rd., the oldest house in Asheville, was built in 1840 for James M. Smith, said to be the first white child born (1787) west of the Blue Ridge. The brick structure of post-Colonial architecture has 18-inch brick walls, massive end chimneys, and a two-story gallery porch on the front. There is a fan transom over the front door. The original mahogany doors and mantels are retained.

10. MEMORIAL MISSION HOSPITAL, covering a ridge between Biltmore Ave. and McDowell St. (US 25) at Victoria Rd., is a medical center for the mountain counties. A consolidation of the Mission, Biltmore, Victoria, and Asheville (Negro) Hospitals, the 6-story brick building (opened in 1954) has about 350 beds. North on the grounds is the nurses' home and west, the medical library. A building for doctors was to begin on the south in 1954.

11. SITE OF NEWTON ACADEMY, 2 m. S. on Biltmore Ave., on ground now occupied by Newton Elementary School, was founded before 1793 as Union Hill. Later headed by the Rev. George Newton, the school trained many of the region's early leaders.

12. BILTMORE VILLAGE, lying S. of the Swannanoa River at the S. end of Biltmore Ave., now a part of the city of Asheville, was designed and built by George Vanderbilt as a model English-type community of which Biltmore House was the manor. A native of Staten Island, N. Y., Vanderbilt in 1889 began buying land southeast of Asheville, including Mount Pisgah and several other forested mountains and valleys. A village plaza and a score or more of houses were erected, in the medieval half-timber type of construction. All Souls Episcopal Church became the cultural center of the village and Biltmore Hospital, later replaced by a modern structure, the health center and since merged with Memorial Mission. The village proper was sold to an investment company after Mr. Vanderbilt's death. The original architectural style has given way to modern brick stores and filling stations but many of the old houses, the Estate office, stores on the plaza, and the Norman church remain.

13. The BILTMORE ESTATE (*open Apr. 1-Oct. 1, 9-6; Oct. 1-Apr. 1, 9:30-5; adm. $2.40 per person*), entrance on Lodge St. from Biltmore Village, comprises 12,000 acres of farm and forest lands including the landscaped grounds surrounding Biltmore House, the Biltmore Dairy Farms, a reservation for wildlife propagation, and 15 highly developed farms operated by tenants.

In 1892 Mr. Vanderbilt appointed young Gifford Pinchot superintendent of the Biltmore forests, enabling him to institute the first large-scale reforestation project in the United States. On the appointment of Pinchot as chief of the U. S. Division of Forestry he was succeeded in 1895 by Dr. Carl Alvin Schenck, forest assessor of the Grand Duchy of Hesse, whose work as a practical forester and as founder of the Biltmore School of Forestry contributed to the development of scientific forestry in this country. The reforestation project was later made the object of special study by the Appalachian Forest Experiment Station.

In 1916, Mrs. Vanderbilt sold 80,600 acres to the U. S. Government to form the nucleus of the Pisgah National Forest. Later she sold a tract from the estate for development into the Biltmore Forest residential village. The 50 acres immediately surrounding Biltmore House are laid out in terraces and gardens. The front approach is a grass-carpeted esplanade with a circular pool in the center. At the eastern end of the esplanade the Rampe Douce, an ornate stone structure designed in the manner of the one in the gardens of the chateau of Vaux le Vicomte in France, gives access to bridle paths that traverse the thickly wooded slopes. Beyond a hedge are the spring gardens containing one of the most nearly complete collections of trees in the South. The Chauncey D. Beadle collection of Native Southern Azaleas is to the south.

The BILTMORE HOUSE (*guides on duty*), designed by Richard Morris Hunt in the early French Renaissance style of Francis I, recalls the palatial chateaux at Blois and at Chambord. Frederick Law Olmsted, Sr., designer of Central Park in New York City, was landscape architect, and Chauncey D. Beadle, landscape engineer.

Completed in 1895 after 5 years of construction, with skilled artisans from this country and from Europe, the house covers an area of 4 acres with frontage of 780 feet. The façade rises in three distinct stories, graduating in height from the elaborate portal to the finial cresting on the roof. The severity of the mass is relieved by the characteristic French peaked roof with dormer windows and lofty chimney stacks. The walls are of hand-tooled Indiana limestone; the roof is of slate.

The main portal opens into the front hall, 75 feet in height, with Guastavino tile ceiling. At the left of the hall a spiral stairway, modeled after that of the Chateau de Blois, and supported by its own arch construction, leads to the topmost floor.

14. BILTMORE FOREST, a suburban area lying south of Biltmore Village, was developed from a portion of the Biltmore Estate. With its natural wooded setting, landscaped drives, country club, riding academy, and a few shops, this incorporated village, which has its own municipal facilities, is considered one of the most attractive in the South. Near the center is the BILTMORE COUNTRY CLUB and golf course.

15. The LEE H. EDWARDS HIGH SCHOOL, McDowell St. (US 25), was designed by Douglas Ellington in 1927. It is constructed of granite in tones ranging from white through gray to pink. A tower, banded in orange brick and terra cotta, rises above the central rotunda. Besides the class rooms the structure contains an auditorium seating 1,800.

16. MINERALS RESEARCH LABORATORY, 180 Coxe Ave., is operated by N. C. State College through the Dept. of Conservation and Development.

Here tests are made and new recovery methods developed for the chief commercial minerals of the area: feldspar, clays, and mica with related products.

17. ALLANSTAND CRAFT DISPLAY AND MARKETING CENTER, 16 College St., is the outgrowth of the work started by Frances L. Goodrich in 1898. When she retired in 1931 Allanstand was given to the Southern Highland Handicraft Guild.

18. The ST. LAWRENCE CHURCH (*Roman Catholic*), NW. corner Haywood and Flint Sts., completed in 1909, was designed by Rafael Guastavino, whose body rests in a crypt near the entrance of the Chapel of Our Lady. Guastavino, a native of Spain, won a wide reputation for originating a cohesive type of self-supporting arch. He came to Asheville in 1889 as a consulting architect on the Biltmore House. Finding the facilities of the Catholic church inadequate, he proposed construction of a new building to which he contributed his services and part of the funds. The architecture of the brick structure is of modified early Renaissance design. The entrance is flanked by twin towers and surmounted with statues of St. Lawrence, St. Stephen, and St. Aloysius Gonzaga. The auditorium is covered by a large elliptical dome having a clear span of 82 by 58 feet. The self-supporting dome is built wholly of tile, so woven that of its three layers no two joints coincide. The main altar and that of the Chapel of Our Lady were designed by Stanford White. The reredos, in carved walnut, was obtained from an old church in northern Spain. Surrounding the reredos are figures of the saints in polychrome terra cotta by Guastavino.

19. In RIVERSIDE CEMETERY, entrance on Birch St., is the GRAVE OF WILLIAM SYDNEY PORTER (O. Henry), short-story writer (1862-1910), whose second wife was Sarah Lindsay Coleman of Weaverville. O. Henry did some of his writing while living near Weaverville, 9 miles north of Asheville.

A MONUMENT marks the grave of 18 interned German sailors who died of typhoid fever during World War I in the U. S. Hospital, Kenilworth. With several hundred others, they were held in an internment camp at Hot Springs after being taken from German merchant ships in U. S. harbors. The monument was erected in 1932 by the Kiffin Rockwell post of the American Legion, and other legionnaires throughout the State.

Here also is the GRAVE OF THOMAS L. CLINGMAN (1812-97), Representative in Congress and later U. S. Senator, who served as brigadier general in the Confederate Army. After the war he measured several mountain peaks in western North Carolina and assisted in developing the mineral resources of the section. Clingmans Dome in the Smokies bears his name—Clingmans Peak in the Blacks.

The GRAVE OF GOV. ZEBULON BAIRD VANCE is marked by a rough block of granite, and nearby is the GRAVE OF GEN. ROBERT B. VANCE (1828-99), his brother. Gen. Vance served in the Confederate Army as commander of the military district of Western North Carolina.

The GRAVE OF THOMAS WOLFE (1900-38), is surrounded by those of his family, made famous through his novel, *Look Homeward, Angel.* His epitaph is from his own writings.

20. GROVE PARK INN, off Macon Ave., on the west slope of Sunset Mountain, a resort hotel built in 1912-13 for E. W. Grove, resembles a Swiss mountain hostelry. With a frontage of almost 500 feet, the mass of the building rises in a series of terraces, giving a rambling, horizontal effect. The walls are of native granite boulders. Massive dormer windows lend variety to the red-tiled roof. The lobby is notable for two fireplaces of unusual size.

The BILTMORE INDUSTRIES (*open 9-5 Mon.-Fri., 9-12 Sat.*) adjoining the Grove Park Inn premises, are housed in a group of buildings including work-shops, offices and salesrooms. Here are produced the Biltmore homespuns (piecegoods), made on hand-operated looms from yarns dyed in the wool.

21. SMOKY MOUNTAIN HIGHWAY BRIDGE carries US 19-23 west across the French Broad 95 ft. above the river. At 2.3 m. from Pack Sq. is junction with Louisiana Ave. North 2 m. is RICHMOND HILL (*open daily, except Tues., May-Oct.; adm. $1.20*). Built for Richmond Pearson, U. S. Congressman and minister to Persia, Greece, and Montenegro, the large residence with its period furnishings reflects the charm of bygone days. On display are pictures, letters, and gifts from presidents and foreign potentates during the owner's public career. The hill commands a view southward over the French Broad to Asheville and eastward to the Craggy Range. On the hill's grassy slope the poet Sidney Lanier made his camp when he first came to North Carolina in 1881, trying to regain his health.

Chapel Hill

Information Services: Alumni Headquarters, Carolina Inn; YMCA Bldg., campus; South (Administration) Bldg., campus; Graham Memorial, E. Franklin St.; Chamber of Commerce, Tankersley Bldg., E. Franklin St

Railroad Station: Nearest passenger station at Durham, N. C., **10 m.**; nearest freight station at Carrboro, **1 m.**

Bus Station: 311 W. Franklin St., for Carolina Trailways and Queen City Coach Co.

City Buses: Along regular routes.

Airports: Raleigh-Durham, **14 m.** E. on NC 54 to Nelson, L. .**1 m.** on US 70A, R. **2 m.**, for Capital, Eastern, and Piedmont Airlines; Horace Williams Field, **1 m.** N. on Airport Rd., for private planes.

Radio and Television Stations: WUNC (FM only 9.15), a non-commercial, educational radio station operated by the University, WUNC-TV (channel 4); WCHL (1360), 6 A.M.-sundown.

Newspaper: Chapel Hill Weekly; The Chapel Hill News Leader (bi-weekly).

Swimming: Bowman Gray Memorial Pool, Kessing Outdoor Pool.

Golf: Finley Golf Course, Mason Farm Rd., 18 holes.

Tennis: University courts.

Football: Kenan Stadium.

Baseball: Emerson and Fetzer Field.

Basketball, boxing, and wrestling: Woollen Gymnasium.

Fishing: University Lake, **3 m.** W. of Carrboro; Eastwood Lake, **2 m.** E. on US 15-501.

Annual Events: State-wide Dramatic Festival and Tournament of the Carolina Dramatic Assoc., April; Annual High School Debating Contest, April; Garden Tour, April; Carolina Folk Festival, June; University Day, Oct. 12.

CHAPEL HILL (501 alt., 9,177 pop.), seat of the original University of North Carolina, first state university to open its doors, is situated on a granite elevation 250 feet above the eastern coastal plain and is near the center of the State. The town takes its name from the little New Hope

Chapel of the Established Church of England that stood in the late 18th century at the northern intersection of the crossing of the great road from Petersburg south with the road from New Bern to Salisbury.

With no industries and no commercial interest other than to serve the University community, Chapel Hill has remained a friendly town, its sociability interwoven with intellectual liberalism. The business section consisted of one long block on Franklin Street until World War II. To meet the expanded needs, new business houses were built westward along Franklin Street. Under the guidance of the Chapel Hill Planning Board, the majority are Georgian Colonial in style. Notable among the new structures are the Town Hall, Carolina Theater, Harriss-Conners Chevrolet Co. Inc., Colonial Store, Fowler's Food Store, the Bus Station, and the Carl Smith building.

On the 552-acre campus are dignified ivied buildings bearing the names of men and women outstanding in State and University affairs. Pleasant streets are shaded by lichened oaks, hickories, hollies, cedars, flowering fruit trees, redbud, and dogwood. Homes, old and new, are set in shady yards and banked with flowers and shrubs. Stone walls clad with ivy or rambler roses border the University as well as private property. Fraternity houses, mostly Georgian, cluster about the edges of the campus among the village churches, the post office, and the Carolina Inn. The Inn, whose portico is reminiscent of Mount Vernon, was presented to the University by an alumnus, John Sprunt Hill of Durham. Forested Battle Park, with brooks, springs, and picnic grounds, is at the east end of the campus.

In 1776 the Halifax convention framed a constitution which provided that "all useful Learning shall be duly encouraged and promoted in one or more Universities." Sponsored by Gen. William R. Davie, "Father of the University," a charter issued by the general assembly in 1789 stipulated that the University should not be "within five miles of the seat of government or of any place holding courts of law or equity." In 1792 the commissioners, "because of its healthiness," chose this hill where "the flat country spreads out below like the ocean," and where "an abundance of springs of the purest and finest water—burst from the side of the ridge." The first trustees, with Gen. William Lenoir as president, were men who had been or later became governors, legislators, senators, and State and Federal judges.

The village grew with the new institution. On Oct. 12, 1793, Davie as grand master of Masons laid the cornerstone of Old East, the first building, and the first town lots were sold. Oct. 12 is annually celebrated as University Day.

On the opening day, Jan. 16, 1795, in spite of bitter weather and almost impassable roads, many prominent men, including Gov. Richard Dobbs Spaight, assembled at Chapel Hill. The first student, Hinton James, who walked part of the 170 miles from Wilmington to Chapel Hill, did not arrive until Feb. 12; for two weeks he was the student body. By the end of the second term there were 100 students. Although the young institution was accused of being "aristocratical," tuition fees were low and living conditions primitive. The boys seldom saw a newspaper and weeks intervened between letters. The only way to travel the red clay roads was by horseback, cart, "chairs," or double sulkies. Feather beds were rented from the steward for $24 a year or the boys slept on hard boards; meals at commons were $40 for the year. Some of the boys brought body servants from home to forage for firewood, carry water, and sometimes cook their meals.

The University's original endowment consisted of old claims on sheriffs and other officers, and escheats, including unclaimed land warrants granted to Continental soldiers, collection of which was uncertain and often made enemies for the new school. By constant struggle and periodic appeals for private benefactions, the institution grew despite general poverty, opposition to taxation, denominational hostility, and sectional controversies between the east and west. The general assembly did not appropriate public funds for its maintenance until 1881.

Joseph Caldwell came from Princeton in 1796 to accept the chair of mathematics, and until he was elected the first president in 1804, the school was under a succession of "presiding professors." Notable in Caldwell's regime (1804-12, 1817-35) was the erection in 1830 of a modest observatory, the first in connection with an American university, to house instruments he had purchased in London. Under Caldwell, the institution grew from a small classical school into a creditable college. He was succeeded by David Lowry Swain, youngest governor of the State (1832-35), an astute politician and practical financier who did much to popularize the University over the whole State and to build up its endowment before the termination of his long tenure (1835-68).

The University remained open during the Civil War, although as each Southern State seceded its student sons summarily departed until, at the 1865 commencement, there were but 4 graduates and 10 or 12 students. Union troops protected college property when they occupied the village in April, 1865. Unable to weather the storms of Reconstruction, its endowment dissipated in worthless securities, the institution was closed by a carpetbag administration in 1868. It was not successfully reopened until 1875 after a heroic fight led by Cornelia Phillips Spencer and friends and alumni headed by Kemp Plummer Battle. Mrs. Spencer, after whom the first women's dormitory was named, climbed to the tower of South Building and rang out the glad tidings when word was received that the University would reopen. The LL.D. conferred upon Mrs. Spencer in 1895 was the first honorary degree bestowed upon a woman by the University. Among her many writings was *Last Ninety Days of the War* (1866), written at the request of Gov. Zebulon B. Vance. Dr. Battle, president (1876-91), established the first summer normal session in the South (1877) and wrote a comprehensive two-volume history of the University.

During the administration of Dr. Francis Preston Venable (1900-14) the University's finances were set in order, student athletics were encouraged, and creative scholarship was required of the faculty. Venable Hall, the chemistry building, recalls his eminence in that field.

The brief administration of Edward Kidder Graham (1914-18) was notable for the enlargement of the University's service to the State at large, increased resources for administrative and building purposes, and a strengthening of student morale and honor standards. During his regime, Mrs. Robert Worth Bingham (Mary Lily Kenan Flagler) endowed the Kenan professorships in memory of her parents and her uncle. Under Pres. Harry Woodburn Chase (1918-30), the University achieved an international reputation for high standards of scholarship and for freedom in research and teaching. In 1922 the institution was elected to membership in the Association of American Universities and in 1931 to its presidency.

Under Pres. Frank Porter Graham (1930-1949) the administrative consolidation of the University of North Carolina, the North Carolina College for Women at Greensboro, and the North Carolina State College of Agriculture and Engineering at Raleigh into the University of North Carolina was effected in 1932. New schools and divisions were added at Chapel Hill—Library Science in 1931, the General College in 1935, and Public Health in 1936. The Institute of Government became a part of the University in 1942, the Communication Center was established in 1945, and the School of Education reestablished in 1948. New departments were added—City and Regional Planning in 1946, Radio in 1947, Religion in 1947, and Astronomy in 1950 in connection with the $3,000,000 Morehead Building and Planetarium which was completed in 1949.

The Division of Health Affairs was organized in 1949 and includes the schools of Medicine, Public Health, Pharmacy, Nursing, and Dentistry, and the Memorial Hospital. It was established for the purpose of integrating the work of all of the health professional schools and the hospital in their teaching and research programs within the University at Chapel Hill.

In 1950 a School of Social Work and a School of Journalism were established and the School of Commerce became the School of Business Administration.

In the development of the consolidation process, Robert B. House was selected by Pres. Graham to serve as Dean of Administration of the University of Chapel Hill, which title was changed to Chancellor in 1945.

On March 22, 1949, Gov. Scott appointed Pres. Graham to the United States Senate. Pending the selection of a new president, Controller W. D. Carmichael, Jr., was designated as Acting President. Under Pres. Gordon Gray (1950-   ) the University has continued to make long strides forward.

Growth of the University at Chapel Hill is depicted in enrollment figures. In 1920 students numbered 1300; in 1930, 2700; in 1941, 4108; and in 1948-49, under G. I. Bill, etc., a high of 7603. In 1953 the enrollment leveled off, and there were 5218 students in residence. There were in 1953 about 800 members of the faculty and 77 permanent buildings.

The Carolina Playmakers, now under the direction of Samuel Selden, have made a distinguished contribution to American folk drama in recent decades. Their founder and former director, the late Frederick H. Koch, came to the University in 1918. The Playmakers annually present 5 major plays and 6 experimental productions (written and directed by students). Koch also organized the Bureau of Community Drama and helped organize the State-wide Carolina Dramatic Association. Each summer many Playmakers act and assist in off-campus productions, such as *The Lost Colony, Unto These Hills,* and *Horn in the West.* Among "Proff" Koch's students here were Paul Green, Shepperd Strudwick, and Thomas Wolfe.

The University Press publishes annually about 20 books and issues 5 periodicals and technical journals. The press specializes in books about the South and also publishes books in the general scholarly field.

Notable among those in the writers' colony in Chapel Hill are Paul Green, Noel Houston, and Betty Smith. Faculty members have achieved international distinction by their contributions to a number of fields.

POINTS OF INTEREST

(Unless otherwise stated, all University buildings are open during school hours.)

1. The OLD WELL, in a little classic temple on maple-shaded Cameron Ave., in the heart of the campus, is the shrine and symbol of the University and center for outdoor "pep" meetings, though for years its chief mission was to furnish the only water available to students. In 1954 it was reconstructed along its original lines, the surrounding grounds were landscaped, and brick walks laid.

2. SOUTH (*MAIN*) BUILDING, opposite the well, modeled after Princeton's Nassau Hall, is a three-story brick building with a Westover River Front entrance and a two-story Ionic porch at the south. In 1798 its cornerstone was laid, and walls for a story-and-a-half building erected. Students made little huts in the structure, which remained roofless until a lottery and Pres. Caldwell's canvass of the State in his stick-back gig provided money for its completion (1814). When the University was closed in 1868, horses and cows were stabled on the lower floor. Remodeled (1926), South Building houses administrative offices.

3. OLD EAST, flanking the well on the E., is the country's oldest standing State university building. Designed and built by the "mechanic," James Patterson, its cornerstone was laid Oct. 12, 1793. It is a simple well-proportioned three-story brick building, without architectural distinction. Originally intended as the south wing of a larger structure to face east along a mile-long avenue, Old East was two stories high and had 16 rooms, each accommodating 4 students. Bricks were burned from clay with wood taken from University lands. Sea shells given by a Wilmington friend were brought by boat to Fayetteville and thence by wagon to Chapel Hill where they were converted into lime. In 1824 Old East was lengthened and made one story higher to conform to Old West, built in that year. In 1924 the danger of collapsing walls and foundations entailed remodeling the interior of Old East, but the work did not destroy the original lines.

4. OLD WEST (1824), flanking the well on the W., matches Old East, and also serves as a dormitory.

5. The DAVIE POPLAR, N. of the well in the heart of the old campus, is a great ivy-covered tree named for the Father of the University. Under it

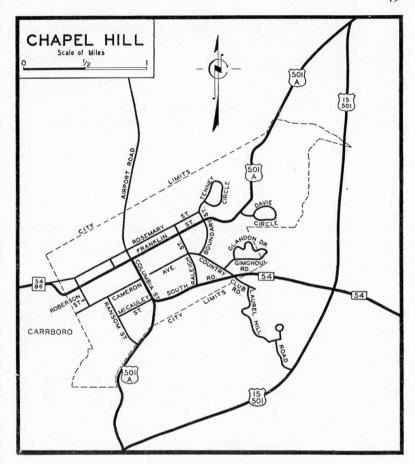

the commissioners supposedly paused to eat lunch when they were inspecting the site for the new University. Contrary to popular belief, Davie was not one of these commissioners.

6. GERRARD HALL, between Memorial Hall and South Building, built in 1822, is a small rectangular brick structure, which served for many years as a chapel. It was named for a University benefactor, Maj. Charles Gerrard. There was formerly a classic portico on the south side intended to face an east-west avenue, abandoned when merchants complained that it would divert traffic from Franklin Street. It is now used to accommodate small audiences and religious groups.

7. MEMORIAL HALL, opposite New West, is a white-columned, buff-painted brick convocation hall. Erected in 1931, it contains memorial tablets

to war dead, prominent alumni, and benefactors of the University. One honors James Knox Polk, 11th President of the United States, who was graduated with the first honors of his class in 1818 and "never missed a duty while in the institution." He attended the 1847 commencement while he was President.

8. NEW WEST, W. of Old West, was begun in 1857, as was its companion building, New East, to provide much-needed accommodations, when, after the gold rush, the enrollment increased from 170 students in 1850 to 456 in 1858. It is a three-story building of stuccoed brick and sandstone trim, with a large central pavilion flanked by wings. The architecture is of Italian influence with a well-executed detail. NEW EAST is similar in design but has 4 stories. New West houses the department of psychology and has on its 3rd floor the DIALECTIC SOCIETY HALL (*open on application to janitor*). The "Di" and the "Phi" literary societies, organized in 1795, were long in charge of all student activities, and expulsion from the society was tantamount to dismissal from the University. Their tradition of violent political disagreement arises from the fact that the Di was for western and the Phi for eastern students. Sectionalism still plays a part in the choice of members, but the organizations are largely forensic and parliamentary.

9. PERSON HALL, W. of the poplar, first chapel of the University, was started in 1793 and finished in 1797 through the gift of Gen. Thomas Person. It was built in three sections, the original laid in Flemish bond with carefully designed post-Colonial details. The H-shaped one-story building is, architecturally, one of the most notable structures in Chapel Hill. It now houses the PERSON HALL ART GALLERY.

10. HILL MUSIC HALL, NW. of Person Hall facing the poplar, is a white sandstone and buff brick building originally the Carnegie Foundation Library (1907-29). Through the gift of alumnus John Sprunt Hill and his wife, it was remodeled as a center for University musical activities. The auditorium seats 796, has a 4-manual pipe organ, and can accommodate a chorus of 125 and a 60-piece orchestra.

11. ACKLAND MEMORIAL ART MUSEUM, S. Columbia St., now under construction, is the gift of William Hayes Ackland, of Washington, D. C. Constructed of red brick with limestone trim, it will be along Georgian lines and will house exhibitions of art (including the Ackland Collection), the department of art, and the art reference library.

12. GRAHAM MEMORIAL (1932), off Franklin St. on the old campus, student union and major center of student activity, was a gift to the University from alumni and friends, including an anonymous donation of $80,000. The red brick building has an 8-columned portico with balustraded parapet. It was named in honor of Edward Kidder Graham, whose portrait hangs in the lounge with those of other University presidents.

13. The MOREHEAD PLANETARIUM, 2nd block, E. Franklin, the gift of engineer-industrialist John Motley Morehead (class of '91), houses the

Zeiss Planetarium instrument in its 68-foot hemispherical steel dome, exhibits in astronomy and allied sciences, and art exhibits in the galleries and in the Memorial Rotunda. The permanent collection of paintings in the Rotunda includes the famous "porthole pictures" of George and Martha Washington; Rembrandt's portrait of his sister, Liesbeth van Rijn; de Gelder's painting, *The Scribe;* Raeburn's portrait of John Andrew MacDonnel; and others, including the lovely portrait of Genevieve Morehead, by Nic Michailow. Also in the Rotunda is a large aneroid barometer by Henry Browne and Son and a great clock by Howard. The pendulum of this clock is more than 13 feet long. Automatic chimes strike the hours and quarters, and a different peal is heard each day of the week. Respectively from Monday through Sunday, the peals are those of the cathedrals and churches of Silchester, Whittington, Tennyson, Derby, Guilford, Winchester, and Fort Augustus.

On the floors above the Rotunda are rooms for special purposes, not normally open to the public, although times of open house frequently make it possible for those who visit the building to see the Faculty Lounge, the University Room, and the Dining Room, reserved for University functions.

On the floors below the Rotunda level, there are exhibit rooms for displays to make clear and interesting many of the facts and principles of the universe. A large orrery, or mechanical planetarium, one of only two of its type in the world, shows the visitor how the planets revolve around the sun, while their "moons" revolve around them, and the planets themselves rotate on their axes.

Public demonstrations are given at 8:30 each evening and at 3 P.M. on Saturdays and 3 and 4 P.M. on Sundays.

14. NEW EAST, NE. of the Playmakers Theater and erected in 1857, houses the geology and geography department. On the 1st floor is the GEOLOGICAL MUSEUM (*open 8:30-4:30, Mon.-Fri.; 9-1, Sat.; and on special occasions*). In the collection are specimens of rare North Carolina gems, fossil wood from sedimentary rocks, and itacolumite, flexible sandstone from Stokes County. On the 4th floor is the PHILANTHROPIC ASSEMBLY HALL (*open on application to janitor*).

15. DAVIE HALL, E. of New East, built in 1908 and named for the University's founder, houses the botany and zoology departments. In the building are many specimens of mounted plants and animals and the HERBARIUM (*open 9-5, weekdays*), one of the largest in the South.

16. The COKER ARBORETUM, NW. corner Cameron Ave. and Raleigh St., is a 5-acre University garden transformed from a boggy cow pasture by Dr. W. C. Coker. It is one of the most complete botanical gardens of its kind in America and contains almost every shrub or tree that grows in the temperate zone. A loose rock wall marks its boundaries, and a wistaria trellis borders Cameron Avenue.

17. The PLAYMAKERS THEATER, E. of South Building, when built in 1849, was called the Smith Building for Gov. Benjamin Smith, first benefactor of the University, who gave land warrants for 20,000 acres. It

was designed by Alexander J. Davis at the height of the Greek Revival and has a portico of the Corinthian order. The column capitals are designed with ears of corn and other grains in place of the traditional acanthus leaves. This was the first Library of the University (used only by faculty and visitors) and scene of the annual commencement balls. After a period as the law school it was converted into the experimental theater of the Carolina Playmakers who also maintain a Forest Theater for occasional outdoor productions on Country Club Road in Battle Park.

18. The UNIVERSITY LIBRARY (*open 7:45* A.M.-*11* P.M., *weekdays; 2-6, Sun.*), erected in 1929, at the end of the quadrangle behind South Building is an impressive limestone structure with monumental granite steps, a Corinthian portico, and a low dome. The interior, conservatively decorated in the classic style, is finished in plaster and travertine. The 675,000 volumes constitute one of the largest book collections in the South. As a result of an addition to the library in 1952, space has been doubled. Special collections of importance include the Southern Historical Collection of more than 2,500,000 manuscripts; the N. C. Collection of 145,000 items relating to the State; and the Hanes Collection recording the development of the book, including 650 incunabula titles and over 1200 manuscripts Additional recent features are the Rare Book Room; the Sir Walter Raleigh Rooms with 17th century furnishings; the Early Carolina Rooms, with 18th century furnishings; the enlarged Bull's Head Bookshop; and the expanded Library Extension Department with its State-wide lending services. Union catalogues show the holdings of the Library of Congress, Duke University Library, and other libraries in the State.

19. Rising behind the dome of the library, facing Raleigh Rd., is the MOREHEAD-PATTERSON BELL TOWER, erected in 1931, an imposing Italian Renaissance campanile in a setting of boxwoods, presented by John Motley Morehead and Rufus Lenoir Patterson. Names of their families, long associated with the University, are inscribed on the bells. Each afternoon at 5 o'clock the chimes ring out old hymns, University songs, and, occasionally, popular music.

20. KENAN STADIUM, behind the bell tower, built in 1927, is approached by roads and paths through the woods that encircle it. This concrete amphitheater nestles in a natural bowl and seats 24,000 in its permanent stands and 20,000 in temporary stands. The end walls of the oval are terraced in native shrubs and slope down to a gateway on the western end and a field house on the eastern end. The stadium was the gift of William Rand Kenan, Jr., in memory of his parents. It is used for major athletic events and commencement exercises and in the summer for plays, pageants, and concerts.

21. WOOLLEN GYMNASIUM, Raleigh Rd. and Raleigh St., built of brick and steel and completed in 1937, consists of the main front three-story wing, the Gymnasium wing, and the Bowman Gray Memorial Pool. Just

south is the Women's Gymnasium (1943) and the Kessing (outdoor) Pool (1943). These buildings and pools are among the finest in the country.

22. The INSTITUTE OF GOVERNMENT faces the intersection of Raleigh and Country Club Rds. The three wings of this graceful Georgian building (under construction) will house classrooms, library, and dormitory facilities as well as staff and administrative offices. When completed in 1956 the building will bear the name of Joseph Palmer Knapp whose interest in the government of North Carolina counties, cities, and towns led the Knapp Foundation to contribute half the cost of construction.

Unique in its field, the Institute of Government grew out of the law classes of Prof. Albert Coates in the 1920's, developed during the 1930's, and became an integral part of the University in 1942. Its staff members make continuous comparative and analytical governmental studies. The results of their work are published, taught in training schools, and demonstrated by practical application. The objectives are constant: to bridge the gap in knowledge and experience between outgoing and incoming public officials; to co-ordinate the work of officials in overlapping governmental units by reducing friction and duplication of effort; and to bridge the gap between citizens and officials through a continuing program of education.

23. MEDICAL CENTER, Pittsboro Rd., south of the main campus, consists of the Schools of Medicine, Dentistry, Pharmacy, Public Health, and Nursing and the North Carolina Memorial Hospital, which were established in 1949 by means of a State appropriation of $14,000,000. The Hospital, including psychiatric and tuberculosis units, was opened in 1952. It has 600 beds and facilities for 100,000 out-patient visits per year. The Dental Clinics, activated in 1952, provide care for 50,000 patient visits per year. The Schools of Pharmacy and Public Health have been in full operation for many years. The Schools of Medicine and Dentistry graduated their first students in 1954. The School of Nursing holds its first commencement in 1955. Because of the physical inter-connection of all primary health education and service programs, this is one of a handful of "complete" medical centers in the world. Extensive research programs are in progress. It is especially significant that the Health Division was created in part to assist the various communities of North Carolina raise the level of their health programs. Much of the creative energy of the Health Center will, therefore, be spent in work at the community levels.

24. The METHODIST CHURCH, E. Franklin St., formed in 1853, is of colonial style and is constructed of red brick with limestone trim. Its steeple, 210 feet high, can be seen from afar. The pulpit and the interior of the sanctuary are especially notable for their simplicity. The building was designed by James Gamble Rogers, New York, who designed the Sterling Memorial Library and the Harkness Memorial Quadrangle at Yale University, the Chicago group of Professional Buildings at Northwestern University, and others.

25. The SPRUNT MEMORIAL PRESBYTERIAN CHURCH (1918), opposite Graham Memorial, is a noteworthy example of village church

architecture, designed by Hobart B. Upjohn in the Wrenn tradition. An oval stairway connects the parish house with the main body of the church.

26. The CHAPEL OF THE CROSS (*Episcopal*), Franklin St. adjoining Spencer Hall, has three buildings connected by a cloister. The original church, built with slave labor (1842-46), is a small brick building in the Gothic Revival style and contains an old slave gallery. The new church building and the parish house, designed by Hobart B. Upjohn in the same style and built in 1924-25, were the gift of the Durham industrialist, William A. Erwin, in memory of his grandfather, Dr. William R. Holt. The brick parish house forms the rear of the garth, connecting the two church buildings. The new buildings were constructed of pink Mount Airy granite; the stained-glass windows were designed by Bacon, of London.

27. The PRESIDENT'S HOUSE, SE. corner Franklin and Raleigh Sts., built in 1909, is a large dwelling with colonnaded portico and porches on three sides, erected in Pres. Venable's regime on the site of Pres. Swain's former home.

28. The STONE COTTAGE (*private*), NE. corner Franklin and Hillsboro Sts., was originally the law office of Judge William H. Battle and Samuel F. Phillips, later U. S. Solicitor General. Italian in style it is of field stone construction covered with stucco. Here in 1845 began the University's first professional school, that of law.

29. The WIDOW PUCKETT HOUSE (*private*), 501 E. Franklin St., built about 1799 for John Puckett, is one of the few remaining houses with the narrow front porch and open-work "veranda supports" peculiar to early Chapel Hill dwellings. A characteristic loose rock wall borders the lawn. For many years this was the home of the Rev. Dr. James Phillips, mathematics professor and father of Cornelia Phillips Spencer. It is now the home of Chancellor Robert B. House.

30. The HOOPER HOUSE (*private*), SE. corner Franklin St. and Battle Lane, was built in 1814 for William Hooper, grandson of the signer of the Declaration of Independence of the same name and once professor at the University. The original lines and proportions of the frame structure are well preserved. It has a gambrel roof and end chimneys which step back unattached above the second story. It is now the home of Kay Kyser.

31. The MONOGRAM CLUB, Country Club Rd., across from the Forest Theater, built as a reception center for the Navy Pre-Flight School during World War II, is now used as a public restaurant and meeting place. The mirrored soda fountain room contains an interesting "round-the-world circus parade" designed by William Meade Prince and carved in wood by Carl Boettcher.

32. GIMGHOUL CASTLE, on Point (Piney) Prospect, Gimghoul Rd., is a turreted, native stone structure which affords a sweeping view of the countryside. It belongs to the Gimghouls, a junior social order. Beneath

Dromgoole Rock at the castle entrance, according to college legend, is the grave of Peter Dromgoole, killed in a duel with a fellow student over his sweetheart and buried secretly by the terrified survivor and the seconds.

33. A new residential development, GLEN LENNOX, is located 1½ miles east of town on NC 54. This settlement comprises 440 apartments, a dozen commodious dwelling houses, and a shopping center of a dozen modern stores. All constructions are one-story, except that the administrative offices and a number of doctors' and dentists' offices are on the second floor of the commercial area.

At the northern end of the development an 8-acre lake is now under construction. Across the highway from the commercial buildings is a 3-acre plot which has recently been made into a park—to be enjoyed by the faculty and children of the new elementary school, as well as by residents of the apartments.

Charlotte

Information Services: Chamber of Commerce, 222 S. Church St.; Carolina Motor Club, 701 S. Tryon St.; State Auto Assoc., Selwyn Hotel.

Railroad Stations: 215 E. 6th St., for Norfolk and Southern Ry.; 401 W. 4th St., for Piedmont & Northern Ry.; N. Tryon at 13th St., for Seaboard Airline R. R.; 601 W. Trade St., for Southern Ry.

Bus Stations: Union Terminal, 418 W. Trade St., for Atlantic Greyhound, Carolina Coach Co., Carolina Scenic Stages, Carolina Transit Lines, Queen City Coach Co., Queen City Trailways; and 316 W. Trade St. for Sharon Coach Co.

City Buses: Along regular routes.

Airports: Douglas Municipal Airport, **7 m.** W. on US 74-29, for Capital, Eastern, and Piedmont Airlines; Southern Airways and Southern Flight Service; Cannon Airport, 2½ m. W. on Tuckaseegee Rd., for private planes; Delta Aircraft Service, Albemarle Rd., for private planes.

Radio and Television Stations: WAYS (610), WAYS-TV (channel 36), WBT (1110), WBT-FM (99.9), WBTV (channel 3), WGIV (1600), WIST (930), WMIT-FM (106.9), WSOC (1240), WSOC-FM (103.5).

Newspapers: Charlotte News (eve. except Sun.), *Charlotte Observer* (morn. and Sun.), and *Mecklenburg Times* (weekly).

Educational Institutions: Charlotte College (*coed*); Queens College (*women*); Johnson C. Smith University (*Negro, coed*).

Recreational Facilities: 31 parks and playgrounds, 7 swimming pools, 3 community centers.

Golf: Carolina Golf Club, **3 m.** SW. on US 74-29, 18 holes; Carmel Country Club, **6 m.** SE. on US 16, 18 holes; Charlotte Country Club, Country Club Lane, 27 holes; Eastwood Golf Club, Plaza Rd., 18 holes; Hillcrest Golf Club, **2 m.** E. on US 74-27; Municipal Golf Course, Barringer Dr., 9 holes; Myers Park Country Club, Roswell Ave., 18 holes; Sharon Golf Club, **3 m.** SE. on NC 262, 9 holes.

Baseball: Griffith Park, Magnolia Ave., South Atlantic League (Class A).

Football: Municipal Stadium, N. Cecil St. and Park Dr.

Riding: Lakeside Stables, 2045 Wilmount Rd., and Meadowbrook Stables, Providence Rd.

Annual Events: Carolina Carrousel, Nov.; Carolina Ginners Assn., Feb.; Carolina Golden Glove Boxing Tournament, Feb.; Carolina Motor Club Travel Show, April; Carolina-Virginia Fashion Show, Nov.; Debutante Ball, June; Food Show, Sept.; Garden Club Show, May; Kennel Club Show, April; Shrine Bowl Game, Dec.; Southern States Fair, Oct.; Textile Show, autumn.

CHARLOTTE (732 alt., 134,042 pop.) is the largest city in the Carolinas and dominates the piedmont area, a broad rolling plateau extending from the foothills of the Appalachians to the Atlantic coastal plain. The city is the nucleus of a galaxy of prosperous, expanding piedmont cities. The "Queen City" is blessed with a pleasantly temperate climate throughout the year. Because of its rapidly developing wholesale business, amounting to over $1,260,000,000, it is becoming best known as the key distribution city in this area. Similarly, it is the outstanding retail center and one of the leading textile manufacturing centers.

Its growth has been amazing. In 1750, the present County of Mecklenburg numbered, perhaps, 100 inhabitants, excluding Catawba Indians. In 1850, the village of Charlotte had 1,065 residents. In 1950, there were nearly 200,000 in "Greater Charlotte." In the first 30 years of the 20th century, the city quadrupled in size. Between 1940 and 1950, there was an increase of 33%.

Independence Square, formed by the intersection of Trade and Tryon Sts., is the center of the city, within 6 blocks of which are tall office buildings, hotels, and the principal stores. The residential sections of W. Trade and N. Tryon, formerly the charm of the community, are already all but absorbed by expanding business.

Eastward of the city are several residential sections: the Country Club area, Eastover, Myers Park, and Dilworth, where many of the finer homes are now situated. Beautiful landscaping, large trees, and careful maintenance characterize these developments. Beyond these are large estates, marking the trend of the wealthy toward the country. The bulk of the city's population lives in smaller homes on attractive, tree-shaded streets in the newer suburbs.

An interesting development of the last few decades is the disappearance of the company-owned mill village which formerly provided housing for the majority of the white operatives. The small houses have been sold to private individuals. Many have been replaced by more modern homes and light industry.

Charlotte's 37,531 Negroes, 28% of the total population, live in scattered, segregated districts. Two government-owned developments, Fairview and Southside Homes, provide low-cost living accommodations of a superior type. Double Oaks, on the north of the city, is privately owned and is equipped with its own swimming pool and recreational features. Other privately owned developments include Southview and Brookhill. Biddleville, the western suburb where Johnson C. Smith University is situated, contains the homes of many of the business and professional groups. Lying between S. McDowell and S. Brevard Sts. is Blue Heaven, typical of the sections inhabited by the poorer Negroes. Although the bulk of the Negro population is employed in common labor and in domestic service, the race is well represented in business and in the professions.

The present Charlotte area was occupied by the Catawba Indians when the first permanent settlers began arriving about 1748—Scotch-Irish and Germans coming down through Pennsylvania and Virginia, and a few Englishmen from Virginia, were met by another stream of Scotch-Irish, English, and a few Swiss and Huguenots coming up from Charleston, S. C. The inhabitants soon organized the notable 7 colonial Presbyterian congregations of Mecklenburg, several of them with good classical schools for boys. Colonial Lutheran and German Reform congregations, mostly in areas now separated from Mecklenburg, were also organized during the colonial period. From the beginning, the Scotch-Irish took the lead in political affairs.

Catawba and passing Cherokee Indians gave the settlers trouble, and there were skirmishes with some hostile northern Indian allies of the French. In 1761 the Catawba withdrew into the territory that had been assigned them just inside the South Carolina line. By 1763, the settlers were no longer molested by the Indians, but many Mecklenburgers fought in the Cherokee campaign of 1776 in the western parts of the State.

The section was a part of Anson County until 1762 when Mecklenburg County was formed. The original conveyance of 360 acres for the town site was made by Henry E. McCulloch, agent for George A. Selwyn, in 1765 for "ninety pounds, lawful money." The county seat was built around a small courthouse, probably log, and chartered in 1768. Town and county were named for Queen Charlotte of Mecklenburg-Strelitz, wife of George III.

Fertility of the soil brought more settlers and prosperity to the region. In 1771, Queens College for boys was established, an outgrowth of an earlier classical school at Sugaw Creek Church, and the first college south of Virginia. The disallowance of the charter of Queens by the English crown (owing to Whig and Presbyterian influences on its board of trustees), the imposition of ever-increasing taxes, and the interference in local government by the King's party in the capital made the area around Charlotte a focal point of dissatisfaction with British rule. Finally, news that the blood of colonists had been shed by redcoats at Lexington and Concord was climaxed by a meeting of 27 representative men, called by Col. Thomas Polk, the county militia leader, member of the general assembly, and a great-uncle of Pres. James K. Polk. The session convened May 19, 1775. On the following day, according to local history, the delegates affixed their signatures to a declaration of independence (the Mecklenburg Declaration). It supposedly met with wild acclaim by the excited crowd milling about the courthouse. The date is inscribed upon the State flag and upon the Great Seal of North Carolina and is observed as a State holiday.

Capt. James Jack was chosen to take the message to Philadelphia where Congress was then sitting. After a hazardous ride on horseback, partly through Tory country, he arrived at the Congress only to meet with refusal on the part of the members to consider the measure. The records containing the Declaration were destroyed by fire in 1800.

Because of the controversy that later arose over the authenticity of the Mecklenburg Declaration, Capt. Jack issued a statement attesting that he rode to Philadelphia with the document. This statement, along with those of surviving delegates and witnesses, is believed by many to establish proof of the genuineness of the first declaration of independence in the Thirteen Colonies. However, other historians hold that there is no evidence of the May 20, 1775, meeting. Proof exists of a meeting in Charlotte on May 31, 1775, which adopted a set of resolves more moderate in tone than those of the so-called declaration.

On Sept. 26, 1780, Charlotte was occupied by the British under Cornwallis but not until the invader's advance had been hotly contested by the partisan band of Col. William R. Davie. The State troops, under the command of Brig. Gen. William Lee Davidson, harassed the British outposts, and a number of skirmishes took place in the vicinity. The most famous of these was the skirmish at McIntyre's or Bradley's Farm on Oct. 4, 1780, the Whigs being led by local captains. So inveterate was the animosity of the Mecklenburgers, that Lord Cornwallis is reputed to have called the section a "damned hornet's nest." The epithet, minus the expletive, is perpetuated on the city's seal and is proudly borne by many local organizations.

The British remained in Charlotte Town for less than a month, but in January of 1781, Cornwallis again invaded North Carolina. Gen. Nathanael Greene left Gen. William Lee Davidson to slow up the British advance on the Catawba River. On Feb. 1, the redcoats forced a crossing at Cowan's Ford, killed Gen. Davidson, dispersed his militia, and moved on from Mecklenburg County for the battle with Greene at Guilford Courthouse.

Mecklenburg's Revolutionary history has been a favorite subject for historical novelists. At least 5 have settings centered in the "Independence County": *The Hornet's Nest* by E. P. Roe (1886), *The Master of Appleby* by Francis Lynde (1902), *Alexandriana* by LeGette Blythe (1940), *Raleigh's Eden* by Inglis Fletcher (1940), and *The Ragged Ones* by Burke Davis (1951).

Two presidents of the United States spent part of their boyhood in Charlotte. Andrew Jackson was born in the Waxhaw settlement, a part of which extended into Mecklenburg, and he attended school (probably briefly) in Liberty Hall. James Knox Polk was born in the county near Pineville, and the Polk family were among the first citizens of Charlotte.

George Washington visited the town in 1791, received a flattering ovation, but was unimpressed by any future possibilities. Pres. Woodrow Wilson, who had spent his freshman year at Davidson, made the May 20th address in Charlotte in 1916.

At the end of the 18th century, Charlotte was the center of a gold rush, and until the discovery of gold in California in 1848 this was the most productive region in the country. A branch of the United States Mint was built in Charlotte in 1836, and with the exception of the years of the Civil War, was operated until 1913.

During the ante-bellum period, Charlotte was the court and buying center for the planters and farmers of the county. A handsome neo-classic courthouse and an impressive Neo-Gothic Presbyterian church were then show-places of the village. The county contained many prosperous plantations with such names as "Cedar Grove," "Rural Hill," "Rosedale," "Glenwood," "Oak Lawn" and "Holly Wood."

Charlotte and Mecklenburg County sent several units to the Confederate Army, including the Charlotte Grays, the Hornets' Nest Rifles, and officers of the Bethel Regiment. The last full meeting of the Confederate Cabinet was held in the town in the home of William Phifer on N. Tryon St. At the end of the war, there were 1,200 soldiers in local hospitals. While in Charlotte, Pres. Jefferson Davis learned of Lincoln's assassination (April 15, 1865).

The abolition of slavery and the introduction of wages into the economy of farming changed the principal occupation of this and other sections of the piedmont from agriculture to manufacturing. Development of enormous quantities of hydroelectric power on the Catawba River, which flows a short distance west of the city, aided the expansion of industry.

Charlotte is the center of the nation's textile industry. The piedmont region of the Carolinas has become known as the Land of Textiles. Charlotte has a tremendous stake in the future of the mills which spin the cotton or fibre and weave the cloth that clothes America and a considerable portion of the world. Practically all the large textile companies in the United States handle their entire business in the South through offices and plants in Charlotte. The American Cotton Manufacturers Institute, formerly located in New York City, is now located in Charlotte. There are more than 40 textile plants located in Charlotte. Within a 50 mile radius there are more than 4,600,000 spindles. More than 650 cotton mills are located within a 100-mile radius.

Charlotte is headquarters for the Duke Power Company's system in North and South Carolina, serving 211 communities, with 5,620 miles of high-tension transmission lines. Since World War II, Duke Power Company has invested an additional $270,000,000 in capital expansion.

Churches have played a prominent part in Charlotte's life. Founded by staunch Presbyterians at a time when the Church of England dominated the ecclesiastical and educational life of the coast, this has always been a Calvinist stronghold. Not until 1766, however, were Presbyterian ministers allowed to perform marriage ceremonies. Virtually all denominations are now well represented.

The 20th century, and especially the last decade or two, has witnessed a remarkable growth in Charlotte's cultural activity. Music, in particular, has taken long strides forward. Charlotte now has (1) The Community Concert Assn. which is responsible for bringing many world-famous artists to the city (2) The Charlotte Symphony of about 70 members which presents 5 pairs of concerts yearly (3) The Charlotte Opera Assn., complete with orchestra and scenery, presents 4 operas annually with local artists (4) The Oratorio Singers, 60 voices, presents two programs a year, both classical and modern (5) The Charlotte Choral Society, 75 voices, primarily popular and semi-classical performances. Queens College, Johnson C. Smith University, and Davidson College in the county all have excellent musical organizations.

The Charlotte Writers' Club is an active group for the encouragement of creative writing. It awards an annual prize for the best short story submitted. Half a dozen authors listed in *Who's Who in America* reside in Charlotte or Mecklenburg County.

Art is sponsored by the Mint Museum of Art, drama by the Little Theatre, and a beginning for an historical museum by the Alexander Rock House.

POINTS OF INTEREST

1. INDEPENDENCE SQUARE, at the intersection of Trade and Tryon Sts., is the SITE OF THE FIRST COURTHOUSE, indicated by a circular iron marker at the center of the intersection. The courthouse during the Revolution was described by Joseph Graham as "a frame building raised on eight brick pillars ten feet from the ground, which was the most elevated place. Between the pillars was erected a wall of rock three and a half feet high and the open basement answered as a market-house for the town." Here, it is claimed, the "Mecklenburg Declaration of Independence" was read by Col. Thomas Polk. Around this courthouse took place "the battle of Charlotte," a skirmish in which the advance of Lord Cornwallis was delayed by Col. William R. Davie, Sept. 26, 1780. Cornwallis occupied the town and established his headquarters in the "White House" of Col. Thomas Polk, the SITE OF CORNWALLIS' HEADQUARTERS being now marked by a plaque in the sidewalk at the northeast corner of Trade and Tryon Sts.

2. A MONUMENT TO CAPT. JAMES JACK, 211 W. Trade St., marks the site of the tavern conducted by Patrick Jack, father of the redoubtable Capt. James Jack who bore the news of Mecklenburg's independence to the Continental Congress in Philadelphia. The North Carolina delegates there quashed the movement as "too premature." The gray stone marker with a bronze plaque shows a rider in bas-relief and lists the roster of membership of the Capt. James Jack Chapter of the Children of the American Revolution who subscribed for the monument. Mary Groome McNinch's poem, "The Ride of Captain Jack—1775," tells the story of this Revolutionary exploit.

3. The FIRST PRESBYTERIAN CHURCH, W. Trade St., between N. Church and Poplar Sts., occupies the site of the first church built in the village of Charlotte. The original church, completed in 1823, served all denominations, though the Presbyterians predominated. That denomination purchased the property in 1841 and in 1857 replaced the small brick building with a stuccoed brick church of Norman Gothic design, in outward appearance essentially that of the present church. Fundamental alterations (a re-building except for the entrance) took place in 1894, the present Sunday School building was added in 1916, and further additions (a section to

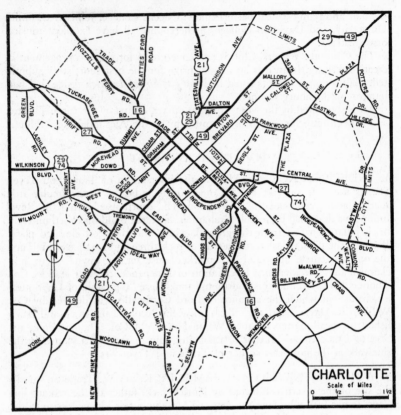

join the Fellowship Hall, originally the manse) were made in 1951-52. The McAden Memorial Window, a copy of Sir Edward Burne-Jones' painting, *Hope,* won a prize at the Chicago Fair of 1894. The church occupies an entire city block in the heart of the business section. Its spire, rising above old trees shading a broad yard, once dominated the town.

The OLD CEMETERY, lying at the rear of the church and fronting on W. 5th St., served the town as a common burying-ground until about 1854 and was used by the Presbyterians until 1870. During Reconstruction it is believed that the Ku Klux Klan held meetings here, many of Charlotte's first citizens being members. Within two years, the group became convinced that the organization was getting out of hand and many resigned. Among the outstanding citizens buried here are Gov. Nathaniel Alexander (1805-07), Col. Thomas Polk, and Gen. George Graham. Many of the headstones are now difficult to decipher. One epitaph reads: "Her Breach in the Social Circle Will Long be Severely Missed."

4. The SHIPP MONUMENT, corner S. Mint and W. 4th Sts., at the rear of the post office, commemorates the military reinstatement of the Southern States after the Civil War. Lt. William Ewen Shipp, the first Southerner graduated from West Point after the conflict, chose service with the 10th Cavalry (Negro) and was killed in the Battle of Santiago, Cuba, July 2, 1898. His body was interred at Lincolnton. Subscriptions to defray the cost of the 30-foot, 15-ton granite shaft were made by school children throughout the State.

5. The BIRTHPLACE OF JULIA JACKSON (*private*), 834 W. 5th St., is a two-story frame structure built in the 1850's for James P. Irwin. The portico is a later addition, the interior marble mantel and curved staircase are original. The house was once the center of a 300-acre plantation. Here the wife of Gen. "Stonewall" Jackson came from Virginia to live with her sister, Mrs. Irwin. And here the General's only daughter, Julia, was born Nov. 23, 1862. Mrs. Jackson was the daughter of Dr. Robert Hall Morrison, first president of Davidson College. Two of her sisters also married men who became Confederate generals: D. H. Hill and Rufus Barringer.

6. The PUBLIC LIBRARY OF CHARLOTTE & MECKLENBURG COUNTY (*open 9-9, weekdays; 2-6, Sun.*), 310 N. Tryon St., has been located in a Carnegie building since 1903. (A new Main Library building is planned for this location. Construction is expected to begin in 1954. Temporary quarters will be at 315 N. College St.). Serving all of Mecklenburg County, the Library operates a system of branch and mobile libraries and has excellent collections in textiles, religion, family relationships, serials, and educational films and fair collections in genealogy and regional history. Non-fiction holdings are listed in the Union Catalog at the University of North Carolina. The Library has the Library of Congress printed catalogue and a wide collection of periodical indexes.

7. The LITTLE THEATRE OF CHARLOTTE, INC. (*open, apply to Managing Director*), 501 Queen's Rd., occupies its own building (constructed 1941) in one of the most exclusive residential districts of the city. The auditorium seats approximately 300. The organization has about 3,000 members and each season produces 6 plays, which run for a minimum of two weeks. *Curtain Call,* the theatre magazine, is published monthly during the season. The Little Theatre of Charlotte was founded in 1925 under the title of the Drama League.

8. The PUBLIC BUILDINGS, 600-700 blocks of E. Trade St., erected in the early 1920's and designed by C. C. Hook, are in a landscaped setting. The CITY HALL, of modified classic design with limestone exterior and fireproof construction, houses the offices of mayor, city manager, and various departments and contains the council chamber. Three other buildings of the municipal group are of gray brick with limestone trim, standing behind the city hall and harmonizing in design. The COUNTY COURTHOUSE, of neoclassic design, contains the county executive offices, superior and county courtrooms, and the county jail. In the plaza at the entrance is a MONU-

MENT TO THE SIGNERS OF THE MECKLENBURG DECLARATION, a granite shaft erected in 1898 and moved from the former courthouse to the present site.

9. The SITE OF THE CONFEDERATE NAVY YARD is indicated by a marker on the wall of the railway underpass near 226 E. Trade St. In May, 1862, it was decided to move the center of naval ordnance from Norfolk, Va., to Charlotte, which had the advantage of safety from invasion from the sea yet rail connection with the port of Wilmington.

10. The SITE OF QUEENS COLLEGE (COLONIAL) is commemorated by a marker at the SE. corner of 3rd and S. Tryon Sts., now occupied by a filling station. Until the early 1920's the county courthouse stood on the site. In December, 1770, Gov. Tryon suggested to the assembly that a school for higher learning was needed in the back country. Within a month a bill was enacted providing for the establishment of Queen's College in Charlotte. Controversy over land titles and the Regulator movement hampered progress. In June, 1773, Gov. Martin issued a proclamation to the effect that the King had disallowed the charter. A local historian states that "the King objected to the number of dissenting ministers among the trustees," and complained that "a College under such auspices was well calculated to ensure the growth of a numerous democracy."

The school continued in spite of fruitless efforts to obtain a charter under the name of Queen's Museum. It is said that the meetings that led to the drafting of the Mecklenburg Declaration were held in the building. Diplomas were issued under the name of Queen's Museum in 1776, but soon after, for patriotic reasons, the name was changed to Liberty Hall Academy, and thus it was incorporated in 1777. When Cornwallis conquered the town in 1780, his forces occupied and damaged the building. The institution was never able to re-establish itself after the Revolution on its old footing. Many notable men were at one time or another enrolled as students: Pres. Andrew Jackson, Gov. William R. Davie, Gen. Joseph Graham, Col. William Polk, and Gov. John Adair of Ky.

The present Queens College in Charlotte is, like its namesake, a Presbyterian institution, but is a college for women.

11. The MINT MUSEUM (*open 10-5, Tues.-Sat.; 3-5, Sun.*), corner Hampstead Place and Eastover Rd., now an art gallery, was reconstructed from materials of the original branch of the U. S. Mint, being an almost exact reproduction. The original building, situated on ground now occupied by the U. S. Post Office on W. Trade St., was designed by William Strickland (1787-1854) of Philadelphia, who was architect for the U. S. Customhouse, the Masonic Temple, and the Merchants Exchange in Philadelphia. Designed in the Federal style, the two-story structure is T-shaped in plan, the stem of the letter forming a long well-proportioned gallery on the main floor. The cross arm is formed by the foyer with rooms to the right and left of the entrance. The interior has vaulted ceilings and walls of local stone.

The long façade of the central section is broken by a severe pedimented portico approached by a flight of steps. Beneath the sloping eaves of the pediment a golden American eagle is perched with outspread wings. Stuart Warren Cramer, Sr., assayer of the mint (1889-93), wrote: "This eagle was a landmark in Charlotte when I first came here and a pet of Charlotte people, as well it might be, for it was perhaps the largest eagle in the world, being 14 feet from tip to tip, and five feet high. When I had to redecorate it, it took over 165 books of gold leaf and 10 books of silver leaf to cover it."

The Charlotte Mint, a very useful arm of the Treasury, served the gold-producing districts of the southern Appalachian region—at that time the only gold-yielding territory in the country. Five million dollars were coined here between 1837 and 1861. In 1844 the building was almost totally destroyed by fire but was rebuilt on the original plan. During the Civil War, operations were suspended, and the Mint was used as a Confederate headquarters and hospital. When it was reopened after the war, coinage was discontinued, but the government used it for assaying until 1913. When the government ordered the demolition of the Mint in 1932 to make way for the left wing of the Post Office, enough money was raised by patriotic citizens to buy the materials from the old building, the present site was donated by Mr. E. C. Griffith of Charlotte, and on Oct. 22, 1936, the Mint Museum of Art was formally opened.

The Mint plays an important part in the cultural life of Charlotte. Classes in painting, ceramics, and handicrafts, for both adults and children, are held during the 10 months' season—Sept. 1 to July 1. Concerts and lectures are established features of the regular program. In the galleries are exhibited historic relics, ceramics, the work of local artists, and outstanding traveling art shows. Among the many fine canvases in the Mint's permanent collection are Ridolfo Ghirlandaio's *Madonna and Child with Four Saints* and *Madonna and Child* by Francesco Granacci, both gifts of the Samuel H. Kress Foundation. The Mint also houses a CHILDREN'S NATURE MUSEUM.

12. The MARTIN L. CANNON RESIDENCE (*grounds open by permission*), 400 Hermitage Rd., is the former home of James B. Duke, tobacco and power magnate (*see* DURHAM). The original house, erected by Z. V. Taylor about 1915, was purchased in 1920 by Mr. Duke who enlarged and remodeled it. In recent years, equally elaborate homes have been built in and around the city, but for a while the Duke house occupied the position of primacy in Charlotte comparable to the "White House" of Col. Thomas Polk during the colonial period and the William Phifer house during the late ante-bellum period. The Cannon property is a 10-acre estate which from early spring to fall blooms with flaming azalea, pink and white dogwood, and other plants and shrubs.

13. COVENANT PRESBYTERIAN CHURCH BUILDINGS, in the triangle between Morehead St. and Dilworth Rd., were erected 1950-53 and comprise one of the largest church plants in the State and one of the most noteworthy groups of church edifices in the country. The Gothic buildings, laid out around a center court, are constructed of native gray and tan granite from the Salisbury quarries and are dominated by the 170-foot stone tower

of the sanctuary, which is similar to St. Andrews at Heckington in Lincoln-shire, England. The Gothic details of the exterior are all carved in limestone. The massive exterior doors of solid mahogany, adorned with intricate wrought iron, the stained-glass windows, the long marble aisle, and the mahogany lacework of the chancel are all noteworthy. The pews, seating 1200 persons, are also mahogany.

14. DILWORTH METHODIST CHURCH, 603 E. Boulevard, a lime-stone structure of English Gothic design with lofty twin towers, was erected in 1922 with funds raised by private subscription and augmented by a con-tribution of the Duke Foundation.

15. QUEENS COLLEGE (*women; buildings open during school hours*), between Queens Rd. and Radcliffe Ave., has 12 buildings of dark red brick trimmed with white stone, on a large wooded campus. Its sorority houses are of the bungalow type. The institution was founded in 1857 as the Char-lotte Female Institute and first occupied a building on N. College St. In 1895, it became the Presbyterian Female College. In 1912, the name was changed to Queens College, in honor of the colonial Presbyterian institution in Charlotte for men, and the college was moved to its present site. Chicora College of Columbia, S. C., was consolidated with it in 1930. Operated by the Presbyteries of Mecklenburg, Kings Mountain, and Greenville in the Synods of North and South Carolina, the college has an enrollment of 400, with 300 in the Evening College, and is fully accredited.

16. The TULIP GARDENS (*open during blooming season*), at the resi-dence of J. B. Ivey, 1638 E. Morehead St., contain about 20,000 plants in numerous varieties that bloom usually the last two weeks of March. Plant-ings of tulips border the walks and driveway. Each variety is marked for the information of visitors.

J. B. Ivey is sponsoring a garden at the Methodist Home for the Aged, situated about one mile from the city limits of Charlotte. Tulips bloom from the last of March till the first of May, jonquils from the last of March, roses in April and May, peonies the last of May, anemones during March and April, pansies during March and April. There is also an herb garden con-taining about 80 varieties.

17. The RUDISILL GOLD MINE (*closed*), corner of Gold and Mint Sts., produced from 40 to 60 tons of ore per day averaging about $12 a ton until the company suspended work in 1938 because of the low gold content. Having operated from 1826 until the California rush, the mine lay inactive until 1934 when operations were resumed.

18. JOHNSON C. SMITH UNIVERSITY (*Negro; buildings open during school hours*), entrance on Beatties Ford Rd., between Martin and Mill Sts., occupies an 85-acre wooded campus with 23 buildings most of which are of Greek Revival design. Degrees are conferred in liberal arts, science, and theological courses. A premedical course is under supervision of a branch of the American Medical Association. Students from other colleges make

use of the well-equipped laboratories. The senior division of the College of Liberal Arts is coeducational. The library has an extensive musical collection, including facsimiles of the original manuscripts of Stephen Collins Foster. Although controlled by the Presbyterian Church of the U. S. A., the university is nonsectarian. Student enrollment is about 600.

The first land acquired was by gift of Col. William R. Myers, a former slave owner, who saw the need of educational facilities for the Negro race. When founded in 1867 the school was known as Biddle Memorial Institute. In recognition of a substantial endowment made by the widow of Johnson C. Smith of Pittsburgh, Pa., the present name was adopted in 1923. James B. Duke made a large contribution to the institution in 1925.

Durham

Information Services: Chamber of Commerce, Washington Duke Hotel, 207 N. Corcoran St., Market St. entrance; Carolina Motor Club, 111 W. Parrish St.; Duke University, Main Lobby, Union Bldg. (*open 24 hrs. daily*).

Railroad Station: Union Station, S. Church St., for Southern Ry., Seaboard Air Line, Norfolk Southern, Norfolk & Western, and Durham & Southern R. R.

Bus Station: NW. corner Dillard and Main Sts., for Carolina Trailways, Atlantic Greyhound, Virginia Trailways, Queen City Trailways, and Southern Coach Co.

City Buses: Along regular routes.

Airport: Raleigh-Durham Airport, **12.5 m.** SE on US 70, for Eastern, Capital, and Piedmont Airlines.

Radio and Television Stations: WDNC (620), WDNC-FM (105.1), WTIK (1310), WSSB (1940), Duke University Station WDBS (*student-operated; broadcasting area limited to campuses*), WTVD (channel 11).

Newspapers: Durham Morning Herald (Daily & Sun.); *Durham Sun* (Eve. except Sun.); *News-Journal* (Thurs.).

Educational Institutions: Duke University and North Carolina College (*Negro*).

Swimming: Duke Park, end of N. Mangum St., US 501; Forest Hills Clubhouse, 1639 University Dr.; Hope Valley Country Club, **4 m.** SW. off NC 751; Long Meadow Park, Liberty St.; Hillside Pool, Pine St.

Golf: Hope Valley Country Club, 18 holes; Hillandale Golf Club, **2 m.** NW. on US 70A, 18 holes.

Tennis: Forest Hills Park, Duke Park, Hope Valley Club, Duke University Courts.

Hunting and Fishing: Inquire Chamber of Commerce.

Baseball: Durham Athletic Park, N. end of Morris St., for baseball, football, soft ball, rodeos, auto stunt shows, singing conventions, and model airplane exhibits; Duke University Ball Park, West Campus.

Football: Duke Stadium.

Municipal Parks: 11 municipal parks with 192.8 acres.

Gardens: Sarah P. Duke Memorial Gardens, West Campus, Duke University (*open daily, 8 A.M. to 8 P.M.*).

Annual Events: Kennel Club Show, Apr.; Flower Show, May; Carillon Recitals, throughout the year; County Fair, 3rd wk. Sept.; Duke University Commencement, week of first Sun. in June; Duke University Founders Day, Dec. 11.

DURHAM (405 alt., 71,311 pop.), is a modern industrial city in the eastern piedmont. The universal demand for tobacco, coupled with the genius of the Duke family and other business leaders, is exemplified in long rows of factories where thousands work daily, filling whole trains with their products. Here was created the fortune that endowed Duke University.

Three streets converge at FIVE POINTS, center of the business district, which in the 1860's was a country crossroads. A few skyscrapers along the principal streets tower above crowded rows of lesser buildings. The great tobacco factories lie close to the heart of the business district, and the railroad tracks that serve them cross up-town streets.

Many of the finer homes are in the southwest part of the city and beyond in the Forest Hills and Hope Valley subdivisions. Commonplace dwellings throughout the town house the families of mill and factory workers. In South Durham is a section known as Hayti, where 27,000 Negroes live and operate their own business firms.

The two campuses of Duke University lie to the northwest and west of the city's center. Throughout the town are parks and playgrounds for both races.

Often the air is permeated by the pungent scent of tobacco from the stemmeries and the sweetish odor of tonka bean used in cigarette manufacture. From 9 to 5 o'clock Durham's streets reflect the activity of its business houses and professional offices. When the American Tobacco and the Liggett and Myers whistles blow, an army of workers pours forth—men and women, white and colored. Buses and trucks, heavily laden, rumble along the thoroughfares. For an hour or two the streets are alive with the hurry and noise of a big city. Then the bustle subsides and relative calm is resumed.

The region around Durham was occupied by the Occoneechee, Eno, Schoccoree, and Adshusheer Indians, who had migrated elsewhere before 1750 when the first white settlers, of English and Scotch-Irish extraction, secured land grants from the Earl of Granville. The section was then a part of Orange County and by 1777 contained only a few hundred inhabitants.

Durham is new by North Carolina reckoning, dating from the 1850's when a settlement known as Prattsburg contained wheat and corn mills serving the farmers. Construction of the North Carolina Railroad in 1852-56 gave some impetus to growth. William Pratt, a large landowner, refused to give a right-of-way or land for a station. Dr. Bartlett Durham offered 4 acres about two miles west of Prattsburg and the station was named for him. The railroad detoured around Prattsburg and the Pratt property.

The town of Durham was incorporated in 1867, and when Durham County was created from Orange and Wake in 1881, it was made the seat. In 1865 there were fewer than 100 people in Durham, but by 1880 the number had increased to 2,041. In the spring of 1865 Gen. Joseph E. Johnston surrendered to Gen. William T. Sherman at the Bennett House near Durham. There has been erected, through the gifts of the Samuel T. Morgan family, and maintained by the State, a suitable marker at the site of the surrender, in the midst of a 30-acre park.

The rise of the tobacconists marked the beginning of the town's industrial life. As early as 1858 Robert F. Morris was manufacturing tobacco. Sherman's soldiers liked the product of this factory, which in 1865 was being operated by John R. Green, originator of the Bull Durham blend; later William T. Blackwell and Julian S. Carr joined the business.

Meanwhile Washington Duke, mustered out of the Confederate Army in 1865, walked 137 miles to his old farm near Durham to start life over again. He began grinding tobacco, which he packed, labeled Pro Bono Publico, and sold to soldiers and others. This venture proved so successful that soon he was joined by his three sons, Brodie, Benjamin N., and James B. (Buck); by 1874 all four were established in Durham as manufacturers of smoking tobacco. To escape the sharp competition in this field, "Buck" Duke decided to start making cigarettes, which by 1880 had become important. A few years later the installation of cigarette machines increased daily production from 2,500 to 100,000 and made possible large-scale exportation to Europe.

After a period of sharp competition, during which Blackwell and others were gradually absorbed, the Duke organizing genius formed (1890) the American Tobacco Company, embracing practically the entire tobacco industry in the U. S., with James B. Duke as its guiding spirit. The advertising campaign inaugurated about that time was unusually comprehensive. Billboards, signs, and even cliffs displayed the giant figure of the Bull of Durham. When Anne Thackeray called upon Lord Tennyson "she found the poet laureate peacefully smoking Bull Durham."

In 1911 the American Tobacco Company was dissolved into smaller units as a result of a decree by the U. S. Supreme Court, but by that time the Duke fortune was firmly founded, and Durham was established as the world's tobacco capital. The city manufactures about one-fourth of all the cigarettes produced in this country, and 9 warehouses conduct sales of leaf tobacco. In addition to this domestic supply, several million pounds of foreign-grown tobaccos are imported annually.

James B. Duke did with tobacco what Rockefeller did with oil and Carnegie with steel. Through bartering at crossroads he became adept at trade. Unwilling to spend much time in school, he did not consider college training essential to success. After amassing a fortune, however, he provided the means for establishing a great university. In the latter part of his life he engaged in the development of water power in the piedmont and mountain sections of North and South Carolina. The Southern Power System (the Duke Power Company and its subsidiaries) was the result.

In December, 1924, the Duke Endowment of $40,000,000 for numerous benefactions, including aid for hospitals but particularly for Duke University, was announced. Mr. Duke died the following October, and by the provisions of his will the endowment was increased to nearly $80,000,000.

CHOWAN COUNTY COURTHOUSE, EDENTON (HIGHTON)

INTERIOR, SMALLWOOD-WARD HOUSE, NEW BERN (HIGHTON)

SPIRAL STAIRWAY, POWELL HOUSE, NEAR TARBORO (HIGHTON)

ORTON PLANTATION, NEAR WILMINGTON (WOOTTEN)

STATE CAPITOL, RALEIGH   STATE CAPITOL, RALEIGH

STATE CAPITOL, RALEIGH

MARSH HOUSE, BATH (WOOTTEN)

BELLAMY HOUSE, WILMINGTON (HIGHTON)

BROTHERS' HOUSE, WINSTON-SALEM (FRANK JONES)

BELO HOUSE, WINSTON-SALEM (OLD SALEM RESTORATION HEADQUARTERS)

LIBRARY, BILTMORE HOUSE, ASHEVILLE (ASHEVILLE CHAMBER OF COMMERCE)

BILTMORE HOUSE, ASHEVILLE

BURKE COUNTY COURTHOUSE, MORGANTON (MORGANTON CHAMBER OF COMMERCE)

CITY HALL, CHARLOTTE (CHARLOTTE CHAMBER OF COMMERCE)

This benefaction is the largest emanating from the South and the largest yet made for the exclusive benefit of the region.

The other large industries of Durham are cotton-textile and hosiery mills. In all some 110 manufacturing establishments employ 25,375 persons. This does not include the Duke University $7,000,000 payroll. The city is also an important medical center, with 6 hospitals and a total of 1637 beds: Watts Hospital (*public, white*), Duke Hospital (*public*), Lincoln Hospital (*public, colored*), McPherson Hospital (*private, eye, ear, nose, and throat*), North Carolina Cerebral Palsy Hospital, and the Veterans' Administration Hospital with 500 beds which opened in 1953 at a cost of $8,000,000.

Notable in Durham is the status of the Negro population. The Negroes have a college and operate business firms, a large insurance company, schools, newspapers, a library, a hospital and the Mechanics and Farmers Bank of Durham and Raleigh. In 1887 Negroes owned but two lots in the city. In 1953 their business assets aggregated $51,329,278.12. Negro industry has expanded since 1865 from a single blacksmith shop owned by Lewis Pratt, a former slave. Gen. Julian S. Carr lent the Negro John Merrick money to start his business career, first as a barber then as a real estate investor. Washington Duke gave the printing press used in publishing the first Negro newspaper. White bankers helped organize the first Negro bank.

The North Carolina Mutual Life Insurance Company has grown from a small beginning in 1898 into the largest Negro insurance company in the world, operating in 9 states and the District of Columbia and employing 1235 persons. Oldest among the 40 churches for Negroes in the city are St. Joseph's African Methodist Episcopal and the White Rock Baptist.

POINTS OF INTEREST

1. The DURHAM HOSIERY MILL (*not open to public*), 109 S. Corcoran St., manufactures full-fashioned and seamless nylon hosiery and cotton socks. A branch mill on Walker St. spins synthetic yarn. The mill produces 8,400,000 pairs of ladies' hose a week. About 650 persons are normally employed.

2. TRINITY M. E. CHURCH (1922), N. Church St., was designed in the Neo-Gothic style by Ralph Adams Cram. It is built of rough local stone with semicircular steps and stained glass windows.

3. The DURHAM PUBLIC LIBRARY (*open 10-9 Mon.-Fri.; 9-6 Sat.*), 311 E. Main St., erected in 1921, contains about 60,000 volumes. It was first opened at Five Points in 1898. Bookmobile service is carried to outlying communities in the county and edges of the city.

4. The EPHPHATHA EPISCOPAL CHURCH, NW. corner Geer and North Sts., is one of few churches in the U. S. built exclusively for deaf-mutes. Services are in the sign language.

5. The LIGGETT & MYERS TOBACCO COMPANY (*open 8-11:15 A.M. and 1-3:30 P.M. Mon.-Fri.; guides*), at the corner of W. Main and

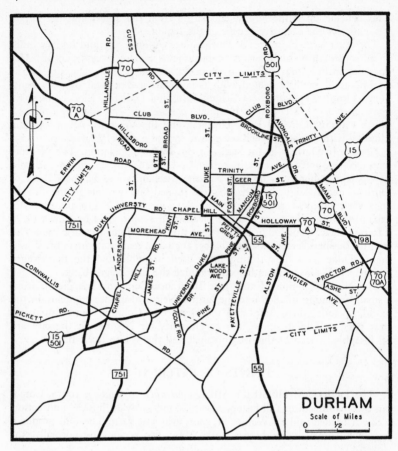

S. Duke Sts., produces Chesterfield, Fatima, L & M, Home Run, Picayune, and Piedmont, as well as smoking tobaccos. Tours are conducted through a modern 6-story brick building. Acres of brick buildings, from two to 6 stories in height, contain the mass of machinery that processes the tobacco from redrying the "hands" to the packed products. After aging in storage for two or three years the tobacco is carefully blended and placed in the hoppers of cigarette machines where it is encircled by cigarette paper and issues as a continuous cylinder to be cut into proper lengths. Each machine turns out 1,200 cigarettes a minute. After inspection the cigarettes are transferred to another machine for packaging and then to another for incasing in cellophane covers. Finally cases filled with cartons are loaded into freight cars from conveyor belts.

6. The ERWIN MILLS, INC. (*not open to public*), between 9th and 14th Sts., Mulberry St. to Hillsboro Rd., manufacture wide sheeting, sheets, and

pillow cases. Denims are made at the company mills in Erwin and Stone-wall, Miss.; sportdenim, outing and inter-lining flannels, luggage fabric, twills, drills, and jeans are made in the mill at Cooleemee. The three local mills employ 2,000 workers, some of whom occupy company-owned houses around the mills. Since 1892, when the Erwin chain of mills began making muslin tobacco bags, it has become one of the largest concerns in the State manufacturing cotton goods.

7. The DUKE MEMORIAL M. E. CHURCH (1914), W. Chapel Hill St., of cream-colored pressed brick with limestone trim, is designed in a modified English Gothic style. Chimes in the tower were given by Mrs. J. Edward Stagg, granddaughter of Washington Duke, as a memorial to her husband. They are played each day at noon.

8. In MAPLEWOOD CEMETERY, both sides of Kent St., S. of Duke University Rd., is the MAUSOLEUM OF THE DUKE FAMILY and the GRAVE OF GEN. JULIAN S. CARR (1845-1924), who made a fortune in the tobacco business, contributed to Trinity and other colleges, helped equip and maintain two Durham companies in the Spanish-American War, and was prominent in the affairs of the Methodist Church, the Democratic party, and the Confederate Veterans.

9. THE AMERICAN TOBACCO COMPANY PLANT (*open 9-11 A.M. and 1-2:45 P.M. weekdays; guides*), SW. corner Pettigrew and Blackwell Sts., manufactures Bull Durham smoking tobacco, Lucky Strike, Pall Mall, Herbert Tareyton, and some 15 other brands of cigarettes and smoking tobacco. It employs about 3,000 persons. The plant, which is entirely mechanized, manufactures approximately 20 million cigarettes per hour.

10. DURHAM CONTAINER COMPANY (*open, apply at office*), 2002 E. Pettigrew St., manufactures corrugated shipping containers consuming approximately 18,000 tons of paper per year. It employs 125 persons and operates its own fleet of trucks for delivery to N. C., S. C., Va., and Tenn.

11. The STANFORD L. WARREN PUBLIC LIBRARY for Negroes (*open 10-8 Mon.-Fri., 10-2 Sat.*), 1201 Fayetteville St., was established by Dr. A. M. Moore in 1913. From a small Sunday school library in the White Rock Baptist Church it has grown to over 40,000 volumes.

12. The NORTH CAROLINA COLLEGE FOR NEGROES (coeducational), 1911 S. Fayetteville St., is housed in 35 buildings on a 55-acre campus. The school was begun in 1910 as a training school for ministers, through the efforts of the late Dr. James E. Shepherd, who raised funds by subscriptions. The name was changed to National Training School in 1916. Ownership was transferred to the State in 1923. A faculty of 125 teaches a student body of about 1,500. The college confers A.B., B.S., B.S. in Home Economics, B.S. in Public Health Nursing, and B.S.C. degrees. In graduate work the following degrees are conferred: M.A., M.S., M.S. in Public Health, M.S. in Home Economics, and Ph.D. in Education. The college

mixed chorus of 85 members gives concerts and broadcasts. The college maintains its own library which contains over 62,000 volumes.

13. B C REMEDY COMPANY (*not open to public*), SW. corner Morris and Corporation Sts., has its home office here. B C originated in 1910 behind the prescription counter of the old Five Points Drug Store. It has grown into a modern 4½-story building employing 150 persons and has salesmen that cover the nation.

14. WRIGHT MACHINERY COMPANY (*not open to public*), Holloway and Calvin Sts., designs and builds automatic and semi-automatic packaging machinery as well as contract machine work for other industries. The machinery is mainly used for bakery products, food, candy, and the whiskey industry. Organized in 1893, it normally employs 700 persons and is a subsidiary of the Sperry Corp., New York.

15. The TOBACCO WAREHOUSES (*open during season*), Morgan St., N. of Main St. in the center of the bright-leaf belt, sold an average of 43,763,894 pounds of tobacco a season during the past 5 years. The season opens about the first of Sept. and closes about 10 days after Thanksgiving. Buyers representing the large manufacturers and independents purchase tobacco at daily auctions.

DUKE UNIVERSITY

(Buildings open during school hours unless otherwise indicated)

Duke University, largest private educational institution and the only private university in North Carolina, lies at the edge of the 7000-acre Duke Forest, 5-minutes' drive from the business district of Durham.

The University's two separate campuses with their contrasting styles of architecture represent one of America's most beautiful universities. The EAST CAMPUS, site of the Woman's College, is of Georgian architecture. Buildings of red brick and limestone are arranged along a half-mile grassy mall, dominated by a large domed auditorium. A private drive leads 1.5 miles to the west to the main or WEST CAMPUS. Here buildings of Collegiate Gothic architecture, flagstone walks, and box hedge are reminiscent of Oxford and Cambridge, England. The multi-colored stone is quarried in nearby Hillsboro. The dominant feature of the West Campus is the CHAPEL, rising 210 feet above the quadrangles. It is one of the most famous structures in the South and the symbol of the institution.

Duke University traces its ancestry back to a one-room log cabin, "an elementary subscription school," known as Brown's School House, in the northwest corner of Randolph County. From this start in 1838, Methodists and Quakers founded a private academy known as Union Institute. In an unbroken history the institution became Normal College (1851), a state-affiliated training school for teachers (believed to be the first institution in the South empowered to grant degrees in teacher training); then Trinity College, a liberal arts college affiliated with the North Carolina conferences of the Methodist Episcopal Church, South (1859-1924). In 1892 through the efforts of Pres. John F. Crowell and public-spirited citizens of Durham, Trinity was moved to Durham and located on the present site of the Woman's College.

Rapid expansion of the college and increased benefactions followed until 1924, when James B. Duke established the magnificent Duke Endowment providing for philanthropies to colleges, hospitals, retired ministers, and orphans through the two Carolinas. Trinity College became Duke University and the University the principal beneficiary of the Endowment.

Leaders of Trinity College and its predecessors were Brantley York, Braxton Craven, Dr. John F. Crowell, and Bishop John C. Kilgo. Presidents of Duke University have been William Preston Few (1910-40) who was president of Trinity College at the time of the endowment; Robert Lee Flowers (1941-48); and the present head of the institution, Arthur Hollis Edens (1948-).

Among its most outstanding alumni are Gordon Dean (former chairman, Atomic Energy Commission), Vice-Pres. Richard M. Nixon, George V. Allen (foreign diplomat and Ambassador to India), Walter Hines Page (Ambassador to Great Britain, 1913-18), and Daniel C. Roper (Sec. of Commerce, 1933-38).

One of the most famous incidents involving academic freedom in the country occurred here in 1903. The noted historian, John Spencer Bassett, then a Trinity College professor, in an article on race relations, stated that Robert E. Lee and Booker T. Washington were the two greatest Southerners. Despite a heated attack led by Josephus Daniels, editor of the (Raleigh) *News and Observer,* the faculty, trustees, and students staunchly defended him. This vigorous tradition of academic freedom is still maintained.

Today Duke University enrolls slightly less than 4900 students and is committed to holding its enrollments to this figure. The student body in 1954 represented all 48 states and 33 foreign countries. The total number of faculty members was 601. Expansion after World War II to over 5,000 students was contrary to the University's long-time policy of maintaining small classes and maintaining a high student-faculty ratio. Annual Loyalty Fund Drives, beginning in 1948, and a large-scale Development Program have been committed to aims of making the University "better not bigger." The Development Program was in progress from 1949-51 and a total of 9 million dollars was subscribed. Immediate goals today are funds for more scholarships, fellowships, research, and endowed professorships.

Duke University divisions include the liberal arts colleges for undergraduate students: Trinity College for men and the Woman's College, as well as the College of Engineering. Graduate and professional schools are the Schools of Divinity, Medicine and Nursing, Law, Forestry, and the Graduate School of Arts and Sciences. Other divisions are the Marine Laboratory at Beaufort, N. C., and the Highland Hospital at Asheville.

Facilities of special reputation are DUKE HOSPITAL and the LIBRARY. The University's 600-bed teaching hospital (131 beds for Negroes) is a regional diagnostic and teaching center, providing post-doctoral and ancillary training programs. The hospital admits some 17,000 patients per year from all 48 states and many foreign countries. Out-patient clinic visits total more than 160,000 per year.

The University Libraries include the General, Woman's College, Divinity, Engineering, Law, Medicine, Biology-Forestry, Chemistry, and Mathematics-Physics which contain a total of 1,130,000 volumes and about 2,000,000 manuscripts; 3,950 periodicals and 70 newspapers are received currently. The General Library (*open 8 A.M. to 11 P.M. daily except Sat. and Sun. when its hours are from 9-6 and 2-6*) ranks 13th in the nation and 51st in the world.

The Rare Book Room of the General Library contains the Trent collection of Walt Whitman, rare pieces of Southern Americana from the George Washington Flowers collection, several significant collections in English literature, examples of early printing and bookmaking, Biblical manuscripts, association volumes, and other book treasures of the University.

The University maintains a symphony orchestra, concert band, chamber arts society, numerous choral groups, in particular the Chapel Choir and the Men's Glee Club, and a wide selection of other cultural and artistic offerings. The Arts Council and Concert Series bring famous musicians, artists, and speakers to the city throughout the year.

The DUKE STADIUM, S. of the West Campus, seats 40,000 in its permanent stands. It is of horseshoe shape and is built in a natural hillside amphitheater.

The SARAH P. DUKE MEMORIAL GARDENS (*open daily 8 A.M. to 8 P.M.*), are located on the right of the main entrance to the West Campus. Perennially beautiful, they reach their peak of brilliant color and fragrance in the spring.

Edenton

Information Service: Carolina Motor Club, 101 E. Water St.

Guide Service: Edenton Tea Party Chapter, N. S. D. A. R.

Railroad Station: Broad and W. King Sts. (freight only).

Bus Station: Broad and W. King Sts. for Carolina Trailways, Norfolk Southern Bus Corp., and Seashore Transportation Co.

Airport: Nearest at Elizabeth City, 32 m., for Capital Airlines.

Accommodations: 1 hotel; 5 motor courts; boarding houses.

EDENTON (16 alt., 4,468 pop.), seat of Chowan County and one of the three oldest communities in the State, is a placid town on a peninsula formed by Pembroke and Queen Anne's Creeks near the western extremity of Albemarle Sound. Here lived men who helped shape the colony's destiny and made the town a political, commercial, and social center. Its citizens played important parts in defying the British Parliament, assisting the Revolutionary forces, and launching the new State.

The business section occupies fewer than a dozen blocks along or near Broad Street, which bisects the town from the bay front to the fork of the Virginia and Hertford roads. Once distinguished by three rows of great elms, the thoroughfare has been modernized to provide parking space. Fish houses, packing plants, and oil storage tanks edge the bay, built on filled-in land where the old wharves used to be. Intersecting Broad Street are King, Eden, Queen, Church, Gale, Albemarle, and Carteret streets, named long before the Republic was established. Along the sound and the Chowan River are old plantations that have always been a part of the life of the community.

In 1622 John Pory, secretary of the Virginia colony, explored the rich bottom lands to the Chowan River, and by 1658 settlers had come down from the Jamestown area. In 1712 the General Assembly passed an act "to build a Courthouse and House to hold the Assembly in . . . in the forks of Queen Anne's Creek," and appointed commissioners to lay off a town. It was not until 1714 that the first lot was sold, to Edward Moseley, who within a year built the first house in the future town. Sixteen years later

Dr. John Brickell reported there were 60. By 1777 there were 135, about a dozen of which are still occupied. The village was called simply "ye town on Queen Anne's Creek" until 1722, when it was incorporated as Edenton in honor of Governor Charles Eden, who had just died. The inscription on his tombstone states that he had administered the affairs of the province for 8 years "to ye great satisfaction of ye Lords Proprietors and ye ease and happiness of ye people"—an opinion not universally held by "ye people." Because the Governor lived nearby, and because the Assembly met here rather more often than in New Bern or Wilmington, Edenton was an unofficial capital of the colony for nearly 40 years.

Early shipbuilders, most notable of whom was Joseph Hewes, did a thriving business. So did the merchants who exported pitch, tar, turpentine, lumber, tobacco, corn, and salt meat and fish. Almost 50 years after the Revolution, the weekly paper still reported a fair number of ships docking and sailing. By then, however, many merchants were aware that the Port of Roanoke was doomed, by its distance from the nearest inlet, Ocracoke, and by the shallow waters below Roanoke Island, which made an increasingly difficult passage for larger ships.

Edenton was one of the three North Carolina ports to which supplies from all over the colony were sent, in the summer of 1774, for the relief of the closed port of Boston. Three months later, women from at least 5 counties gathered in Edenton to sign resolutions supporting the protest of the Provincial Congress against British injustice to the colonies. The Edenton Tea Party was the first known political activity of women in the American colonies. The Test signed by the Vestry of St. Paul's Church in 1776 makes it clear that the citizens of Chowan County considered themselves loyal subjects of the King, and *for that reason* determined not to put up with the injustices imposed by His Majesty's Parliament. Four names will show the measure of their patriotism and ability: Joseph Hewes, signer of the Declaration of Independence; James Iredell, associate justice of the first Supreme Court; Samuel Johnston, continental congressman, governor (1787-89), and first United States Senator from North Carolina; and Hugh Williamson, surgeon-general of the North Carolina militia (1780-1782), signer of the Federal Constitution, congressman, and author of a two-volume history of the State. Only once during the Revolution was the town believed to be in any danger. After the battle of Guilford Court House, when Cornwallis' forces, victorious but badly crippled, had turned eastward, Edenton, though well out of his path, was suddenly seized with panic. Dozens of families loaded all their goods on barges and fled to Windsor. In the early summer raiders swept down from the direction of Suffolk and pillaged plantations along the river and sound, and a few privateersmen appeared by water; but all of them were put to flight without undue difficulty. One sensible gentleman who had refused to move his family observed that it would have been easier, cheaper, and safer to defend the town than to flee.

Colonial and Revolutionary Edenton and the surrounding Albemarle region have been the subject of 7 novels, known collectively as "The Carolina Series," by the adopted North Carolina novelist, Inglis Fletcher, who lives at nearby Bandon Plantation (*see below*).

Edenton was less fortunate in the War between the States than in the Revolution. From October to December, 1861, while it was headquarters for several companies of the 19th North Carolina Battalion, Capt. William Badham organized an artillery unit, the Bell Battery, composed of Chowan and Tyrrell men. Its cannon were cast from the bells of the town: the "St. Paul," the "Fannie Roulhac," the "Edenton," and the "Columbia." However, the defenses of Albemarle Sound were dangerously weak. On Jan. 12, 1862, an Edenton lady wrote President Davis that Gen. Hill had not had time to fortify the bay and that the forts at Roanoke Island were too poorly armed to stop light-draft gunboats; nearly every man of service age was gone, and the harvested corn and cotton would be "a rich prize to the Yankee invaders." After Roanoke Island fell, exactly three weeks later, the town was at the mercy of the gunboats, and finally became Union headquarters.

From the earliest days to recent years, shad and herring fisheries were Edenton's principal occupation, and they still account for an important part of its business. Nearby waters also afford good angling for bass and perch. Cotton, corn, soybeans, tobacco, early and late truck, cantaloupes, and watermelons are shipped out by boat, train, and truck. The most important crop produced from the fine, loamy soil of the region is Jumbo peanuts; the town is the largest peanut market in the State and the second largest in the country. There are storage warehouses, two raw processing plants, and two finishing plants, shipping annually nearly half a million 90-pound bags. There are three lumber yards and one veneer plant. The 20,800-spindle textile mill is the largest cotton yarn plant east of Tarboro.

POINTS OF INTEREST

1. BARKER HOUSE, (*open*) S. Broad St. on waterfront, built about 1782, was the home of Thomas and Penelope Barker. Thomas Barker, long prominent in colonial affairs, served as a London agent for the colony for about the last 10 years before the Revolution. His wife, according to tradition, presided over the Edenton Tea Party Oct. 25, 1774—the earliest known instance of political activity on the part of women in the American colonies. In 1830 the house was bought by Augustus Moore, whose law office was known as "the Judge Shop," from the number of his students who became judges. His descendents owned the house until 1952 when it was bought and presented to the town by Mr. Haywood Phthisic for a community house. It was moved from its original site at 213 Broad St. at that time.

2. The traditional SITE OF THE EDENTON TEA PARTY, Colonial Ave. facing the W. side of the green, is marked by a large bronze teapot mounted on a Revolutionary cannon. Here, at the home of Mrs. Elizabeth King, the Tea Party was believed for some years to have taken place. In

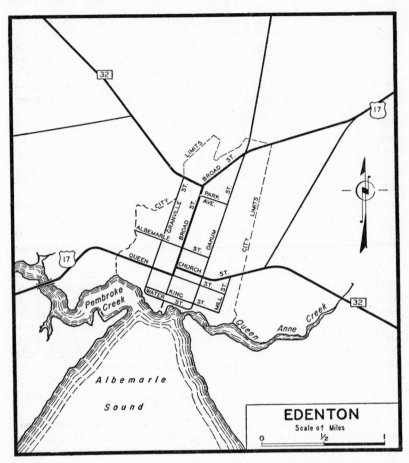

EDENTON

Scale of Miles

0   ½   1

1904, however, the list of signers, printed in two British newspapers, along with the text of the resolutions and a news letter, was found in the British Museum. Mrs. King's name does not appear in this list.

3. EDENTON GREEN, facing the Courthouse, has been part of the Courthouse property ever since the town was laid off in 1712. Equipped with stocks, rack, and pillory, it was early used as a drill ground for the militia and was known as the "Publick Parade." By 1718 it was the site of the first Chowan County Courthouse, the "Council Chamber" built especially for meetings of the General Assembly of the colony. The grassy commons, shaded by arching oaks, slopes gently down to the bay. On the sea wall are three of a shipment of 45 of REVOLUTIONARY CANNONS purchased in France for the Continental Army by Thomas Benbury and Thomas Jones,

Edenton patriots, and supposedly brought to Edenton in 1778 by William Borritz, captain of a French ship, *The Holy Heart of Jesus*. These three, along with several others, were saved when the ship was wrecked in Albemarle Sound. Several are now used as corner markers in Edenton and two are mounted on Capitol Square in Raleigh. Those left in Edenton were put out of commission in 1862 by the Federal commander who observed "there was more danger standing behind them than marching in front."

The JOSEPH HEWES MONUMENT, S. edge of the green, commemorates Hewes's services in the Continental Congress and his labors as chairman of the committee of marine. As such he was the first executive head of the U. S. Navy, in which capacity he appointed John Paul Jones a naval officer. Jones wrote his patron: "You more than any other person have labored to place the instruments of success in my hands." Hewes's presentation of North Carolina's Halifax Resolves to the Continental Congress on May 27, 1776, was the first utterance for independence in that body. He died in 1779 while attending Congress and is buried in Christ Churchyard, Philadelphia.

The CONFEDERATE MONUMENT, N. edge of the green, commemorates the Chowan County men who died in the Civil War. The cross walks are reminiscent of their flag.

4. EAST CUSTOM HOUSE and BOND HOUSE (*private*), Court St. and Courthouse Green, were built about 1805 as the office and house of Joseph Blount Skinner, whose younger brother, Thomas Harvey Skinner, was pastor of the Brick Presbyterian Church, New York, and one of the founders of Union Theological Seminary there. About 1846 both buildings were bought by Henry Bond, who occupied the larger house and used the smaller for a customs office.

5. EDMUND HATCH HOUSE (*private*), also known as O'Malley's Ordinary, E. King St., is believed to have been built about 1744 for André Richard, a French barber, as a gift for his daughter Lucy and her husband Edmund Hatch. Later owners were Dr. Samuel Dickinson (1774-77), Col. James Blount (1777-78), Josiah Collins (1786-1800), and Myles O'Malley's daughters, Mary and Ann. After 1814 it was used as an ordinary. A kitchen wing was added ca. 1800 and there have also been very recent alterations.

6. HORNIBLOW'S TAVERN, E. King St., stood on the site of the present Joseph Hewes Hotel. The tavern is familiar to readers of James Boyd's *Drums* and the novels of Inglis Fletcher. Mrs. Horniblow was required to post bond as a guarantee that the house would not "on the Sabbath day suffer any person to tipple or drink more than is necessary."

7. CHOWAN COUNTY COURTHOUSE, E. King St., has been described by the architect, Thomas Waterman, as "perhaps the finest Georgian courthouse in the South." Built in 1767, probably by Gilbert Leigh, it has been in continuous use ever since and is the earliest of the permanent public buildings in the State. Constructed of warm red brick with white trim, its general plan, with central courtroom and flanking offices is typical of Tide-

water Virginia. Mr. Waterman continues: "The origin ... can certainly be found in the Capitol in Williamsburg. . . . Even the judge's chair and paneled wainscot ... are parallel to these features of the Williamsburg Capitol. . . . There is no precedent for the fine two-story facade, with central, pedimented pavilion, nor for the beautifully designed cupola. . . . The second floor contains what is said to be the largest paneled room in the colonies, only exceeded in size possibly by the ballroom at Hampton-on-the-Santee, South Carolina, and in beauty by the great room in the Newport, Rhode Island, Colony House. . . . There are facing fireplaces and a pair of doors to one side, leading to the stair hall and Masonic room. The room is simply though vigorously paneled, in two ranges of panels below and above a chair rail. The paneling is crowned by a full entablature with pulvinated frieze and dentiled cornice."

The MASONIC LODGE, which uses a room opening into the paneled room, owns a chair once used by George Washington as master of the Alexandria, Virginia, lodge.

8. JAMES IREDELL HOUSE, 107 E. Church St., was occupied by Iredell from 1778 until his death in 1799. He came to North Carolina in 1767 at the age of 17 as deputy collector for the Port of Roanoke. In 1778 he became attorney general of the State, and 1789 he was appointed an associate justice of the first U. S. Supreme Court. An ardent defender of the Federal Constitution, he and William R. Davie financed the publication of the *Debates* of the Hillsboro Convention and in 1791 he published *Iredell's Revision*, the most comprehensive compilation of N. C. statutes up to that time. His son and namesake was governor of N. C. (1827-28).

James Wilson of Pennsylvania, a signer of the Declaration of Independence, and also an associate justice of the U. S. Supreme Court, died here while on a visit to his friend. He was buried at Hayes (*see below*), but in 1906 his remains were removed to Pennsylvania and a cenotaph was placed at the original grave.

Iredell's house was used, from about 1853 on, as a rectory for St. Paul's Church, during much of which time it was occupied by Iredell's cousin, the Rev. Samuel Iredell Johnston. Saved in 1949 by the Edenton Chapter of the N. S. D. A. R., the house is now in the care of the James Iredell Association, Inc., and the Edenton Tea Party chapter, N. S. D. A. R., under agreement with the State Dept. of Conservation and Development.

9. BLAIR HOUSE (*private*), E. Church St., built about 1775, was originally owned by the Blair family. From 1852 to 1856 it was the home of Thomas C. Manning (1825-1887), later brigadier general in the Confederate Army, chief justice of the Louisiana Supreme Court, and minister to Mexico, 1886 till his death in 1887.

10. The CUPOLA HOUSE, S. Broad St., was described by Thomas Waterman as "the outstanding house of the region. . . . No more important example of Jacobean design [exists] south of Connecticut, except Bacon's Castle, in Surry County, Virginia." The date assigned to the house until recently was 1758, based on the fact that the initials of Lord Granville's

agent, Francis Corbin, and this date have been applied, not carved, on the gable finial. The real date of its construction, based on its peculiar architectural features, would seem to be about 1712. The bold, overhanging, second story with its hewn brackets, the high gables with their carved finials, and the great projecting chimneys with weathered offsets are typical of the finest Jacobean houses in America. Waterman, moreover, believes that these are probably the first sash windows used in North Carolina. The oval window of the front gable, he states, "is perhaps unique in American timber building." The octagonal cupola, or "lantern" used for sighting incoming ships and supposedly illuminated on the King's birthday, public holidays, and other festive occasions, bears every evidence of being original. The interior of the cupola "is simply treated with a wood cornice dado and moulded window frames." The entire house was so trimmed until the regrettable sale of the paneling of the first floor to the Brooklyn Museum.

The first floor contains the SHEPARD-PRUDEN MEMORIAL LIBRARY, with a small collection of early Caroliniana. On the second floor is the EDENTON MUSEUM of relics and documents, including an original treaty with the Tuscarora Indians (1712), the tea set used at the Tea Party, a portrait of Mistress Penelope Barker, and a large iron fireback bearing the likeness of George II and the royal arms in bas-relief.

11. JOSEPH HEWES HOUSE (*private*), 105 W. King St., probably built ca. 1725, was owned by George Blair and his wife Jean Johnston from 1769 to about 1782. Blair and Hewes were business partners. It was the birthplace of William Allen, Congressman, Senator (1837-49), and Governor of Ohio (1874-76).

12. JAMES IREDELL, JR., HOUSE (*private*), W. King St., built about 1800, is the last remaining business property of the early 18th century, having been used as a store by Edmund Hoskins, 1806-20. In 1820 James Iredell, Jr., who had bought it 4 years before, took it over and used "an apartment" as his law office until he sold the house when he became governor in 1827.

13. The ELLISON HOUSE (*private*), W. King St., now remodeled beyond recognition, was owned by Benjamin Ellison, a Tory, from 1760 to 1776 when it was confiscated. From 1816 to 1827 it was the home of James Iredell, Jr. before he became governor.

14. BEVERLY HALL (*private*), W. King St., was built for John Bonner Blount in 1810 as a combined bank and dwelling. In 1816 it became one of the first three branches of the State Bank. The great brick vault is still intact, with walls two feet thick and steel bars reinforcing floor, walls, and roof. The two-pound key is a curiosity.

Surrounding the Georgian Colonial structure of white-painted bricks are magnolias, cape jessamine, Japanese cherries, and weeping willows. The main porch on the east elevation has slim Doric columns and a delicate second-floor latticed rail. The central columns extend to the hip roof forming a two-story portico over the entrance. Four great chimneys are enclosed.

15. The WESSINGTON HOUSE (*private*), W. King St., also called the Graham and the Dr. Tom Warren house, was headquarters for the Federal Army during the occupation of Edenton, 1862-65. Waterman states that this house "ushered the Romantic Revival into Tidewater North Carolina" and is "a large-scale, Italian-villa style house," with galleried porch and possessing "well-designed and well-placed detail."

16. The CUSTOM HOUSE, Blount St., was probably built for Wilson Blount, who bought the site, owned for a time by Francis Corbin, Lord Granville's agent, in 1772. It was used as the Customs House certainly from 1799 to 1828.

17. The POLLOCK HOUSE (*private*), W. Eden St., was built around 1765, probably for George Blair and his wife, Jean, the sister of Samuel Johnston, on property owned in 1723 by Christopher Gale, soon to become chief justice of North Carolina. In 1783 Mrs. Blair and Samuel Johnston sold it to Stephen Cabarrus, who sold it in 1787 to Cullen Pollock, wealthy Bertie planter, and his wife Ann Booth, who owned it until 1821. In 1824 it was bought by Dr. James Norcom.

18. The CHARLTON HOUSE or SAWYER HOUSE (*private*), W. Eden St., was built about 1765, for Jaspar Charlton and his wife Abigail, the first signer of the Tea Party resolutions. It later belonged to Samuel Tredwell (1815-21) and to William D. Lowther, son of Penelope Johnston (1821-53). It is an early three-bay, gambrel roof house perhaps adapted from the French Mansard.

19. The TREDWELL HOUSE (*private*), W. Eden St., was built about 1787, for William Borritz, captain of the *Holy Heart of Jesus,* which brought cannons from France for the Revolutionary forces. From 1799 to 1828 it was the home of Samuel Tredwell, Collector of the Port of Roanoke, and his wife Helen Blair, whose daughter Frances married her cousin, Gov. James Iredell, Jr.

20. The LITTLEJOHN HOUSE (*private*), W. Eden St., built before 1790, was the home of William and Sarah Blount Littlejohn. She was a signer of the Tea Party resolutions.

21. The LEIGH HOUSE (*private*), W. Queen St., was probably built by Gilbert Leigh, believed to be the architect of the Courthouse, who owned the property from 1756 to 1771. In 1774 it was owned by William Bennett, hatter, and his wife Lydia, one of the Tea Party signers.

22. ST. PAUL'S CHURCH, NW. corner Broad and Church Sts., is a rectangular brick building, with an elliptical apse containing the chancel, and a square entrance tower supporting an octagonal, tall, shingled spire. An "unusually complete survival of early church building," it represents "an ideal in village churches, unrivaled in this country except perhaps by Christ Church, New Castle, Delaware." Inside the church, tall aisle columns

support side galleries running the length of the barrel vaulted nave. The high box pews, free since 1868, have doors; aisle galleries and certain pews in the body of the church were once set aside "for the use of our people of color." The church was lighted only with candles until 1869 when oil lamps were added.

The church, "possessing much charm and Old World beauty," is set among lovely magnolias, crepe myrtles, elms, redbuds, dogwoods, and boxwood, and a variety of japonica, forsythia, and spirea. Of particular interest is a group of graves under the magnolias, moved to St. Paul's about 70 years ago, from plantation burying grounds endangered by the river or the sound. These include the graves of three Proprietary governors, Henderson Walker, Thomas Pollock, and Charles Eden. Among the chief treasures of the church are vestry minutes dating from 1701 and a silver chalice, procured with a generous gift from Gov. Francis Nicholson, of Virginia, but inscribed as a gift of Col. Edward Moseley.

The parish, organized under the Vestry Act in 1701, has the oldest charter in the State and the second oldest church building. The original wooden building, erected in 1701-02 on a peninsula southeast of Edenton, was the first church in North Carolina. In 1711 the Rev. John Winston wrote that "The Vestry met at an Ordinary where rum was the chief of their business," that the church had "neither floor nor seats," and that, as the key was lost and the door open, "all the Hoggs and Cattle flee thither for shade in the Summer and Warmth in the Winter."

Ground was cleared for the present brick structure in March, 1736, and in 1740 the Assembly levied a tax upon every tithable in the county for its completion and ordered that it be used for vestry meetings as soon as "fit for Divine Worship," under penalty of fine if it met elsewhere. "Ye roof was righted" by 1745, but the first Divine Worship was not until April 10, 1760. The interior woodwork was not finished until 1774. For almost 75 years it was under the care of the Society for the Preservation of the Gospel. Extensive repairs were made in 1806-09. Repairs were again being made in 1948-50, when a disastrous fire destroyed the steeple, roof, galleries, and old organ. All interior furnishings and memorials had been removed and were installed again when the church was rebuilt exactly as it had been originally.

Among the rectors have been Clement Hall (1755-59); Daniel Earl (1759-78); Charles Pettigrew (1778-1807), elected the first bishop of North Carolina, but never consecrated; Samuel I. Johnston (1837-65); and Robert B. Drane (1876-1932). Daniel Earl was not allowed to hold services during the Revolution because he combined fiery Revolutionary activities with adherence to the Church of England. A fox-hunting planter and fisherman, he arrived one morning to find a verse attached to the church door:

"A half-built church,
A broken-down steeple,
A herring-catching parson,
And a damn set of people."

Despite the devotion of most members to the American cause, the parish suffered disaster and remained inactive for about 30 years.

23. The BOOTH HOUSE (*private*), SE. corner of Granville and Gale Sts., moved to this site in 1942, was constructed in 1767 and represents the full development of the gambrel-roof house in North Carolina. It was, 1779-91, the home of Willis Williams, captain of the ship *Caswell*, which, with the aid of shore batteries, kept Ocracoke Inlet open during the Revolution, the one channel of supply for the rebels in the State.

POINTS OF INTEREST NEAR EDENTON

1. East from Edenton on Water St. and across Johnston's Bridge to the unpaved Soundside Rd. now called the Indian Trail; R. on this road to HAYES (*private*), 0.5 m., in a beautiful grove (R) on the edge of Edenton Bay. The 1,500-acre plantation was acquired in 1765 by Samuel Johnston (1733-1816), and the mansion was built 1789-1801. One of the finest houses in the Albemarle, it was named for the estate of Sir Walter Raleigh in England. Johnston served as governor (1787-89) and was the first U. S. senator from North Carolina. During his lifetime Hayes was a social, intellectual, and political center.

The two-story central section of the house is surmounted with a large cupola and is connected to the one-story wings by curved, covered passages. One of the smaller buildings contains the library, the other the kitchen. The southwest elevation, facing the bay, has a two-story Doric portico supported upon shallow brick arches and ornamented at the second floor with a wrought-iron railing. The northeast elevation, 5 bays in width, has a small semicircular portico. Fanlights and side lights grace the doorway. The shutters are permanently fixed over the upper halves of the windows to lessen the sun glare. The house contains steel engravings and portraits by Sir Joshua Reynolds and Thomas Sully, and a 5,000-volume library whose catalogue, written with a quill pen, looks like an exquisite engraving.

The GATE HOUSE, near the entrance, was the original house called "Hayes," built for John Rieusset and sold to Samuel Johnston in 1765. After being moved from its original site, it was used as the miller's house. Now, greatly enlarged, but with much of its woodwork unchanged, it is an unusually attractive dwelling.

The Indian Trail passes several beautiful old plantation homes that have existed since colonial times and at the mouth of Yeopim River reaches DRUMMONDS POINT (*fishing boats for hire*), 8 m., named for Gov. William Drummond. In the mouth of the river is BATTS (BATZ) GRAVE or BATTS ISLAND. An early deed (1696) of Chowan Precinct records the sale of 27 acres known as Batts Grave, but tide erosion has completely reduced the land. Early in the 18th century it belonged to George Durant, Jr. The Indians called the island Kalola for the sea gulls that alone disturbed its solitude until Jesse Batts, a hunter and trapper, came here. Batts fell in love with Kickowanna, daughter of a Chowanoke chief, Kilcanoo. She returned his love, spurning the suit of Pamunky, chief of the Chasamonpeaks. For his bravery in helping defeat the Chasamonpeaks, Batts was adopted into the tribe. Thereafter the couple lived on the upper waters, but Batts made frequent visits to his island home. Kickowanna often went in her canoe to visit him there. One night in a raging storm she was drowned. Batts never left the island again and died a brokenhearted man.

2. Right from Edenton on NC 32, which follows the old stagecoach route known for years as the Virginia Rd.

At WINGFIELD, 10 m., on the banks of the Chowan River is the SITE OF THE UNION FORT, a stockade built by a group of Buffaloes (Union sympathizers) in the fall of 1862 and destroyed, along with Wingfield plantation house, by Confederates sent out three months later by Lt. Gen. D. H. Hill.

BANDON (*private*), 15 m., a plantation home, is located on land used as a camp site by Ralph Lane, Governor of Roanoke Island, who made an expedition up the Chowan River as far as Winton in 1585. This expedition was described in Hakluyt's *English Voyages*. Original grants were to Thomas Bray, 1717, and Edward Moseley, 1719, by Lord Granville. Later it was known as Boydsburgh, for an early owner. It was bought in 1769 by the Rev. Daniel Earl ("Parson Earl"), rector of St. Paul's Church (1759-78) (*see* EDENTON) who renamed it "Bandon" for his native village in Southern Ireland. Of the early dependencies, three buildings remain, the old kitchen, smoke house, and school house, where the parson and his daughter Ann conducted a classical boarding school for boys, among whom were the two sons of Baron von Pollnitz, former chamberlain to Frederick the Great.

The main block of the present house was built for Earl's son-in-law, Charles Johnson, Vice Pres. of both the Hillsboro (1788) and the Fayetteville (1789) conventions, and U. S. Senator during Jefferson's administration. Later additions were made about 1825 by Johnson's son, Charles Earl Johnson. It is now the home of Inglis Fletcher, novelist (*see* EDENTON), and her husband, John Fletcher.

3. MULBERRY HILL, 7 m. E. of Edenton on Air Station Rd., was patented in 1684 by Capt. James Blount. One of the most interesting houses in the county, the distinguished 4-story brick house, built before the Revolution, has an enormous fanlight (radius 5 feet) made from one piece of wood. The interior woodwork is probably the most beautiful in the Albemarle section.

Elizabeth City

Information Service: Chamber of Commerce, Virginia Dare Hotel Arcade.

Railroad Station: Burgess & Water Sts., for Norfolk-Southern R. R. (*freight only*).

Bus Station: SW. corner Fearing and Poindexter Sts., for Virginia Dare Transportation Co. and Carolina Trailways.

Airports: Municipal, **3 m.** S., for private planes; U. S. Coast Guard Air Station, **3 m.** SW. on NC 170, for Capital Air Lines.

Piers: Norfolk-Southern docks at foot of Burgess St.

Radio Stations: WGAI (560), WCNC (1240).

Newspapers: Daily Advance (eve. except Sun.); *Independent Star* (morn. except Sat.).

Educational Institutions: Elizabeth City State Teachers College (*Negro*).

Swimming: Carter Perry Swimming Pool, S. Road St.; river beaches.

Golf: Elizabeth City Country Club, **3 m.** N., US 17 and NC 158.

Hunting and Fishing: Inquire Chamber of Commerce.

Annual Events: International Moth Boat Class Association National Regatta, 3 days in Oct.; Outboard and Inboard Motor Boat Regatta, July and early fall; Potato Festival, late in May.

ELIZABETH CITY (8 alt., 12,685 pop.), shipping point and retail trade center for a large section of northeastern North Carolina and seat of Pasquotank County, is connected with outside markets by water, rail, and highway. It is the only town on the 40-mile length of the Pasquotank River, and its landlocked harbor at the head of the State's great system of sounds is 30 miles from the ocean in a direct line. The town is a convenient base from which to visit the duck-hunting country of Currituck, the game grounds of the Dismal Swamp, historic and vacation spots along the sounds and ocean, and sport-fishing waters off the banks and inlets.

Pasquotank River is a link in the Intracoastal Waterway and at Elizabeth City forms one of the finest inland harbors along the Atlantic seaboard. Good wharfage, marine railways, and fresh water, free from teredos and barnacles, induce many yachtsmen to winter their craft here. The 5th District U. S. Coast Guard maintains a small craft shipyard and a supply depot for its district land station in Elizabeth City. Other important Coast Guard and Naval installations are located south of the town (*see Points 12 and 13*).

Visible from any of a half-dozen streets that sweep down to the water or parallel the shore, the river mirrors moving or anchored craft. The harbor is the home port of freighters, tugs, barges, cruisers, yachts, bugeyes, and catboats, as well as the locally developed moth boat. Elizabeth City is one of the largest fish-marketing centers in the South. Fish houses, shipyards, and other marine facilities cluster about the water front.

The business district extends from the Pasquotank River west to Pool St., north to Elizabeth St., and south to Church St. To the north and northwest is the industrial section, with its lumber, veneer, cotton, and hosiery mills. The Negroes, representing 37% of the population, live in scattered sections, but are chiefly concentrated in the southern and southwestern districts.

The harvesting of the Irish potato crop about the middle of June brings an influx of buyers, inspectors, and truckers, impartially referred to by the townsfolk as "potato bugs." A similar situation exists during the May pear and early fall sweet potato seasons. Cotton, corn, peanuts, and soybeans are the staple crops. The latter are grown mainly for seed purposes and are gathered with harvesters manufactured locally. Lumber and cotton manufactories are the chief industries.

As early as 1666 Bermudians established themselves on the Pasquotank River where they engaged in shipbuilding. In 1672 Pasquotank County, named for an Indian tribe in the region, was constituted a precinct in the Great County of Albemarle and the first courts were held at Relfe's Point. William Edmundson and George Fox made Quaker converts through the section the same year. In 1706 the first meetinghouse of that faith in the State was erected in the county near the earliest school. Blackbeard roved these waters for a time and traditionally maintained headquarters at the Old Brick House, but recent research indicates that it was not built until after Blackbeard's death. Trading vessels called at the port and customs inspections were held as early as 1722 at the Narrows of Pasquotank, as the town site was then called. In 1739 the county of Pasquotank was formed.

The West India trade, spurred by the cutting of the Dismal Swamp Canal in 1790, and the attendant swarm of "shingle-getters" who came to grub out the swamp timber, led to the formation of the town. The 50-acre Narrows Plantation of Adam and Elizabeth Tooley was conveyed to the town commissioners to be laid off in small tracts and assigned by lot. First incorporated (1793) as Reading, the name was changed to Elizabeth Town, either in honor of Elizabeth Tooley or of Queen Elizabeth. In 1799 it replaced Nixonton (Old Town) as county seat and in 1801 was named Elizabeth City.

In the early 1800's ocean-going vessels crowded the docks where Negro slaves loaded shingles, barrel staves, and ship parts to be exported to the West Indies, or unloaded cargoes of molasses, rum, sugar, and tropical fruits. Three shipyards did a thriving business—building, overhauling, and repairing sailing vessels. Many of the builders, blacksmiths, and caulkers were Negro slaves. Oak bark stripped from staves was used to tan leather, and William Steiger's combined tannery and bakeshop at Canal Bridge gave the name Leather Hill to the slight rise at the south end of town. Stage-coaches made regular stops, traveling along the canal bank from Nor-folk, Va.

Federal occupation of the town in 1862 was a "grand, gloomy, and peculiar time." The sheriff and many citizens set fire to their own houses at the approach of the Federal fleet, and the brick courthouse was also burned.

Elizabeth City experienced a slow but steady growth after the Civil War, particularly in connection with the farming, lumbering, and fishing interests in the surrounding territory and the establishment of cotton and hosiery mills. However, in this period the town's interests, like those of all the section east of Chowan River and north of Albemarle Sound, were much more closely linked with those of neighboring Virginia cities than with the rest of North Carolina. Before 1921 a north-south railroad and a few sound steamers formed the only outlet. The construction of good roads began in 1921. The Chowan River Bridge (1926), and the Albemarle Sound Bridge (1938) connected the town and the surrounding section economically with North Carolina, and the Albemarle country was "bought back from Vir-ginia, which long had held it as hostage."

POINTS OF INTEREST

1. The PUBLIC SQUARE, bounded by Main, Martin, and Elliott Sts. and Colonial Ave., is a broad double square of grassy lawn shaded by beautiful trees and shrubbery. A bandstand (E. of courthouse) is used for concerts by the famous Elizabeth City High School Band, which has, for the past 15 years, had the financial and moral backing of Miles Clark, local business man. The CONFEDERATE MONUMENT stands in the center of the square.

The U. S. POST OFFICE and COURTHOUSE, NW. corner Main and Martin Sts., erected in 1906 and enlarged in 1938, occupies half the square. It is of later Italian Renaissance style.

The COUNTY COURTHOUSE (*open 9-5 weekdays*), NE. corner Main and Elliott Sts., was designed and built by A. L. West in 1882 of red brick heavily trimmed with granite. The columned and pedimented porch, at the Main St. entrance, is surmounted by a cupola with a clock and bell. The latter strikes the hours, rings the alarm for fires, and sounds the summons to court. Deed books date from 1700 and will books from 1752.

Behind the courthouse and facing Colonial Ave. is the AGRICULTURAL BUILDING, a red brick structure in the Georgia Colonial style, erected 1938. It houses county offices and the COUNTY PUBLIC LIBRARY (*open 9-6, week-days; 9-9, Mon.*)

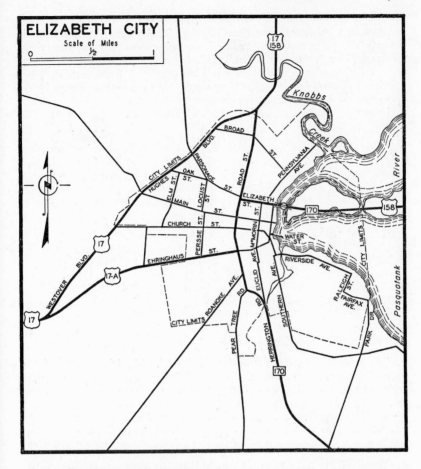

2. The JUDGE SMALL HOUSE (*private*), 204 E. Colonial Ave., long the Pool-Greenleaf home, was erected about 1800 on the site of the Post Office Bldg., but was moved to its present location in 1902. A weatherboarded frame house with Doric columns, it has a second-story balustraded gallery. Its interior is notable for hand-carved mantels, wainscot, and arched doorways. It was used as the Federal Army Headquarters during the Civil War.

3. The NASH HOUSE (*private*), NW. corner Colonial Ave. and Martin St., is a large white weatherboarded structure with massive chimneys, many-paned windows, dormers in the gabled roof, and a two-story Doric portico. It was erected in the early 1800's and was originally owned by Benjamin Anderson, a Quaker, who in 1834 published the *Herald of the Times,* "a family newspaper devoted to news, literature, science, morality, agriculture, and amusements."

4. The SITE OF TOOLEY'S GROG SHOP, 112 S. Water St., is now occupied by a hardware store. Here Elizabeth Tooley catered to the Dismal Swamp "shingle-getters," her tippling house being one of several, also called "doggeries" or "three-cent shops." Thieving slaves found them a ready market for plunder, according to a petition presented to the legislature by aggrieved planters in 1859. The grog shops, however, met strong competition from the grocery stores, whose proprietors kept a free whiskey barrel and plenty of honey and sugar to mix with the liquor.

5. CHRIST CHURCH (*Episcopal*), SE. corner Church and McMorine Sts., a Gothic Revival building was built in 1856 and is the oldest in town. The original was erected in 1825 on ground deeded to the parish in 1790 by the descendants of Isaac Sawyer, who in 1761 purchased a 250-acre tract from Lord Granville for 10 shillings. Eighteen beautiful stained-glass windows depicting the life of Christ are said to be the most complete story of the Bible in stained glass in the State.

6. The FEARING HOUSE (*private*), SE. corner S. Road and Fearing Sts., is the oldest residence in the town. The original portion was built about 1740 by Charles Grice, a shipbuilder from Germantown, Pa. After the War of 1812, Isaiah Fearing, a New Englander, married the 6th Mrs. Grice. Their descendants still own and occupy the house. The original part of the house includes 4 large rooms and two hallways with hand-carved paneling and hand-hewn heartwood timbers, fastened with wooden pegs and hand-wrought nails. The south ell was added in 1825 and the two-story columned portico and the north ell shortly after the Civil War.

7. The CHARLES HOUSE (*private*), 710 W. Colonial Ave., was built in the early 1800's for William Charles. This Greek Revival mansion was formerly the manor house of a large plantation and was approached from W. Main St. by a double row of elms and boxwoods. The facade is adorned with a two-story Doric portico with 6 columns. Inside are hand-carved mantels and two mahogany stairways, one of which terminates in a graceful "monkey tail." The house was used as a hospital during the Civil War.

8. The BIRTHPLACE OF J. C. B. EHRINGHAUS, 300 E. Church St., is now used as the WOMAN'S CLUB. Ehringhaus was governor, 1933-37, friend of education, member of the general assembly, and solicitor.

9. The PASQUOTANK RIVER YACHT CLUB, Riverside Ave. at the Charles Creek Bridge, is near the junction of Pasquotank River and Charles Creek. It is the headquarters of the yachting fraternity and the moth boat enthusiasts. The moth boat is a small sailing yacht conceived and built by Capt. Joel Van Sant in 1929. An 11-ft. craft with a 15-ft. sail and center board, it is easy to maneuver and transport. The annual International Moth Boat Regatta is held in the Pasquotank River in early autumn.

10. The ELIZABETH CITY SHIPYARDS (*open to public*), 800 block Riverside Ave., extends along the Pasquotank River shore for 1000 ft., on what has been a shipyard site since the early 1800's. The marine railway

accommodates boats up to 200 ft. and 800 tons. There are facilities for repairing machinery and hulls of wooden and steel vessels.

11. The ELIZABETH CITY YACHT BASIN (*open to public*), 800 block Riverside Ave., one of the largest yacht basins between New York and Florida, attracts many luxurious crafts, some of which make this their home port.

12. ALBEMARLE HOSPITAL, at head of Riverside Ave., facing Pasquotank River, is a Duke-endowed hospital, consisting of 100 beds and owned by the town and the county.

13. ELIZABETH CITY STATE TEACHERS COLLEGE (*Negro*), ½ m. SE. on Southern Ave., was established in 1891 in a single wooden building. The school now occupies 17 buildings and has an electrically-lighted athletic field. About ⅕ of the 500 students are male. The 4-year course is for teacher training.

14. U. S. COAST GUARD AIR STATION, 3 m. SE. on NC 170, on the shores of the Pasquotank River, is the chief Sea and Air Rescue Station for the 5th Coast Guard District and employs helicopters and other new devices for peace and wartime rescues. It contains hangars, barracks, and landing fields. Also located on the reservation is the Coast Guard Aviation Repair and Supply Station for the East coast. Capital Air Lines also use the Coast Guard landing fields.

15. The U. S. NAVAL AIR FACILITY, 6 m. out NC 170, L. 1 m., is the Navy's Anti-Submarine Air Patrol, which uses both blimps and helicopters for coastal patrol. Here is said to be the world's largest wooden building lacking girder support, and the steel hangar is said to be the largest structure in the State.

LOCAL TOUR FROM ELIZABETH CITY

Elizabeth City—Weeksville—Halls Creek; NC 170. **17.5 m.**

NC 170 branches southeast from US 17 (*see* TOUR *1a*) in ELIZABETH CITY, **0 m.**

At a country church, **1.5 m.**, is the junction with a dirt road.

Left on this road to ENFIELD FARM (*private*), **2 m.**, also known as the Winslow House, on the bank of the Pasquotank River. Here was erected in 1670 the home of Thomas Relfe, provost marshal of the general court and one of the first vestrymen of Pasquotank Parish. Two rooms of the original building, with brick walls 3 feet thick, are incorporated in the present farmhouse.

Enfield Farm was the SCENE OF THE CULPEPER REBELLION in 1677. When Acting Gov. Thomas Miller attempted to stop settlers from getting necessary supplies unless the customs tax was paid, John Culpeper, former surveyor general of South Carolina, George Durant (*see* TOUR *1a*), and other planters, seized Miller and 6 members of the council and imprisoned them at Enfield. They then convoked a legislature, appointed courts, and for two years exercised all the rights and powers of government. When Culpeper went to London to defend his conduct the Lords Proprietors declined to punish him.

COBBS POINT, formerly called Pembroke, on Enfield Farm, was the scene of a minor naval battle in 1862. Visible are the remains of a rude fort, hastily thrown up to defend the harbor when Federal gunboats came up the river from Roanoke Island.

BAYSIDE (*private*), 3 m., also known as the Hollowell House, is a Classical Revival plantation house on the highest point of land along the Pasquotank River. It was built for John Hollowell about 1800. The white-columned mansion faces the highway, in a setting of wide lawns, spreading trees, and spacious gardens. The greater part of the plantation was acquired by the U. S. Coast Guard during World War II and converted into an air base; the main house, the overseer's house, slave cabins, and a small area around them were excluded.

WEEKSVILLE, 7.5 m. (10 alt., 200 pop.), on New Begun Creek, is the center of one of the most fertile farming areas in northeastern North Carolina. Here are also located the U. S. NAVY LIGHTER-THAN-AIR STATION (with preservation and storage facilities for several hundred aircraft) and a U. S. COAST GUARD STATION.

At SYMONS CREEK, 11 m., is the SITE OF THE FIRST QUAKER MEET-INGHOUSE IN NORTH CAROLINA (1706). A marker indicates the SITE OF THE FIRST SCHOOL IN NORTH CAROLINA, established in 1705 by Charles Griffin, a lay reader of the Established Church sent out by the Society for the Propagation of the Gospel. He was the first professional teacher in North Carolina of whom there is record.

NIXONTON, 14.8 m. (50 pop.), on Little River, originally Old Town, was the seat of Pasquotank County until 1793. Nixonton was the center of a flourishing trade with the West Indies in the early 1800's.

The OLD CUSTOMHOUSE (*private*), on a hill sloping to the river, is a one-story wooden structure built in 1745 and now serving as a dwelling. The original structure contained three rooms; two rooms and two porches have been added. The paneling in the original three rooms has been removed to the North Carolina Room in the University Library at Chapel Hill.

At HALLS CREEK, 17.5 m., opposite Halls Creek Church, is a memorial tablet marking the SITE OF THE GRAND ASSEMBLY OF THE ALBEMARLE (1665), the first assembly of settlers ever held in North Carolina. It convened by order of William Drummond, North Carolina's first Governor; George Catchmaid was speaker. The assembly petitioned the Proprietors to allow the North Carolinians to hold their lands under the same conditions as the Virginians. Accession to this request was made in what is known as the Great Deed of Grant (1668). Tradition relates that one of the bylaws of the assembly provided that "the members should wear shoes, if not stockings" during the session of the body and that they "must not throw their chicken and other bones under the tree."

Fayetteville

Information Service: Chamber of Commerce, Old Market House.

Railroad Stations: 470 Hay St., for Atlantic Coast Line R. R.; 319 Rankin St., for Norfolk Southern Ry.; Russell St., for Aberdeen & Rockfish R. R.

Bus Station: Union Bus Station, 304 Gillespie St., for Greyhound Lines and Queen City Trailways.

City Buses: Along regular routes.

Airport: Grannis Field, Ft. Bragg, **10 m.**, for Piedmont Airlines.

Radio Stations: WFAI (1230), WFLB (1490), WFNC (1390), WFNC-FM (98.1), WBBO (780).

Newspapers: The Fayetteville Observer (daily).

Educational Institutions: Fayetteville State Teachers College *(Negro, coed)*.

Swimming: Fayetteville Country Club Pool; Lamon St. Municipal Pool; Rainbow Lake *(Negro)*; Seabrook Municipal Pool *(Negro)*; YMCA Pool, Old St.

Golf: Fayetteville Country Club, 18 holes.

Tennis: Lamon St. Park; Cape Fear Courts *(Negro)*, Old Wilmington Rd.

Annual Events: Camellia Show, Feb.; Flower Festival, spring; Fall Flower Show, Oct.; Dairy Cattle Show, Sept.; Cumberland County Fair, Oct.; Lady Lions Minstrel, Oct.

FAYETTEVILLE (107 alt., 34,715 pop.), seat of Cumberland County, lies on the west bank of the Cape Fear River. The most conspicuous point of interest is the century-old Market House, standing "where all roads meet," and containing the old bell that still rings the curfew at 9 o'clock every night.

Business houses line Gillespie, Green, Hay, and Person Sts. at the foot of the Haymount Hills. Older residential sections contain tree-shaded structures more than 100 years old. Sherwood Forest, in the western suburbs, has some of the finer homes. Negroes of the city live in several communities, the largest of which is Murchison Heights, on the north side of town. Fayetteville State Teachers College, located there, has exerted an important cultural influence upon the Negro race.

Fayetteville dates from 1739 when Scots, led by Col. Alexander McAllister, settled Campbelltown, whose orderly streets are still distinguishable in the eastern part of town along the river. In 1746-47, a group of expatriated Scots, men who had escaped "the penalty of death to one of every 20 survivors of Culloden," established a gristmill and village at Cross Creek, a mile northwest of Campbelltown, where they found two streams crossing.

For a few months in 1774 Fayetteville was the residence of the celebrated Highland heroine, Flora MacDonald, and her husband, Allan, who fought with the Highland Scots against the Whigs at the Battle of Moore's Creek Bridge (*see* TOUR *17*). Whigs also met here, at Liberty Point, June 20, 1775, and signed resolutions pledging themselves to "resist force by force" and to "go forth and be ready to sacrifice our lives and fortunes to secure freedom and safety."

The preponderance of Tories in Cumberland County during the Revolution made Fayetteville the center of an area characterized by internecine warfare. A number of minor encounters took place in and about Fayetteville, and in 1781 Cornwallis occupied the town en route to Wilmington. In 1783 the settlements of Campbelltown and Cross Creek united and were incorporated as Fayetteville, the first community so honoring the Marquis de Lafayette.

Fayetteville served as the State capital from 1789 to 1793. Here on Nov. 21, 1789, the second State ratification convention ratified the Federal Constitution, which had been rejected the previous year at Hillsboro. Also in Nov., 1789, the general assembly, meeting in Fayetteville, chartered the University of North Carolina.

In 1790 the first book of poetry printed in the State was issued by Sibley and Howard, Fayetteville printers: *The Monitor: or a Poem on Dancing, addressed to the Ladies and Gentlemen of the Fayetteville Assembly.* There is no extant copy and no key to the author's identity, though he was probably a North Carolinian.

By 1823, with a population of 3,532, Fayetteville was second only to Wilmington in size and commerce. The town was accessible to vessels of light draft that brought imports from the Atlantic and carried back products of the fields, looms, potteries, and forges. A network of roads radiated from the town, the most important being the noted Plank Road of timbers upon heavy stringers, which ran 129 miles northwest to Bethania.

On March 4-5, 1825, Lafayette was the guest of Fayetteville. He stayed at the home of Duncan McRae on the site of the present courthouse.

On May 29, 1831, the most destructive fire in the United States up to that time destroyed 600 homes, 125 business houses, several churches, and the convention hall where sessions of the general assembly had been held. In 1865 Sherman occupied the town, wrecked the only printing press, and burned some of the mills.

Railroads aided the town's growth after 1870, and the advent of the textile mills offset the decline of the turpentine and lumber industries. River traffic was suspended in 1923, but in 1936 a lock and dam built at Tolar's Landing made a 9-foot slack-water channel available to Fayetteville. A dock and terminal were built to provide facilities for revival of the river trade. Today, textile and lumber mills are the largest industries. Others include tobacco sales warehouses and furniture, food, cotton seed, processing, fertilizer, brick, concrete, and stone companies. The proximity of Fort Bragg (*see below*) has materially changed the appearance and tempo of the town.

George Herman Ruth hit his first home run in professional baseball and acquired his nickname "Babe Ruth" in Fayetteville, while training with the Baltimore Orioles in 1914.

POINTS OF INTEREST

1. The MARKET HOUSE (*open*), Market Sq., at the intersection of Green and Gillespie, Person and Hay Sts., houses the Chamber of Commerce. This three-bay brick building has a hipped-roof central section surmounted by a tower whose clock has run accurately since 1838, when the building was erected. Three arched passageways pierce the central section and Ionic pilasters on the upper walls separate the many-paned arched windows. Single-story arcaded wings with balustraded roofs flank the central. section. The bell in the cupola is rung each day at 7:30 for breakfast, at 1 p. m. for dinner, at sunset, and at 9 p. m. for curfew. The building served originally as a produce market, where slaves were occasionally sold. Later it housed a public realty exchange and the town hall.

The Market House occupies the SITE OF CONVENTION HALL, destroyed by the fire of 1831. Here was held the convention that ratified the Federal Constitution (1789) and sessions of the general assembly (1789-93). On Mar. 4, 1825, Gen. Lafayette addressed a large crowd of people from a stage erected at the door, thanking them for naming the town in his honor. On the northwest corner is a bronze tablet commemorating events that took place on the site.

2. The WOMAN'S CLUB, 225 Dick St., formerly known as the Sanford House, is a two-story weatherboarded structure, painted white, with a hip roof. It rests on high brick basement walls. The porch is 4 columns wide with Ionic details superimposed upon Doric. The upper doorway has the original fanlight and side lights but the lower door has been remodeled. The building housed a bank as early as 1807 and the vault is intact in the basement. Lafayette was entertained here in 1825. In one of the rooms is a marble mantel with a hand-carved design of two doves in the center and vases of flowers on the posts. Here Elliott Daingerfield (1859-1932), the painter, lived as a boy.

3. LIBERTY POINT, Person and Bow Sts., was the scene of a meeting of 39 patriots who pledged resistance to Great Britain, June 20, 1775. A boulder with names of the signers marks the spot.

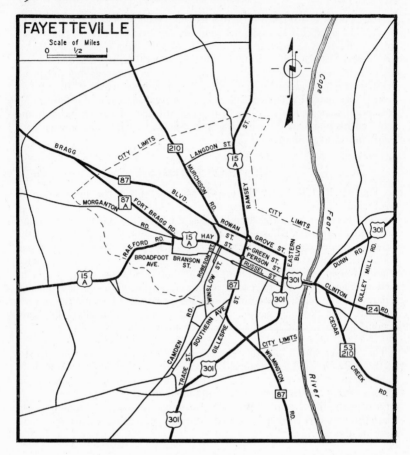

4. The FIRST PRESBYTERIAN CHURCH, E. corner Bow and Ann Sts., was built about 1816, gutted by fire in 1831, and rebuilt with the original walls in 1832. This oblong brick building has a spacious portico with 6 square columns and a simple steeple. In the vestibule are a marble-topped mahogany table and sacramental silver dating from 1824. For many years whale oil was burned in the ornamental chandeliers. The south wing of the church and the spire were designed by Hobart B. Upjohn, N. Y. architect, in 1922. A second addition, the Fuller Memorial Building, was erected in 1945.

5. The MACKETHAN HOUSE (*private*), Cool Spring St. and Cool Spring Lane, built in 1778, was originally the Cool Spring Tavern. This handsome, white-painted frame house has a two-story porch across the front. The steep-pitched roof is flanked by massive end chimneys.

6. COOL SPRING, NW. corner Cool Spring St. and Cool Spring Lane, on the bank of Cross Creek, was a source of drinking water before the Civil War. It was at the head of the steps leading to the spring that Flora MacDonald, according to legend, spurred the Highland Scots to fight for England before the battle of Moore's Creek Bridge.

7. The SITE OF PEMBERTON'S (McNEILL'S) MILL, Cool Spring St. opposite the spring, is occupied by a water-driven machine shop. In 1861 a mill that manufactured gray cloth for Confederate uniforms stood here.

8. The SITE OF CROSS CREEK is visible from the intersection of Grove and Kennedy Sts. The name derives from two small creeks, Cross from the west and Blount from the south, that met and apparently separated, forming an island of some size. It was said that the streams, when swollen from the rains, actually crossed each other in their rapid course.

9. The JAMES DOBBIN McNEILL MONUMENT, SE. corner Green and Bow Sts., is a rough-hewn, flat-faced boulder carved with fire hose winding around small bronze tablets surmounted by a bronze eagle. A central tablet bears a profile and record of James D. McNeill (1850-1927), 6 times mayor, commander of the Fayetteville Division of N. C. Naval Reserves, captain of the Red Shirts (see WILMINGTON), and organizer and president for 26 years of the State Firemen's Association.

10. The SITE OF FLORA MacDONALD'S HOME, NE. corner Green and Bow Sts., where she supposedly lived for a few months 1774-75, is now occupied by a filling station. Born in the Hebrides in 1722, Flora, a member of the Clanranald branch of the MacDonald clan, is famous for her support of Bonnie Prince Charlie, last of the Stuart pretenders to Britain's throne. After his defeat at Culloden in 1746, the royal fugitive, with a price on his head, fled to the Hebrides. Determined to save him, Flora disguised the prince as a servant girl and smuggled him safely across the water to the Isle of Skye whence he escaped to France. Her ruse discovered, she was arrested, but her courage and beauty won public sympathy. After her release she became a toast of London society. In 1750 she married Allan MacDonald, son of the Laird of Kingsborough, and in 1774 the MacDonalds emigrated to N. C. and settled first at Cross Creek. A few months later they resided at Mount Pleasant (see LOCAL TOUR, below), now called Cameron's Hill, in Harnett County, before moving to a place on Cheek's Creek, in Mont-gomery County. As a result of Allan's participation in the battle of Moore's Creek Bridge, he was imprisoned at Halifax and later exchanged in New York. Flora, after the confiscation of her property, sojourned some months near present Pinehurst and then joined her husband in New York. She, a broken old woman, sailed for Scotland from Nova Scotia in 1779. A college at Red Springs is named for her.

11. ST. JOHN'S EPISCOPAL CHURCH, 242 Green St., was erected in 1817, burned in 1831, and rebuilt with the original walls in the Gothic Revival style. The 1817 structure, one of the most elaborate brick churches of the period, had a fine organ, clock, and bell.

12. The MASONIC BUILDING (*open to members only*), 221 Mason St., home of Fayetteville Masons since it was built in 1858, is a two-story clapboard structure with small porches on two sides, painted gray and trimmed in white. When organized and chartered in 1760 by the Grand Lodge of Masons in Scotland, it was called Union Lodge; in 1788 its name was changed to Phoenix Lodge.

13. The ARMORY (*open for dances, boxing matches, etc.*), 214 Burgess St., a one-story white brick building erected in 1933, is headquarters for the Fayetteville Independent Light Infantry, organized in 1793 and reputed to be the second oldest military organization in continuous service in the U. S. The unit has served in every national war (except World War II) since its founding and was a part of the 30th Division in World War I. Its motto is: "He that hath no stomach to this fight, let him depart."

14. The METHODIST CHURCH, NW. corner Hay and Old Sts., dedicated in 1908, is the red brick steepled edifice of a Methodist organization that originated in the late 1770's from a weekly "preaching" by Henry Evans, a free Negro shoemaker. White members of the congregation erected a chapel for themselves in 1803, and their Sunday school, organized in 1819, is the earliest Methodist Sunday school in the State of which there is authentic record.

15. THE HALE (McNEILL) HOME (*private*), NW. corner Hay and Hale Sts., is a two-story brick dwelling built in 1847 and first called Greenbank. The mahogany rails and posts of the interior stairway were made in Scotland. Two rooms have mantels of black marble, fanciful heavy moldings, and gas fixtures. The thick doors are dressed with huge locks. All timbers are mortised and fastened with wooden pins.

16. The SITE OF THE CONFEDERATE ARSENAL, SW. corner Hay St. and Maple Ave., destroyed by Union troops during Sherman's occupation in 1865, is identified by a marker.

17. FAYETTEVILLE STATE TEACHERS COLLEGE, Murchison Rd. at NW. city limits, is the oldest normal school for any race in the South. In 1867, 7 Negroes bought a lot for a school site and prevailed upon Gen. O. O. Howard of the Freedmen's Bureau, to build the Howard School on this lot. In 1877 Gov. Zebulon Vance induced the legislature to take it over for the education of teachers for the Negro race. Thus the "Fayetteville State Colored Normal School" continued to grow. After several moves, it located permanently in 1908 on this 92-acre campus, where the value of its plant is now estimated at two million dollars. In 1939 its name was changed to the present one and its course of study from two to 4 years. There are more than 600 students and a faculty of 60. On the campus is a marble tablet to Dr. E. E. Smith, who served as principal (1883-1933), U. S. Minister to Liberia, and an adjutant in the Spanish-American War. Charles W. Chestnutt (1852-1932), one-time principal, was the author of short stories and novels. The excellent library was named for him.

18. CROSS CREEK CEMETERY, Grove St. between Ann St. and Cross Creek, shaded by ancient cedars and pines, contains the graves of many Scottish settlers. Confederate soldiers are buried around the CONFEDERATE MONUMENT, erected Dec. 30, 1868. It is a 10-foot octagonal shaft on a white marble base surmounted by a cross, designed by George Lauder. Here also is the grave of the artist, Elliott Daingerfield.

19. ST. JAMES SQUARE, the intersection of Ramsey, Green, Rowan, and Grove Sts., is on the site of the first Cumberland County Courthouse, built about 1755. The square was named for James Hogg, a prominent early citizen.

20. JOHN A. OATES HOME (*private*), NE. corner of St. James Sq., a handsome two-story white house, was built prior to 1800.

21. NIMOCKS HOUSE (*private*), 309 Dick St., is a one-story, clapboard house with 4 dormer windows. Built in 1805 for Duncan McLeran, a lawyer, it is one of the interesting smaller early houses.

22. The ROBERSON HOUSE, 321 Person St., now operated as Faircloth Florist, is considered the oldest house in town. A rectangular, two-story white clapboard house, with interesting dentil work, its original façade has been recently altered.

LOCAL TOUR FROM FAYETTEVILLE

Fayetteville—Fort Bragg—Manchester—Spout Springs; NC 87. **23 m.**

This route parallels the Wilmington-Sanford branch of the Atlantic Coast Line, built in the early 1860's to transport coal from the Egypt mines (now Cumnock) on Deep River to the Cape Fear River port at Fayetteville and originally designated The Western Railroad. The route through Manchester and Spout Springs lies upon the route of the old Western Plank Road which extended from Fayetteville to Salem, the longest road ever constructed of planks, completed about 1852. Through coaches of 4 horses each operated from Warsaw to Salem, and relay points were spaced at 12-mile intervals. The last coach trip ended in Fayetteville on April 28, 1864. The driver, David Brown, is said to have seated himself in the line's office and cried.

NC 87 branches northwest from Fayetteville (*see* TOUR 3) in FAYETTE-VILLE, **0 m.**

At **4 m.**, in a grove, is the NOTT HOUSE (*private*), an ante-bellum plantation house sheathed with wide clapboards and having broad, double galleries at the front and rear. Hand-made iron hinges and fasteners are attached to solid paneled doors and shutters.

BUENA VISTA (*private*), **6 m.**, the Alexander McPherson home, was built about 1845. A two-story, white clapboard house, it was used by Gen. Atkins Clark as his headquarters in 1865.

FORT BRAGG, U. S. MILITARY RESERVATION (*open*), **10 m.** (*for information concerning artillery practice and directions to Long Street Church inquire at headquarters*), one of the largest in the United States, is three times the size of the District of Columbia and covers an area of 130,000 acres, 28½ miles long and 14½ miles wide.

Gen. Francis Marion, the Swamp Fox, made this site his headquarters while he harassed British forces. Cornwallis, after the Battle of Guilford Courthouse (*see* TOUR 9), maintained headquarters here.

Fort Bragg has a complete system of municipal and recreational facilities, chapels, and a school for children; the buildings are modern, built of brick and stucco.

Originally planned as an artillery training area, the Fort is known today as "The Home of the Airborne." Named after a North Carolinian, Confederate Gen. Braxton Bragg, the present site was purchased by the government in 1918 and became a permanent installation in 1922. The XVIII Airborne Corps has its headquarters on the post. There are also several Army schools, including: Parachute School; Advanced Leadership School; and the Psychological Warfare School, the only one of its kind in the Armed Forces. At one time during World War II there were 160,000 men at Fort Bragg, and today it ranks in population as one of the top 10 cities in North Carolina.

POPE AIR FORCE BASE, one of the nation's early military flying fields, was established during World War I and named in honor of Lt. Harley Halbert Pope, who died in an aircraft accident on the Cape Fear River near Fayetteville, Jan. 7, 1919. The airbase has played an important part over the years in the development of the nation's air might. By 1934 the air field was recognized as an important air base, and the Air Corps' first mass flights of aircraft were staged from Pope Air Force Base. At the present time the Ninth Air Force, controlling air bases and fighter-bomber wings over the nation, locates its headquarters here. Today the Ninth Air Force, which flew more tactical missions during World War II than all other Allied and Axis tactical forces combined, is a center of the nation's tactical air training.

LONG STREET CHURCH, organized in 1758, is on the old Yadkin Rd. within the reservation. Highland Scots settled the region as early as 1736. The Rev. Hugh McAden, a Presbyterian missionary, first held services at the home of Alexander McKay in 1756. Two years later Long Street, Old Bluff, and Barbecue Churches were organized, with the Rev. James Campbell, a native of Argyllshire, as first pastor. For 137 years services were held continuously in Long Street Church, whose name is believed to refer to the settlements lining the road for a mile or more. The simple hip-roof structure was built (1845-47) of hand-dressed long-leaf pine timbers. The church is entered through two front doors, and the pulpit stands between them, set high up against the wall.

Near Long Street Church is the SITE OF THE BATTLE OF MONROE'S CROSS-ROADS (Mar. 10, 1865). Maj. Gen. Judson Kilpatrick commanded the Federals and Lt. Gen. Wade Hampton the Confederate forces. Upon the arrival of Federal reinforcements the Confederates retreated.

Beyond the rock wall of the church cemetery a stone marks the graves of 30 unidentified men who fell in the battle. Highlanders and their descendants are also buried here.

In MANCHESTER, 13 m. (165 alt., 850 pop.), once a turpentine shipping point on Lower Little River, is the SITE OF HOLLY HILL, now occupied by a story-and-a-half house. It was the Murchison family seat from the days when Kenneth Murchison, a Revolutionary soldier, erected his home in a magnificent grove of hollies. A tombstone, erected to one of his former slaves, bears the following inscription: "Reverend Jack Murchison, born 1795, died 1922."

Across Little River bridge, 13.5 m., (R) stands the chimneyed DANIEL McDAIRMID HOUSE, now known as the Black place. Daniel McDairmid was the son of an immigrant Scottish minister, the Rev. Angus McDairmid, pastor of the original three Presbyterian churches of the Cape Fear Valley: Bluff, Long Street, and Barbecue.

At 17.6 m. is the junction with a dirt road.

Left on this road to OVERHILLS (197 alt., 30 pop.), 1.2 m., the Avery Rockefeller Estate, which at one time covered 147,000 acres, now greatly reduced. The rambling, red brick mansion with tile roof and iron balcony was erected in 1928. There is a smaller, white-painted brick house, and a golf course.

Visible on both sides of the highway at 22 m. is a rare variety of pyxie plant, the flowering moss (*Pyxidanthera brevifolia*). Apparently a relic of an almost extinct family, it survives in compact mats, 3 to 5 feet wide, of tiny white wheel-shaped flowers, closely overlapped on slender, branching stems. It was discovered in 1928 by Dr. B. W. Wells, head of the Botany Department of State College, Raleigh, and is believed to exist only within a 6-mile area around SPOUT SPRINGS, 23 m. (333 alt., 25 pop.).

At Spout Springs NC 87 forms a junction with NC 27.

West from Spout Springs NC 27 crosses the crest of a prominent hill, at 3 m., formed of fine red soil in surprising contrast to the coarse white sand forming the lower and longer ridges surrounding it on all sides. This eminence was called by original settlers MOUNT PLEASANT, settled by Allen Cameron who came from Argyllshire in Scotland and secured title to the hill through royal grant.

At the western base of the hill flows the FLORA MacDONALD SPRING, used by the heroine during her stay here while her husband, Capt. Allan MacDonald of Kingsburgh, negotiated the purchase of some 500 acres upon Cheek's Creek in Montgomery County (*see* FAYETTEVILLE).

Greensboro

Information Services: Chamber of Commerce, 225 N. Greene St.; Carolina Motor Club, 107 S. Davie St.; Greensboro Industries, Inc., 519 W. Washington St.

Railroad Station: E. Washington and Forbis Sts., for Southern Ry.

Bus Station: Union Terminal, 312 W. Gaston St. for Carolina Coach, Atlantic Greyhound, and Queen City Coach Cos.

City Buses: Along regular routes.

Airport: Greensboro-High Point, **9.4 m.** on US 421, for Eastern, Capital, and Piedmont Airlines.

Radio and Television Stations: WBIG (1470); WGBG (1400); WCOG (1320), WCOG-TV (channel 57); WFMY-FM (97.3), WFMY-TV (channel 2), WPET (950).

Newspapers: Greensboro Daily News (morn.); *Greensboro Record* (eve. except Sun.).

Educational Institutions: Woman's College of the University of North Carolina; Greensboro College (*women*); Agricultural and Technical College of North Carolina (*Negro, coed*); Bennett College (*Negro, women*); Immanuel Lutheran College (*Negro, coed*).

Swimming: Lindley Park Pool; Hamilton Lakes, **3 m.** W. on US 421; Greensboro Country Park, **5 m.** NW. on US 220, R. **.5 m.**; Nocho Recreation Park (*Negro*), E. Bragg St. and Benbow Rd.; Ritter's Lake, **5 m.** S. on US 220; Oakhurst Swimming Pool, W. on old High Point Rd. at city limits.

Golf: Sedgefield Country Club, **6 m.** near US 29-70, 18 holes; Starmount Forest Golf Club, Hamilton Lakes, **3 m.** W. on US 421, 18 holes; Greensboro Country Club, 18 holes; Gillespie Park Municipal Golf Course, 18 holes; Green Valley Public Golf Course, 18 holes; Nocho Park Golf Course, 18 holes (*Negro*).

Tennis: Memorial Stadium, Bagley and Dewey Sts.; Greensboro Country Club; Sedgefield, **6 m.** W. near US 29-70. The city maintains 30 other courts; call City Recreation Dept. to reserve court for 1 hour.

Baseball and Football: Memorial Stadium, Bagley and Dewey Sts.; Greensboro Senior High School Stadium, Westover Terrace.

Riding: Sedgefield Riding Academy, **6 m.** W. near US 29-70, on Groometown Rd.; New Hunt Riding Academy, **4.1 m.** W. near old High Point Rd., E. on Yow St.

Shooting: Skeet Club, **6 m.** W. on US 29-70.

Hunting and Fishing: Lake Brandt (*municipal*), **10 m.** NW. off US 220; Greensboro Country Park, **5.5 m.** NW. near US 220; inquire Chamber of Commerce or game warden, county courthouse.

Annual Events: State High School Music Contest, 3rd week April; Garden Club Show, around May 15; golf tournaments, GGO in spring for men, spring and fall for women, championship for men in fall; Kennel Club Show, fall; Central N. C. Fair, fall; State High School Track Meet, fall.

GREENSBORO (838 alt., 74,389 pop.) at the eastern point of the triangle of close-lying cities that includes Winston-Salem, the tobacco town, on the west, and furniture-hosiery manufacturing High Point at the southern apex, is typical of the industrial piedmont from which the community draws its raw materials, electric energy, manpower, and trade. The city is an educational and textile-manufacturing center, though its diversified industries also produce structural steel, chemicals, terra cotta, cigarettes, etc.

In the business section the Jefferson Standard Life Insurance Company Building dominates the skyline and marks the city's center at Jefferson Square, where Market and Elm Sts. cross. The streets are broad and in the residential sections are shaded by stately pines, oaks, maples, and other trees.

The new homes are in such subdivisions as Sunset Hills, Westerwood, Lake Daniel Park, Fisher Park, Latham Park, and Irving Park within the city, and Hamilton Lakes, Starmount Forest, Friendly Acres, Guilford Hills, Garden Homes, Pinecroft, Lamrocton, and Sedgefield beyond the city limits; many fine old houses lie along the city's original streets. Trim lawns and gardens are everywhere in evidence, and public parks and playgrounds are numerous.

The industrial areas stretch along the railroads for several miles on each side of town. Mill communities in the northeast section indicate the importance of the textile industry.

The city's Negroes, 25% of the total population, live in more or less scattered, segregated areas but are most concentrated in Warnerville, in the southwest part of the city. Professional and cultural groups occupy many attractive homes in the eastern part of the city. They maintain their own library, theatres, dramatic and literary societies, and have recreational facilities such as ball parks, swimming pools, and playgrounds.

The earliest settlers around Greensboro were English and Welsh Quakers, German Calvinists and Lutherans, and Ulster Scot Presbyterians. They were small freeholders, whose zeal for religious, economic, and political freedom dotted the region with churches, wrested prosperity from the wilderness, and helped win independence from the British Crown.

The city occupies part of the original grant (1749) from John Carteret, Earl of Granville, to the Nottingham Company, for settlement of a colony of Ulster Scot Presbyterians on the waters of North Buffalo and Reedy Fork creeks. To the east, on Stinking Quarter Creek, a German colony settled at the same time, and to the west, along Deep River and its tributaries, two groups of Quakers took up lands.

In 1771 Guilford County, also known as Unity Parish, was created from portions of Orange and Rowan counties. The name honors Frederick, Lord North, Prime Minister of England and later Earl of Guilford. The first courthouse was built 5 miles northwest of Greensboro in 1774. Around it grew up the straggling village of Guilford Courthouse whose name, after the Revolution, was changed to Martinville in honor of Alexander Martin, Governor of North Carolina (1782-85; 1789-92), and delegate to the Constitutional Convention in Philadelphia. Of this village there is hardly a remaining trace.

Men from Guilford County played a prominent part in the Battle of Alamance in 1771, where Regulators clashed with Gov. Tryon's troops. Cornwallis, who invaded the county in 1781, suffered a Pyrrhic victory at the Battle of Guilford Courthouse on March 15. This battle proved to be the turning point of the Revolution in the South, paving the way for the Battle of Yorktown the following fall which resulted in American Independence. Such leaders as Colonels John Paisley, William Dent, and Arthur Forbis commanded troops recruited from the region.

After Rockingham and Randolph, originally part of Guilford, were set up as separate counties, Martinville was not centrally located. Accordingly, the general assembly in 1808 authorized commissioners to purchase and lay off a tract of 42 acres at the geographic center of the county on land purchased from Ralph Gorrell. The new town was named Greensboro, in honor of Gen. Nathanael Greene, commander of the colonial forces at Guilford Courthouse.

Two companies were recruited for the War of 1812. People of the county were generally opposed to secession in 1860, but when North Carolina took its stand with the Confederacy, 180 men marched away with the Guilford Grays, besides those who enlisted in other units. The city served as a Confederate depot for supplies and specie. Jefferson Davis, fleeing southward after the fall of Richmond, met Gen. J. E. Johnston here to decide on surrender to Sherman and also held here a meeting with his cabinet in April, 1865. Nearly 7,000 Confederate troops were paroled in Greensboro after the surrender.

Early in the 19th century there were factories for making chairs, carriages, wool and fur hats, and tobacco products. About 1833 the first steam cotton mill, the nucleus of the textile industry, was in operation.

After the Civil War, the Negro district known as Warnerville was founded by Yardley Warner, a Northern Quaker, who purchased 34 acres, divided the land into half-acre tracts, and sold them to the freedmen on liberal terms. In later years the land has been divided, added to, and resold.

Since 1890, when the city's population was 3,317, Greensboro's progress has been rapid. The Cone Mills (textile) were followed by other mills and factories, including Burlington Mills with home offices in Greensboro; Blue

Bell, the world's largest work-clothing manufacturers with home offices in Greensboro; J. P. Stevens & Company with southern offices in Greensboro; and Mojud Hosiery Company, Southern Webbing Mills, Blue Gem Overall Company, and others. Greensboro is also the home of Vick Chemical Company, world famous drug and cosmetics manufacturers. Other large industries are P. Lorillard and Company with the most modern cigarette factory in the world, Western Electric, Carolina Steel & Iron, and Truitt Manufacturing Companies. Greensboro is perhaps the largest insurance center in the South. Here are the home offices of the Jefferson Standard, Pilot, and Southern Life Insurance Companies.

Since Dr. David Caldwell established his "log college" classical school in 1767 in what is now Starmount Forest, Greensboro has encouraged learning. It now has 6 colleges in the city or immediate environs, three of them for Negroes. Minister, physician, teacher, and statesman, Dr. Caldwell served as a delegate to the first constitutional convention in Halifax in 1776. His log college had an enrollment of about 50 and served as "an academy, a college, and the theological seminary." From it were graduated men who became leaders in this and neighboring states. In 1838 the Greensboro Female Academy (Greensboro College) was founded, and other academies, boarding schools, and seminaries soon followed.

The Euterpe Club, organized in 1889 as the Coney Club, has helped develop music appreciation, and the Civic Music Association brings noted musicians to the city. Woman's College sponsors an annual North Carolina High School music contest. Well-trained glee clubs are maintained by the Woman's College, Greensboro College, and by two of the Negro colleges, Bennett and the Agricultural and Technical College.

William Sydney Porter (O. Henry, 1862-1910) was born in Greensboro and as a boy worked in a local drug store. About 1880 he was playing second violin in a string orchestra formed primarily for serenading the young women of Greensboro Female Academy. The *Greensboro Record* quoted an associate of Porter's: "I can see Will Porter right now with his foot on a stump and his fiddle across his knee saying to Charlie Collins, 'Charlie, gimme your A'.... One number we sure could play—the old Saltello Waltz—because we played it at every concert.... The funny thing about this waltz was that so far as we knew it had no stopping place, no end. We just kept on playing and playing until Charles Collins would say, 'Look out fellows, I'm going to stop!' "

Other literary figures associated with the city are Wilbur Daniel Steele (born in Greensboro in 1886), 4 times winner of the O. Henry Memorial Award, and Albion Winegar Tourgée, a prolific writer of Reconstruction days and a former Federal soldier who came to Greensboro in 1865, spent a decade there, and is best known for his *A Fool's Errand*. The Rev. Eli W. Caruthers, ante-bellum biographer and historian of the Revolution, and Calvin H. Wiley, author and first State superintendent of schools (1853), were important 19th century literary figures in Greensboro. Today, William T. Polk, Burke Davis, and Lettie Rogers carry on the literary tradition. Significant contributions are also made by faculty members of the Woman's

College. J. Larkin Pearson, poet laureate of the State, and Dorothy Gilbert, historian, are at nearby Guilford College.

Richard Berry Harrison, Negro actor who played "De Lawd" in Marc Connelly's play, *The Green Pastures*, was for 7 years head of the dramatic department at Agricultural and Technical College. Charles Winter Wood, his successor in the role and organizer of the first professional stock company for Negroes in America, was head of the drama department at Bennett College.

The celebrated radio commentator, Edward R. Murrow, was born and lived 6 years in the Center community south of Greensboro.

POINTS OF INTEREST

1. The JEFFERSON STANDARD LIFE INSURANCE COMPANY BUILDING (1923), Jefferson Sq., NW. corner Market and Elm Sts., is a 17-story structure of modified Gothic design and is the tallest building in the city. The top floor gives a panoramic view of the surrounding country.

2. The MASONIC TEMPLE (*open 9-11, 2-5, daily*), 426 W. Market St., is a two-story marble and granite structure of neoclassic architecture. It was built in 1926-28 by the Masonic Temple Company under the presidencies of J. E. Latham, James R. McClamroch, and Julian Price. A marker in front recalls that the building stands on the SITE OF O. HENRY'S BIRTHPLACE. The MASONIC MUSEUM, founded in 1933, contains Masonic relics.

3. The SHERWOOD HOME (*private*), 426 W. Gaston St., erected in 1843, is a red brick dwelling with white colonnaded portico, built for M. S. Sherwood, who once published the Greensboro *Patriot,* founded in 1826. William Swaim, a later editor, and his daughter, Mary—mother of O. Henry —lived here.

4. The main building at KEELEY INSTITUTE, 447 W. Washington St., is BLANDWOOD (*open; telephone for permission*), a rectangular two-story structure of gray stuccoed brick. At the entrance is a square flat-topped tower of three stories with arches in three sides of the first story. Built in 1825, Blandwood was originally the home of John Motley Morehead, Governor of North Carolina (1841-45). Gen. Pierre G. T. Beauregard and his staff, moving troops to join Lee in Virginia, were guests here for several days in 1865. In 1897 the house was converted into a sanitarium. The east and west wings were added in 1905.

5. GREENSBORO COLLEGE, main entrance on W. Market St. between S. Cedar St. and College Pl., is one of the oldest Methodist colleges for women in the world. Its ivy-colored brick buildings are set in a 25-acre, tree shaded campus. The present enrollment is about 400.

A year before the charter was obtained (1838) the trustees of the Greensboro Female College purchased 210 acres west of Greensboro, 40 of which they reserved, while the rest eventually was sold for nearly enough to pay the original purchase price. The cornerstone of the first building was laid

GREENSBORO
Scale of Miles

in 1843, and the school opened in 1846 with the Rev. Solomon Lea of Leasburg as head of the first faculty. After a disastrous fire in 1863 the school was rechartered in 1869, though not reopened until 1873.

The MAIN BUILDING (1904) is a three-story brick structure of wide proportions trimmed with white stone. From the central rotunda, supported by Doric columns and topped with a low open cupola, wings extend in three directions. FITZGERALD HALL, erected in 1912 and named for J. W. Fitzgerald, is a two-story brick building ornamented with three Doric porticoes. HUDSON HALL, built in 1917, a duplicate of Fitzgerald Hall, was named in honor of Mrs. Mary Lee Hudson. ODELL MEMORIAL BUILDING, containing the college auditorium (*open for school entertainments, etc.*), on College Pl. just off the campus, erected in 1922 by J. A. Odell in memory of his wife, Mary, is a two-story brick building with a Roman arched entrance. Atop the structure is a flat balustraded promenade. The most recent buildings are the JAMES ADDISON JONES LIBRARY (1950), the ARTS AND SCIENCE BUILDING (1950), and the HANNAH BROWN FINCH CHAPEL (1954).

6. The OLD BUMPASS HOME (*private*), 114 S. Mendenhall St., was erected in 1847 for the Rev. Sidney Bumpass, prominent Southern Methodist minister. The red brick structure of modified Georgian Colonial architecture is fronted by a portico with 4 limestone Doric columns and is shaded by great oaks. A Methodist paper, the *Weekly Message,* was published here, and the house was used for religious meetings. After the death of the Rev. Mr. Bumpass in 1857, his widow continued the work. Because of her active participation in the temperance movement, community betterment, and the religious life of the region, the section around this house became known as Piety Hill.

7. The WOMAN'S COLLEGE OF THE UNIVERSITY OF NORTH CAROLINA (*buildings open during school hours unless otherwise noted*), main entrance from Spring Garden St. on College St., is one of the largest women's colleges in the United States and has a 110-acre campus. It was founded by Dr. Charles D. McIver and opened in 1892 as the State Normal and Industrial School. Later it became known as the North Carolina College for Women, and, in 1931, it was made a unit of the University of North Carolina. The college, which confers 7 undergraduate degrees, is organized into the College of Liberal Arts, the School of Music, the School of Education, and the School of Home Economics.

A driveway runs (R) from College St. past the ADMINISTRATION BUILDING, constructed in 1892 of red brick with Mount Airy granite and limestone trim. Towerlike structures flanking the entrance and containing bay windows rise to the roof level where they terminate in low spires. The McIVER BUILDING, built in 1908, is a three-story structure of red brick with limestone trim. A pedimented two-story Ionic portico rises from the second-story level. The building contains lecture rooms, laboratories, and offices. On the front lawn is the life-size, bronze MONUMENT OF CHARLES DUNCAN McIVER, founder, a replica of the one on the capitol grounds at Raleigh.

The ALUMNAE BUILDING, erected in 1935 of red brick and marble trim, houses offices of the alumnae, student government association, and student publications. Three brick walks approach the marble entrance portico, adorned with Corinthian columns and a classic entablature.

SPENCER HALL, built in 1904, is a succession of red brick buildings trimmed with granite. On the Walker Ave. façade is a Georgian Colonial portal, and on the College St. side are gabled entrances with colonnaded porticoes and arched dormers.

West of the dormitory group is the new athletic field and the new COLEMAN GYMNASIUM (1951). The AYCOCK BUILDING (*open for chapel, lectures, plays, etc.*), corner Tate and Spring Garden Sts., contains offices and auditorium. The most recent buildings include the library (1950), home economics school (1951), Elliott Hall (Student Union, 1952), and the infirmary (1953).

8. The BUFFALO PRESBYTERIAN CHURCH, Church St. Ext. at northern city limits, commonly called Old Buffalo, was built in 1827, the third church on the site. The congregation was organized in 1756. The structure of handmade brick is of Southern post-Colonial architecture. It was originally designed as a one-story building, but space was added before the Civil War for a loft, just over the entrance, to be occupied by Negroes, and a portico with 4 white columns was erected across the front. The fine oaks surrounding the structure are older than the church. The old burying ground behind the church contains the graves of the first pastor, Dr. David Caldwell, Guilford County's first first-citizen, and other Revolutionary patriots including Col. Daniel Gillespie.

9. WORLD WAR STADIUM, on Bagley St. between Dudley St. and Park Ave., with seating capacity of 10,000, was erected by citizens of Guilford County in honor of local residents who lost their lives in World War I.

10. The CONE TEXTILE MILLS (*not open to public*) are situated in the northeastern section of the city, in a 2½ square-mile area north of E. Bessemer Ave. and east of N. Elm St. The Cone Mill Community, once outside the corporate limits, is now incorporated with the city. The mills, established in 1895 by Moses and Ceasar Cone, are Greensboro's largest industry, one of the most important textile-manufacturing groups in the South, and the largest denim mill in the world. In one year the mills produce enough denim to make 25,000,000 pairs of overalls, or if the strips were placed end to end, they would reach around the earth three times.

11. DUNLEITH (*private*), 677 Chestnut St., the home of Judge Robert P. Dick, built in 1857, stands in a beautiful grove of elms, oaks, cedars, and Norway pines. The white frame house is of three sections. The central towerlike portion contains the main entrance, a Georgian Colonial doorway with a fanlight and side lights. The portico, rising to the second story, is surmounted by an iron balustrade. There are two-story gabled wings, extending north and south from the central section.

Gen. William R. Cox occupied the residence for a period during the Civil War, when tents of Union soldiers dotted the spacious grounds. Robert P. Dick was a member of the North Carolina Supreme Court (1869-72) and later served as Federal district judge. For many years, with Judge John H. Dillard, he conducted a private law school.

12. CIVIC CENTER, Summit Ave. and Church St., reconstructed in 1938 from the old First Presbyterian Church and Smith Memorial Building, was presented to the city of Greensboro by Mrs. Lunsford Richardson, Sr., and her three daughters. The original tower and exterior of the church are preserved, and a new structure unites the two buildings to form a single

composition. The center houses the public library, art center, and historical museum, besides providing quarters for social welfare organizations.

The Presbyterian congregation was organized in 1824 with 4 slaves among the 12 original members. The building, erected in 1892, third on the site, was vacated in 1928 when a new church was built on Fisher Park Circle. The adjacent cemetery contains many old graves including that of the second pastor, John A. Gretter (d. 1853). The JOHN M. MOREHEAD MONUMENT marks the grave of this prominent citizen who became governor.

The GREENSBORO PUBLIC LIBRARY (*open 9-6, weekdays*) includes a valuable collection of books on North Carolina with full sets of Colonial and State records and the complete O. Henry collection of C. Alphonso Smith. In the latter is an original manuscript.

The GREENSBORO HISTORICAL MUSEUM, the largest and finest in the State except the State Museum in Raleigh, was organized in 1924. It contains a pioneer room of Indian and colonial relics; items from the Battle of Guilford Courthouse; and relics of all the wars in which the United States has participated. There is also a replica of the Porter Drug Store (with many original furnishings) in which O. Henry worked.

13. The AGRICULTURAL & TECHNICAL COLLEGE OF NORTH CAROLINA (*Negro, coed.*), a standard 4-year college, occupies a 28-acre campus lying between Laurel, Dudley, Lindsay, and E. Market Sts. The institution was established in 1891 by an act of the general assembly for the instruction of Negroes in agriculture and the mechanical arts. The course was later expanded to include the liberal arts. The present enrollment is 4350, with a faculty of 250.

The buildings, two and three stories in height, are of brick with sandstone trim, arched doorways, balconies, and balustrades. By World War II, the college had made such conspicuous progress that it was among the first Negro institutions to be used by the various branches of the Federal government for defense and war training programs. Today an army ROTC and an air ROTC unit are maintained here. Since 1949, 17 major buildings have been authorized by the State. Included among these are the modern, functional LIBRARY (1954); the ENGINEERING BUILDING (1954); W. KERR SCOTT HALL (1951), which houses 1010 students; and the CHARLES A. HINES HALL (1950), the chemistry building.

14. BENNETT COLLEGE (*Negro, women*), on E. Washington and Gorrell Sts., between Macon and Bennett Sts., occupies a beautiful landscaped campus of 40 acres. Established as Bennett Seminary in 1874 by the Methodist Church, the institution became Bennett College (*coed.*) in 1889, and Bennett College for Women in 1926. It was named for Lyman Bennett of Troy, N. Y., its first benefactor. The college has a capital endowment of over a million dollars, an enrollment of 500, and is a member of the Association of American Colleges. The A.B. and B.S. degrees are conferred. The Bennett College Dramatic Club has won a reputation for the excellence of its presentations, and the glee club frequently makes public appearances.

The Georgian, brick buildings, most of them built since 1922, include the Thomas F. Holgate Library (1939), the Annie Merner Pfeiffer Chapel, and the Student Union.

15. OUR LADY OF GRACE CHURCH (Roman Catholic), SE. corner W. Market and Chapman Sts., was given (1950-52) by Julian Price and his children as a memorial gift in honor of Mrs. Ethel Clay Price. The architect, Henry V. Murphy, of Brooklyn, N. Y., followed a free rendering of the French Gothic style. The structural material is Salisbury granite. Pyramided against the sky is the graceful tower surmounted by a delicate lead-over-steel fleche that rises 116 feet above the street level.

The interior walls are done in a golden buff blend of face brick. The stained windows made in Canada are of pastel colors giving a bright, cheerful illumination. The main altar, shrines, and baptismal font are of white Carrara marble; the floor of the sanctuary is made of Vermont marble. The interior is distinguished by wood carvings depicting various church and architectural symbols. Conspicuous in the sanctuary is an episcopal throne and kneeling bench, formerly used by Cardinal Gibbons in the Baltimore Cathedral.

Just east of the church, the parochial school, designed by the Rev. Michael McInerney, Benedictine Monk of Belmont Abbey, harmonizes with the adjacent church.

High Point

Information Services: Chamber of Commerce, 329 N. Main St.; Carolina Motor Club, 116 College St.

Railroad Stations: W. High and S. Main Sts., for Southern Ry.; High Point, Randleman, Asheboro, & Southern R.R.; High Point, Thomasville and Denton R.R. *(freight only).*

Bus Station: Union Terminal, 100 Lindsay St., for Carolina Trailways, Atlantic Greyhound, and Queen City Coach Co.

City Buses: Along regular routes.

Airport: Greensboro-High Point, US 311 to NC 68, R. **9 m.** to Friendship, R. on US 421, **0.6 m.**, for Eastern, Capital, and Piedmont Airlines.

Radio Stations: WMFR (1230), WMFR-FM (99.5), WHPE (1070), WHPE-FM (95.5), WNOS (1590), WNOS-FM (100.3).

Newspaper: High Point Enterprise (daily & Sun.).

Educational Institutions: High Point College (coed.).

Swimming: City Park Lake, **1.5 m.** E. on US 29-70; Negro Park, Gordon St.

Golf: Emerywood Country Club, Country Club Dr. and Hillcrest Dr., 9 holes; Blair Park links *(municipal)*, S. Main St. (US 311) at city limits, 9 holes; Sedgefield Country Club, **8 m.** E. on US 29-70, 18 holes.

Tennis: Blair Park, S. Main St. at city limits; City Lake Park, Jamestown; Negro Park, Gordon St.

Hunting and Fishing: Quail, dove, and squirrel hunting in season, inquire Chamber of Commerce; fishing at City Lake Park.

Riding: Sedgefield Riding Academy, **8 m.** E. on US 29-70.

Shooting: Skeet Club, **5 m.** W. on US 311.

Annual Events: Southern Furniture Exposition *(open to trade only)*, Jan. and July.

HIGH POINT (940 alt., 39,973 pop.), an industrial center on a level plateau in the piedmont, is known chiefly for its large-scale production of furniture and hosiery. The city, rectangular in shape, is divided north and south by railroad tracks, and east and west by the 100-foot-wide Main Street, with the railroad station in the center.

On Main Street, from the railroad crossing, the retail business section extends for several blocks on both sides of the tracks. On the northwest in Emerywood, a recent development with landscaped grounds, are many of the finer homes. The streets of the city are shaded by great oaks and elms extending to the outer edges of the business section. Scattered about the city are 15 parks with a total of 132 acres.

Covering about 4 square miles on the south are scores of furniture factories, hosiery and silk mills, and other manufacturing plants. One of the cotton mills has its own village containing small modern cottages for the factory workers, churches, community buildings, and playgrounds.

Uptown streets show constant activity, for this industrial community is visited by salesmen, buyers, and factory representatives. Several large conventions are held here every year. On Friday and Saturday afternoons the streets take on a carnival appearance and sidewalks are jammed with pedestrian traffic.

The city's 7,946 Negroes, 20% of the city's total population, live in scattered sections on East Washington St., Kivett Drive, Welch St., Fairview St., and on Burns Hill, where many own their own homes. They have a well-equipped park on Gordon St. in the eastern part of town.

The High Point area was originally settled by Quakers about 1750, but the town was not laid out until 1853 when the State-built North Carolina Railroad was brought through. In that year Solomon Kendall sold part of his farm for $5,000 for a town site which was laid out exactly square, two miles long and two miles wide. So intent were the surveyors on making the town of precise dimensions that they ran the eastern boundary "through the doors of Jane Parson's house."

The new village was named "High Point," because it was the highest point on the railroad line between Goldsboro and Charlotte. It soon became an important trading center with completion in 1854 of the plank road between Salem and Fayetteville. This road, 130 miles long, followed part of the old Indian trail and pioneer wagon road from the mountains to the Cape Fear River and was the most important highway in the State. Mileposts were placed along the west side of the road, with the mile numbers carved instead of painted, so night travelers could feel the figures. One of the old mileposts is in the Quaker Museum at Springfield Meetinghouse.

High Point was incorporated in 1859 and soon became the trading center of surrounding farm communities. In the 1880's it had two tobacco factories and three warehouses, but this industry was overshadowed by its rapid expansion in neighboring cities. In 1888 furniture manufacturers were attracted by the abundance of hardwood timber available, and the quiet country town quickly changed into a modern industrial center. Since then the population has increased manyfold. The city limits were extended in 1923.

High Point's Negroes were at first employed in the tobacco plants. In later years large numbers were attracted from Georgia and South Carolina by an expanding program of local public works. Many are now engaged in business and professions. In 1891 the Society of Friends founded a school to provide education for Negroes.

POINTS OF INTEREST

1. The GIANT BUREAU (*open 8-12, 1-5 weekdays*), 508 N. Hamilton St., symbolizing the city's position as a furniture-manufacturing center, was formerly the office of the Chamber of Commerce. It was built in 1925 of wood painted white, is 32 feet high, 27 feet long, and 14 feet wide. A square screen on the top represents a mirror. The front of the building is designed to simulate a bureau with drawers and knobs. This building was presented to the Junior Chamber of Commerce by the Chamber of Commerce in 1951.

2. The WORLD WAR MEMORIAL, W. Broad and College Sts., a gift to the city by Mr. and Mrs. M. J. Wrenn, was sculptured in Italy by Maurecinni from stone quarried at Flatresanti, and erected in 1923. The statue is of a soldier, facing west. On the base are names of High Point men who served in World War I.

3. The HIGH POINT PUBLIC LIBRARY (*open 9-9 weekdays*), S. Main St., is next to YMCA.

4. The SOUTHERN FURNITURE EXPOSITION BUILDING (*open to trade only*), 209 S. Main St., now occupies the entire width of the block between Main and Wrenn Sts. and contains almost half a million square feet of floor space. The original 10-story, red brick structure, trimmed in granite, limestone, and marble, was built in 1921. Four stories were added in 1940 and the new million-dollar 10-story addition was completed in July, 1950. Its floor space is rented to furniture manufacturers who maintain permanent exhibits there and who twice a year, in Jan. and July, bring out their new lines for inspection and sale.

5. OAKWOOD CEMETERY, at the N. end of Steele St., contains the graves of many Confederate soldiers. Here is the GRAVE OF LAURA WESSON, called the Florence Nightingale of the Civil War. As a girl in her teens she enrolled as a nurse in the Wayside Hospital, where 5,000 Confederate soldiers were treated. When a smallpox epidemic broke out, Laura Wesson served the segregated patients until she contracted the disease and died (April 25, 1865).

6. The JOHNSON FARMHOUSE (*private*), 102 Louise Ave., bears the date of construction (1824) on an original chimney. Although additions have been built, much of the old house, with its low beamed ceilings, remains. The two-story, white frame residence has a portico with 10 Doric columns arranged in clusters of two and three. Old elms, magnolias, and large boxwoods grace the lawn.

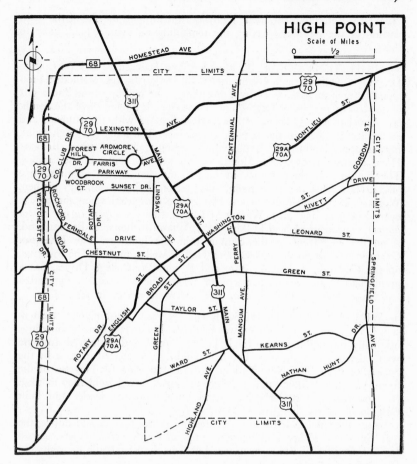

Across the street, on a site occupied by an apartment house, was Johnson's Camping Ground. Its position on the plank road between Fayetteville and Salem made it popular with travelers in the early 19th century. Around a blazing campfire news of the day was exchanged, ballads and hymns were sung, and horses and other chattels were swapped. Construction of railroads put an end to the camping grounds.

7. On the SITE OF WELCH'S INN, 1425 E. Lexington Ave., a section of the original building remains. Probably used as a dining room, it is now a residence (*private*). The oblong building of hand-made brick, erected in 1786, has a single story with gabled roof. Welch's Inn was a tavern on the stagecoach road from Raleigh to Salisbury during the early 1800's and was noted for its comfortable beds and palatable food. A sign proclaimed

"J. Welch, Entertainment." The highway runs through the site of the main portion of the building, leaving the remaining ell upon a bank close to the road.

8. HIGH POINT COLLEGE, Montlieu Ave. between E. and W. College Dr., was established as a coeducational institution by the Methodist Protestant Church in 1920, aided by a donation to the building fund and a gift of 52 acres by the city of High Point. The college is a member of the Southern Association of Colleges and Secondary Schools with 680 students and 40 faculty members in the 1953-54 school year. The long, red brick buildings occupy a landscaped campus with winding walks and drives. ROBERTS HALL, erected in 1922, faces Montlieu Ave., near the center of the campus. The building is three stories in height and houses the administrative offices, classrooms, assembly room, laboratories, dining room, and kitchen. WOMAN'S HALL and McCULLOCH HALL were completed when the college opened in 1924. The M. J. WRENN MEMORIAL LIBRARY (*open during school hours*), erected in 1936-37 by Mrs. M. J. Wrenn in honor of her husband, is on the east front of the campus near the highway. The HARRISON GYMNASIUM, just north of McCulloch Hall, is well equipped. The STADIUM, on the field near Lexington Ave. and E. and W. College Drives, has a grandstand with a seating capacity of 3,000. The MEMORIAL AUDITORIUM AND MUSIC HALL and the SCIENCE BUILDING were erected in 1953-54.

9. WILLIAM PENN HIGH SCHOOL (Negro), Washington St. extension 0.5 m. from center of city, was established in 1923 when the buildings originally belonging to the High Point Normal and Industrial Institute were taken over by the city. The first building was erected in 1892 by the Society of Friends of New York to provide education for Negroes of the town. James A. Griffin, the first Negro principal, served from 1897 to 1923. In 1900 the men students made and burned 200,000 bricks and built Congdon Hall for the girls.

Before the Civil War the site was used as a slave market and during the war, for Camp Fisher, mobilization camp for Confederate soldiers, named for Col. Charles E. Fisher, who was killed in the first Battle of Manassas. Four regiments were trained here.

10. BLAIR PARK, S. Main St. at city limits, 86 acres in area, includes the municipal golf course, clubhouse tennis courts, and children's playgrounds. The land was a gift to the city of High Point by the Blair family.

11. The original LOG HOUSE of the Blair family, S. Main St. at city limits, stands across the highway from Blair Park, adjacent to the present Blair home. Erected in 1798, the house remains as first built except for a brick chimney and new floors.

New Bern

Information Service: Chamber of Commerce, 301 Hancock St.

Guide Service: Chamber of Commerce and the Attmore-Oliver House, 513 Broad St. (US 17).

Railroad Station: Hancock and Queen Sts., for Atlantic Coast Line, Norfolk Southern, and Atlantic and East Carolina R. R.

Bus Station: 812 Broad St., for Seashore Transportation Co.

Airport: Simmons-Nott Municipal, **1.5 m.** E. of city (US 70), for National and Piedmont Lines.

Waterways: 12 ft. mean channel, Neuse and Trent Rivers.

Radio Stations: WHIT (1450), WOOW (1490).

Newspaper: Sun Journal (daily).

Golf: New Bern Golf & Country Club, **4 m.** W. on Pembroke Rd.

Swimming: Trent Pines Club, river beaches at Minnesott (**25 m.** E., NC 55).

Hunting and Fishing: Inquire Chamber of Commerce.

Boating: Eastern Carolina Yacht Club.

Annual Events: Motor Boat Races, Beagle Dog Trials, Garden Tours.

NEW BERN (18 alt., 15,812 pop.), the second oldest town in North Carolina, retains the flavor of past centuries. Spread across a bluff at the confluence of the Neuse and Trent rivers, 35 miles from the Atlantic Ocean, it has an atmosphere of charm based primarily on its distinctive architecture. Massive brick town houses, stately Georgian residences, and wistaria-laden clapboard cottages line narrow streets shaded by oaks, poplars, elms, and pecan trees. Many of the old streets retain their original brick pavements. Along residential East Front St. are old homes, three lines of arching trees, and a wide promenade along the Neuse River sea wall.

Named for Bern, Switzerland, the city was settled in 1710 by a colony of German Palatines, some Swiss, and a few English, who were seeking religious, political, and industrial freedom and advancement in the New

World. Under the leadership of the Swiss Baron Christopher de Graffenried, and aided by a gift of £4,000 from Queen Anne of England, two ships with about 650 colonists were sent out in January, 1710. John Lawson, Surveyor General of Carolina and author of *A New Voyage to Carolina,* 1709, and Christopher Gale, to be chief justice of the State in 1712, were in charge. As a result of storms, disease, and the capture of one of the ships by a French vessel in Chesapeake Bay, only a sickly remnant reached the Chowan River, where Thomas Pollock, a wealthy planter, provided "certain necessaries" and transportation to the future New Bern.

In September, 1710, de Graffenried himself arrived with 156 Swiss. He purchased 17,500 acres from the Lords Proprietors at 20 cents an acre and also recompensed King Taylor, Tuscarora Indian chief, and John Lawson, the Surveyor General. The town was laid out, probably by Lawson, with the principal streets "in the form of a cross, one arm extending from river to river, and the other, from the point, back indefinitely."

In September, 1711, the settlement was almost wiped out by a Tuscarora uprising. Lawson and de Graffenried were taken to the Indian fort, Nohoroco, where Lawson was executed and de Graffenried held prisoner for 6 months until ransomed. The war raged intermittently for two years, and the colonists were reduced to such desperation that in 1713 many of them returned with de Graffenried to Switzerland.

The settlement made a new start under the leadership of Col. Thomas Pollock, Proprietary Governor (1712-14, 1722), who had acquired de Graffenried's interests. In 1723 it was incorporated as a town and made the seat of Craven County, named for William, Earl of Craven, one of the Lords Proprietors.

Sessions of the colonial assembly met here from 1745 to 1761, with the exception of 1752 and from 1770-74 it was the seat of the royal governors. In July, 1774, Col. John Harvey, speaker of the House of Commons, and other Cape Fear leaders called an extra-legal convention to meet in New Bern, August 25. This First Provincial Congress, the first anywhere in America to be called and held in defiance of British orders, met in Tryon's Palace and elected Harvey moderator. It "fully launched North Carolina into the revolutionary movement," declaring that "any act of Parliament imposing a tax is illegal and unconstitutional," by adopting a nonexportation agreement, and by electing William Hooper, Richard Caswell, and Joseph Hewes as delegates to the First Continental Congress. The following April, the royal governor, Josiah Martin, ordered dissolution of the assembly and Second Provincial Congress, which also met in Tryon's Palace, fled aboard a British man-of-war, thereby ending royal rule in North Carolina.

After the Revolution shipbuilding became an important activity, and timber, iron, and rope were produced locally. Race tracks, fox hunts, and balls made New Bern noted for its gay social life. Trade was carried on chiefly with the New England ports of Salem and Boston; exports consisted mostly of leaf tobacco, molasses, lumber, and naval stores. The Bank of New Bern was chartered by the assembly in 1804.

Such commerce perhaps explains the late 18th-century character of many

New Bern houses, which have been preserved through a series of favorable circumstances. The town was spared the ravages of the Civil War because of continued Federal occupation after Gen. Ambrose E. Burnside's defeat of Confederate Gen. L. O'Bryan Branch on Mar. 14, 1862. Unsuccessful attempts to retake the town were made Mar. 14, 1863, and Feb. 1 and 5, 1864. New Bern also escaped the effects of rapid progress. With the advent of the railroad in 1858, its importance as a port and distributing point declined and it gradually subsided into a placid river port. A 40-block, three-day fire in 1922 was confined to the Negro section.

New Bern has many small industries, including lumber, boat building, needle trades, plywood, machine and foundry, dairy products, wood-working, tobacco processing, printing, silk screening of textiles, chemical, canning plants, fertilizer, feed mills, grain storage elevators, and meat packing. Nearby waters afford year-round fishing and there is good hunting for duck, goose, quail, turkey, deer, bear, squirrel, opossum, rabbits, and other game. New Bern is connected with the Intracoastal Waterway by the Neuse River.

Prominent early citizens include Richard Dobbs Spaight and his son of the same name, and Abner Nash, governors; Martin Howard, provincial chief justice (1767-73), who presided at all the Regulator trials; and Elizabeth Shine, mother of Admiral David G. Farragut. Later figures were William Gaston, eminent jurist and orator; Gabriel and George W. Rains, prominent Confederate officers; and Furnifold M. Simmons, U. S. Senator (1901-31). John Cook, brought to the town as a slave in 1805 and later freed, devoted his life to charitable works. Upon his death in 1856 he was buried in the white cemetery and a monument raised to his memory by popular subscription. His body was moved to Greenwood Cemetery in 1916.

Negroes, who represent 42.7 % of the city's population, work in the mills, on the farms, and in domestic service, though a few are engaged in business and professional activities. The first public schools for Negroes in North Carolina were established at New Bern in 1862, when soldiers of a New England regiment volunteered as teachers.

POINTS OF INTEREST

The city has identified its points of interest with numbers and signs of the Bear of Bern. These numbers are indicated in parentheses.

1. (1) UNION POINT, E. Front and S. Front Sts., the juncture of the Neuse and Trent rivers, is where King Taylor of the Tuscarora Indians is said to have lived with his tribe at a village they called "Chattawka," from which the now-famous Chautauqua, N. Y., derived its name. At this point, de Graffenried erected a government house and fort in 1710. The site was converted into a public park by the Woman's Club, in cooperation with the city. The Woman's Clubhouse there is used for club and civic affairs.

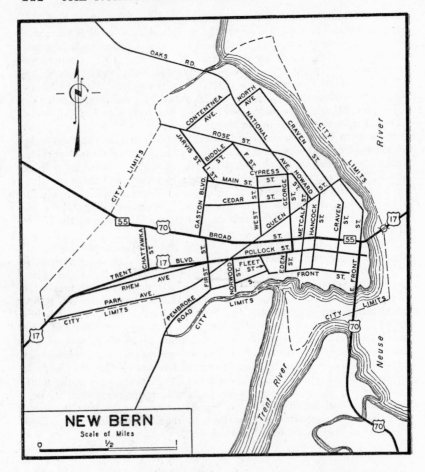

NEW BERN
Scale of Miles
0   ½   1

2.   (2) SITE OF TREATY TREE, E. Front and Pollock Sts., is the spot, tradition relates, where de Graffenried and the Indians made an important treaty under a live oak tree, which was burned in the great fire of 1842. On the southeast corner stands the SIMPSON-DUFFY HOUSE (*private*), built for Samuel Simpson about 1810 and originally like the adjoining Sparrow-Daniels residence. In the late 1860's Capt. Appleton Oaksmith, shipper and trader, bought the place, redesigned it after Morro Castle, Havana, Cuba, and placed over the Pollock St. entrance a stone panel, carved with the figureheads of a woman and two lions. An interesting myth ascribes the panel to de Graffenried and the woman's head as a representation of Queen Anne, with whom he was supposedly in love. During the Civil War, the residence was used by the Federal provost marshal as an office and guard house.

3. (3) HASLEN-WEST HOUSE (*private*), 305 E. Front St., now modernized and improved, was formerly a brick kitchen for the former Haslen mansion started in 1761 on the corner lot. Considered the oldest brick house still standing in the town, the kitchen has been converted into a Dutch-type house of two stories with a gambrel roof. John Bird Sumner, later Archbishop of Canterbury (1848-62), is said to have stayed there while on a visit with his mother, Dr. Haslen's sister.

4. (4) FIRST PRINTING PRESS, E. Front and Broad Sts., was long operated on this site, having been moved from Pollock St., adjoining the Episcopal Church. Here James Davis, the first State printer, soon after setting up his press in 1749, printed the first newspaper, the first pamphlet, and the first book in the province.

5. (7) HISTORIC CANNON, E. Front River Shore, unearthed several years ago in the center of town, is believed to be one of the originals from Tryon's Palace. Across the street on the corner is the HOME OF FURNIFOLD M. SIMMONS, U. S. Senator (1901-1931). The FIRST POST ROAD from New England to Charleston over which mail was first carried regularly in North Carolina, 1738-39, passed near this spot.

6. (8) EMORY-BISHOP-BREWER HOUSE (*private*), NW. corner E. Front and New Sts., now modernized, is said to have been the residence of James Coor, talented architect and prominent statesman. Pres. James Monroe and Vice-Pres. John C. Calhoun were entertained here in 1819 when it was owned by wealthy Sir George Pollock. Later it was the home of Matthias Manly, Supreme Court Justice of N. C. (1860-65). Dormer windows and broad porches have been added and small-paned windows replaced with single-paned ones. The interior hand-carved mahogany staircase, cornices, and wainscot are retained.

7. (9) GULL HARBOR (*private*), E. Front and Short Sts., the Tilghman-Justice home, was frequently visited by Elizabeth Shine, born June 7, 1765, in the section, and mother of Admiral David Glasgow Farragut (1801-70), famous naval hero.

8. (10) The SITE OF THE JOSEPH LEECH HOME, SW. corner E. Front and Change Sts., is identified by a marker. Col. Leech (1720-1803) was a member of the First Provincial Congress, the General Assembly, the Council of Safety, and the State Constitutional convention, as well as State treasurer, custodian of Tryon's Palace, and mayor of New Bern during Washington's visit.

9. (12) The LOUISIANA HOUSE or VAIL-MOULTON HOME (*private*), NW. corner E. Front and Change Sts., a wooden dwelling built in 1776, originally had in the rear a double porch similar to the one still in the front, resembling ancient structures in Louisiana. William Attmore, a Philadelphia merchant, wrote in 1787 that "this Method of Building is found convenient on account of the great Summer Heats here." Mary Bayard Devereux Clark, poet, lived here until her death in 1886.

10. (13) The SMALLWOOD-WARD HOUSE (*private*), 95 E. Front St., built about 1815, has definite affinities to Connecticut buildings and is listed in New York as a perfect type of Georgian architecture. Constructed of red brick, laid in Flemish bond, the house has beautiful wood carving in the slender, pedimented porticoes, interior cornices, and mantels. The front and side porches are considered the finest of all the beautiful New Bern porches. The interior is noted for its broad stair hall, whose winding stair is cut from the entrance hall by a graceful elliptical arch. On the first floor are the counting room, now used as a drawing room, and the dining room. On the second floor are two bedrooms and the original drawing room converted into a bedroom. The chair rails and pedimented overmantels in the dining and drawing rooms display exceptional craftsmanship. The nautical rope molding in the cornices and door trim gives credence to the theory that James Coor, an English naval architect, is responsible for much of this work.

Under the CYPRESS TREE (11), at rear of house, near Neuse River, Indian treaties and Revolutionary parleys were held. One of the first ships built in North Carolina was launched within the tree's shadow. George Washington, Edward Everett, and other notables have viewed the river from under this thousand-year-old cypress, one of 20 trees in the Hall of Fame of American Trees.

11. (14) JARVIS-SLOVER-HAND HOUSE (*open to public*), E. Front at Johnson Sts., is another fine brick, Georgian Colonial house, built about 1811 and bought by Moses Jarvis in 1812. The house has a notable sheltered and recessed doorway, 46-inch wide doors, 7-inch keys, and distinguished hand-carved interior woodwork. Now an antique shop, it was used during the Civil War by Federal Staff officers, including Gen. John G. Foster.

12. SLOVER-GUION HOUSE (*private*), SW. corner E. Front and Johnson Sts., erected 1838 and said to have taken three years for construction, this early Republican house served as Dept. Headquarters for Federal Gen. A. E. Burnside and other local commanders of the Federal Dept. of N. C., after their capture of New Bern on March 14, 1862. Its modernized antique brick kitchen and slave house in the rear yard on E. Front St. is now the Bynum home.

13. (17) RICHARDSON or CAPTAIN'S WALK HOUSE (*private*), SE. corner Johnson and Craven Sts., dating back to 1838, is a massive 4-story frame house, with a captain's walk, also called a catwalk, or widow's walk. The railed platform between the chimneys, reached by a trap door in the roof, was used to sight approaching ships. During the Civil War it was used as a hospital for the 9th N. J. Infantry and as barracks for Company B, 45th Mass. Regiment.

14. The JERKINS-DUFFY HOUSE (*private*), SW. corner Johnson and Craven Sts., occupies a lot once owned by Dr. Alexander Gaston, father of William Gaston (1778-1844), N. C. Supreme Court Justice, composer of the State song "The Old North State," and the man largely responsible for

the constitutional amendment (1835), permitting Catholics to hold State offices. Gastonia and Gaston County are named for him.

The white clapboard house, built about 1818, is L-shaped in plan. It has an entrance with carved pediment and fanlight, flanked by slender columns and approached by shallow steps on both sides. A captain's walk is between the chimneys at the west end of the house.

15. (19) The COOR-GASTON-WALKER HOUSE (*private*), SW. corner Craven and New Sts., is an unusual L-shaped house with verandas possessing Chinese Chippendale balustrades. Built by James Coor soon after he acquired the land in 1767, it may have been designed by John Hawks, architect of Tryon's Palace. This was the home of N. C. Supreme Court Justice William Gaston for many years. In the rear yard stood his law office, now moved to a lot adjoining City Hall.

16. On the COURTHOUSE LAWN, W. side of Craven, between New and Broad Sts., is the WASHINGTON OAK (20), planted in 1925 as a memorial of Washington's visit, and a MARKER (21) with bronze memorial tablets to the three New Bernians, who were state governors: Richard Dobbs Spaight, Richard Dobbs Spaight, the younger, and Abner Nash, all three of whom are buried across the Trent River. Inside the courthouse are portraits of the first Richard Dobbs Spaight; the Earl of Craven, the Lord Proprietor for whom the county was named; and other distinguished leaders. On the west lawn is a memorial shaft erected Nov. 12, 1944, to Craven citizens who died in World Wars I and II.

17. (21A) WILLIAM GASTON OFFICE, on lot adjoining City Hall, originally stood near his home on Craven St. It has been recently reconstructed by the New Bern Garden Club in cooperation with the N. C. Garden Club.

18. (22) CITY HALL (*open 9-5 weekdays*), NW. corner Craven and Pollock Sts. (erected as a post office in 1897, remodeled in 1935) is of yellow brick trimmed with terra cotta. Over its arched entrances are two copper black bears, symbols of the town. Inside hangs a framed bear banner, gift of the Burgesses of Bern, Switzerland, in 1896, after New Bern had adopted the armorial bearings and colors of the patron city. Here also are original parchment grants to de Graffenried, who was given the title of "Landgrave of Carolina and Baron of Bernburg."

19. (24) TAYLOR-WARD HOUSE (*private*), 228 Craven St., built 1792 for Isaac Taylor, this brick residence has a graceful doorway, beautiful interior woodwork, and rare recessed window seats. It was 45th Mass. Regimental Headquarters during the Civil War.

20. (25) GASTON HOTEL, S. Front between Craven and Middle Sts., is one of the oldest hotels in continuous service in the South. Honoring William Gaston, its original name was Gaston House in 1855, then was changed to The Chattawka, the name of the early Indian settlement. The arch at the right of the entrance used to be a driveway for stage coaches.

21. (26) FIRST BAPTIST CHURCH, Middle St. between S. Front and Pollock Sts., a Gothic Revival brick structure, was built in 1848, though the congregation was organized in 1809. Meredith College, Raleigh, N. C., and Furman University, Greenville, S. C., took their names from former local pastors, the Reverends Thomas Meredith and Richard Furman, Jr. *The Biblical Recorder,* State Baptist publication, was started here Jan. 5, 1835, by Meredith. William Hooper, a leader in founding Wake Forest College and its second president, and Samuel Wait, its first president, were also pastors here. The church was enlarged and redecorated in 1942-43 and again redecorated following a fire in 1947. President Harry Truman worshipped here Nov. 7, 1948, the first Sunday after his triumph in the election.

22. (27) CHRIST EPISCOPAL CHURCH, Pollock and Middle Sts., erected in 1873 upon the site of two earlier churches, is a weathered red brick edifice with a lofty, gold-crowned spire. The parish was organized in 1715, and the first church was built in 1750. George II gave the parish a silver communion service, Bible, and prayer book in 1752. The grave of the first rector, James Reed, early advocate of public schools, is in the churchyard. There is a tradition that when he prayed for George III, lads, prompted by patriot parents, drummed at the door and shouted "Off with his head!" The church was razed during the Revolution, reputedly because the brick had been brought from England. The second church was erected in 1825, and its outer walls were used to construct the present building. Two dioceses have been organized here: North Carolina in 1817 and East Carolina in 1887. Extensive repairs were made in 1949 to the church, parish house, and church school building.

In a corner of the churchyard fence is the LADY BLESSINGTON CANNON (28), taken from the British ship, *Lady Blessington,* captured during the Revolution by a privateer belonging to John Wright Stanly, New Bern patriot.

23. (29) SITE OF OLD COURTHOUSE and MARKET HOUSE, Middle and Broad Sts., is the spot where, on May 31, 1775, patriots adopted resolutions pledging their support to the cause of independence. At the May term of court, 1786, the celebrated case of *Bayard vs. Singleton,* was decided. This was the first decision ever handed down under a written constitution which declared a legislative act unconstitutional. This principle, applied by Chief Justice John Marshall in *Marbury vs. Madison* in 1803, is now a fundamental principle of American law.

24. (31) FEDERAL BUILDING, SW. corner Middle and New Sts., erected in 1933-35, of Colonial design, is on the original site of the John Wright Stanly home. New Bern had the first postal service in N. C. The first post office in the State under the Republic was started here June 1, 1790, with Francis Xavier Martin as postmaster. Murals in the courtroom (*open in court season or upon request*) depict the Bayard case, de Graffenried and the Old World settlers, Davis and the first printing press, and the first provincial convention.

25. (33) ST. PAUL'S ROMAN CATHOLIC CHURCH, Middle St. between New and Johnson Sts., was erected in 1841. The parish, the first of the Catholic faith in the State, was organized in 1821, comprising about all east Carolina. Cardinal Gibbons often visited here while Bishop of North Carolina. Father Thomas F. Price, local priest, founded the Catholic orphanage at Raleigh and the American Foreign Missionary Society at Mary Knoll, N. Y.

26. (36) JOHN WRIGHT STANLY HOUSE, New St., between Middle and Hancock Sts., now a PUBLIC LIBRARY and MUSEUM, was "almost certainly designed" by John Hawks, the architect of Tryon's Palace, according to the architect Waterman. Built, probably in the 1770's on the lot now occupied by the Federal Building, it was moved to its present site and remodeled in 1935-36 by the New Bern Library Association. Closely resembling Hudson River mansions, it has no counterpart in the State. The main block of the frame house with its corner quoins and flush siding is rectangular in plan with a continuous cornice. The door and lower windows are pedimented. Its Georgian hip roof has three hipped dormers and a flat deck, surrounded by a balustrade. The stairway, with balustrade and baroque Chippendale brackets of walnut or mahogany, is considered the finest in North Carolina of the period.

This was the home of John Wright Stanly, merchant and patriot, who supposedly lost 14 privateers in the Revolution. Washington spent two nights here in 1791. It was also the home of Stanly's son, John Stanly, State legislator and congressman, and the birthplace (1817) of John Stanly's grandson, Brig. Gen. Lewis Addison Armistead, who led his brigade of Pickett's division in the charge at Gettysburg in 1863 and was killed at the peak of the Confederate advance. This was also Gen. Burnsides' first headquarters in New Bern.

27. (37) FIRST PRESBYTERIAN CHURCH, New St., opposite the Stanly House, was supposedly built by Uriah Sandy (1819-22), while the congregation was organized in 1817 by John Witherspoon, a grandson of a signer of the Declaration of Independence. This white weatherboarded meetinghouse, with fanlighted door, a graceful Ionic portico, and a square tower diminishing in 5 stages to an octagonal cupola, has a hand-carved pulpit and a sloping floor. Mrs. Eunice Hunt, a charter member, was the daughter of the great Congregational minister, Jonathan Edwards. This is the oldest Presbyterian organization and church building in any town in eastern North Carolina. The original church deed and communion service and other relics are preserved.

28. (38) NEW BERN ACADEMY, New and Hancock Sts., housing a section of the city schools, is a late Georgian Colonial structure, erected in 1806 on the site of the original building burned in 1795. The classic semicircular entrance portico was restored in 1935. New Bern Academy, the first incorporated school in the State, opened in 1764 and received its charter in 1766. It was partially maintained by a tax of a cent a gallon

on all liquors brought up the Neuse River. The high school building is named for Moses Griffin, who in 1816 left property for the education of needy boys and girls, one of the earliest of such bequests.

29. (39) MASONIC TEMPLES and THEATER (*open 9-12, 1-5 daily*), Hancock at Johnson Sts., form a rare combination of the old and the new. The old Masonic Temple, completed in 1808, is one of the oldest still in use. The brick building of Classical Revival architecture has a shallow surface arch of elliptical outline in the stuccoed wall, corner quoins, and prominent voussoirs over the flat-arched windows. The second-floor lodge room contains notable hand-carved paneling and Masonic relics. St. John's Lodge, No. 3, A. F. and A. M. was chartered Jan. 10, 1772, by Joseph Montfort, only Provincial grand master for America. The MASONIC THEATER on the first floor is the oldest theater still operating in the U. S.; it has been used regularly since 1805. In the rear is the SITE OF THE DUEL (Sept. 5, 1802) between Gov. Richard Dobbs Spaight, the elder, and John Stanly, the younger. Their frequent clashes, as rival leaders of the Republican and Federalist parties, led to a duel, as a result of which Spaight was mortally wounded on the fourth fire and died the next day. Criminal proceedings were instituted against Stanly, but he was pardoned by Gov. Benjamin Williams.

The handsome new $300,000 SCOTTISH RITE TEMPLE on the corner, dedicated Nov. 17, 1949, is one of the most modern in the South.

30. (40) The SITE OF THE RAINS HOUSE, 411 Johnson St., is now occupied by the Presbyterian manse (*private*). Here, in June, 1803, was born Gen. Gabriel J. Rains, Supt. of the Confederate Torpedo and Harbor Defense Bureau, whose submarine explosive inventions held Federal fleets at bay. His brother, Col. George Washington Rains, inventor and author, made these torpedoes effective through fuse priming, built Confederate munitions factories, and held many steam engine patents. The manse was built in 1842.

31. (41) CEDAR GROVE CEMETERY, NE. corner Queen and George Sts., was opened in 1800 by Christ Church and turned over to the city in 1854. The weeping arch entrance of coquina shell holds moisture, and there is a superstition that if water drops on a person he will be the next carried there in a hearse. The CONFEDERATE MONUMENT, a 15-foot marble shaft, identifies a mass Confederate grave. Interred in the cemetery are William Gaston, whose law desk and chair are supposedly buried with him; William J. Williams, painter of the Mason portrait of Washington in the Alexandria, Va., lodge; Moses Griffin, Mary Bayard Clarke, and other notables.

32. (42) KAFER PARK, NW. corner Queen and George Sts., is the city athletic field, part of the area taken over by the city after a 40-block fire Dec. 1, 1922. It is the home diamond of the New Bern Bears, who in 1951 won the Coastal Plains Baseball League Pennant.

33. (43) The NATIONAL CEMETERY, N. end of National Ave., contains the graves of over 3,500 Union soldiers from 20 states. N. J., Conn., R. I., and Mass. have monuments.

34. (44) The SITE OF JAMES GILL'S SHOP, Broad St., between George and Burn, is where Gill, a locksmith and silversmith, invented in 1829 an early revolver, a percussion weapon with 14 chambers, first of its kind.

35. (46) The JONES-LIPMAN HOUSE (*private*), SW. corner Pollock and Eden Sts., a small frame structure, was one of the Federal prisons. Here Emeline Pigott, Confederate spy, was imprisoned after being arrested for trying to slip through the lines into New Bern without a pass. Her story that she was taking a chicken to her sick mother failed to impress the questioning officer. Released from jail without trial and given a military escort to her home in Carteret County, she later admitted having swallowed incriminating papers when arrested.

36. (47) The STEVENSON HOUSE (*private*), Pollock at George Sts., built in 1805, is notable for its carved woodwork, century-old fence, and captain's walk. It was used as one of the several Federal hospitals during the Civil War.

37. (48) The BRYAN-ASHFORD HOUSE (*private*), 605 Pollock St., was built for Joseph Bryan in 1802 and later used by Washington Bryan. This handsome two-and-a-half story brick home has rare rosewood folding doors and Sheffield doorknobs. The adjoining law office, built in 1824, has an entrance of perfect symmetry, with hand-carved pediment and sunbursts in the center of the front gabled façade.

38. (49) The STANLY-GREEN-WINFIELD HOUSE, Pollock at Hancock Sts., was built in 1850 for Edward Stanly, Congressman and Governor of the Federal Dept. of N. C. Recently restored, it is now used as a USO service center.

39. (50) TRYON'S PALACE, 223 George St., is now in the process of complete and authentic restoration, based upon physical and documentary research. The original walls of the west wing are all that remain of the original group. Reconstruction was made possible through the generosity of the late Mrs. Maude Moore Latham, of Greensboro, a native of New Bern, who donated more than a million dollars for the purpose. The necessary land was purchased by the State. The N. C. Dept. of Conservation and Development and the Tryon's Palace Commission are sponsoring the work.

Tryon's Palace, "the most beautiful building in the Colonial Americas" was erected in 1767-70 by Royal Governor William Tryon. Its architect, John Hawks, an Englishman, was the "first professional architect to remain in America." The Palace combined the governor's residence and statehouse, containing assembly hall, council chamber, and public offices. Here was the seat of government under royal Governors Tryon and Martin; N. C.'s First Provincial Congress in defiance of royal authority (1774); the first constitutional general assembly (1777); the inauguration of Richard Caswell, first constitutional governor; and the frequent seat of government until the capitol was moved to Raleigh in 1794.

Tryon was able to secure the appropriation for the erection of the palace from an assembly now tractable because of the recent repeal of the unpopular Stamp Act. Wide disapproval of the appropriation of over £16,000 was a factor in precipitating the War of the Regulation, in which Tryon resorted to armed force to quell the Regulators.

The Hawks design included a brick house of two main stories, 87 feet wide and 59 feet deep, with two outlying wings of two lower stories each, connected with the main block by semicircular colonnades. One wing contained servants' quarters and a laundry, the other, granary and hayloft. Written accounts describe the construction from the shingled roof "More beautiful than slate or tyle" down to "two wells with Pumps Compleat."

The traveler, William Attmore, in 1787 described the "grand Staircase lighted from the Sky by a low Dome, which being glazed kept out the weather," and noted that "the King of G. Britain's Arms are still suffered to appear in a pediment at the front of the Building; which, considering the independent spirit of the people averse to every vestige of Royalty appears Something strange." In 1791, when Washington was tendered a magnificient ball, his horses were stabled in the executive offices, and he described the palace as "now hastening to ruin."

In 1798, a Negro woman, searching for eggs in the cellar with a lighted torch, started a fire that destroyed all but the west wing, which has since served as warehouse, dwelling, stable and carriage house, parochial school, and chapel, before it was converted (1931) into an apartment house.

40. The SITE OF FORT TOTTEN is at the western edge of town, between US 17 and 70. Here stood one of the forts built around New Bern by Union forces after they seized the town in March, 1862. Trenches were built across New Bern from the Neuse to the Trent River, and a fort was erected at each terminus and in the center.

Raleigh

Information Services: Chamber of Commerce, 23 W. Davie St.; Carolina Motor Club, 230 W. Hargett St.

Railroad Stations: 400 W. Cabarrus St., for Southern Ry.; Seaboard Ave., for Seaboard Air Line R. R.

Bus Station: Union Bus Station, 217 W. Morgan St. for Atlantic Greyhound, Carolina Coach, Southern Coach, Queen City Coach, and Seashore Transportation Companies.

City Buses: Along regular routes.

Airports: Municipal, **3.5 m.** S. on US 15-A, for private planes and training field; Raleigh-Durham Airport, US 70, **13 m.** NW. of Raleigh, for Eastern, Capital, and Piedmont Airlines.

Radio and Television Stations: WPTF (680), WPTF-FM (94.7), WRAL (1240), WRAL-FM (101.5), WNAO (850), WNAO-FM (96.1), WNAO-TV (channel 28).

Newspapers: The News and Observer (daily, morn.); *The Raleigh Times* (daily, eve. except Sun.).

Educational Institutions: N. C. State College (*coed*); Meredith College (*women*); Peace College (*women*); St. Mary's School (*women*); Shaw University (*Negro*); St. Augustine's College (*Negro*); also King's Business College, Hardbarger's Business College & Payne's Business and Secretarial School. Special schools located in Raleigh: State School for the Blind, Methodist Orphanage, and Catholic Orphanage. The three private institutions: Ravenscroft School, Sacred Heart Catholic School, and St. Monica Convent (*Negro*).

Swimming: Pullen Park, approached from Hillsboro St. or US 64; John Chavis Memorial Park (*Negro*), Lenoir St. at city limits; Hayes Barton Pool, Scales St.

Golf: Raleigh Golf Assn., **4 m.** S. off US 15-A on county road S. of Municipal Airport, 18 holes; Cheviot Hills, **9 m.** NE. on US 1, 9 holes; Raleigh Country Club, Peartree Lane, 18 holes; Carolina Country Club, Glenwood Ave. Ext., 18 holes.

Tennis: Pullen Park, approached from Hillsboro St. or US 64.

Boating: Gresham's Lake, **6 m.** N. on US 1.

Baseball and Football: Riddick Stadium and Red Diamond, N. C. State College.

Annual Events: Southern Conference Basketball Tournament, March; Engineers Fair, State College, spring; Flower Show, Raleigh Garden Club, May, Oct.; Farmers Convention, July; 4-H Club meeting, July; Debutante Ball, Sept.; State Fair, 3rd week, Oct.; State Literary and Historical Assn., State Folklore Society, State Art Society, 1st week Dec.

RALEIGH (363 alt., 65,679 pop.), the capital and fifth largest city of North Carolina, has experienced since the outbreak of World War II the greatest population growth percentagewise of any major Tar Heel city. Originally constructed from a wooded wilderness in the eastern piedmont, it has expanded considerably from its original limits in the southeastern or downtown portion of the modern city. In this section, Capitol Square, dominated by the stately old Capitol Building and surrounded by State departmental buildings, forms a hub from which the principal streets radiate.

Capitol Square, covering 6 acres and shaded by some 50 varieties of trees, was one of 5 squares designated in the original plan of Raleigh. The remaining 4, located in each quarter of the city, were originally set aside as public parks. Only two of these areas, Nash and Moore squares in the southwest and southeast respectively, still serve their initial purpose. Caswell Square, on the northwest, is now occupied by State departmental buildings and Burke Square, on the northeast, contains the Governor's Mansion.

Fayetteville Street, running south from Capitol Square to Memorial Auditorium, was once the Sunday promenade for Raleigh's beaux and belles. Now it is the chief commercial artery, lined with stores, hotels, theaters, the Federal Building, courthouse, and city hall. The streets paralleling and crossing Fayetteville form the main business section of downtown Raleigh.

Until recent years Raleigh was predominantly a city of comfortable, unpretentious homes with broad lawns and gardens beneath old trees. Older residential areas such as Cameron Park, Mordecai, and Boylan Heights perpetuate the names of prominent early families; Hayes Barton was named for the home of Sir Walter Raleigh in England. Raleigh was largely a community of southern tradition and charm, and its families had been neighbors for generations.

With the city's rapid growth as a manufacturing, retail, and distribution center, it has been transformed into a modern progressive city. Many of the older homes have been converted into apartments or rooming and boarding houses. Newer subdivisions, such as Anderson Heights, Budleigh, Cameron Village, Country Club Hills, Glenwood Village, and Longview Gardens, have been developed to accommodate families of varying incomes.

Most significant of the new subdivisions is Cameron Village, located on what was formerly a 158-acre tract of wooded land lying in the heart of one of Raleigh's residential sections. During the 5-year period from 1948 to 1953, 90 private homes and apartment houses containing 560 units were constructed in the area. In 1948 the apartment project won first prize in the National Association of Home Builders' contest for "ingenuity, originality and soundness of design and construction, and suitability of the project to its location."

By 1954 Cameron Village's shopping center, the largest such suburban project in the Southeast, boasted 40 stores and 38 business and professional offices on a 36-acre tract lying in the center of the subdivision. Among its outstanding features are: extra-wide walkways covered by a canopy; free parking space for over 1,500 cars; enforced sign control forbidding projecting or colored neon signs; underground wiring; and the designing of all stores on a street-floor level. The material for the buildings consists mainly of Crab Orchard stone, Roman brick, and California redwood.

The atmosphere of Raleigh reflects its varied functions as a governmental, educational, commercial, and social center. Possessing 6 colleges, a historical museum, natural museum, art gallery, and such active organizations as the Raleigh Little Theatre and the Civic Music Association, it enjoys a rich cultural life. Each December the State Literary and Historical Association, the State Art Society, the North Carolina Society for the Preservation of Antiquities, and other statewide cultural organizations hold their annual meetings in the Capital City.

Every two years, when the general assembly is in session, Raleigh assumes an even more lively air. Social life attains its gayest tempo, hotel lobbies swarm with delegations, and hotel rooms glow with midnight conferences. Every 4 years, when a new governor assumes office, the inauguration festivities are attended by visitors from all parts of the State. Each fall the N. C. State Fair attracts hundreds of thousands of other persons to the city.

The 17,871 Negroes of the city, approximately 27% of the total population, own and operate hotels, newspapers, banks, and a savings association. They have two colleges, libraries, municipal playgrounds, churches, hospitals, and other institutions. Many are represented in the professions, although the bulk of the Negro population is employed in business establishments. Most Negroes live in the southern and eastern sections of the city.

In 1771 when Wake County was formed from parts of Cumberland, Johnston, and Orange counties, a courthouse and jail were erected on the hillside in front of the residence of Joel Lane, who, with his brothers Joseph and Jesse, had come here several years previously. This home became so popular with travelers that the owner built a tavern and helped to erect a log church, the Asbury Meetinghouse. The settlement was known as Wake Courthouse. The county was made coextensive with St. Margaret's Parish, and both were named for Margaret Wake, wife of the royal governor, William Tryon.

Despite objections from North Carolina's principal towns, the State convention in 1788, seeking a central location for an "unalterable seat of government," resolved that the site should be within 10 miles of Isaac Hunter's plantation. Hunter's land was among the 17 tracts considered, but the commission of legislators purchased 1,000 acres of Joel Lane's land for £1,378, and it has been suggested that Lane's excellent punch played a part in the transaction.

The town was laid out by William Christmas in April, 1792, with Union (now Capitol) Square reserved for the statehouse. The 4 parks were named for the first three governors under the constitution and for Attorney General Alfred Moore. The streets were named for the State's 8 judicial districts, each (except Morgan) identified by the name of its principal city, for the commissioners, and for other prominent citizens. In pursuance of instructions the commissioners built a brick statehouse "large enough for both houses of the assembly," and upon completion of the building Raleigh was taunted with being a "city of streets without houses."

In 1799 two newspapers championed the rival creeds of the Federalist and Republican parties. By 1800 the population numbered 669, and during that year Methodist Bishop Francis Asbury held a "big meeting" in the statehouse, which at that time was used for religious gatherings, balls, and public meetings.

With State aid, the Raleigh Academy for boys and girls was established on Burke Square in 1801. Casso's Inn, opened before 1800 at the corner of Morgan and Fayetteville Streets, was an early political rendezvous. The town bell hung at this corner. The Indian Queen Tavern, on the site of the present Federal Building, advertised in 1803 that it was the best in town with "13 rooms, 9 of which have fireplaces."

Destructive fires occurred in 1818, 1821, and 1831. In the last the statehouse was destroyed and with it the $10,000 marble statue of George Washington by the Italian sculptor, Canova, reputed to have been at the time the most expensive work of art in the United States.

In 1840, a three-day celebration, with parades, orations, and subscription balls, marked the completion of the new statehouse and the entrance of the first train over the Raleigh & Gaston Railroad, first standard-gage railway in the State. The Raleigh Guards, organized in 1846, served in the Mexican War. During the legislative session of 1850-1851 the *Raleigh Register* published the first daily newspaper in North Carolina.

Although Union sentiment was strong in Raleigh, 100 guns were fired on Capitol Square, and bells were rung when the State convention adopted the secession ordinance on May 20, 1861. The city became a concentration point for Confederate troops, and gunpowder and other supplies were manufactured here. Saltpeter was stored in the Capitol rotunda. When Sherman's army entered without resistance, April 14, 1865, University president David L. Swain, in the absence of Governor Vance, delivered the keys of the Capitol to the victorious Union general.

During Reconstruction confusion and disorder prevailed in Raleigh, as indeed throughout the State. During the late 1860's the Radical Republicans, consisting of Northern "carpetbaggers," native "scalawags," and uneducated Negroes, controlled the general assembly. The legislators indulged in lavish expenditures, voted themselves salaries of $8 per day and 20¢ per mile for travel, and installed an open bar in the west wing of the Capitol, which was dubbed the "third house." Nicks in the Capitol steps remain where whiskey barrels were rolled in and out. In 1877 Zebulon B. Vance returned to the Capital City as governor. Reconstruction was at an end.

During the late 19th century Raleigh shared in the industrial develop-

RUBENS "THE HOLY FAMILY WITH ST. ANNE," IN STATE ART MUSEUM, RALEIGH

ST. THOMAS, BATH

ST. PAUL'S EDENTON (HIGHTON)

ST. PHILIP'S CHURCH RUINS, BRUNSWICK COUNTY

OLD BETHABARA CHURCH, OLD TOWN, NEAR WINSTON-SALEM

MORAVIAN CHURCHYARD WINSTON-SALEM

CHRIST CHURCH, RALEIGH   FIRST PRESBYTERIAN CHURCH, NEW BERN
(HIGHTON)

ST. LAWRENCE CATHOLIC CHURCH, ASHEVILLE (ASHEVILLE CHAMBER OF COMMERCE)

HOME MORAVIAN CHURCH AND SALEM COLLEGE, WINSTON-SALEM (WOOTTEN)

CEDAR GROVE CEMETERY, NEW BERN (HIGHTON)

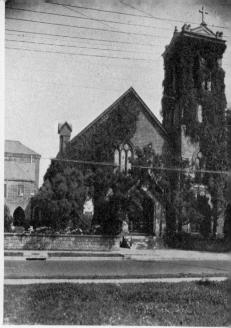

ST. JOHN'S-IN-THE-WILDERNESS, FLAT ROCK
(HISTORIC AMERICAN BUILDING SURVEY)

ST. PETER'S CHURCH, WASHINGTON
(WASHINGTON CHAMBER OF COMMERCE)

FIRST PRESBYTERIAN CHURCH, GREENSBORO (ART SHOP)

INTERIOR OF ST. JOHN'S, WILLIAMSBORO, AS RESTORED, 1955

UNION METHODIST CHURCH, CRICKET COMMUNITY, WILKES COUNTY

ment of the State. By 1900, when the city's population was 13,743, cotton and knitting mills, a tobacco warehouse, and an electric power plant had been established. A union passenger station was built for the railroads serving the city.

Raleigh's greatest growth has occurred during the 20th century, particularly in the period since the outbreak of World War II. Its population now includes some 7,000 State and 1,000 Federal employees. Over 120 manufactories in or near the city make food and kindred goods, stone, concrete, chemicals, and electronics and textile, metal, and lumber products. Large printing establishments publish books and periodicals. Three insurance companies now have their home offices in the city. In addition, Raleigh has become the largest retail and distribution center on US 1 between Richmond, Va., and Jacksonville, Fla. By 1952 the business done by Raleigh's more than 800 retail establishments exceeded $110,000,000 annually; sales by the city's wholesale distributors were estimated at over $200,000,000.

Raleigh's literary history began in 1792, the year of its founding, with "On the Seat of Government," a poem probably written by Thomas Harminson Hall of Edgecombe County. The first novel by a resident of the State was *Matilda Berkely* (1804) by Winifred Marshall Gales (1761-1839), wife of Joseph Gales, editor of the *Raleigh Register*. The first children's book written by a North Carolinian was *A Wreath from the Woods of Carolina* (1859) by Mary Ann Mason (1802-81), wife of the rector of Christ Church. Raleigh poets include Theophilus Hunter Hill (1836-1901), whose *Hesper* (1861) was the first book published under copyright of the Confederate States; Henry Jerome Stockard (1858-1914); Lilla Vass Shepherd (1881-1953); Edwin McNeill Poteat (b. 1892); and Lucy Cherry Crisp. Samuel A. Ashe (1840-1938) was author of *A History of North Carolina* (1902, 1925). Josephus Daniels (1862-1948), journalist, wrote among other works a 5-volume autobiography. His son Jonathan Daniels (b. 1902) has published many books, including *A Southerner Discovers the South* (1938), *Tar Heels* (1941), and *The End of Innocence* (1954). Clarence Poe (b. 1881) editor of the *Progressive Farmer,* has written on agriculture and travel. Anne Preston Bridgers (b. 1891) co-authored *Coquette* (1928), a Broadway success starring Helen Hayes. Charlotte Hilton Green (b. 1889) is a nature writer. Carl Goerch (b. 1891) and Bill Sharpe (b. 1903), editors of *State* magazine, have issued several informal books about life in North Carolina.

POINTS OF INTEREST

1. The STATE CAPITOL (*open 8:30-5:30, Mon.-Fri.; 8:30-12:30, Sat.*) rises in impressive simplicity from the center of Capitol Square at the N. end of Fayetteville St. Solid and imposing, yet of graceful lines, the structure is an excellent example of the Grecian Doric mode. The building is illuminated at night by tinted floodlights. Sentimental attachment to the century-old building has resisted efforts to replace it with a larger modern structure. The capitol was authorized by the general assembly in 1832. W. S.

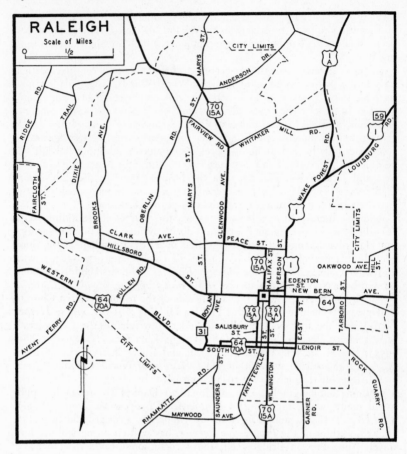

Drummond and Col. Thomas Bragg were the architects, with Ithiel Town, then at work on the New York Customhouse, as consultant. Through Town, David Paton was secured in 1834 to take complete charge. Paton imported stonemasons from Scotland, whose cutting and finishing he personally directed. The cornerstone was laid in 1833, and the building was completed in 1840 at a cost of $530,684.

The cruciform structure, 160 feet long north to south, 140 feet east to west, and 97½ feet high at the center, is constructed of rectangular granite blocks of irregular size, quarried a mile southeast of the site. In 1952 the exterior walls were sandblasted, restoring them to their original light grey color. The Raleigh Experimental Railway, first in North Carolina, ran from the east portico of the capitol to the quarry to haul the stone. Horse-drawn cars were operated over this strap-iron tramway, and a passenger car was run after working hours "for the accommodation of such ladies and gentlemen as desired to take the exercise of a railroad airing."

Doric porticoes on the east and west wings and the weathered green copper roof and dome with its crownlike cresting provide the dominant architectural motifs of the exterior. The difficulty of adapting the Doric order to a three-story building was overcome by using the first story as a base and permitting the columns to run through the upper stories to an adequate pediment. Paton employed Greek methods of construction, stone-cutting, and finishing. No color was applied, but an adjustment of light and shadow was obtained by recessing the windows between simple piers. In the entrance hallways are worn stairs with wrought-iron handrails, uneven flooring of slabs, and monolithic Ionic columns, all of granite. Wood was used for the heavy studded doors and light window frames.

The carved ornamental detail in the halls and public rooms is Greek, employing Ionic and Corinthian forms, but the private offices show touches of the English Gothic. The vestibules are decorated with columns and pilasters similar to those of the Ionic Temple on the Illissus, near the Acropolis. The remainder is groined with stone and brick pilasters of the Roman Doric order. In 1952 an elevator was installed in the east vestibule.

At the intersection of the principal axes of the plan is a rotunda crowned by a low dome which, despite its stylistic inconsistency, harmonizes with the Doric detail of the exterior. The interior of the rotunda has a maximum height of 93½ feet. Bronze plaques on the walls of the first floor commemorate important events or personages in North Carolina history. There are niches containing busts of John M. Morehead, William A. Graham, Matt W. Ransom, and Samuel Johnston. All were sculptured by F. Wellington Ruckstuhl between 1900 and 1912.

The floor of the rotunda at the second story is in the form of a gallery around a 17-foot circular well, overhanging the lower floor about 9 feet and without apparent support. Mortised curving stone stairs to the third floor, at the north of the west entrance, are supported by their own construction.

On the first floor are offices for the Governor, Secretary of State, State Treasurer, and State Auditor. The second floor contains the senate chamber and the hall of the house of representatives. The plan of the hall of the house is that of a Greek amphitheater, with a semicircular Greek Doric colonnade. The senate chamber, with columns of similar order, is cruciform in plan with a rostrum at the north side.

The third floor, containing galleries and rooms used for clerical purposes, is finished in the florid Gothic style. The lobbies as well as the rotunda are lighted with cupolas.

On the east grounds is a monument to Andrew Jackson, James K. Polk, and Andrew Johnson, "Three Presidents North Carolina Gave the Nation," by Charles Keck. In 1948 President Truman made the principal address at the ceremony dedicating the monument. Behind the monument are fountains in two lily ponds, and in front of it are two mortars from Fort Macon. To the southeast of the capitol is a statue of Charles D. McIver sculptured by Ruckstuhl and erected in 1911. On the south, within an iron fence, is a bronze copy of Houdon's Washington from the original in the capitol at Richmond, Va., placed here in 1858. It is flanked by a pair of French-cast cannon made in 1748, mounted at Edenton in 1778, and brought here in 1903.

To the south of the Washington monument is Memorial Mall, an area 216 feet long (from east to west) and 30 feet wide. On the eastern end is a statue to Zebulon B. Vance by Henry Ellicott, originally erected on the east grounds in 1903 and moved to its present location when the Three Presidents monument was placed in 1948. On the western end of the Mall is a statue to Charles B. Aycock by Gutzon Borglum, erected in 1924.

At the southwest corner of Capitol Square, facing Morgan St., is a monument to the women of the Confederacy by Augustus Lukeman. To the southeast of the capitol is a statue by W. S. Packer of Ensign Worth Bagley of Raleigh, first American officer killed in the Spanish-America War. Beside it is a Spanish gun, mounted here in 1908. On the northwest is Borglum's statue of Henry Lawson Wyatt, first North Carolina soldier killed in action in the Civil War, at Bethel Church, June 10, 1861. Nearby is a tablet, erected in 1940, honoring Samuel A'Court Ashe (1840-1938), North Carolina soldier, historian, legislator, and editor. Dominating the west grounds is a reproduction of Muldoon's Confederate Monument, a 70-foot shaft surmounted and flanked with bronze figures of Confederate soldiers. Two 32-pounders, cast in 1848, are mounted beside the monument.

2. The STATE LIBRARY BUILDING, facing the capitol on Morgan St. between Salisbury and Fayetteville Sts., is a 4-story limestone structure of modified French Renaissance design. Completed in 1913, it houses several State departments. The STATE LIBRARY (*open 9-5, Mon.-Fri; 9-1, Sat. in winter; half-hour earlier in summer*) on the 1st floor and part of the basement and 2nd floor, originated in a miscellaneous collection of books for the use of legislators and State officials. It contains about 90,000 volumes and is a general reference library specializing in North Caroliniana, Southern history, and genealogy. Offices of the Secretary of State annex, containing land-grant records, are located on the 2nd floor, and the Utility Commission has offices on both the 2nd and 3rd floor. The N. C. Library Commission occupies the 4th floor.

3. The JUSTICE BUILDING, facing the capitol on Morgan St. between Fayetteville and Wilmington Sts., is a 5-story steel and concrete structure with outer walls of Mount Airy granite. Completed in 1939, it houses the offices of the Attorney General, the Adjutant General, Supreme Court, Supreme Court Library, and other State departments. Built with Federal aid, it occupies the site of Peter Casso's Inn, erected before 1800.

4. NORTH CAROLINA MUSEUM OF ART, E. Morgan St. (*open 9-5 weekdays; 2-5 Sat. and Sun.; free*), is a 4-story brick building, formerly the State Highway Building (1921-53). In 1953, the general assembly allocated

it for renovation for its present use. Collections: 200 paintings (purchased by an appropriation of $1,000,000 by the general assembly of 1947—largely through the efforts of Robert Lee Humber of Greenville), mainly 15th to 18th century, representing 8 major schools of western art and including important works by Peter Paul Rubens, Hans Memling, Van Dyck, Rembrandt, Lochner, Crespi, Bellotto, Boucher, Gainsborough, Raeburn, Romney, Gilbert Stuart, Copley, Moran, Ryder, and others; State Art Society's collections of Phifer bequest paintings, ancient glass from George Pratt gift, and Contemporary North Carolina Artists' Purchase Award paintings and sculpture; Jugtown Pottery; North Carolina textiles; other miscellaneous gifts. A collection of paintings, valued at $1,000,000, is to be added by the Samuel H. Kress Foundation gift to match the 1947 State appropriation. There is a regular schedule of changing exhibitions, October through June.

5. The HIGHWAY BUILDING, facing the capitol on Wilmington St. between New Ave. and Morgan St., is a 5-story granite building harmonizing with the neoclassic design of the Justice Building. Completed in 1953, it houses the offices of the State Highway and Public Works Commission and the Division of Purchase and Contract.

6. The AGRICULTURE BUILDING (1923), with the main entrance at NW. corner Edenton and Halifax Sts., is a 4-story limestone structure designed in the neoclassic style with a three-story Ionic colonnade above a rusticated first story. It houses the Dept. of Agriculture, Board of Public Buildings and Grounds, and the Board of Elections. A 6-story annex, forming an ell extending to Salisbury St., was completed in 1954. Here is housed the STATE MUSEUM (*open 9-5, weekdays; 1-5, Sun.*), with entrances at 101 Halifax St. and 102 N. Salisbury St. The museum, established in 1851, is devoted to the natural history and natural resources of the State. Exhibits cover the geological history of the State with consequent mineral and soil resources; the large variety of plant life, with timber resources; and the varied animal forms from the primitive to the prehistoric American Indian. Early agriculture is depicted by tools and implements.

7. The EDUCATION BUILDING (1938), NW corner Salisbury and Edenton Sts., is a 5-story white granite structure of modern design. Most of the main floor is occupied by the State Dept. of Archives and History. The HALL OF HISTORY (*open 9-5, weekdays; 2-5, Sun.*) is a museum containing items dating from the Indians and the Roanoke Island colony, works of art, literature, sculpture, manufacturing, handicraft, and commerce, and archives and relics of the wars in which North Carolina has participated. There is also a copy of Canova's statue of George Washington. State departments and commissions occupy the other floors.

8. CHRIST CHURCH (*Episcopal*), SE. corner Edenton and Wilmington Sts., is probably the most noteworthy Gothic Revival building in the State. It was designed by Richard Upjohn, architect of Trinity Church in New York, and erected between 1848 and 1853. The design is based upon that of an English medieval parish church. The main block is of local red-gray

stone neatly squared and faced. Joined to it by a three-arched cloister is a square bell tower of gray stone, accented with darker red-gray stone and with three levels of small windows. A slender octagonal spire tapers from the tower to a height of about 100 feet. Its weathercock is said to be the only chicken Sherman's army left in Raleigh. The subdued interior is dominated by the altar and reredos of Caen limestone carved in France. A slave gallery extends across the western end of the nave. Built partly with slave labor, the church replaces an 1829 structure. Records of the parish date from its organization in 1821. The first rector was John Stark Ravenscroft, first Episcopal Bishop of North Carolina.

The Parish House and Chapel of the Annunciation (1913) is connected by a cloistered walkway to the north and east of the church. Designed by Hobart Upjohn, grandson of the church's architect, and constructed of granite from the same quarry, it harmonizes with the old church.

The Old Rectory (*private*), 111 Newbern Ave., the oldest building of the church group, was erected about 1818. It is of brick with granite lintels and sills and has double-gallery porticoes on the east and west elevations. It was originally constructed as the N. C. State Bank and the residence of its president. The vault was removed when the parish acquired the property in 1873. The lower floor at present is used for the Wake County Cerebral Palsy Clinic. The upstairs is used for parish teaching and for the home of the assistant.

9. The RICHARD B. HAYWOOD HOUSE (*private*), 127 E. Edenton St., was built in 1854 of bricks made by family slaves for Dr. Richard Benehan Haywood, whose descendants own and occupy it. The rectangular two-story structure has a hip roof, 4 chimneys, and a 4-column Doric portico. This house was commandeered during Federal occupation as headquarters for Maj. Francis P. Blair, Jr., a classmate of Dr. Haywood at the University of North Carolina, and was visited by Gens. Sherman and Grant.

10. The TREASURER HAYWOOD HOUSE (*private*), 211 Newbern Ave., was built about 1794 for John Haywood, State Treasurer. It is owned and occupied by one of his descendants, remaining much as it was when built and containing many of the original furnishings. The house is of Classical Revival design, finished with beaded weatherboarding. A small double-gallery entrance porch, with Doric columns and single wrought-iron railing flanking the steps, rises to a level dentiled cornice beneath the gabled roof. There is a wing on the left and two great end chimneys. Lafayette dined here in 1825.

11. The GOVERNOR'S MANSION (*telephone capitol hostess for appointment*), 210 N. Blount St., stands on Burke Square, which in 1792 was suggested as a "proper situation for the Governor's house." The red brick and sandstone building was authorized by the assembly in 1885 and finished with convict labor in 1891. Gustavus Adolphus Bauer, the designer, employed numerous gables, patterned roof, paneled chimneys, and lathe-turned

porches in the then-fashionable style. There were extensive renovations and redecoration in 1949.

12. The HENRY CLAY OAK, North St. 110 ft. NW. of Blount St., is 6 feet in diameter and believed to be between 500 and 600 years old. Under this tree while he was a guest of Kenneth Rayner, Henry Clay is said to have written the well-known Raleigh letter to the *National Intelligencer* which, because of its evasive treatment of the question of admitting Texas as a slave state, was a factor in his defeat for the presidency (1844).

13. PEACE COLLEGE, N. end of Wilmington St., in a 10-acre grove, was opened in 1872 by the Rev. Robert Burwell after it had been organized in 1857 as a Presbyterian girls school by the Rev. Joseph M. Atkinson and William Peace, prominent Raleigh merchant who donated the site. During the Civil War the partially completed main brick building was used for a Confederate hospital and afterwards housed a Freedmen's Bureau. From 1907 to 1952 the Presbyterian Church of North Carolina has owned and controlled the institution, which is an accredited Grade A junior college and high school with a faculty of 17 and a student body of 225. Today it is under the control of the Synod of North Carolina.

14. The MORDECAI HOUSE (*private*), NW. corner Wake Forest Rd. and Mimosa St., is a Greek Revival mansion of heart-pine timbers painted white with green blinds. In 1758 Joel Lane gave the older portion, with its hand-hewn timbers and wooden pegs, to his son, Henry. The 4 front rooms, the two-story columned portico, and the east portico were added in 1824 by Moses Mordecai, whose descendants own and occupy it. Lafayette stopped here in 1825, and in 1860 Gen. Joseph Lane, grandson of one of Raleigh's earliest settlers, and then a vice-presidential candidate, was a guest.

15. In OAKWOOD CEMETERY, NE. corner Linden and Oakwood Aves., are buried 6 N.C. governors: Aycock, Bragg, Fowle, Holden, Swain, and Worth.

16. ST. AUGUSTINE'S COLLEGE, NE. corner Oakwood Ave. and Tarboro Rd., was founded in 1867 by the Episcopal Church for the education of Negro youth. Its 20 buildings stand on a 35-acre campus. There are 371 students and 27 teachers. The curriculum includes a preparatory course, a 4-year college course leading to A.B. and B.S. degrees, and the Bishop Tuttle School of Religious Education and Social Service. St. Agnes Hospital and Training School is affiliated with the college. According to tradition, Willie Jones, commissioner for the state-at-large when Raleigh was founded, and one of the framers of the State constitution, is buried in an unmarked grave on the grounds, once a part of his plantation.

17. NATIONAL CEMETERY, SE. corner E. Davie St. and Rock Quarry Rd., established in 1867, covers 7 acres and contains the graves of 1,274 Union soldiers (many of whom were originally buried on Bentonville Battlefield in 1865) and soldiers of other wars.

18. The SITE OF THE BIRTHPLACE OF ANDREW JOHNSON, 123 Fayetteville St., is indicated by a granite marker. At the head of this street stood Casso's Inn, early political meeting place. In the innyard was the home of Jacob Johnson, hostler, janitor, and town constable, whose wife, Polly, did the weaving for the inn. There is a legend that on Dec. 29, 1808, when pretty Peggy Casso was attending her wedding ball in the statehouse, a little girl summoned her. "Come quickly, Ma'am! Polly the weaver wants you." Polly had a baby son and wouldn't Peggy name him? Dropping on her knees beside the infant, she said: "I name thee, on this my wedding night, Andrew." Sixteen years later the *Star and North Carolina Gazette* advertised a reward of $10 for the return of two runaway apprentices, William and Andrew Johnson, brothers. Andrew worked as a tailor's apprentice at Carthage and later settled in Tennessee. On his return to Raleigh in 1867, President Johnson called first on Mrs. Peggy Stewart, his godmother.

19. The RICHARD B. HARRISON PUBLIC LIBRARY (*Negro; open each weekday*), 214 S. Blount St., was founded in 1935 by an interracial group and the State Library Commission and named for the Negro actor. The library contains 21,680 volumes, 90 periodicals, and 551 recordings.

20. The WAKE COUNTY COURTHOUSE, 316 Fayetteville St., stands on property conveyed to the county for 5 shillings by Theophilus Hunter and James Bloodworth in 1795 for erection of a "large and eligant" wooden building. The present courthouse is a rectangular, 4-story building of granite and terra cotta designed in the neoclassic style with recessed loggias in front and rear elevations fronted by Corinthian columns. The Wake County jail is located on the 4th floor.

21. The MEMORIAL AUDITORIUM, S. end of Fayetteville St., harmonizes with the Greek Revival design of the capitol which it faces. Erected in 1932 by the city and designed by Atwood and Weeks, it memorializes Wake County citizens who served in various wars. Of white brick and marble, it contains an auditorium seating 4,000, committee rooms, banquet hall, kitchen, and a fire station. The auditorium, converted into a ballroom, is the scene of the annual Debutante Ball in Sept., when young ladies from all sections of the State make their bows to society. The Governors' inaugural balls are also held here, which was the site of the old governor's palace (1818-65).

22. SHAW UNIVERSITY (*Negro, coed.*), SE. corner E. South and Wilmington Sts., had its beginning in Dec. 1865, in a theological class for freedmen conducted by Dr. Henry M. Tupper, Union Army chaplain, and his wife. Chartered in 1875 under its present name, the university is supported by the Negro State and Northern Baptist conventions. It has 549 students and grants the degrees of A.B., B.S., B.D., and B.S. in Home Economics. Ten red brick buildings of eclectic design occupy a 25-acre wooded campus.

23. The SACRED HEART CATHEDRAL (*open daily, guide service*), NW. corner Hillsboro and McDowell Sts., was erected in 1924 by the Rev.

Thomas Griffin, as a parish church. Two months later it became the first cathedral of the Diocese of Raleigh and the residential parish of the first bishop, The Most Reverend William J. Hafey, D.D. The first Catholic parish in Raleigh dates back to 1821. The Cathedral Parish is the residence of the third bishop of Raleigh, Most Reverend Vincent S. Waters, D.D., whose jurisdiction as bishop extends over 99 counties of the State. The Bishop's House is in the rear of the Cathedral (15 N. McDowell). The Cathedral is constructed of gray granite in a modified Gothic style, having a low tower at the corner with a slate roof, and having exceptionally good stained glass windows. The Cathedral School built in 1937 of Salisbury granite stands on an adjoining lot on Hillsboro St. and accommodates 350 grammar and high school students. The Convent facing on Edenton St., built in 1927 of the same stone as the church, is the residence of the Sisters of St. Dominic of Newburgh, N. Y., who teach in the school.

24. The ST. PAUL A.M.E. CHURCH, NW. corner Edenton and Harrington Sts., originated in 1849 when Negro members of Edenton Street Methodist Church organized as the city's first Negro congregation. In 1853 they acquired the old Christ Church building, which they moved to this site on rollers at night amid singing and shouting. The present red brick, steepled edifice was erected in 1884.

25. The JOEL LANE HOUSE (*open; resident caretaker*), 728 W. Hargett St., built before 1771 for Joel Lane, is the oldest house in Raleigh, though 150 feet removed from its original site. This Dutch Colonial structure has a gambrel roof, dormer windows, a vine-covered entrance stoop, and great end chimneys. The rear wing is a later addition, and the whole has been remodeled. Refurnished in the style of its period, the house serves as headquarters for the Wake County Committee of the Colonial Dames.

26. ST. MARY'S SCHOOL, 900 Hillsboro St., founded in 1842 by the Rev. Aldert Smedes, was conducted successively by him and his son, the Rev. Bennett Smedes, as an Episcopal school for young ladies until 1897, when it was acquired by the Episcopal Church. St. Mary's, the largest Episcopal high school and junior college in the United States, is fully accredited and has a student body of 300 and a faculty of 28. On the shady 20-acre campus are 21 buildings. Smedes Hall, the main building, is a substantial red brick structure with white columned portico and broad steps, flanked by wistaria-covered East and West Rock Buildings. The little frame cruciform Chapel, with a hooded entrance, was designed by Richard Upjohn. Ravenscroft, 802 Hillsboro St., at the E. end of the grove, is the residence of the Episcopal Bishop of the Diocese of North Carolina.

27. The NORTH CAROLINA STATE COLLEGE OF AGRICULTURE AND ENGINEERING OF THE UNIVERSITY OF NORTH CAROLINA (*buildings open during school hours unless otherwise noted*), Hillsboro St. at Oberlin Rd., has 64 buildings in a tract of 2,199 acres which includes the campus and adjoining research farms. The plant is valued at approximately $30,000,000. Eight additional experimental test farms are

maintained in different parts of the State in cooperation with the State Dept. of Agriculture.

With a teaching staff of over 560, the college annually enrolls about 4,000 resident students and offers undergraduate and graduate training for technical, scientific, and professional service in 48 academic departments. It includes the Schools of Agriculture, Education, Design, Forestry, Engineering, Textiles, and the Summer School. The college has an Extension Division with 7,000 students enrolled in correspondence, short courses, and night classes. The college also operates the North Carolina Agricultural Experiment Station and the North Carolina Agricultural Extension Service. Units of the army and air force ROTC give 4 years' instruction in military and air science and tactics.

Opened in 1889 as the North Carolina College of Agriculture and Mechanic Arts, the college was established through the efforts of the Watauga Club, an organization of young Raleigh men interested in the establishment of an industrial school, and Col. L. L. Polk, whose *Progressive Farmer* sponsored a farmers' movement for an agricultural college. One of the first buildings, HOLLADAY HALL (1888), named for the first president, serves as the administration building. It was erected on land donated by R. Stanhope Pullen and accommodated the original student body of 72 and their 8 teachers. In 1917, the name was changed to North Carolina State College of Agriculture and Engineering. In 1932, it became a unit of the University of North Carolina, but through all these changes it has been popularly referred to as State College.

Dominating the Hillsboro St. campus entrance is the TOWER, a 116-foot campanile of white Mount Airy granite, designed by William Henry Deacy. Conceived by alumni in 1921 as a monument to the 33 State College men who lost their lives in World War I, it was completed in 1937. Alumni are now completing plans for an Alumni Memorial Building to be dedicated to former students who died in World War II.

The State College opened its magnificent new D. H. HILL LIBRARY BUILDING (*open 8 a. m.-10 p. m., Mon.-Sat.*) in the fall of 1954. This modern library provides shelving for 400,000 volumes and is designed to seat 900 readers. The book collection is primarily scientific and technological, but there is also an extensive general collection.

The WILLIAM NEAL REYNOLDS COLISEUM (1949) is the college's largest building and one of the largest of its type in the South. It has accommodations for 12,400 at indoor contests, public meetings, ice shows, and dances.

The FRANK THOMPSON GYMNASIUM (1924) seats 2,500 at indoor contests, and Riddick Stadium seats 15,000 or 20,000 with temporary stands.

The RALEIGH RESEARCH REACTOR, the first privately owned and operated nuclear reactor, is located on the State College campus. The reactor is housed in the Burlington Laboratory Building, a modern one-story structure 110 feet square. Laboratories for students and research workers are also in this building.

Adjoining the campus is the ANDREW JOHNSON HOUSE (*admission upon application to keeper*), a tiny, gambrel-roof frame structure, the birthplace

(1808) of the 17th President of the United States. It was removed from its original site on Fayetteville St. to Pullen Park and in 1937 was moved here.

28. The RALEIGH LITTLE THEATRE, Pogue St., near State College, has an amphitheatre, seating 3,000 people, which is used during the summer for vesper services, community sings, concerts, and plays. Its Little Theatre, seating 300 people, presents 9 plays during the winter months.

29. CHAVIS PARK, on Chavis Way, in SE. Raleigh, is one of the finest Negro parks in the South. Named for John Chavis, a slave who became a famous educator, the park has a modern swimming pool, picnic areas, and recreational facilities.

30. The STATE SCHOOL FOR THE BLIND (*admission upon application at the superintendent's office*), coeducational, S. end of Ashe Ave., occupies 16 buildings on an 85-acre tract. Operated for the benefit of visually handicapped children between 6 and 21, it was established in 1845 and moved to its present site in 1923.

31. The STATE SCHOOL FOR THE BLIND AND DEAF (*Negro*), 4 m. out US 70, was opened in 1868 and moved in 1931 to its present location, where it occupies 15 brick buildings on a 300-acre tract. Negro children, deaf or visually handicapped, are admitted between the ages of 6 and 21.

32. CENTRAL PRISON (*no visitors except prisoners' relatives*), N. end Morgan St., authorized by the legislature in 1869, is a battlemented structure that required 14 years to erect. Its 12-acre area is surrounded by a gray granite wall. The prison contains the only lethal gas execution chamber east of the Mississippi.

33. The STATE HOSPITAL AT RALEIGH, located on Dix Hill, Boylan Dr. at Boylan Ave., was authorized in 1848 by the general assembly at the instigation of Dorothea Lynde Dix, pioneer reformer in the treatment of mental cases. Located on a forested tract of 1,248 acres, the main building, designed in the Gothic Revival style by Alexander Jackson Davis, was opened in 1856. The central wing of this building was replaced in 1954 by a 6-story Hospital and Admissions Building.

34. MEREDITH COLLEGE, 3.5 m. out US 1-64, is a 4-year Baptist college with a student body of over 600. First opened to students in 1899 as the Baptist Female University and located in the heart of Raleigh at the corner of Edenton and S. Blount Sts., the name was changed to Meredith College in 1909 (in honor of Thomas Meredith, longtime Baptist leader in the State), and the college itself moved to its present location in 1924. The red brick buildings, at the end of a tree-lined avenue, are surrounded by a campus of 170 acres.

35. The STATE FAIRGROUNDS, 5 m. out US 1-64, has been located on its present 225-acre site since 1929. The first State fair was held in 1853.

An annual 5-day N. C. State Fair, usually held the 3rd week in October, has been conducted by the N. C. Dept. of Agriculture since 1937. Annual attendance is around 500,000. The grounds contain exhibit buildings, Youth Center, race track with 4,500-seat grandstand, and 4 lakes. In 1953 the STATE FAIR ARENA (*open each day*), was constructed. Variously described as "one of the most remarkable buildings ever constructed" and "the most significant new building in this country," it was designed by the late Matthew Nowicki in collaboration with W. H. Deitrick of Raleigh. Constructed at a cost of $1,600,000, the Arena is of parabolic design, with a roof supported on cables suspended between 90-foot concrete arches and walls entirely of glass. Its seating capacity is 9,500. It is available for livestock shows and sales, trade shows, rodeos, circuses, conventions, exhibits, and other entertainments. It received the Gold Medal by the Agricultural League of New York as the outstanding achievement in engineering in 1952 and the 1953 award of the American Institute of Architects.

Salisbury

Information Service: Salisbury Chamber of Commerce, N. Main St.

Railroad Station: Liberty & Depot Sts., for Southern Ry.

Bus Station: Union Terminal, 226 N. Main St., for National Trailways and Queen City Coach Co.

Airports: Smith Reynolds Airport, Winston-Salem, **38 m.**, for Eastern, Capital, and Piedmont Airlines; Municipal Airport, Charlotte, **42 m.**, for Eastern, Piedmont, Capital, and Southern Airlines.

Newspaper: The Salisbury Post (eve.).

Educational Institutions: Catawba College (*coed*); Livingstone College (*Negro, coed*); Salisbury Business College; Salisbury Commercial College.

Swimming: Mirror Lake, **2 m.** E. on Old Faith Rd.; Granite Quarry Lake, **6 m.** E. on US 52; Salisbury Country Club, just off US 70 at City Lake; Bank Street Pool (*Negro*); High Rock Lake, **8 m.** E. on Trading Ford Rd.

Golf: Salisbury Country Club, 18 holes; McCanless Course, 9 holes, **2 m.** E. on Dunns Mt. Rd.; Alexander's Course, 9 holes, **2 m.** E. on Stokes Ferry Rd.

Tennis: Boyden H. S., Monroe and Allen Schools, Catawba College (hard surface, all-weather courts, play by permission of school officials).

Baseball and Football: Newman Park and Shuford Park in western Salisbury.

Hunting and Fishing: High Rock Lake, bass and bream, **8 m.** E. of Salisbury; small game hunting in isolated areas between Salisbury and Albemarle, inquire at local sporting goods stores.

Annual Events: Regional High School Music Contest, March; Golf Tournaments, seasonally; Rowan County Fair, fall; Garden Club Shows, May.

SALISBURY (764 alt. 20,102 pop.), one of the oldest towns in the piedmont, is the seat of Rowan County. The county, formed in 1753, first extended westward to the South Seas. It has sired 6 counties and grandsired 26 others.

Old deeds attest to the fact that Salisbury was in existence as the trader's "camping site" long before the first courthouse (1755) was erected. From the time that early commerce was carried on between Fort Henry in Virginia and the Indians of the interior of the Carolinas and Georgia the Trading Path was the principal highway. It stretched from Petersburg, Va., through present-day Warrenton, Hillsboro, Asheboro, to the Trading Ford on the Yadkin and thence towards Concord where it branched, one fork leading to Augusta, Ga., the other to the Cherokee villages in western North Carolina. Seven miles from Trading Ford the traders pitched their camp on high level ground, fed by numerous nearby springs. This "camping ground" was later selected by the first justices of the Rowan Court as the location of the courthouse, which was the westernmost court center in America.

During the colonial period thousands of Scotch-Irish and German immigrants made their way down the "Great Wagon Road" from Pennsylvania into the piedmont region where they met the Trading Path which carried them across the Yadkin into Rowan County. These land-hungry racial groups fanned out in all directions taking up generous offers of land made by the McCulloh Land Company and the Earl of Granville. As the land became settled, Salisbury continued for many years to serve as the outpost of civilization to these immigrants. Here was located the nearest court center, the nearest land office, the only stores where merchandise could be purchased, and the center for all social contact in the western part of the colony. In 1765 Gov. Tryon reported that more than 1,000 wagons passed through Salisbury in a year.

By 1790 it was the only county in the State to have a population of 15,000. Among these were the sturdy ancestors of Pres. Dwight D. Eisenhower, Adlai Stevenson, Senator Alben Barkley, Pres. James K. Polk, and such bold spirits at Kit Carson and David Crockett. Other notables were born, have lived, or were educated here: Andrew Jackson, Daniel Boone, Gov. William R. Davie, Gen. William Lee Davidson, Gov. Alexander Martin, John Brevard, the Hon. Charles Fisher, and the prominent Henderson family. Two of its sons became governors: John W. Ellis (1859-61) and Montford Stokes (1830-32), though the latter was elected from Wilkes County. It was from Salisbury that Daniel Boone was sent by Richard Henderson and Company (later the Transylvania Company) to blaze a trail into the "lands beyond the mountains" in the present state of Kentucky. From the borders of Rowan went Christopher Gist in 1751 to explore what is now the region drained by the Ohio River. Gen. James White, a Rowan native, left the bounds of Center Church to found Knoxville, Tenn., in 1786. His son, Hugh Lawson White, ran for president in 1836.

Salisbury's importance lay in the fact that it was one of the 6 borough towns in the colony in 1766 and served as the center of the Salisbury District (created 1777) made up of the counties of Anson, Mecklenburg, Tryon, Surry, and Guilford. Rowan took the lead in drafting the first resolves designed to enforce the non-importation agreement against Great Britain and struck the highest note of any resolve passed in the colony when she called for an "indissoluble union" of the colonies. Rowan formed the first committee of safety in the State and played an important part in the Revolution. She furnished 4 of the leading commanders of the patriot forces when Cornwallis invaded Carolina in 1780-81: Matthew Locke, Francis Locke, Griffith Rutherford, and William L. Davidson. It was also while studying law here that William R. Davie received his first commission (*see* TOUR *3*). According to the Minute Docket of the Rowan Court, the court did not meet on Saturday, Feb. 27, 1781, as Cornwallis "marched into town Saturday evening preceding the February term and left late Monday night or early Tuesday morning."

Rowan's contribution to the Revolution may be surmised from the remark of Lt. Col. Banastre Tarleton, Cornwallis' dashing subordinate, "that the Counties of Mecklenburg and Rohon (Rowan) were more hostile to England than any others in America."

One of Rowan's favorite stories is the contribution of Mrs. Elizabeth Steele who presented a bag of specie to Gen. Nathanael Greene, who had stopped, discouraged and retreating before Cornwallis, at her tavern in Salisbury on Feb. 2, 1781. Greene, greatly encouraged by this gesture and warmed by a good meal, took a picture of King George from the wall and wrote on the back: "O George, hide thy face and mourn."

At the conclusion of hostilities many Tories were forcibly ejected from their lands, and these tracts were sold to land speculators. One group of Highland Scots who resided in the "Nottingham Settlement" just east of China Grove were removed altogether, and their lands became the property of German farmers who lived adjacent to them.

George Washington paid Salisbury a visit in May, 1791. The ordinary in which he spent the night has long since been torn down, but the stone steps from which he supposedly spoke have been removed to the Library lot.

Gen. John Steele, U. S. Congressman (1789-93) and first Comptroller of the Currency (1796-1802) lived here, and Gen. William R. Davie (*see* TOUR *3 and* CHAPEL HILL) studied law here under Judge Spruce Macay (pronounced Macoy). James K. Polk, whose mother was a native of Rowan, visited here frequently.

After the Panic of 1819 Rowan's population remained static because of migrations to the southwest and northwest. Renewed prosperity followed the coming of the North Carolina Railroad, completed in 1855, from Salisbury to Charlotte. Cotton factories, increased trade, and the booming mining town of Gold Hill, in lower Rowan, were halted by the Civil War.

Gov. John W. Ellis, a native and resident of Rowan and an ardent secessionist, replied to Lincoln's call to Federal arms by a call to Confederate arms and informed Lincoln he would get no troops from North Carolina.

During the Civil War, the Confederate Government maintained here a prison for Federal prisoners, where over 12,000 died. When Federal Gen. George Stoneman captured Salisbury in April, 1865, he used the same prison for Confederate prisoners.

Salisbury was the home of Frances Fisher (1846-1920), who married James M. Tiernan, a Marylander. Under the pen name, Christian Reid, she wrote about 40 novels. Her charming novelette, *The Land of the Sky* (1876), describing a summer trip through western North Carolina, gave that section its lovely name. Also born here was Hope Summerell Chamberlain, author of the delightful books, *This Was Home* (about Salisbury) and *Old Days in Chapel Hill*.

Today its industrial enterprises include Stanback headache powder, textile plants, granite quarries, and the giant Buck Plant of Duke Power Company on the Yadkin River nearby. A new $21,000,000 Veterans' Hospital was completed in 1953.

POINTS OF INTEREST

1. ROWAN COUNTY COURTHOUSE, N. Main St., built in 1926, has records dating back to 1753 and includes such names as Daniel Boone, Andrew Jackson, Gen. Francis Locke, and Governors William Tryon, Richard Caswell, Alexander Martin, Richard Dobbs Spaight, William R. Davie, and Zebulon B. Vance. A superior court entry of Nov. 6, 1787, shows that Andrew Jackson was admitted to the bar on that date.

2. The COMMUNITY BUILDING, next to the courthouse, was formerly the old courthouse, built 1854-57. It is a two-story Greek Revival edifice, with a fine Doric entablature and 6 Doric columns on the front two-story portico. Now used as a community center, it houses the Chamber of Commerce, Red Cross headquarters, etc.

3. The congregation of ST. JOHN'S EVANGELICAL LUTHERAN CHURCH, NE. corner W. Innis and Church Sts., was organized between 1747 and 1768 and housed in a log structure, the first church erected in Salisbury. The present building, of Gothic design, is constructed of brick trimmed with stone.

The OLD LUTHERAN CEMETERY, N. Lee St., was established, along with the first Lutheran Church, in 1768 by John Lewis Beard. Among the prominent people buried here is Archibald Henderson (1768-1822), U. S. Congressman (1799-1803), whom Archibald D. Murphey called "the most perfect model of a lawyer the bar of North Carolina ever produced," and whose monument was erected by the N. C. Bar. Also buried here are Confederate Col. Charles F. Fisher, President of the N.C. Railroad, and Nathaniel Boyden, Associate Justice of the N. C. Supreme Court and introducer of the ordinance which declared the secession ordinance of May 20, 1861, null and void.

4. Near the center of Salisbury is a NATIONAL CEMETERY containing the graves of 12,216 soldiers. During the Civil War 11,700 Federal soldiers who died in the Salisbury prison were buried here. Only the boundaries of the burial trenches are marked, though a record of the names has been kept. Robert Livingstone, son of David Livingstone, the missionary to Africa, lies here. Veterans of later wars are also buried here.

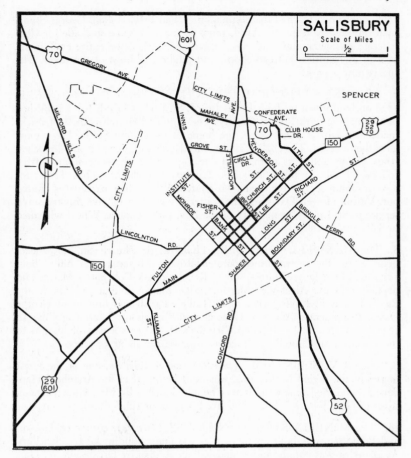

5. The CONFEDERATE MONUMENT, at Innis and Church Sts., erected in 1909, is a reproduction of the Baltimore, Md., monument by Frederick Ruckstuhl.

6. The SITE OF THE SALISBURY PRISON, Horah St., was one of the 4 largest maintained by the Confederate Government. First intended as a prison for Confederate deserters and others awaiting court martial, it was converted into a camp for Union prisoners. In Oct., 1864, 10,000 prisoners arrived to be crowded into a space sufficient for only 2,000. Some built mud huts for themselves or burrowed into the earth. Food, clothing, and sanitary provisions were inadequate. Serving as guards were the State Junior Reserves, boys under 17, and the Senior Reserves, men over 45 (later over 50) since all others were supposed to be bearing arms. Of the 2,800 prisoners who began the march to Wilmington when a transfer was ordered in Feb.,

1865, only 1,800 reached the destination. When Federal Gen. George Stoneman captured Salisbury in April, 1865, he used the same stockade for Confederate prisoners, and when he departed he burned the entire equipment, as well as factories, railroad shops, and public buildings of the town. The site is now a park.

7. ST. LUKE'S EPISCOPAL CHURCH, W. Council St., was erected in 1828 on land given by John Lewis Beard. St. Luke's Parish was established in 1753, along with Rowan County. The dignified church is built of bricks made in a kiln at Steeleworth, the home of Gen. John Steele. His widow gave the material. The chalice, paten, and flagon were made from "brooches, rings, chains and gifts from loved ones," given, at the suggestion of Mrs. Jefferson Davis, by the ladies of St. Lazarus Church, Memphis, Tenn., for a communion service for their own church. When their parish was blotted out, Varina Howell Davis and the scattered parishioners gave this treasured service to St. Luke's, in memory of the Rev. John Thomas Wheat who died in Salisbury in 1888.

8. The MAXWELL CHAMBERS HOUSE, S. Church St., now headquarters for the recently incorporated ROWAN MUSEUM, was built about 1819 for Judge James Martin, son of Revolutionary Col. James Martin and nephew of Gov. Alexander Martin. Judge Martin sold it in 1836 to the Rev. Thomas F. Davis, rector of St. Luke's Parish and brother of George Davis, Confederate Attorney General and Bishop of South Carolina. In 1847 it was bought by Maxwell Chambers II and was a part of his gift to the Presbyterian Church. It served as a manse for about 55 years.

9. The GOV. ELLIS HOME (*private*), 200 S. Ellis St., one of the finest homes of the period in this area, was built before 1822 for Archibald Henderson, who died that year. It was bought in 1849 by Mrs. Giles Pearson, sister of Gov. John W. Ellis, who lived here until Ellis' death in 1861.

10. The McNEELY-STRACHAN HOUSE (*private*), corner of Jackson and Bank Sts., was built about 1815 as the main building of the Salisbury Academy. It was bought and remodeled about 1859 by Dr. Joseph W. Hall who added the beautiful iron-work of the double galleries and the picturesque iron-work gateway. The rooms are imposing, with 12-foot ceilings on the first floor and 14-foot ceilings on the second. It was used as army headquarters during Federal occupation. In recent years a third story was added.

The SALISBURY ACADEMY, originally Queens Museum and later Liberty Hall in Charlotte (*see* CHARLOTTE), was moved, through the efforts of Dr. Samuel Eusebius McCorkle, to Salisbury in 1784 and operated until 1792. It was revived in 1807 and in 1812 the Thespian Society, a local theatrical group, took over its charter and soon built this house as the main building. In 1822 John Fulton, wealthy merchant and active civic leader, erected the GIRLS' SCHOOL for the young ladies of the academy on S. Fulton St. (now the residence of Sidney Blackmer, the well-known actor and native son). The BOYS' SCHOOL, opposite the Frank B. John School, is now vacant. The third floor, designed for the theatre of the Thespian Society, has a sloping floor, but the stage has been removed. It later belonged to Gen. Thomas G. Polk and following that to Hon. Francis E. Shober.

11. ROWAN MEMORIAL LIBRARY, Fisher St., the gift of the Burton Craige family, is an attractive Georgian building (1952) which occupies the site once occupied by the homes of Judge Spruce Macay and Archibald Henderson. The law office of Judge Macay, where Andrew Jackson, William R. Davie, and others studied, was sent to the Centennial Exposition in 1876, but the nearby WELL, from which Jackson and Cornwallis drank, is still in use.

In the northeast corner of the lot is the LAW OFFICE OF ARCHIBALD HENDERSON (*see 3 above*), perhaps the oldest unaltered structure in Salisbury.

12. OAK GROVE or OLD ENGLISH CEMETERY, N. Church St., dates back to 1769. Here are buried American and British Revolutionary soldiers; also Mrs. Elisha Mitchell whose husband's name is perpetuated in Mount Mitchell; Gov. John W. Ellis; and Burton Craige, U. S. Congressman (1853-61), Confederate Congressman (1861-62), and introducer of the ordinance of secession in the N. C. Convention of 1861.

13. In CHESTNUT HILL CEMETERY are buried U. S. Sen. Lee S. Overman (1903-30), a leading supporter of Wilson's war policies; John Steele Henderson who served as U. S. Congressman (1885-95) and introduced the first appropriation for Rural Free Delivery (1893); Gen. John Steele whose body was removed from the graveyard at Steeleworth; and Christian Reid, famous novelist.

14. The VETERANS' HOSPITAL, SW. of the city, completed in 1953, at a cost of $21,000,000, employs about 675 people in its modern, functional buildings.

15. LIVINGSTONE COLLEGE, Monroe St., housed in 10 brick buildings, on 315 acres, incorporated in 1879, is a coeducational institution with 400 Negro students.

16. CATAWBA COLLEGE, 2 m. out US 70, is a 4-year coeducational institution maintained by the Evangelical and Reformed Church. The administration building is a three-story brick structure of Tudor design with central entrance tower and battlemented roof. Established at Newton in 1852, the college was brought here in 1925. Present enrollment is about 600.

17. STEELEWORTH, known for a time as Lombardy and Cedar Walk (*private*), in the NE. section of the city, was built in 1799 by Gen. John Steele, Federalist leader, U. S. Congressman (1789-93) and Comptroller of the U. S. Treasury (1796-1802). Originally the center of a great plantation, its garden was particularly beautiful. The floor plans for the house, now greatly altered, are in the Southern Historical Collection at Chapel Hill. The interior contains interesting woodwork and two Adam mantels. Archibald Henderson, biographer, historian, and mathematician, was born here.

POINTS OF INTEREST NEAR SALISBURY

1. ALEXANDER LONG HOME, 2 m. NE. of Spencer, near the Yadkin River, was built in 1783 by Alexander Long, a wealthy planter, who used it as an inn for those who used his ferry, 1 m., across the Yadkin. Washington crossed here on his way to Salem in 1791. The large two-story frame house is paneled with walnut. It has large double brick chimneys which bear, in glazed headers, the letters "A. L." and "E. L.," the initials of Alexander and Elizabeth (his second wife) Long. Above are heart-shaped patterns; diamond-shaped motifs are also used in the chimney.

2. Right on NC 150 to THYATIRA PRESBYTERIAN CHURCH, 9 m., which was founded in 1752, though the present building was completed in 1860. Here are buried the ancestors of Senator Alben W. Barkley and Pres. James Knox Polk. Also buried here is Francis Locke, judge of the Superior Court (1803-14), who was elected U. S. Senator in 1814 but decided, after setting out in his gig for Washington, that the trip was too rough. He turned back and refused to qualify. Among others buried here were the Rev. Samuel E. McCorkle, who operated one of the first schools, Zion Parnassus Academy, here; and Elizabeth Maxwell Steele (*see above*).

3. Right from Salisbury on the Beatties Ford Rd. to the old ORGAN CHURCH, 10 m. This Evangelical Lutheran Church, originally Zion's Church, is one of the three mother churches of the denomination in North Carolina. It was organized shortly after 1747. Hickory Church, the first building, was owned and used jointly by the Lutheran and German Reformed congregations. The present sturdy two-story stone structure erected in 1791 is the third used by the Lutherans. The building no longer contains the old pipe organ for which the church was named, nor the old goblet-shaped pulpit with high soundboard and winding steps. The organ was built in the church entirely by hand by a member of the congregation, named Steigerwalt (Stirewalt) and was the first organ in any Lutheran church in North Carolina.

GRACE REFORMED CHURCH, 12 m., was built (1795-1811) by members of old Hickory Church when they separated from the Lutherans. It was commonly called the Lower Stone Church because it was built of the same kind of stone as the old Organ Church but on a lower site on Second Creek.

Wilmington

Information Services: Carolina Motor Club, Hotel Cape Fear Bldg.; New Hanover Historical Commission (tel.); Merchants Association, Chamber of Commerce, 4th and Princess Sts.

Railroad Stations: Union Station, Redcross and Front Sts., for Atlantic Coast Line R.R.; end of Brunswick St. for Seaboard Air Line R.R.

Bus Station: Walnut and 2nd Sts., for Greyhound, Queen City, and Seashore Transportation.

Airport: Bluethenthal Field, **3 m.** N. on US 117, **1 m.** E. on Airport Rd., for commercial and private planes and for National and Piedmont Air Lines.

Piers: N. C. State Ports Authority, with $5,000,000 river front terminals, S. end of harbor; Sprunt Corporation, Heide & Company, and Seaboard Air Line terminals, N. end of harbor.

Radio and Television Stations: WMFD (650), WMFD-FM (96.3), WMFD-TV (channel 6), WGNI (1340).

Newspapers: The Wilmington Morning Star (daily & Sun.); *Wilmington News* (daily except Sat.); *The Sunday Star-News* (Sun.).

Educational Institutions: Wilmington Junior College; St. Mary's Roman Catholic parochial school.

Swimming: Greenfield Lake, S. end of 4th St.

Golf: Municipal Golf Course, **4 m.** E. on US 76, 18 holes; Cape Fear Country Club, on US 76 E., in city limits, 18 holes.

Tennis: Municipal playgrounds: Pembroke Jones Park, Market and 14th Sts.; Wallace Park, 21st and Market Sts.; Robert Strange Playground, 8th and Nun Sts.; Greenfield Park.

Hunting and Fishing: Inquire Chamber of Commerce, Southeastern North Carolina Beach Association, New Hanover Fishing Club, and Sheriff's Office.

Annual Events: Azalea Festival; Azalea Professional Golf Tournament, late March each year; Easter Carols; Annual Outing, Junior Police Bureau; Municipal Christmas Tree.

WILMINGTON (32 alt., 45,043 pop.), seat of New Hanover County and chief deep-water port of the State, is situated at the head of a narrow peninsula between Cape Fear River and the Atlantic Ocean, 30 miles from the river mouth. The gateway to many popular play areas, a year-round vacation and resort atmosphere pervades this two-century old town, with its historic buildings and elaborate gardens. The surrounding country is a region noted for the variety of its vegetation.

The river, thickly lined with piers and warehouses, is visible only at street ends and at the customhouse wharf. Several residential streets have landscaped parkways where palmettos grow in profusion. Fine old homes, many surrounded by informal gardens and some enclosed by high walls, are sheltered by oaks, maples, and magnolias. Fountains and monuments mark many street intersections.

In 1732, about 5 years after the settlement of Brunswick, lower down the river, Wilmington was settled by English yeomen who built log shacks on a bluff east of the junction of the Northeast and Northwest Branches of the river. This settlement soon admitted colonists from the lower peninsula, who sought better harbor facilities and protection from pirates. Originally it was called New Liverpool, but early deeds, 1733-36, show that adjacent settlements were called New Carthage and New Town, or Newton. Gov. Gabriel Johnston settled here in 1734, and the following year the colonial council and courts were held here. In 1739 Johnston changed the name to honor his patron, Spencer Compton, Earl of Wilmington. The town rapidly became the commercial center of the entire Cape Fear region. Fort Johnston, authorized by the Assembly in 1745 and completed in 1764, was constructed at the mouth of the river as a protection against Spanish privateers.

Resentment against the Stamp Act reached a climax in Wilmington in 1765 when funeral rites of Liberty were performed on Market Street, and the stamp master was forced to resign. At Brunswick, His Majesty's Ship *Diligence* was prevented from unloading the obnoxious stamps. This resistance antedated the Boston Tea Party nearly 8 years.

Wilmington's Revolutionary heroes include Cornelius Harnett, colonial statesman, Gen. Robert Howe, trusted friend of Washington, and William Hooper, signer of the Declaration of Independence. The British, under Maj. James H. Craig, held the town from Jan. to Nov., 1781. Sporadic raids were made on the Cape Fear region during this occupation. After the battle of Guilford Courthouse, Cornwallis retreated to Wilmington to repair his damages before marching on to Yorktown and defeat.

Innes Academy was established in 1783, with funds bequeathed by Col. James Innes "For the use of a free school." In 1804 the Bank of Cape Fear was incorporated. Women of the town organized the Female Benevolent Society in 1817. After a slave uprising in 1831, six of the leaders were tried and hanged.

During the Civil War, Wilmington, protected by Forts Fisher, Caswell, and Johnston at the mouth of the river, was the chief port of entry for Confederate blockade runners. In 1862 they brought in yellow fever from

Nassau, causing hundreds of deaths. When the two forts and the town fell to Union forces in Jan., 1865, the last port in use by the Confederacy was gone. The fate of the South was soon sealed. Many homes, churches, and warehouses were destroyed by the disastrous fires during and after the war.

The Wilmington *Star*, North Carolina's oldest daily newspaper to have continuous existence to the present day, was founded Sept. 23, 1867 by Maj. William H. Bernard. Between 1875-1881, government engineers, under Henry Bacon, closed New Inlet, which had been deepened by a hurricane in 1871. This saved Wilmington's harbor by insuring a sufficient depth over the main bar. The dam is known as the Rocks.

Wilmington suffered under carpetbag rule until 1876, when the Democrats regained control. A fusion of Republicans and Populists won in 1895 and elected or appointed several Negroes to municipal offices. Resentful Democrats organized the Red Shirts, who, in 1898, so intimidated Negro voters that a sweeping victory was won. As a result, the Red Shirts compelled the resignation of the mayor and councilmen and all Negro officeholders for successors of their own choosing. After a Negro printing office was burned, a general riot started and 9 or more Negroes were slain. Restriction of the franchise for Negroes and the unquestioned supremacy of the Democratic party ensued.

Until 1910 Wilmington was the largest city in North Carolina. The shallow channel and the distance from the sea limited its development, and its industry and trade failed to match the more spirited stride of inland cities. During World War I three government shipyards were built here and about 30 vessels were launched for naval duty. Later deepening of the channel brought a resurgence of trade to the city. In World War II the government-owned North Carolina Shipbuilding Company built 145 mammoth cargo ships in 4 years. Terminals for oil companies, fertilizer plants (which produce about 600,000 tons annually), lumber mills, creosoting plants, shirt factories, and carpet and wood pulp plants are the most important industries.

The harbor handles more than two million tons of cargo annually and port revenue collections exceed $15,000,000 a year. The controlling depth is 34 feet over the ocean bar and 32 feet in the river channels, with a 34-foot depth in the anchorage basin. The city is accessible to the Intracoastal Waterway through the Cape Fear River where, at the old Liberty Shipyard property, there is a free yacht basin. Wilmington is an important railroad center, with the general offices of the Atlantic Coast Line and division headquarters for the Seaboard Air Line.

The Thalian Association, one of the earliest theatrical organizations in North Carolina, was formed prior to 1788. The group was revived in 1814 and again in 1846, continuing until the Civil War. In 1929 a new theater group assumed the old name. Today full-length plays are presented, including the works of members. The Brigade Boys Club, outgrowth of a semi-military organization known as the Boys Brigade, maintains a club building, library, and gymnasium and conducts a character-building program for local youths. A social center, Harmony Circle, is maintained by Jews of the city.

The majority of the city's 14,000 Negroes, about 40 per cent of the total population, are employed in manual and domestic labor, though many are engaged in the skilled trades and a few are represented in the professions.

POINTS OF INTEREST

1. THE U. S. CUSTOMHOUSE, Water St. between Princess and Market Sts., stretches the length of a city block. Designed by James A. Wetmore and built in 1914-16 of natural sandstone, its three stories are marked by classic simplicity. It is enhanced by a recessed court and esplanade in front. From the wharf, where the U. S. Coast Guard cutter *Mendota* docks, there is a wide view of the river. Across the river on the Eagle Island shore is the SITE OF BEERY'S SHIPYARD, also called the Confederate Navy Yard. Here in 1862 the ironclad *North Carolina* was built. Upstream the water front is crowded with docks and warehouses and plants and facilities for handling the export-import trade. Downstream are more docks and warehouses for cotton, chemical, cooperage, and other concerns. Farther south are the tanks of many oil companies, which annually distribute millions of gallons of petroleum products. Wilmington is the second largest Atlantic port for distribution of such products.

2. The SITE OF THE OLD COURTHOUSE, NE. corner Front and Market Sts., is now occupied by business structures. Here, on Nov. 16, 1765, Dr. William Houston, the royal stamp master, was forced to resign by the militia, which also prevented the landing of stamped paper. Here too the safety committees met, which adopted a defense pledge June 19, 1775.

3. The SITE OF CONFEDERATE HEADQUARTERS, NW. corner Market and 3rd Sts., is now occupied by an automobile service station. This was the military center when Wilmington was a strategic port as the "life line of the Confederacy." Here John C. Calhoun was entertained as Secretary of War on April 12, 1819. It was torn down during World War I.

4. The GEORGE DAVIS MONUMENT, Market and 3rd Sts., commemorates Wilmington's Confederate States Senator and Attorney General. An heroic portrait statue of bronze on a granite pedestal, it was executed by Francis Herman Packer and erected in 1911.

5. The CORNWALLIS HOUSE, SW. corner Market and 3rd Sts., is State headquarters of the N. C. Society of the Colonial Dames of America, who have established a museum of colonial furniture and relics in the building. Built in 1771, this two-story, white, weatherboarded structure, shaded by huge magnolias, has a gabled roof, and the front porches are carried on two superimposed ranges of Ionic columns. The central bay of the colonnade, slightly wider than the rest, is surmounted by a pediment. The first floor of the house is raised well above the ground on a high latticed basement. The double cellars have apartments locally referred to as dungeons. Tradition tells of a tunnel leading two blocks west to the river. Cornwallis supposedly maintained headquarters here while in possession of the city in April, 1781,

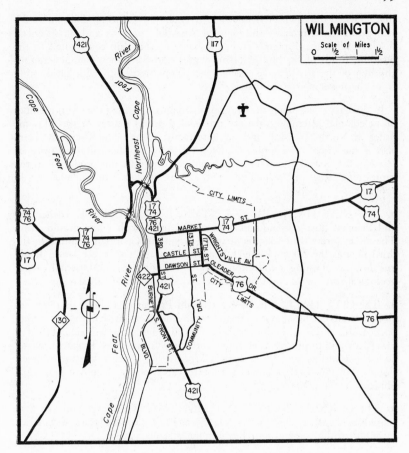

and used the basement as a military prison. The original floor boards bear marks reputedly made by British muskets.

6. ST. JAMES' CHURCH (*Episcopal*), SE. corner 3rd and Market Sts., of Gothic Revival design, built by T. U. Walter, architect of the United States capitol dome, was erected in 1839 near the site of an earlier church built in 1751, materials from which were used in the new structure. The parish was founded in 1735. Until the Civil War the interior had galleries around three sides of the nave "for the use of our people of color." A transept was added in 1879. The wooden altar and reredos were carved by Silas McBee and his sister, of Sewanee, Tenn. It was used for a hospital during Union occupation of the town.

In the vestry room hangs a painting of the head of Christ, *Ecce Homo* (Behold the Man), artist unknown, taken from a captured Spanish ship that attacked the town of Brunswick in 1748. The painting, done on wood, was given the church by the General Assembly in 1754 and has been on display ever since. Proceeds from the booty of this ship contributed to the building funds of St. Philips (Brunswick) and St. James. For generations children of the parish have greeted the rising Easter sun with carols sung from the tower above the belfry.

In the CHURCH YARD is the grave of Cornelius Harnett (1723-81), member of 13 colonial assemblies, deputy provisional grand master of the Masonic order in North America, and delegate to the Continental Congress. Here also is the grave of Thomas Godfrey (1736-63), author of the *Prince of Parthia,* the first drama written by a native American and produced on the professional stage. Published in 1765, it was produced in Philadelphia in 1767.

7. The NEW HANOVER COUNTY COURTHOUSE, SE. corner 3rd and Princess Sts., was built in 1892 of red brick with white granite trim. The annex, erected in 1925, is of white granite in Georgian design. On the third floor is the NEW HANOVER COUNTY MUSEUM (*open 3-5 Mon., Wed., and Fri.*), containing a collection of early Wilmingtoniana, Oriental curios, geological specimens, and Confederate and World War I relics.

8. The CITY HALL, NE. corner 3rd and Princess Sts., built in 1855, has 18-inch walls surfaced with cream stucco and is fronted by a Corinthian portico. In addition to municipal offices the building contains THALIAN HALL, an auditorium seating 1,000 and the WILMINGTON PUBLIC LIBRARY (*open 9-8 weekdays except June 1-Sept. 1, 9-7*), with 55,000 volumes. Founded in 1760 as the Cape Fear Library, this is one of the oldest municipal libraries in the country.

9. The CORNELIUS HARNETT MONUMENT, Market and 4th Sts., is a white obelisk erected by the N.C. Society of Colonial Dames of America in honor of the colonial and Revolutionary statesman.

10. The HEBREW TEMPLE, SE. corner E. Market and 4th Sts., built in 1875, is the first temple erected by Jews in North Carolina. The design is based upon Oriental tradition, employing Saracenic detail.

11. The WILMINGTON LIGHT INFANTRY ARMORY, Market St. between 4th and 5th Sts., a two-story structure of pressed brick and marble, built in 1852, served as a residence until acquired by the Wilmington Light Infantry in 1892. Fixtures include a built-in stove and wall safe. This fine building was deeded to the city in 1952 by the Reserve Corps and will be the future home of the Wilmington Public Library. The basement has been reserved as a club room for the Reserve Corps until the last member has died.

The company, organized in 1852, was equipped by Jefferson Davis, Secretary of War under President Pierce. During the Civil War the unit occupied Forts Johnston and Caswell, but in World War I its members were assigned to various regiments.

12. The BELLAMY MANSION (*private*), NE. corner Market and 5th Sts., is a "flamboyant, late Classic-Revival house whose ornate details herald the coming of the Victorian period." Built in 1859, it has a massive Corinthian portico which borders three sides of the wooden structure. The wide entrance door with its segmental, pedimented heading is carved in a design of roses and leaves. The original carpets and furnishings are still on display. The front yard is enclosed by an elaborate cast-iron fence. During Union occupation in the spring of 1865, it served as headquarters.

13. HUGH MacRAE HOUSE (*private*), E. Market St. between 7th and 8th Sts., a Gothic Revival house designed in the style of a Tudor baronial castle, was built about 1850 by James Post and remodeled in 1902 by Henry Bacon, designer of the Lincoln Memorial in Washington. The ivy-clad brick building with brown stucco and stone trim has a series of pointed arches beneath the main cornice. The south elevation has a conservatory with wrought-iron supports surmounted with a wrought-iron balustrade. The yard is enclosed by a wrought-iron fence with wide gates, designed by Bacon, at both north and south carriage entrances. During the Civil War the house was used by Federal troops as a hospital.

14. St. MARY'S CATHEDRAL (*Roman Catholic*), NW. corner Ann and 5th Sts., of Spanish Renaissance design, is the work of Rafael Guastavino and was built (1912-13) under the supervision of Rafael Guastavino, Jr. Graceful towers flank the front entrance and a dome spans the main section of the glazed-brick building. The interior walls are decorated with mosaic figures of the saints in varicolored tiles. The stained-glass windows were made by Franz Meyer in Munich, Germany.

15. The COUNCIL TREE, near SE. corner 4th and Ann Sts., is a great oak, which in 1740 marked the town boundary and under whose shade, according to tradition, political and other gatherings were held.

16. The SITE OF THE BIRTHPLACE OF ANN WHISTLER, SW. corner 4th and Orange Sts., is occupied by a residence. She was the subject of the world-famous painting, *My Mother,* by the artist, James Abbott McNeill Whistler.

17. The FIRST PRESBYTERIAN CHURCH, NE. corner 3rd and Orange Sts., was erected in 1928 after a design by Hobart Upjohn. The body of the church, granite with limestone trim, is English Gothic with a clerestory. The front with its spire suggests the French Gothic, particularly the Cathedral at Chartres, while the brick Sunday school building is Tudor. A previous church on this site was served by the Rev. Joseph Ruggles Wilson, father of Pres. Woodrow Wilson. In the vestibule a mosaic tablet, placed by the Stamp Defiance chapter, D. A. R., memorializes the 28th President, who, as a boy, was a member.

18. The GOVERNOR DUDLEY MANSION (*private*), SW. corner Front and Nun Sts., was constructed about 1832 of red brick, since painted white. This Federal style house has a two-story main block, flanked by recessed

wings. Twin stone steps, with iron railings, rise to a small landing in front of the porticoed, fanlighted doorway. At the rear is a two-story conservatory, from which stone steps lead to the garden, terraced broadly down to the water's edge. An iron railing marks the Front Street entrance, behind which are luxuriant palmettos. It was originally the home of the first popularly elected governor of North Carolina, Edward B. Dudley (1836-41), who is credited with the famous "It's a long time between drinks" reply to Gov. Pierce Butler of S. C. Here Gov. Dudley entertained Daniel Webster in 1847, and James Sprunt entertained Pres. William H. Taft in 1909. Here also the Wilmington & Weldon Railroad was organized about 1836, which, when completed in 1860, distance 160 miles, was the longest railroad in the world. It is now owned by the Wilmington Lodge of Elks.

19. The CONFEDERATE MEMORIAL, 3rd and Dock Sts., designed by Francis H. Packer, is a bronze pair of soldiers in bas-relief set against polished white granite, given by Gabriel James Boney as a memorial to his comrades.

20. ST. THOMAS' CHURCH (*Roman Catholic*), Dock St., near 2nd, now a mission and school for Negroes, conducted by the Sisters of Mercy, was built in 1845 as St. Thomas Pro-Cathedral. James, Cardinal Gibbons, as a young bishop, served this church. In a reading room at the rear of the altar he began his famous religious treatise, "The Faith of Our Fathers." He secured in Europe several valuable religious paintings which are displayed at the rear of the altar. Father Thomas F. Price, Wilmington native and co-founder of Mary Knoll Mission, N..Y., was an acolyte under Bishop Gibbons.

21. The DeROSSETT HOUSE (*private*), NE. corner 2nd and Dock Sts., supposedly designed by James Post and built about 1850, is of modified Georgian design with façade of fluted Doric columns and a hip roof crowned with a cupola. A 6-foot openwork brick wall surrounds a terraced garden.

22. HILTON PARK, N. end of 4th St. at the river, on the site of the estate of Cornelius Harnett, is a 3-acre park named for William Hilton, Cape Fear explorer. Here is what is claimed to be the World's Largest Christmas Tree, a live oak festooned with moss, 70 ft. high, 15 ft. in circumference at the base, its limbs spreading 115 ft. It is decorated for the Christmas season, when nightly religious services are held.

23. OAKDALE CEMETERY, N. end of 15th St., is shaded with live oaks draped with Spanish moss, brightened in the spring by dogwood blooms. Here are buried a number of interesting people:

Dr. W. W. Wilkings, the last man killed in a political duel in N. C. (1857).

Henry Bacon, designer of Lincoln Memorial. His brother designed his gravestone from a pattern of honeysuckle buds that Henry Bacon had admired in Egypt.

Mrs. Rose O'Neill Greenhow, a Washington society matron who served as a Confederate secret agent, whose message revealing the Federal order for McDowell's advance on Manassas is credited with enabling Confederates to forestall a surprise attack and win the first battle of Bull Run. Arrested by Allan Pinkerton, Federal detective, in August 1861, she was imprisoned until April, 1862, when she was sent to Richmond, Va. Later returning from England aboard the Confederate blockade runner, *Condor,* she was drowned when her small boat capsized after the ship grounded off New Inlet near Wilmington.

Capt. William A. Ellerbrook and his dog, Caesar, buried in the same casket. The dog died trying to rescue his master from a burning building. A community monument commemorates master and dog.

Nancy Martin, whose grave is marked by a simple granite cross bearing the name "Nance." When she died at sea in 1857 her father seated her body in a chair and enclosed both in a cask of rum.

Lizzie B. Turlington, a deaf mute teacher in the State school for the deaf and dumb. Her monument records she was "Murdered by W. L. Bingham," her fiance, also a deaf mute. When she wanted to postpone their marriage, he persuaded her to take a ride with him. Her body, found a few days later, was buried here on Christmas day, 1866. Bingham's fate is unknown.

24. In the NATIONAL CEMETERY, Market and 20th Sts., along the banks of Burnt Mill Creek, are buried 2,200 Union soldiers, many of whom were disinterred from battlefields and moved to this reservation.

25. GREENFIELD PARK, S. end of 3rd St., surrounding Greenfield Lake, originally a mill pond, has a sunken garden of native flowers. The insectivorous Venus's flytrap also grows here. A playground, bathing beach, and boating facilities are maintained. Wild fowl find shelter here during the winter months. There is a 5-mile drive around the lovely lake.

BEACH TOUR

US 76 leaves downtown Wilmington, at 0 m., and continues through the suburbs to the junction with the Masonboro Loop Rd., 5 m.

Right on this road to MASONBORO SOUND, 4 m. Here is ESCHOL (*private*), the summer home (1760) of Gen. Alexander Lillington, a prominent figure before and during the Revolution (*see* TOUR *17A*); it is occupied by his descendants. All along Masonboro are old summer homes and sites of homes that served distinguished families of the Colonial and Revolutionary periods. George Moore cut a road from his plantation at Rocky Point on the Northeast Cape Fear River to Masonboro, over which his wife and 28 children traveled on horseback each summer to the coast. Luggage and household belongings were transported the 25 miles on the heads of Negro slaves. On many of the old estates are pans used during the Civil War for obtaining salt from sea water. Signs indicate small resorts where roasted oysters are served duing the winter months.

From BRADLEY'S CREEK, 7.5 m., Wrightsville Beach is visible (R) in the distance.

AIRLIE (*private; open; small admission fee*), 8 m., is a rambling white frame house with green blinds and a green roof. A broad porch on the southeast overlooks the sound.

In the landscaped gardens of the estate are found almost every known variety of azalea and the Topel tree, an unusual hybrid developed by R. A. Topel, who grafted the yaupon on another holly. It has broad, shiny, dark-green leaves without sharp points, and clusters of brilliant red berries, about three times the size of the holly berry.

On the bank of Bradley's Creek is the MOORINGS, the estate to which Capt. John Newland Maffitt, one of the most noted of the Confederate blockade runners, retired after the Civil War.

US 76 runs along Wrightsville Sound to WRIGHTSVILLE SOUND STATION, 9 m.

Left from Wrightsville Sound Station on a marked road is the BABIES HOSPITAL (1928), a model institution.

At 9.5 m. US 76 unites with US 74 and crosses a bridge and causeway over Wrightsville Sound and the Intracoastal Waterway to HARBOR ISLAND, where is located an important experimental PLANT OF THE INTERNATIONAL NICKEL COMPANY.

WRIGHTSVILLE BEACH, 10 m. (711 pop.), a year-round island beach resort (*surf, sound, and channel bathing; yachting, motorboating, deep-sea fishing, and dancing*), has an average summer population of 4,000. Many business and fraternal organizations hold conventions here. There are hotels, inns, and cottages and the headquarters of the Carolina Yacht Club.

US 74 turns left and goes up the northern end of the island, 0.5 m.; US 76 turns right and goes to the southern end, 1.8 m.

Boats are available for deep-sea fishing or for pleasure trips. At the southern end of the island is LUMINA (*dance pavilion, picnic grounds, and bathhouses*). Grounded upon the sands off Wrightsville Beach are the skeletons of the *Emily* and *Fanny and Jenny,* Confederate blockade runners scuttled during the Civil War.

LOCAL TOUR FROM WILMINGTON

Clarendon—Orton—Old Brunswick—Southport—Supply; NC 130. 47 m.

This tour of historic sites and homes along the lower Cape Fear River begins 4 miles west of Wilmington at the junction of US 17 and NC 130.

Behind the SPIRITINE PLANT, 0 m. (R), are the REMAINS OF BELVEDERE, where Gov. Benjamin Smith entertained George Washington for breakfast.

The high brick building, set above terraces banked with ballast stones, overlooks the Brunswick River.

NC 130, known as the Old River Road, branches south and parallels the Cape Fear's western branch through woodlands shaded by century-old oaks. Possibly the first white men to visit the Cape Fear River were the members of a Spanish expedition which landed in 1526 under the leadership of Lucas Vasquez de Ayllón numbering 500 men and women and 100 horses. On entering the river, which he named "Jordan" in honor of the captain of one of his vessels, he lost one ship and built a *gabarra* to replace it. This is the first recorded shipbuilding in the present limits of the United States.

WILMINGTON RESERVE FLEET, 1 m., using the Brunswick River to moor several hundred World War II Liberty Ships now in mothballs, can be seen from the road and presents a strange sight among the trees covered with Spanish moss.

CLARENDON (*open*), 8 m., a 1,000-acre cotton and tobacco plantation, is one of the few fine old Cape Fear plantations which has retained its identity. The oldest building standing is a small, square building of distinctive brick bond believed to be late 17th century. The two-story, antebellum house built for the Watters family in the mid-19th century has been moved but is in good repair. The big house was built in the 1920's. It is here that Inglis Fletcher wrote *Lusty Wind for Carolina*. The most unusual feature of Clarendon is a canal 50 feet wide that runs straight from the steps of the big house, .5 m., to the Cape Fear River which at one time was named the Clarendon River. One bank of this canal is being bridged for visitors to walk out into the oldest rice fields on the river. Ruins of the rice mill lie below the old mill pond on the edge of which can be found the Venus's-flytrap (*see* TOUR 1b). There is an unidentified avenue of ruins and live oaks leading to an Indian field where many different pieces of Indian pottery have been found. Clarendon and the River Road area abound in wild game. Alligators can be seen in the canal, deer in the thickets, and occasionally wild turkeys in the trees.

TOWN CREEK, 9 m. (30 pop.), is the site of the first settlement on the Cape Fear River, when a party of New Englanders in 1660 attempted to settle here. In 1661 and 1663 exploring parties from Barbados, headed by Capt. William Hilton, paved the way for the party of royalists who, in 1664, established a settlement at the mouth of Town Creek, which they called Charles Town (also known as Old Town) in the County of Clarendon. At that time the two Carolinas were divided into three counties, Albemarle to the north, Clarendon in the center, and Craven to the south. Clarendon extended from the west bank of the Cape Fear River to Cape Romain and westward to the South Seas. The first settlers were joined the following year by other Barbadians, among them Sir John Yeamans, who had been appointed their governor. These Barbadians planted cotton and exported boards, staves, and shingles. The settlement numbered 800 persons in 1666. In 1667 Massachusetts made a general contribution by order of court for the relief of the colony; nevertheless, it was abandoned in the same year. In 1670 Yeamans became one of the founders of the Charles Town on the Ashley River in South Carolina.

PLEASANT OAKS (*private*), **10 m.**, a 4,000-acre estate spectacularly planted with azaleas, was granted to the widow of John Moore in 1728, from whom, it is believed, the "Widow Moore's Creek" (*see* TOUR *17*) took its name. An ante-bellum house stands on the point of land made by Town Creek and the Cape Fear. The big house stands ½ mile lower down the river between a large artificial lake and the river.

On the SITE OF LILLIPUT (*private*), **13 m.**, was one of the earliest plantations on the river, owned by Eleazar Allen, receiver general of the colonies for the southern district (1745-48). According to his tombstone, he was serving as chief justice of the colony at his death. Lilliput later became the property and for a time the residence of Sir Thomas Frankland, a great-grandson of Oliver Cromwell. At the time of the Revolution, Lilliput was owned by Gov. William Tryon and was confiscated along with the property of other Tories. Since Tryon did not acquire the property until a few months prior to moving into the Palace at New Bern, it is doubtful that he ever lived at Lilliput.

ORTON PLANTATION (*adm. to grounds, $1; camellias bloom in Jan. & Feb.; azaleas in late Mar. & Apr.*), **14 m.**, a 5,500-acre estate, is part of one of the three earliest grants on the Cape Fear. In 1725 a grant for 1500 acres was issued to Maurice Moore. Three years later Maurice sold 500 of these to his brother, Roger "of Berkeley County in South Carolina," later known as "King Roger," because of his imperious manner and his opulence. Orton House stands within the bounds of this 500-acre tract.

The lower central bay of the mansion was built for Roger sometime after 1734 and was used as his residence until his death in 1751. The house was later occupied by Roger Moore's grandson, Gov. Benjamin Smith (1810-11). After a dispute between Benjamin and his brother, James, the latter dropped the name Smith to assume his grandmother's name of Rhett, went to South Carolina, and became the founder of the Rhett family of that State.

Entrance to the magnificent estate is marked by massive gray stone pillars surmounted by iron spread-eagles. The drive winds between tall trees and past ponds once planted with rice. Across the diked marshland were rails for a small car on which visitors rode to the house from the river.

On a high bluff overlooking the river is the MANSION, shaded by moss-draped live oaks, some estimated to be more than 500 years old, and surrounded by extensive gardens of both formal and informal design. Hundreds of varieties of camellias and azaleas, native and imported, bloom from the first of January until May, and other flowers and shrubs bloom the year round. A COLONIAL GRAVEYARD on the estate contains the tombs of Roger Moore, his wife, and members of the family. The tombs are of hand-made brick, some with slabs bearing lengthy inscriptions. The mansion is of brick, painted white, almost square in plan, with a Doric portico. Above the heavy wooden entrance door is a small balcony. Dimensions of the original building were about 60 by 75 feet, but about 1840 the upper story and the columns were added, and in 1910 the two wings were added by James Sprunt, whose family still owns it. The lovely mansion is the subject of a full wall mural in the dining room at Blair House in Washington, D. C.

On Orton Estate, half a mile southeast of the mansion, is OLD PALACE FIELD, the site of Russellborough. This 55-acre tract was bought from Roger Moore's estate in 1751 by John Russell, captain of H. M. Sloop *Scorpion,* which was stationed in the Cape Fear. Russell began construction of a residence here but died before its completion. In 1758 it was sold to Arthur Dobbs, Governor (1754-65), who completed the structure and lived there until his death in 1765. Two years later it was acquired by William Tryon, Governor (1765-71), who lived here until he moved to the newly completed Palace at New Bern in 1770. In 1771 Tryon sold Russellborough to William Dry, Collector of the Customs at Port Brunswick, who changed the name to Bellfort. As a result of Dry's ardent espousal of the American cause, his home was burned by the British when they invaded the river in 1776 under Lord Cornwallis and Gen. Clinton.

A rubble of ruins, almost hidden by trees and vines, is all that remains of the winter mansion occupied by Tryon when he was in Brunswick. Here a marker, of brick and stone from the ruins, commemorates the STAMP ACT DEFIANCE. When the British Parliament passed the Stamp Act, citizens of the region demanded and received the resignation of Stamp Master William Houston (*see* WILMINGTON) and by ordered demonstrations so evinced their dissatisfaction that when H.M.S. *Diligence* arrived in Nov. 1765 with the stamps, they were not unloaded. Incited by the seizure of two ships whose papers had not been stamped, 1,000 partly armed citizens, headed by Speaker John Ashe and Col. Hugh Waddell, proceeded to Brunswick. On Feb. 19, 1766, in defiance of two armed British vessels, the *Diligence* and the *Viper,* and despite garrisoned Fort Johnston at the river's mouth, the mob forced the release of the seized ships and the resignation of William Pennington, His Majesty's comptroller, who agreed to issue no more stamped paper. Two months later Parliament repealed the act.

Just south of Old Palace Field is the SITE OF OLD BRUNSWICK, 15 m., founded by Col. Maurice Moore. Plans for this town were completed as early as June, 1726, when Moore sold two lots to Cornelius Harnett, the father of the Revolutionary hero of the same name. However, there is no positive evidence of a dwelling in the town prior to June, 1728. Brunswick was the trading center for the new settlement, and upon the establishment of New Hanover County in 1729, the village became the county seat. In 1731 Dr. John Brickell, in his *Natural History of North Carolina* wrote: "Brunswick Town is most delightfully seated, on the South-side of that Noble River Cape Fear; and no doubt but it will be very considerable in a short time, by its great trade, the number of Merchants, and rich planters, that are settled upon its banks."

Despite this prediction, Newton, later to become Wilmington, founded about 1732, soon overshadowed Brunswick as a center of trade. When

Wilmington was incorporated in 1740, all governmental offices, which had been located at Brunswick, were transferred to Wilmington. However, a shoal in the river, at the mouth of Town Creek, prevented the passage of large vessels, and, as a result, practically all naval stores, the principal staple of the Cape Fear region, were shipped out of Brunswick. By the time of the American Revolution more naval stores, in the form of pitch, tar, and turpentine, were shipped out of Brunswick than from any other port in the British Empire.

When Brunswick County was established in 1764, the village again became a county seat and remained so until 1778 when governmental functions were moved to the comparative safety of Lockwood's Folly. Between 1757 and 1776 Brunswick was one of the 8 borough towns of North Carolina, which entitled it to send a representative to the provincial legislature.

In 1776 Brunswick's deep water harbor became a liability rather than an asset. When the British invaded the river in 1775-76 the people of Brunswick abandoned the town and fled to Wilmington and other points, and much of the village was burned by the British. The war also brought an end to the British naval stores market, and so Brunswick was never again occupied by more than three or four families. After about 1825 it apparently was completely abandoned.

Brunswick was never a large town, but its population of approximately 250 to 300 was not insignificant for that time. Physically the town stretched along the river for about a half-mile and back from the river about a quarter-mile. Within this area were located about 40 dwellings, along with various shops, the church, and other buildings.

Possibly the most dramatic incident in the life of Brunswick took place in 1748 when the town was captured by a large group of Spaniards who entered the river on Sept. 4, 1748. Two days later the inhabitants, aided by seamen on friendly vessels in the harbor, recaptured the town, but only after great damage had been done. One of the Spanish vessels was blown up, and the surviving Spaniards sailed away on the remaining privateer. The invaders were not pirates but were privateers, legitimately engaged in assisting Spain in war against England.

Funds derived from the sale of slaves and goods captured from the Spaniards were applied, in part, to the cost of constructing St. Philip's Church in Brunswick and St. James' Church in Wilmington.

Old Brunswick has now been taken over as a State Historical Park, but is as yet undeveloped. Future plans include restoration of St. Philip's Church and partial restoration of the Town of Brunswick.

ST. PHILIP'S CHURCH (1754-68) is Brunswick's most noted ruin. Cedar trees grow within the 33-inch-thick brick walls which survived the Federal bombardment of Fort Anderson. The chancel windows, slender and arched, are flanked by doorways. The side walls have 4 windows each, 15 feet high and 7 feet wide. At first utilizing a mere shed, Brunswick churchmen improved their place of worship until finally in 1768 this once-handsome little edifice was sufficiently completed for services. Built of English brick combined with some locally made, it was His Majesty's Chapel in the

Colony, and the royal Governors, Dobbs and Tryon, had their pews raised above the others. The exact date of its destruction is not known, but it was probably burned during the Revolution when much of Brunswick was burned by the British. Only the walls were standing when the Methodist missionary, Francis Asbury, visited the scene in 1804. Behind the church lie many of Brunswick's citizens. Among them are Arthur Dobbs, royal Governor (1754-65), and Alfred Moore, Justice (1799-1805) of the U. S. Supreme Court.

At **18 m.** is the SITE OF FORT ANDERSON, part of the defense line of Wilmington, captured by Union troops after a severe bombardment, Feb. 17-19, 1865. Only grass-clad ruins mark the spot.

HOWES POINT, **19 m.**, is the site of the plantation of Job Howe, birthplace of Gen. Robert Howe (1732-86), aide of George Washington. The plantation was plundered by British troops under Cornwallis, May 12, 1776. After destroying mills in the vicinity, the British embarked for Charleston. Their advance upon Orton's mill was halted at a small spring-fed lake since called LIBERTY POND.

The SUNNY POINT MILITARY RESERVATION, containing 14,000 acres, extending 7 miles along the Cape Fear River, at a point 2.5 miles above Southport is the site of an enormous ocean general-purpose shipping terminal now under construction. Owned by the Army, Navy, Marines, Air Corps, and Coast Guard, it will have three docks large enough to accommodate 9 Liberty-type ships at once. Extensive dredging and the building of a railroad from Leland (*see* TOUR *16*) are now under way.

SOUTHPORT, **26 m.** (26 alt., 1,748 pop.), the seat of Brunswick County, is situated on a beautiful estuary of the Cape Fear River (*bathing beaches; still- and deep-water fishing; hunting*). When founded by Gov. Benjamin Smith (*see above*) and others in 1792 it was called Smithville; the present name was adopted in 1889. In one year nearly 2,000 boats, including 500 yachts, touched at Southport, which is midway between New York and Florida on the Intracoastal Waterway. Sea breezes make the summers cool, and proximity to the Gulf Stream tempers the winters. The town is attractive with groves of wind-swept live oaks, spiny Mexican poppies growing along the streets, and a profusion of western gaillardia and sea evening primrose. Neat old houses, some with two-story galleries and "widow's walks," line the water front or the picturesque streets. A STEEL TOWER, built by the Pilots Association, rises above the town. From it watchmen look for ships desirous of being piloted up the river to Wilmington.

FORT JOHNSTON, on a 6-acre bluff, was the first fort built in North Carolina, named in honor of Gabriel Johnston, Governor (1734-52). It was completed in 1764 and in 1775 it became the refuge of Josiah Martin, Governor (1771-76), who remained until patriots forced him to flee, July 19, 1775, on which date it was destroyed by fire. The State owned the property until 1794 when it was ceded to the government on condition that a new fort be built. The substantial brick masonry then erected is in good repair. It was seized by Confederates in 1861.

It is now used by Army Engineers as a base for dredge crews and survey parties, and by the Lighthouse Service for crews working on lighthouses and buoys.

The RUINS OF FORT CASWELL are 3 miles by water and 8 miles by land south of Southport. Constructed in 1825, the fort was manned during the Civil, Spanish-American, and World Wars. It is now owned by the N. C. Baptist Association and used as a recreational area. Outside the area of the fort stretches CASWELL BEACH, a residential development of about 30 cottages, on the strand of which are unusual pieces of driftwood and old cypress knees jutting up through ancient peat, showing that the coast line has been receding for many years.

LONG BEACH, 2 m. below Caswell Beach (*furnished cottages, rooming houses; pavillion, bath houses, small boats for inside fishing*), stretches for several miles along a sandy beach. Begun in 1939, it has about 300 cottages.

The forts at the mouth of the Cape Fear River afforded protection to blockade runners during the Civil War, giving access to the port of Wilmington and constituting the "life line of the Confederacy." Because of the configuration of the coast, it was difficult to effect a close blockade. The blockade-running ships were designed for speed and easy maneuvering, usually side-wheelers armored with iron and rigged as schooners. They would reach the coast and steam noiselessly along at night until the protection of the forts was reached. If overhauled, they had orders to ground and fire the boat rather than submit to capture. More than 30 such ships were scuttled between Topsail Inlet and Georgetown, S. C., a few of which are still visible at low tide.

SMITH ISLAND, sometimes called Bald Head, about 17,000 acres in area, is available by boat from Fort Caswell, 2 m., or from Southport, 4 m. The extreme tip of the island forms the dread CAPE FEAR, the "promontorium tremendum" of DeBry's map. FRYING PAN SHOALS, 20 miles off Cape Fear, marked by a lightship, are among the most dangerous along the coast. Cape Fear is described by George Davis (*see* WILMINGTON), in "An Episode in Cape Fear History" in the *South Atlantic Magazine,* Jan., 1879:

"Looking then to the Cape for the idea and reason of its name, we find that it is the southernmost point of Smith's Island, a naked bleak elbow of sand jutting far out into the ocean. Immediately in its front are Frying Pan Shoals pushing out still farther 20 miles to sea. Together they stand for warning and woe; and together they catch the long majestic roll of the Atlantic as it sweeps through a thousand miles of grandeur and power from the Arctic towards the Gulf. It is the playground of billows and tempests, the kingdom of silence and awe, disturbed by no sound save the sea gull's shriek and the breakers' roar. Its whole aspect is suggestive, not of repose and beauty, but of desolation and terror. Imagination cannot adorn it. Romance cannot hallow it. Local pride cannot soften it. There it stands today, bleak and threatening and pitiless, as it stood three hundred years ago when Grenville and White came near unto death upon its sands. And there it will stand bleak and threatening and pitiless until the earth and sea give up their dead. And as its nature, so its name, is now, always has been, and always will be the Cape of Fear."

Pirates including Blackbeard, Stede Bonnett, and Richard Worley preyed upon shipping in this region. Finally Robert Johnson, Governor of South Carolina (1717-19), sent Col. William Rhett against Bonnett. A desperate encounter occurred within Southport Harbor during the summer of 1718. Bonnett's vessel escaped up the Cape Fear to the Black River, where it was overtaken by Rhett's ship. Bonnett at last surrendered with 40 survivors of his band. They were taken to Charleston, S.C., for trial. Bonnett managed to escape in woman's apparel but was soon recaptured. All were hanged and their bodies buried in Charleston Harbor below the high-water line. While awaiting execution, Bonnett wrote an appeal asking to be spared that he might devote the remainder of his life to good works.

From Southport NC 130 runs in a northwesternly direction through a farming section and forests of scrub oak and pine to SUPPLY (*see* TOUR *1b*), where it forms a junction with US 17 (*see* TOUR *1b*).

Winston-Salem

Information Services: Chamber of Commerce, 106 N. Cherry St.; Winston-Salem Automobile Club, Hotel Robert E. Lee Bldg., 5th and Marshall Sts.

Railroad Station: Union Station, 300 S. Claremont Ave., for the Southern Ry. and Norfolk & Western R. R.

Bus Station: Union Station, 418 N. Cherry St., for Atlantic Greyhound Lines, Queen City Coach Co., and Wilkes Transportation Co.

City Buses: Along regular routes.

Airport: Smith Reynolds Airport, **3 m.** N. of Courthouse on Liberty St. Ext., for Piedmont, Eastern, and Capital Airlines.

Radio and Television Stations: WSJS (600), WSJS-FM (104.1), WSJS-TV (channel 12), WAIR (1340), WTOB (1380), WTOB-TV (channel 26), WAAA (980), WAAA-FM (93.1).

Newspapers: Winston-Salem Journal (daily, morn.); *Twin City Sentinel* (daily, eve.); *Winston-Salem Journal-Sentinel* (Sun.).

Educational Institutions: Salem Academy and College (*women*); Bowman Gray School of Medicine; Winston-Salem Teachers College (*Negro, coed*); and, in the fall of 1955, Wake Forest College (*coed*).

Swimming: Crystal Lake, Reynolda Rd., US 421, **2 m.** W. of city limits; Camp Dorker, Peace Haven Rd., **3.4 m.**; Reynolds Memorial Park, Reynolds Park Rd., **.9 m.** outside city. The City Recreation Dept. has numerous indoor and outdoor pools. The YMCA, 315 N. Spruce St., has an indoor pool.

Golf: Public: Hillcrest Golf Club, US 158, **2½ m.** W., beyond city limits, 18 holes; Reynolds Memorial Park, Reynolds Park Rd., **.9 m.** beyond city, 18 holes. Private: Forsyth Country Club, Country Club Rd., 18 holes; Old Town Club, Kent Rd., 18 holes. Driving Ranges: Smith's, US 158, **1 m.** W. beyond city; Merriwether's, Polo Rd., **2.6 m.** W., beyond city.

Tennis: City Recreation Dept. has numerous courts at its many recreation centers in the city. Reservations made through the City Recreation Dept.

Baseball: Southside Park, Waughtown St.

Basketball: Various high school gymnasiums. Hanes Hosiery Mills Gymnasium, home of the Hanes Hosiery Girls Basketball Team, National AAU Champions for three consecutive years.

Annual Events: Moravian Watch Night Service and Memorabilia, New Year's Eve; Moravian Easter Sunrise Service; Candle Teas, early Dec.; Moravian Christmas Love Feasts and Candle Services, Christmas Eve; Piedmont Bowl, Nov.; Tobacco Market opening, Sept.; Arts Council Follies, May; Winston-Salem Preaching Mission, Feb.; Winston-Salem Fair and Dixie Classic Livestock Exposition, Oct.; Salem College May Day.

WINSTON-SALEM (884 alt., 87,811 pop.), in the north-central section of the North Carolina piedmont, is the leading industrial city of the two Carolinas and is considered one of the important manufacturing centers of the South.

Salem was founded in 1766 and Winston in 1849; the two towns united in 1913. The minutely accurate records of the first Moravian settlers hold the key to an understanding of the modern city. In 1752 the Moravian bishop, August G. Spangenberg, led a surveying party on horseback across North Carolina from Edenton to the Blue Ridge Mountains and over the mountains at Blowing Rock. The return was made down the Yadkin River valley, and in Jan. 1753, Spangenberg camped at the "three forks of Muddy Creek" where he wrote of the land in that area, "This is the best land we have found that is not yet taken in North Carolina." Here a tract was chosen for settlement.

From Lord Granville the Moravians bought 98,985 acres and called the tract "Wachau" after the ancestral Austrian estate of Count Zinzendorf, patron and able leader of the Moravian Church. The name became Wachovia when the English language was employed. The deed was made to James Hutton of London "in trust for the Unitas Fratrum," as the Moravians were called. To finance their settlement they organized a land company in which each stockholder received 2,000 acres and bore his proportionate share of the expense of colonization.

On Oct. 8, 1753, 15 Moravian men set out on foot from Pennsylvania, 12 of whom were to remain as settlers. The records show that they were well chosen for usefulness in a pioneer community. The little company arrived at the Wachovia tract on Nov. 17, 1753, and took possession of an abandoned hunter's cabin near a meadow. For this shelter and their safety they "rejoiced heartily," holding their first Carolina love feast, or fellowship meeting, while the wolves howled in the forest about them. Thus was founded the first settlement, Bethabara, or House of Passage, later familiarly known as Old Town (*see* TOUR *17*), 3½ miles from the present Winston-Salem.

They were welcome in a frontier country that lacked ministers, doctors, and skilled craftsmen. Where scattered settlers were of different religious faiths, the Moravians held fast to their own church customs. On New Year's Eve they observed Watch Night by reading the Memorabilia, or annual record of community and world events. Love feasts were occasions for rejoicing. The Easter Sunrise Service proclaimed the Christian's triumph over the grave. Nor would they do without musical instruments in the crude surroundings of Bethabara. Soon after their arrival a wooden trumpet was made from the hollowed limb of a tree. Later they brought in French horns, trombones, a violin, and even an organ.

In spite of hardships, the Bethabara settlement, enlarged by families from Pennsylvania and Europe, grew and prospered. In 1758 Indian alarms drove the settlers from many scattered farms into Bethabara for food and protection. Crowded conditions and a desire to discard the communal system led to the founding of a new settlement, Bethania, in 1759 (*see* TOUR *17*), 6 miles from the present Winston-Salem.

When the Wachovia tract was bought, a town was planned for the center of it. Tradition says that the name Salem, meaning "peace," was selected by Count Zinzendorf before he died in 1760. In Jan., 1766, 12 men went to the new town site and began cutting logs for the first house, singing hymns as they worked. This cabin stood until 1907; its heavy door and inner stairway are preserved by the Wachovia Historical Society.

By the end of the year 1771, Salem had several family houses and community buildings. Civil and religious affairs were under the supervision of congregation boards whose control was facilitated by a lease system. No lots in Salem were sold outright, but were leased for one year subject to renewal as long as the tenant was satisfactory.

During the War of the Regulators there were disturbances in the surrounding country. After the Battle of Alamance, Gov. Tryon brought troops with their prisoners to Wachovia.

The Salem diary gives a stirring account of Revolutionary days. Some members claimed exemption from military service on the grounds of conscientious objections. Heavy fines and threefold taxes were collected in lieu of service. A legislative act confirmed the validity of property titles, endangered by the Confiscation Act of 1777. The years 1780 and 1781 were particularly trying. Detachments of Colonials poured into Wachovia for supplies. Although the Moravians raised no troops, they furnished aid to the patriots, and Traugott Bagge, a Salem merchant, acted as purchasing agent for the army in this section. After the Battle of Kings Mountain (*see* TOUR *17*) British prisoners were brought to Wachovia, chiefly to Bethabara. Whigs engaged a party of Tories at Shallow Ford, 12 miles west of Salem, in 1780. Cornwallis came this way in pursuit of Greene, spending the night of Feb. 9, 1781, in Bethania, where the British army destroyed much property, and then passed on through Bethabara and Salem. For the colonial troops a storehouse for ammunition was built in Salem, and a hospital was provided to care for wounded soldiers.

President Washington visited Salem in 1791 and was lodged in the new tavern. The Salem band greeted the President on his arrival and serenaded him at night. He and his secretary, with Governor Martin, attended a Moravian song service "to their great edification." A little girl played the piano in the girls' school for his entertainment. Washington inspected the town, "seeming especially pleased with the waterworks," and wrote a complimentary note to the citizens of the town. Matthew Miksch was the first tobacconist, opening a "shop for tobacco" in 1773. In 1828 John Christian

Blum established a printing shop and began publication of his famous Blum's *Almanac*. Wool-carding machinery was introduced by Vaniman Zevely in 1815. Salem's first cotton factory was built in 1836. The Fries family was prominent in operating a wool mill and a cotton mill.

When Forsyth County was formed out of part of Stokes County in 1849, Salem lay near the center of the new county and was the natural choice for a courthouse site. The congregation agreed to sell the land just north of Salem for a county town on condition that the courthouse should be placed on the crest of a hill and that the streets of the new town should be continuous with the streets of Salem. For two years the county seat had no separate designation, but in 1851 the legislature named the new community for Maj. Joseph Winston of Kings Mountain fame. During the building of the courthouse, the Forsyth courts were permitted to meet in the Salem Concert Hall on condition that no whipping posts be placed within the town limits. In 1854 the plank road to Fayetteville, 129 miles long, was completed.

Salem was incorporated by the assembly of 1856-57; Winston by the assembly of 1859. Incorporation marked the separation of town and church affairs in Salem.

At the outbreak of the Civil War, the younger generation of Moravians, free from scruples against bearing arms, enlisted with their neighbors. The Forsyth Rifles were uniformed at the wool mill of Francis Fries. Wachovia saw Union soldiers only when Stoneman's raid reached Salem, and when the 10th Ohio Cavalry was quartered there after the war.

Following the war, the little town of Winston grew rapidly and soon became a center of business and industry. Salem had long been known for the Nissen Wagon Works, founded 1787, and the F. and H. Fries Woolen Mills, founded 1840. However, gradually the trade and business of the two communities centered in Winston, until today Salem has become mainly residential.

In the years prior to and around the turn of the century, great industries were founded in Winston and have grown until today they are world leaders in their fields. The year 1872 was particularly significant for Winston as it marked the opening of the first tobacco factory and the first tobacco auction. In 1875 R. J. Reynolds founded in Winston the R. J. Reynolds Tobacco Company, which has grown from a little factory until today it is the largest cigarette manufacturing plant in any one city in the world. Its world-famous products, Camel, Cavalier, and Winston cigarettes and Prince Albert Smoking Tobacco, are made only in Winston-Salem.

In the 1870's John Wesley and Pleasant Henderson Hanes, two brothers, came to Winston and founded a tobacco factory which they later sold to Reynolds. Pleasant Henderson Hanes then founded the P. H. Hanes Knitting Company in 1901, which today makes men's and boys' knit underwear, sportswear, and sleepwear and is the world's largest manufacturer of men's and boys' knit underwear. John Wesley Hanes in 1900 founded the Hanes Hosiery Mills Company, which is today the world's largest producer of ladies' seamless nylon hosiery and the world's largest circular-knit hosiery mill under one roof.

In 1946, another giant industry came to Winston-Salem, the radio shops of Western Electric Company. In addition to these largest industries, there are some 300 other industries, making a wide range of items, although Winston-Salem's primary products are in tobacco, textiles, electronics, and furniture.

In addition to its manufacturing industries, Winston-Salem is also a center of commerce and trade. It is the home of the largest bank between Washington and Atlanta, the Wachovia Bank and Trust Company. Winston-Salem is a large tobacco market with over 20 warehouses selling about 60,000,000 pounds annually.

Since World War II, Winston-Salem has done much to renovate its environment. A new City-County Library was completed in 1953, as was a new Negro YM-YWCA, and a new Boys Club. A tremendous Memorial Coliseum is now underway.

A recent development of great significance to the community is the program underway to restore and preserve Old Salem. Already several of the old buildings are open to the public (*see* POINTS OF INTEREST), and Old Salem will undoubtedly become one of the major tourist and historical attractions of the State.

Another movement of importance which has developed since the war is the Arts Council, which coordinates the arts, music, drama, and other cultural activities of the community. The Council, founded in 1949, was the first in the South and at the time of its founding, one of three in the country. The Council maintains an Arts Center and conducts an annual fund-raising drive to support its activities and aid those of its 16 member groups.

POINTS OF INTEREST

1. HANES HOSIERY MILLS CO., 518 W. 14th St., is the world's largest producer of ladies' seamless nylon hosiery. The knitting and finishing processes are completed in the modern plant covering an area between 12th and 14th Sts. on Ivy Ave. About 2,200 persons, most of them skilled operatives, are employed in the plant.

2. REYNOLDS OFFICE BUILDING, NE. corner N. Main and 4th Sts., was designed by Shreve, Lamb, and Harmon, designers of the Empire State Building. It is the tallest structure (22 stories) in N. C., with the pinnacle of its tower 315 feet above street level. From a distance the building has the appearance of a fluted column, crowned by a stepped pyramid. Floodlighted at night, the tower is an outstanding landmark in the city.

3. R. J. REYNOLDS TOBACCO CO. PLANT, with offices in the Reynolds Building, forms the largest cigarette and tobacco manufacturing plant in any city in the world. All products of R. J. Reynolds Tobacco Co. are made in Winston-Salem. In addition to Camel and king-size Cavalier cigarettes, the company produces a number of brands of smoking and chewing tobaccos. Three "Reynolds" brands—Camel cigarettes, Prince

Albert Smoking Tobacco, and Days Work, a flat plug chewing tobacco—are America's largest-selling products in their fields.

Richard Joshua Reynolds was just 25 years old when he opened a little factory in Winston, in 1875, and began to produce chewing tobaccos. That original building—which then housed all the manufacturing and storage facilities, and the office space as well—at first covered less ground than a tennis court. There were only two regular employees in the beginning. The many buildings now required in the operations of R. J. Reynolds Tobacco Co. have a combined floor space of well over 10,000,000 square feet—or more than 250 acres. The number of regular employees has grown to about 11,500, and in addition the company supplies seasonal work to several thousand other employees.

Miles of modern machinery enter into the production today, and on the average working day "Reynolds" pays the U. S. Treasury more than

$1,500,000 for federal tax stamps to use on its products. If all the Camel cigarettes produced in any one recent year were placed end to end, the line would be long enough to encircle the earth at the equator well over 170 times.

Each year, many thousands of visitors are welcomed by Reynolds Tobacco Co. on guided tours in its plant. (*Tours are available each working day. The starting point is the manufacturing personnel office in the Reynolds Office Building—corner of 4th and Main Sts.*)

An average of more than a mile of freight cars and highway trucks combined are required per working day for the company's shipments in and out of Winston-Salem.

4. P. H. HANES KNITTING CO., 601 N. Main St., manufactures men's and boys' underwear, sportswear, and sleepwear. The company also operates a spinning plant at Hanes, N. C., where the raw cotton is manufactured into yarn. The Winston-Salem units knit, finish, cut, and sew the cloth into finished products. About 3,800 persons, most of them skilled operatives, are employed in the plants. The company was founded in 1902 and has marketed the *Hanes* brand on a nationwide scale since 1913. It also operates a branch sewing plant at Sparta, N. C.

5. TOBACCO WAREHOUSES (*open in season*), between 5th, Trade, Liberty, and 9th Sts., and on Patterson Ave., are humming centers of activity from the middle of Sept. until the end of Dec., as the Old Belt flue-cured tobacco of this section is brought in for sale. As much as a million pounds is sold in a single day from over 20 warehouses, nearly 60,000,000 pounds being an average season's turnover. Visitors are welcome to visit the warehouses and see the famous auction system in action.

6. NISSEN BUILDING, SW. corner 4th and Cherry Sts., designed by W. L. Stoddard, is 18 stories high and was completed in 1927. Built of buff brick laid in Flemish bond, the mass is relieved by granite, marble, and limestone facings. This structure was financed by a business that can be traced back to 1787, when the first Nissen wagon was built.

7. THE JOURNAL-SENTINEL BUILDING (*open on application at office*), 420 N. Marshall St., designed by Harold Macklin, and built in 1927, is in keeping with the simplicity of the old Moravian architecture. The design of the cupola on the roof and the Palladian window in the front and center of the second story are based upon those of Independence Hall, Philadelphia.

8. CITY-COUNTY LIBRARY (*open 9-9, Mon.-Sat.*), corner W. 5th and Spring Sts. (1953), designed by Northup and O'Brien, architects, is considered one of the finest public libraries in the South.

9. The RICHARD J. REYNOLDS MEMORIAL AUDITORIUM (*open for school assemblies, entertainments, etc.*), N. Hawthorne Rd. (1924), designed by Charles Barton Keene, was the gift of Mrs. Katherine S. Reynolds as a memorial to her husband, Richard J. Reynolds, founder of the R. J. Reynolds Tobacco Co. Standing on an eminence known as Silver

Hill, the auditorium is connected by a walkway with the Reynolds High School. The structure seats 1,030 on the main floor and 1,087 in the balcony. Six huge Corinthian columns of Indiana limestone support the roof of the portico. The structure, of modified Georgian Colonial design, is built of red brick with limestone cornices and trim. In the lobby are two marble statues, the *Discus Thrower* and the *Wrestlers,* made in Florence, Italy, and given to the high school by a citizen of Winston-Salem.

10. WESTERN ELECTRIC CO., Chatham Rd. Plant, moved to the city in 1946, where it manufactures communication equipment. The radio shops have several plants over the city. In 1953-54 a $8,000,000 permanent plant was built on Old Lexington Rd.

11. THE WINSTON-SALEM TEACHERS COLLEGE (*Negro, coed*), in Columbia Heights at the end of Wallace St., occupies a campus of 62 acres valued at more than two million dollars. It was founded by Dr. S. G. Atkins in 1892 as the Slater Industrial Academy, in a one-room frame building housing 25 pupils. Today it is a Grade A, 4-year institution, with 600 students. The State assumed full control of the school in 1905, and the school was given its present name. It was the first Negro institution in the U. S. to grant degrees for teaching in the elementary grades.

12. THE ARTS CENTER (*open to the public*), 822 W. 5th St., is the headquarters for The Arts Council and its 16 member organizations, representing the music, arts, drama, and other cultural activities of the community. The Arts and Crafts Workshop and art galleries are also located in the building.

13. WAKE FOREST COLLEGE, entrance off Reynolda Rd. (US 421 W.) is about one mile west of city limits. This 120-year-old Baptist institution, a 4-year coeducational college, is being moved from its present site near Raleigh to Winston-Salem. A new campus is being constructed on 300 acres of the beautiful Reynolda estate, at an estimated cost of $17,500,000. The college expects to open at the new location in the fall of 1955. Visitors are welcome to drive through the new campus.

14. THE REYNOLDA GARDENS, on the Reynolda estate, entrance off Reynolda Rd. (US 421 W) about ½ mile beyond city limits, are lovely in the spring. The cherry trees, which bloom in April or May, are considered among the finest in the country.

15. BOWMAN GRAY SCHOOL OF MEDICINE OF WAKE FOREST COLLEGE, corner S. Hawthorne Rd. and Everett St., opened its doors in Winston-Salem in the fall of 1941. It is an expansion of the Wake Forest College two-year medical school which was located at the college from 1902 until 1941. The name was changed on the opening in Winston-Salem from the Wake Forest College School of Medical Sciences to the present name. The 4-year medical college in Winston-Salem had been made possible by the Bowman Gray Foundation. When the school opened in Winston-Salem, it had a student body of 73; today the student body numbers over 400. It is today recognized as one of the leading medical schools in the country.

OLD SALEM

Old Salem is a unique survival of an early American planned community. Founded in 1766 by Moravians as a religious, cultural, and trades center, this quaint village centered about a public square on approximately 20 city blocks. Forty of the old buildings are still standing.

The Moravian Church and Salem College have owned much of the property, and, together with the Wachovia Historical Society, have been largely responsible for the splendid state of preservation until the spring of 1950 when a formal restoration program was begun by Old Salem, Inc., a non-profit organization made up of the people of Winston-Salem.

Through the restoration program, it is hoped to recapture the flavor of the old village and to portray as a living picture lesson the pioneer life in America of a people who represent the essence of that quality which stimulated men to brave the wilderness of the early days, to carve for themselves a new life of freedom and human dignity, and to retain and emphasize the deep religious significance that Salem can give to the world—to teach the manner of their arts, their skills, and the products of their labors.

Because of the careful building methods and voluminous detailed records the Moravian Brethren kept from the beginning, Old Salem has more to preserve and less to reconstruct than almost any other similar project in the country. With materials from native soil and forests, the Brethren built their church, schools, shops, and homes.

The settlers of Salem came from England, the Palatinate, Denmark, Switzerland, Moravia, Saxony, Alsace, Württemburg, and the Black Forest. With them came their customs in building, and they substituted innovations where scarcity of materials required.

The old community reflects a dignified simplicity, with great warmth of character and a love of good materials and workmanship. There is a harmonious blending of foreign ideas by master craftsmen, with nothing of the elegant decoration so popular in the early days.

Although the Moravians were always conscious of the appearance of the structures they built, they frequently placed windows, doors, and chimneys for functional needs rather than for balance in design. The buildings of brick, frame, and logs were erected to conform to certain spacing and alignment along the streets.

Some of the remaining unusual architectural features to be seen in the old village are: the rich, ruddy orange-brown, beavertail-shaped shingle tile roofs; double-tiered dormer windows; the uniformly steep pitch of the gabled roofs with the slight change of pitch at the gutter; the lime plaster strip which separates the chimney from the chimney cap; and segmental and semi-circular arched hoods supported on handsomely shaped brackets.

Other interesting features are the unusually large brick, customarily laid in Flemish bond; rather flat elliptical arches using rowlock brick over windows and doors; masonry walls which had been plastered and lined to simulate coursed stone; octagonal and round wrought-iron railings with their graceful termination and extreme simplicity; interesting hardware used throughout Salem, such as several types of door latches, including the elbow latch intended to be used by the elbow for opening; and the tiered-top fireplaces and the hearths, raised 8 inches.

In restoring the old village, as many of the shops of the craftsmen are being re-established as feasible. Most of the dwelling houses are being preserved and restored as such, with a number of the buildings to be used as exhibition buildings. The dwellings, except for the exhibition buildings, will have restored exteriors and remodeled interiors, and are being rented to suitable tenants. Suitable landscaping is being done and gardens developed.

Headquarters for the restoration are located at 614 S. Main St., opposite Salem Square, and here information pertaining to the village and restoration may be had.

Among the first key buildings which are being restored and opened to the public are: Wachovia Museum, housed in Boys' School, 1794; Salem Tavern, 1784; John Vogler House and Shop, 1819; Lick-Boner Block House, 1787. The home Moravian Church and "God's Acre," or Moravian Graveyard, also hold much interest for the visitor.

Interesting old buildings still lining the streets of the old village are: "FOURTH HOUSE" (*private*), 450 S. Main St., built in 1768, was the fourth house to be erected in the village and is the oldest house still standing in Salem. The home of an early saddlemaker, it was restored in 1940 by the Forsyth County Com. of the Colonial Dames.

BELO HOUSE (*apartment house*), 455 S. Main St., is a handsome building with a Corinthian portico and elaborate cast-iron grille. It belongs to the middle portion of 19th-century Salem, having been built in 1849 by Edward Belo. The grille work and iron animals were made at the Belo foundry near Salem. Belo's store was on the first floor of the building, and his family dwelling was on the second floor with entrance facing Bank St. The house, at one time a well known Inn, now belongs to the Moravian Church.

CAPE FEAR BANK (*private*), SW. corner S. Main and Bank Sts., was built in 1847 as a branch of the Cape Fear Bank of Wilmington, N. C., and was the first bank in Salem.

VORSTEHER'S HOUSE, SE. corner Bank and S. Main Sts., built in 1797, now houses the Moravian Church Archives and the voluminous records of the early Moravian settlers. The Vorsteher was the town warden, treasurer of the Salem Congregation.

HENRY LEINBACH HOUSE (*private*), 508 S. Main St., was built in 1822 for a residence and shop by Leinbach, a shoemaker. Owned by descendants of the builder since construction, it is now occupied by the builder's great-granddaughter.

WINKLER'S BAKERY (*business house*), 527 S. Main St., was built in 1800 by Thomas Butner, a baker, for a dwelling and shop. It was famous until 1927 as a bakery.

TOBACCO SHOP (*business house*), 534 S. Main St., was built in 1770 and is the third oldest building still standing in Salem. The home of the first tobacconist in Salem, it was here the Winston-Salem tobacco industry began. The building has been radically changed from its original appearance.

WACHOVIA MUSEUM, NE. corner S. Main and Academy Sts., has one of the largest collections of local antiquities in America. The collection is housed in two buildings, part being in the old Boys' School, built in 1794, and the other in a new building, erected in 1937. The Wachovia Museum exhibitions were promoted by the Wachovia Historical Society until leased in 1953 by Old Salem, Inc., for operation. The Boys' School is still under its original tile roof.

LICK-BONER BLOCK HOUSE, 512 S. Liberty St., was built by an early Salem carpenter who had much to do with the building of Salem houses prior to 1800. The house, restored in 1952, was the first restoration project of Old Salem, Inc. It was in this house in 1845 that the North Carolina poet, John Henry Boner, was born. One room is set up as a memorial to Boner, and this and the entrance hall of the house are furnished and open to the public. The house represents the less pretentious type of dwelling of the old village.

BROTHERS' HOUSE (*Moravian Church Home*), 600-04 S. Main St., is built in two sections. The frame portion was built in 1769 and the brick portion in 1786. It is the second oldest building standing in the village. Here, at the hub of the industrial life of the town, the young boys would enter at the age of 12 or 14 to become apprenticed to a master craftsman to learn a trade. They would continue to live in the house until they married, and if they did not marry, they remained there and were called the Single Brothers. It is in the sub-basement of this building that the colorful annual Christmas Moravian Candle Tea is held.

SALEM SQUARE, in the heart of the village, was originally placed one block north of the present site, but was moved by the early Brethren in 1768. A restoration of the Square is planned with a white clapboard fence around it, and structures to be replaced will be a firehouse and market, a cistern, and a sun-dial. Brick walks will be laid in early fashion.

OLD SALEM RESTORATION HEADQUARTERS, 614 S. Main St., is the INFORMATION CENTER. A scale model of Salem as it looked in the early days is on display; also current exhibits of antiquities belonging to the village.

The COMMUNITY STORE, 624 S. Main St., was erected in 1775 as the village trading center and residence for the store keeper. The building, radically changed in two major alterations, is being restored to its original appearance.

JOHN VOGLER HOUSE (*House Museum*), SW. corner of S. Main and West Sts., was built in 1819 by John Vogler, a silversmith and clockmaker, for a dwelling and shop. Restoration was begun in 1954 to return it to its early appearance, complete with shop and dwelling furnishings typical of Vogler's early occupancy. Many of his original furnishings are being used.

ANNA CATHARINA HOUSE, West St. behind John Vogler House, was the home of Anna Catharina Antes Kalberlahn Reuter Heinzmann Ernst, whose fascinating diary was developed by Dr. Adelaide L. Fries into a historical novel, called *The Road to Salem*. The charming little house was built in 1772 by Anna Catharina's second husband, Christian Reuter, surveyor of Salem. The house is being reconstructed.

CHRISTOPH VOGLER HOUSE, 708 S. Main St., built in 1797 for Christoph Vogler, a gunsmith, is the oldest brick dwelling in Salem. The initials of the master builder, Johann Gottlieb Kraus, who built the house, are on the south wall. The house is being restored.

JOHANN BLUM HOUSE (*private*), 724 S. Main St., was built by an Old Salem pioneer publisher and banker. It was here that Blum with a second-hand, hand press began to publish Blum's *Almanac,* the publication which Tar Heel agriculturists banked upon for advice for the tilling and planting of their crops.

JOSHUA BONER HOUSE (*private*), 723 S. Main St., was built in 1844 by Boner, a hatter, who was mayor of Salem at one time. The building served as Union Headquarters during Civil War occupation.

EBERT-REICH HOUSE (*private*), 731 S. Main St., built in 1793, was the home of tin and coppersmiths. It was restored in 1939 under private direction.

SALEM TAVERN (*House Museum*), 800 S. Main St., built in 1784, was the first brick structure in Salem and replaced an earlier frame one which was destroyed by fire. George Washington was entertained here in 1791 while on his southern tour.

DAVID BLUM HOUSE (*Salem College Faculty House*), 803 S. Main St., erected in 1842 by David Blum, was an inn at one time and was called the Zevely House.

KUHLN HOUSE (*private*), 901 S. Main St., was built in 1830 by Dr. Christian David Kuhln, prominent Salem doctor. It was restored in 1947 under private direction.

JOHN D. SIEWERS HOUSE (*private*), 832 S. Main St., was built in 1844 by Siewers, a cabinetmaker, who used it for his home and shop. It was restored in 1940 under private direction.

EBERHARDT HOUSE (*private*), 935 S. Main St., was built in 1831 by Lewis Eberhardt, a village locksmith. It was restored under private direction in 1951.

SISTERS' HOUSE (*Salem College Dormitory*), Salem Square at West St., was erected in 1786 to house the Single Sisters of the community and the young girls who entered for schooling in the household arts. The building is under its original tile roof.

GIRLS' BOARDING SCHOOL (*Salem College Dormitory*), built in 1804, the first building erected for the Girls' School, developed into Salem College, one of the oldest girls' schools in the South and the oldest in continuous operation.

HOME MORAVIAN CHURCH, Salem Square, built in 1800, has long been the heart of the Salem community and is the center of Moravian activities of the Southern Province.

INSPECTOR'S HOUSE (*office, Pres. of Salem College*), NW. corner Academy and S. Church Sts., was erected in 1810 to house the Inspectors (Principals) of the early Girls' School. It was restored in 1934.

VIERLING HOUSE (*private*), 463 S. Church St., was built in 1800 by Dr. Samuel Vierling, an early Salem physician. One of the finer houses in Salem, it is now occupied by a great-great-great grandson of the builder.

GOD'S ACRE, or Moravian Graveyard, Cedar Ave., contains more than 3,000 graves, all having similar, flat white-marble markers to symbolize the equality and brotherhood of man. There are no family plots. It has been used by Moravians in the city since 1771 and is the closing scene of the Moravian Easter Sunrise Service. This service has been held for over 180 years and attracts around 25,000 people annually.

SALEM ACADEMY AND SALEM COLLEGE, Church St. facing Salem Sq., are two of the most historic educational institutions in the nation. In 1772 the Moravians opened a day school for the daughters of the Salem community. Originally known as Salem Female Academy, it was the only school of its kind for young women in the South. Arrangements were made in 1802 for accepting students in residence, and girls began arriving by stagecoach and horseback from distances as great as Texas and the "Indian Territory." The growth of the school was rapid, and during the Civil War and Reconstruction it was taxed with the problem of caring for its over-flowing student body. In the latter half of the 19th century Salem received a charter permitting the award of college degrees, and the school was later divided into two separate institutions under one governing body.

Salem Academy students now reside in imposing buildings (1931) on the east side of the beautiful 56-acre campus. A preparatory school, it includes grades 9-12, with its enrollment limited to 87 residents and 12 day pupils.

To the west and facing Salem Square are the distinctive red brick, tile-roofed buildings of Salem College. To a student body of approximately 330, Salem offers degrees in the Liberal Arts, Sciences, and Music, and provides teacher-training courses from kindergarten through the secondary school level.

Part III

TOURS

NOTES ON THE USE OF PART III

A departure has been made in certain instances from the type of material included in the former *Guide*. Such changes and omissions were believed valid because of the increased development of the State and because of the ephemeral nature of some of the information.

1. Adequate accommodations in various places may be assumed unless stated to the contrary. *Collins Travelbook of North Carolina,* published annually (obtainable without cost from the State Tourist Bureau, Raleigh), furnishes complete information on hotels, motels, inns, and restaurants.

2. All roads mentioned may be assumed to be good paved roads, unless otherwise indicated.

3. The description of the main routes are, of course, valid in the reverse direction.

4. Cumulative mileages have been used throughout; the same system is used for side tours, with mileages counted from the junctions with the main route.

5. It is suggested that travelers read in advance the description of the sections they expect to tour and to mark those points they wish to view.

6. Population figures are those of the U.S. Census (1950) where available; for unincorporated towns and towns of less than 1,000, the *Rand-McNally Commercial Atlas and Marketing Guide* (1954) was used.

7. Figures for altitudes above sea level were derived from a report, "North Carolina Place Names Origins," completed in 1939 by the Writers' Project of the Works Projects Administration.

Mountain altitudes were taken from the *Official Data on 223 Highest Mountain Peaks,* compiled by George W. McCoy.

TOUR 1 *(US 17)*

(Portsmouth, Va.)—Elizabeth City—Edenton—Williamston—Washington
—New Bern—Wilmington—(Myrtle Beach, S. C.).
Virginia Line—South Carolina Line, **285 m.**

US 17, known as the 1,000-mile Ocean Highway, is the shortest route between the
New York City region and Florida. Branching south from US 1 in the industrial
area of New Jersey, it traverses flat country never far above sea-level. It crosses the
N. C. line 19 miles south of Portsmouth, Va., having followed the banks of the
Dismal Swamp Canal from Deep Creek, Va. Between Deep Creek and South
Mills, N. C., the route is known as the George Washington Highway.

Section a. VIRGINIA LINE *to* WILLIAMSTON; **86 m.**

This route, entering Camden County, N. C., runs through the ancient
Albemarle region, passing level stretches of truck farms, penetrating dense
swamps, crossing picturesque bridges, and skirting the great indentations of
coastal sounds and broad river estuaries. The section is famous for duck
hunting and sport fishing.

Possession of the section was wrested from the Indians by the English.
Troublous times marked the regime of the 8 Lords Proprietors (1663-1729)
and that of the Crown (1729-76). Pirates sailed the sounds and rivers spreading terror in their wake. There was fighting here during both the Revolution
and the Civil War.

The GREAT DISMAL SWAMP has been reduced by drainage from
2,200 to 750 square miles. It is 30 miles long north to south and varies in
width. With its northern border a little south of Norfolk, Va., the swamp
covers parts of Norfolk and Nansemond counties in that state and in North
Carolina extends through portions of Currituck, Camden, Pasquotank, and
Gates counties. The Dismal Swamp Canal, dug by Negro slaves, although
authorized by the legislature, was constructed (1790-1822) by private subscription. The Albemarle and Chesapeake Canal also connects Albemarle
Sound with Chesapeake Bay.

In the dense forests of bald cypress, black gum, and juniper, the sunlight
filters down upon a tangle of woodbine and honeysuckle. Game is still

plentiful, especially in the almost inaccessible Coldwater Ditch section, where bear, deer, opossum, and raccoon occur. The swamp is also a haven for many species of birds, among them the rare ivory-billed woodpecker. In summer the canal bank is a mass of honeysuckle, reeds, myrtle, and Virginia creeper.

Fire and ax have made ruthless attacks on the swamp without materially altering it. It is virtually an unbroken wilderness, owned by lumber companies who operate sawmills along the borders. There are miles of scattered clearings where the peat has burned down 8 or 10 feet to the sand and clay.

LAKE DRUMMOND, connected with the canal by the 3-mile Feeder Ditch, is a fresh-water lake in the heart of the swamp. Although on the Virginia side, it is named for William Drummond, first Governor of North Carolina (1663-67), who supposedly discovered it. The Irish poet, Thomas Moore, visited the lake in 1803 and wrote a melancholy ballad, the *Lake of the Dismal Swamp*.

The swamp water, colored by the leachings of gum, cypress, maple, and juniper, resembles old Madeira wine. Pure juniper water is considered delicious and healthful, and was once carried by ships on long sea voyages. Juniper tea, made from steeped cedar "straw," was once a common beverage in swamp lumber camps and was believed to give immunity from malaria.

On the Virginia-North Carolina Line, 0 m., is the SITE OF THE HALFWAY HOUSE. Built about 1800, half in North Carolina and half in Virginia, the house was a stagecoach stop. There was much gambling in the taproom and the place was notorious as a dueling ground and hide-out. Fugitives from Virginia rested as contentedly on the North Carolina side as did North Carolina fugitives on the Virginia side. An unsupported legend is that while visiting here Edgar Allan Poe wrote "The Raven."

SOUTH MILLS, 8 m. (9 alt., 479 pop.), was formerly named New Lebanon, to distinguish it from Old Lebanon in the Horseshoe area. A 120-foot drawbridge crosses the canal near the locks. South Mills was formerly known as Gretna Green, where many couples came over from Virginia to be married.

ELIZABETH CITY, 22 m. (*see* ELIZABETH CITY).

Points of Interest: Public square, Judge Small House, Fearing House, Charles House, Shipyards and Yacht Basin, Beveridge House, and others.

Elizabeth City is at the southern junction with US 158 (*see* TOUR *12*) and the junction with NC 170 (*see* ELIZABETH CITY—LOCAL TOUR).

WINFALL, 38 m. (16 alt., 421 pop.), is a village in the bend of the highway, shaded by ancient trees arching overhead, its calm undisturbed by the busy hum of its 8-stack sawmill.

Right from Winfall on NC 37 is BELVIDERE, 6 m. (101 pop.), a village settled by Quakers in the early 18th century. Strong believers in education, the Quakers founded here one of the State's earliest schools, Belvidere Academy.

At **6.8 m.** is NEWBY'S BRIDGE over the Perquimans River. The earliest highway from Pasquotank to Virginia crossed at this point.

At **6.9 m.**, R., stands the EXUM NEWBY HOUSE, situated in a beautiful grove. Built in 1767, it has a gambrel roof and interesting moldings and woodwork.

South of Winfall US 17 crosses the broad Perquimans River, which rises in the Great Dismal Swamp and flows southeast to Albemarle Sound. The hard-surfaced highway is built on what was formerly a corduroy road that had as its foundation a causeway placed by the Indians. The road is bulwarked on both sides by curved sheets of corrugated iron, bombproofs salvaged from World War I supplies. The causeway leads to a modern drawbridge. As early as 1784 there was a floating bridge here supported on whisky barrels.

HERTFORD, 40 m. (15 alt., 2,096 pop.), seat of Perquimans County, is a picturesque, old peninsula town in the bend of the river. It was first called Phelps Point for the owner of the site, and was a port of entry as early as 1701. When incorporated in 1758 it was renamed for the Marquis of Hertford.

The EDMUNDSON-FOX MEMORIAL (L), south of the bridge, erected (1929) by the North Carolina Yearly Meeting of Friends, bears an inscription claiming that here was held "the first religious service on record in Carolina." This claim ignores the baptisms of Manteo and Virginia Dare on Roanoke Island, services in Charleston, S. C., and other claims.

In 1672 William Edmundson, follower of George Fox, the founder of the Religious Society of Friends, preached a sermon to the settlers on the *Work of God*. In Sept. of the same year Fox spent 18 days "in the north of Carolina" and had many "meetings among the people."

The PERQUIMANS COUNTY COURTHOUSE, Main St., is a Georgian Colonial structure of kiln-burned brick with a columned entrance portico and a clock cupola above the fanlighted window in the gable. The original building, probably constructed in 1731 or earlier, was of one story with the jury room detached. In 1818 the Masons added the second story in return for which they were allowed the use of the large upper room. In an 1890 remodeling, extensive changes were made. In 1932 Clinton W. Toms, tobacco-manufacturing executive, made possible restoration of the building. Small paned windows, interior paneling, and heavy inside wooden shutters were again installed, the clock cupola was added, and the original worn red bricks were painted a warm buff.

County records are unbroken from the first deed book, dated 1685, and include the Durant deed, oldest on record in North Carolina. On Mar. 1, 1661 (1662), George Durant acquired from Kilcocanen, chief of the Yeopim Indians, a tract of land known as Wecocomicke. Durant's deed mentions a still earlier purchase of adjoining lands by Samuel Pricklove, giving support to the contention that the earliest permanent settlements in the State were on Durants Neck. However, there is evidence of an earlier settlement between the Roanoke and Chowan rivers.

The SITE OF THE OLD EAGLE TAVERN, which was razed in 1920, covered 6 lots in the heart of town. It is known to have existed as early as 1754. George Washington was supposedly a guest while in the vicinity surveying the Dismal Swamp Canal. Tradition says William Hooper, signer of the Declaration of Independence, once lived here.

The HARVEY HOME (*private*), Main St., built before 1800, has a two-story porch fronted by tall columns. The hand-hewn heart pine timbers are fastened with wooden pegs. Beneath an old tree shading the house is a spot believed to be KILCOCANEN'S GRAVE. The sidewalk, flanked by markers, crosses the grave.

SIDE TOURS FROM HERTFORD

1. North of Hertford on US 17 at **1.4 m.**, R. to DURANTS NECK, between Little and Perquimans (per-quim'-ans) rivers. The peninsula was named for George Durant, whose land title is the oldest recorded in the State.

NEW HOPE, **9.2 m.**, a farm settlement, adjoins the HECKLEFIELD FARM, estate of Capt. John Hecklefield, prominent in the affairs of the Albemarle Colony. The Albemarle assembly and the county courts frequently met here in the early 1700's.

At **15.2 m.** is the LEIGH MANSION, one of the most pretentious of the manor houses of this area and situated on an estate which includes the major portion of the Durant grant. The mansion, of red brick burned on the place by slaves, has a double-gallery porch front and rear with an immense ballroom on the third floor. The separate kitchen is reached by a balustraded walk raised on brick piers.

In the yard is a stone slab, said to be the gravestone of Seth Sothel, North Carolina's "most despised governor." Appointed in 1678, he was captured by pirates on his way to Carolina. He served as governor, 1683 to 1689, when he was seized and banished by the colonists who had become incensed over his corrupt conduct. Buried in the mud under an old elm tree is a slab supposed to have marked George Durant's grave.

2. Left from the center of Hertford, at the point where US 17 swings R., a branch road runs into HARVEYS NECK, a peninsula 12 miles long. Here was the colonial seat of John Harvey, Gov. of North Carolina (1679) and Thomas Harvey, Gov. (1694-99). The latter's son, Col. John Harvey (1725-75), was active in behalf of independence while speaker of the assembly, a post which he held at his death. Col. Harvey, known as Bold John, was moderator of the First Provincial Congress (*see* NEW BERN).

At **9.7 m.** is the junction with a cedar-lined lane leading (L) to the RUINS OF ASHLAND, the last Harvey home, which was destroyed by fire a few years ago.

At **10.5 m.** are the RUINS OF BELGRADE MANSION, home of the Harvey family until burned during the Civil War. In the family burying ground is the GRAVE OF GOV. THOMAS HARVEY. The tombstone bears the date 1729. Thomas and Miles Harvey, also buried here, were members of the general assembly, 1776.

A number of 18th and early 19th century houses still stand in this peninsula, among which are the Newbold-White House, the Harrell House on Yeopim Creek, and "Cedar Grove," the old Gatling home.

EDENTON, 53 m. (*see* EDENTON).

Points of Interest: St. Paul's Church, Beverly Hall, Cupola House, Iredell House, Chowan Courthouse, Edenton Green, and others.

South of Edenton on US 17 (L) at PEMBROKE CREEK, **53.5 m.**, is a U. S. FISH HATCHERY (*open*), where shad, herring, bass, and other fishes are propagated. Here is the SITE OF THE HOME OF STEPHEN CABARRUS (1754-1808), a Frenchman who came to America during the Revolution. He became a member of the general assembly in 1783, and for 10 of the 15 years that he served was speaker of the lower house. He was also a member of the first board of trustees of the University of North Carolina. A North Carolina county and a street in Raleigh bear his name.

At **57.2 m.**, the highway crosses the Chowan River Bridge and enters Bertie County. At the southern end of the bridge is EDENHOUSE POINT, the site of the home of Gov. Charles Eden (1714-22) and of Gov. Gabriel Johnston (1734-52), both of whom were buried in a grove of willows nearby. Eden's remains were later reburied in St. Paul's Churchyard (*see* EDENTON).

There is strong evidence that the earliest permanent settlement in North Carolina was on a point of land between the mouths of the Chowan and Roanoke rivers and that some form of government existed before the Durant purchase. The first recorded exploration to the Chowan River was John Pory's in 1622. In 1653 the Virginia assembly granted to Roger Green, who had just explored the region, 1,000 acres for himself and 10,000 acres for the first 100 people who would settle on the Roanoke River south of the Chowan "next to those persons who have had a former grant." There is no record that Green's grant was ever settled, but its language, according to Connor, the historian, "leads irresistibly to the conclusion that when it was issued there were already settlers along the waters of the Chowan." On the Nicholas Comberford map of 1657 is shown a neatly drawn house, marked "Batt's House," at the west end of Albemarle Sound, at the mouth of Salmon Creek, at what is now called "Avoca." This lends weight to an entry in George Fox's *Journal* (1672), in which he mentions meeting in Connie-Oak (Edenton) Bay "Nathaniel Batts, who had been Governor of Roanoke. He went by the name of Captain Batts, and had been a rude, desperate man." Batts may have been appointed Governor of South Albemarle by Sir William Berkeley, a Lord Proprietor and Governor of Virginia. Batts is the first known permanent white resident of North Carolina.

Left from Edenhouse Point on a dirt road to EDENHOUSE BEACH (*bathing, boating, fishing*), **1 m.**, a quiet resort on the banks of the Chowan, near its entrance to Albemarle Sound.

At **60 m.** and **2 m.** N. stood the home of Edward Hyde, a cousin of Queen Anne and first Governor of the separate Province of North Carolina, 1712 (having been Deputy Governor of Carolina, 1710-12).

At **60 m.** and **2 m.** S. stood BAL GRA, the home of Thomas Pollock, acting governor (1712-14, 1722), governor's councilman, and one of the wealthiest and most prominent men of the colony.

At **62.2 m.**, US 17 crosses Salmon Creek, along whose banks was the plantation and home of Seth Sothel, tyrannical governor of the Albemarle Colony (1678, 1682-89), who is supposedly buried on the plantation. Later this plantation, known as MILL LANDING FARM, was owned by Sir Nathaniel Duckenfield's family, Tories, who returned to England. The present house, AVOCA, **6 m.** L., was built prior to its purchase by Cullen Capehart in 1828.

At **63.3 m.** is the junction with NC 45.

Right on this road **13 m.** to COLERAIN. Between this road and the Chowan River are a number of century-old plantations: Black Rock, Willow Branch, and Hermitage. MT. GOULD, at **6.5 m.**, was originally called Mount Galland for its owner Penelope Galland, the step-daughter of Gov. Charles Eden. The present house was built about 1800 by George Gould, former Surveyor-General of the colony.

COLERAIN (367 pop.) was founded by John Campbell, a member of the colonial legislature and Speaker of the House. His home, LAZY HILL, formerly stood on the Chowan River. Here is also the HARDY HOME, one-time residence of the Hardy family who came to Bertie County about 1690 and from whom is descended Gen. Douglas MacArthur, through his mother, Mary Pinckney Hardy.

At Colerain and farther down the Chowan River are important commercial fisheries and processing companies for herring.

Left on NC 45 to SCOTCH HALL (**7 m.**, ask directions at MERRY HILL, **1.7 m.**), beautifully situated between the Roanoke River and Albemarle Sound and possessing an impressive boxwood avenue from the house to the water's edge. This property has belonged to William Maule, Surveyor-General under Gov. Eden (1714-22), and his widow, Penelope Galland, who is frequently mentioned in historical novels of Inglis Fletcher. Here Charles Pettigrew, first bishop-elect of the N. C. Episcopal Church, also lived. The present handsome house, built about 1835 by the Capehart family, who still own it, was besieged by Federal gunboats during the Civil War.

WINDSOR, **74 m.** (10 alt., 1,781 pop.), on the Cashie (cah-shy') River, was a port of entry before the Civil War. Merchandise was relayed from here to the interior by wagons over the old Halifax Road. The town boasted a Million Dollar Bank, branch of the State Bank. The three main streets are King, Queen, and York. Windsor became the seat of Bertie County in 1774.

Surrounding plantations grow cotton, tobacco, peanuts, and truck produce. The town has sawmills, barrel mills, and tobacco warehouses. Fishing with seine, net, and hook and line is available in the vicinity. Game includes deer, squirrel, quail, wild goose, and duck.

WINDSOR CASTLE (*private*), Belmont Ave., originally an 8-room log house built by William Gray, was later rebuilt near its earlier site, in 1850 by Patrick Henry Winston. Here were born his 4 distinguished sons: George Tayloe Winston, President of the University of North Carolina, N. C. State College, and the University of Texas; Patrick Henry Winston, Jr., prominent lawyer in Washington State; Robert Watson Winston, Superior Court judge and noted biographer; and Francis Donnell Winston, Superior Court judge and Lt. Governor of N. C.

ROSEFIELD (L) (*private*), at the southern limits of the town, overlooks the beautiful valley of the Cashie. Originally the property of John Gray, who donated the town site in 1768, it was the birthplace of his grandson, William Blount, member of Continental Congress, signer of the Federal Constitution, governor of the South West Territory, and U. S. Senator from Tennessee. The frame house, still owned by direct descendants, has had many additions.

Right from Windsor on NC 308 to the BIRTHPLACE OF GOV. LOCKE CRAIG (1913-17), a modest dwelling.

At **3.5 m.** is HOPE, the birthplace of Gov. David Stone (1808-10). Built prior to 1770 by his father, Zedekiah Stone, this house, one of the most impressive ones built in colonial North Carolina, is now occupied by Negro tenants. The second-floor drawing room and library (beautifully panelled) and the wooden gutters are especially significant.

South of Windsor the route runs through green swampland and a forest of pine and cedar.

At **77 m.** (R) is JORDAN FARM, the oldest known house standing in Bertie County. A small brick house, built by Joseph Jordan in 1713, it is typical of the 17th-century Virginia country houses [cf. "Pinewoods" or the Warburton house (c. 1690) in James City County, Va.]. The fine panelled interior was destroyed by fire in 1928.

At **81.2 m.** is the junction with a marked dirt road.

Right on this road to the tract known as INDIAN WOODS, **5 m.**, a reservation set up in 1717 for the Tuscarora Indians remaining after the war of 1711-13. They lived here until 1803 when they entered into a 99-year lease with some of the settlers and left to join their kinsmen in New York. About 1857 their descendants came from New York to make final settlement with the heirs of the lessees.

US 17 crosses Conine Swamp and the Roanoke River over a long bridge and causeway. Framed by hedges of honeysuckle, the causeway passes over tangled swamp abounding in gnarled and moss-draped cypresses.

WILLIAMSTON, **87 m.** (60 alt., 4,975 pop.), seat of Martin County, lies on the southern bank of the Roanoke River and was incorporated in 1779. First called Skewarky, the town was later named in honor of Col. William Williams of the Martin County militia. The county was named for Josiah Martin, last royal governor (1771-76). A port of entry before the Revolutionary War, the town had an old courthouse built in 1774 on stilts over the river. To enter the courthouse people climbed ladders from their boats. When court was declared in session the ladders were removed and no one was permitted to leave.

Williamston, a tobacco-marketing town, has also a peanut factory, fertilizer plants, lumber mills, chemical and irrigation equipment distribution plant, plywood plant, meat packing plant, a tobacco stemmery, and woodworking shops.

The Asa Biggs Home (*private*), Church St., is a square structure distinguished by a railed balcony under each second-story window. Judge Biggs (1811-78) was prominent in the State's political life and was U. S. Congressman (1845-47), U. S. Senator (1855-57), and Federal and Confederate district judge.

Right from Williamston on NC 125 to Rainbow Banks, **10 m.**, site of an old fort where Union gunboats were driven from the Roanoke River. The old dirt fort presented a formidable obstacle to the Federal gunboats which attempted to navigate up the river. Perched on the 100-foot cliffs for almost a mile along the river banks, heavily armed Confederate troops manned cannon which commanded all access to the river. The moment a Federal gunboat came around the bend, it was at the mercy of the strategically-placed cannon.

Section b. WILLIAMSTON *to* SOUTH CAROLINA LINE: **197 m.** US 17

In this section are relics of provincial rule, ivy-grown colonial houses and forts thrown up during the Civil War. The route runs through forests of longleaf and loblolly pine, traverses cypress swamps where black-water creeks meander, and crosses broad rivers that empty into island-bound, braçkish sounds to the east.

Forests and fields run with game; most of the streams teem with fish. Several State parks, game preserves, and resorts are close at hand. Rivers and sounds offer boating, fishing, and bathing; beaches for surf bathing line the outer banks.

South of WILLIAMSTON, **0 m.**, US 17 passes fields planted with potatoes, tobacco, corn, cotton, peanuts, and garden produce. Brightleaf tobacco is the principal crop. Almost every farm has a small fruit orchard. At **10 m.** the route crosses Great Swamp, overgrown with brush, scrub pine, and scattered gum and cypress.

WASHINGTON, **23 m.** (19 alt., 9,698 pop.), seat of Beaufort County, is on the north bank of the Tar-Pamlico River. Narrow streets, parallel with or at right angles to the river, indicate an 18th-century plan, though the town has few old houses as a result of the Civil War. The town was taken by Federals, March, 1862, and Confederate efforts to recapture it in 1862-63 failed. It was almost wiped out by burning and shelling by evacuating Federals in April, 1864. The river laps at foundations of mercantile establishments on Water St. and borders yards and gardens.

The scuppernong grape and related varieties are indigenous to the region. The Mish (originally Meish) grape was developed in Beaufort County by Albert Meish, who came from Westphalia, Germany. Washington is a marketing center for cotton, tobacco, and garden produce.

Originally Beaufort County was part of Pamtecough (Pamticoe) Precinct of the County of Albemarle, which in 1696 became the Great County of Bath. Pamtecough was the name of a tribe of Indians in the region. In 1705 Bath was divided, the portion north of Pamtecough River constituting Pamtecough Precinct. The name was changed to Beaufort in 1712, honoring

Henry Somerset, Duke of Beaufort, who had inherited the proprietary rights of the Duke of Albemarle.

On Nov. 30, 1771, the general assembly authorized James Bonner to establish a town at the Forks of Tar River, which Colonel Bonner later named for his commander in chief. Earliest recorded mention of the place as Washington is in an order of the council of safety at Halifax dated Oct. 1, 1776.

The BEAUFORT COUNTY COURTHOUSE, SW. corner 2nd and Market Sts., is a square two-story structure of brick painted white, built about 1800. A modern annex in the rear is of red brick. The clock in the cupola antedates the building. In the courthouse is a will, inscribed in French and dated 1820, which indicates that Col. Louis Taillade lived in Washington at that time. Taillade accompanied Napoleon from Elba to France when the ex-Emperor attempted to regain his lost domains.

At the SE. corner Bridge and 2nd Sts. was the SITE OF THE DE MILLE HOUSE, a three-story red brick house built by Thomas De Mille, early vestryman of St. Peter's. His grandson, William C. De Mille, born here, was a celebrated 19th-century playwright who collaborated with David Belasco in such successes as *The Wife, The Charity Ball, Lord Chumley,* and others. William C. was the father of Cecil and William, prominent in the motion picture industry. The latter was also born here.

The HOLLADAY HOUSE (*private*), 706 W. 2nd St., is a two-story frame house distinguished by curving porch steps at each end of the square-columned, one-story front porch. The first-floor windows extend down to the floor, and all windows have louvered shutters. Modillions ornament the level cornices of the porch and of the hip roof. The house was used as a hospital when Federal troops occupied the town; soldiers destroyed all but one of several marble mantelpieces.

"ELMWOOD" (*private*), 731 W. Main St., a large two-story house, moved from its original site, was built about 1820 by an English architect for Col. Joshua Tayloe. It was written up in *Harpers Weekly* in the 1850's as a Southern home of unusual beauty. A spiral staircase and Chinese wall paper in the dining room are particularly interesting.

The OLD WARREN PLACE (*private*), 612 W. Main St., an attractive one-story house built flush with the street and high off the ground was built in the early 19th century and bought in 1850 by Edward Jenner Warren, the grandfather of Lindsay C. Warren, U. S. Congressman (1925-40) and U. S. Comptroller General (1940-54). Curving steps lead to a stooped entrance to the principal floor. Beneath are an old kitchen with a Dutch oven and great fireplace with hanging cranes; an English "housekeeper's" room; and a sewing room.

The RODMAN HOUSE (*private*), 520 W. Main St., built in 1848 by John Grist and bought by Judge William Blount Rodman after the Civil War, is a large, square, white house with upper and lower balustrades of wrought-iron grillwork and enormous high-ceilinged rooms. There are original chandeliers and black marble mantelpieces in the parlor and dining room and etched red Venetian glass panels on each side of the front door.

The FOWLE HOUSE (*private*), 412 W. Main St., built in 1797 and containing a beautiful spiral staircase, is a three-story house opposite the buoy yard on West Main St. The Fowle family have occupied it since 1888, and the Misses Mary and Annie Fowle now live there. Originally the home of the ancestors of Capt. Samuel A. Ashe, it has also served as hospital, boys' school, and hotel. In the late 19th century the house was moved back from the street and remodeled.

The HAVENS HOUSE (*private*), 404 W. Main St., is an ante-bellum house, said to be the replica of a house seen by the builder in the West Indies. A curving latticed breezeway, reminiscent of Mount Vernon, leads to the old brick kitchen in the rear, now used as an antique shop.

The FIRST PRESBYTERIAN CHURCH, 121 Gladden St., on the site of the original which was built in 1824 and burned by the Federals, was rebuilt along original lines in 1867. Graceful fluted columns, supporting the old slave gallery, were removed about 1900, but were restored in 1953. It has one of the most charming interiors in the State.

OLD BANK OF WASHINGTON, 216 W. Main St., now the West End Branch of the Bank of Washington, built about 1859, has 18-inch brick walls, a portico supported by 4 Ionic columns, and original iron shutters for windows and doors. These shutters have twice prevented complete destruction by fire.

On E. Main St. is the SITE OF THE DIMOCK HOUSE (*private*), onetime home of Dr. Susan Dimock (1847-75), first woman admitted to the N. C. Medical Society (1872). After studying at Vienna and Zurich, she became a resident physician at the New England Hospital for Women and Children in Boston. Here she established the first course in scientific nursing in the U.S., and a Boston street is named for her. At the age of 28 she was drowned in a shipwreck off the Scilly Isles.

ST. PETER'S EPISCOPAL CHURCH, NE. corner Bonner and Main Sts., is a vine-clad Gothic Revival structure erected in 1868. It is of weathered brick with a large square tower. The original wooden church (1822) was destroyed in 1864 by a fire that started when a citizen burned valuable documents to prevent their being taken by Federals. As the tower burned, heat caused the bell to toll until it fell from its supports. After the bronze had melted an old Negro carried it in a wheelbarrow to his home. After the war, he returned the metal, and proceeds from its sale were added to the building fund. In the NW. corner of the churchyard is the GRAVE OF COL. JAMES BONNER.

The MYERS HOUSE (c. 1814) and the TELFAIR HOUSE (c. 1818) (*private*), Water St. next to the NE. corner of Bonner St., are square old town houses with stoops close to the street, after the New England fashion. They are of frame construction, two stories on a brick foundation, and topped with a shingle roof. During the Civil War a shell passed entirely through the Telfair house. Both houses are owned by descendants of the builders.

At the foot of Market St. stands the OLD MARKET HOUSE, which opens on the City Dock where the oyster boats come in. One block E. stood the old shipyard in which the James Adams Floating Theatre was built in 1913. This was the original Showboat on which Edna Ferber spent some time gathering material for her novel of that name. Although the locale of *Showboat* was the Mississippi, she used Beaufort County names and legends and copied verbatim an inscription in St. Thomas' Church, Bath.

An unusual organization, "Tarheels Afloat," has an annual Memorial weekend cruise down the Pamlico River to Bath, oldest town in the State. Requiring no dues, ownership of a boat is the only prerequisite.

A square frame house painted white, 219 Harvey St., was formerly at 242 E. Main St. This is the BIRTHPLACE OF JOSEPHUS DANIELS, Secretary of the Navy (1913-21); Ambassador to Mexico (1933-41). Also born in Washington was Churchill C. Cambreleng (1786-1862), Minister to Russia during the Van Buren administration. At 203 W. Main St. was the home of Gov. Daniel G. Fowle (1889-91), Confederate officer, State legislator, and Superior Court Judge.

Washington is at the junction with US 264 (*see* TOUR *14*).

South of Washington US 17 crosses the Pamlico River and passes ROD-MAN QUARTERS, an ante-bellum plantation bequeathed by John Gray Blount to his grandson, Judge W. B. Rodman, who, after the war, found it so desolated from Union and Confederate occupation that he never went there again.

At CHOCOWINITY (*MARSDEN*), **26 m.** (35 alt., 500 pop.), is TRIN-ITY EPISCOPAL CHURCH, a small, square, one-story frame building, founded in 1775 by the Rev. (Parson) Nathaniel Blount.

Chocowinity is at the junction with US 264 (*see* TOUR *14*).

At VANCEBORO, **41 m.** (753 pop.), is the junction (R) with NC 43 and NC 118.

In BRIDGETON, **56 m.** (8 alt., 805 pop.), on the Neuse River, are lumber mills and a crate factory.

Left from Bridgeton on NC 55 through forest lands, swamps, and potato fields is GRANTSBORO, **11 m.** (20 alt., 1,000 pop.), a shipping point for Irish potatoes, at the junction with NC 306. Right, through ARAPAHOE (273 pop.) and a sandy ridge tobacco farming country, to MINNESOTT BEACH, **23 m.** (*picnic tables, rental cottages and apartments, dance pavilion, a summer café; trout and croaker fishing; duck, goose, and brant shooting*), on the Neuse River. A few hundred yards down-river is WILKINSON'S POINT, the southernmost tip of the Old Pamlico Road, on the site of an Indian trail to Corepoint on Pamlico River. To the right is CAMP SEA GULL, owned and operated by the Raleigh YMCA.

Retracing NC 306 from Minnesott, at **2.3 m.**, R., a road leads through scenic country, following the shoreline of the Neuse River and passing near CAMP DON LEE (Methodist) and CAMP CAROLINA (Christian) to ORIENTAL (590 pop.), **11.1 m.**, a quaint town near the junction of the Neuse with the Pamlico Sound. Through here pass thousands of tons of fish, crabs, and shrimp yearly. (*Accommodations are limited to 2 houses*).

At Oriental is the junction with NC 55 which leads to BAYBORO (453 pop.), the seat of Pamlico County, formed in 1872. Named for the extremely luxuriant bay tree, Bayboro is on the Bay River, a link in the Intracoastal Waterway. Commercial fishing, oyster culture, and raising potatoes are the principal occupations.

NC 55, L., leads back **4 m.** to Grantsboro.

US 17 makes a sharp (L) turn across the Neuse River bridge.

NEW BERN, **58 m.** (*see* NEW BERN).

Points of Interest: Smallwood-Ward House, Slover-Guion House, John Wright Stanly House (*public library*), First Presbyterian Church, Tryon's Palace, and others.

New Bern is at the junction with US 70 (*see* TOUR *15*).

At **70 m.** (L) is the FOSCUE HOUSE, an old brick plantation dwelling built in the early 18th century. House and lands are traditionally haunted.

POLLOCKSVILLE, **71 m.** (13 alt., 400 pop.), on the banks of the narrow Trent River, was named for Col. Thomas Pollock (*see* NEW BERN), a large landowner and proprietary governor of North Carolina (1712-14, 1722). In colonial days this town was surrounded by plantations on which remain a few houses of faded splendor. The town is dependent on farming and lumber milling.

At **73 m.** is the junction with NC 12.

Right on NC 12 is TRENTON, **10 m.** (28 alt., 469 pop.), the seat of Jones County, formed in 1779 from Craven and named for Willie Jones, Revolutionary patriot and Anti-Federalist leader (*see* HALIFAX). Trenton is built around Brock Mill Pond, whose mill has operated continuously since before the Civil War. Huge gnarled cypresses, shrouded with Spanish moss overhang unruffled blue water. George Washington was entertained at the OLD SHINGLE HOUSE (*private*), then a colonial tavern. The first county court was held in the THOMAS WEBBER HOUSE (*private*), a modernized two-story wooden building. The second courthouse was burned by Federal troops in 1863. The third, of wood, was abandoned when a modern brick one was completed in 1939.
Great Dover Swamp lies in the northern part of the county and Whiteoak Swamp in the south-central. Small game, deer, and fish are plentiful. The principal occupation is raising tobacco, corn, cotton, peanuts, soybeans, and hay.

MAYSVILLE, **78 m.** (41 alt., 818 pop.), the largest town in Jones County, depends on farming and lumber milling. In colonial days rice was grown in the savannas and shallow ponds. Today, marl deposits nearby are mined extensively. The border of the CROATAN NATIONAL FOREST

THE OLD WELL, CHAPEL HILL (COMMUNICATION CENTER)

PLAYMAKER'S THEATRE, CHAPEL HILL (WOOTTEN)

WEST CAMPUS, DUKE UNIVERSITY, DURHAM

EAST CAMPUS, DUKE UNIVERSITY, DURHAM (HIGHTON)

MEMORIAL TOWER, STATE COLLEGE, RALEIGH   CHAPEL, DUKE UNIVERSITY, DURHAM
(STATE COLLEGE NEWS BUREAU)

MOREHEAD BUILDING, CHAPEL HILL (NORFOLK & WESTERN RAILWAY)

COTTON MILLS ON TAR RIVER, ROCKY MOUNT (ROCKY MOUNT CHAMBER OF COMMERCE)

MINT MUSEUM OF ART, CHARLOTTE (HIGHTON)

JEFFERSON STANDARD BUILDING, GREENSBORO
(GREENSBORO CHAMBER OF COMMERCE)

REYNOLDS BUILDING, WINSTON-SALEM
(WINSTON-SALEM CHAMBER OF COMMERCE)

AYCOCK AUDITORIUM, WOMAN'S COLLEGE, GREENSBORO (GREENSBORO CHAMBER OF
COMMERCE)

TRYON STREET, LOOKING NORTH, CHARLOTTE

CHAMBERS BUILDING, DAVIDSON COLLEGE (FRANK JONES)

MODEL OF NEW WAKE FOREST COLLEGE CAMPUS, WINSTON-SALEM

CUSTOM HOUSE, WILMINGTON

ASHEVILLE FROM BEAUCATCHER MOUNTAIN (ASHEVILLE CHAMBER OF COMMERCE)

(*see* NATIONAL FORESTS), first created in coastal North Carolina, is near the eastern edge of the town.

1. Left from Maysville on the Catfish Rd. to CATFISH LAKE, 3 m., one of 5 lakes within the forest. Deer and other game occur in the bog lands of this LAKES POCOSIN AREA. "Pocosin" is derived from an Algonquian term for *swamp* or *dismal*. The permanently saturated peaty soil is overlain with sand or sandy loam bearing a sparse growth of trees, mostly black pine, and a dense undergrowth of evergreen shrubs and vines. In places the streams are coffee-colored.

2. Left from Maysville on the Maysville-Swansboro Rd. to YELLOWHOUSE FIELD, 4.5 m., site of the home of Col. John Starkey (d. 1765), staunch defender of the colonists' rights and pioneer advocate of a public school system. At 7 m. is the three-story frame HOME OF GOV. DANIEL RUSSELL (*private*), (1897-1901). Gov. Russell, a kinsman of Col. Starkey, is buried on Hickory Hill nearby.

At BELGRADE, 81 m., shell-marl and limestone deposits are quarried.

The route passes through HOFMANN FOREST, an 83,000-acre experimental area, managed by N. C. State College as a training ground for students in forestry and as a hunting preserve for deer, bear, etc.

JACKSONVILLE, 95 m. (23 alt., 3,960 pop.), seat of Onslow County, stands on baylike New River. The earliest mention of Watland's Ferry, which preceded Jacksonville, is in a record of court held there in July, 1757.

Onslow was formed (1734) from the Great County of Bath, and named for Arthur Onslow, then Speaker of the British House of Commons. Most of the settlers were English and German. Spanish buccaneers and pirates beset the region in the 1740's.

This is one of the few coastal counties of the State whose mainland borders the ocean without an intervening sound, and it gives its name to the long curve between Beaufort Harbor and Cape Fear. Holly Shelter Swamp is in the southern portion. New River, whose upper reaches are lost in Whiteoak Swamp, is the only large river in North Carolina with head-waters and mouth in the same county. It is 5 miles wide at the mouth, where extensive oyster beds are under cultivation. New River oysters are large, grow singly instead of in clusters, are finely flavored, and command a high price in the markets. Tobacco is the chief money crop. Onslow County hams are famous.

The proximity to Camp Lejeune, begun 1942, has transformed the village of Jacksonville into a bustling town and the county into the fastest growing one in North Carolina (1940-50). Its progress is reflected in a new COURT-HOUSE (1948), the ultramodern DR. CLYDE A. ERWIN SCHOOL (1953), and the GEORGETOWN (Negro) HIGH SCHOOL (1953). Edward B. Dudley, first popularly-elected governor of North Carolina (1836-41) and first president of the Wilmington and Weldon Railroad, was born one mile north.

Along US 17, S., and NC 24, E., lies CAMP LEJEUNE, the largest all-purpose Marine base in the world. Named for Lt. Gen. John A. Lejeune, noted World War I Marine Commandant, it was originally known as New

River Marine Base, for the river (3 to 5 miles wide) which bisects it. Construction (begun in 1942) on the 173-square mile reservation, of which 26,000 acres are under water, has been carefully planned along modern lines and has resulted in an attractive post.

Across from the MAIN ENTRANCE (*admission by permit at gate*), **5 m.** E. of Jacksonville on NC 24, is MIDWAY PARK, a modern housing project community of around 4,000 civilian employees and military personnel.

At **19 m.** on NC 24 is SWANSBORO (559 pop.), on the Intracoastal Waterway. The oldest town in Onslow County, it is now a small fishing resort (*accommodations for fishermen*). Three miles south was the BIRTHPLACE OF OTWAY BURNS, a shipbuilder and a celebrated privateersman in the War of 1812.

South of Camp Lejeune US 17 runs through well-wooded country with few farms. Natural gardens of wild flowers cover many acres displaying blooms every month but January. Here grow insectivorous pitcher-plants, including the rare Venus's-flytrap.

FOLKSTONE, **111 m.** (70 alt., 125 pop.), is at the junction with NC 172.

Left on NC 172 is SNEADS FERRY, **9 m.** (500 pop.), on New River (*limited accommodations and boats for "outside" fishing*). A drawbridge crosses New River, leading through Camp Lejeune to Swansboro, **29 m.**, along the famous fishing grounds of Onslow Bay.

At HOLLY RIDGE (1,082 pop.), **115 m.**, site of war-time CAMP DAVIS, is the junction with a paved road.

Right on this road, across Topsail Sound and the Intracoastal Waterway to SURF CITY, **4 m.** (*accommodations limited*) and R. **8 m.** to NEW TOPSAIL BEACH.

At **129 m.** is HAMPSTEAD (56 alt., 350 pop.).

Left from Hampstead a road leads through woods to the water, **1 m.** (*boats and guides available*). TOPSAIL INLET nearby is a favorite spot for angling for bluefish, drum, sheepshead, and mackerel.

South of Hampstead is (R) the WASHINGTON TREE, a large live-oak marked by the D. A. R. as the tree under which the first President stopped to rest on his way to Wilmington in 1791.

Passing BAYMEADE, 140 m., US 17 enters a plantation where the resinous sap of longleaf pine trees is gathered and then along an avenue of spreading moss-strewn oaks set in thick, subtropical vegetation.

WILMINGTON, **146 m.** (*see* WILMINGTON).

Points of Interest: Customhouse, Cornwallis House, St. James Church, Bellamy Mansion, Hilton Park, Greenfield Park, and others, and LOCAL TOURS of the beaches and historic sites in the vicinity.

Wilmington is at the junction with US 421 (*see* TOUR *17*).

US 17 crosses the Cape Fear River to EAGLES ISLAND. Some of the numerous flowers along the causeway were brought here from foreign ports in the soil used as ballast by ships calling for cotton and naval stores. The waterlily, marsh bluebell, marsh aster, spiderlily, marshmallow, and numerous other plants thrive on the marshy land. The highway, along the course of the first toll road authorized by the legislature, has been successively a corduroy, plank, and rock-ballast road and has carried traffic for two centuries. Bridges span Alligator Creek and the Brunswick River.

At **150 m.** is the junction with the Old River Rd., NC 130 (*see* LOCAL TOUR FROM WILMINGTON).

At **151 m.** is the junction with US 74-76 (*see* TOUR *16*).

In SUPPLY, **175 m.** (37 alt., 134 pop.), guides are available for deer and quail hunting.

SHALLOTTE, **183 m.** (33 alt., 493 pop.), is on the Shallotte River (*fishing; boats and guides available*). In 1729, according to the Pennsylvania *Gazette* of April 29, 1731, this settlement was known as Shelote, but there is no record of its origin. George Washington spent the night here with "one Russ" in an "indifferent house."

THOMASBORO, **193 m.** (30 alt., 50 pop.), is at the junction with the Pea Landing Rd.

Left on this road to CALABASH, **4 m.** (30 alt., 100 pop.), called Pea Landing from the great number of peanuts raised by the principal planters of this section until 1873 when the name was changed to Calabash (*fishing, hunting, boats, and guides available*). On a bluff overlooking the Calabash River stands the old FRINK HOUSE dated on the chimney 1801 and called Hickory Hall. Legend says it was named for a large hickory stump around which the house was built.

US 17 crosses the South Carolina Line 23 miles north of Myrtle Beach, S. C.

TOUR 1A *(US 158)*

Elizabeth City—Kitty Hawk—Nags Head—Manteo—Fort Raleigh—Oregon Inlet—Hatteras Inlet; US 158. 117 m.

This route, known as the Virginia Dare Trail between Elizabeth City and Fort Raleigh, runs along the picturesque banks, which are narrow strips of sand that form the eastern boundary of the State, separating the ocean from the sounds. The Indians called the banks "out islands." Along this treacherous, wreck-strewn stretch of the Atlantic coast, is the site of the first successful airplane flight and of the first English settlements in America.

US 158 branches northeast from US 17 (*see* TOUR *1*) in ELIZABETH CITY, 0 m. (*see* ELIZABETH CITY), and crosses Pasquotank River drawbridge. At night the illumination from moored craft and the streets of Elizabeth City, topped by the beacon on the water tank, is visible for several miles. A causeway, 1.5 miles long, begins at the east side of the bridge and crosses small MACHELHE ISLAND, known locally as Goat Island. Its owner combined the first two letters of the names of his four children—Mary, Charles, Eloise, and Helen—to form the name. A deep but narrow cut is spanned by Stinking Gut bridge and thence the road crosses FERRY SWAMP. The first course over this swamp was a corduroy road flanked by bogs that meant death to anyone who fell into them. After piles had been driven down 100 feet, only to disappear, the State decided to "float" a road. A 16-foot-wide jointed strip of concrete was suspended on steel netting. For a time this rose and fell with the tides, but eventually settled below tidewater. Later the problem was finally settled by the present asphalted roadbed, elevated on pilings joined by steel cables. The fragrant swamp woodlands of pine and cedar are gay in spring with dogwood, honeysuckle, wild rose, and Carolina yellow jessamine; cattails rise from the waving reeds and smilax twines around the taller trees.

CAMDEN, 4 m. (9 alt., 200 pop.), a rural community, is the State's smallest county seat. Originally called Jonesboro, the village was named for Charles Pratt, Earl of Camden, as was the county when it was cut off from Pasquotank in 1777. The CAMDEN COUNTY COURTHOUSE, with a portico of 4 massive columns on brick piers, was built in 1847. Originally the ground floor was used to quarter horses. Potatoes are grown extensively in the section. During the harvest season, people work day and night digging and shipping the crop.

Camden is at the junction of US 158 and NC 343.

1. Right from this junction to the GATLING HOUSE (*private*), **1.3 m.**, known earlier as the Earle Plantation, which is noteworthy for its spiral staircase and interior woodwork. Alfred Moore Gatling, the original owner, represented Edenton in Congress (1823-25).

2. Left from Camden on NC 343 to the junction with the dirt Shipyard Ferry Rd., **3.5 m.**; L. on this road **0.5 m.** to the SAWYER HOUSE (*private*), probably built in the 1740's for Thomas Relfe, the original grantee and believed to have been used as a hospital and refuge during the Civil War. It is a rectangular, two-story brick house, with concealed end chimneys, a one-story porch, and a small frame ell in the rear.

3. Right from Camden on NC 343 to the junction with the old dirt Indiantown Rd., **2 m.**; L. on this road **0.5 m.** to FAIRFIELD, also called the Brick House. The mansion, built in the mid-1700's, was the home of Brig. Gen. Isaac Gregory, who led the gallant N. C. brigade at the Battle of Camden, Aug. 16, 1780, in which he suffered two bayonet wounds and had his horse shot from under him. The interior paneling and front stoop of the house have been removed.

SHILOH BAPTIST CHURCH, at SHILOH, **12 m.** (500 pop.), bearing the date 1727, is the oldest organized Baptist Church in the State. The building, erected in 1848-49, is a hand-hewn pine, joined with pegs. On the floor are marks made by musket butt plates when the church was used as a Federal arsenal. In the churchyard is the GRAVE OF DEMPSEY BURGESS, major and later lieutenant colonel in Gregory's Continental brigade and a member of the Provincial Congress in 1775-76 and of the Fourth and Fifth U. S. Congresses (1795-99).

OLD TRAP, **16 m.** (300 pop.), a truck-marketing village, was the scene of bustling maritime activity in colonial days. Earliest grant on record there is 1681. Men going to the windmill and to the busy wharves often tarried at the grog shops which were also frequented by loose women. Housewives dubbed the crossroads "The Trap," which later became Old Trap.

At BELCROSS, **6 m.**, NC 170 swings north.

At **6 m.** on NC 170 is SHAWBORO (15 alt., 135 pop.), a rural village. Here (L) is a TWIN HOUSE, consisting of two story-and-a-half gabled houses built one in front of the other about 10 feet apart and connected by a one-story gabled structure. The first was built about 1820 and the other added, according to one version, after a quarrel between the husband and wife, who decided to live apart.

SLIGO, **9 m.**, a rural community, was named by Edward Drumgoole, Methodist circuit rider, from Sligo, Ireland, who visited here in 1783.

Sligo is at the junction of NC 170 and NC 34.

1. Left on NC 170 is the village of MOYOCK, **10 m.** (originally called Shingle Landing), the commercial center of this area. Left from Moyock on a dirt road **11 m.** to PUDDING RIDGE, on the edge of the Dismal Swamp. From 1907 to 1935, an Amish-Mennonite colony, called "hook-and-eye" Mennonites, because

they wore no buttons, was here. This custom, like that of shaving the upper lip, was adopted by their progenitors when they were opposing civil authority in Switzerland, where buttons and mustaches were taxed.

Church rules decreed that no member could serve on a jury, bring a lawsuit, hold public office, swear oaths, attend theaters, or use tobacco or liquor. The men wore long hair, flowing beards, and straight-hanging coats. The women wore a quilted or slatted bonnet except on Sunday when they put on the "prayer covering," a white bonnet trimmed with lace and frills and tied under the chin. From infancy children were appareled like their elders. They spoke the "Pennsylvania Dutch" dialect, but church services were conducted in German.

NC 34 runs southeast from Sligo to CURRITUCK (*boats and guides available*), **4 m.** (8 alt., 200 pop.), a commercial fishing center. The name of the town, the county, and the sound which borders it is from Coratank (Indian, *wild geese*). Its first settlement may be traced to the year 1663 when Lord Berkeley granted to John Harvey 600 acres of land "lying in a small creek called Currituck (probably Indian Creek), falling into the river Kecoughtancke (North River), which falls into the Carolina River (Albemarle Sound), the land being granted Mr. Harvey for bringing into the colony twelve new settlers."

Currituck was formerly a part of the Great County of Albemarle. Its early settlers were said to be jubilant when, in 1728, following the boundary dispute between North Carolina and Virginia, the line was established to include them in North Carolina.

CURRITUCK COURTHOUSE, built in 1876, is of weathered red brick. This is the governmental center, as there are no incorporated towns, and local affairs are administered by the county. People of the section refer to the town as "the courthouse."

South of Courthouse Point, on a little rise (R) overlooking the sound, is PILMOOR MEMORIAL METHODIST CHURCH, a neat structure of red brick with small steeple and white trim, erected in 1928 on or near the spot where Joseph Pilmoor, on Sept. 28, 1772, preached the first Methodist sermon ever delivered in North Carolina.

Currituck Sound is a link in the Intracoastal Waterway. Its eastern shore is separated from the Atlantic Ocean by "the banks," an elongated reef or belt of sand which girds the entire coast of North Carolina, except for a few inlets. Currituck Sound was once a salt-water body, whose inlet, described by William Byrd, was the starting point for the line "betwixt North Carolina and Virginia" in 1728. Soon afterwards this inlet was choked up and another, 5 miles south, gave access to the sea until 1828. Today the first inlet is Oregon Inlet, 40 miles south.

The whistling swan (*Cygnus columbianus*) breeds in Alaska and northwestern Canada but winters on Currituck Sound. When full-grown they weigh from 12 to 16 pounds. They seem to mate for life and are accompanied by their young during the first winter.

Timothy Hanson in 1720 brought to Currituck County the seeds of the grass (*Phleum pratense*) which he developed into the fodder grass, timothy.

Around Currituck firesides is still told the legend of 16-year-old Betsy Dowdy's ride in December, 1775. The bankers feared that if Gen. William Skinner did not go to Col. Robert Howe's aid at Great Bridge, Va., the British would defeat the small American force there, invade North Carolina, and pillage their homes. On her wiry banker pony Betsy rode all night from the dunes of Currituck to Gen.

Skinner's headquarters in Perquimans, 50 miles distant. Meanwhile the Battle of Great Bridge was won, Dunmore evacuated Norfolk, and eastern Carolina was saved from British invasion.

Across the sound from Currituck is KNOTTS ISLAND, **6 m.**, approached only by boat or by a road from Virginia. On this peninsula, 5 by 3½ miles, the last of North Carolina's "lost provinces," live 416 residents who are tied commercially to Virginia by the only road, but politically to Currituck County. Designated as "Knot Isle" on the Comberford Map of 1657, it is described by William Byrd in 1728 as having a "good" soil and being a "Plentiful Place for Stock, by reason of the wide Marshes adjacent to it, and because of its warm Situation. But the Inhabitants pay a little dear for this Convenience, by losing as much Blood in the Summer Season by the infinite number of Mosquetas, as all their Beef and Pork can recruit in the Winter."

In the western portion, MACKEY ISLAND, is the summer HOME OF JOSEPH P. KNAPP, who before his death was owner of the Crowell Publishing Co. and benefactor of Currituck County and the Institute of Government at Chapel Hill.

At Barco, **9 m.**, NC 34 rejoins US 158.

COINJOCK, **20 m.** (5 alt., 216 pop.), a small neat town, is on the bank of the Albemarle and Chesapeake Canal, a link in the Intracoastal Waterway. Near the draw bridge across the canal are three wharves, a marine railway, and a lodge (*rental boats available*).

BERTHA, **26 m.** (26 pop.) is at the junction with NC 3.

Left on NC 3 is POPLAR BRANCH (*boats on charter to the banks*), **2 m.**, a scattered settlement in the woods and a carp-shipping village.

At JARVISBURG, **32 m.** (15 alt., 550 pop.), stands the BIRTHPLACE OF THOMAS JARVIS, Governor of North Carolina (1879-84).

At POINT HARBOR, **42 m.**, the highway crosses the three-mile-long WRIGHT MEMORIAL BRIDGE, marking the confluence of Albemarle and Currituck sounds and near the sounds of Croatan and Roanoke. This leads into Dare County and the northern extremities of the Outer Banks, a peninsula beginning near the Virginia line and extending south to Oregon Inlet, where the next link in the Outer Banks-Hatteras Island begins. A picturesque wooden arch spans the east end of this bridge as the road enters Dare County, the birthplace of the nation (1584) and of aviation (1903).

Dare, youngest of Albemarle region counties, was founded in 1870 from Hyde, Currituck, and Tyrrell and named for Virginia Dare, the first white child born of English parents in the New World. Its area includes 300 square miles of land and 1,200 square miles of water.

Once there were Coast Guard stations about every 7 miles along the 110-mile stretch of beach from the Virginia line to Hatteras Inlet. Some, which have been decommissioned, were operated as lookout, beach patrol, and lifeboat stations as late as World War II; several were assigned to other governmental use or were converted into summer residences. While lookouts and radio and electronic watches are maintained in most of the stations now remaining active, regular beach patrols are no longer necessary, because modern highways run along much of the Outer Banks, and shipwrecks seldom occur along the coast today. During severe storms the Coast Guard render a valuable service in warning summer and year-around residents in the area. The "rescues" of today are more likely to be assistance to a fishing craft that needs to be towed into port rather than the old time shipwrecks which gave the waters of the area generally the name "graveyard of the Atlantic" of sailing ship days.

From the bridge the highway passes for nearly a mile through a dense forest in which pine and dogwood predominate and crosses a great ridge of dunelands. Suddenly the blue waters of the Atlantic are dead ahead. After crossing the hilltop, a highway branches to the left through the residential area of seaside SOUTHERN SHORES with its modern cottages on both sides of a highway extending for 4 miles or more parallel with the ocean. Under Federal agencies during the mid-Thirties, sand fences were built and grasses planted along much of the ocean-side area, stopping the movement of some dunes and effectively curtailing beach erosion. This stabilization has made possible the recent development of long stretches of ocean front.

At 2 m. on this route, a new paved highway branches north-westward and leads into Duck, giving an alternative route to this village.

East of the bridge, at less than a half-mile, is the Duck-Kitty Hawk cross roads.

1. North on this improved road through a picturesque forest, sometimes along the eastern shore of Currituck Sound, to the fishing village of DUCK, 5 m. From here the sandy road leads, via the U. S. Naval Aviation Target range, to CAFFEYS INLET COAST GUARD STATION. From Caffeys Inlet (no longer an inlet except in name), deep sand trails (*recommended only for motorists experienced in driving the dry sands on the beach at low tide*) lead to COROLLA (75 pop.), 16 m., the site of CURRITUCK BEACH LIGHTHOUSE, generally known as the Whaleshead. The lighthouse is of rough unpainted brick, 163 feet high, with a light of 160,000 candlepower. It was erected in 1875 to fill a dangerous unlighted gap between Cape Henry to the north and Bodie Island to the south, where southbound ships keep well inshore to avoid the north-flowing current of the Gulf Stream. Behind the lighthouse are large sand dunes, two of which, WHALESHEAD BARCHANE (variant of *barkhan,* East Turkish for "moving forward") and POYNERS HILL, are almost as large as those at Kitty Hawk. The former hill has been found to move 20 feet in one year.

On Jan. 31, 1878, the *Metropolis,* formerly a Federal gunboat, *The Stars and Stripes,* was wrecked 3 miles south of the lighthouse with a loss of nearly 100 lives. This wreck caused a nation-wide scandal and greatly enhanced the reputation of the bankers as ship-wreckers.

Near Corolla is the famous WHALESHEAD CLUB, a three-story, multi-gabled mansion built as a hunting lodge for a wealthy railway executive. It is complete with canals, a tiny harbor, and lawns.

North of Corolla is a place known as WASH WOODS, where substantial tree trunks, washed by the tide, give evidence that at one time a great forest came right up to the ocean.

Something of the type of inhabitants living along the Outer Banks in 1728 may be gleaned from William Byrd's description of a "Marooner, that Modestly call'd himself a Hermit, tho' he forfeited that name by Suffering a wanton Female to Cohabit with Him. His Habitation was a Bower, cover'd with Bark after the Indian Fashion which in that mild Situation protected him pretty well from the Weather. Like the Ravens, he neither plow'd nor sow'd, but Subsisted chiefly upon Oysters, which his Handmaid made a Shift to gather from the Adjacent Rocks. Sometimes, too, for a change of Dyet, he sent her to drive up the Neighbour's Cows, to moisten their Mouths with a little Milk. But as for raiment, he depended mostly upon his length of Beard, and She upon her Length of Hair, part of which she brought decently forward, and the rest dangled behind quite down to her Rump, like one of Herodotus's East Indian Pigmies. Thus did these Wretches live in a dirty State of Nature, and were mere Adamites, Innocence only excepted."

2. South from this junction an unpaved but improved road leads along a scenic route with overhanging branches of pine and hardwoods, sometimes laden with Spanish moss, to Kitty Hawk (*see below*).

US 158 swings right and parallels the ocean beach, lined for many miles with summer and year-around residences, modern shops, hotels, motels, and newly created beach residential developments extending westward to the shores of the sounds. An ocean fishing pier is located on the beach here.

KITTY HAWK, 50.5 m. (9 alt., 300 pop.), originally hidden in the windswept woodlands westward of US 158, now has approximately 5 miles of ocean beach development. It was in the soundside village, now reached by a modern paved highway from ocean-side US 158, that the postmistress, during the summer of 1900, received a letter from Dayton, Ohio, asking information about the topography of the section with reference to proposed "scientific kite-flying experiments" which Wilbur and Orville Wright planned to make during their September vacation. Capt. W. J. Tate, whose wife was postmistress, answered the letter and served as host when they arrived. Over a period of three years the Wrights carried on glider experiments in the Kitty Hawk and nearby Kill Devil Hills area. In 1903 the brothers built a special craft, designed somewhat like their experimental gliders, and equipped it with a gasoline motor.

On May 22, 1928, there was unveiled at Kitty Hawk, in the immediate area where the Tates had lived and where the Wright brothers had first boarded following their arrival in 1900, a commemorative marker erected with contributions solely from Kitty Hawk citizens and their friends and inscribed: "On this spot, September 17, 1900, Wilbur Wright began the assembly of the Wright Brothers' first experimental glider which led to man's conquest of the air." Actually this was not the "first experimental glider" as the Wrights had conducted previous scientific kite-flying experiments at their home in Ohio.

The name "Kitty Hawk," according to some local folklore adherents, is derived from the mosquito hawks which swarm here at certain seasons. Another colorful legend is that the name comes from the cry of the wild goose. It is said that the Indians evolved killy from kill, and computed the white man's year "Fum a Killy Hauk to a Killy Hauk," the time between the killing of the first goose of one season and the first goose killed during the next season. A more logical explanation would be that the name is derived from Chickahauk which appeared on a map prepared for the Lords Proprietors in 1729. While the woodlands village of Kitty Hawk on Kitty Hawk Bay, an eastern reach of Albemarle Sound, achieved international fame as the spot where the Wright brothers came to conduct glider experiments which led to powered flight within three years, the picturesque town with its winding roads, quaint houses, and waterfront anchorages is also noted for commercial and fresh water sports fishing, duck and goose hunting. The Dare Beaches area from Wright Memorial Bridge southward to Oregon Inlet has recently become a highly developed summer resort area along about 20 miles of ocean front. A modern paved highway parallels the ocean beach, with cottages, shops, or recreational facilities on both sides of the route and at intervals residential areas extending to the sound shore on the west, places such as Avalon Beach, Croatan Shores, Delray Beach, Roanoke Shores, and others.

At **51 m.** are the northern limits of KILL DEVIL HILLS, incorporated as a municipality during the 1953 general assembly. In area its limits, extending from the ocean to sound shores, include many thousands of acres. Along the entire stretch of developed resort areas are numerous hotels, motels, restaurants, and stores or shops, in addition to recreational facilities.

At intervals along the stretch of beach from Southern Shores and Kitty Hawk southward to Oregon Inlet are the skeleton-remains of many shipwrecks. In 1927 the Greek steamer *Kyzikes* broke in two when she foundered on this beach. A year later the *Carl Gerhard* was driven ashore in approximately the same location. Only remnants of these two wrecks remain today, but the skeletons of many other ships, mostly vessels of sail, may be seen half buried in the sands along the surf.

At **54.8 m.** is the junction with a government road.

Right on this road the WRIGHT BROTHERS NATIONAL MEMORIAL, **1 m.** (R), erected by the Federal Government in 1932, rises from the top of Kill Devil Hill. The surrounding 314-acre park is a landscaped spot in the barren expanse of glaring dunes. Native wire grass and transplanted sod were used to anchor the hill. Several spiral walks lead to the summit of the 90-foot dune. The triangular pylon, of Mount Airy granite, 60 feet high, has a star-shaped base resting on a sunken foundation 35 feet deep. On the outer walls are wings in bas-relief, and the inscription: "In commemoration of the conquest of the air by the brothers Wilbur and Orville Wright conceived by Genius, achieved by Dauntless Resolution and Unconquerable Faith." At night the monument is illuminated by floodlights.

Within the monument massive bronze doors lead to a memorial room of Salisbury pink granite, which has a central niche for a small model of the original Wright plane, and on each side niches for busts of the Wright brothers. Engraved on a stainless steel table is a map, charting notable flights in the first 25 years of aviation. Inscriptions record the date of the first flight of a power-driven airplane, Dec. 17, 1903. Curving inner stairs ascend to the observation platform atop the monument, which affords an extensive view of the surrounding area.

North of the monument, 600 feet, is the granite boulder marker erected by the National Aeronautic Association, unveiled Dec. 17, 1928, the 25th anniversary of the flight. It stands on the spot where the crude and fragile machine left the earth under its own power. Four flights were made, the brothers alternating at the controls, until a sudden gust of the 21-mile wind rolled the machine over, damaging it so that further experiments were impossible. Orville was at the controls on the first flight when the plane stayed in the air 12 seconds, traversing 120 feet. On the fourth flight, with Wilbur at the controls, it was flown 852 feet in 59 seconds.

During the 50th anniversary celebration of the first flights, Dec. 14-17, 1954, held under the sponsorship of the National Park Service, Kill Devil Hill Memorial Society, Air Force Association, and the North Carolina 50th Anniversary Commission, there were dedicated exact replicas of the Wright brothers' hangar and quarters buildings on the original site. These buildings are furnished exactly as pictures show them furnished at the time of the famous flight experiments.

KILL DEVIL HILL, one legend relates, was named for a brand of Medford rum so potent that it was considered strong enough to "kill the Devil." Tribute to the power of this liquor was paid in the *Ballad of Kill Devil Hills* or the *Ballad of Medford Rum,* and according to William Byrd, in his *History of the Dividing Line:* "Most of the Rum they get in this country comes from New England, and it is so bad and unwholesome, that it is not improperly call'd 'Kill Devil.'" It is logical to assume, however, that the early settlers, who called bodies of water "kills" and ridges of land "devils" (*see* Webster), appropriately called these ridges "Kill Devil Hills."

Right from the monument **1 m.** on a road to the FRESH PONDS, the largest of which covers 125 acres. Lying on this narrow sand bar between the salt waters of ocean and sound, these pools are covered with pond lilies and contain fresh-water fish. They are popularly considered bottomless, and the mystery of their existence has been variously explained; an inlet may have once existed at this point, connecting the ocean with Kitty Hawk Bay.

Left from the monument on a road **1.2 m.,** across two free bridges are LITTLE and BIG COLINGTON (200 pop.), fishing villages on Colington Island between Kitty Hawk Bay and Roanoke and Albemarle sounds. Originally named Carlyle Island, it was granted in 1663 to Sir John Colleton, a Lord Proprietor. Some believe this to be the Trinity Harbor of DeBry's map. Most of the inhabitants are of English descent.

At **56 m.** is NAGS HEAD BEACH where two ocean fishing piers have been constructed along the recently developed area.

The WRECK OF THE HURON is indicated by a marker recalling the disaster of Nov. 24, 1877, when 108 lives were lost. For years the tank, boiler, and bell were visible about 175 yards offshore. The wreckage swarms with fish, particularly sheepshead.

NAGS HEAD, **57.2 m.** (45 pop.), has been a resort for more than a century. Until 1929 the sound side was the site of the larger cottages and hotels, and cottagers and Sunday excursionists came by boat to a long pier jutting out into Roanoke Sound. Opening of the Virginia Dare Trail and the Wright Memorial Bridge has directed development along the ocean boulevard.

A romantic explanation for the name "Nags Head" is that in the early days of the settlement "land pirates" deliberately sought to wreck ships. On a stormy night a lantern was tied to the neck of an old nag, which was then ridden along the beach. Mistaking the light for a beacon, ships were lured to the treacherous reefs, there to be boarded and looted by the wily shoremen. Those who hold to this story should try tying a lighted lantern around the neck of a banker pony. A more reasonable explanation is that it was named for one of the highest points on the Scilly Islands, off the coast of Devon—the last sight of old England.

In the folklore of this coast are a headless horseman who gallops silently over the dunes and an everlasting stain on the sandy beach from the blood of a banker woman slain by her husband who found her in the embrace of another and did not wait to learn that the stranger was her long-absent brother.

The White Doe, reincarnation of Virginia Dare, supposedly still roams the hills, visible to humans only on the stroke of midnight. According to one tale, the Lost Colony was adopted by an Indian tribe. Virginia was loved by the young brave Okisco and by the magician Chico. To thwart his rival, Chico changed the young woman into a white doe. Wenando, magician of another tribe, gave Okisco a silver arrow that would magically restore the maiden to human form if it pierced the heart of the white doe. When Okisco shot the doe through the heart, a mist arose revealing the form of Virginia Dare—dead.

It is generally believed that the beautiful Theodosia Burr, daughter of Aaron Burr and wife of Joseph Allston, Governor of South Carolina (1812-14), perished off the coast here. On Dec. 30, 1812, she sailed from Georgetown, S. C., on the *Patriot,* a small pilot boat, to visit her father in New York and was never seen again. The boat was then believed to have been wrecked off Hatteras during a storm.

In 1869, Dr. W. G. Pool was called to attend a poor banker woman, who gave him a portrait from her wall for a fee and told him its story. In 1812 a small pilot boat, with sails set and rudder lashed, drifted ashore at Kitty Hawk. There were no signs of violence or bloodshed on the deserted ship— an untouched meal was on the table, and silk dresses hung within a cabin. On the wall was the portrait of a young and beautiful woman, painted in oil on polished mahogany and set in a gilded frame. The bankers stripped the boat, and the portrait fell to the woman's sweetheart, who gave it to her. The bankers believed the pirates had forced all on board to walk the plank, only to be frightened away before they could plunder the ship.

Upon comparison, Dr. Pool was impressed by the resemblance of his portrait to a picture of Aaron Burr; photographs of the portrait were sent to members of the Burr and Edwards families, who, almost without exception, proclaimed the likeness that of Theodosia. Compared with the Sully portrait, features and expression were found to be similar. The Nags Head portrait is in a private museum in New York City.

Legendary confessions round out the story. Years later, two criminals, later executed, admitted they were members of a pirate crew that boarded the *Patriot* and forced passengers and crew to walk the plank. A dying beggar in a Michigan almshouse confessed he was one of the pirates and that he had been haunted by the face of the beautiful woman who pleaded for her life that she might go to her father in New York.

The sea constantly encroaches at Nags Head and steadily the span of sandy beach between cottage line and ocean grows narrower; at other places along the coast, the land is building out. Also, the shore is building up on the sound side so that cottages, originally erected on pilings over the water, stand on dry sand. JOCKEY'S RIDGE (138 feet high) is the highest coastal sand dune on the Atlantic or Gulf coasts. ENGAGEMENT HILL, more than 100 feet high, SEVEN SISTERS, and lesser dunes farther south are hardly less imposing.

At intervals paved roads lead (R) to the sound side. High dunes give way to rolling beachland and flat meadows. At **65 m.** is a junction. Here US 64 (*see* TOUR *13*) and US 264 (*see* TOUR *14*) begin, and here is the beginning of the new all-paved Hatteras Highway (*see* DRIVE ALONG THE BANKS, after this section).

The route branches R. across 2.5 miles of causeway and bridges over Roanoke Sound, to enter ROANOKE ISLAND, **67.5 m.**, 12 miles long with an average width of 3 miles.

At **69 m.** is a junction with NC 345. At the junction is the site of a skirmish during the Civil War. After the fall of Hatteras, Roanoke Island was the only hope of defense for Albemarle Sound and its tributary rivers. Ships, the wrecks of which still snag fishermen's hooks, were sunk in the sound to impede the Federals, but Gen. Ambrose E. Burnside with 15,000 troops sailed up Croatan Sound and landed on the island. The Confederates under Col. Henry M. Shaw engaged the Federals but were forced to retreat and finally to surrender on Dec. 7, 1862.

Left on NC 345 is WANCHESE, **4 m.**, which has one of the busiest harbors in the section and is a trading point for northern Pamlico Sound. It was once the center of Dare's shad-fishing industry in which 90 per cent of the county's population were employed. The tourist business is the chief source of income today.

Right from the junction on NC 345 is MANTEO, **70.5 m.** (635 pop.), seat of Dare County and its only incorporated town. The village was named for the Indian Chief, Manteo. Old docks line the water front. Manteo (*guides and boats available for fishing and hunting*) has limited water commerce other than fishing. Government surveys show a greater variety of fishes in Dare County waters than in any other county in the United States. Game fish attract sportsmen the year around. Channel bass weighing 50 to 75 pounds are frequently taken. Other varieties are bluefish, speckled or gray trout, rock or striped bass, pigfish, blackfish, and several kinds of perch.

Numerous varieties of waterfowl migrate to this natural feeding ground— the white swan and many species of wild duck and wild goose. Shore birds, such as golden plover and yellowlegs, furnish sport for hunters. The section also affords quail and snipe shooting.

They say that Roanoke hominy, commonly called big or lye hominy, is still prepared in some rural sections as the Indians made it. Tradition says they served it to Amadas and Barlow in 1584.

At 71 m. is the junction with a dirt road.

Right on this road to MOTHER VINEYARD (*open to public*), **0.5 m.** Here is an unusually fine scuppernong grapevine, covering more than an acre. Local tradition is that the vine was planted by Amadas and Barlow from roots brought from the Scuppernong River. Another theory claims discovery of the vine in Tyrrell County, near Columbia (*see* TOUR *13*).

FORT RALEIGH (*open daily, 8:30-5:00*) **74 m.**, is the site of the first attempted English settlement in America, the "Citie of Ralegh" (or New Fort) in what was then Virginia. Between 1584 and 1591 seven separate English expeditions visited Roanoke Island (*see* HISTORY).

On July 4, 1584, Amadas and Barlow touched the present North Carolina coast, planted the arms of England, and took possession of the continent for Sir Walter Raleigh under his patent from Queen Elizabeth. After two months of exploration they returned to England, taking with them the Indians, Manteo and Wanchese, and samples of the strange products of the land, including tobacco and potatoes. In 1585, Sir Richard Grenville brought over a Raleigh colonizing expedition of 108 persons under Gov. Ralph Lane, landing on Roanoke Island, Aug. 17. Grenville returned to England, and the colonists built a fort. Trouble with the Indians and near-starvation ensued, and when Sir Francis Drake's fleet appeared in 1586 the Lane colonists departed with him. Two weeks later Grenville returned with supplies and, finding the Lane colony gone, left 15 men to hold England's claim.

Gov. John White's expedition arrived in 1587 and found no trace of the men except an unburied skeleton, the fort and dwellings in ruins. They rebuilt the fort and restored friendly relations with the Indians, aided by Manteo, who, on Aug. 13, 1587, was baptized and, by order of Sir Walter Raleigh, invested with the title, Lord of Roanoke. This is the first recorded celebration of a sacrament by English-speaking people in America.

Among the colonists was Gov. White's daughter, Eleanor, wife of Ananias Dare. The daughter of this couple, born on Aug. 18, 1587, was the first white child born of English parents on American soil. The following Sunday, Aug. 25, she was christened Virginia, for the colony was then called Virginia.

On Aug. 27, 1587, John White sailed for England "for the present and speedy supply of certain known and apparent lacks and needs, most requisite and necessary for the good and happy planting of us, or any other in the land of Virginia." White was detained in England by the Spanish Armada and not until Mar. 20, 1591, was he able to embark to America. He arrived at Roanoke Island Aug. 15, 1591, searched for two days, and "found the houses taken down and the place very strongly enclosed with a high palisade of great trees, with curtains and flankers, very fortlike; and one of the chief trees or posts at the right side of the entrance had the bark taken off, and five feet from the ground, in fair capital letters were graven CROATOAN, without any sign or cross of distress." So ends the romantic story of that tragic Lost Colony of 116 men, women, and children. There have been numerous conjectures as to their ultimate fate, but the truth has never been discovered. John Lawson wrote in 1709: "I cannot forbear inserting here a pleasant story that passes for an uncontested Truth amongst the inhabitants of this Place; which is that the Ship which brought the first Colonies, does often appear amongst them under sail, in a gallent posture, which they call Sir Walter Raleigh's Ship; and the truth of this has been affirmed to me by men of the best Credit in the Country."

Gov. White made minute and careful drawings, now in the British Museum, of the activities of the colonists and their Indian neighbors. These drawings, as well as other pertinent records of the time, were consulted in the reconstruction of the fort and other buildings.

In 1941 FORT RALEIGH NATIONAL HISTORIC SITE was established to commemorate the earliest attempt at English colonization within the limits of the continental United States and the birthplace of Virginia Dare, first white child of English parentage born in the New World. The area (16 acres) embraces part of the settlement sites of 1585 and 1587. Ralph Lane's "new Fort in Virginia," located within the site, was partially uncovered during archeological explorations in 1947. The village site, presumably close to the fort, has not yet been located.

Small blockhouses flank the entrance to the palisaded reservation and rise from the 4 corners. Unofficial reproductions of the colonists' log houses stand among the pine, oak, dogwood, and holly. They are built of split, unpeeled juniper logs and are chinked with Spanish moss, though this type of log construction was not used by the first English settlers, who used a wattle-and-daub type of construction. The stone used for foundations and fireplaces is ancient ballast rock, recovered from the waters around the island (*see* ARCHITECTURE).

The FORT was built by Ralph Lane, governor of the 1585 expedition sent out from England by Sir Walter Raleigh. In recent years, the earthen fort of the colonists has been located and restored, but the remains of the houses of the settlers have not yet been located. Here is a stone monument erected in 1896 in memory of the Lost Colony. The MUSEUM contains implements used in colonial days. Each year, on Aug. 18, the Roanoke Island Historical Association, Inc., a State agency, celebrates the birthday of Virginia Dare at Fort Raleigh. The 350th anniversary took an elaborate form in 1937.

At the WATERSIDE THEATER, a symphonic drama, *The Lost Colony,* written by North Carolina Pulitzer Prize winner, Paul Green, has, since 1937, dramatized the story of the English settlers. The first of a bumper crop of outdoor dramas, this play has run every summer (*late June-early Sept.*), barring the interruption when the coast was blacked out during World War II, and has been seen by over a half million people.

The ELIZABETHAN GARDEN, adjacent to Fort Raleigh, a project of the North Carolina Garden Clubs, is a two-acre formal garden illustrating the land the first colonists left behind and the land they found upon arrival here. The famous collection of antique garden ornaments, some dating back to the 16th century, from the Jock Whitney Estate in Georgia, have been erected here, and work is progressing towards completion of the project.

NC 345 continues to WEIR POINT, 75 m., at the tip of Roanoke Island. Here, in 1902, Reginald A. Fessenden, of the U. S. Weather Bureau, built an experimental wireless station and established communication with a ship similarly equipped. He subsequently completed his experiments elsewhere and secured patents for his system.

A ferry now runs between Roanoke Island and Manns Harbor (*see* TOUR *13*), but a $3,500,000 bridge, 2.5 miles long, to replace the ferry, is now under construction.

DRIVE ON THE BANKS

From eastern terminus of US 158 to Hatteras Inlet, 69 m.

A recently completed paved highway from the terminus of US 158 leads to a free ferry across Oregon Inlet, then by a paved road to Hatteras village (*sand and beach trails lead to Hatteras Inlet*). Hotels, cottages, motor courts, and guest houses are available at all places along the route.

Though the Outer Banks run from the Virginia Line to Cape Lookout, this section from Bodie Island to Hatteras is not only the most accessible, but it is of great interest to the traveler.

The CAPE HATTERAS NATIONAL SEASHORE RECREATIONAL AREA extends southward along the Outer Banks some 70 miles from Whalebone Junction. Outside the National Seashore is the developed beach section along the highway for the first 5 miles and the picturesque villages of Hatteras and Ocracoke Islands. The area is composed of 28,500 acres in public beach and dune lands and is unique as the first and only unit of such character in the National Park System. At 5.5 m. is HEADQUARTERS (*information and other services*).

Plans are now underway for an Outer Banks Highway running from Virginia Beach to connect with US 158 at Southern Shores.

BODIE (Body) ISLAND LIGHTHOUSE (*active*), 5 m., was built in 1872. There are tentative plans to use Park Headquarters and the lighthouse as a tourist facility and a natural history interpretive center. The first light here was erected in 1848 to mark the dangerous stretch of low-lying coast between Capes Henry and Hatteras. Rebuilt in 1859, it was destroyed during the Civil War. When rebuilt it was placed on a new site north of the inlet that had recently been opened. Five sailing vessels were wrecked in the vicinity while the tower, finished in 1872, was under construction. The lighthouse is 163 feet high and throws a 160,000-candlepower beam visible for 19 miles.

OREGON INLET, 8 m., a mile wide, is crossed by a free ferry (*22-car ferries are in continuous operation daily*). This is one of the best points on the coast for drum (channel bass) fishing and is a center for Gulf Stream fishing. While drum and bluefish are running, scores of fishing boats with shining lures trailing astern pass through the inlet, and anglers come here to catch channel bass, blues, Spanish mackerel, trout, flounder, and other sound, inlet, and surf-feeding game fishes. *

The 6,500-acre area between Oregon Inlet and Rodanthe constitutes the PEA ISLAND MIGRATORY WATERFOWL REFUGE (HEADQUARTERS *at* 15 m.) under control of the U. S. Fish and Wildlife Service; it is a part of the Cape Hatteras National Seashore Recreation Area. A dyke has been constructed to impound water for wintering ducks, geese, and other birds, especially the gadwall and the snowgoose.

NEW INLET, 17 m., opened in 1933 by a severe northeast storm and ocean tides, is now closed. On the beach nearby are fragments of wrecks, many of them barely discernible above the sand.

RODANTHE, 21 m. (70 pop.), on the most easterly point of the North Carolina coast, is a soundside fishing village, where the older folk celebrate the birth of Christ on Jan. 5, Old Christmas, or Twelfth Night. The village is locally called Chicamacomico, for the COAST GUARD STATION (now used as a National Park Service base for maintenance operations on Hatteras Island), which operated here for 80 years. Here is the surfboat in which, on Aug. 16, 1918, Capt. John Allen Midgett and a crew of 5 braved a sea of blazing oil and gasoline to rescue 42 persons from the British tanker, *S. S. Mirlo,* torpedoed by a German submarine. For this deed Congress awarded them bronze Medals of Honor. Close by the station is the burial mound of 10 British seamen drowned in the wreck of the *Strathairly,* Mar. 4, 1891, in which only 7 lines were saved and 9 bodies were never recovered.

In World Wars I and II, this station and others in the area saw more warfare than any other part of the United States. German U-boats, particularly during the Battle of the Atlantic, prowled these waters, often surfacing in sight of land to destroy ships. Strict censorship has precluded figures on exact losses in World War II, but it is definitely known that 29 ships were sunk in these waters.

WAVES, 23 m., and SALVO, 27 m., are small fishing, soundside settlements, where fig trees grow in abundance. The gnarled oaks and abundant vegetation contrast sharply with the barren, wreck-strewn beaches.

AVON, 39 m., (500 pop.), a fishing village also known by the Indian name, Kinnakeet, is the site of the LITTLE KINNAKEET STATION, recently decommissioned and now used as a ranger station. Tons of bluefish and trout are caught here every season. Fruit trees, vineyards, and truck gardens grow along its winding streets, shaded by gnarled oaks, cedars, and yaupon bushes.

On CAPE HATTERAS, 45 m., and Hatteras Island wildlife is abundant. For years herds of wild ponies, cattle, and hogs ranged at will, till the

Federal program of sand fixation by grass plantings necessitated a strict stock law. In winter the waters are dotted with ducks and geese, and there is frequently the gleam of a white swan. Sandpipers and gulls feed in flocks, undisturbed by scurrying sand fiddlers. Eagles and ospreys wheel above the water on the lookout for prey, and schools of porpoises sport just beyond the breakers of the roaring Atlantic.

At the tip of the cape, 1,200 acres, including the gently shelving beach on the south, were given to the Federal Government by J. S. Phipps, as a part of the National Seashore Area. Within the area is CAPE HATTERAS LIGHT-HOUSE (*open 1 to 3 P.M., Thurs.-Mon.*), abandoned in 1936, but reactivated in 1951, the tallest brick lighthouse in America. Spirally painted black and white, the structure is 191 feet high and commands a view of a great wreck area, with ship skeletons protruding from the sands. The first lighthouse, authorized by Congress in 1794 and built in 1798, was blown up by the Federal fleet in 1861. The present one was built two miles inland in 1869-70, but when the encroaching Atlantic reached its very foot by 1936 it was abandoned in favor of a steel tower to the east. However, the CCC and WPA moved in in 1936 with a sand-anchoring project and as a result of their labors the historic light shines again from its old home.

After the classic engagement between the *Merrimac* and the *Monitor* in Hampton Roads, Mar. 9, 1862, the *Monitor* was dispatched to Charleston Harbor Dec. 29 in tow of the side-wheeler *Rhode Island*. The following night the unseaworthy little "cheese box" sank in a gale off Hatteras, with a loss of 4 officers and 12 men; 49 of her crew were saved by the *Rhode Island*.

Within the shadow of the Hatteras Lighthouse is the MARITIME MUSEUM, in which the heroic story of the sea in this "graveyard of the Atlantic" is the major theme. The two-story 20-by-65-foot building was opened in 1954.

DIAMOND SHOALS, most treacherous shallows on the coast, extend 25 miles out to sea from the cape. Few ships stranded on these vast shifting ridges of sand are ever refloated, but the *Maurice R. Thurlow* proved an exception when she ran aground during a storm on Oct. 13, 1927. Her crew of 9 signaled for help, and coast guardsmen took them ashore in a surfboat. The Coast Guard cutter *Mascoutin*, which was dispatched from Norfolk, Va., could find no trace of the schooner and reported her lost. Thirteen days later the Dutch tanker *Sleidrecht* sighted the schooner in the North Atlantic. A general order to run down the modern Flying Dutchman was broadcast. Every few days the sea wanderer was reported in a different place, but she was never overtaken, and her fate is unknown.

The shoals are marked by DIAMOND SHOALS LIGHTSHIP, moored 13 miles off the tip of Cape Hatteras. With radio signals and a beacon visible for 14 miles, the ship serves continuously for a year, when she and her crew of 16 are relieved by another "wave wallower."

Early efforts to maintain a lightship here proved futile, but there has been one since 1897 except for brief intervals. One such interval occurred on Aug. 8, 1918, when a German submarine opened fire on a merchant ship about a mile and a half away. The lightship wirelessed a warning to vessels in the vicinity, and the submarine located and sank her. The crew escaped in small boats to Cape Hatteras.

West of the cape the road passes sand hills whose thickly forested ridges are clothed with loblolly pine, live oak, and holly including the yaupon (yo'pon). The trees incline westward (*see* NATURAL SETTING), and the woods contain deer and small game. Yaupon (*Ilex cassine* and *Ilex vomitoria*) is a dark evergreen with bright red berries. The small glossy leaves are dried and used for tea, emetic to those unaccustomed to it, though it contains much caffeine. It was called the "black drink" when used by the Creeks at their annual "busk" or green-corn thanksgiving for ceremonial purification.

BUXTON, 46.5 m., is a delightful village where Spanish moss hangs from the ancient live oaks and the yaupon bushes are abundant. Many yards contain a grapefruit or orange tree. It is said the first citrus tree grew by accident when a grapefruit seed strayed from a bag of garbage.

South of Buxton the road winds through woods where palmettos, hung with Spanish moss, grow in profusion and the vegetation is generally sub-tropical. The open beach is strung with wrecks, giving rise to the grisly joke that Hatteras' chief importation is wrecks.

At FRISCO, 50 m. (100 pop.), are neat white houses with bright blue blinds and dooryards gay with flowers and picket fences.

Southwest of here the route emerges onto a wide flat beachland, with sound and ocean in sight.

HATTERAS, 54 m. (700 pop.) (*boats available for trips to the Gulf Stream, 20 miles offshore*), vies with Ocracoke as the largest community on the banks. Sportsmen interested in Gulf Stream fishing have materially aided its development. Houses, some flamboyantly painted, nestle among scrubby, stunted live oaks and waterbushes teeming with mockingbirds. The people are weathered and bronzed, possessed of a sturdy independence and self-reliance. Occupations were limited almost entirely to fishing and boating and to Government employment in the Lighthouse Service and the Coast Guard until the recent influx of tourists.

Here the people, as elsewhere along the banks, speak with a broad accent said to have been brought over from Devon. Many older families believe they are descended from shipwrecked English sailors. The picturesque old words, phrases, and accent are fast disappearing, but occasionally old timers will delight the tourists (*comers n'goers*) with tales of uncommon *hoigh toids* (high tides), of a trip from his *neighborhood* (town) to *the country* (the mainland), or of a *couthy* or *witty* (capable) boy who found some duck *nesties* in the marsh at *calm daylight* (daybreak).

HATTERAS INLET, 55 m., is famous for angling. Dolphin, amberjack, tarpon, sailfish, marlin, and yellow-fin tuna provide sport for deep-sea fishermen (*fishing best from late April to Oct.*).

Where the marsh and beach converge at the inlet are traces of FORT HATTERAS and its outlying flank defense, BATTERY CLARK. Col. W. F. Martin was in charge of Fort Hatteras when, on Aug. 27, 1861, a Federal fleet appeared, equipped with Dahlgren guns, secure beyond the range of the old-style smooth-bore pieces of the Confederate defenders. Federal amphibious operations led to the surrender of Fort Hatteras Aug. 29 and gave Union forces an effective entrance into North Carolina.

From Hatteras a private ferry leads across Hatteras Inlet to OCRACOKE ISLAND, 16 miles long and about 2 miles wide at its broadest (*only about 4 paved miles at present; only the experienced driver should attempt this trip*).

At the eastern end is the HATTERAS INLET COAST GUARD STATION. Except for this and a few club houses, there are no residences on the island outside the village itself.

The island's shoreline, like the other Outer Banks, is dotted with skeletons of wrecked ships. The ghost ship, *Carroll A. Deering,* a 5-masted schooner, was found stranded on Diamond Shoals in 1921, with food still warm in the galley pots and on the mess tables, but with no crew on board. Recognized as a menace to navigation, she was blown up by the Coast Guard and her bow washed ashore about halfway between the village of Ocracoke and Hatteras Inlet where some of the wreckage may still be seen. No trace was ever found of the crew.

OCRACOKE (800 pop.) is a picturesque commercial fishing and shrimping village (*small hotel, cottages, camps, and tourist homes; advisable to make reservations in advance; taxi service available for bathing, fishing, and exploratory trips; fishing, clamming, crabbing, and oystering are popular*). The old town, a favorite of those wishing to get an atmosphere of content, is partly built around symmetrical SILVER LAKE, a natural lake which has been dredged to a depth of 14 feet with a channel opening into Pamlico Sound. Water oaks and yaupon overhang the winding streets of sand. Islanders, coast guardsmen, and sportsmen live peacefully here. Until Naval construction during World War II, there was no civil officer of the law on the island. Since then there has been a deputy sheriff (mostly a tax collector) and a justice of the peace. Infrequent hurricanes, hardly one in a decade, strike with great force. The village was inundated in 1933 and 1944.

The OCRACOKE LIGHTHOUSE, rising above the village, was built in 1823, replacing an earlier one built in 1798 on Shell Castle Island. Standing 76 feet above ground, it has an 8,000-candlepower beacon, which shows a fixed white light for 14 miles.

OCRACOKE COAST GUARD STATION (*open*), built in 1941, and used as a Naval Station for anti-submarine warfare during World War II, has now reverted to the Coast Guard.

In spite of the evidence against it, the legend persists locally that Theodosia Burr Allston was rescued from a shipwreck near the island and lived at Ocracoke until her death (*see* TOUR *1A*).

Ocracoke, one legend says, was named by the pirate Blackbeard (*see* TOURS *1A and 14A*), who dropped anchor one day in the inlet and before unloading his booty surveyed the coast to make sure that it was clear. There was nothing to break the still stretches of sand and calm of the shallow sea. He suddenly shook his fist and yelled into the unbearable stillness, "Oh, crow, cock!" However, Lamb's map of 1676 and Hark's of 1680 show an Okok, and Lawson's of 1709 shows an Occacock.

Tradition says a house (now completely gone) in the village known as "Blackbeard's Castle" or the OLD PIRATE HOUSE was his home and the hiding place for plunder. At TEACHS HOLE, in the inlet near the village, the buccaneer tarred and caulked his ships. This was also the scene of the battle in which Blackbeard met his fate in 1718.

Before the Civil War Ocracoke was an important port of entry. In the 1700's large storage warehouses were maintained here. The most famous was on Shell Castle, a small island of shell rock in the inlet, owned by John Gray Blount, merchant prince and landowner. A pitcher in the Blount Collection in the Hall of History (*see* RALEIGH) bears a sketch of Shell Castle. Here ships were loaded with cargoes of tar, pitch, and turpentine and returned with staples and manufactured articles. The captain of a Spanish ship once offered to cover Shell Castle with Spanish doubloons, but Blount refused to sell at any price.

After the royal Governor, Josiah Martin, had been driven out of the colony, he wrote the home government from New York: "The contemptible Port of Ocracock ... has become a great channel of supply to the Rebels while the more considerable Ports of the Continent have been watched by the King's ships," but concluded that "Commodore Hotham the Naval Commander ... will no doubt take all proper measures for shutting up that Avenue of succour to the Rebels."

Cattle, hogs, and many shaggy wild ponies once roamed Ocracoke and other islands of the banks. The few remaining ponies and cattle are branded and turned loose on a common range. No hogs remain. The ponies are said to have been descendants of Barbary ponies brought by Sir Walter Raleigh's colonists, or by Portuguese sailing vessels, but an old banker superstition would have them evolved from sand fiddlers. Lack of fresh water on the banks impelled a curious cooperation among the ponies. Gathered in a circle, they would paw broad shallow water holes in low spots and lie prone to drink. An annual pony roundup is held on July 4.

Ocracoke may be reached daily by mail boat (*no cars*) from Atlantic (*see* TOUR *15*).

TOUR 2 (US 258)

(Franklin, Va.)—Murfreesboro—Scotland Neck—Tarboro—Kinston—Junction with US 17. **155 m.**

This route traverses a section of the coastal plain where bright-leaf tobacco is the staple crop. Small farms lie between pine forests containing a few maple, ash, gum, oak, and hickory trees. The highway crosses several rivers which in spring and fall rise to torrential proportions and at times rage through fertile bottom lands.

US 258 crosses the North Carolina Line, **0 m.**, 12 miles south of Franklin, Va., and enters Hertford County. Col. William Byrd made his survey of the dividing line "betwixt North Carolina and Virginia" through here in 1728. Early 19th-century homes are scattered through this section.

At **4.5 m.**, 400 yards N., stands the BIRTHPLACE OF RICHARD J. GATLING (b. Sept. 12, 1818), the inventor of the Gatling Gun and of numerous agricultural implements.

MURFREESBORO, **10 m.** (2,140 pop.), in an agricultural and lumbering area, is a college town on the Meherrin River. Its charming old homes and large trees indicate its 18th-century origin. A gay resort town in the early 19th century, its Indian Queen Tavern, now gone, entertained Lafayette in 1825. One of the largest basket factories in the world is located here.

William Murfree gave the land surrounding Murfrees Landing in 1787. From here, tobacco, naval stores, corn, pork, and lumber were shipped down the Meherrin to the Chowan River, thence across Albemarle Sound to the ocean. The yellow brick MURFREE HOME (*private*) is the mansion of the founder's family. The porch columns were added in recent years. Murfreesboro, Tenn., was named for his son, Col. Hardie Murfree, Revolutionary patriot.

CHOWAN COLLEGE, oldest Baptist women's school in the State, founded in 1848 as Chowan Baptist Female Institute, did not close its doors during the Civil War or Reconstruction, but did during World War II. It is now a coeducational junior college. The ADMINISTRATION BUILDING, built in 1851, is an impressive 4-story brick and concrete structure with massive columns and a broad double-veranda.

At Murfreesboro is the junction with US 158 (*see* TOUR *12*). At **12 m.** US swings south, entering Northampton County.

At **21 m.** is WOODLAND (590 pop.), founded by Quakers. Their descendants worship at CEDAR GROVE MONTHLY MEETING HOUSE (1904).

RICH SQUARE (971 pop.), **27 m.**, was referred to in a 1766 deed to Marmaduke Norfleet as "a tract of land called the rich square." Here was the site of a Friends Meeting House, 1758.

At Rich Square is a junction with NC 305.

Left on this road **3 m.**, in the locality of the first Quaker settlers, is the WILLIAM COPELAND HOUSE (*private*). This three-story, 18th-century, brick house with secret stair from attic to cellar is built in a style common to the earliest domestic houses to be found in the Albemarle region (N. C.) and the lower James River region (Va.). The roof line is often referred to as Dutch Colonial. For years before and during the Civil War the Quakers maintained here an underground depot for fugitive slaves.

At **29 m.** is a junction with NC 308.

Left on this road, **3 m.**, to the GRAVE OF LEMUEL BURKITT, pastor of the Sandy Run Baptist Church (1773-1807), founder of the Kehukee Baptist Association, and member of the N. C. Ratification Convention (1788).

At **5 m.** is ROXOBEL (394 pop.). In the immediate vicinity are several fine ante-bellum homes (*private*): WOODBOURNE (c. 1810), built in the style of Palladio's Roman country house and with ancient boxwoods in front; OAKLANA (c. 1825), a typical planter's home of the period; and LIBERTY HALL (1805), which contains a fine panelled wainscot and Adam-styled mantel.

At WOODVILLE, **11.5 m.**, are several other fine plantation homes of the ante-bellum period: the PUGH-WALTON-MIZELLE-URQUHART HOUSE (1801), the YELLOW HOUSE (1815), the LEWIS THOMPSON HOUSE (1842), and the HINTON-AVERETTE-PUGH-THOMPSON HOME (c. 1820). All of these houses are in an excellent state of preservation and most of them are occupied by the descendants of the builders.

The route crosses the Roanoke River, **34 m.**, on Edwards Ferry Bridge, built in 1926 and named for an early ferry run by Cullen Edwards, holder of a pre-Revolutionary land grant. Here the hull of the Confederate iron-clad ram *Albemarle* was built (*see* TOUR *13*). It was then towed to the Navy Yard at Halifax, where the armor plate from the Tredegar Iron Works in Richmond, Va., was shipped by the Wilmington and Weldon Railroad. It then sailed down to Plymouth where the machinery was installed.

KELVIN GROVE (R), **39 m.**, is an ante-bellum home, the original part of which was moved from Edwards Ferry in 1824. The pedimented central portion with two-story wings at each end was very popular in this section.

MAGNOLIA (*private*) (L), **39 m.**, built 1845-50, is a good example of the Greek Revival style. The landscaping was done by Dr. Cheshire, the father of Bishop Joseph Blount Cheshire.

WOODSTOCK (*private*) (R), **39.7 m.**, built in 1793, was remodeled in 1840 in the Victorian "Italian Villa" style, with arched windows. These grounds were also landscaped by Dr. Cheshire.

OLD TRINITY EPISCOPAL CHURCH (L), **40 m.**, was built in 1855 of deep-toned red brick of modified English Gothic, after designs by Frank Wills, noted New York architect. The church was organized in 1832 out of the Kehukee Chapel of Edgecombe Parish (built prior to 1738 on a hill 4 miles SE. of Scotland Neck). In the gardenlike cemetery is the TOMB OF WHITMEL HILL (1743-97), colonel in the Continental army, one of the framers of the N. C. Constitution of 1776, and member of Continental Congress (1778-81).

Right, at **40.3 m.**, to the SALLIE BILLIE HOUSE (*private*), **1 m.**, an interesting variation of the Morris-plan house, used in the Randolph-Semple House in Williamsburg, Va. There is only one window in the two-story central-pedimented section. Inside is fine carved woodwork and a Chinese Chippendale stairway.

SCOTLAND NECK, **41 m.** (103 alt., 2,730 pop.), on a fertile neck of land in the bend of the Roanoke River, was settled in 1722. Some claim its name was derived from John Nairn, a Scot who owned a large tract of land here; others point to the fact that many of the early settlers were from Surry County, Va., where there is a "Scotland Neck" across the James River from Jamestown. The first settlers in this "Neck" lived along the river, but about 1800 the planters began moving up to the present location on the "piney woods" section to escape the malaria, or "bad air" of the river. The town is chiefly an agricultural center, but it has some textile and lumbering interests.

Here is the HOME OF CLAUDE KITCHIN (*private*), Congressman (1901-23) and Democratic majority leader (1915-19). Opposed to the declaration of war in 1917, he later supported Woodrow Wilson's policies. His brother, Gov. W. W. Kitchin (1909-13), also a Congressman, is buried just north of the town on US 258.

Legend has it that after the Stuart restoration, John and Edward Cromwell, brothers of the Protector, fled to America (1675). While on the ocean they decided to change their names to escape possible persecution and performed a solemn ceremony of writing their names on paper and cutting the letter M from the Cromwell and casting it into the sea. The brothers first landed in New Jersey, but later settled near Scotland Neck, at what is still called Crowell's Crossroads.

At **49 m.** US 258 crosses Deep Creek, whose waters are darkened by passage through upland swamps of cypress and juniper.

PRINCEVILLE, **61 m.** (58 alt., 919 pop.), is one of the country's few incorporated villages politically dominated by Negroes. Chartered in 1885, it has an all-Negro administration including a volunteer fire company. The place is really a suburb of Tarboro, where most of its male inhabitants are employed.

At Princeville is the junction with US 64 (*see* TOUR *13*), which joins US 258 between Princeville and Tarboro.

TARBORO, 62 m. (58 alt., 8,120 pop.), seat of Edgecombe County, is a tobacco-selling and cotton-manufacturing center on the western bank of Tar River. The county, named for the Earl of Edgecombe, British commissioner for trade and plantations, was formed as a precinct of old Albemarle in 1732, but was not given official status by the assembly until 1741. The town was laid out in 1760 on or near the site of an earlier Tar Burrow established by people of English descent from Virginia. At the insistence of the rector of St. Mary's Parish, such names as St. John, St. Andrew, and St. Patrick were given to the shady winding streets branching from Tarboro Common.

Tarboro was one of several towns that played host to North Carolina's itinerant legislature in its early days. The 1787 session, with 180 members in attendance, met here. About 50 legislators were packed into Toole's Tavern; others were quartered in private homes. William Attmore, a Philadelphia merchant in Tarboro at the time, notes in his journal: "Every family almost received some of the members; Beds were borrowed from the Country, 3 or 4 placed in a room and two of their Honors in a bed." After the fuel had been exhausted at the tavern, the members resorted to "Drams of some kind or other before Breakfast; sometimes Gin, Cherrybounce, Egg Nog, etc."

The assembly met at the courthouse; it had a long room for the commons and a smaller room for the senate. Every member sat with his hat on except when addressing the chair. Members gambled in a tavern at an "E.O. table" brought thither by a Mr. Faulkner of Philadelphia, and at other games, one New Bern trader losing £600 in a night.

In providing entertainment for the visitors, attempts were made to "represent dramatic pieces, but with very bad success. . . .Two of the actresses were adventuresses from Charleston." One Billy Ford emerged from a "jovial meeting" of the legislature wearing a silk handkerchief to hide a black eye caused by a swiftly hurled orange skin. "Somebody also threw the leg of a Turkey which miss'd him, but fell not guiltless to the floor, giving Toole a violent blow on the back," in which connection Attmore remarks that at the tavern they "invited me to go upstairs to be introduced to some great Men, but I was engaged!" Washington spent the night of April 18, 1791, here and described it as "less than Halifax, but more lively and thriving."

Edgecombe County's principal crops are tobacco, peanuts, and cotton; Tarboro factories manufacture cotton cloth, cottonseed products, veneers, corn meal, and feed. The municipality operates a creamery and maintains a high standard for its milk supply.

TARBORO COMMON, a shaded park in the center of the business section, contains a monument to Col. Louis D. Wilson (1789-1847), who represented Edgecombe County for 19 years in the general assembly. In the course of a speech urging North Carolina's participation in the war against Mexico, a younger senator remarked that it was well enough for Wilson to favor "this contemptible war," as he was too old to go. Wilson rallied a volunteer militia from Edgecombe, and proceeded to Mexico. He died of fever at Vera Cruz. Wilson and Wilson County bear his name (*see* TOUR 3). Other monuments honor Confederate soldiers of Edgecombe County and Henry L. Wyatt, slain at Bethel Church, June 10, 1861, whose death was remembered by his Confederate comrades as the "First at Bethel" (*see* RALEIGH). An old cotton press has been moved here from the Norfleet plantation.

Local legend places the BARK HOUSE (*private*), 501 W. Wilson St., on the site of an early fort built by settlers as protection against Indians, who were numerous in the region until about 1720. The frame structure is covered over with slabs of bark.

DR. J. P. KEECH'S OFFICE (*open*), 115 E. Church St., contains a collection of early novels and school texts, Indian relics, old weapons, and wooden gavels from a community house erected by Thomas Blount in 1808.

CALVARY EPISCOPAL CHURCH, NE. corner Church and David Sts., was organized as St. Mary's Parish in 1741. The present building, third on the site, was begun in 1860, though not completed until 1867. Its twin towers are green with English ivy. In the wall-enclosed churchyard is the GRAVE OF WILLIAM DORSEY PENDER (1834-63), killed at Gettysburg, youngest major general in the Confederate Army. Here also is the GRAVE OF COL. WILLIAM LAWRENCE SAUNDERS, Secretary of State of North Carolina (1879-91) and compiler of the *Colonial Records of North Carolina*. His tombstone bears the statement, "I decline to answer," made by Col. Saunders when questioned in a Ku Klux Klan investigation (*see* TOUR *8*).

At 71 m. is the junction with NC 43.

Left on NC 43 to the junction with an improved road, 1 m.; L. 1 m. on this road to BRACEBRIDGE HALL (*private*), birthplace and lifetime residence of Elias Carr, leader in the agrarian movement in the 1890's and Governor of North Carolina (1893-97). The two-story mansion with Doric portico, set in a grove of oaks, was probably built in 1826. An icehouse, dairy, and slave quarters are among the dependencies.

FARMVILLE, 87 m. (86 alt., 2,942 pop.), is an agricultural and tobacco-marketing center with warehouses scattered about the town.

Farmville is at the junction with US 264 (*see* TOUR *14*).

At 96 m. is a bronze tablet on a boulder marking the course of the OLD HULL RD., cut by British troops during the Revolution. A second tablet on the boulder indicates the GRAVE OF GEN. THOMAS HOLLIDAY, Greene County soldier of the War of 1812.

SNOW HILL, 99 m. (74 alt., 946 pop.), seat of Greene County, is an agricultural center in a prosperous tobacco-producing area. It was founded in 1799 but not incorporated until 1855.

Snow Hill is about 5 miles southeast of the site of the Indian town of Cotechney, the Tuscarora stronghold, to which in 1711 were brought the captives John Lawson and Baron de Graffenried, founders of New Bern (*see* NEW BERN). Lawson, who as surveyor general of North Carolina had disposed of large areas of land claimed by the Indians, was tortured to death. Legend says his captors thrust lightwood splinters into his flesh and set them afire. De Graffenried was released after 6 weeks' imprisonment.

Greene County, named for Revolutionary Gen. Nathanael Greene, was laid out in 1791 from the now extinct Dobbs County. It was first named for James Glasgow, but was renamed in 1799 after Glasgow had been convicted of fraud in connection with the issuance of land grants.

When Samuel Ashe, Governor (1795-98), heard of Glasgow's plans to remove incriminating records and burn the statehouse at Raleigh, his comment was, "An angel has fallen." A special court of circuit judges found Glasgow and his associates guilty. He was fined £2,000, but the Negro, who at his behest had attempted to burn the statehouse, was hanged. This special court, directed by an act of 1799 to sit at Raleigh, was the nucleus of the State's highest tribunal, an act in 1805 constituting it the State supreme court. Glasgow's body was moved to an unmarked grave in Raleigh.

Greene County was settled about 1710 by families from Virginia, Maryland, and North Carolina counties to the north. Though one of the smallest counties in the State, it is one of the richest agriculturally, yielding abundant crops of tobacco, corn, and cotton.

The GREENE COUNTY COURTHOUSE (1935) is the third to serve the county. Constructed of brick and limestone, it is two stories in height with a third-story attic. The symmetrical façade is designed with a portico of four Doric columns and consonant Greek detail. The first courthouse was erected in 1806.

The EPISCOPAL CHURCH is a simple 4-bay structure with white overlapped vertical siding. A rude, unpainted cross surmounts the peak of the front gable and a bell rack stands to the left rear of the church in the yard.

A marker at the principal business intersection designates the Granville Line, surveyed in 1743. Snow Hill lies on the southern boundary of the "one-eighth part" of Carolina retained by Lord Granville in 1729 when the other Lords Proprietors surrendered their charters (see HISTORY). This marker also commemorates an Indian battle at Fort Nohoroco, a Tuscarora fortress nearby on Contentnea Creek. On Mar. 20-23, 1713, in perhaps the severest battle fought with the Indians up to that date, Col. Maurice Moore broke the power of the Tuscarora and their allies in North Carolina. The Tuscarora surrendered 20 of their chief men to Moore and later emigrated to New York to join the Five Nations.

Right from Snow Hill on NC 102 to the junction with a dirt road, **5.7 m.**; L. **0.4 m.** on this road to the junction with a lane; R. **0.2 m.** up the lane to the HENRY BEST HOUSE (*private; open on request*). This was the home of a Greene County soldier of the Revolution and was built probably in the early 1800's. It is a two-story, clapboarded house, one room deep, with end chimneys and ell at the rear. A two-story porch, the length of the front, is supported on two ranges of square columns, vaguely Doric in detail, which are a later addition. There is a fine dentiled and modillioned cornice at the rear. The upper gallery of the porch is enclosed by a delicate wood railing. Inside, a wainscot with beveled paneling runs around the hall and the two lower rooms; the staircase has a spiral newel.

KINSTON, **114 m.** (46 alt., 18,336 pop.), located on the northern bank of the Neuse River, is the seat of Lenoir County. Established as a trading post for planters in 1740 by William Heritage, a prosperous and prominent planter and jurist, the site was originally known as "Kingston." About 1750, Richard Caswell, a native of Maryland, chose "Kingston" as his home. He later became the first Governor of North Carolina under the State Constitution. Establishment of the town was officially authorized by Royal Gov. Arthur Dobbs in 1762. First trustees of "Kingston" were: Richard Caswell, Francis McLewean, Simon Bright, Jr., John Shine, and David Gordon, who laid out the town and named its first streets for themselves, and for William Heritage, except the main street, Queen Street, named for Queen Charlotte, wife of King George III, and King Street, named for King George III. Shortly after the American Revolution, zealous patriots dropped the "g" and adopted the name "Kinston."

Lenoir County, named for Revolutionary Gen. William Lenoir (*see* TOUR *19*), was formed in 1791 from Dobbs County, but before 1759, it was part of the Great County of Bath.

Before the Civil War, the Dibble family established a buggy factory here and operated a fleet of freight and passenger boats to New Bern. Among the earliest industries was the shoe-manufacturing plant of John Cobb Washington and George Washington, relatives of Pres. Washington. The section near the factory was called Yankee Row when Federal troops were quartered there, Dec. 13-14, 1862.

On the SE. corner of Gordon and Heritage Sts. is the SITE OF THE BIRTHPLACE OF DR. JAMES AUGUSTUS WASHINGTON, who with Dr. Isaac E. Taylor in 1839-40 first administered medicine with a hypodermic needle.

The LENOIR COUNTY COURTHOUSE (1940), SE. corner Queen and King Sts., a modern 4-story concrete building, replaced three earlier ones. The first, of wood (1792), was burned. A brick building erected in 1845 was set afire by the clerk of the court in 1878. The few records that could be saved were removed to a store building which the determined clerk fired a few nights later. The incendiary served a term in the penitentiary, but Lenoir is without its early records. The third was torn down in 1938.

On the courthouse green is a MONUMENT TO RICHARD CASWELL (1729-89), a Maryland surveyor who came to North Carolina with letters to Gov. Johnston. After serving as deputy surveyor of the Colony and clerk of Orange County Court, he started his long career in the general assembly (1754-71), where he evinced vigorous interest in court reforms. Caswell commanded Tryon's right wing at Alamance (*see* TOUR *15B*) and led a patriot force at Moore's Creek Bridge (*see* TOUR *17A*). He was a delegate to the Continental Congress (1774-76) and first Governor under the State Constitution (1776-80), during which time he helped organize and equip troops. In 1780 he was elevated to a major-generalship in command of the entire State militia. He served as Governor a second time (1785-87) and died in 1789 while Speaker of the assembly at Fayetteville. His body was returned to Kinston, where he had resided for 25 years.

The PUBLIC LIBRARY (*open 9-5 weekdays*), 109 King St. opposite the courthouse, is supported jointly by the city and its civic organizations. The central section of the house, two stories in height, is flanked by one-story wings. Usually referred to as the Peebles House, it is the oldest in Kinston, having been built by a man named Lovick and sold to Abner Nash in 1824. Remodeling has changed its original appearance.

At Kinston the ram *Neuse,* Confederate ironclad boat built higher up the river at White Hall, was grounded and burned by Confederates in 1865. Its hull still lies on the bottom of the river within the city limits of Kinston.

Kinston's bright-leaf tobacco market is one of the 4 largest bright-leaf tobacco markets in the world. This industry began in 1895 when Jesse W. Grainger grew and marketed the first bright-leaf tobacco in the country and later established the first tobacco auction house. Kinston now has 14 tobacco auction warehouses with a total floor area of 35 square acres. The 7 stemming and redrying plants employ more than 3,000 persons in the fall.

The Kinston DACRON PLANT of E. I. DuPont de Nemours & Co., Inc., is located 6 m. NE. of Kinston on NC 11. At Kinston are also a large textile plant, three shirt factories, paper box manufacturing plant, lumber manufacturing, dairy products industries, food processing enterprises, and the State's first federally inspected meatpacking plant.

Kinston is at the junction with US 70 (*see* TOUR *15*).

At **115 m.** US 258 crosses the Neuse River.

At **115.8 m.** is the junction with NC 55.

Left on NC 55 to the junction with NC 12, **0.7 m.**; R. **14.2 m.** on NC 12 to the junction with a dirt road; R. **2.7 m.** on the dirt road to the WHITAKER PLANTATION HOUSE (*private*), a story-and-a-half structure, sloping in the manner of a New England "salt-box" to one story at the rear, with extended front porch on square piers. The pegged frame house is covered with weatherboarding. The massive right chimney is still standing, but only the base of the left remains. Plainly visible in the one-story section are holes made by a cannon ball which went through the house during the Civil War. Here on March 8, 1865, Gen. Braxton Bragg repulsed Federal forces led by Gen. Cox, capturing many prisoners. This was one of the last Confederate victories, since Federal reinforcements forced Bragg to retire immediately to Goldsboro. Twelve days later these same Confederate troops met defeat in the "last stand of the Confederacy" at Bentonville (*see* TOUR *18*).

TOWER HILL, 4 m. out NC 55, E., and **1.5 m.** R., the plantation of Gov. Arthur Dobbs (1754-65), was selected as the colonial capital and named George City by an act of the assembly in 1758. The London Board of Trade repealed the act before it was executed. Here stands the JOHN TULL HOUSE (*private*), originally the home of William Heritage, the first settler of Kinston. Subsequently the house was occupied by three generations of Tulls.

RICHLANDS, 143 m. (65 alt., 877 pop.), is a sawmill and farming town that grew up on Avirett, ante-bellum plantation of James Battle, who owned the 7-mile stretch of land from this point to Catherine Lake.

At **155 m.** is the junction with US 17 (*see* TOUR *1*), 1 mile west of Jacksonville.

TOUR 3 *(US 301)*

(Emporia, Va.)—Weldon—Halifax—Rocky Mount—Fayetteville—Lumberton—(Florence, S. C.)
Virginia Line—South Carolina Line. **196 m.**

US 301, known as "The Tobacco Trail," begins at Baltimore, Md., carries the tourist through the tobacco area in Maryland, Virginia, North and South Carolina, and Georgia, and ends in Sarasota, Fla. It avoids large cities (including Washington, D. C.), by-passes many towns, and is considered the most popular North-South route on the East Coast. A limited-access highway, with north and south lanes separated by a grass plot, is now being planned by State and Federal officials.

Section a. VIRGINIA LINE *to* WILSON; 64 m. *US 301*

Between the Virginia Line and Wilson, US 301 runs through the coastal plain, traversing a countryside broken by pine forests, stands of hardwood, and occasional swamps. Intersecting roads lead into farming country that produces peanuts, tobacco, cotton, potatoes, and corn. Rivers on the lower slopes of the piedmont plateau have been developed into power sources for manufacturing enterprises.

US 301 crosses the Virginia-North Carolina Line, **0 m.,** 11 miles south of Emporia, Va., and enters Northampton County.

The route follows part of the old Petersburg-to-Halifax highway used by Cornwallis' army in 1781, and over it Confederate troops hauled supplies during the siege of Petersburg in 1864-65.

GARYSBURG, **7 m.** (145 alt., 344 pop.), is a farm village at the junction with US 158 (*see* TOUR *12*). Here (R) is the OLD GARY HOUSE (*private*), long used as an inn. A two-storied rectangular frame house, built in 1820 of virgin timbers, with a "dog-run" through the center, its builder, Roderick Gary, represented Northampton County in the House of Commons (1821-36), longer than any other man (from 1777 to 1850).

At **8 m.** a steel and concrete bridge spans the Roanoke River, 100 feet below and crosses into Halifax County.

US 301 by-passes Weldon; US 301-A goes through the town.

WELDON, 9 m. (78 alt., 2,295 pop.), the market town of a peanut-growing district, began to assume importance after railroad links from Virginia had been built in 1832-34. When these terminals were connected with Wilmington on completion of the Wilmington & Raleigh Railroad, in 1840, the 161.5-mile stretch was described as the longest railroad in the world. The line, renamed the Wilmington & Weldon Railroad in 1854, played an important part as a supply line to Gen. Robert E. Lee at Richmond, Va.

In 1835 a 9-mile canal was chartered from Rock Landing to Weldon's Orchard in which the masonry in the three original locks is still sound. Power is developed from the Roanoke River. Weldon has peanut and cotton-seed processing factories, tobacco warehouses, a brick plant, and lumber-yards. Forests and streams of the vicinity abound with game and fish. It is known as the "Rockfish Capital," because of the fine striped bass fishing here in the spring.

Weldon is the center of an area of large farms, and a number of its residents have large holdings along the Roanoke River, whose rich silt has made this one of the richest agricultural sections in the State. The recently constructed Kerr Dam and Reservoir (see TOUR 12) was designed primarily to prevent the disastrous floods which have frequently inundated the lowlands along the river.

Here is the birthplace and residence of Ovid Williams Pierce (1910-   ), author of the recent novel, *The Plantation*.

Throughout this section peanuts are plowed out before the first frosts and, still attached to their vines, are stacked in the fields to cure for several weeks. The actual harvest is marked by clouds of dust attending the operation of the giant mechanical "pickers" as the threshing-machines are called that dot the fields among the black stacks.

At Halifax, US 301 skirts the western part of the village; NC 113 goes through it.

HALIFAX, 15 m. (135 alt., 346 pop.), ancient borough town and seat of Halifax County, was the scene of North Carolina's first constitutional convention. Men whose names live in the State's early history walked beneath the oaks and sycamores along narrow, crooked King, Dobbs, and Granville streets in the days when Halifax was noted for its gay social life.

As early as 1723 settlers were established in this region, and when the county was set up in 1757, it was named for the second Earl of Halifax, president of the British board of trade, which then administered colonial affairs. In 1758 Halifax succeeded the older Enfield as the county seat. In 1760 Halifax was made a borough and from 1776 to 1782 nearly every session of the general assembly was held here. Not only was it a political center, but, according to contemporary accounts, it was "a pretty town," situated in the "wealthiest region of North Carolina" and its soil was "rich and highly cultivated." Its society was "considered among the most polished and cultivated in the State." Numerous visitors commented on its grace, gaiety, and opulence. A wedding in 1790 was celebrated by "twenty-two consecutive dinner parties, in so many different houses, the dinners being regularly succeeded by dances and all terminated with a great ball." By 1791 its importance was waning. George Washington, on his Southern tour, noted that "it seems to be in a decline and does not it is said contain a thousand Souls."

The COURTHOUSE GREEN, part of the 4 acres set aside for public buildings when the town was laid out in 1758, is at the intersection of King (Main) St. and the Weldon Rd. The HALIFAX COUNTY COURTHOUSE (1910), a brick structure with a Corinthian portico and surmounted with a dome, succeeds two previous buildings (1759 and 1847). In the archives is a complete set of will books, beginning in 1759. Here on Apr. 4, 1776, 139 delegates to the Provincial Congress met. Samuel Johnston, of Chowan County (see EDENTON), as president of the congress, appointed a committee to "take into consideration the usurpation and violences attempted and committed by the King and Parliament of Britain against America." On April 12 the committee reported, designating Joseph Hewes, William Hooper, and John Penn as North Carolina's delegates to the Continental Congress, ". . . to concur with the delegates from the other Colonies in declaring Independency, and forming foreign alliances, reserving to this Colony the sole and exclusive right of forming a Constitution and laws for this Colony. . . ." These Halifax Resolves constitute the *first official action by any Colonial legislature for absolute separation from Great Britain and for national independence.* In recognition of this fact the North Carolina flag bears the date, and April 12, Halifax Day, is a State holiday.

From a platform in front of the first courthouse, on Aug. 1, 1776, Cornelius Harnett (see WILMINGTON) read the Declaration of Independence (its first proclamation in the State) to the assembled citizens who carried him through the streets on their shoulders.

Three months later, Nov. 12, 1776, an elected congress met in Halifax (presumably here), adopted the Constitution of 1776 (which had been drafted in the nearby Constitution House), and elected Richard Caswell the first Governor of the State of North Carolina (see TOUR 2).

Before leaving here in May, 1781, Lord Cornwallis, on his way to Yorktown, Va., condemned two of his men to death for "rape and robbery" the preceding evening.

On the green is a marker honoring Brig. Gen. Junius Daniel (1828-64), gallant Halifax officer killed at the Battle of Spotsylvania and buried in an unmarked grave in the Colonial Cemetery.

The OLD GAOL (Jail), two blocks NE. of the courthouse on King St., is a high, square brick structure authorized by the colonial assembly in 1764. The most substantial prison in the colony, with two-foot-thick brick walls, it was used in March, 1776, to confine 41 Highland Scot leaders after their defeat at Moore's Creek Bridge (see TOUR 18). Among them was Maj. Allan MacDonald, husband of the celebrated Scottish heroine who had helped Bonnie Prince Charlie escape. Efforts are now being made to preserve it as a museum or State Park.

Adjacent to the jail is the old CLERK's OFFICE, now used as a county library. A picturesque, one-story, red brick building with swinging iron shutters, constructed about 1780, it was also used as the printing office of Abraham Hodge, who came from New Bern to Halifax in 1784 to publish a weekly newspaper, the *Halifax Journal,* one of the State's most important papers in the Federal period.

Below the Clerk's Office, occupying the rest of the block towards the river, is the SITE OF THE EAGLE HOTEL. This old hostelry served as headquarters for members of Provincial congresses and assemblies that met in Halifax. According to tradition, many notables have been entertained or lodged here: Cornwallis and Tarleton when the entire British army was quartered in Halifax for several days in May, 1781, on their way to Yorktown; George Washington, on April 17, 1791; and Lafayette, on Feb. 27, 1825. Lafayette was entertained by a banquet "where the usual thirteen toasts were drunk," addressed by Maj. Allen Jones Davie (son of Gen. Davie), and fêted with a ball.

Around 1845 part of it was removed 4 blocks south by its owner, Michael Ferrall, for his residence, and is now known as the GARY HOME (*private, open by appointment*). The interior and exterior woodwork is hand made. The hand-blown glass panels around the double entrance doors are framed by facings ornamented with sunbursts, which are repeated at the corners of the roof and in one of the over-mantels.

Across the road from the Clerk's Office are the COLONIAL CHURCHYARD and the SITE OF THE COLONIAL CHURCH OF ENGLAND. The church, with only 6 pillars now remaining, was used by all denominations between 1820 and 1830. Buried in the churchyard are many early Halifax citizens, including Hodge (1755-1805), Gen. Daniel, and Mrs. Sarah Jones Davie, wife of Gen. Davie and daughter of Gen. Allen Jones (*see* TOUR *12*).

The MASONIC TEMPLE (*not open*), Weldon Rd. W. of the courthouse, a two-story clapboarded structure, 30 by 30 feet, home of the Royal White Hart Lodge, organized in 1769. It is one of the oldest Masonic temples built for that purpose and still in use in the United States. The first floor was used for a schoolroom until 1829. The Royal White Hart Lodge held its first meeting in 1764, though not chartered until 1767. The master's chair was installed in 1765, silver candlesticks in 1784, and the handsome ballot box in 1820. A bell, cast in 1810, hangs between 10-foot posts in the yard.

In the adjoining sedge field is a fenced enclosure; the plaque on the gate bears the inscription: "The GRAVE OF MONTFORT. This gate swings only by order of the Worshipful Master of Royal White Hart Lodge." Col. Joseph Montfort (1724-76) was clerk of Halifax court from 1758 until his death, clerk of the district court, town commissioner, and a member of several colonial assemblies. In 1772 he received from the Duke of Beaufort, grand master of Masons of Great Britain, an appointment as Provincial grand master of North America.

Across from the Lodge is an old house (*can be visited*) which was used as a Confederate hospital. Pronounced by Waterman as "a perfect example of Dutch Colonial architecture," it has interesting paneling and mantels.

Northwest of the Masonic Temple on the Weldon Rd. (L) is LORETTA (*private*), a clapboard house with sharply pitched roof, central gable, and portico. It has been restored as it was when it was the Halifax home (1783-1805) of Gen. William R. Davie (1756-1820), except the left wing has been added. Davie was one of North Carolina's 5 delegates to the 1787 Constitutional Convention in Philadelphia; he was instrumental in securing from the general assembly in 1789 an act to establish the University of North Carolina; and as grand master of Masons in the State laid the cornerstones of the University's first two buildings (*see* CHAPEL HILL). In 1798 Davie was elected Governor, but resigned in 1799 to become Minister Plenipotentiary to France. After his defeat for a seat in Congress, he retired in 1805 to Tivoli plantation near Landsford, S. C., where he remained until his death in 1820.

ST. MARK'S EPISCOPAL CHURCH, King St., was built in 1854 on the Grove property to replace the Colonial Church. It is of wood, painted gray, 4 bays long with steeply pointed roof and belfry at front. The vertical siding has overlapped joints. The building was at one time damaged by fire and has been remodeled. The old Register, still extant, describes it as "a perfect Tudor Gothic."

CONSTITUTION HOUSE was restored in 1920, moved from its original site behind the Colonial Churchyard to the Grove property, and furnished with period furniture and household articles. It is a small, square, clapboarded building raised on brick piers, with a narrow front porch, well-proportioned doorways, and two outside brick chimneys. In this house was drafted the Constitution of 1776 (Nov. 13-Dec. 6, 1776) by a 9-man committee appointed by the provincial congress which presumably met in the courthouse. The framers were Willie and Allen Jones, Samuel Ashe, Richard Caswell, Cornelius Harnett, Thomas Person, Griffith Rutherford, and Archibald Maclaine.

The GROVE, in the SW. part of Halifax, was the property of Willie (pronounced Wiley) Jones (1741-1822). His colonial mansion, built in 1765, closely resembled the Randolph-Semple House in Williamsburg, Va. Famous for its lavish hospitality, racing stable, and track, nothing remains of the house but a brick chimney. Jones, planter, legislator, and one of the framers of the first State Constitution, acted as Governor of North Carolina in 1776 while president of the council of safety. He served several terms in the Continental Congress and, as the ultra states'-rights advocate, opposed ratification of the Federal Constitution by the Hillsboro convention; though elected to the Federal Constitutional Convention (1787), he declined to serve. His political power, as head of the Anti-Federalist forces, was unchallenged; he has become known as the "Jefferson of North Carolina—a liberal aristocrat."

There is a strong tradition, unsupported by documentary evidence, that

John Paul Jones, the "father of the American Navy," was befriended here by Willie Jones and that in appreciation he assumed Willie's last name. It is a known fact that John Paul, as he was then known, had killed the ringleader of a mutiny on his ship in 1773 and had fled to America. It is also known that through the offices of Joseph Hewes of Edenton he had obtained his first commission in the American Navy.

Lafayette called on Mrs. Willie Jones, Feb. 28, 1825. The local paper described his visit: ". . . the meeting of the General and this venerable lady, was truly affecting; there was not a dry eye in the room—the aged frame of Mrs. Jones was convulsed with feeling and the General sunk in a chair overpowered with various and conflicting emotions."

In 1781 Cornwallis quartered a portion of his troops at the Grove; during the Civil War, Confederate Col. McRae camped on the estate with an entire regiment, and Union soldiers occupied the house at the close of the war.

Across Quanky Creek from the Grove is the SITE OF QUANKY PLACE, the plantation of Col. Nicholas Long (1728-98), a wealthy planter who served as commissary general of the North Carolina Revolutionary forces. Colonel and Mrs. Long erected workshops here to make implements of war, clothing, and other supplies for the soldiers. Tradition says the Longs entertained Pres. Washington at Quanky Place in 1791.

In June, 1954, the Historical Halifax Restoration Committee was organized to promote the restoration of the many 18-century buildings here.

At **16 m.,** NC 561 (L) forms a junction with US 301.

Left on this road to GLEN BURNIE (*private*), **6.5 m.,** the old Tillery house. Built in 1800 by Thomas Blount Hill and originally called "The Hermitage," this is one of the finest examples of the Morris-plan house in North Carolina.

ENFIELD, **26 m.** (113 alt., 2,361 pop.), the oldest town in Halifax County, has plants for the manufacture of peanut products. From 1745 until supplanted by Halifax in 1758, Enfield, then known as Huckleberry Swamp, was the seat of Edgecombe County. As a protest against British oppression, in 1759 Francis Corbin (*see* EDENTON) and Joshua Bodley, agents of Lord Granville, were seized by armed men and lodged in jail at Enfield until the agents readjusted their captors' tax levies.

At the COLUMBIAN PEANUT PLANT (*open*) peanuts are stored, cleaned, shelled, and packed in jute bags for shipment.

Right from Enfield on a gravel road to BRANCH PLANTATION (*private*), **0.7 m.,** home of John Branch, Governor of North Carolina (1817-20). He served as U. S. Senator (1823-29), Secretary of the Navy under Andrew Jackson, Congressman, and Governor of the Territory of Florida (1843-45). The two-story house, painted gray, is one room deep with one end chimney at the left and two at the right. The eave is lined with a coarse dentiled cornice. Gen. Lafayette is said to have addressed admirers from the upper porch in 1825. Gov. Branch is buried in the family graveyard 100 yards east of the house.

Right on NC 481 from Enfield to SHELL CASTLE (*private*), **2 m.** Built in 1790 by Matthew Cary Whitaker, Revolutionary patriot, it is still owned by his descendants and is furnished in period style. The house is very tall, with 4 dormers across. The formal garden has been kept as originally; the enormous English boxwoods must be coeval with the house.

At **27 m.** is the junction with an avenue of oaks.

Right on this road to the EAST CAROLINA INDUSTRIAL TRAINING SCHOOL, **0.3 m.**, a college established for Negroes whose 4 red brick buildings stand at the corners of a grassy court.

At **28 m.** US 301 crosses FISHING CREEK near which bones of an ichthyosaurus were excavated some years ago. On the creek bank is a large flat stone impressed with human and animal footprints and intricate designs.

WHITAKERS, **33 m.** (134 alt., 962 pop.), was named for Richard and Elizabeth Carey Whitaker, the first white settlers to venture into this Tuscarora stronghold. They settled on Fishing Creek and in 1740 built Whitakers Chapel between Enfield and Scotland Neck. This Church of England chapel was used by Methodists in 1786 when Bishop Asbury preached there.

BATTLEBORO, **38 m.** (135 alt., 329 pop.), started (1840) as a railroad stop in a rich agricultural area. The station was named for James and Joseph Battle, stockholders in the Wilmington and Raleigh Railroad.

At **44 m.** is the junction with NC 95.

Left on NC 95 to the junction with a lane, **4.5 m.**; R. on the lane to the BATTLE HOMESTEAD (*visitors welcome*), property of the Battle family since c. 1742 when Elisha Battle purchased this rich Tar River bottom land, then a part of Cool Spring Plantation, from the Earl of Granville. Elisha Battle was a member of the Halifax convention in 1776 and chairman of the committee of the whole in the assembly at Tarboro in 1787 for consideration of the Federal Constitution, adoption of which he opposed in 1788 at Hillsboro.
The one-and-a-half story house has a gambrel roof and massive end chimneys. In the eastern chimney was a brick dated 1742, lost in repairing. Three dormers in front, a porch the length of the house, and additions to right and rear are later alterations. The wide-paneled doors, the 12-light windows, and the interior paneling are excellent examples of 18th-century craftsmanship. The east façade has two 8-light windows on each side of the chimneys, set high so that a person sitting in the room could not be shot from ambush.

US 301 crosses Tar River, **45.5 m.**, on a high concrete bridge. Legend recalls that Cornwallis' soldiers, fording the river near here, found their feet black with tar that had been dumped into the river. Their observation that anyone who waded North Carolina streams would acquire tar heels is said to have given North Carolinians the nickname of "Tar Heels."

ROCKY MOUNT, **46 m.** (121 alt., 27,697 pop.), the third largest brightleaf tobacco market in the world and an industrial and railroad center, was named for the mounds near the site at the Falls of the Tar. At the Falls, on the north bank of the Tar, was the first settlement and the SITE OF DONALDSON'S TAVERN (*indicated by a bronze tablet*) where Lafayette spent the night of Feb. 28, 1825. Here also stood the FALLS PRIMITIVE BAPTIST CHURCH (built in 1757), which was said to have been burned by a nearby barkeeper when he learned of a legislative act prohibiting selling spirits so close to a place of worship.

When the tracks of the Wilmington and Weldon Railroad were laid through near here in 1840, a town grew up around the freight platforms and gradually merged with the village around the cotton mill at the Falls. The town, incorporated in 1867 with 50 inhabitants, lies half in Nash and half in Edgecombe counties, the Atlantic Coast Line tracks bisecting Main Street and marking the county boundary, so that citizens living on one side of the street have to attend court in Nashville while those on the other side go to Tarboro.

Rocky Mount has several tobacco-redrying plants and 16 tobacco-auction warehouses with a combined capacity of 70,000,000 pounds. The output of its many manufacturing establishments includes cotton yarns, pile fabrics, broad silks, shirts, overalls, cottonseed oil and meal, fertilizer, cordage, and lumber products. From a station on the pioneer Wilmington & Raleigh Railroad (1846) the town has developed into a modern railroad center and division point with repair shops and yards for 4 divisions of the Atlantic Coast Line, the largest single employer in the county. It also has the largest livestock market in eastern North Carolina. A new residential section, "West Haven," with many fine homes, has grown up around the lake in the southwestern part of the city.

The ROCKY MOUNT COTTON MILLS (*not open to public*), 1151 Falls Rd., one of the largest in the State, were established by Joel Battle in 1818 and have been continuously under the management of the Battle family. During the first of the Civil War, they made cloth for the Confederate government. The original building, burned in 1863 by Federal forces, was rebuilt after the war only to be destroyed by an incendiary. Rebuilt in 1871, the plant has been enlarged and modernized. The output is cotton yarns. THE MILLS, built by Col. Benjamin Dorsey Battle, son of the founder of the mills, was one of the few homes to escape burning during the Civil War.

MANGUM'S WAREHOUSE, covering a city block, is the scene of the annual all-night June German (*2nd Fri. in June*), given by the Carolina Cotillion Club, and attended by thousands of guests from several states. This ball has been an important social event since 1880 when a group of young men formed the club. On Saturday night after the ball Negroes use the same warehouse and decorations for their June German.

The THOMAS HACKNEY BRASWELL MEMORIAL LIBRARY, near the junction of US 301 and NC 43, given in 1923 by Dr. Mark Russell Braswell in memory of his son, contains a collection of Indian artifacts, paper money, old records, and curios. The red brick building with white limestone trim is of one story with end pavilions and a central portico.

Rocky Mount is at the junction with US 64 (*see* TOUR *13*).

Right from Rocky Mount on NC 43 to the LEWIS HOME (*private*), 1.3 m., built in 1839 by Bennet Bunn on the western bank of Tar River. A three-story brick mansion, it has a hip roof and an entrance with a simple fanlighted doorway on the second floor level. The balcony and the 4-column portico, resting on a raised arcaded brick basement, are modern. According to legend, a silver dollar and a quart of brandy were constructed in each corner, so that the owner would never be broke or dry.

On NC 43 at **5.4 m.** is the DORTCH HOUSE (*private*). The old part, moved from a nearby field to be added as a kitchen ell at the rear, was built c. 1798; it has a steep roof, small windows, heavy chimney, and fireplace with beveled panels.

On the lower floor, front and rear, are Palladian windows framed with Ionic fluted pilasters and entablature. The modillioned cornice returns at the corners and follows the raked line of the gable. Interior woodwork includes a mahogany stair rail, paneled wainscot and mantelpieces, and finely carved door and window casings with arabesque panels above. This part of the house was built c. 1803.

The COOPER HOUSE (*private*), **12 m.**, formerly the Battle home, is the oldest known house in Nash County. The kitchen, dining room, and parlor connected by a passageway are later additions to the original small wooden building, which was mortised and assembled with wooden pegs. The house stands on a little hill on a mile-square tract purchased by William Battle from the State in 1779 for 50 shillings per 100 acres.

At **62 m.**, L., **2 m.**, is the JOSHUA BARNES HOME (*private*), a square, antebellum house, erected c. 1845 by Joshua Barnes, Confederate Brig. Gen. of the N. C. Militia, State Senator, and called the "father of Wilson County."

US 301 by-passes Wilson in its western suburbs; 301-A goes straight through the town.

WILSON, **64 m.** (147 alt., 23,010 pop.), the largest bright-leaf tobacco market in the world and the seat of Wilson County, was named for Col. Louis D. Wilson (*see* TOUR 2). The county, formed in 1855, was settled largely by English families who came from Virginia after 1840.

Uptown, Nash is a narrow and bustling business street. West of Pine Street it broadens into a mile-long, tree-shaded arcade through a section of comfortable homes surrounded by landscaped lawns and gardens. The industrial section has cotton and fertilizer factories, 10 stemmeries and redrying plants, and 19 tobacco warehouses, including sprawling Smith's Warehouse, called the world's largest (*Free conducted tours of auction sales leave from the Chamber of Commerce, 10:30 each morning, Mon. through Fri. from mid-Aug. to about Thanksgiving*).

Tobacco, the State's first commercial crop, originally produced only for export, was packed in huge hogsheads and rolled through the woods to water-edge inspection houses where sailor-buyers broke open the casks for examination before bargaining. This gave rise to the warehouse auction system still used and the practice of terming it a "break," though the loose-leaf method is now employed.

When the graded tobacco "hands" are "in order," the farmer hauls them to market. The warehouses are one-story buildings with plenty of open floor space and numerous skylights to allow natural lighting, as tobacco is judged for color as well as for texture and aroma. Lots are piled in shallow baskets and arranged in rows down which pass the auctioneer and buyers. The procedure moves so swiftly that more than 400 lots are sold in an hour and 89,000,000 pounds have been sold in a season. However, a visitor may watch the sale without understanding a word of the auctioneer's patter and without hearing a single word spoken by a buyer, as a mere gesture or change of expression indicates a bid to the watchful seller. A tobacco festival and exposition are held annually in August.

Wilson's manufactured products include cotton yarns, cottonseed meal and oil, fertilizers, bale covering, bus and refrigerated truck bodies, wagons, agricultural implements, shirts, food products, and laundry supplies.

The WILSON COUNTY COURTHOUSE, Nash and Goldsboro Sts., three stories and attic high, was built in 1924 in neoclassic design, replacing a building erected in 1855.

Fronting on Whitehead and Lee Sts. is the 12-acre campus of the ATLANTIC CHRISTIAN COLLEGE, incorporated in 1902, a coeducational institution with about 500 students, operated by the North Carolina Christian Church. The buildings, of brown brick, are of various styles.

Between Vance and Academy Sts., facing the railroad, stood the WILSON FEMALE ACADEMY (built in 1859), which supplanted two earlier ones. From the spring of 1863 until April, 1865, it was used as a Confederate Military Hospital, where wounded soldiers from Fort Fisher, New Bern, and Plymouth were sent. It later became the WILSON COLLEGIATE INSTITUTE. Among its students were Gov. Charles B. Aycock (*see* TOUR *4*) and Josephus Daniels. The latter lived here as a boy; his mother was postmistress of the town (1866-83).

In MAPLEWOOD CEMETERY is the GRAVE OF REBECCA M. WINBORNE (1831-1918), maker of the original "Stars and Bars." The flag was designed by Maj. Orren R. Smith of Franklin County and was first displayed, Mar. 18, 1861, at Louisburg.

Natives of Wilson were Dempsey Bullock (1863-1928), local poet and historian, and Henry Groves Connor (1852-1924), Associate Justice of the North Carolina Supreme Court and Federal district judge. Two sons of Judge Connor attained prominence: George W. Connor, Associate Justice of the North Carolina Supreme Court (1924-38), and Robert D. W. Connor, first U. S. Archivist (1934-41). At the old railroad depot here the song "Ho! For Carolina!" was written by Dr. William Bernard Harold. Wilson was also the western terminus of the Greenville and Raleigh Plank Road. Its construction was stopped here in 1853.

Wilson is at the junction with US 264 (*see* TOUR *14*) and NC 58.

Section b. WILSON *to* SOUTH CAROLINA LINE; *132 m. US 301*

Between Wilson and the South Carolina Line US 301 swings along the edge of the fertile piedmont plateau. Forests of longleaf and shortleaf pine are sprinkled with oak, maple, ash, and gum. Shallow streams have worn sloping ravines in many places.

At **5 m.** is the junction with US 117 (*see* TOUR *4*).

SELMA, **26 m.** (179 alt., 2,639 pop.), is an industrial town (incorporated in 1873) with textile mills, chemical plants, and other industries. The Southern and Atlantic Coast Line Railways cross at Selma. Mitchiner's Station, on the old North Carolina Railroad, about a mile north of the present town of Selma, served Johnston County before the Civil War, as citizens of Smithfield did not want trains coming into their town.

At **28 m.** is the northern junction with US 70 (*see* TOUR *15*).

SMITHFIELD, **31 m.** (140 alt., 5,574 pop.), seat of Johnston County, is a tobacco-market town on a bluff above the Neuse River. The Assembly of 1746 created the county, named for Gabriel Johnston, governor under the crown (1734-52). At the same time St. Patrick's Parish, Church of England, was established co-extensive with the county; 10 years later the parish was divided, that part above the mouth of Mill Creek becoming St. Stephen's Parish. In 1758 when Dobbs County was formed from Johnston only St. Stephen's Parish remained—St. Patrick's going to Dobbs County. The first county court met "at the dwelling of Francis Stringer at the ferry on Neuse River" near present-day Kinston, but from 1746 to 1759 gathered at Walnut Creek near present La Grange. Between 1759 and 1771 court met at HINTON'S QUARTER at a site now on the Round House Farm one mile south of Clayton. In March, 1771, the county seat was finally established on John Smith's property on the banks of the Neuse River in the present town of Smithfield. Since 1797 the courthouse has been at its present site.

Smithfield was named for Lt. Col. John Smith (1736-90) who, in 1762, had purchased the tract of land on which the town was laid out in 1777. Smith was a lad of 4 or 5 when his father emigrated to this section from Virginia. He was a delegate from Johnston County to the Provincial Congress which convened at Hillsboro on Aug. 20, 1775.

On May 3, 1771, Gov. William Tryon and the colonial militia, marching from New Bern to the frontier to quell the Regulator uprisings, camped at Smith's Ferry, near the courthouse. Here he was joined by Johnston County troops, and in a meadow by the river a review of the whole militia was staged. In May, 1779, the general assembly convened here.

The JOHNSTON COUNTY COURTHOUSE (1920) is a three-story granite and limestone structure of neoclassic design. The main façade is adorned with Roman Doric columns and pilasters, forming an entrance loggia. On the lawn is a statue of a soldier dedicated to the citizens of the county who died in World War I and a fountain to veterans of the same conflict.

At HOLTS LAKE, **33 m.**, a recreation center (*fishing, swimming, boating*), is the junction of US 301 and 701 (*see* TOURS *3* AND *18*).

BENSON, **46 m.** (245 alt., 2,102 pop.), is the center of a tobacco-farming area. A sport shirt factory, two lumber companies, and a veneer plant comprise its industry. The Benson Community Sing (*4th Sun. in June*) is a day-long program of group singing. Now (1954) in its 34th year, it is one of the oldest "grass roots" events and draws around 25,000 people annually.

DUNN, 53 m. (210 alt., 6,316 pop.), a marketing center, was founded by descendants of early English and Scottish settlers. Near here, at AVERAS-BORO, 4 m. W., Sherman's Army was temporarily checked by Hardee's Confederates, in March, 1865. At Dunn is the HOME OF MAJ. GEN. WILLIAM C. LEE (U. S. Army 1917-48), who was a pioneer in organizing Army airborne units.

Dunn is at the junction with US 421 (*see* TOUR *17*).

At GODWIN, 61 m., is the junction with a marked road.

Left on this road to FALCON, 2.7 m. (245 pop.), a settlement and gathering place of the Pentecostal Holiness Church, which maintains an orphanage and school and conducts annual camp meetings in August. The work is interdenominational.

At 64 m. is the junction with a marked road.

Right on this road 0.6 m. to the junction with a dirt road; L. 0.6 m. on the dirt road to OLD BLUFF (Presbyterian) CHURCH (*key available at last house before reaching church*), named for a high point of land on which it stands. Built in the 1840's the well-preserved, white weatherboarded structure, with pedimented gable ends and recessed entrance loggia, is used for services only once a year (*4th Sun. in Sept.*). The interior has galleries on three sides. Near the church is a monument to its founder, the Rev. James Campbell, a Scottish missionary sent from Philadelphia in 1757, who in three years organized Old Bluff, Barbecue, and Long Street Churches.

FAYETTEVILLE, 78 m. (*see* FAYETTEVILLE).

Points of Interest: Market House, First Presbyterian Church, Cool Spring, Site of Cross Creek, Site of Flora Macdonald's House, and others.

Fayetteville is at the junction with US 15A (*see* TOUR 6) and NC 27 (*see* LOCAL TOUR FROM FAYETTEVILLE).

Left from Fayetteville on NC 27 to the junction with a dirt road, 28 m.; L. 0.3 m. on the dirt road to the PURDY HOUSE (*private*), a two-story brick mansion with porches across the front and rear at both floor levels. The porches and kitchen have been added to the original structure. It was erected in 1808 by James S. Purdy on land granted the Purdy family by George III before the Revolution. The brick of the 16-inch walls is laid in Flemish bond. Notable features of the interior are a fireplace with Ionic detail, wainscot of beveled paneling, and a cornice in the right-hand room.

Between Fayetteville and the South Carolina Line US 301 penetrates part of the cotton kingdom. Spring plowing turns up dull red soil, sometimes making the earth seem cloud-shadowed even on bright days. Grown men do the plowing, but at chopping time in midsummer women and children, black and white, ply their hoes. Cotton-picking time in the autumn brings out entire families. Mechanical cotton pickers are being used increasingly.

LUMBERTON, 111 m. (137 alt., 9,186 pop.), seat of Robeson County, is on both sides of the Lumber (Lumbee) River, originally called Drowning Creek. Here are textile mills, a fertilizer factory, 22 tobacco warehouses, a gigantic Carolina Light and Power Co. plant, a new $2,000,000 hospital, and one of the 4 cancer hospitals in the United States. The town is also a shipping point for truck produce, and farmers' cooperatives are represented in stores, groups, and a curb market.

Robeson County (second largest in the State) is half-humorously, half-seriously called "The State of Robeson." One of the richest agricultural counties in the United States, it has also been one of the most progressive, being one of the first to install agricultural and health departments.

Robeson County was formed in 1787 from Bladen. Col. Thomas Robeson, Whig hero of the Battle of Elizabethtown (see TOUR 18) and later State senator, opposed its creation until it was suggested it be named for him. The first court was held in 1787 at the home of John Willis, the "founder of Lumberton," a captain in the Revolution, later a brigadier general, and a member of the legislature and of the conventions of 1788-89. The present COURTHOUSE (1908), the third to be built, of Italian Renaissance design, has a complete series of will and deed books from 1787.

Early inhabitants of this section were Croatan Indians who, some contend, descend from survivors of Raleigh's Lost Colony (see TOUR 1A); others claim that they are descended from Portuguese traders who came here from Florida. Today the Indians comprise one-fourth of the population—more than any county in eastern America. The first white settlers (c. 1730) were English and a few French, who chose the southern portion. A few years later Highland Scots settled the northern and western parts.

By the latter half of the 18th century Lumberton had become a trading center for timber and naval stores, which were floated down the Lumber River to Georgetown, S. C. Later Robesonians turned to farming and cattle raising.

During the Revolution, the section seethed with conflict between Whig and Tory factions. Francis Marion, the "Swamp Fox," a South Carolina partisan leader, was active in this region and wrote many letters from "Red Bluff," the home of Gen. John Willis in Lumberton.

The oft-quoted political battle-cry, "As you love your state, hold Robeson," was telegraphed to Col. William French, Robeson County Democratic Chairman, on Aug. 3, 1875, by the State Democratic Chairman, Gen. W. R. Cox, in the heroic struggle of that party to gain control of the State Convention from the Republicans and thus end Reconstruction in the State.

Lumberton was the home of Angus W. McLean, Governor (1925-28) and Assistant Sec. of the Treasury (1920-21). Born near Maxton, he practiced law and is buried here.

Lumberton is at the junction with US 74 (see TOUR 16).

ROWLAND, 129 m. (145 alt., 1,293 pop.), formerly called Plainview and later Alfordsville, is a cotton and retail center named for Col. Alfred Rowland, II, Confederate officer. The GRAVE OF DR. JAMES ROBERT ADAIR is pointed out by a marker. A surgeon, soldier, Indian explorer, and author who came to Robeson in 1770, he spent nearly 40 years among the Indians, chiefly the Chickasaw, and published in 1775 the *History of the Indian Tribes,* a book expounding his theory that the Indians were descendants of the Lost Tribes of Israel. Its intimate account of the habits and customs of the tribes is valuable. The song, *Robin Adair,* written by Lady Caroline Keppel, is supposedly based on his travels.

Right from Rowland on US 501 to ASHPOLE PRESBYTERIAN CHURCH, **1.5 m.,** successor to a log church built here in 1796. The present building, third on the site, was partly completed during the Civil War. Simple lines are accentuated by a small belfry over the front entrance. The gallery, whose east side was reserved for slaves, remains unchanged. Timbers are hand-hewn, mortised with wooden pegs. Weatherboarding, flooring, and seats are hand-planed and put together with hand-made nails. The origin of the name is accredited to John Cade, one of the early settlers, who built bridges of ash poles across the millrace just below his dam.

Once the church gave all members in good standing a small metal disc or token, which allowed them to partake of communion. The principal event of the year was the Spring Sacrament, which persists as Homecoming Day (*3rd Sun. in May*).

ASHPOLE CEMETERY, in use for more than 150 years, is on the eastern side of Mitchell's Creek, near the site of the old Adair home.

At **132 m.** US 301 crosses the South Carolina Line, 26 miles north of Florence, S. C.

TOUR 4 (US 117)

Junction with US 301—Goldsboro—Warsaw—Wilmington; US 117. 109 m.

US 117 crosses eastern North Carolina flat lands where shadowy cypress swamps are almost as common as tobacco fields. Cotton farms are numerous though truck is also produced in large quantities.

US 117 branches south from its junction with US 301, **0 m.** (*see* TOUR 3), 5 miles south of Wilson.

At **2.1 m.** the highway spans Black Creek, a mile north of where Cornwallis crossed during his retreat from Wilmington in 1781 over Old Fort Road, now called Cornwallis Trail.

FREMONT, **9 m.** (154 alt., 1,395 pop.), incorporated in 1867, is an active cotton buying and shipping point.

At **10 m.**, is the BIRTHPLACE OF CHARLES B. AYCOCK (**2/3 m. E.**), Governor (1901-05) and crusader for universal education. Taken over as a State Historical Park in 1949, the remains are being restored.

US 17 skirts the western part of Goldsboro; US 17-A goes through the town.

GOLDSBORO, **21 m.** (111 alt., 21,399 pop.), seat of Wayne County, is in the center of eastern North Carolina's bright-leaf tobacco belt. Although chiefly a retail and commercial center, the city has 46 small diversified manufacturing plants employing 2800 people.

Wayne County, established in 1770 from part of Dobbs and named for "Mad Anthony" Wayne, Revolutionary hero, has the soil and climate suitable to diversified farming. Tobacco, cotton, corn, Irish and sweet potatoes, green beans, wheat, and soy beans are the principal crops. Dairying and live stock production have become important in recent years.

Goldsboro, incorporated in 1847, was named for Maj. Matthew T. Goldsborough, a civil engineer for the Wilmington and Weldon Railroad (now part of the Atlantic Coast Line) which passed through here. To take advantage of this railroad, the county seat was moved from Waynesboro on the Neuse River in 1847. Many houses and stores were torn down and rebuilt at Goldsboro. Goldsboro's importance increased when it became the eastern terminus of the North Carolina Railroad, built by the State (1851-56) from Goldsboro to Charlotte. In 1858 the Atlantic and North Carolina (the Old Mullet line) reached Goldsboro from the coast. On Dec. 17, 1862, Goldsboro was attacked by Federal troops, led by Gen. J. G. Foster, on a raid from New Bern. In March, 1865, three armies of Union forces met in Goldsboro under the respective command of Generals Sherman, Schofield, and Terry.

Of interest to the visitor are warehouses for tobacco auction sales, the Wayne County Memorial Community Building, erected as a memorial to heroes of World War I, the 18-hole municipal golf course, Seymour Johnson Air Base, and the Odd Fellows Orphans' Home.

The STATE HOSPITAL FOR NEGRO INSANE (2 m. W. of the city), established in 1884, was the first mental hospital for Negroes in the world. It has been completely modernized since World War II at the expenditure of millions of dollars. A $4,500,000 school for mentally defective Negro children is being added to the hospital.

Goldsboro is justly proud of its public school system, one of the first in the State. Here Gov. Aycock began his educational evangelism. Goldsboro was also the scene of the early career of the noted educator, E. A. Alderman, who later became President of the University of North Carolina, of Tulane University, and Chancellor of the University of Virginia. Other eminent educators who served as superintendents of the Goldsboro schools were E. P. Moses, well-known school administrator and organizer of the Goldsboro public school, P. P. Claxton, later U. S. Commissioner of Education, J. Y. Joyner, later State Supt. of Public Instruction, J. I. Foust, later President of Woman's College (see GREENSBORO), and E. C. Brooks, later State Supt. of Public Instruction and President of State College (see RALEIGH).

The BORDEN HOUSE (*private*), 111 S. George St. (c. 1857), originally a "Southern plantation" type house with porches on three sides, but remodeled in 1921 along Georgian lines, was the headquarters of Gen. Schofield during Yankee occupation.

The MASONIC HOME, cor. N. William and E. Mulberry Sts., was the HOME OF COL. WILLIAM T. DORTCH, Confederate Senator, speaker of the State House of Representatives, and head of the committee to codify the State laws in 1883.

ST. STEPHENS EPISCOPAL CHURCH, N. James St. (built 1856), is an English Gothic brick and granite structure. Here Gen. Schofield presented an offering taken from his soldiers, after finding that no offering was taken at the service because of impoverished conditions.

HERMAN PARK, E. end of Park Ave., is a 19-acre city park given by the Weil family. In addition to tennis courts and other recreational facilities, it has recently been beautified with roses and azaleas by the Men's Garden Club. The park is one of the many contributions of the Weil family, prominent business men and civic leaders. Among their other gifts was one of their homes, which houses the GOLDSBORO PUBLIC LIBRARY, W. Chestnut St.

Goldsboro is at the junction with US 70 (*see* TOUR *15*).

Left on US 70 is junction with NC 110, **4 m.** Right on this road, at **14 m.**, and left at **15 m.** is the CLIFFS OF THE NEUSE STATE PARK. (*A 12-acre lake for boating and swimming, picnicking area, refreshment stands, limited camping facilities, hiking, and a park museum.*) The gift of Lionel Weil, of Goldsboro, and others in 1945, it includes 321 acres on both sides of the Neuse River. The cliffs, rising 90 feet above the river, are a unique geological feature in this section. It is very interesting botanically, because of the unusual mixture of plants, trees, and shrubs. Mountain laurel and galax contrast with Spanish moss.

NC 110 at **14 m.** leads straight to junction with NC 55, at **16 m.** Left on this road to SEVEN SPRINGS, **20 m.**, down the Neuse River from the Cliffs. First known as Whitehall, Seven Springs was settled in 1743 by William Whitfield and became a favorite local spa in 1880 when a hotel (*now private*) was built here. The 7 mineral springs, each giving water of a different chemical content, are within an area 15 feet square and have been widely patronized for their medicinal qualities.

At **23 m.** on the northern bank of Neuse River is the SITE OF WAYNESBORO, former seat of Wayne County (1782-1847), first known as the Court House. Dr. Andrew Bass, delegate to the Provincial Congress of 1775 and to the Hillsboro convention of 1788, who owned the land on which Waynesboro stood, is believed to have been its founder. Waynesboro disappeared after removal of the seat to Goldsboro.

At **23.1 m.** the route crosses the muddy Neuse River. Along these shores, on Dec. 14, 1862, Gen. Evans repulsed Federal troops under Gen. Foster, who had won a skirmish two days earlier at Kinston.

At **31 m.** is a marker indicating the former GRAVE OF EZEKIEL AND MARY SLOCUMB, Revolutionary figures of the Battle of Moore's Creek Bridge, who were buried on the Slocumb farm here until they were moved to Moore's Creek Battlefield (*see* TOUR *18*). Lieut. Slocumb made a leap on horseback over a wide ditch and high wall on this farm to escape British soldiers. Mrs. Slocumb, left at home with an infant when her husband departed for Moore's Creek, had a dream in which she beheld her husband lying mortally wounded. She saddled a mare and rode 75 miles until she heard the sound of the cannon. Quickening her pace, she arrived at a clump of woods. ".... Just then I looked up, and my husband, as bloody as a butcher and as muddy as a ditcher, stood before me." She spent the remainder of the day succoring the wounded on the battlefield.

MOUNT OLIVE, **35 m.** (165 alt., 3,732 pop.), is in a farming area that produces bright-leaf tobacco, cotton, vegetables, berries, cucumbers, and melons. It has one of the largest pickle plants in the world and is referred to as "the pickle capital of the South." Mount Olive was founded with the coming of the railroad in 1839-40. Confederate troops were encamped here for a few days in March, 1865, prior to the Battle of Bentonville (*see* TOUR *18*).

Here is the home of Sam Byrd, actor and author, most famous for his portrayal of Jeeter Lester in the long-run Broadway hit, *Tobacco Road*. This is also the birthplace of Marion Hargrove, author of *See Here, Private Hargrove*. A nearby farm was the birthplace of Gov. Curtis H. Brogden (1874-77).

In 1953 the MOUNT ALLEN JUNIOR COLLEGE, operated by the Free Will Baptist Church, opened its doors.

FAISON, 42 m. (166 alt., 768 pop.), is one of the largest cucumber markets in the world. A local pickle plant (*open; apply at office*) annually uses about 70,000 bushels of cucumbers besides cauliflower, onions, and sweet peppers. Strawberries and produce are shipped.

The FAISON HOME (*private*) was built prior to 1785, as the residence of Henry Faison, first settler and founder of the town. The white frame house with green blinds has lost its early character through remodeling. Here is the birthplace of Brig. Gen. Samson L. Faison, who was decorated for helping to break the Hindenburg Line in World War I.

Right from Faison on NC 403 to the WILLIAMS HOME, **0.3 m.**, a square frame two-story structure erected in 1853. A 6-column portico rises to the eaves, and there are two one-story wings. The fine proportions are said to be the result of the influence of an aunt who was deeply interested in Ruskin's writings on art. Gen. Terry of the Union Army maintained his staff here in 1865. In the WILLIAMS ART GALLERY OF PLANTATION LIFE (*open by permission*) is a collection of paintings by Mrs. Marshall Williams (b. 1866), including ante-bellum scenes and portraits.

East of Faison are level piney uplands penetrated by streams bordered with swamps; south and southeast are pocosins.

WARSAW, 51 m. (160 alt., 1,598 pop.), is a truck market center bordering on the cotton belt. Three miles west was the home of James Kenan (*see* KENANSVILLE, *below*).

At Warsaw is the junction with NC 24.

Left on this road to KENANSVILLE, **9 m.** (127 alt., 674 pop.), seat of Duplin County. The town was named for the family of Col. James Kenan (d. 1810), who in 1765 led a force of volunteers from Kenansville to Brunswick to oppose enforcement of the Stamp Act. He served as county sheriff, trustee of the University of North Carolina, councilor of State, and for many years was in the general assembly.

The county, formed in 1750 from New Hanover and named for Lord Duplin, British nobleman, was first settled by Ulster Scots who came over under the patronage of Henry McCulloch, wealthy London merchant who received vast tracts of land in the colony from George II.

Grove Academy was conducted here in the middle 1800's. Among its students were William R. King, Vice Pres. of the United States (1853-57), and F. M. Simmons, U. S. Senator from North Carolina (1901-31). A school for young women, known as the Female Seminary, was operated here until the 1920's. An early philanthropist was Alexander Dickson (d. 1814), who bequeathed most of his large estate to the poor children of his county.

The first church built by Scotch-Irish settling here about 1736 was near what is now the old Rutledge Cemetery. The GOLDEN GROVE CHURCH, the congregation's third, near the center of town, is weatherboarded, painted white, and has a square tower and pointed windows.

In the Duplin County jail, in Sept. 1831, Dave Morisy, a Negro, was incarcerated for fomenting a plot in which insurgent slaves were to murder all the white people between Kenansville and Wilmington, and then to seize Fort Caswell at Smithville (Southport). The revelation of the plan caused intense excitement. Some 15 Negroes were arrested, and prominent citizens asked Gov. Montfort Stokes for militia to guard the jail. Dave confessed, implicating David Hicks, a Negro preacher. The two were convicted and publicly hanged. Their heads were cut off and placed on poles at highway intersections and slaves were marched by to gaze upon them. Dave's head was placed on the Wilmington Road (now US 117), which became known as the Negro Head Road.

WALLACE, 71 m. (51 alt., 1,622 pop.), is the marketing center of a large strawberry-raising section. An auctioneer conducts the sale of berries in a shed, open on all sides. An annual Strawberry Festival is held early in June. Nearby was the home of Thomas Larkin, U. S. Consul at Monterey, Cal. (1844-48). He played an important part in winning California for the United States at the beginning of the Mexican War.

Left from Wallace on NC 41 is TIN CITY, 1 m., a farm village. Here the British, led by Maj. James H. Craig, occupier of Wilmington, defeated the N. C. militia Aug. 2, 1781, at the Battle of Rockfish.

At 73 m. is the junction with NC 11.

Right on this road is WILLARD, 1 m. (50 alt., 100 pop.), and the NORTH CAROLINA COASTAL EXPERIMENT STATION, conducted by the State in cooperation with the Federal Government. Here experiments are being carried on to produce a variety of scuppernong grape that will bear in clusters, thus facilitating transportation. The scuppernong, a member of the muscadine family, is a white grape of delicious flavor, probably the oldest cultivated native American variety. It is common in the Cape Fear River section, originating, it is believed, along the banks of the Scuppernong River in Tyrrell County (see TOUR 13). A field day for farmers is held annually.

To the south of the experiment station is PENDERLEA FARMS, a project inaugurated by the Division of Subsistence Homesteads and managed for a time by the Farm Security Administration. Some of the families selected were removed from submarginal land taken out of cultivation by the Government, others were promising but impoverished tenant farmers. The project contains approximately 10,500 acres, which have been sold to different individuals, and there are a number of A-grade farms and dairies, as well as the Robbins Nursery and bulb farms. The up-to-date school serves as a community center.

At 81 m. is the "Welch Tract" set apart by the Lords Proprietors in 1725 for Welch settlers. Among these was John James, father of Hinton James. His son, born and reared here, rode horseback nearly to Chapel Hill and sold his horse and walked the rest of the way to the University, where he was the first student to matriculate when the University of North Carolina opened in 1795. One of 7 men of the first graduating class, July 4, 1798, he became a civil engineer and was made assistant to the Chief Engineer, who was brought from Scotland to improve navigation of the Cape Fear. He is buried in the old Hopewell Presbyterian Churchyard.

BIG SAVANNAH, 83 m., is a railroad station in an area noted for the variety of its wild flowers and shrubs. Here grow the wild orchid and several insectivorous plants including the bladderwort, the pitcherplant, and the rare Venus's-flytrap, which is found only near the Carolinas' coast. This, described by Darwin as "the most wonderful little plant in the world," grows to a height of from 4 to 12 inches and produces a white showy flower in early May. In a group of three near the center of each half of the leaf are triggers which, when touched, cause the leaf to close like a trap. Insects thus caught are digested by enzymatic juices secreted by the plant.

In the swamps the prevailing trees are the bald cypress and juniper (white cedar), usually festooned with Spanish or gray moss, which is not moss nor a parasite but is related to the pineapple and the aerial orchids of the tropics.

BURGAW, 85 m. (49 alt., 1,613 pop.), is the seat of Pender County, which was formed from New Hanover in 1875 and was named for William Dorsey Pender (1834-63), youngest major general of the Confederacy. On the courthouse lawn in Burgaw stands a monument to Gen. Pender, placed there by the United Daughters of Confederacy of Pender County. Burgaw was named for the Burghaw Indians by the Wilmington & Weldon Railroad who donated 50 acres to the County Commissioners for a site. Tobacco, blueberries, lumbering, and dairying are the principal sources of income.

Here is the HOME OF S. S. SATCHWELL, who was the founder of the State Medical Society (1849), head of the Confederate Hospital at Wilson (*see* WILSON), and first President of the State Board of Health (1879).

Left from Burgaw on NC 51 to a sand clay road leading to the state-owned HOLLY SHELTER GAME REFUGE 15 m. Around 15,000 of the 35,000 acres were used as public hunting grounds where bear, deer, quail, and waterfowl are taken in season; in 1953 the legislature closed this refuge to all hunters for three years. The refuge is in Holly Shelter Pocosin, which covers more than 100 square miles in the eastern central section of Pender County.

ST. HELENA, 87 m. (55 alt.), is the first of several agricultural colonies developed for immigrants by Hugh MacRae, Wilmington realtor. The land was cut into small farms of 10 acres or as large as wanted. These farms were improved, equipped, and sold to the colonists on easy terms. Now this property is owned individually, and there are many truck farms and dairies which ship produce to northern markets the year around. Scientific methods of agriculture are used, and all farmers are members of the Farm Bureau Organization of Pender.

ROCKY POINT, 94 m., a small farming community, was the seat of many prominent colonial families. At 3 m. E. is the GRAVE OF SAMUEL ASHE, President of the Council of Safety (1776), one of the first three State judges, and governor (1795-98). At 3 m. SE. is the HOME OF JAMES MOORE, commander of the Whigs at Moore's Creek Bridge (*see* TOUR *18*) and a brigadier general of N. C. troops at Charleston. At 9 m. NE. is the GRAVE OF ALEXANDER LILLINGTON, a Revolutionary leader and Whig colonel at Moore's Creek. His home, Lillington Hall, once a showplace, burned several years ago.

At 98 m. the route crosses the Northeast Branch of the Cape Fear River.

CASTLE HAYNE, 100 m. (20 alt., 513 pop.), is the center for one of several agricultural colonies developed in this region by the late Hugh MacRae, Wilmington real estate operator and financier. Though the St. Helena colony (*see* TOUR *4*) was the first, Castle Hayne, a 6,000-acre development, is the most widely known for the horticultural achievements of its 75 families, 40 of whom are from the Netherlands.

Many thousands of cartons of flowers are marketed each season: paper white narcissi, daffodils, tulips, Dutch irises, peonies, and gladioli. Several years ago when one of the growers placed his bulbs in cold storage the temperature was accidentally allowed to go below the usual degree, and as a result the plants bloomed earlier. By this treatment, Castle Hayne bulbs are made to bloom at any time desired. Products include early spring vegetables, strawberries, corn, forage, and cover crops, the soil being in productivity throughout the year.

US 117 terminates at WILMINGTON, 109 m. (*see* WILMINGTON).

Points of Interest: Customhouse, Cornwallis House, St. James Church, Bellamy Mansion, Dudley Mansion, Hilton Park, Greenfield Park, and others.

TOUR 5 *(US 1)*

(South Hill, Va.)—Henderson—Raleigh—Southern Pines—Rockingham—
(Cheraw, S. C.)
Virginia Line—South Carolina Line. **180 m.**

Section a. VIRGINIA LINE *to* RALEIGH; **66 m.**

This route, which begins in Maine and ends at Key West, Fla., runs
through North Carolina cotton, corn, and tobacco farm lands and occasional
pine and oak forests. US 1 crosses the Virginia-North Carolina Line, **0 m.**,
15 miles south of South Hill, Va.

At NORLINA, **8 m.** (438 alt., 874 pop.) is the northern junction with
US 158 (*see* TOUR *12 for this route and for a side tour of Kerr Dam*). Near
here passed the Great Trading Path, dating from the early 17th century, from
Petersburg, Va., to the Catawba and Waxhaw Indians along the Catawba
River.

Between Norlina and Henderson lies part of the State's "black belt,"
populated by descendants of slaves, numerous in this plantation region.
Many Negroes bear the names of the families to whom their ancestors
belonged. Operating in this section prior to the Civil War were groups of
white men called by the Negroes "paddyrollers." The name referred to the
patrols of 6 men from each militia company established by legislative acts,
whose duty it was to patrol each district at least once every two weeks,
apprehending and punishing Negroes found outside their masters' plantations without passes or making themselves otherwise objectionable. In Negro
dialect the patrols became "patteroles," or "patter-rollers," which forms are
used by Joel Chandler Harris in *Uncle Remus* and by Charles W. Chesnutt
in the *Conjur Woman*. As the common punishment was to place the
offender across a barrel and apply a paddle instead of the legal lash, and
as the barrel was apt to roll under the impact, the administrators became
facetiously known as "paddle-rollers," and finally "paddyrollers."

At **9.8 m.** is the junction with a road.

Right on this road to the junction with a dirt road, **1.4 m.**; R. **2 m.** on this
road to POPLAR MOUNT (*private*), in a grove of great oaks (R). The rambling
story-and-a-half house is covered with beaded weatherboarding, with entrance

door protected by a low gabled porch. There are two end chimneys at the right end, beyond which are several additions. On the left is a small office building with hip roof and a small porch supported by octagonal posts.

Poplar Mount was built as the home of Weldon Nathaniel Edwards (1788-1873), Congressman (1815-27), State Senator (1833-36, 1850-54), Speaker of the State Senate (1850-54), leader in the organization of the secession party early in 1861, and President of the North Carolina secession convention in 1862. Edwards practiced scientific agriculture. Instead of planting cotton he concentrated on the growing of grain, hay, fruit, and tobacco, and the breeding and improvement of stock. Game chickens were his pride and joy and furnished entertainment for his numerous guests. The house was sold by his nephew, Marmaduke Hawkins, to a colony of Germans after the Franco-Prussian War.

RIDGEWAY, 10 m. (422 alt., 250 pop.), is in a region of prosperous small farms producing vegetables, berries, fruits, and Ridgeway cantaloups. Most of the farmers came here in the 1880's from southern Germany by way of New York and Pennsylvania. Since the beginning of the settlement, when most of the people spoke no English, the Lutheran Church has been the center of social life. The church served also as a schoolhouse and, until the children began attending State schools, both English and German were taught. Part of the church services are still conducted in German.

MANSON, 12 m. (428 alt., 50 pop.), is a community of farmhouses. About 1850 the Roanoke Ry. built a line from this point to Clarksville, Va. During the Civil War, Gen. Longstreet's soldiers took up the entire railroad and laid it between Greensboro and Danville, Va., to transport supplies from western North Carolina to Richmond.

MIDDLEBURG, 17 m. (494 alt., 217 pop.), a farming community founded in 1781, was midway between terminals of the Raleigh & Gaston R.R. Dr. Joseph Hawkins established one of the State's earliest medical schools at his home here in 1808. Several granite quarries are operated in the vicinity.

At 17.5 m. is the junction with a road.

Right on this road to PLEASANT HILL (private), 0.6 m., a two-and-one-half-story clapboarded house with gable roof, dormers, and twin end chimneys. The low wings on each side of the central section and some of the ornaments in the cornice, notably the Greek fret, are possibly additions of the 1850's when the house changed ownership. An inappropriate porch with rough stone columns was added in 1869.

Pleasant Hill was erected by Col. Philemon Hawkins, Jr. (1752-1833). Hawkins fought alongside his father, Tryon's chief aid at Alamance (see TOUR 15B), but father and son later became ardent patriots. The son was a colonel in the Provincial militia, member of Provincial Congresses and of the 1789 convention that ratified the Federal Constitution (see FAYETTEVILLE). Pleasant Hill in 1777 was the birthplace of Colonel Hawkins' son, William Hawkins, Governor of North Carolina (1811-14) and Speaker of the House of Commons (1810-11).

At Middleburg, road (R) leads to DREWRY, 7 m. Left here to Bullocksville Landing and Park (undeveloped) and the banks of Kerr Reservoir (Bugg's Island Lake).

Straight north from Drewry to Va. Line, **13.7 m.**, and the JOHN H. KERR DAM, **16.7 m.** The Dam and Reservoir is a 117,300-acre, multiple-purpose project of the U. S. Army Corps of Engineers. About 23,000 acres are in North Carolina, principally in Vance County. The dam provides flood control for the lower 178 miles of the Roanoke River and a hydro-electric powerhouse for distribution of electric power to local power companies. The Dam creates a 48,900-acre lake, with an 800-mile shoreline (*Nearest N. C. hotel and motel facilities at Henderson, Norlina, Oxford, and Wise. Concessions along the route include rental boats, docking and mooring for private boats, bait, tackle, and refreshments; excellent fishing, hunting, swimming, and picnic grounds*). The Dam is 144 ft. high at the central portion (the equivalent of a 14-story building) and is over half a mile wide.

At **21 m.** is a junction with a road.

Right on this road to ASHLAND (*private*), **4 m.** This two-story house, three bays wide, has a doorway on the right-hand bay and a story-and-a-half addition on the right with end chimneys matching the twin chimneys on the left side of the main house. The beaded weatherboarding is painted white, and both eaves and window headings have well-designed cornices. A later porch extending across the entire façade is supported by Roman Doric columns, supplemented by log posts. Ashland was built in 1746 by Samuel Henderson, farmer and miller. He was one time high sheriff of Granville County and became the father of Richard Henderson.

Near Ashland is the GRAVE OF RICHARD HENDERSON (1735-85), judge of the Crown who was driven from the bench at Hillsboro by the Regulators (*see* TOUR *15*); they later burned his home. Judge Henderson was the founder and president of the Transylvania Colony, organized in 1775 to form a new State in the Indian territory that later became Tennessee and Kentucky. Daniel Boone helped in the negotiations with the Indians for the purchase of the land and, with 30 axmen, went ahead to cut a passage through the tangled laurel thickets for the emigrants. His tombstone states that he was "Founder of Nashville, Tennessee, and Boonesville, Kentucky, and author of the Cumberland Compact."

At **5 m.** is TAR HEEL MARINA at Satterwhite Point, on Bugg's Island Lake (*For recreational facilities and accommodations, see Kerr Dam, above*).

On return trip, an alternate route, on dirt road, leads to NUTBUSH CREEK BRIDGE and INDIAN CREEK PARK, **1 m.** (*boat access area*), and continues to NC 39 (*see side tour after Henderson, below, for a continuation of tour around the lake*).

HENDERSON, **23 m.** (513 alt., 10,996 pop.), is an industrial town in the bright-leaf tobacco belt. It is the seat of Vance County, which was created in 1881 and named for Gov. Z. B. Vance. The town's huge warehouses bustle with activity in the fall as tobacco farmers bring in their crops by automobile, truck, and wagon. Auction sales of tobacco are held in the fall (*Mon.-Fri., Sept. to Christmas*). Industrial plants include cotton mills, hosiery mill, a fertilizer plant, a motor truck factory, and the world's largest manufacturer of jute. Granite and tungsten mines and the Kerr Reservoir in the northern part of the county have added to the town's importance. Henderson is also the home of the great chain of Rose's 5-10-25¢ Stores, which operate in 6 states.

On the courthouse lawn is a MONUMENT TO LEONARD HENDERSON (1772-1833), Chief Justice of the State Supreme Court, for whom the town was named when laid out in 1840.

Right from Henderson on NC 39, across Cross Flat Creek to WILLIAMSBORO WAYSIDE, 5 m., on right (*picnic and boat access area, fishing and swimming*).

At 7 m. is WILLIAMSBORO, settled about 1740 and called Nutbush until 1780 when Col. Robert Burton renamed it for his father-in-law, Judge John Williams, who had given him the land. An important political and social center about 1800, it had perhaps the finest race track in the State.

The SITE OF THE SNEED MANSION is on one of the original town lots. The mansion was such a favorite with lawyers and judges that, until about 1860, court was often said to have "adjourned to Sneed Mansion House."

ST. JOHN'S EPISCOPAL CHURCH is the only colonial church building standing in the Diocese of North Carolina. It was built by the Lewis family of Granville County in 1757, 9 years after the parish was established. Waterman, an authority on colonial architecture, described St. John's as being "a remarkable survival of a colonial church of its period. While simple in form, the woodwork, both exterior and interior, is extensive and well preserved. It constitutes the best exemplar of colonial church woodwork in North Carolina, as the other churches of the period have lost their interiors through alteration or fire. In form the building is rectangular, with its main axis east and west. Of frame construction, it is set on a high basement, all of original brickwork laid in Flemish bond.... The super-structure has high sidewalls and a gable roof, trimmed with a fine modillioned cornice at the eaves." Interesting features are its barrel ceiling, box-type pews with doors, and windows glazed with 18th-century English crown glass. The church has recently undergone extensive repairs, including a new tile roof and the removal of the cupola and porch which had been added in the 19th century.

Although services were held here much earlier, no clergyman was resident in the parish until 1769 when the Rev. James McGartney was appointed rector by Gov. William Tryon. Bishop John Stark Ravenscroft was rector of St. John's, 1828-30.

At Williamsboro was also the first location of the famous Bingham School, founded in 1826 by D. H. Bingham. The first military school in North Carolina, it was moved to Littleton in 1829.

On the south side of Main St. is a long lane leading to CEDAR WALK (*private*), hidden from view by a few of the cedars that gave the place its name. It was built in 1750 by Hutchins Burton for a boarding school, and called Blooming Hope. Burton hanged himself from the attic stairwell and visitors testify to the presence of his ghost. The house is two stories high with a central door flanked by pilasters. The wing at the left, a later addition, has a fine dentiled cornice, the detail of which resembles the work at Burnside and Prospect Hill (*see below and* TOUR *12*).

1. Right from Williamsboro 1 m. on a stone-surfaced road to the RUINS OF OAK-LAND, the summer home occupied about 1820 by James Turner, Governor of North Carolina (1802-5), and U. S. Senator (1805-16).

2. Left from Williamsboro 0.9 m. on a road to the junction with a dirt road; R. 1.3 m. on this road to the junction with a marked lane; R. 0.6 m. on the lane

to BURNSIDE (*private*). This two-story weatherboarded house has a dentiled cornice and upper and lower doorways with semicircular fanlights and side lights. A brick in the east end chimney bears the date 1801. The interior carved woodwork, designed with varying detail, is characteristic of the Classic Revival period.

Tradition is that in 1760 this was the home of Col. Memucan Hunt, first State treasurer, and later that of his son, Dr. Thomas Hunt, who inherited the place about 1820. It was named Burnside in 1824, after Dr. Hunt had sold it to Patrick Hamilton, one of 5 brothers who came here from Scotland about 1806. The Hamiltons were born in Burnside, Lanarkshire, according to the tombstone of William Hamilton (1779-1840) in St. John's Churchyard.

Left from Williamsboro to NINE OAKS (*private*), **2 m.**, a colonial house built by Maj. Bromfield Ridley, a Continental soldier. Some of the ceilings were executed by an Italian artist. The interior carving is among the finest in the State.

·On NC 39 at **12.7 m.** in TOWNSVILLE (421 alt., 219 pop.) is the SITE OF NUTBUSH PRESBYTERIAN CHURCH (1805), whose congregation was organized in 1754. This little church, burned in March, 1941, was one of the few churches for white people where John Chavis often preached between 1809 and 1832. Chavis, a free Negro, displayed unusual intelligence as a child and was sent to Princeton—according to tradition—to demonstrate whether a Negro could acquire a college education. He became a Presbyterian minister and taught school in Raleigh and other North Carolina towns. Among his pupils were Charles Manly, Governor of North Carolina (1849-51), and the sons of Chief Justice Leonard Henderson.

1. Left from Townsville, **3 m.**, are extremely valuable tungsten mines. Operated since 1942, when tungsten was discovered here, the output of these mines is valued at over 9 million dollars annually. Tungsten, valuable for its extreme hardness (next to diamonds) and its heat-resistancy, is primarily used in radios, television, electric lights, and war products.

2. Right from Townsville, **2 m.**, is the TOWNSVILLE LANDING, at the Lake, and the VANCE COUNTY WILDLIFE CLUB CONCESSION.

At **15 m.** is ROCK SPRING CHURCH. Right on this road to HENDERSON POINT, **4 m.**, or PARADISE POINT, **6 m.**, both dead-end roads at the lake. Plans for development are in progress.

NC 39 leads to ISLAND CREEK DAM, **22 m.**, and continues to intersection with US 15, at **26 m.** (*see* TOUR 6).

At **24 m.**, R. 1½ m. is LOCUST HILL, built in 1740 by Col. William Eaton, who came from Petersburg, Va., with 11 white and 16 Negro servants. The house was later used as a county home for the poor.

KITTRELL, **31 m.** (372 alt., 189 pop.), surrounded by flowering fields and rows of evergreens, is the home of the CONTINENTAL PLANT CO., a general plant nursery. Here was located the Davis Hotel, the famous glass house built in 1871 which catered to tuberculosis patients. A famous 19th-century health resort and social center was located at **0.5 m.** W. at KITTRELL SPRINGS. Here was one of the first and greatest resort hotels in the State. It was used as a Confederate hospital during the Civil War and burned in 1885.

Right from Kittrell on the graded Lynbank Rd. to RUIN CREEK, 2 m., SITE OF POPCASTLE INN, a colonial tavern and gaming house operated until about 1860. It is said to have been built by a nobleman, a political refugee from Europe, and later owned by Captain Pop, a pirate who supposedly hid gold nearby.

At 35 m. US 1 crosses Tabbs Creek on which John Mask Peace lived in 1713. Peace, the first known white settler of this region, migrated here from near Snow Hill after the Tuscarora War. He was the ancestor of William Peace, for whom Peace College in Raleigh was named.

At 39 m. US 1 by-passes Franklinton; US 1-A goes through the town.

FRANKLINTON, 40 m. (432 alt., 1,414 pop.) is a textile-manufacturing and lumber-milling town as well as a shipping point for cotton and bright-leaf tobacco. Sterling Mills and a branch of Burlington Mills are located here.

Left from Franklinton on NC 56 is LOUISBURG, 10 m. (226 alt., 2,545 pop.), seat of Franklin County. This town, the "old fords of the Tar," was first settled in 1758, and in 1764 was named in commemoration of the capture by American forces of the French fortress of Louisburg, Nova Scotia. The town is situated on the old stage road between Richmond and Raleigh. Aaron Burr is believed to have spent a night here on his way from South Carolina to New York. On the way to Warrenton next day he supposedly enforced his demand that the stage driver be more careful by laying a pistol across his knees.

Louisburg is the birthplace of Edwin W. Fuller, author of the *Angel in the Cloud and Other Poems* and *Sea Gift* (1873), a novel once so popular at the University of North Carolina that it was known as the Freshman's Bible. Here stands the HOME OF GOV. THOMAS W. BICKETT (1917-21), the first governor in the State to be nominated by a Democratic primary.

Dependent to a large extent on farm trade, Louisburg is a tobacco marketing center and claims the distinction of being the world's largest tobacco market for one year prior to World War II. The manufacture of feeds, lumber products, and aluminum moldings for store fronts are the principal industries.

LOUISBURG COLLEGE, in a 10-acre oak grove, is a Methodist coeducational junior college, with a student body of about 300. The buildings of red-painted brick are scattered about the administration center (1855), which has a Greek Doric portico; the later wings have small Roman Doric porticoes. A chimney, remains of a building erected in 1814 and burned in 1928, bears a tablet with the date 1802. The school was chartered as the Louisburg Female Seminary in that year when it was decided to separate the male and female departments of the Franklin Academy for Males and Females, whose first building was erected in 1779.

In 1855 the school was reorganized as a private college. In 1891 it came into the possession of Washington Duke, who operated it until his death in 1905, his son, Benjamin N. Duke, gave it to the North Carolina Methodist Conference.

The DRINKING FOUNTAIN AND MARKER, Courthouse Sq., was erected to commemorate the designing by Orren Randolph Smith, a North Carolinian, of the *Stars and Bars*—first of the Confederacy's 4 flags—and its first display in North Carolina at Louisburg, Mar. 18, 1861.

1. Left from Louisburg on NC 561 to the junction with a road, 2.5 m.; L. 2 m. to the JOHN ALLEN PLACE (*private*) on the left. The house is covered with beaded weatherboarding and fronted by a one-story bracketed porch. The east chimney is said to date from 1818, but the part belonging to this date has been incorporated

with the rest of the story-and-a-half structure and is indistinguishable. The west chimney bears the date 1837.

Inside are beautiful old furniture and interesting relics. John Allen was known as "Spelling John" because of his phenomenal memory. He could spell a word and tell where it stood by page and line in the old blue-back speller. The family has a lustre goblet that he won as the best speller in North Carolina, and a letter signed by Robert E. Lee testifying to the excellence of John Allen's scholarship at Washington (later Washington and Lee) College. The family also has a book of calculations used for dictation in the schools when textbooks were not available; it was written about 1814 with a goose quill and illustrates the "rule of threes." John Allen's half-brother, Orren Randolph Smith, was living here when his Confederate flag was first displayed.

On NC 561 is (R) the OLD COLLINS PLACE (*private*), **9.4 m.**, a two-story house, two rooms wide, with two stone end chimneys. Every opening in the façade is designed with a Palladian motif. An upstairs ballroom, 24 feet square, has never been completed. Caleb Allen, who acquired the property about 1896, is said to have been the only owner who paid money for it; others acquired it as a gambling debt or through inheritance.

2. South from Louisburg on NC 39 to the HOME OF GREEN HILL (*private*), **1 m.**, where Bishop Coke held the first North Carolina Methodist Conference in 1785. This well-preserved white frame farmhouse has dormer windows, three great brick end chimneys, and high porches. Green Hill was prominent in State as well as Methodist affairs, represented Bute County in 4 Provincial Congresses (1774-76), and was a major of the Bute militia in the Revolution. He moved to Tennessee in 1799 and established a new home, Liberty Hall, south of Nashville. One of his descendants is the author of the popular children's stories based on the adventures of Miss Minerva and William Green Hill.

3. North from Louisburg on NC 39 to the junction with a dirt road, **2 m.**; L. **2 m.** on this road to the point where Lynch's Creek enters Tar River, the SITE OF THE HANGING OF MAJOR LYNCH (1767). This British officer, commissioned to collect taxes in the frontier Colony, was here summarily executed, carrying out the sentence of a mock court; the term "lynch law" is believed by some to have so originated. One of the last remaining bands of Tuscarora Indians in North Carolina was exterminated here in 1725. Skeletons and relics have been found at the site on Tar River at the mouth of Toole's Creek.

4. On NC 39 at INGLESIDE, **5 m.**, is the HOME OF FENTON FOSTER, who experimented with the linotype machine, perfecting his invention too late to obtain a patent, which had just been granted to Mergenthaler. Pieces of type have often been found on the grounds nearby.

5. South from Louisburg on NC 59 to junction with a dirt road, **3¼ m.** Left on this road to CASCINE, **1 m.**, a house which has been unaltered since its erection about 1750 and which has been owned by 5 generations of Perrys, whose progenitor first settled here in 1746. A race track in the back was so situated that ladies could watch the finish from the porch of the old house.

At **44 m.** US 1 by-passes Wake Forest; US 1-A goes through the town.

At **49.5 m.** US 1 follows a boulevard whose grassy parkway is planted with dwarf magnolias and shrubs. In WAKE FOREST, **50 m.** (400 alt., 3,704 pop.), a college town, the streets are bordered with fine trees, and old houses harmonize with the ivy-grown buildings on the wooded campus of WAKE FOREST COLLEGE (Baptist) in the heart of the village. When Wake Forest Institute opened in 1834, each of its 16 students was required to bring an ax and a hoe in addition to two sheets and two towels.

Reorganized as a college in 1838, Wake Forest in 1894 added a school of law and in 1896 a department of religion, first in connection with an American college of liberal arts. The standard four-year course leads to degrees of B.A. and B.S., and graduate work is offered leading to the M.A. degree. A summer school is conducted.

The college buildings occupy a beautiful 25-acre campus shaded by magnolias, oaks, maples, elms, and cedars. Wait Hall, erected in 1839 and named for the institution's first president, Samuel Wait, was destroyed by fire in 1933. A building program in the 1930's included a new WAIT HALL, three-story brick building in modified Georgian Colonial style; the WILLIAM AMOS JOHNSON MEMORIAL MEDICAL BUILDING; a combination gymnasium and auditorium; concrete stadium and field house. The OLD DORMITORY, built about 1839 by Capt. John Berry (see ARCHITECTURE), was burned in 1934 but has been rebuilt. Off the campus are the CALVIN JONES HOUSE (1820); the NORTH BRICK HOUSE (1838) which served as the home of early presidents; and the SOUTH BRICK HOUSE (1838).

After the removal of Wake Forest College to Winston-Salem (see WINSTON-SALEM), the College's old campus will be used exclusively by the Southeastern Theological Seminary (Baptist).

The marked SITE OF ISAAC HUNTER'S TAVERN, which Hunter operated in 1788, is at 60 m. The North Carolina General Assembly ruled that the State Capital should be placed within 10 miles of this point.

RALEIGH, 66 m. (see RALEIGH).

Points of Interest: State Capitol, Christ Church, Site of the Birthplace of Andrew Johnson, Joel Lane House, N. C. State College of Agriculture and Engineering, and others.

Raleigh is at the junction with US 15-A (see TOUR 6), US 64 (see TOUR 13), and US 70 (see TOUR 15).

Section b. RALEIGH *to* SOUTH CAROLINA LINE: 114 m.

This route swings into thickly wooded farming country where cotton, corn, and tobacco are the predominant crops.

METHOD, 4 m. (444 alt., 350 pop.), Negro village, was developed by Berry O'Kelly (d. 1932), Negro educator, merchant, and leader, who founded the school which bears his name. The plant includes three large brick buildings and a church.

STATE HIGHWAY SHOPS, 5.1 m., a group of sprawling, barnlike buildings (R), include a supply depot, garage, and repair shop.

At 8 m. US 1 unites with US 64 (see TOUR 13).

At **8.5 m.** on US 1-64 is CARY (496 alt., 1,446 pop.), a suburban community founded about 1852 by A. Frank Page, father of Walter Hines Page, the author, editor, and wartime Ambassador to Great Britain (1913-18). The BIRTHPLACE AND HOME OF WALTER HINES PAGE (*private*) is across the railroad tracks, half a block from Academy St. The two-story white dwelling now in poor repair, stands in a grove of elms, surrounded by a picket fence. Page as a boy of 12 is said to have walked the railroad tracks 8 miles to Raleigh to hear Pres. Andrew Johnson speak.

At **14 m.** US 64 (*see* TOUR *13*) branches R.

At **16 m.** on US 1 is APEX (504 alt., 1,065 pop.), which received its name in the early 1870's when a survey for the Raleigh & Augusta R.R. showed this to be the highest point on the right-of-way between Norfolk and Sanford. After North Carolina had adopted prohibition in 1907, Apex was used by the Baldwin gang as headquarters for distributing liquor run in from Virginia.

The route crosses the Haw River, **30 m.**, through a region where the hills attain the elevations of small mountains, and the landscape takes on a rugged aspect seldom found in the piedmont. Swift-flowing streams, Rocky River, Robinson, and Bear Creeks, furnish power for many small mills that grind the wheat grown in the region.

US 1 crosses the Deep River, **31.5 m.**, a narrow stream that twists through green valleys. High abrupt banks in places become hanging cliffs with a drop of 100 feet or more. Rabbits, squirrels, and birds are abundant. Deep River joins the Haw a mile to the southeast, their confluence forming the Cape Fear.

LOCKVILLE, **41 m.**, formerly known as Ramseys Mill, was the scene of a British encampment after the Battle of Guilford Courthouse (*see* TOUR *9*). Cornwallis' troops remained only long enough to build a bridge across Deep River.

Between this point and **52 m.**, US 1 unites with US 15-501 (*see* TOUR *7*).

South of Lockville US 1, called the Jefferson Davis Highway, has bronze and granite markers placed at 10-mile intervals by the United Daughters of the Confederacy to honor the President of the Confederacy.

At **42 m.** the highway crosses the GRANVILLE LINE (*see* TOUR *2 and* HISTORY).

SANFORD, **46 m.** (375 alt., 10,013 pop.), seat of Lee County, on the edge of the pine belt bordering the Sandhill section, is the market town for 4 counties and seat of a highly diversified industrial life, including textiles, textile machinery, furniture, capacitors, and cotton and tobacco warehouses. Local brick-making industries supply the State with 40% of its brick. Lee County, not formed until 1907, is interesting geologically. A great sandstone and shale belt of Triassic formation has been bared; coal mining along

Deep River was important before the Civil War. Many "brownstone front" mansions of Philadelphia and New York were built from the stone of this section.

At the NORTH STATE POTTERY (*open*), one of the largest and best known in the State, potters pursue their ancient craft using an old-time kick wheel and mule-power grinding mills.

Sanford is at the junction with US 421 (*see* TOUR *17*).

At 47.5 m. is the junction with a country road.

Left on this road a short distance to BUFFALO PRESBYTERIAN CHURCH. The white-frame Victorian Gothic building, erected between 1878 and 1880, is the fourth to serve the congregation. The Highland Scottish congregation was organized before April, 1796. This marks the northern-most penetration of this race. Originally, morning services were held in English; afternoon services in Gaelic.

CAMERON, 57 m. (304 alt., 284 pop.), is one of the largest dewberry markets in the world.

VASS, 61 m. (287 alt., 757 pop.), is likewise a dewberry market.

At 62 m. the route crosses Little River. Beyond are the dry, white ridges of the Sandhills. Shortleaf pines give way to the lighter green, longleaf variety. The region abounds with fox, raccoon, opossum, squirrel, rabbit, quail, and dove. Many deer stray into this section from the game refuge at Fort Bragg (*see* LOCAL TOUR FROM FAYETTVILLE).

SOUTHERN PINES, 72 m. (516 alt., 4,179 pop.)

Transportation: Seaboard Air Line R. R.; Piedmont Airlines Service.
Accommodations: 11 modern hotels, most of them open only during winter season; motels, tourist homes, and boarding houses; rates slightly higher in winter.
Information Service: Chamber of Commerce.
Golf: Mid-Pines Country Club, 18 holes; Pine Needles Golf Club, 18 holes; Southern Pines Country Club, one 18-hole course and one 9-hole course.

ANNUAL EVENTS

Golf Tournaments: On all courses in season. *Horse Events:* Moore County Hounds Hunter Trials; Stoneybrook Steeplechase and Race Meet in Feb. and March; horse shows and gymkhanas held Sunday afternoons in spring season; Moore County Hunt, live and drag, three times weekly Thanksgiving to April. *Tennis:* Local, county, and junior tournaments on municipal courts starting in May; Sandhill Invitational in Aug.

This winter resort, whose golf courses attract the foremost professionals and amateurs of the country, was established primarily as a health resort in 1880. Exploitation of the mild dry climate, coupled with the adaptability of the Sandhills to peach growing and truck raising, helped to develop this region of pine barrens, which, after the exhaustion of its hardwoods, had almost reverted to a wilderness.

During the season Southern Pines' population swells to about 6,500 residents. Broad Street, running parallel with the tracks, is a one-way boulevard with a parkway of magnolias, pines, and blossoming shrubs. Here are gift shops, book stores, newsstands, and specialty shops.

The writers' colony at Southern Pines had as its founders the late James Boyd, author of *Drums,* and his wife, Katharine Lamont Boyd, who influenced the authors, Struthers Burt and Katherine Newlin Burt, to join them there. Other well-known writers have lived and visited in Southern Pines from time to time. Among those now living there are Wallace Irwin, novelist and journalist, and his novelist wife, Laetitia McDonald Irwin, also Miss Lockie Parker, writer and editor of children's books. At Pinebluff, a short distance away, lives Glen Rounds, author-illustrator of children's books.

Among its many attractions is the SHAW HOUSE (*open in season*), an attractively restored cottage home of the mid-19th century, operated by the Moore County Historical Association. In addition to the museum, herb garden, and 200-year-old cabin, a tearoom is open in season.

Southern Pines is at the junction with NC 2, which leads to Pinehurst, 7 m. (*see* TOUR 5*A*).

ABERDEEN, 76 m. (339 alt., 1,603 pop.), is a trading town and shipping point for tobacco, truck, and fruit. A. Frank Page, a miller, and father of Walter Hines Page, came here from Wake County. The family built the railroad that is now part of the Norfolk Southern. Originally called Blues Crossing, the town became Aberdeen when it was incorporated in 1893. Many of the early settlers in this section were Scottish.

Left from Aberdeen on NC 5 to OLD BETHESDA CHURCH (*adm. by permission of Mrs. Belle Pleasants whose house is 100 yds. R. Homecoming usually 4th Sun. in Sept.*). 1 m. The church (1860), a rectangular white clapboarded structure with tower and spire in the center of the façade, contains an old slave gallery with a separate entrance. At the close of the Civil War, part of Gen. Sherman's army encamped in and around the building.

The congregation, organized in 1790 by the Philadelphia Presbytery, built its first church that year in the midst of a 5-acre tract which had been granted in 1766 by King George III to John Patterson. This is the third church on this site.

In BETHESDA CEMETERY is the TOMB OF WALTER HINES PAGE. On a simple slab of gray granite is inscribed only his name and the dates Aug. 15, 1855—Dec. 21, 1918. Here also is the GRAVE OF FRANK PAGE, his brother, first chairman of the North Carolina Highway Commission, which started the State's present highway system. Beneath the cedars in the older portion of the cemetery lie crumbling, crude, and stained monuments to early settlers. One is inscribed: "In Memory of COLIN BETHUNE (an honest man). A native of Scotland by accident, but a citizen of the U.S. from choice who died Mar. 29, 1820. Aged 64 years.

> "His dust must mingle with the ground
> Till the last trump's awakening sound
> It will then arise in sweet surprise
> To meet its savior in the skies."

PINEBLUFF, 80 m. (307 alt., 575 pop.), is a small winter resort and residential village. The large hotel was converted into a club, later into a sanatorium.

At 84 m. the route crosses the Lumber River and runs through the Sandhills into a region of dark pine forest and darker cypress swamp, draped in vines and Spanish moss.

HOFFMAN, 88 m. (428 alt., 398 pop.), re-incorporated in 1952, is the center for the SANDHILLS GAME MANAGEMENT AREA, consisting of 57,000 acres administered by the State Wildlife Resources Commission. Begun as the Sandhills Land Utilization Project under Franklin D. Roosevelt's administrations, this submarginal farm land and cutover-forest area was developed as a recreation, forestry, and wildlife reservation. Today, no hunting is allowed on the refuge, which serves as a production unit for deer, wild turkey, and quail.

Within this refuge are 7 lakes (*open to fishing*) including INDIAN CAMP RECREATION PARK (*small swimming pond and picnic facilities*), on the shore of 65-acre LAKE McKINNEY (*boating, bathing*). The McKINNEY LAKE HATCHERY (*picnic facilities*), operated by the U. S. Fish and Wildlife Service, propagates bass, bream, and crappie and is the source of stocking for 64 North Carolina counties.

ROCKINGHAM, 102 m. (211 alt., 3,356 pop.), the seat of Richmond County, was established in 1784 and named for Charles Watson Wentworth, Marquis of Rockingham, British Prime Minister (1765-66, 1782). The county, formed in 1779, was named for Charles Lennox, Duke of Richmond. Many of the inhabitants are descendants of original settlers, and the town has a quiet, conservative air, despite its industrial plants.

Within a radius of 4 miles are 6 large cotton mills. The first cotton mill, erected in 1837, was burned by Kirkpatrick's cavalry, a part of Sherman's army, which passed through here March 4-7, 1865, on its march from Savannah to Goldsboro. In addition to textile plants, Rockingham has a hosiery mill, foundry, paper mill, and three food industries. Tobacco, cotton, peanuts, and peaches are the chief farm products.

Rockingham is at the junction with US 220 (*see* TOUR 9) and US 74 (*see* TOUR 16).

At 108.5 m. is a marker indicating the GRAVE OF WILLIAM HENRY HARRINGTON, 1 m. NW. An energetic patriot brigadier general of militia, his home was burned by Tories. He served as a State senator and a commissioner to locate the State capitol. A large planter, he owned 60 slaves in 1790.

South of Rockingham US 1 parallels the Pee Dee River and at 114 m. crosses the South Carolina Line, 10 miles north of Cheraw, S. C.

TOUR 5A (*NC 2*)

Southern Pines—Pinehurst; NC 2. 7 m.

Resort hotels, many open only in winter.

NC 2, known as Midland Rd., branches northwest from its junction with US 1 in SOUTHERN PINES, 0 m. (*see* TOUR 5). Midland Rd., a boulevard with pine-planted central parkway, is paralleled in stretches by bridle paths.

The residential section, KNOLLWOOD, 1 m., is composed of country estates, winter cottages, and year-round residences.

At 2.5 m. is the junction with a marked paved road.

Right on this road to KNOLLWOOD AIRPORT, 2.5 m.

At 2.6 m. is the junction with a marked sand road.

Left on this road is the CAROLINA ORCHIDS, INC. GREENHOUSES (*open weekdays; adm. $1; proceeds to charity*), 100 yds. The climatic conditions of the tropics are maintained for the many rare orchids grown here.

PINEHURST, 6 m. (536 alt., 1,600 pop.).

Railroad Station: South edge of village at US 15-501 for Norfolk Southern R.R.
Airport: Knollwood Airport, 5 m. east on NC 2 and paved road.
Accommodations: 5 large hotels; rates higher Oct. to May.
Information Service: Pinehurst, Inc., 1 Dogwood Rd. at Market Sq., or E. C. Mignard, Hotel Ambassador, New York City.
Golf: Pinehurst Country Club, four 18-hole courses; greens fee, $1 to $2.50.
Tennis: 6 sand-clay courts.

ANNUAL EVENTS

Golf Tournaments: Mid-South Professional Tournament, mid-Nov.; Seniors Tournament, 2nd wk. Mar.; United North and South Open Championship, 3rd wk. Mar.; North and South Invitation Championship for Women, last wk. Mar., 1st wk. Apr.; North and South Invitation Amateur Championship, 2nd wk. Apr. *Races:* Stoneybrook Steeplechase and Racing Assn. meet, 3rd Sat. Mar. *Horse Show:* Pinehurst Jockey Club, Mar. 28-29. *Field Trials:* Continental Field Trial Club, late Nov.; Pointers Club of America membership events, 1st wk. Dec.; open events, 2nd wk., Dec.; Pinehurst Field Trial Club, 2nd wk. Jan. *Kennel Show:* Pinehurst Kennel Club, auspices American Kennel Club, early Apr.

Pinehurst is a winter resort, resembling a country village. Roads and drives ramble past great estates, many of which are open the year around, comfortable hotels and inns, and numerous smaller residences and cottages designed in a modified Georgian Colonial style. Aymar Embury II, of New York and Pinehurst, set the architectural style of the colony. Frederick Law Olmsted, landscape architect, laid out the parks and open spaces, ornamenting the curving roads with evergreens, hollies, and flowering shrubs. Sweet-scented longleaf pines give the village its name.

The Market Place, Pinehurst's business district, is the focal point of the village, which does not depend on the surrounding country for patronage or supplies. While tennis courts and country club verandas attract gay throngs, groups of elderly ladies take the air in old-fashioned tallyhos or victorias, and children pile into wagonettes when they go on picnics.

James W. Tufts, of Boston, in 1895 bought 5,000 sandy acres from the family of Walter Hines Page for $1 an acre. His early plans for using some of his millions to build a health resort did not materialize but later he established a recreational and sports center here. The founder's son, Leonard Tufts, further developed the resort.

Pinehurst, not incorporated as a town, is a private business enterprise operating under the corporate laws of North Carolina. A special charter in 1911 granted the owners the right to exercise police powers. The village regulations prohibit locomotives from operating at night, dogs from howling at night, and roosters from crowing.

The VILLAGE CHAPEL (*nonsectarian, Episcopal ritual; Sun. services during winter season; frequent organ recitals*), one block south of Market Sq., is a pale red brick structure suggestive of old New England meetinghouses. The façade is marked by a portico of 4 Corinthian columns supporting a simple pediment. A square tower in the Wren tradition, with a 4-faced clock, diminishes in stages to a slim octagonal spire that rises high above a background of dense foliage. There are urns on each set-back of the tower. Hobart Upjohn's design for this church (*see* ARCHITECTURE) was awarded a Diploma of Merit at the International Exhibit at Turin, Italy, in 1926, the year of its completion.

The WOMAN'S EXCHANGE, opposite the chapel, occupies a log cabin, built about 1820 and once the kitchen of the early plantation house of James Ray, on Nicks Creek. Moved here to serve as a museum, the cabin is a clearing house for home products of Moore County, including needlework and antiques.

The PINEHURST COUNTRY CLUB, two blocks southwest of the chapel, is a center of social and sporting life. Broad verandas and terraces overlook the 4 golf courses. Donald Ross, golf architect whose home is in Pinehurst, planned the courses. Number Two is used for championship play. Number One was designed especially for ladies and Number Four for beginners.

CLARENDON GARDENS, with 20 acres of fine winter plants, has been recognized by the American Holly Society as one of the nation's top collections of growing holly. There are 185 varieties.

FONTANA DAM AT THE EDGE OF THE GREAT SMOKIES

TOBACCO AUCTION (FARM SECURITY ADMINISTRATION)

WEAVING ON OLD-FASHIONED LOOM, BURGESS

POTTER AT WORK, JUGTOWN

STATE HIGHWAY BUILDING, RALEIGH

CHAIR MONUMENT, THOMASVILLE

MAKING CIGARETTES, WINSTON-SALEM (R. J. REYNOLDS)

COTTON PICKERS AT WORK

UNLOADING COTTON AT GIN, SMITHFIELD (FARM SECURITY ADMINISTRATION)

MODERN HOME, DURHAM (WEBB & WEBB)

STATE FAIR ARENA (LEWIS P. WATSON)

NET FISHING AT VANDEMERE

SAW MILL ON DISMAL SWAMP CANAL (WOOTTEN)

HATCH MILL NEAR COLUMBUS

OLD MILL WHEEL, DILLINGHAM (ASHEVILLE CHAMBER OF COMMERCE)

CIGARETTE FACTORY, DURHAM (LIGGETT & MYERS)

WEAVE ROOM IN TEXTILE PLANT, GREENSBORO (BURLINGTON INDUSTRIES, INC.)

TOUR 6 (US 15-15A)

(Clarksville, Va.)—Oxford—Creedmoor (15-A)—Raleigh—Fayetteville—Laurinburg (US 15)—(Bennettsville, S. C.); US 15, 15A, 15. Virginia Line—South Carolina Line. 164 m.

Section a. VIRGINIA LINE *to* CREEDMOOR, 32 m., US 15.

Between the Virginia Line and Creedmoor, US 15 traverses rolling countryside and elevated flat lands where tobacco and corn are produced on small farms. The route is marked by granite squares and bronze tablets every 10 miles to designate this as part of the Jefferson Davis Highway.

US 15 crosses the Virginia-Carolina Line, 0 m., 6 miles south of Clarksville, Va., and enters Granville County.

At .9 m. is the junction (L) with NC 39 (*see* TOUR 5 FOR TOUR OF KERR RESERVOIR).

STOVALL, 7 m. (478 alt., 410 pop.), is dependent on the growing of tobacco and vegetables.

Left from Stovall on an unpaved road to the marked SITE OF THE HOME OF JOHN PENN, 4 m., a N. C. signer of the Declaration of Independence; Penn came from Virginia in 1774 and resided here until his death in 1788. He was buried here until 1895 when his remains were moved to Guilford Battleground (*see* TOUR 9); the body of his wife, Susannah Lyne, lies in the family burying ground.

At 8 m. is the junction with a narrow concrete road.

Left on this road to the HOME OF COL. WILLIAM T. GREGORY (*private*), 1 m. Near his home Col. Gregory (1868-1932), an eccentric landowner and tobacco planter, operated a general store where he gave away rather than sold articles.

At 17 m. is the northern junction with US 158 (*see* TOUR *12*), which unites with US 15 between this point and Oxford.

OXFORD, 18 m. (476 alt., 6,685 pop.), seat of Granville County, is a manufacturing town and tobacco market where autumn sales are conducted in 10 large warehouses. The State's first tobacco sales warehouse devoted solely to aging cured leaf tobacco was built here in 1866.

Oxford was founded in 1764 when Bute County was formed from Granville and the seat of Granville was moved to Samuel Benton's plantation, called Oxford. The town was laid out in 1811-12 and incorporated in 1816. Granville County had been formed in 1746 and named for John Carteret, Earl of Granville, who retained his domain when the other Lords Proprietors surrendered their charters to the Crown in 1729. The Oxford Academy, authorized in 1811 when the general assembly empowered trustees to raise funds by means of a lottery, was established in 1817 and existed until 1880. At the eastern city limits on US 158 is the SITE OF HORNER MILITARY SCHOOL, established in 1855 by James Hunter Horner and moved to Charlotte in 1914. Horner had come to Oxford in 1851 as principal of the Oxford Male Academy.

OXFORD ORPHANAGE, College St., occupies the site of St. John's College, a Masonic seminary for male students that existed between 1858 and the Civil War. The orphanage, opened in 1873 by the Grand Lodge of Masons in North Carolina, provides academic courses and vocational training for about 400 children. The OXFORD COLORED ORPHANAGE, founded by Negro Masons in North Carolina, is maintained by the State.

The GRANVILLE COUNTY COURTHOUSE, built in 1838, with additions in 1891 and 1937, contains county records from 1746. At Capehart Cleaners, opposite the courthouse, is a COLLECTION OF INDIAN RELICS found in this section. In the 17th and early 18th centuries, Granville County was the home of 17 Indian tribes, most powerful of whom were the Tuscarora.

Between Oxford and Creedmoor the route passes fields of tobacco and corn.

At **28 m.**, across the railroad to the L., is HESTER (80 pop.), a farm village dominated by the meeting hall of Hester Grange, a farmers' club.

Right from Hester on a sand-clay road to INDIAN GRAVE HILL, **1 m.**, where many Indian relics have been found and carried away by amateur archeologists.

At **32 m.** is CREEDMOOR (358 alt., 852 pop.), where one of the largest mule markets in the State is conducted. The town is sustained by a small lumber mill and a farm trade.

At Creedmoor US 15 leads to Durham, **15 m.** (*see* DURHAM *and* TOUR 7); tour 6 branches left and follows US 15A.

Section b. CREEDMOOR *to* SOUTH CAROLINA LINE; **132 m.** US 15A, 15.

Between Creedmoor and Laurinburg US 15A winds along the eastern slopes of the piedmont plateau. Thick forests of cedar, holly, and stubby-leaved slash pine rise over growths of dogwood and redbud in the northern portion; longleaf pine dominates the southern. Fields are planted with tobacco, cotton, and occasionally vegetables.

Between **9 m.** and **15 m.** is the HARRICANE SECTION, once notorious for the illicit manufacture of corn liquor in stills concealed among the hills and pine woods.

RALEIGH, 24 m. (*see* RALEIGH).

Points of Interest: State Capitol, Christ Church, Site of the Birthplace of Andrew Johnson, Joel Lane House, N. C. State College of Agriculture and Engineering, and others.

Raleigh is at the junction with US 64 (*see* TOUR *13*), US 1 (*see* TOUR *5*), and US 70 (*see* TOUR *15*).

South of Raleigh US 15A passes through a section that contains some of the most productive farming land in North Carolina. Peach orchards blossom along the route in spring, and in summer miles of cotton fields show their delicate blooms.

CARALEIGH, 26 m. (355 alt., 600 pop.), is a village centering around the American Woolens Mills plant.

At 27.5 m. is the entrance (R) to CAROLINA PINES, a recreational development (*hotel, clubhouse, restaurant, golf course, lake, tennis courts, riding stables*). Frogs are propagated here and mineral water bottled.

At 28.1 m. a tablet imbedded in a boulder commemorates the Ramsgate Road. This highway between Wake Crossroads, now Raleigh, and Orange County was built by Gov. William Tryon in 1771 before his expedition against the Regulators (*see* TOUR *15B*). The route, so named for the old Ramsgate Road in England over which pilgrims to Canterbury journeyed centuries ago, was nicknamed Ramcat or Rhamkatte in derision of Tryon.

FUQUAY-VARINA, 43 m. (420 alt., 1,992 pop.), a tobacco-market town, was once a health resort. It has a mineral spring covered by a springhouse in a wooded park.

At 55 m. is the northern junction with US 421 (*see* TOUR *17*).

The highway crosses the deep Cape Fear River at 55.5 m.

LILLINGTON, 56 m. (325 alt., 1,061 pop.), the seat of agricultural Harnett County, was named for Revolutionary Col. Alexander Lillington (*see* TOUR *6*).

At the McKINNON HOUSE (R), 75 m., during the Civil War, Federal soldiers hanged McKinnon for refusing to reveal where he had hidden his share of the money distributed by directors of the local banks when Union troops were approaching. After the soldiers had left, a slave cut down and revived his master.

At 76 m. is the junction with an unpaved road.

Left on this road to CARVERS FALLS, 0.5 m. Here the Cape Fear River is 60 feet wide and drops 18 feet. The falls serve as shower baths for youngsters who use the thick forest and ravine for bathhouses.

TOKAY VINEYARD, 80 m., once the site of a large winery, was replanted in 1934 after a long interval of neglect.

The PARAPET, 82 m., is the name given to ruins of breastworks thrown up during the Civil War by Gen. Joseph E. Johnston's army in anticipation of a Federal attack on Fayetteville.

FAYETTEVILLE, 83 m. (see FAYETTEVILLE).

Points of Interest: Market House, First Presbyterian Church, Cool Spring, Site of Cross Creek, Site of Flora MacDonald's House, and others.

Fayetteville is at the junction with US 301 and NC 28 (see LOCAL TOUR FROM FAYETTEVILLE).

Southwest of Fayetteville whites and Negroes of all ages work in the cotton and tobacco fields along the road. Occasionally in late summer, when immediate harvest is necessary to prevent cotton rotting on the stalks, girls and women incongruously dressed in shorts work in the fields.

The DUNCAN SHAW HOUSE, 92.5 m., built in 1860, is a plantation dwelling with a two-story front porch supported by columns made to simulate stone. Beams and clapboards are pegged together.

LAKE RIM, 93 m., has a 240-acre STATE FISH HATCHERY and GAME FARM, established in 1924. The hatchery propagates large-mouthed black bass, blue bream, and crappie; the game farm, quail, pheasants, and wild turkeys. Demonstration and experimental areas are planted with Asiatic chestnuts, pines, and black locusts.

RAEFORD, 105 m. (262 alt., 2,030 pop.), is the farming and industrial center of Hoke County, which was formed in 1911 and named for Confederate Gen. Robert F. Hoke. The northern part of the county is largely occupied by Fort Bragg (see LOCAL TOUR FROM FAYETTEVILLE). One mile SW. of Raeford is the SITE OF EDINBURGH MEDICAL COLLEGE, one of the first medical schools in the State. Founded in 1850 by Dr. Hector McLean, it flourished for 15 years and graduated several famous physicians. Dr. McLean's office is still standing.

At Raeford is the junction with NC 211.

1. Left from Raeford on NC 211 to the ANTIOCH PRESBYTERIAN CHURCH (L), at a bend in the road, 6.9 m. This weatherboarded building painted white is 6 bays long. Above the entrance doors are 4 rectangular windows, with a quatrefoil opening in the gable. Galleries run around three sides of the interior. The church was built about 1883 near the site of an older building whose pews were used by Union soldiers to build a bridge over Raft Swamp River. In the church cemetery are the graves of early Scottish settlers including that of the Rev. John McIntyre (1750-1852), who came to America in 1791, was ordained in 1809, and preached in both English and Gaelic at several churches in this area. He was one of the organizers of the Fayetteville Presbytery in 1813 and the Synod of North Carolina at Alamance Church the same year. Local legend says he preached a sermon on his 100th birthday.

Right from Antioch Church 2 m. to a granite marker, indicating the SITE OF THE BATTLE OF McFALL MILL or RAFT SWAMP, Sept. 1, 1781. Less than 100 Whig

patriots under Colonel Wade met a much larger number of Tories under Colonels
Ray, McDougal, David Fanning, and "Sailor" Hector McNeill. The Continentals
were defeated and pursued by Fanning, who killed 19 Whigs and captured 54
prisoners. The Tory loss was negligible.

On Oct. 15, 1781, McNeill, encamped on the edge of the swamp, heard that
Rutherford was resting at McFall Mill, and proceeded to take up the causeway.
When Whig dragoons under Maj. Graham launched a surprise attack the Tories
fled, their horses floundering through the water; many were overtaken and killed.
This marked the end of armed Tory opposition in this section.

2. Right from Raeford on NC 211 is TIMBERLAND, **4 m.** (75 pop.), an agricultural village and winter resort. McCAIN, **10 m.** (200 pop.), is a small village
in which is the NORTH CAROLINA SANATORIUM FOR THE TREATMENT OF TUBER-
CULOSIS, established in 1907 and maintained by the State since 1909. A tablet at
the entrance to the main building honors the founder and first superintendent,
Dr. James E. Brooks. The modern $3,000,000 plant accommodates 550 resident
patients. There is a separate Negro division. The institution issues a monthly
paper, the *Sanatorium Sun.*

Across a ravine about 200 yards at **108.6 m.** is BETHEL PRESBYTERIAN
CHURCH, whose society was organized in 1776. In the church Bible are
entries reputedly indited by Gen. Sherman but probably written by some
wag in the Federal Army:

"Mr. McNeill will please preach a sermon on the illusions of pleasure and
hope.

"Mr. McNeill will please prove the absurdity of the Universalist doctrine.

"Mr. McNeill will please preach a sermon from the First Epistle of John,
4 Chapter.

"Mr. McNeill will please pray for Old Abe.

"By order of W. T. Sherman, Major Genl. Comd. U. S. Forces."

WAGRAM, **115 m.** (397 pop.), on the edge of the Sandhills, is a shipping point for peaches, melons, and general farm produce.

Right from Wagram to the SITE OF THE OLD SPRING HILL BAPTIST CHURCH,
0.8 m. In the church cemetery is the GRAVE OF JOHN CHARLES MCNEILL (1874-
1907), author of *Songs Merry and Sad,* and *Lyrics from Cotton Land.*

Near the cemetery is the small brick HEXAGON HOUSE, in the 1860's a meeting
place of the Richmond County Temperance and Literary Society. The hexagonal
building has a window on each side and a door facing the road. On the hip roof
is a wooden goblet, turned upside down.

At **121.5 m** is the junction with the Wire Rd., so named when a tele-
graph line was run beside the road; it was part of the ante-bellum stage
route between Cheraw, S. C., and Fayetteville.

Right on this road to the LAUREL HILL CHURCH (R) **2.6 m.,** a weatherboarded
building with an octagonal cupola and two doors in the front gable end. One of
Gen. Sherman's buglers carved his name in the belfry in 1865.

In the graveyard is buried Duncan McFarland, Congressman (1805-7) and
wealthy landowner. Tradition relates that he once rode horseback all the way to
Washington, but slaves had to cut a bridle path to the road before he could set
out on his journey.

LAURINBURG, 125 m. (227 alt., 7,134 pop.), seat of Scotland County, was founded in the 1870's. The county was formed from Richmond County in 1899 and named for the homeland of its first settlers.

The SCOTLAND COUNTY COURTHOUSE (1901-2), Church St., is a square building with a Corinthian portico. In the yard is the WILLIAM GRAHAM QUAKENBUSH MONUMENT, an obelisk on a granite base. Quakenbush was principal of the Laurinburg High School (1879-1900). The CONFEDERATE MONUMENT is a 30-foot column supporting the figure of a soldier.

At McDougald's Funeral Home, half a block south of the courthouse, hangs the MUMMY OF FERRENZO CONCEPIO, an itinerant Italian musician who was murdered with a tent stake at Laurinburg in 1909. The undertaker embalmed the body but has waited in vain for relatives or friends to claim it.

The privately owned LAURINBURG INDUSTRIAL INSTITUTE, occupying several brick buildings, offers its Negro students academic and vocational training.

Laurinburg is at the junction with US 74 (see TOUR 16), and US 15-501 (see TOUR 7).

At 126 m. US 501 branches off to the left.

Left on US 501 to STEWARTSVILLE CEMETERY, 3 m., an old Scottish burying ground. Many of the monuments are ornamented with thistles.

Buried here is the Rev. Colin Lindsay, born in Scotland, according to the story, several years after the supposed death of his mother. After Mrs. Lindsay had apparently died, she was interred in the family vault. Roused by grave robbers seeking valuables, she lived to regain her full health and some years later to become the mother of Colin. He came to America in 1792 and shortly afterward settled in this region.

US 501 continues to ROWLAND, 19 m., where it forms a junction with US 301 (see TOUR 3).

At 132 m. US 15 crosses the South Carolina Line, 10 miles north of Bennettsville, S. C.

TOUR 7 *(US 501-15)*

(South Boston, Va.)—Roxboro—Durham—Sanford—Carthage—Pinehurst
—Aberdeen—Laurinburg—(Junction with US 15A), US 501, 15.
Virginia Line—Laurinburg. **151 m.**

Between the Virginia Line and Durham US 501 crosses generally level
terrain; between Durham and Pittsboro the country is broken by ridges
and ravines utilized for woodland and pasture. Bordering the highway are
fields of tobacco and corn interspersed with pine and oak forests. Beyond
Sanford the route traverses the heart of the Sandhills (*see* TOUR 5).

US 501 crosses the Virginia-North Carolina Line, **0 m.**, 14 miles south
of South Boston, Va., and enters Person County. Near here Gen. Nathanael
Greene, pursued by Cornwallis, crossed the Dan River into Virginia, in
Feb. 1781. Later he recrossed the river a few miles west and the two armies
met Mar. 15, 1781 at Guilford Courthouse (*see* TOUR 9).

ROXBORO, **13 m.** (671 alt., 4,321 pop.), a cotton-manufacturing and
tobacco-marketing center, is named for Roxburgh in Scotland; it is the seat
of Person County, formed in 1791 and named for Revolutionary Gen.
Thomas Person (*see* TOUR *12 and* CHAPEL HILL). This region is an extension
of the Virginia Blue Wing copper district, containing novaculite, a quartz
used for whetstones; silver; and in the western part, granite valuable for
building.
Manufactured products include toweling and upholstery and drapery
fabrics.
The town was founded when the temporary seat of Person County was
moved here from Payne's Tavern, and a courthouse was erected between
two springs. John R. Green, a Roxboro native, originated Bull Durham
tobacco (*see* DURHAM). William W. Kitchin, U. S. Congressman (1896-
1908) and Governor of North Carolina (1909-13), was practicing law here
when he was elected governor.
The white stone, box-shaped PERSON COUNTY COURTHOUSE was built in
1930. On the lawn is a square granite block inscribed with the names of
the county's Confederate soldiers, and honoring Capt. E. Fletcher Satter-
field (1837-63), killed at Gettysburg. The hotel across the street is on the

SITE OF THE EDWIN G. READE HOME. Reade was a U. S. Congressman (1855-57), Confederate Senator, President of the State Convention (1865), and Justice of the N. C. Supreme Court (1865-78).

Roxboro is at the junction with US 158 (*see* TOUR *12*).

South from Roxboro on the sand-clay Hurdles Mill Rd., which was the colonial route between Virginia and Hillsboro, to the SITE OF PAYNE'S TAVERN, **4 m.** Local tradition asserts that this was the birthplace of Dolly Payne Madison, wife of Pres. James Madison, though records of New Garden Meetinghouse (*see* TOUR *15B*) fix her birthplace there. A farmhouse occupies the tavern site, but there are traces of a brick wall that once surrounded the tavern. At this inn—referred to as Payne's "onery," presumably a corruption of "ordinary"—Cornwallis passed a night in 1781. After the death in Philadelphia in 1793 of her first husband, John Todd, and one of her two children, Dolly is said to have returned here with her small son while James Madison visited at the Taylor home near the tavern.

At **27 m.** US 501 passes (L) the edge of ROUGEMONT (500 pop.), whose name (Fr., *red mountain*) was suggested by the color of the soil on nearby Riggs Mountain.

QUAIL ROOST FARM (*open*), **29 m.** (R), is a model 1,500-acre dairy farm stocked with purebred Guernseys.

At **30 m.**, beside the junction with a paved road, is a highway MARKER TO WILLIE (Wiley) PERSON MANGUM, whose home site and grave is **6 m.** NE. Mangum was a U. S. Senator for 18 years and president pro tempore (1842-45). An ardent Whig leader, he also served in Congress and in 1837 received the 11 votes of South Carolina for president.

Left on this road to 4-mile-long LAKE MICHIE, **3 m.**, Durham reservoir. Shrubs, holly trees, and wild flowers line the shore. This territory, in which many Indian relics have been found, was the home of the Occoneechee, Eno, and Adshusheer Indians until about 1750.

An arrowhead (R) **35 m.**, bearing a bronze tablet, points out part of the INDIAN TRADING PATH. A natural outcropping of rock nearby is shaped like a horseshoe. Here, tradition says, an Indian chief came frequently to invoke the assistance of the war god for his tribe.

At **39 m.** is the junction with a marked road.

Right on this road to the DUKE HOMESTEAD (*open 3:30-5:30 Sun., Apr.-Dec.*), **1 m.**, a small white clapboarded dwelling built in 1851 by Washington Duke, founder of the Duke tobacco industry (*see* DURHAM). The walls and floors are of hand-hewn pine. The house has been restored and the original furniture, with supplementary pieces also used in the 1860's, has been placed in the rooms.

At BRAGGTOWN, **40 m.**, is the junction with a marked road.

Left on this road to FAIRNTOSH PLANTATION (*grounds and out-buildings open*), **7 m.** The square, green-shuttered manor house, of white clapboards and fronted by a broad porch, was built in 1802 by Duncan Cameron, who defended North Carolina landowners when the heirs of Lord Granville sued for recovery of property confiscated by the State at the outbreak of the Revolution. The house contains much of the original furniture. In the carriage house is the Cameron carriage and nearby are the old kitchen, and white-painted law office of the master, a school-house, and a row of buildings including dairy house, smoke house, ration house, and weaving house. A gray frame chapel containing a hand-made walnut altar and pews is lighted by a cluster of stained-glass windows.

DURHAM, 43 m. (*see* DURHAM).

Points of Interest: Durham Hosiery Co. Plant, Liggett & Myers Tobacco Co. Plant, Erwin Cotton Mills, American Tobacco Co. Plant, Duke University, and others.

Durham is at the junction with US 15 which unites to form US 15-501 (*see* TOUR 6) and US 70 (*see* TOUR 15).

At 51.6 m. US 15-501 by-passes Chapel Hill (*see* CHAPEL HILL); US 15-501-A goes through the town.

Points of Interest: Old East, University Library, Kenan Stadium, Playmakers Theatre, Coker Arboretum, Gimghoul Castle, Morehead Planetarium, Ackland Art Museum, and others.

For several miles US 15-501 traverses a shallow valley called the Triassic Sea by geologists.

At 53.7 m. the highway crosses an overhead bridge over NC 54.

Left on NC 54 to the junction with NC 55, 5 m.; R on NC 55 to the O'KELLY CHURCH, 4 m., a two-story white clapboard structure with a small steeple. A monument marks the grave of James O'Kelly (1757-1826), founder of the O'Kellite sect. O'Kelly objected to the episcopal powers of Bishops Coke and Asbury and, in 1792, followed by a group of dissenting ministers, broke away from the Methodist Episcopal Church. This schism was known as the Republican Methodist, but the name was later changed to the Christian Church. In 1932 it merged to become the Congregationalist-Christian Church.

PITTSBORO, 72 m. (409 alt., 1,094 pop.), is the seat of Chatham County, which was formed in 1771 and named for the Earl of Chatham, who, as William Pitt, championed the rights of the American colonies in the British Parliament. Primarily an agricultural county, it produces tobacco, grain, cotton, poultry, and dairy products. The town's chief industries are lumber, textiles, and furniture. Named for the Earl of Chatham's second son, William Pitt the Younger, it was incorporated in 1787. It received its greatest growth in the 1820's and 30's when many families moved from the Cape Fear. Prior to the Civil War it was considered a summer resort for those who lived in the coastal plain.

CHATHAM COUNTY COURTHOUSE (1882), a three-story square structure with a raised basement, a pedimented portico, and red-painted brick walls having stuccoed white columns and pilasters, is topped with a tower and octagonal, domed belfry. On July 16, 1781, when Pittsboro was still called Chatham Courthouse, David Fanning with a party of Tories raided the town while a court martial was in progress, capturing 44 persons. Fanning terrorized a wide area (*see* TOURS *13 and 15*). Cornwallis spent the night at Chatham Courthouse in the course of his march to Wilmington after the Battle of Guilford Courthouse.

The YELLOW HOUSE (*private*), now on the south side of the square, is probably the oldest house in town. The right end of the house, which has weathered clapboards and sagging sills, survives from the house built by Patrick St. Lawrence, early town commissioner and trustee of Pittsborough Academy, which was so luxurious that it bankrupted both St. Lawrence and his contractor. A device for fastening folding doors to the ceiling allowed the entire lower floor to be thrown into a ballroom.

The WADDELL HOUSE (*private*), Salisbury St., a two-story yellow frame house with red brick end chimneys, was the birthplace of Capt. James Iredell Waddell (1824-86), commander of the Confederate cruiser, *Shenandoah,* which carried the only Confederate flag that ever went around the world. After the collapse of the Confederacy, Waddell, then in the Pacific, sailed around Cape Horn to England where he remained until the members of his crew were granted amnesty.

ST. BARTHOLOMEW's EPISCOPAL CHURCH (1833), Salisbury St., is a small rectangular building, its entrance marked by a low square tower and steeple on the right of the façade. A veneer of red brick was applied (1938) over the original clapboard construction. The congregation was organized in Revolutionary days. Within the building, finished in stained pine, are a slave gallery and furnishings carved from native walnut by one of the rectors, the Rev. R. B. Sutton. The communion service was made of family silver given by communicants. In the old graveyard are the graves of John Owen, Governor of North Carolina (1828-30); Abraham Rencher, U. S. Congressman (1829-39) Chargé d'Affaires to Portugal (1843-47), Governor of The Territory of New Mexico (1857-61); and Edward Jones, Solicitor General of North Carolina (1791-1827).

The PITTSBOROUGH ACADEMY BUILDING (*private*), a gabled white frame structure of one room, is now incorporated into a residence. Erected in 1886, it once housed the academy, established by legislative act in 1787. William Bingham was its first principal, and among its pupils were John Owen and Charles Manly, Governor of North Carolina (1849-51).

The MASONIC LODGE (1838), East St., is a two-story frame building with an overhanging second story in front, supported by square stucco columns. The order itself, organized many years prior, sent a delegation to the laying of the cornerstone of Old East Building at Chapel Hill in 1793 (*see* CHAPEL HILL).

Pittsboro is at the junction with NC 93.

Right on NC 93 to the junction with a country road, **8 m.**, and right again to ROCK REST, **3 m.**, the home of Capt. Johnston Blakeley (1781-1814), commander of the U. S. sloop *Wasp*, during the War of 1812. Blakeley captured the *Reindeer, Avon, Atlanta,* and many other British ships. The *Wasp* and all aboard disappeared in Oct. 1814, leaving no clue to its fate.

At the village of LOCKVILLE, **85 m.**, US 15-501 unites with US 1 for 11 miles (*see* TOUR 5).

At **96 m.**, US 15-501 swings right from US 1 to Carthage, **106 m.**

CARTHAGE, **106 m.** (1,194 pop.), seat of Moore County, is the trading center of the surrounding clay country and contains textile, hosiery, and lumber plants. Formerly called Fagansville for Richardson Fagan in whose home the court was originally held, the town was incorporated in 1796. Internecine warfare was waged in this section during the Revolution between Whigs and Highland Scot Tories.

In Carthage the modern MOORE COUNTY COURTHOUSE (*apply here for admission to quail farm; see below*) dominates the town from its gardened setting. On the lawn is a marker in honor of a man who once worked here as a tailor, Andrew Johnson, later President of the United States. West of the courthouse is a marker to James McConnell of the French Flying Corps (d. 1917). The MEMORIAL HOSPITAL also bears his name.

The main street of Carthage was the route of the Fayetteville-to-Bethania plank road, a toll road 129 miles long, which was built in 1849-54.

Right from Carthage on a graveled road **11.2 m.** to the junction with a second graveled road; R. **0.5 m.** on this road to the WILLIAMS BURYING GROUND near Governors Creek. Here is the GRAVE OF BENJAMIN WILLIAMS, member of the Provincial Congress, the U.S. Congress, both houses of the general assembly, Governor of North Carolina (1799-1802, 1807-8), and a member of the original board of trustees of the University of North Carolina.

Continue on the first graveled road from the junction with the second graveled road **0.1 m.** to the junction with a third graveled road. Left **0.1 m.** on this road across the Deep River on a high steel bridge to HORSESHOE FARM, a plantation at a wide bend in the stream. At **0.2 m.** (L) is the PHILIP ALSTON HOUSE (*private*), known also as the House in the Horseshoe, a pre-Revolutionary, two-story frame house, with brick end chimneys and a front porch. Bullet holes in the weatherboarding are evidences of the Whig-Tory skirmishes of 1780-81.

During his occupancy of Wilmington, British Major Craig aroused the Highland Scots and other Tories until the region between the Haw and Yadkin rivers was virtually in a state of civil war. Upon one occasion Colonel Alston and 25 Whigs were trapped in the Alston house by Tory David Fanning and his men (*see* TOURS *13 and 15*). After brisk shooting Alston was forced to surrender.

Across the road from the Alston house is a commercial QUAIL FARM (*adm. restricted; apply at Carthage Courthouse*), where hundreds of quail and wild turkeys are raised annually.

On the third graveled road at **2.7 m.** is the junction with a dirt road; R. **0.5 m.** on this road to the only ANTHRACITE COAL MINE south of Pennsylvania, most of the product being used locally.

Carthage is at the junction with NC 27.

Right on NC 27 to CROSS HILL, **1.5 m.**, where the Tories rendezvoused in Feb., 1776, under Gen. Donald MacDonald and Maj. Allen MacDonald, husband of the celebrated Flora MacDonald (*see* TOUR *18 and* FAYETTEVILLE), before going down to Cross Creek (Fayetteville) and on to defeat at Moore's Creek Bridge (*see* TOUR *18*). Here (R) is also the GRAVE OF DR. GEORGE GLASCOCK, Revolutionary surgeon, whose mother, Patty Ball, was a kinswoman of George Washington. Glascock's murder in 1787, attributed in his son's affidavit to the instigation of Col. Philip Alston, cost Alston his seat in the general assembly until he was reinstated after acquittal at a later trial.

At **6 m.** is the junction with NC 22.

1. Right on NC 22 to the "ghost" town of PARKWOOD, **2 m.** (R), buried deep in pine woods and deserted for over half a century. In the 1880's it was the flourishing village of a millstone factory, even boasting of the first telephone system in the county. Parkwood's main thoroughfare is now overgrown. Wistaria and honeysuckle creep into the French windows of the old hotel, whose last guest registered Apr. 2, 1891. The factory walls guard machinery rusting under rotting shingles; unused millstones lie beside the stream.

McCONNELL, **6 m.** (40 pop.), is the center of the Moore County gold fields, unworked since about 1900 because the low gold content made operations unprofitable.

At **9 m.** is the junction with a dirt road, marked Pinehurst and Mt. Carmel.

1. Left on this road to the junction with another dirt road at Mt. Carmel Church, **4.3 m.**; R. **2.3 m.** on this road to the PETRIFIED WOOD. On both sides of the road for some distance are sections of wood petrified when air pockets in them became filled with silica.

At **10.2 m.** is the junction with NC 705.

1. Right on NC 705 is ROBBINS, **2 m.** (425 alt., 1,158 pop.), built on the old Plank Road from Fayetteville to Bethania, whose main street is an elbow in the highway. Originally called Mechanicsville for David Kennedy, a famous gunsmith and mechanic, it later was known as Elise, then Hemp for the vast amount of rope produced here. Since 1948 it has been named Robbins for the head of the mills here and at Aberdeen. Time and progress are beginning to make a change in the housekeeping, farming methods, and customs in some of the isolated regions of this section.

2. Left from Robbins, **2 m.**, on an unimproved road to the GERHARDT MINE (*no visitors below surface*), the largest pyrophyllite mine in the world, though referred to locally as a talc mine. Here the deposit is 200 feet underground. Grinding mills pulverize the material for use as talcum powder and as a filler in roofing, linoleum, and fertilizer.

US 15-501 turns left from Carthage and enters the Sandhills. At **110 m.** (L) is a MARKER TO MAJ. ALEXANDER McLEOD, illegitimate son of the 18th chieftain of McLeod and son-in-law of Flora MacDonald. His home, GLENDALE, stood 1½ miles west. The celebrated Flora lived for a period after Moore's Creek Bridge at the nearby home of Kenneth Black.

At **117 m.** is Pinehurst (*see* TOUR *5A*).

US 15-501 continues to Aberdeen (*see* TOUR *5*), crosses the Lumber River at **128 m.**, and joins 15-A at Laurinburg, **151 m.** (*see* TOUR *6*).

TOUR 8 *(US 29)*

(Danville, Va.)—Reidsville—Greensboro—Salisbury—Charlotte—Gastonia
—(South Carolina Line); US 29, 29-A, 29.
Virginia Line—South Carolina Line, **178 m.**

This route across the piedmont runs over gently rolling land, wooded or planted with corn, tobacco, small grains, and other crops.

US 29 crosses the North Carolina Line, **0 m.**, 5 miles southwest of Danville, Va.

PELHAM, **2.5 m.** (740 alt., 500 pop.), a trading center in rural Caswell County, lies in a region well adapted to the culture of bright-leaf tobacco. This was a local Gretna Green when North Carolina marriage laws were more convenient than those of Virginia.

Southwest of here the road follows a high ridge through a region of farms marked by tobacco barns, crude log affairs which nevertheless appear more substantial than the cabins of the tenant croppers. The distant sky line is pierced by the brick smokestacks of Reidsville's tobacco factories. Storage warehouses of the American Tobacco Co., **15.4 m.**, border the highway for more than a mile (L).

REIDSVILLE, **18.3 m.** (841 alt., 11,708 pop.), is an industrial city with wide streets, one of North Carolina's three tobacco-manufacturing centers. Other factories manufacture cotton, silk and rayon textiles, shoe polishes and leather preservatives, concrete forms, food products, feedstuffs, and auto batteries.

The town grew out of a settlement which began in 1815 when Reuben Reid and his family purchased a farm and built their home on the Danville-Salisbury road. His son, David S. Reid, was Governor of North Carolina (1851-54), and U. S. Senator. William Lindsey established the first tobacco factory here in 1858 and produced the brand, Lindsey's Level Best. In 1863 the Confederate Government built the Piedmont Air Line for transporting troops and supplies to Lee's and Johnston's armies. Maj. Mortimer Oaks and James Allen entered the tobacco business in 1871, and three years later F. R. and S. C. Penn came from Virginia and opened a tobacco factory here that steadily expanded.

The American Tobacco Co. Plant (*open Mon.-Thurs. 9-4:15; Fri. 9-12*), an outgrowth of the Penn factory, covers an entire city block. The air-conditioned brick buildings are equipped with machinery capable of producing 200,000,000 cigarettes a day. The principal product is Lucky Strike cigarettes. Because of the large quantities of Turkish tobacco and cigarette paper imported by the company, Reidsville was made a port of entry.

In the Federal Building (1936), weekly receipts averaging $4,000,000 indicate the revenue derived from the tobacco industry. This striking brick and limestone structure has monumental entrances flanked by chrome and frosted-glass lamps and surmounted by gilt eagles.

In the old Settle Family Graveyard is the ivy-covered marble Tomb of Mrs. Stephen A. Douglas, first wife of Abraham Lincoln's political antagonist. Following her death in 1852 in Washington, D. C., the body was brought in a horse-drawn hearse to her girlhood home. The party did not reach the cemetery until after dark and the tradition is that the last rites were held by the flare of lightwood torches.

Reidsville is at the junction with US 158 (*see* tour *12*).

Left from Reidsville on NC 87 to Citty's Store, **9.1 m**; R. **1.5 m.** to High Rock Farm, a handsome, 3-story, brick house said to have been built from plans originally drawn by Peter Jefferson, father of Thomas. It was also said to have been used later as a tavern. Near here, at High Rock Ford, Gen. Greene gathered his army together prior to the battle of Guilford Courthouse.

Right from Reidsville on NC 65 to the junction with a dirt road, **3 m.**; R. **2 m.** on this road to an old Iron Works Mill originally called Troublesome Iron Works. A marker recalls that at different times Greene and Cornwallis camped here during the Revolution before the battle of Guilford Courthouse. Greene also retired here after the battle and fortified the area, expecting an attack by Cornwallis. On his southern tour, Washington breakfasted here June 3, 1791.

At **10 m.** is MONROETON, a crossroads settlement. Left **8.5 m.** from the crossroads to the old Cunningham (Patrick) Mill, erected in 1816. Members of the Ku Klux Klan gathered here (*see* tour *13*). The mill, powered by an overshot wheel, still grinds meal. Carved over the door of a springhouse near the mill is the name of the builder, "J. Patrick, 1824."

South of Reidsville US 29 runs through a hilly, wooded section, crossing Troublesome Creek at **24.7 m.** and Haw River at **25.5 m.** At **30 m.** is MONTICELLO, a rural section settled by English Calvinists after the organization of Guilford County (1771).

GREENSBORO, 42 m. (*see* greensboro).

Points of Interest: Woman's College, Greensboro College, Greensboro Historical Museum and Library, Masonic Temple and O. Henry Birthplace, Gov. Morehead Home, Sedgefield, the Lorillard Cigarette Factory, Jefferson Standard Building, Cone Textile Mills, and others.

Greensboro is at the junction with US 70 (*see* tour *16*), US 421 (*see* tour *17*), and US 220 (*see* tour *9*).

US 29 unites with US 70 between Greensboro and High Point. Between Greensboro and Charlotte is a 4-lane boulevard.

At **49 m.** is the entrance to SEDGEFIELD (100 pop.), a resort. SEDGE-FIELD INN, a rambling Tudor-style building, stands in a 3,600-acre woodland park. Here are attractive country homes and the VALLEY BROOK GOLF COURSE (*18 holes*), scene of open, amateur, and professional matches.

JAMESTOWN, **53 m.** (779 alt., 748 pop.), has two distinct sections. The business buildings are in the newer settlement. In old Jamestown, settled by Quakers in 1757, are shady lawns and gardens around old homes, some of which are in ruins. The village was named for James Mendenhall, a Pennsylvania Quaker who came to North Carolina in 1759.

Gold and copper were discovered about 1815 in the granite hills along Deep River, 5 miles south of town. Several mines were operated but the cost of production finally exceeded the value of the ore, and, except for copper mining during the Civil War, the mines were abandoned. The dumps, tunnels, and dilapidated buildings remain. A girls' school was founded in Jamestown about 1812, and for several years after 1820 George C. Mendenhall conducted the Tellmont Law School, one of the earliest in the State. Early agricultural and religious papers were published here, and in 1839 an attempt was made to grow silkworms in this section.

The HIGH POINT CITY PARK (R), **54 m.**, contains a 40-acre lake, covering sites of a pre-Revolutionary tannery, a Quaker hat factory, and a woolen mill. A swimming pool (*open in summer*) is nearby. The dam and spillway are illuminated at night. An outdoor amphitheater seats 2,500 persons.

Near the reservoir is an OLD QUAKER MEETINGHOUSE, now a museum, that was erected about 1819. It has hand-hewn timbers and hand-made red brick laid in Flemish bond upon a heavy stone foundation.

At the entrance to the High Point City Park is (R) the MENDENHALL HOUSE, an ivy-covered brick ruin, built in 1824 by Richard M. Mendenhall and used for a store once run by a slave. The initials R M M are carved on a stone slab under the eave line in the gable.

Opposite the entrance to the park is (L) the STEELE HOUSE (*private*), a brick building, erected in 1811, remodeled and painted dull yellow.

Beyond the Steele House is (L) the COFFIN HOUSE (*private*), a weather-boarded building, painted white, that was erected before 1820 by Dr. S. G. Coffin, who here conducted a school in which young gentlemen "read medicine." In the late 1830's the house was remodeled and Greek Revival details added. From about 1840 to 1850 the school was conducted by Dr. Madison Lindsay. Dr. J. L. Robbins, a pupil and later associate of Dr. Coffin's, assumed direction in 1854. In 1856, in the presence of several students, he used an anesthetic in a successful operation for removal of an abdominal tumor, the first use of a general anesthetic in North Carolina.

At **56 m.** US 70 skirts High Point; US 70A-29A goes through the city.

At **56 m.** US 70-29 forms a junction with NC 68 and the Wallburg Rd.

Straight ahead **1 m.** on the Wallburg Rd. to the junction with a dirt road; L. **3.5 m.** on the dirt road to BRUMMELS INN (*private*) on Rich Fork Creek. This weatherboarded building painted white with green trim has end chimneys and stands in a small grove of maples. The old stage road formerly passed close to the inn, operated by the wealthy slave-owning Jacob Brummel. The house was originally a one-room log structure on a stone and brick foundation. It was later a two-story frame building with a one-story ell at the right end. Three doorways open in from a porch extending the length of the house. The central door, in the old log section, formerly led into the dancing room of the tavern; a chimney with a slab inscribed "J. B. 1814" stands between this room and the ell. The tongue and groove doors are battened and have HL hinges.

Among other relics in the tavern is an old conch shell formerly used for calling the slaves. One slave girl could blow a blast strong enough to be heard 6 miles away. A tale is still told about a stranger named William D. Weatherford, who appeared at the inn during the winter of 1854, announced he had buried a satchel of gold in the woods "between two trees," and, a few hours after his arrival, died. He was buried in the graveyard behind the inn. The Brummels were never able to identify the stranger or to find the gold.

HIGH POINT, 59 m. (*see* HIGH POINT).

Points of Interest: Tomlinson Furniture Plant, Southern Furniture Exposition Building, High Point College, Blair Park, and others.

High Point is at the junction with US 311 (*see* TOUR *9A*).

Left from High Point on Kivett Dr. to the HAYWORTH SPRINGS PICNIC GROUNDS (*tables, water*). A footpath leads **0.5 m.** over the hill to the OLD GOLD MINES, where the ruins, pumps, and water dam are half-hidden in a dense growth of oak and pine. Three mines were opened here following the discovery of gold in North Carolina. Although the ore assayed more than $23 a ton the vein disappeared before the mines had begun to yield a profit.

At **61.7 m.** is the junction with the High Point by-pass (*see above*).

THOMASVILLE, 66.7 m. (853 alt., 11,154 pop.), founded in 1852 by John W. Thomas, is located on both sides of the North Carolina Railroad (now operated by the Southern Railway). The BIG CHAIR (the world's largest), located on the commons, proclaims Thomasville as "The Chair City," the first chair factory in the State having been built here in 1879. Complete lines of furniture are produced in large quantities, and since 1910 cotton and hosiery mills have been established here.

An advanced form of City Council-Manager government is in operation, Thomasville having been the third city in North Carolina to adopt such a system.

The MILLS HOME, in the southwest section of Thomasville, is headquarters for, and one of the homes of, the Baptist Orphanage of North Carolina, Inc. Founded in 1885 by John H. Mills, it has developed into one of the largest child-caring institutions in the South.

Four blocks northeast of the Big Chair is a large 4-story brick building constructed in 1856 by John W. Thomas for Glen Anna Seminary, later known as THOMASVILLE FEMALE COLLEGE. This imposing structure, with additions, is now occupied by the Ragan Knitting Company.

On NC 109 is GLEN ANNA (*private*), ½ m., which was from 1849 to 1857 a boarding school for girls called Sylva Grove Seminary and later Glen Anna Seminary.

At 3 m. on NC 109 is CEDAR LODGE, the home of John W. Thomas from 1825 until he founded Thomasville. It was renovated and additions built in 1902 to 1905.

US 29-70 forms a junction with US 52 (*see* TOUR *10*) and US 64 (*see* TOUR *13*), all of which by-pass Lexington.

LEXINGTON, 78 m. (811 alt., 13,552 pop.), manufacturing town and seat of Davidson County, was settled in 1775 and later named for the Revolutionary battle site. Three open plots and the courthouse square were reserved for public buildings when Lexington became the county seat in 1824. The CONFEDERATE MONUMENT is now on the plot where the public well was for many years. The first courthouse stood in the center of the crossing of the streets now known as Main and Center Sts. The present COURTHOUSE, a temple-like Classical Revival structure on the SW. corner of the square was built about 1840 and rebuilt in 1870 using the walls of the older structure. It was renovated in 1918. Six stone Corinthian columns rise across the front elevation; on the roof is a square clock cupola. Slave auction blocks flank the entrance steps.

Lexington has a diversity of industries, including textile products, wood furniture, garments, and dairy products. The first roller mill in North Carolina, erected by Grimes Brothers in 1879, is still in operation near the center of town.

The CALDCLEUGH HOUSE (*private*), now located on Salisbury St., was built before 1824 for Alexander Caldcleugh, State Senator and one of the founders of Lexington. He deeded the original 25 acres for 50¢ each to the county seat. His log house stood on the corner of Davie (now Main St.) and the old Raleigh Road. Some years after his death in 1833 the log house was covered over with weather-boarding and ceiled with wide boards and an addition as large as the original house was built. In 1913 it was moved to lots on Salisbury St., and two houses were made out of this residence.
Therefore, the original Caldcleugh House is preserved intact but located on a different site. Noteworthy architectural features are the beautiful doors and frames, small windows, wide flooring, and thick walls.
The original site of the Caldcleugh house is now occupied by CENTURY OAKS, the John T. Lowe residence. In the yard are 4 registered oaks nearing 200 years old, which Mrs. Lowe has named Daniel Boone, Gen. Greene, Vance-Settle, and Col. R. Opie Lindsay.

Right from Lexington on NC 150, at a right-angle bend overlooking the Yadkin River, is a junction with a dirt road, 5 m.; L. on this road to the BOONE MEMORIAL PARK and BOONE'S CAVE, 1 m. Here is the marked site of a cabin built by Daniel Boone. A MUSEUM OF RELICS in a reproduction of the log cabin includes a stone inscribed "D. Boone." About 100 yards from the cabin is what has been known for generations as Boone's Cave, or the Devil's Den, where Daniel is said to have hidden from the Indians. The opening, about 2 feet wide, overlooks the river and is obscured by the surrounding forest. The cave, 3 to 5 feet high, runs into the solid rock, 80 feet in one direction and 45 feet in another.

A marker (L), **88.5 m.**, designates the SITE OF OLD TRADING FORD, covered by the waters of High Rock Lake. In colonial times settlers annually met the Indians to trade, especially for shad, near here on the Yadkin River. After Gen. Greene, retreating before Cornwallis, crossed the river here on Feb. 2-3, 1781, a sudden rise of the water prevented the British from following and permitted the Americans to escape.

The highway crosses the Yadkin River, **89.5 m.**, at the upper end of HIGH ROCK LAKE over a bridge more than 1,000 feet long. The lake serves as a fresh-water reservoir for Salisbury, and the hydroelectric plant at High Rock Dam furnishes power for the Carolina Aluminum Co. High Rock is one of several great power developments on the Yadkin. Below its confluence with the Uharie River at the upper end of Lake Tillery, it is called the Pee Dee. It was said that Daniel Boone's desire to explore the upper Yadkin led him westward to the "Kintuck" country (*see* TOUR *19*). The Pee Dee was said to be the river of Stephen Foster's song until he substituted the Swanee as being more euphonious.

SPENCER, **92 m.** (3,242 pop.), is a division point of the Southern Ry. Twenty-five hundred persons, some of whom live in Salisbury, are employed here in the railroad offices, roundhouses, and shop.

SALISBURY, **96 m.** (*see* SALISBURY).

At **98 m.** are the ROWAN COUNTY FAIRGROUNDS (R).

The marked SITE OF THE HOME OF BETSY BRANDON (R) is at **100 m.** While Gen. Washington in 1791 was on the way to Salisbury he stopped at the farm home of Squire Richard Brandon. All the family except 14-year-old Betsy had gone to Salisbury to see the President. He told her that if she would give him breakfast she should see Gen. Washington before any of the others.

CHINA GROVE, **104 m.** (821 alt., 1,491 pop.), is a manufacturing town with a branch of the Cannon Mills.

China Grove is at the northern junction with US 29-A, now the route.

Left here on US 29 and NC 601, an alternate and shorter route by-passes China Grove, Landis, Kannapolis, and Glass and leads to Concord, **12 m.**

Right on US 29-A; KANNAPOLIS, **110 m.** (765 alt., 28,448 pop.), is the largest unincorporated town in the State, owned by CANNON MILLS, INC. (*not open to the public*), whose factories, offices, stores, and warehouses line both sides of the highway for more than a mile.

James William Cannon and his brother, David Franklin Cannon, built a yarn mill at Concord in 1877. At first the rough cotton yarn was sent to Northern mills for weaving; however, it was not long before the enterprising Cannons were producing cloth woven in their own mills. Until the Southern women began to buy ready-made clothing at the turn of the century, the famous "Cannon cloth" was a necessity in practically every home in the South. Towels were not made by Cannon Mills until 1898. In that year a mill in Concord turned out the first cotton hand towel ever finished in the South, and James W. Cannon became a pioneer in the manufacture of towels. The Cannon Mills are now the largest producers of household textiles in the world, with plants scattered throughout the South and extensive sales offices in New York City. Towels, blankets, and sheets are made in Kannapolis, where the heaviest production is concentrated. The two plants in Kannapolis consist of 10 complete mills which employ approximately 19,000 workers.

The town was built on a 600-acre tract of abandoned cotton land purchased by Mr. J. W. Cannon in 1906. The next year a "mill village" sprang up around the towel plant and the company's new offices. Today the "mill village" is a prosperous and thriving city of more than 28,000 inhabitants dependent upon the textile industry for their living. They have comfortable homes, progressive schools, many fine churches, modern theatres, community baseball, and a large Y.M.C.A. Its buildings follow one general architectural theme—Williamsburg colonial. A vast program of remodeling, begun in 1937, is still in progress.

A familiar landmark which rises above the factory system is a large illuminated neon sign representing a cannon.

The JACOB STIREWALT HOUSE, 112 m., also known as Mill Hill, is one of a number of houses built by John, or his son, Jacob Stigerwalt (Stirewalt), the only real architects in the piedmont in the early days. This house, whose construction was begun in 1780 and completed in 1820, has a well-detailed Greek Doric porch and beautiful interior woodwork, including finely carved mantels.

MT. OLIVET METHODIST CHURCH, US 29-A, 113 m., near Cook's Crossing, one of the oldest churches in the Kannapolis area, was organized about 1760. First services were held under a brush arbor near the present cemetery and were conducted by a "circuit rider" who served the congregation during its early years. The early preachers were entertained by George and Martha Rodgers at their home just back of the present church where the little band of worshippers was fostered. The first church, built of logs, in 1780, was located on the site of the present parsonage.

The CABARRUS MEMORIAL HOSPITAL, US 29-A, 115 m., on a large tract given by Mrs. James W. Cannon, is the result of the vision and generosity of Mr. and Mrs. Charles A. Cannon. Its recent addition, designed by J. N. Pease and Co., Charlotte, makes it one of the finest hospitals in the State.

CONCORD, 117 m. (704 alt., 16,486 pop.), the seat of Cabarrus County, was so called because two factions (Germans and Scotch-Irish), disagreeing over the exact location of the county seat, finally reached a harmonious settlement at this spot. The literal meaning of the word was further implanted by being called the main street—"Union"—which it still is. The major part of the business district is located on Union Street. Concord produces cotton goods, cotton seed oil, lumber, flour, mattresses, and hosiery. Four plants of the Cannon Mills, Inc. are located here.

The FIRST PRESBYTERIAN CHURCH, N. Union St., is a red brick reproduction of a church in New Haven, Conn. Its carillon can be heard throughout the city. The cemetery, behind the old Presbyterian Church on S. Depot St., has been converted into a MEMORIAL GARDEN, a quiet and lovely spot in which many of the original residents of Concord are buried. The cemetery, started in 1804, is one of the oldest in the piedmont section of the State. Beyond the west wall many slaves and old-time servants are buried.

In the HOUSTON HOUSE, 25 N. Union St., Confederate Pres. Jefferson Davis spent the night of Apr. 18, 1865.

Concord is at the southern junction with US 29.

1. Right from Concord on the Popular Tent Rd. to the SITE OF THE PHIFER HOME, **1 m.**, where Pres. Washington was the overnight guest of Col. Martin Phifer, Jr., on May 29, 1791. The house, then one of the show places of the State, was built by Col. John Phifer, of Revolutionary fame, who entertained Gov. William Tryon here in 1768 and was later a member of the famous Mecklenburg Convention of 1775 (*see* CHARLOTTE). The Phifer Long Tavern on the plantation was torn down during World War II.

POPULAR TENT PRESBYTERIAN CHURCH, **7 m.** W. on Popular Tent Rd., one of the first churches between the Yadkin and Catawba Rivers, was formed by Scotch-Irish immigrants from Pennsylvania and Cecil County, Md., who called their settlement "Popular Tent," because a tent was used as a church for a long time. One of the original members of the Orange Presbytery, established in 1770, its congregation was organized in 1764 or 1765 with the Rev. Hezekiah James Balch as the first pastor. He served the church until his death in 1776 and is buried in the church graveyard—resting place of many early Presbyterians of this section.

At **10 m.** an iron cross marks the SITE OF CABARRUS BLACK BOYS ACTION in their Gunpowder Plot. During the conflict between Gov. Tryon and the Regulators (*see* TOUR *15B*), the Governor had ordered a shipment of gunpowder, flints, blankets, and other military supplies sent from Charleston, S. C., to Gen. Hugh Waddell at Salisbury. A group of 9 local young patriots, knowing that the supplies were to be used in oppressing their own people, blacked their faces, overtook the wagon train camped on Phifer's Hill, and captured it (May 2, 1771). They smashed the kegs of powder, tore the blankets into strips, and Maj. James White fired a pistol into the train, causing a tremendous explosion. When Gov. Tryon offered a pardon to anyone who would give evidence against the other, two half-brothers, each unknown to the other, turned informants. Their treachery forced the other Black Boys to flee to Georgia, where they joined the army. At the close of the war they returned to Cabarrus to live.

2. Right from the square at Concord on the old Charlotte Rd. (present US 29) to SMITHVILLE, later known as the Morehead Place (*private*), **8 m.**, family

home of Col. Robert Smith. This pre-Revolutionary structure overlooking the Rocky River is a large square house to which wings have been added. Windows and doors are irregularly placed, and the broad thick chimneys have their original tops. In the family burying ground slabs are held by mortar in brick foundations. Slaves were buried in a plot nearby.

Pres. Washington, with Maj. William Jackson, his aide and secretary, dined at noon here on Sunday, May 29, 1791. Local tradition relates that the President, while making his toilet before dinner, discovered he had left his powder puff in Charlotte the previous night. After dinner he continued on his journey to the Phifer home. Traveling in a coach of pale ivory and gilt, bearing designs painted to represent the 4 seasons, as well as the coat of arms of the Washington family, the President noted in his diary that "the lands between Charlotte and Salisbury are very fine, of a reddish cast and well timbered, but very little underwoods. Between these two places are the first meadows I have seen on the road since I left Virginia, and here also we appear to be getting into a wheat country."

3. Left from Concord on NC 73 to St. John's Church, **6 m.**, one of the first three Lutheran churches in North Carolina. The first building, a rude hut of unhewn pine logs, without floor, windows, or chimney, was owned jointly by the Lutheran and German Reformed denominations. It was used for both church and school and called Dutch Buffalo Creek Church. In 1771 the Lutherans withdrew peaceably, adopted the name of St. John's, and erected the old Red Meeting-house. The Rev. Adolph Nussman came over from Germany in 1775 to be the first regular pastor of St. John's. A monument over his grave is on the church grounds. The first ecclesiastic assembly of the Lutheran Church of North Carolina was held at St. John's on May 20, 1794. The fifth and present brick structure was erected in 1845 and extensively remodeled in 1888. The roof is steeply pitched, and the tall windows evenly placed. The educational building was added in 1937.

4. Southeast from Concord on NC 601 and NC 200 to the REED GOLD MINE, **10 m.** In 1799, 12-year-old Conrad Reed found, while wading in Meadow Creek, the first gold nugget ever discovered in the United States. The original nugget weighing 3½ pounds was used for a door-stop in the Reed home for several years before anyone knew what it was. On a trip to Fayetteville in 1802 Joel (John?) Reed, Conrad's father, sold the nugget to a jeweler for the "big price" of $3.50. The Reed mine yielded a large quantity of "pretty rocks" varying in size. Old records indicate that the largest nugget taken from the mine weighed 28 pounds and was worth about $8,000. This series of events started the first gold rush in the United States, and for a half century Cabarrus County provided the country with its chief source of the precious metal. Close to a dozen sizeable mines sprang up in later years. Remnants of the Reed mine can still be found on the property, including the old tunnel. Few people in recent years have ventured into the entire depth of the cave, although it is a favorite haunt of school children on picnics and other outings.

Between **120 m.** and **122 m.** on US 29-A in a section known as ROCKY RIDGE are huge gray and weathered rocks on both sides of the highway. These range in size from small stones to 100-ton boulders and in the same places form vast ledges which serve as back yards or side entrances of houses.

The Stonewall Jackson Training School (R), **121 m.**, was chartered in 1907 by the general assembly and financed with funds offered Mrs.

Jackson as a pension and declined by her. The boys are housed in 16 three-story cottages grouped about an administration building.

SUGAW (*SUGAR*) CREEK PRESBYTERIAN CHURCH, 126 m., a one-story brick building with a low-pitched gable roof, was erected in 1868-69, and is the fourth church on this site. The exterior walls are adorned with brick pilasters. In the rear is a two-story brick addition. The congregation of this church, organized in 1756, is the oldest in Mecklenburg County.

Here is a marker to Capt. Joseph Graham (1759-1836), who was wounded (1780) in a skirmish with the British at this crossroads in the retreat from the Battle of Charlotte (*see* CHARLOTTE). Capt. Graham, although left for dead, was cared for overnight by Mrs. Susan Alexander, who found him at the spring where he had crawled to drink and bathe his wounds. The following night he returned to his own home on horseback and within two months had recovered sufficiently to rejoin his command. Capt. Graham's Revolutionary reminiscences include an account, from memory, of the adoption of the Mecklenburg Declaration (*see* HISTORY).

ROCKY RIVER PRESBYTERIAN CHURCH, 3.5 m. SW. from the intersection of US 29-A and NC 47, was organized about 1751 and was the first of 7 Presbyterian churches established in what was originally Mecklenburg County. In the spring of 1758, Rocky River called the Rev. Alexander Craighead as its regular pastor. At that time he was the solitary minister between the Yadkin and the Catawba. Here he passed the remainder of his days in the active duties of a frontier minister of the Gospel and ended his successful labors in 1766. Mr. Craighead instilled principles of civil and religious liberty in the people he served, and in the decade of the 70's members of Rocky River congregation took a leading part in the movement for separation from the mother country. One of his daughters married the Rev. David Caldwell (*see* GREENSBORO), one married the Rev. William Richardson (maternal uncle of William R. Davie), and one was the first wife of John C. Calhoun's father. The present handsome, brick sanctuary with brick pilasters and tall windows, was erected in 1861.

CHARLOTTE, 139 m. (*see* CHARLOTTE).

Points of Interest: Independence Square, First Presbyterian Church, Site of Confederate Navy Yard, Mint Museum, Martin Cannon Residence, and others.

Charlotte is at the junction with US 21 (*see* TOUR *9*), US 74 (*see* TOUR *16*), and NC 27.

Between Charlotte and Kings Mountain US 29 unites with US 74 (*see* TOUR *16*); between Charlotte and Gastonia it is a landscaped 4-lane highway known as Wilkinson Blvd.

At 142.2 m. is a marker on the SITE OF CAMP GREENE (R), used as a cantonment during World War I.

At 143 m. is the junction with a marked road.

Left on this road is DIXIE, 4 m.; L. 1.5 m. from Dixie to the STEEL CREEK PRESBYTERIAN CHURCH, erected in 1818 after 4 earlier churches on the site had been destroyed by fire. The rectangular church of red brick and white-painted wooden trim has Gothic windows and a large gallery across the front. The plant includes an educational building, community house, and manse. The congregation was organized in 1762. The first bench of ruling elders (1767) of which there is a record includes Col. Robert Irwin and Zaccheus Wilson, members of the Mecklenburg Committee. Markers show the names of 13 Revolutionary soldiers buried in the church cemetery.

At **145 m.** is a side road.

Left on this road to WAYSIDE COTTAGE (*open*), **100 yds.**, a 6-room brick and frame cottage, headquarters of an organization working among shut-ins. Founded in 1926 by Harold C. (Old Wayside) Brown (d. 1942), ex-soldier of the British Army, poet, actor, himself confined to a wheel chair, the movement reached nearly 1,000 physically handicapped persons in all parts of the world. Activities included marketing of articles made by shut-ins, publication of a magazine, radio broadcasts, and much correspondence.

At **145.2 m.** is the entrance (L) to the CHARLOTTE MUNICIPAL AIRPORT.

At **149.8 m.** Wilkinson Blvd. crosses the Catawba River over the SOLDIERS MEMORIAL BRIDGE, honoring the World War dead of Gaston and Mecklenburg counties.

At **150 m.** is the junction with NC 7.

Left on NC 7 is BELMONT, **2 m.** (685 alt., 5,330 pop.), a textile manufacturing town and educational center. The site was settled in 1850 and was first called Garibaldi, reputedly for the builder of a railway water tank; later it was changed to honor August Belmont, a benefactor of the college.

Belmont is the seat of three institutions operated by orders of the Roman Catholic Church: SACRED HEART ACADEMY AND JUNIOR COLLEGE (1899), a girls' boarding school with an enrollment of 100, conducted by the Sisters of Mercy; ST. LEO'S SCHOOL (1910) for boys between 6 and 8 years of age, with about 100 pupils, and BELMOT ABBEY COLLEGE, conducted by the Benedictine Order, with an enrollment of 250. The college comprises a preparatory department, junior college, and schools of philosophy and theology. The Gothic church with twin towers has a Munster window.

BELMONT ABBEY occupies the site of the old Caldwell plantation, presented to Bishop (later Cardinal) Gibbons in 1876 by the Rev. Jeremiah O'Connell who had secured it immediately after the Civil War. A group of Benedictines came to establish a monastery in what was then a wilderness.

The frame chapel dedicated in 1877 to Mary, Help of Christians, later became known as Maryhelp. A small brick college building was erected, the beginning of the first Roman Catholic college in the middle South for the education of boys. The mission was made independent in 1884, and the community of Belmont received the official title Maryhelp Abbey.

Another honor came in 1910 when Pope Pius X formed an Abbey Nullius from 8 counties of the region. Bishop Leo Haid, in recognition of whose 25 years' administration Belmont Abbey was raised to the status of a cathedral, chose as the heraldic symbol of the institution the fir tree, with the motto Crescat (Lat., *let it grow*).

At **2.5 m.** is GOSHEN PRESBYTERIAN CHURCH, the first of this denomination west of the Catawba River, believed to have been organized in 1764, because in that year the Rev. Alexander McWhorter was sent by the Synod of New York and Philadelphia to "the back parts of North Carolina" to organize churches. The present frame church was built in 1839. Revolutionary patriots are buried in the old cemetery.

At 153 m. US 29-74 skirts CRAMERTON (633 alt., 3,211 pop.), an unincorporated town, whose land and utilities are owned by CRAMERTON MILLS, INC. (*display room and portions of plant open*), textile manufacturers.

At 158.3 m. is the junction with a paved road.

Left on this road to the NORTH CAROLINA ORTHOPEDIC HOSPITAL (160 beds), 1 m., in Babington Heights, one of the three institutions of its kind in the State. It was founded in 1921 by Robert Babington. The Benjamin N. Duke Memorial Ward is a 50-bed unit for Negro children.

GASTONIA, 161 m. (825 alt., 23,069 pop.), seat of Gaston County, is a textile-manufacturing town surrounded by a rich agricultural region. Within Gastonia's corporate limits are several mill communities; these, for the most part, are composed of identical though solidly constructed houses; 62 textile plants produce cotton yarn, tire fabric, bedspreads, sewing thread, knitting yarn, dress goods, upholstery fabrics, hosiery, and other textiles. Other industries include food products, leather, brick, iron and steel products, and automobile accessories. City and county were named for Judge William Gaston (*see* NEW BERN).

During a strike in 1929 at the Loray Mills here, Chief of Police O. F. Aderholt was killed in a skirmish. In a sensational trial at Charlotte 7 organizers were convicted of conspiracy to murder the chief and received sentences varying from 5 to 25 years. Ella May Wiggins, strike sympathizer and mother of 5, was killed when a truck-load of unarmed workers was fired upon. Several novels written about this strike include: *A Stone Came Rolling,* by Fielding Burke (Olive Dargan); *Strike,* by Mary Heaton Vorse; and *To Make My Bread,* by Grace Lumpkin.

Civic projects in Gastonia are a nutritional camp for undernourished children, and an interracial council to promote better understanding between whites and Negroes.

The GASTONIA COMMUNITY CENTER BUILDING, W. 2nd Ave., is centered by MEMORIAL HALL, a two-story building with an octagonal tower surrounded by a one-story arched porch across the front. It was erected by the citizens of Gastonia in memory of veterans of all wars. On each side is a low, one-story building of red brick—the GASTON PUBLIC LIBRARY (R) and the WOMAN'S CLUBHOUSE.

Gastonia is at the junction with US 74 (*see* TOUR *16*).

Right from West Gastonia on a narrow paved road to PISGAH CHURCH, 3 m., whose congregation was organized in 1793 by Associate Reformed Presbyterians who objected to the psalm singing at Goshen (*see* TOUR *16*) and at Long Creek, west of Bessemer City.

At 5 m. is KARYAE PARK, recreation and religious center of the Adelphotia Arachoviton Karyae, a society of Greek-Americans from Arachova, Greece. The organization, formed in 1932, purchased this tract at the foot of Crowders Mountain and built a chapel, pavilion, dining hall, and cottages. A convention is held annually (*Aug.*).

KINGS MOUNTAIN, 170 m. (963 alt., 7,206 pop.), chartered in 1874, is a textile-mill town near the scene of an important battle of the Revolution which bears the same name. In addition to the manufacture of yarn, men's hosiery, drapery, plush, and upholstery material, table damask and bed-spreads, mica and lithium plants are located here.

At Kings Mountain is the western junction with US 74 (*see* TOUR *16*).

At **176 m.** US 29 forms a junction with NC 216.

Left on this road, across the South Carolina Line, to KINGS MOUNTAIN NATIONAL MILITARY PARK, **5 m.** Established by Congress in 1931, the park contains 4,012 acres. On the crest of the ridge (1,040 alt.), 4 monuments have been erected. Notable among them are the CENTENNIAL MONUMENT, dedi-cated in 1880, and the UNITED STATES GOVERNMENT OBELISK, erected by Congress in 1909. Several markers have also been placed by patriotic organizations at his-toric points in the park. A small MUSEUM is located at the main parking area. From here a park road climbs the southwestern slope of the ridge to the upper parking area just below the crest. Foot trails lead to the site of the American troop positions and the British camp. To the east of the park is KINGS MOUNTAIN STATE PARK (*picnicking, swimming, organized camping*).

For 34 years after the Revolutionary battle (Oct. 7, 1780), the field was shunned even by the morbidly curious, but on July 15, 1815, Dr. William McLean, a survivor, with friends and relatives of the men who died there, met at the battlefield to inter the scattered bones and to commemorate with a marker the victory over the British.

The fierce attack of the 910 American frontiersmen composed of North Caro-linians, led by Col. Isaac Shelby, Col. John Sevier, and Maj. Joseph McDowell, and Virginians, led by Col. William Campbell, resulted in the annihilation or surrender of the 1,125 Tory forces of Maj. Patrick Ferguson of Cornwallis' command who had established themselves on the mountain. As the crest of the mountain was comparatively bare of trees, the bright red uniforms of the British and Tories made easy targets for the mountain men. The Whig loss was 28 killed and 62 wounded.

Though relatively isolated in conception and execution from the main course of the Revolution in the South, Kings Mountain is notable as supplying the first definite forewarning of the impending British military disasters in 1781.

The story of this Whig triumph has been written in novel form, *King's Mountain,* and later adapted to an outdoor drama, *The Sword of Gideon,* by Florette Henri. The play has been presented for 4 consecutive seasons (1951-54) in July and Aug. in the BATTLEFIELD AMPHITHEATRE.

US 29 crosses the South Carolina Line, **178 m.,** at the beginning of US 29-A, which leads to Gaffney, S. C., 15 miles.

TOUR 9 *(US 220)*

(Roanoke, Va.)—Greensboro—Asheboro—Rockingham.
Virginia Line—Rockingham, **123 m.**

US 220 follows a scenic route of the Allegheny Mountains to Roanoke, Va., where it swings almost due south to the North Carolina Line. From the North Carolina Line to its terminus at Rockingham it traverses the heart of the industrial piedmont in an almost straight line and drops from hills astir with busy mills to flat, sandy stretches of peach orchards.

US 220 crosses the State Line, **0 m.**, 4 miles south of Ridgeway, Va., and enters Rockingham County. PRICE, **0.5 m.** (1,003 alt., 75 pop.), lies in the bright-leaf tobacco-growing section and is a shipping point for hardwood timber.

At **2 m.** is the junction with a county road.

Left on this road to MATRIMONY CREEK, **5 m.**, which runs through a section referred to as the MEADOWS, being a part of the land granted to the North Carolina surveyors for their service in running the North Carolina-Virginia Line, 1728, and bought from them by Col. William Byrd (*see* TOUR *1a*). The tract embraced 20,000 acres in the valley of the Dan, which Byrd referred to as "an Eden land...a land of milk and honey...a place where everything grows plentiful to supply the wants of man...a land rich even unto the fabled lands about Babylon." However, the story is that he held it so lightly that he lost the land on one turn of the cards.

In his *History of the Dividing Line* Col. Byrd wrote: "About four Miles beyond the River Irvin (now Smith), we forded Matrimony Creek, call'd so by an unfortunate marry'd man, because it was exceedingly noisy and impetuous. However, tho' the Stream was clamorous, yet, like those Women who make themselves plainest heard, it was likewise clear and unsully'd."

STONEVILLE, **5 m.** (823 alt., 786 pop.), produces furniture, plush and upholstery, dresses, and tool handles and has 5 tobacco warehouses.

Left from Stoneville on NC 770 is LEAKSVILLE, **9 m.** (700 alt., 4,045 pop.), which is contiguous to SPRAY (5,542 pop.). These two towns are considered one community, because their textile and manufacturing interests are identical. DRAPER, **15 m.** (3,629 pop.), is a third town in this combination. These towns, known as the Tri-Cities, have three locally owned mills and 8 of Marshall Field

Co.'s plants, manufacturing bedding, curtains, woolen goods, and the Karaston American-Oriental rugs.

At Leaksville, John M. Morehead, later governor (1842-45), and his two sons operated one of the first textile plants in North Carolina. In 1892 Maj. James T. Morehead dropped some calcium carbide into water, while attempting to smelt aluminum in an open furnace. The carbide bubbled and the gas formed burned. Thus a cheap means of making acetylene gas was discovered, which led to the Union Carbide Company. This company is now planning a $30,000,000 Dynel plant between Spray and Draper which will make a wool-like fabric.

US 220 crosses the Mayo River at **8.5 m.**, then parallels it for several miles.

MAYODAN, **10 m.** (594 alt., 2,246 pop.) a cotton-mill town on the summit of Cedar Point Mountain, is named for the Mayo and Dan rivers. The WASHINGTON COTTON MILLS is one of the largest makers of men's and boys' knitwear in the world. A model mill-town, it has its own "city hall," paved streets, and a beautiful recreational area, MAYO PARK, which has a lake, bathhouse, and huge picnic assembly pavillion.

MADISON, **11.5 m.** (577 alt., 1,787 pop.), at the confluence of the Mayo and Dan rivers, is a market town for an agricultural area. It was laid out in 1818 by Randolph Duke Scales and named for James Madison who had relatives living nearby on Mayo River. About 1812 the Roanoke Transportation Co., organized by eastern capitalists to make the Dan navigable this far, created a boom in real estate. Its enterprises include tobacco auction warehouses, textiles, and hosiery mills.

BOXWOODS (*private*), Academy St., built in 1820 for Randolph Duke Scales, is a much remodeled red brick mansion, two and a half stories high. An addition has been built on the north end. The house stands upon an eminence overlooking the Dan River and the fields where the owner used to watch his slaves at work. The doorway in the original front of the house has a fanlight and reeded ornamentations. In 1846 Scales left the house, then called Rural Retreat, upon a sudden impulse, and with his family and slaves moved to Mississippi. The beautiful boxwoods were brought as slips from Pittsylvania County, Va., about 1850.

Madison is at the junction with US 311 (*see* TOUR 9A).

At **12.5 m.** is the junction with NC 704.

Left on NC 704, **4 m.** and **0.5 m.** E., is the SITE OF ALEXANDER MARTIN'S HOME. Martin was governor (1782-85; 1789-92), officer in the Revolution, and member of the Federal Convention.

MULBERRY ISLAND FARM (*private*), **6 m.**, is a white-painted mansion with columned veranda, surrounded by pines and oaks. On the 1,104-acre estate is a stable for show horses. The house was built by Judge Thomas Settle (1831-88), a member of the N. C. Supreme Court during the Reconstruction period.

Moore's Knob (R) and Hanging Rock (R), of the Sauratown Mountains, are conspicuous from the highway at **17 m.**

At **20.5 m.** is the junction with US 158 (*see* TOUR *12*).

At **25.5 m.** is a junction with NC 150 and with an unnumbered road.

At the SW. corner of the crossroads is an OLD BRICK HOUSE (*private*), dated 1840 by a deed to Alexander S. Martin, son of Gov. Martin.

Right on NC 150 to the OLD SANDERS HOUSE (*private*), **1 m.**, a two-story, 4-room house, built in 1815, faced with the original beaded weatherboarding. The brick chimney at the right end of the house is laid in Flemish bond with glazed headers in a diamond pattern. The exterior has been altered past recognition with a central gable and brackets and a modern porch and door. The most notable original features are wide tongued and grooved wall boards, 12-light windows, and HL hinges. This house was once Hezekiah Sanders' inn where stagecoaches changed horses. In 1822 Sydney Porter of New England breakfasted here and remained for a while to teach in a community school. Later he moved his family to Greensboro, where his son, O. Henry, was born.

SUMMERFIELD, **26.5 m.** (881 alt., 700 pop.), was originally called Bruce's Crossroads for Charles Bruce who owned the site, but in 1812 it was named Summerfield in honor of a visiting evangelist.

The BRUCE PLANTATION was the colonial homestead of Charles Bruce, a member of the committee that framed the N. C. Constitution. His home served as the meeting place of the Friends of Liberty prior to the Revolutionary War. During a skirmish between "Light-Horse Harry" Lee and Col. Tarleton, Feb. 12, 1781, Lee's bugler, a boy named James Gillies, was killed. He is buried here in the Bruce family graveyard. The British soldiers who slew this unarmed boy were later captured, executed, and buried near the crossroads. The Bruce house was burned shortly after his death, and another was built on this site.

In front of the Summerfield public school building is a MEMORIAL TO CHARLES BRUCE AND JAMES GILLIES.

Albion Tourgée, who came to North Carolina from New York, drew his character of the Negro blacksmith in *A Fool's Errand* from an ex-slave on the Purcell plantation in this vicinity.

The OLD McNAIRY HOUSE (R), **31 m.**, was built about 1761 by Francis McNairy, a Revolutionary patriot. John McNairy, who was appointed the first federal judge in the Tennessee territory, was born here, and Andrew Jackson lived here with the McNairy family adjacent to the village of Guilford Courthouse during the first year following his reading law under Judge Spruce Macay at Salisbury. He was appointed first U. S. Attorney for the territory of Tennessee and left for Tennessee with Judge John McNairy. Jackson is said to have first practiced law at Guilford Courthouse, and he probably "rode the circuit" to appear in the courts of the neighboring counties. While in Guilford, Jackson is said to have enjoyed the sports of cock fighting and horse racing, and his racing paths were in the neighborhood of the McNairy house and the village of Guilford Courthouse. The house, narrow in proportion to its height, is weatherboarded but probably had simple flat siding of wide boards, some of which are visible around the entrance. There are two small rooms on each of the two floors, and the boards of the inside walls are finely tongued and grooved. In the lower left room is a fireplace unusually elaborate for so modest a building, with the design composed entirely of reeded paneling.

At **32.5 m.** is the junction with a marked road.

Left on this road to LAKE BRANDT (*stocked with perch, bream*), **2 m.**, source of Greensboro's water supply.

US 220 at **33 m.** enters the 119-acre GUILFORD COURTHOUSE NATIONAL MILITARY PARK, scene of the Battle of Guilford Courthouse on Mar. 15, 1781. Here, between Hunting and Horse Pen Creeks, Cornwallis' 2,000 trained soldiers met the Americans under Gen. Nathanael Greene, 1,420 veterans and 2,984 raw recruits. Though Cornwallis held the field, Connor says that Greene's men "outmarched, outmaneuvered, and outfought their better-equipped adversaries," and the encounter so crippled the British that it paved the way for the surrender at Yorktown. After the Revolution the settlement at Guilford Courthouse was named Martinville in honor of Gov. Alexander Martin (*see above*).

Within the park are monuments to many Revolutionary heroes. The GENERAL GREENE MEMORIAL is an equestrian statue, modeled by Francis Herman Packer and erected by the U. S. Government in 1915. The statue is mounted on a granite shaft surrounded by a granite platform.

The COLONIAL COLUMN has 4 large shields bearing historic items, a bronze figure representing a Continental soldier, and a tablet portraying a man with a rope around his neck representing the Regulators hanged after the Battle of Alamance (*see* TOUR *15B*). The WINSTON MONUMENT, erected in 1893 by Gov. Thomas M. Holt, honors the North Carolina troops under Maj. Joseph Winston who remained fighting the Hessians and Tarleton's cavalry after the Continental Line had withdrawn from the battle. The MARYLAND MONUMENT, a rough granite shaft bearing the State seal, was presented by the historical society of that State in memory of the Maryland soldiers who fell here.

Other monuments honor John Penn and William Hooper, North Carolina signers of the Declaration of Independence, whose remains were reinterred here in 1894; Gillies, the bugler; Dr. David Caldwell; the famous giant, "Peter Francisco"; and Judge David Schenck, who organized the Guilford Battle Ground Co. in 1887. In 1917 this company deeded to the Federal Government for a national military park the land with the monuments. The MUSEUM (*open 9-5*), in the administration building, contains relics of the Revolution. This two-story brick structure is in the colonial tradition. A clapboard ell on the left is balanced by a porch on the right.

At **33.2 m.** is the junction with a marked road.

Left on this road to 270-acre GREENSBORO COUNTRY PARK, **0.8 m.**, a recreational development (*water sports*) lying on both sides of Hunting Creek, adjoining the Guilford Courthouse Park boundary.

GREENSBORO, 39 m. (*see* GREENSBORO).

Points of Interest: Woman's College, Greensboro College, Greensboro Historical Museum and Library, Masonic Temple and O. Henry Birthplace, Gov. Morehead Home, Sedgefield, Lorillard Cigarette Factory, Jefferson Standard Building, Cone Textile Mills, and others.

Greensboro is at the junction with US 421 (*see* TOUR *17*); US 70 (*see* TOUR *15*), and US 29 (*see* TOUR *8*).

RANDLEMAN, 59.3 m. (712 alt., 2,066 pop.), is a textile and hosiery manufacturing center. It also was the home of Naomi Wise, whose murder at Naomi Bridge about 1800 by her treacherous lover furnished the theme for the ballad, the *Sorrowful Fate of Naomi Wise.*

South of Randleman the route traverses a hilly region.

At **59.5 m.** is the junction with US 311 (*see* TOUR *9A*).

From this point there is a panorama of the Uharie (Uwharrie) Mountain Range. Through the valley to the west winds the Uharie River.

ASHEBORO, 65 m. (879 alt., 7,701 pop.), seat of Randolph County, was named for Samuel Ashe, Governor of North Carolina (1795-98), and the county for Peyton Randolph of Virginia, President of Continental Congress. When the county was formed in 1779, the site of the town was a wilderness. The first courthouse was at a place called Cross Roads, until 1788 when it was established at Johnstonville, named for Gov. Samuel Johnston (*see* EDENTON). After 14 years it was moved to Asheboro. Jesse Henley conveyed two acres upon which the first courthouse was built.

Asheboro owes its early industrial development to water power furnished by two rivers, the Deep and the Uharie, along which several mills were built. The 40 or more industrial units include hosiery mills, a chemical company, lumber and furniture plants, box, mattress, garter, and broom factories.

This section was the home of the Keyauwee, the Saponi—for whom the Deep River was once called the Sapong—and several other small tribes of Indians before the coming of the white man. The Indian Trading Path between Virginia and Salisbury passed just north of Asheboro. Along this path near Shepherd Mountain the site of an Indian village was discovered and the burial ground nearby excavated in 1936. Numerous skeletons, weapons, and other artifacts found are on display at the University of North Carolina (*see* CHAPEL HILL).

The first white settlers in this region are believed to have been Germans fleeing from the wars of Europe about 1740. Shortly thereafter came English, Irish, and Scots, the latter in the greater numbers. The annual field trials (*late Sept.*) of the Fox Hunters Association of North Carolina and a bench show for fox hounds are held here. Fox hunts are held in the Uharie Mountains to the southwest.

At **68.5 m.** are the RANDOLPH COUNTY FAIRGROUNDS where an annual fair is held in October.

Asheboro was the home of Gov. Jonathan Worth (1865-68) and State treasurer (1862-65). The highway through Asheboro follows the route of the Fayetteville-Bethania Road, a toll road 129 miles long, built in 1849-54.

At **78.5 m.** is the junction with NC 705.

1. Left on NC 705 to the junction with a marked road, **6 m.**; L. **2.8 m.** on this road to JUGTOWN, noted for its pottery. Here the "lost art" of pottery making was revived by the late Mr. Jacques Busbee, a portrait painter, and his wife, Juliana Royster, an art photographer, who since 1915 have dedicated themselves to the re-creation of this art. From information gleaned from local potters, believed to be descended from Staffordshire potters of England, they have faithfully reproduced the shapes and colors ("tobacco-spit brown," "frog skin green," etc.) of pottery used over a century ago. An old-fashioned clay grinding and mixing machine derives its "horse-power" from a mule. The clay is then turned on a kickwheel and the resulting soft dishes, vases, pots, or jugs are allowed to dry, after which they are placed in a kiln where heat from 1,500 to 2,500 degrees is applied.

The crude log cabin in which the pottery is displayed is typical of the early homes of this section. Particularly interesting is the overhang of the roof which protects the clay-and-stone chimney from the rain.

2. Right on NC 705 to the GRAVE OF COL. ANDREW BALFOUR, Col. Balfour, an ardent Whig in the Revolution, was killed by Col. David Fanning, Tory leader (*see* TOURS *7, 13, and 15*).

At **80.5 m.** is the junction with a marked road.

Left on this road to COLE'S POTTERY, **3.5 m.**, one of the oldest in North Carolina and known for unusual glazes.

BISCOE, **91.5 m.** (609 alt., 1,034 pop.), is at the northern end of the peach belt.

Biscoe is at the junction with NC 27.

Right on NC 27, through the northern edge of Montgomery County's peach belt, across Little River, **4.2 m.**, to TROY, **7 m.** (664 alt., 2,213 pop.), a town of unusually broad streets and wide lawns. In 1846 Troy became the seat of Montgomery County, formed from Anson in 1779 and named for Brig. Gen. Richard Montgomery, who fell while attempting to scale the Citadel heights of Quebec on Dec. 31, 1775.

After the present MONTGOMERY COUNTY COURTHOUSE had been erected in 1921, business failed to follow it up the hill where the three-story cream-colored brick building stands in lonely grandeur.

At WADEVILLE, **14.3 m.**, NC 109 leads to MOUNT GILEAD, **5 m.** (421 alt., 1,201 pop.) which serves a fertile farm area and an adjoining power development. Its industries include a large garment factory, two hosiery mills, two lumber plants, and a brick mill.

1. Right from Mount Gilead **4 m.** on NC 731 to HYDRO (55 pop.), employees' village of the Carolina Light and Power Co. This neat village overlooks the waters of LAKE TILLERY, formerly Norwood Lake, a 6,000-acre hydro-electric power reservoir formed by damming the Yadkin River. From the Hydro dam and POWER PLANT (*open; special guides for visitors*), the lake (*stocked with*

white perch, bass, and catfish) extend 18 miles north into the foothills of the Uharie National Forest.

CANDOR, 96.5 m. (729 alt., 617 pop.), is the marketing center for the peach growers of the region that extends west to Aberdeen and south to Rockingham. Here in 1928 the first commercially successful peach orchard in this area was planted by M. R. Clark, who set out 30,000 trees a mile from the town. More than 200 orchards have since that time grown to maturity. Their blossoms (*late Mar. and early Apr.*) delight visitors. Gold was formerly mined at Candor, and the region yields excellent pottery clay.

Left from Candor on NC 211 is SAMARCAND, 4 m. (698 alt., 50 pop), the North Carolina State Home and Industrial School for Girls and Women. *Sand in my Shoes* by Katherine Ball Ripley (1931) recounts the experiences of the author on the peach orchard of Samarcand.

At 97.5 m. is the junction with NC 731 (R).

Right on NC 731; at 6 m. the road passes through a section several miles long, which contains petrified wood. Yellow-brown to steel gray in color, it occurs in pieces as large as 10 inches long and 6 in diameter.

At PEKIN, 10.5 m. an unmarked road to the right leads 1.5 m. to the SITE OF FLORA MACDONALD'S HOME on Cheek's Creek (*see* FAYETTEVILLE). Flora and Allen MacDonald settled here with 8 indentured servants in 1775. The place was abandoned by Flora after Allen was captured as a Tory prisoner at the battle of Moore's Creek Bridge.

NC 731 continues from Pekin to a road (L) at 14.7 m., which leads to TOWN CREEK INDIAN MOUND, now operated as a 53-acre State Historical Park. This ancient center was used by Muskhogean-speaking Indians of the Pee Dee area as a council and burying ground 300 or more years ago. The mound and the palisade surrounding it has been restored, and restoration on the temple on the mound is now underway.

NORMAN, 107.5 m. (300 pop.), containing a large lumber mill, is a marketing town for an agricultural section.

At 112 m. is ELLERBE SPRINGS, one of the old health resorts of the State. Once a mecca for those suffering from asthma and hay fever, it has an old hotel now used by Boy Scouts as a camping ground.

ELLERBE, 113 m. (773 pop.), has a hosiery mill and several cotton gins. The early Highland Scot settlers organized a Scottish Fair here at the foot of the Uharies for games, horse-racing, drinking, dances, and music. As a result, it was long known as the Fair Grounds. Ellerbe, the fruit-packing center of a wide peach-growing area, also has two tobacco auction warehouses and a hosiery and lumber mill.

ROCKINGHAM, 123 m. (*see* TOUR 5), is at the junction with US 1 (*see* TOUR 5) and US 74 (*see* TOUR 16).

TOUR 9A *(US 311)*

Madison—Winston-Salem—High Point—Junction with US 220; US 311.
65 m.

Between Madison and High Point this route penetrates an agricultural
section whose rolling fields are rimmed by the distant Sauratown Mountains.
Through a region of once-popular mineral springs, the highway enters the
industrial area of Winston-Salem and High Point. This stretch is typical
of the piedmont, where the economic structure is a composite of agriculture
and industry.

Southwest of MADISON, 0 m. (*see* TOUR 9), stretches of woodland break
the monotony of the small but thrifty farms, with their chinked-log tobacco
barns.

Between 5 m. and 9 m. the route runs through the fertile bottom lands
of the Dan River.

At 6.8 m. is the junction with NC 772.

Left on NC 772 at 0.8 m. is PINE HALL (*private*), a brick building with a
small white two-story porch built about 1857 by L. W. Anderson. During the
Civil War, Anderson was a major in the Quartermaster Corps, and his home was
used as the collection point in the area for supplies for the Confederate forces.
Agricultural supplies, collected usually by means of a "Tax in Kind," were
shipped down the Dan River to Danville to supply the army in Virginia.
At 7 m. is the town of PINE HALL (579 alt., 400 pop.), which takes its name
from the Anderson Plantation and is the site of one of the largest plants engaged
in the manufacture of face brick and clay products in the State.

Just south of the DAN RIVER PARK (*swimming, picnicking*), 9.6 m.,
a recreational area lying on a hilltop, the highway crosses the river and
low-lying cornfields.

Right at 10.8 m. on a dirt road is SAURATOWN HALL, 1.1 m. (*private*),
originally the home of Peter W. Hairston, who settled here (according to the
family Bible) at 8 o'clock on April 11, 1786. That same year Hairston was
operating, with J. A. Martin, an "Iron Works" (Union Iron Works) on the Dan
River. He represented Stokes County in the legislature in 1792, 1796, 1799, and
1800. In the early 1800's his daughter, Ruth Stovall Hairston, and her husband

built another mansion on the south side of the river, the original one having burned. This brick house, which is T-shaped with two wings set back, has been recently faced with weather-boarding, but it is well preserved and furnished with many of its original pieces. In 1862, when the plantation was perhaps at its height, it included (according to a listing in a Confederate tax book) 14,280 acres of land valued at $98,462 and 379 slaves valued at $125,300. Peter Hairston, II, of Sauratown married Columbia Stuart, the sister of Gen. J. E. B. Stuart, C. S. A., who frequently visited Sauratown Hall. Peter Hairston, II, served as a major on Stuart's staff.

At 12.4 m. is the junction with NC 89 (see TOUR 9B).

WALNUT COVE, 13 m. (634 alt., 1,132 pop.), was first called Lashes or Lash for the Lash family, who settled in the area in the early 1800's. Dr. William A. Lash built an 18-room brick home here in the middle of his fine meadow property. The colored glass windows, bell-shaped turret, and jigsaw scrollwork in the gables belong to the period following the Civil War. The chief industrial establishments of Walnut Cove today are a veneer plant and a lumber company.

Right on NC 65, 4.9 m. is GERMANTON (662 alt., 118 pop.), the county seat of Stokes County (1790-1849). The first courthouse, of log, was replaced with the brick courthouse that still stands in the center of town. Other landmarks include the old METHODIST CHURCH (1851), still in use, which has a slave balcony. The MASONIC LODGE (1850) was later used as a girl's boarding school and is now a private home. Other large homes here such as the Bynum and Hill homes date from the period following the Civil War. Germanton was also the site of the home of Benjamin Forsythe, Revolutionary hero for whom Forsyth County was named; Joseph Winston, war hero and legislator for whom the city of Winston, later Winston-Salem, was named; and Anthony Hampton, great grandfather of Gen. Wade Hampton of South Carolina. The descendants of Gray Bynum, one of the first settlers of Germanton, included Maj. Gen. John Gray Bynum, soldier and U. S. Congressman; his son John Gray Bynum, Jr., Superior Court Judge; and William P. Bynum, Associate Justice of the State Supreme Court. All these men were born in Germanton but later moved to other parts of the State.
Many Indian relics have been found near Germanton, and it is probable that the Saura Indians centered a town near here on the Town Fork Creek before 1700. The term "Upper Saura Town" appears on many old maps and probably refers to this spot, since the land here, well watered and cleared by the Indians, was a natural choice for the first settlers of the county.

Southwest of WALKERTOWN, 22.5 m. (980 alt., 677 pop.), US 311 runs through a section of small homes. Many are occupied by industrial workers employed in Winston-Salem.

WINSTON-SALEM, 30 m. (see WINSTON-SALEM).

Points of Interest: Old Salem, Home Moravian Church, Salem College, R. J. Reynolds Tobacco Plant, Wake Forest College, and others.

Winston-Salem is at the junction with US 52 (see TOUR 10), US 421 (see TOUR 17), and US 158 (see TOUR 12).

Southeast of Winston-Salem US 311 runs through an area where crops are diversified and many of the farmers supplement their incomes by employment in nearby industrial towns.

At **48 m.** is the junction with NC 68.

Left on NC 68 to DEEP RIVER QUAKER MEETINGHOUSE, **5 m.**, a simple, box-like brick structure, 5 bays long, with segmental-arched windows. A chimney occupies the usual position of a tower. The meeting was organized in 1758 and the earliest church on this site, erected in 1778, was used until 1875 when the present building was erected.

HIGH POINT, **49 m.** (*see* HIGH POINT).

Points of Interest: Tomlinson Furniture Plant, Southern Furniture Exposition Building, High Point College, Blair Park, and others.

High Point is at the junction with US 29-70 (*see* TOURS *8 and 15*).

At **51 m.**, two blocks S. of the junction with the new superhighway, US 29-70, is the junction with the Springfield Rd.

Left on the Springfield Rd. **0.5 m.** are the historic grounds and buildings of the SPRINGFIELD MEETINGHOUSE. The community, settled in 1773, is the ancestor of the progressive industrial city of High Point.

The present (third) Meetinghouse, built in 1858, is used as a MUSEUM OF OLD DOMESTIC ARTS. Hundreds of items formerly used in the community have been preserved in this building which was patterned after the second one built in 1800. The shutters used for separating the men from the women during meeting are still to be seen.

The ALLEN JAY HOUSE, built about 1790, stands across the road from the minister's home. It has been restored and is used as an addition to the Museum with two rooms used for a caretaker. It was remodeled in 1867 to be used by Allen Jay, a Friends Minister who came from Indiana to work here during the Reconstruction period.

The fourth Meetinghouse on this site is joined to the Museum by a colonnade. It is a handsome brick structure of colonial design with a smaller facsimile chapel added. Tall grandfather clocks dating back to the early years of the Meeting, each with a history of its own, stand on each side of the pulpit.

In the cemetery, among the old, scarcely legible stones, grow dozens of handsome old English boxwoods. Here are buried Nathan Hunt, founder of New Garden Boarding school, now Guilford College; Tabitha Holton, the first woman lawyer in North Carolina; David H. Blair, U. S. Commissioner of Internal Revenue; John Braselton, William Millikan, and Hannah Blair, revolutionary patriots; as well as many of the early Englishes, Blairs, Tomlinsons, and Haworths.

The first normal school in North Carolina for training teachers was held here, and the old globes used in this school in 1867 may be seen in the Museum. The first MODEL FARM and the first bone mill in the South were also established here, and items from these are preserved in the Museum. The first Sabbath School in North Carolina was also started here.

South of High Point US 311 follows the route of several old roads. This was originally the Indian Trail from the upper Yadkin to the Atlantic Ocean. Then it was used by the Moravians at Salem as a wagon road (*see*

WINSTON-SALEM). A century later it became the Fayetteville and Western Plank Rd., whose 129-mile stretch was the longest ever constructed in the State (*see* HIGH POINT). The plank roads fell into decay during the Civil War and were practically abandoned during Reconstruction days.

US 311 skirts the edge of ARCHDALE, 53 m. (1,218 pop.), established as Bush Hill in 1773 by Quakers. In 1887 it was renamed for the Quaker, John Archdale, Governor of North Carolina (1694-96). Oaks, willows, and elms shade streets lined with comfortable little homes. Though it formerly had its own tanneries and mills it is now virtually a residential suburb of High Point. From 1885 to 1889 the *North Carolina Prohibitionist* was published here.

Right from Archdale on NC 61 is TRINITY, 1 m. (850 alt., 764 pop.), settled in the latter part of the 18th century by Quakers and Methodists. In front of the modern high school is the marked SITE OF TRINITY COLLEGE, established here as Union Institute in 1838. Quaker patronage of the Friends' school at New Garden gave Methodists control of Union Institute, which became Normal College in 1851, and Trinity College in 1859. The school gained a wide reputation for scholarship before it was moved to Durham in 1892, where in 1924 it became the nucleus of Duke University (*see* DURHAM).

In GLENOLA, 57 m. (100 pop.), is a brickyard where fire and building brick are made from the local red and ivory clay.

Left from Glenola to a cemetery containing the GRAVE OF MARTHA BELL, 2 m., Revolutionary heroine. Nearby was the plantation and gristmill of Martha's husband, William Bell, first sheriff of Randolph County. Martha ran both mill and house while he was with the American troops.
Legend relates that when Gen. Cornwallis asked that he might make the Bell house his headquarters and use the mill to grind corn for his soldiers, Mrs. Bell inquired: "Is it your intention, General, to burn the house and mill when you have done with them?" He replied in the negative, whereupon Mrs. Bell remarked that if he had any such intention she would burn them herself. It is said that soon after Cornwallis' departure, Col. "Light Horse Harry" Lee and Col. William Washington arrived and asked her to learn, if possible, when Cornwallis had received his latest reinforcements. Riding into the British lines some distance away, armed with dirk and pistols, Mrs. Bell made a thorough check of the strength of the army and returned to report her findings to the Americans. This was the first of many occasions on which she was able to supply information concerning the movements of the British in the vicinity.

South of Glenola the country is rolling and the low hills of the Uharie Range are referred to locally as mountains. The farms produce cereals, vegetables, and melons.

SOPHIA, 61.5 m. (801 alt., 250 pop.), was settled before 1779 by Pennsylvanians of German ancestry. They named the town for the Electress of Hanover, mother of George I of England. Sophia was established in the midst of hardwood forests, most of which have been cut, leaving only the smaller oak that is hewn into cross ties.

At 65 m. is the junction with US 220 (*see* TOUR 9).

TOUR 9B *(NC 89)*

Junction with US 311—Danbury—Piedmont Springs; NC 89. 11.6 m.

NC 89 branches northwest from its junction with US 311, 0 m., 0.6 miles north of Walnut Cove *(see* TOUR 9*A)*, and crosses low mountains, with Moore's Knob and its Hanging Rock conspicuous on the L.

At **2.6 m.** is the COVINGTON HOME *(private)*, a 10-room frame house built in 1820 with a two-story veranda across the front. Behind the house family graves date from 1780. Since 1948 the house has been completely restored. Col. Matthew Covington, who did much to build up an extensive plantation, operated a plug tobacco factory in a two-story building only 200 yards from his home.

From MEADOWS, **5 m.** (50 pop.), at the intersection with the Germanton Road, is a striking view of the Dan River Valley (R).

DANBURY, **9 m.** (825 alt., 250 pop.), at the foot of the Sauratown Mountains near the Dan River, is the seat of Stokes County, still characterized by a description made by a traveler in 1878 as "that beautiful mountain town where every man takes his time—where there is time for every man." Stokes County, formed in 1789, was named for Col. John Stokes, a Revolutionary officer, member of the original Board of Trustees of the University of North Carolina, and the State's first Federal district judge, appointed by George Washington.

The Union Iron Works was known to have operated here as early as 1786, but no town was established. In 1849 the general assembly divided Stokes County, and despite the contrary wording of the law, the northern half of the county remained Stokes and the lower half became Forsyth County. In 1851 the new county seat of Stokes County was formally named and designated as Crawford, but in 1852 the legislature changed it to Danbury.

Standing on a high bank overlooking the highway is (R) the FULTON BRICK HOUSE *(private)*, built in the early 1800's for Winston Fulton. It has three stories, 10 rooms, and a broad porch. An account book used by Fulton gives side lights on trade from 1850 to 1855. Payment was usually made in labor or with barrels of apples, pounds of wool, deer skins, and other commodities. In 1870, S. B. Taylor built a hotel beside it, and later the house and hotel were joined, as they are today.

The first courthouse, built shortly after 1849 when Forsyth County was separated from Stokes, was replaced in 1902 with the present STOKES COUNTY COURTHOUSE, a brick structure in the center of a shady square surrounded by a few old houses. The MOODY TAVERN (*private*), beside the courthouse, was built about 1841 by Nathaniel Moody. It is a long, narrow, three-story, weatherboarded structure, with a two-storied veranda across the wide front elevation. Since the establishment of Danbury as the county-town the building has been used as a hotel, first as the Moody Tavern and then as the McCanless Hotel. It was here on April 9, 1865 (the day Lee surrendered at Appomatox), that Gen. Stoneman on a raid through western North Carolina made his headquarters.

Many well known lawyers have lived and practiced law in Danbury. Two governors of North Carolina, R. B. Glenn and Thomas W. Bickett, began their law practices here but were elected to the governorship from other towns.

In 1876, Dr. John Pepper began, with his sons, the *Danbury Reporter,* which is still published by the Pepper family and is one of the oldest county weeklies in North Carolina. A fire in the '70's destroyed the original *Reporter* office, but the first press was dragged out of the burning building and leaned against a small tree. A new press was acquired, and the old one was left abandoned against the tree, which today has grown up, imbedding the press in its trunk like a monument.

North Carolina's "tribute block" in the Washington Monument (built 1848-84) in the National Capital was quarried in Stokes County near Danbury, taken by wagon to Fayetteville and by water to Washington.

Right from Danbury to the ROGER'S MAGNETIC IRON ORE DEPOSITS, **2.5 m.,** near the Dan River. Here, during the Civil War, the Confederate Government mined ore and shipped it down the river to a furnace near Danbury. Gen. Stoneman and his Union cavalrymen halted the enterprise. The mine was again in operation in 1939. The old furnace, built of local stone, remains. A tram that ran on rails, similar to the one used in building the State capitol in Raleigh, brought stone from a nearby quarry for construction of the furnace.

At **11.6 m.** is the Piedmont Springs settlement, at the junction with a dirt road.

Left on this road to the once fashionable PIEDMONT SPRINGS HOTEL, **0.2 m.** (L), marked by an abandoned pavilion and a broken fountain. Three summer resort hotels have burned here. The most famous attraction was the spring, which featured freestone and mineral water side by side.

At **1.2 m.** is the junction with a marked road.

Right at **1.6 m.** is a junction with another marked road.

Left on this road **2.3 m.** to HANGING ROCK STATE PARK (*boating, swimming, picnicking, fishing, camping*), a recreational area of 3,865 acres in the heart of the Sauratown Mountains. The land, given by interested citizens, lies wholly within a 40,000-acre State game preserve. The formation for which the park was named is a point of solid rock at the end of a long ridge with a perpendicular drop of 175 feet. A 15-acre lake, bathhouse, and picnic pavilion were completed by C. C. C. labor in 1940. The bathhouse and swimming area have been enlarged since 1948 to accommodate 2,000 bathers at a time. Foot trails (*guides available at Administration Office*) from the swimming area make Cook's Wall, Upper Cascade, Moore's Knob, and Hanging Rock easily accessible. MOORE'S KNOB (2,572 alt.), the highest peak in the Sauratown range, is surmounted by a stone fire tower and during World War I was used for a time as a Signal Corps Observation Point.

Most of the rocks of the Sauratown Mountains were originally sandstone, but, under conditions of great heat and pressure, they were changed to massive quartzites and foliated rocks, such as quartz-schist and quartz-mica schist. Hanging Rock, Cook's Wall, and Moore's Knob owe their greater height to the fact that they are composed of quartzite, which has superior resistance to erosion; the softer surrounding rocks have eroded, leaving these peaks. Here (and in Brazil) is also found a rare and peculiar variety of sandstone, itacolumite, known locally as flexible sandstone, which may be easily bent.

Left at **1.9 m.** on a dirt road to CASCADE FALLS. Beyond the falls a road passes by COOK'S WALL which, though a natural formation, appears to have been man-made. At the foot of Cook's Wall is the famous TORIES DEN, which during the Revolution was supposed to have been a secret meeting place of the Tories. Seepage has filled in much of the cave, but old records describe it as having been of unusual size, made up of naturally formed rooms, one of which was for years filled with bones of animals that had served the Tory food supply.

At **4.1 m.** on the hard surface road is the MOORE'S SPRINGS community. It grew up around the old Moore's Springs resort hotel, now burned down. The mineral spring here still makes the spot a popular tourist stop. Largely of a sulfa type, the water is often bottled and shipped as far as California to people who still attest to its curative powers.

Left at **4.6 m.** on a dirt road is the old MOORE HOUSE (*private*). According to a date on the chimney, the house was built in 1778, which makes it one of the oldest houses in the section. It is a two-story, 8-room house built of brick and shows definite influences of the architecture of Salem. The walls are 8 bricks thick, and the windows on the side are very small. Fireplaces were built in the corner of the rooms with an opening in the wall so that one fire could serve two rooms. Probably built by the Moore family, it was at one time the home of Hardin W. Reynolds, father of Richard J. Reynolds (*see* WINSTON-SALEM). It is situated on a knoll overlooking the Dan River, with a beautiful panoramic view of the entire Sauratown Mountain range.

Right at **4.9 m.** on another dirt road to VADE MECUM SPRINGS (1,800 alt., 100 pop.). The alkaline water is similar to that of Carlsbad. Between 1900-02 two 40-room resort hotels and 11 cottages were built here and for many years operated as the Vade Mecum Springs Hotel. Eventually one of the hotels burned and the development of the automobile popularized more distant vacation spots. The property is now leased to the Episcopal Church for a summer camp. An Indian legend tells that Nikawita, who loved Nanlahwah, was banished by Nanlahwah's chieftain father, because he favored another warrior, Dhonide. Nikawita, however, returned, and the maiden met him at the spring. As they embraced, Dhonide's arrow pierced Nikawita's temple. When Dhonide emerged from his hiding place to take the girl, the waters of the stream rose, engulfed the spring, and carried the two to their deaths. Hence the name, Vade Mecum (Lat., *go with me*). As long as the Saura Indians remained in these mountains the stream flowed over the spring, thus denying the tribe the curative waters in punishment for the sacrilege committed on its banks. About 1850 S. W. Dewey, a New England physician interested in developing the potential mineral resources of the area, diverted the stream, and the spring was reclaimed.

At **8 m.** is the junction with NC 66 near Gap (*see* TOUR *10*).

TOUR 10 (US 52)

(Hillsville, Va.)—Winston-Salem—Salisbury—Albemarle—(Cheraw, S. C.);
US 52.
Virginia Line—South Carolina Line, **152 m.**

Section a. VIRGINIA LINE *to* SALISBURY; 78 m. US 52

This route runs through the Blue Ridge Mountains and the western half of the piedmont plateau, penetrating sections devoted to industrial as well as agricultural pursuits.

Known as the Fancy Gap Scenic Highway, US 52 crosses the North Carolina Line, **0 m.**, 17 miles south of Hillsville, Va. Between the State Line and Mount Airy, apple orchards line the highway, which makes a twisting descent into the "Hollow," a saucerlike depression circled by mountains.

Lying within the Hollow's little plateau is MOUNT AIRY, **5 m.** (1,104 alt., 7,192 pop.), with homes, stores, post office, and churches constructed of the beautiful local gray granite. Besides its quarry the town has textile and hosiery mills and a tobacco auction warehouse.

1. Left from Mount Airy on NC 89 to the MOUNT AIRY GRANITE QUARRY (*open*), **1 m.**, one of the largest and best-equipped open-face granite quarries in the world. One hundred thousand carloads of granite have been shipped for use in such structures as the Wright Memorial at Kitty Hawk (*see* TOUR 1A), the Arlington Memorial Bridge, and the Union Trust Building in the National Capital. A single finished stone often fills a flatcar.

2. Right from Mount Airy on US 601 through hilly country. At **5.3 m.** in WHITE PLAINS (1,150 alt., 550 pop.), on opposite sides of Stewarts Creek, are the HOMES OF THE ORIGINAL SIAMESE TWINS, Eng (meaning *right*) and Chang (meaning *left*) Bunker. Born at Bangesau, Siam, Apr. 15, 1811, of a Chinese father and a Siamese mother, the twins were connected by a thick fleshy ligament joining the lower ends of the breastbones.

They were brought to this country in 1829 by an American ship captain. The surname Bunker was adopted from a bystander at the immigration office when the twins were told they must have a family name. P. T. Barnum exhibited them and gave them wide publicity.

In 1842, in Wilkes County, they married twin sisters, Sallie and Adelaide Yates. They later moved here where they divided their time in three-day periods between the two homes and reared large families. Many of their descendants live in the community. The twins died within an hour of each other in 1874 and were first buried in the garden of one of the homes. Their remains were later moved to the cemetery of the Baptist Church here, where a double monument marks the GRAVE OF THE SIAMESE TWINS.

In DOBSON, **13.8 m.** (1,265 alt., 609 pop.), is the fourth SURRY COUNTY COURTHOUSE (1918), a brick building containing records complete since the county was formed in 1771. At old Richmond in the northwest part of present Forsyth County was Curry County's first courthouse where, on Nov. 12, 1787, Andrew Jackson was admitted to the practice of law. Gen. Stoneman's U. S. Cavalry passed through here on a raid April 2, 1865.

On US 601 at **14.6 m.** is the junction with a graveled road.

1. Left **10.6 m.** on this road to ROCKFORD (834 alt., 150 pop.), the seat of Surry County from 1790 until 1850. Parts of the 16-inch brick walls of the courthouse erected in the 1790's remain.

Southeast of Mount Airy US 52 crosses a hilly, thinly settled countryside where creek bottoms are planted with grains and tobacco, and the distant horizon is shadowed by the bulk of the Blue Ridge. At **7 m.** the road breaks through a narrow defile to reveal Pilot Mountain to the south, Fisher's Peak to the northwest, and Mount Airy in the hollow nearby.

PILOT MOUNTAIN, **17 m.** (1,101 pop.), is the banking and business town of this section.

At **19.5 m.** (R) is the junction with a graveled private toll road.

Right on this road up PILOT MOUNTAIN (2,413 alt.), a curious rock formation rising from country so low to the east and south that it seems to tower over an immense plain. At **2 m.** is the tollgate. Cars must be parked at the top of LITTLE PINNACLE, **4 m.**, whence a footpath leads to the base of BIG PINNACLE. There is a sturdy staircase (106 steps) up the cliff or a ladder to reach the rock-strewn but comparatively level summit (*camping, picnicking; no water nearer than the tollgate*).
On clear days there is a panorama of the uplifts encircling Mount Airy and an extensive section of the Blue Ridge. Pilot is one of 6 mountains in North Carolina bearing the name. The Indians called it Jo-Mee-O-Kee (Ind. *the Great Guide*), because it served them as a landmark.

KING, **26 m.** (1,200 alt., 416 pop.), one of the earliest settlements in what is now Stokes County, is the highest point on the road between Mount Airy and Winston-Salem. The highway in this region has been called successively King's, Hollow, and Old High Road.

At **30 m.** is the junction with NC 66.

Left on NC 66 is a twisting ascent through peaceful farm and dairy country, with Pilot Mountain's uplift conspicuous (L). Right at **5.7 m.** is the SITE OF THE MOUNTAIN VIEW INSTITUTE, which in the last half of the 19th century was a well-known school for boys. The large two-story structure is now a vacant building situated on the high point of the town. At GAP, **12 m.** (20 pop.), where 5 billowing mountain ranges are visible on a clear day, is the junction with a marked road (R), on which are several mineral springs and the entrance to Hanging Rock State Park (*see* TOUR 9B).

At **15 m.** on NC 66 is the junction with a dirt road; L. **2 m.** on this road to the ROCK HOUSE, a vine-covered ruin gutted by fire in 1897. In 1768 Col. Jack Martin settled here on an 8,000-acre grant and in 1770 began to build the ROCK HOUSE, which was not completed for 15 years. It was built by slave labor of local flint stone with walls three feet thick. The huge kitchen fireplace in the basement was large enough to roast an ox. There is a story that the young daughter of Martin's overseer was kidnapped by a band of men and held for ransom in the Old Tory's Den. She removed her petticoat and waved it frantically. Col. Martin saw the distress signal through his spyglass and rallied a party who rescued the girl and punished the kidnappers.

Jack Martin died in 1822 while fighting a forest fire near his home. His grave is in the family graveyard near his home. He was a Revolutionary soldier, member of the House of Commons, and presiding judge of Stokes County court for 30 years. His court was contemporaneously termed "an eternal comedy of errors," owing to Martin's droll humor and occasionally unceremonious procedure.

South of RURAL HALL, **31 m.** (1,002 alt., 900 pop.), a crossroads trading center, the highway pursues a gentle downgrade and at **34 m.** so uniform is the slope that a car can coast for a mile or more.

WINSTON-SALEM, **43 m.** (*see* WINSTON-SALEM).

Points of Interest: Old Salem, Home Moravian Church, Salem College, R. J. Reynolds Tobacco Plant, Wake Forest College, and others.

Winston-Salem is at the junction with US 158 (*see* TOUR *12*), US 311, and US 421 (*see* TOUR *17*).

Right from Winston-Salem on the oil-treated Old Salibury Rd. to the junction with a dirt road, **6 m.**; R. **2 m.** on this road to the FRIEDBERG CHURCH, a white frame structure erected 1823-27, and remodeled in 1904 and later. Nothing of the original building is in evidence except a part of the stone foundations. The first meetinghouse of Friedberg Church was consecrated on Mar. 11, 1769, and the first resident minister was appointed the following year.

At **2.5 m.** on this road is the junction with another road; L. **0.5 m.** down the lane to the ADAM SPACH ROCK HOUSE, the walls of which are standing. It is owned by the Wachovia Historical Society. When erected by Adam Spach it was intended to withstand Indian attacks. The house, built in 1774 of uncut stones laid without mortar, was only one story in height with a full basement and a small attic. A spring in the basement provided water in case of siege, and there was sufficient room in the basement for the cattle. The rooms have loopholes through which muskets could be fired when the shutters were barred.

Adam Spach, a native of Pfaffenhofen, Alsace, settled here in 1754. During the Indian war he took refuge in the fort at Bethabara and afterwards had the Brethren come to his home to hold services. This they did until 1766 when families of Moravians from Pennsylvania had settled in the section in sufficient numbers to form the Friedberg congregation.

ERLANGER, **62 m.**, a company town owned by the Erlanger Cotton Mills, producers of synthetic fabrics, is now incorporated with Lexington.

LEXINGTON, **64 m.** (*see* TOUR *13*), is at the junction with US 64 (*see* TOUR *13*), and US 29 (*see* TOUR *8*), which unites with US 52 between this point and Salisbury, **78 m.** (*see* SALISBURY).

Section b. SALISBURY to SOUTH CAROLINA LINE; 74 m. US 52

Granite quarries, gold and copper mines, mills, and cotton gins mark this portion of the piedmont plateau. Much of the hilly terrain is cut by rapid rivers, which furnish abundant hydroelectric power.

SALISBURY, **0 m.** (*see* SALISBURY), is at the junction with US 29 (*see* TOUR *8*).

GRANITE QUARRY, **4.5 m.** (802 alt., 591 pop.), settled by Pennsylvania Dutch in 1743, is a wayside village in one of the State's leading granite-producing areas.

Left from Granite Quarry on a dirt road, marked Dunn's Mountain Church, to the OLD STONE HOUSE (*open*), **1 m.**, built by Michael Braun in 1766. This austere two-and-a-half-story house has a gable roof and end chimneys. A smooth stone set in the front between two upper windows bears an inscription, the second line of which has never been explained:

"MICHAEL BRAUN-MRICHREDA-BRAU
IO-PE-ME-BE-MI-CH-DA-1766."

The house, surrounded by old cedars and locusts, is on the crest of a hill. Its stone walls, two feet thick, rise two stories from a foundation 12 to 15 feet deep. Floor boards a foot wide, hand-carved wainscoting and moldings, and plastered walls show excellent workmanship, though most of the mahogany paneling has been stripped off and the plaster is covered with the scrawled names and initials of casual picnickers. Tradition relates that when a young Continental officer reconnoitering in the vicinity was pursued by British dragoons, he rode straight through the front door. The mistress slammed the door in the faces of his pursuers and he escaped into the woods at the rear. The house once served as a prison in which the British kept their captives. A young Colonial soldier attempting escape had gained the window sill when the guard saw him and struck with his saber. He missed and the soldier escaped, but the saber marks on the window casing are still visible.

GOLD HILL, **14.3 m.** (764 alt., 249 pop.), is in a mining region where 10 or more gold- and copper-bearing lodes lie within an area of 3.5 square miles. After gold was discovered in 1842, the place became a lively mining camp of 2,000 people, but it later shrank to a quiet country village.

At MISENHEIMER, **17.5 m.** (140 pop.), is the PFEIFFER JUNIOR COL-LEGE, supervised by the Woman's Home Missionary Society of the Methodist Church. There are 11 brick buildings of functional Georgian design, all of which have been erected since 1935, when the name of the school was changed from Ebenezer Mitchell Junior College, in honor of Mr. and Mrs. Henry Pfeiffer, the chief benefactors. The present enrollment is 175 students.

RICHFIELD, **19 m.**, was settled by German Lutherans. One of them, Daniel Ritchie, an early State legislator, opposed an immigration bill by saying: "Mr. Speaker: I am agin this bill. I represent a strong hefty set of folks who can raise their own immigrants!"

NEW LONDON, 23 m. (285 pop.), was once the center of a gold mine section.

ALBEMARLE, 30 m. (505 alt., 11,798 pop.), on the crest of a spur of the Uharie Range, is the seat of Stanly County and a marketing place for the region. The county was named for John Stanly (*see* NEW BERN) when it was formed in 1841. Albemarle's industrial plants manufacture textiles, cottonseed oil, lumber, flour, and bricks.

In 1842, the year the town was incorporated, the first courthouse was built on the intersection of the two main streets but was later moved to a corner lot for which farmer Ned Lowder once refused to trade his fox hound. The move was actuated, the story goes, because various young bloods had attempted to drive their horses and buggies up the courthouse steps. The present COURTHOUSE, on the opposite corner, is a two-story brick structure flush with the sidewalk. Not so many years ago it was the custom for the court crier to lean from the courtroom window and call witnesses and jurors from the street.

WISCASSET MILLS (*open on application*), a Cannon unit (*see* TOUR *12*), is one of the largest full-fashioned hosiery plants in the South.

Albemarle is at the junction with NC 27.

Left from Albemarle on NC 740 to junction with a marked road, 3.8 m.; R. 3.8 m. on this road into MORROW MOUNTAIN STATE PARK (*vacation cabins, boating, swimming, picnic areas, refreshment stand, recreation lodge, and nature trails*), a 4,135-acre tract in the scenic Uharie Mountains, along the banks of the Pee Dee River. The park's panoramic views include Morrow Mountain, Tater Top, and Sugar Loaf. It is geologically interesting, because these mountains are a part of a former range (Old Appalachia), far older than the Appalachians.

At 5 m. on NC 740 is BADIN (2,126 pop.), site of the PLANT OF THE CAROLINA ALUMINUM CO. (*portions of the plant open*), was established in 1913 and named for Adrien Badin, the French industrialist who first started the construction of an aluminum reduction plant on the Yadkin. In 1915 the Aluminum Co. of America took over the town and plant.

Right from Badin 3 m. to a bluff above the YADKIN NARROWS where part of the electric power in the aluminum plant is generated. Here the river is spanned by a spillway dam 210 feet high and 3,700 feet long, with a maximum water head of 187 feet (20 feet higher than Niagara Falls). BADIN LAKE, formed by the dam, offers water sports.

At NORWOOD, 39.5 m. (1,735 pop.), is the giant COLLINS AND AIKMAN CORP. PLANT, makers of upholstery fabrics. The original town, Allenton, 2 m. E., is now under water (Lake Tillery).

Right from Norwood, 5.5 m., at AQUADALE, is the CAROLINA SOLITE CORP. PLANT. The local slate rock or stone is quarried, crushed, and subjected to heat of 2,500 to 3,000 degrees in the giant kilns. The resulting solite is used for concrete construction work and for the manufacture of concrete blocks.

At **41.5 m.** US 52 crosses the ROCKY RIVER, which, 2 miles to the east, joins the Pee Dee River. A few miles southeast of here, at COLSON'S TAVERN, Col. William Lee Davidson's Whig militia defeated Col. Samuel Bryan's Tories, July 23, 1780. Though the Tories were routed, Col. Davidson was seriously wounded.

ANSONVILLE, **48.5 m.** (324 alt., 545 pop.), was founded as a summer settlement in 1844-45 by a group of planters from the lower Pee Dee seeking higher ground to escape malaria. They engaged a Mr. Hatchett from Philadelphia to build their houses and a school for their daughters; the sons were sent away to school. The RUINS OF THE CAROLINA FEMALE COLLEGE, on the northern side of town, a three-story red brick building of Classical Revival design, with ell at the left added later, are used for storing cottonseed. This school operated from 1850 until about 1867 when it was closed by politics and two successive epidemics of typhoid. Diplomas for "proficiency in science and polite literature" were granted, a few of which are still in existence.

Beyond the center of town is (R) the MAJOR COLE HOUSE (*private*), built for Major Cole by Mr. Hatchett (1844-45), and occupied by the former's descendants. The square, two-story, hip-roof house is a brick structure, whose unusually fine cast-iron rails and lacy supports of the front porch are reminiscent of those seen in New Orleans. The curvilinear ironwork, designed with an intricate grapevine motif, was formerly painted; traces of purple and green are still visible.

Opposite the Cole House is (L) the GEN. WILLIAM SMITH HOUSE (*private*), also built by Hatchett (1844-45). It is a white weatherboarded structure with delicately leaded glass in its doorway. Two-story gallery porticoes and other additions were built in the 1880's. Quarters at the rear, arranged approximately in a semicircle, include a dairy, kitchen and ironing room, smokehouse, cabin, and coach house converted into a garage. Behind this group is a red barn with whitewashed sandstone portico of three arches in the Victorian Gothic or Queen Anne style.

In a grove of tall pines on the outskirts of Ansonville is BETHLEHEM CEMETERY, in which is a marker honoring Ralph Freeman, generally referred to as Elder Ralph, who was born a slave, joined the Baptists, had "impressions to preach" and received his license from the church of which he was a member. After the Bear Creek Association bought and gave him his freedom he became an ordained Primitive Baptist minister, traveling and preaching in Anson, Montgomery, Moore, Randolph, and Davidson counties. A white preacher, Joseph Magee, was frequently his traveling companion. Ralph also supplied at times for the Rev. John Culpepper (white) while the latter was representing the district in Congress. Ralph died in 1831.

Tombstones in the cemetery give evidence of the fever epidemic. One bears an epitaph said to have been composed by the departed young lady, which reads:

> The pursuit of Education led me from home
> I bade my Companions Farewell
> I met the contagion and sunk to the tomb
> And now with my Savior I dwell. . . .

At **2 m.** SE of Ansonville is the GADDY WILD LIFE REFUGE (*open Oct. 1-Apr. 1; adm. 52¢*). Here the late Lockhart Gaddy, by infinite patience, won the confidence of a few live decoys. Today 10,000 wild Canada geese come annually to winter. Feeding them is a great tourist attraction.

WADESBORO, 60 m. (433 alt., 3,408 pop.), seat of Anson County and the leading mill town of the region, manufactures outing, hosiery, underwear, thread, and rayon. It lies at the edge of the Sandhill district in the longleaf pine belt. The hills nearby are known as the Carr Mountains. The site of Wadesboro was the gift of Capt. Patrick Boggan, son of the Lord of Castle Finn, who came from Ireland before the Revolution.

Wadesboro's OLDEST HOUSE (*private*), on Wade St., was built about 1800 by Capt. Boggan for one of his daughters. As the marriage of each of his 9 children approached, Boggan became so furious that in 8 cases, the bride and groom chose elopement. Parental forgiveness, when it finally came, was invariably followed by the gift of house, land, and slaves.

Boggan was captain of the Minute Men of the Salisbury District. Once while he was on a secret visit home, Tories surrounded his house and demanded his surrender. The captain placed his wife's flax knife under his coat and meekly followed the Tories out of the house. His captors, though heavily armed, were unprepared for an attack, and so he was able to throw them into confusion, kill three, and escape.

Anson County, formed in 1748, was a county of enormous proportions, reaching from the South Carolina line, where that line crossed what is now the Lumber River, to the Virginia line and westward to the South Seas. Anson County was named for George Lord Anson (1697-1763), the English Admiral and circumnavigator sent to protect the Carolinas' coast from pirates and Spanish raiders between 1723 and 1735. His biographer wrote in 1838 that Anson was popular among the settlers who "gave his name to districts, towns, and mines" and explained that this popularity—according to Mrs. Hutchinson of South Carolina, writing in 1729—was due to the fact that "Anson was free from the troublesome ceremoniousness which often renders many people extremely disagreeable—he is really so old-fashioned as to make some profession of religion and amidst all the scandalous warfare that is perpetually nourished here, he maintains a strict neutrality."

Anson's first courthouse, erected in 1755 at Mount Pleasant or Old Anson, on the Pee Dee, was sold to be used for a church after the county was divided. It was the scene on April 28, 1768 of the first organized act against the Crown in the War of the Regulation which began, according to Gov. Tryon, in Anson. The Regulators marched to the courthouse, while the

Court was in session, took possession of the courthouse, and held a discussion of the injustices of which they were the victims: unlawful exaction of fees and taxes, unequal distribution of the benefits and burdens of the provincial government. This meeting resulted in the drawing up of a petition to Gov. Tryon protesting the injustices under which Anson citizens labored and suggesting that judges should be elected by the people.

Among those opposed to the Regulatory movement in Anson but who later were leaders in the Revolution was Samuel Spencer who became Colonel of the Field Officers of Anson; a delegate to the Provincial Congress in Hillsboro in August, 1775, and one of the three first Superior Court judges elected under the Constitution.

Anson County's second courthouse, built in 1785, was at New Town, later changed to Wadesboro in honor of Thomas Wade, Colonel of the Minute Men of the Salisbury District and delegate to the Provincial Congress at Hillsboro. The old INGRAM HOUSE was where Andrew Jackson stayed when he came to Anson to practice law. The modern brick and stone COURTHOUSE in the center of Wadesboro is of classic design, fronted by a tall colonnade. Built in 1914, it is surrounded by a landscaped square with several memorial monuments and tablets.

Wadesboro is at the junction with US 74 (*see* TOUR *16*).

MORVEN, 69 m. (341 alt., 601 pop.), comprises both an old town and the new one that grew up around the station 2 miles east when the railroad was built here. Old Morven, originally called Sneedsboro, began about 1800 when William Covington built a tavern at a junction on a stagecoach route. Theodosia Burr is reported to have been brought here by her father, Aaron Burr, to meet her fiancé, later Gov. Joseph Allston of S. C. In its OLD SCOTCH GRAVEYARD are buried Covingtons, McKenzies, Fergusons, McReas, and McKays. On his way to Camden, S. C., and defeat, Gen. Horatio Gates stopped here for three days in Aug., 1780.

When Robert F. W. Allston, Governor of South Carolina (1856-58), bought McKenzie's plantation, he brought his sports-loving friends here for horse racing and cock fighting. The Anson Guards, organized at Morven prior to the Civil War, was the first county militia in the State to offer its services. During the occupation by Gen. Judson Kilpatrick and Union troops, Morven was burned.

McFARLAN, 73 m. (297 alt., 136 pop.), is a rural village settled by Scotch-Irish.

US 52 crosses the South Carolina Line at 74 m., 10 miles north of Cheraw, S. C.

TOUR 11 *(US 21)*

(Independence, Va.)—Sparta—Statesville—Charlotte—(Chester, S. C.).
Virginia Line—South Carolina Line, 133 m.

This route, known as the "Great Lakes-to-Florida" route, crosses mountain pastures in the Blue Ridge and runs through the undulating piedmont plateau and fertile plains.

US 21 crosses the Virginia-North Carolina Line, **0 m.**, 4 miles south of Independence, Va., and enters Alleghany County.

TWIN OAKS, **3 m.** (2,430 alt., 75 pop.), is at the junction with US 221.

Between this point and Roaring Gap most of the timber has been cut and mountain pasture lands and plowed fields lie on steep slopes.

SPARTA, **6 m.** (2,939 alt., 820 pop.), the seat of Alleghany County (established in 1859, chiefly by English and Ulster Scots), is a small bustling mountain town which serves as a trading area for the permanent population and for the tourist and vacation colony trade. A shirt and work clothes factory and the largest smoking pipe factory in the South are located here.

At **11 m.** the route crosses the Blue Ridge Parkway (*see* TOUR 20).

ROARING GAP, **13 m.** (3,800 alt., 24 pop.), is a summer resort (*open June 15-Sept. 15*) which occupies a 1,030-acre tract on a high plateau. Most of the property is owned by residents of Winston-Salem (*swimming, boating, horseback riding, and golf*). Left from the main road on Lake Drive, which circles the lake, is a TROUT HATCHERY (*open*) and a picnic ground.

Between Roaring Gap and DOUGHTON, **24.3 m.** (150 pop.), at the foot of the Blue Ridge, US 21 drops 1,600 feet as it runs through timberland where conifers stand out among the deciduous trees. (*Strong fences guard dangerous curves; viewpoint turnouts.*) Southeast of Doughton US 21 enters the piedmont plateau.

STATE ROAD, **32 m.** (300 pop.), named for an early highway, is at the northern end of the Yadkin Valley, a rich grazing country.

Left across a ravine is the HUGH CHATHAM MEMORIAL HOSPITAL, 37 m., opened in 1931 as a memorial to Hugh Gwyn Chatham.

ELKIN, 37.5 m. (891 alt., 2,842 pop.), an industrial town, is said to have been so named because an Indian shouted "Elk in" when the elk he pursued fell into the creek here. An antler allegedly belonging to this same elk is now in the possession of Mrs. Raymond Chatham, great-granddaughter of Richard Gwyn, who in 1829 purchased land here and established a small cotton mill in 1858.

Around Elkin are thermal belts where destructive frosts seldom occur from fruit-blossoming until late autumn. Apples are grown in large quantities.

The RICHARD GWYN HOUSE (*private*), now the E. G. Click residence, W. Main St., was built by Richard Gwyn in 1861-62. Here Federal Gen. Stoneman was an overnight guest in 1865. Because of his cordial reception and the fact that he allegedly was in love with a relative of the Gwyns in California, the house and cotton factory near the house were spared.

The CHATHAM MANUFACTURING CO. PLANT (*open on application at the office*) is one of the world's largest producers of woolen blankets.

In 1878 Alexander Chatham and Thomas Gwyn built a little woolen mill on the banks of Elkin Creek. Farmers brought their fleece over rough mountain roads to the mill where it was made into cloth on a commission basis or was traded for the rough jeans then manufactured at the mill.

The mills, much expanded and moved from the earlier site to be near the railroad, are still owned by the Chatham family. Most of the wool used comes from Virginia and North Carolina, though some is obtained from the West and imported from abroad. This company is one of the largest producers of woolen blankets in the world.

A concrete bridge across the Yadkin River connects Elkin with JONESVILLE, 38.5 m. (998 alt., 1,728 pop.).

South of Jonesville the route runs into a bright-leaf tobacco country in which mud-chinked curing barns appear at intervals (*see* TOUR *11*).

BROOKS CROSSROADS, 48.4 m., is at the junction with US 421 (*see* TOUR *17*).

At 53.8 m. the route enters a fertile countryside where the yards of homes are planted with old-fashioned flowers and shrubs.

The CARSON HOUSE (*private*), 57.5 m., an unpainted, weatherbeaten old frame farmhouse, was the home of Lindsay Carson, father of Kit Carson, the noted frontiersman, before he moved to Madison County, Ky. The land was granted in 1761 to Kit's grandfather, William Carson. Some claim that Kit Carson was born here.

HARMONY, 60 m. (993 alt., 374 pop.), a quiet country village, grew up around the old Harmony Mills Campground, where "protracted meetings" were held annually for many years by members of various churches.

At OLIN, **4 m.** W., stood OLIN HIGH SCHOOL, founded in the early 1850's by Brantley York, founder of the school that became Duke University. The school, a rival of Trinity College (Duke's predecessor), was discontinued and torn down in 1886.

At TURNERSBURG, **65 m.** (791 alt., 75 pop.), the route crosses Rocky Creek on a concrete bridge. A yarn mill, in operation continuously from 1850 to 1950, is now used for storage, being replaced by an electrically driven mill across the road.

At **65.7 m.** (L) is ALLISON'S LAKE (*privately owned; swimming and boating free*), two small bodies of water with an old water wheel near the dam at the lower lake, is the site of an old tannery.

At **67.1 m.** the route crosses the South Yadkin River on a long bridge that spans cultivated fields on both sides of the stream, which is almost dry at times but swells dangerously in floodtime and covers the fields.

At **69 m.** (R) on a hilltop in a grove of oaks is BETHANY PRESBYTERIAN CHURCH, a rectangular, one-story white frame structure erected in 1855. The congregation was organized in 1775 and the first church built near the site of the cabins of the first Ulster Scot settlers from Pennsylvania. This was then part of the hunting grounds of the Cherokee and Catawba Indians; old Fort Dobbs, built for protection against them, stood a few miles to the southwest.

East and north of the church is a CEMETERY enclosed by a wall built from stone taken from a quarry several miles away. "July 1825" is carved on a stone near the gate. Here are buried Revolutionary and Confederate soldiers, pioneers, and their descendants.

Inside the south gate is the marked GRAVE OF DR. JAMES HALL (1744-1826), first pastor of Bethany Church, which he served for 38 years. In 1778 he opened a classical school, Clio's Nursery, in a log building near his home on Snow Creek, using for awhile manuscript textbooks which he wrote. At his home, with the aid of a purchased "philosophical apparatus," he taught the Academy of Sciences, the first attempt in North Carolina to make the sciences a part of academic training. During the Revolution he organized a company of cavalry from the men of his congregations and served as captain as well as chaplain of the regiment.

The EBENEZER ACADEMY BUILDING, at the southern end of the grounds, is a single-story frame structure, weather-beaten and deserted. From its organization by citizens of Bethany in 1822 until it closed in 1857 this was the leading institution of higher education between the Yadkin and Catawba rivers. Students were prepared here for Princeton and later for Davidson College. After the academy closed the building was long used for a public school.

At **72.5 m.** is a marker at the junction with a dirt road.

Right on this road to the marked SITE OF FORT DOBBS, 1 m., built of logs in 1755 as a refuge from Indian attacks. It was named for Gov. Arthur Dobbs (1754-65).

STATESVILLE, 77 m. (925 alt., 16,901 pop.), seat of Iredell County, is a well-planned old town with wide streets and many trees. There are pink dogwoods on Davie Ave., elms on Center St., oaks on Front and West End Aves., myrtles along Sharpe St., maples in the Boulevard section, walnuts on the street named for them, as well as tulip trees, magnolias, and cedars.

Following the organization of the Statesville Audubon Club in 1930, the entire city by ordinance became a bird sanctuary. The birds have responded to this civic welcome by making Statesville their home in increasing numbers.

Scotch-Irish and Germans from Maryland and Pennsylvania came to this region about 1750 and called their settlement and later their church Fourth Creek. Although Statesville was founded on the site in 1789, it was still a small village when a fire in 1852 destroyed most of the buildings. With the opening in 1856 of a college for women and the coming of the Western North Carolina R. R. in 1857, it began to grow rapidly. Textile mills and furniture factories are its most important industries.

Iredell County, formed in 1788, was named for James Iredell, Associate Justice of the first U. S. Supreme Sourt (*see* EDENTON). The county's chief income is derived from livestock and dairy products.

Quincy Sharpe Mills, born in Statesville in 1884, was killed in action at Chateau-Thierry, France, July 26, 1918. His war letters were published in 1923 as *One Who Gave His Life* and his *Editorials, Sketches, and Stories* in 1930.

The IREDELL COUNTY COURTHOUSE (1899), is a two-story building of cream brick in modified Renaissance style, fronted with a portico and topped with a low dome. Elms shade the gardened lawn. In the rear are the county jail and public welfare buildings, both designed to harmonize with the courthouse; LAWYERS ROW, one of the oldest structures in Statesville, a one-story red brick building that has been modernized for county offices; HOME DEMONSTRATION COTTAGE, a center for farmers and their wives; and the STATESVILLE COMMUNITY HOUSE.

The STATESVILLE PRESBYTERIAN CHURCH, corner W. End Ave. and Meeting St., is a substantial modern stone structure on the site of the 18th-century Fourth Creek Meetinghouse. Fourth Creek's congregation was organized in the 1760's.

Across the street is the old FOURTH CREEK BURYING GROUND, surrounded by a low stone wall. In a gardened triangle is the JAMES HALL MARKER, of native granite, to the pioneer preacher, teacher, missionary, and soldier. He was the first regular pastor of Fourth Creek (1778-90), as well as of Bethany.

MITCHELL COLLEGE, W. Broad St., 2 blocks west of the public square, is housed in a group of brick buildings on a wooded knoll. It was founded in

1853 by the Concord Presbytery as Concord Female College. After several changes of name, it was designated Mitchell College in 1917 for Mrs. Eliza Mitchell Grant and Miss Margaret Eliot Mitchell, who taught here from 1875 to 1883. They were daughters of Dr. Elisha Mitchell for whom Mount Mitchell is named (*see* TOUR *18*). Until 1932, when men were admitted as day students, the school was conducted for girls. The enrollment is about 200.

The JOSEPH P. CALDWELL HOUSE is used as a men's dormitory. Caldwell, as editor of the Statesville *Landmark* (1890-92) and the Charlotte *Observer* (1892-1909), was one of the South's foremost liberal journalists.

The ZEB VANCE HOUSE (*open*) W. Broad St., is so called because it was occupied by North Carolina's wartime Governor and was designated as the temporary State capitol and executive mansion when Union troops occupied Raleigh during the closing months of the Civil War. The small, attractive house was moved from uptown to its present site in city-owned Grace Park in 1950 and is now a museum.

WALLACE BROTHERS HERBARIUM (*open*), S. Meeting St., has one of the largest collections of roots, herbs, and other medicinal plants in the world.

At BARIUM SPRINGS, 82 m. (955 alt., 400 pop.), was once a health resort made popular by the mineral springs containing salts of barium, sulphur, and iron, which were discovered and used by the Indians. Since 1891 it has been the location of the PRESBYTERIAN ORPHANS' HOME, situated on a 31-acre campus in an 1100-acre tract of land and owned by the Synod of North Carolina. It cares for 250 children, ages 3-12.

TROUTMAN, 83 m. (955 alt., 631 pop.), founded in 1858, was named for the first settlers who started a wagon shop here. A fair is held here each fall (*harvest time*). Men's work clothes are manufactured here.

In MOORESVILLE, 93 m. (911 alt., 7,121 pop.), incorporated in 1868, the leading industry is cotton manufacturing.

MOORESVILLE COTTON MILLS (*open*) employ 2,400 people in the manufacture of towels and cotton materials. This is one of the few plants that produce the finished articles from raw cotton.

MOUNT MOURNE, 97 m. (844 alt., 200 pop.), a village scattered along the highway, is one of the oldest settlements in this region. Its early history is recorded in the CENTRE PRESBYTERIAN CHURCH (L). The earliest settled minister in the North Carolina piedmont, the Rev. John Thomson, lived in the Centre bounds (1751-53). There was a log meetinghouse in this area in the 1750's, but the name Centre was not used until the 1760's. The present plain rectangular building, of handmade, sun-dried bricks, with tall windows and solid green shutters, was built in 1854. About three sides of the church is a slave gallery. In the vestibule is a white marble marker to members who enlisted in the Revolutionary War, many of whom are buried in the cemetery across the road. Gen. William L. Davidson, killed when trying to block Cornwallis at Cowans Ford, in 1781, was a member of this congregation. The Synod of the Carolinas was organized here Nov. 5, 1788.

Mount Mourne was also the SITE OF TORRENCE'S TAVERN, a Revolutionary ordinary. Col. Tarleton's British cavalry routed a force of American militia here, Feb. 2, 1781.

At 98 m. is the SITE OF CROWFIELD ACADEMY, one of the earliest classical schools. Established about 1760, it was closed by the Revolution, but educated such prominent men as Dr. Ephraim Brevard and Col. Adlai Osborne.

In DAVIDSON, 100 m. (826 alt., 2,423 pop.), is DAVIDSON COLLEGE (L), founded in 1837 by Presbyterians and named for Gen. William Lee Davidson. Its brick buildings, old and new, are sheltered by towering oaks and elms. The original quadrangle at Davidson College was begun in 1836 and was obviously influenced by the University of Virginia architecture. The oldest buildings now standing are the PRESIDENT'S HOUSE (much enlarged since 1836) and two one-story dormitories, OAK ROW and ELM ROW, all of brick. The original Classical Revival chapel at the north end of the quadrangle has been remodelled beyond recognition. The EUMENEAN and PHILANTHROPIC HALLS were built in 1849-1850. The new CHURCH (completed 1952) now closes the south end of the quadrangle.

CHAMBERS BUILDING, completed 1929, is the administration and classroom building, and the largest and most impressive edifice on the campus. It is a brick, Classical Revival building, with Doric portico and dome, owing much in inspiration to Jefferson's "Monticello." It was named for Maxwell Chambers, Salisbury merchant, and largest donor to Davidson College before the Civil War.

FRATERNITY COURT is an interesting arrangement of one-story lodges built in the style of the ante-bellum planters' homes. These are brick with white porticoes. The 11 small houses were completed in 1928 and are used for social purposes only, college regulations forbidding dormitory houses for fraternities at Davidson.

Davidson has a student body of 825 and a faculty of 65. The official seal of the college was designed by the enigmatic Peter Stewart Ney (see TOUR 15B) and has been used continuously since the first diplomas were issued in 1840.

Immediately after the announcement in November 1895 that Prof. William Konrad Roentgen had discovered at Würzburg, Germany, that rays generated in a vacuum tube have the quality of penetrating opaque bodies, Dr. Henry Louis Smith constructed an apparatus at Davidson College that produced X-rays. Dr. Smith, alumnus of Davidson and its president (1901-12), served as president of Washington and Lee University (1912-30).

Other alumni include Woodrow Wilson; R. B. Glenn, Governor of North Carolina (1905-9); Dr. C. Alphonso Smith, founder of the Virginia Folklore Society; Henry Smith Richardson, manufacturing chemist and philanthropist; S. Clay Williams, tobacco-manufacturing executive; Vareen Bell, novelist; and Joseph H. McConnell, President of Colgate-Palmolive-Peet.

At the southern boundary of CORNELIUS, 102 m. (833 alt., 1,548 pop.), a cotton-manufacturing center, is the old white frame MOUNT ZION METH-ODIST CHURCH (L), with a burying ground for Confederate soldiers. Reunion picnics are held here annually.

In HUNTERSVILLE, 107 m. (814 alt., 916 pop.), is a MEMORIAL PLAY-GROUND, established by the Woman's Club. Every tree, shrub, and flower bears the name of some child living in the town.

Right from Huntersville on the Gilead Rd. to CEDAR GROVE, the Torrance estate, 3 m. The three-story structure was built by James G. Torrance in 1831. The sun-dried bricks were made by slaves; lumber was cut and carved on the place; nails were hand-forged. Within are large fireplaces with high mantels. It is the largest of the ante-bellum houses still standing in Mecklenburg.

CHARLOTTE, 120 m. (see CHARLOTTE).

Points of Interest: Independence Square, First Presbyterian Church, Site of Con-federate Navy Yard, Mint Museum, Martin Cannon Residence, and others.

Charlotte is at the junction with US 74 (see TOUR 16), US 29 (see TOUR 8), and NC 27.

At PINEVILLE, 131 m. (575 alt., 1,373 pop.), Nancy Hanks, mother of Abraham Lincoln, is said to have attended school.

Left from Pineville on US 521 across a bridge beside a small Negro cabin, 1 m.; L. 220 yards off the highway is the SITE OF THE BIRTHPLACE OF JAMES KNOX POLK (1795-1849), 11th President of the United States, marked by a rubble-stone pyramid 15 feet high. Polk moved to Tennessee with his family when he was 11 years old, but returned to enter the University of North Carolina (see CHAPEL HILL). He was graduated with honors after three years and two years later com-pleted his law course.

According to one version of the story of what the Governor of North Carolina said to the Governor of South Carolina, the meeting of the two officials took place south of Charlotte, near the State Line (see TOUR 15A).

A 1735 agreement to include Catawba Indian territory in South Carolina is the reason for the irregular course of the boundary between North Caro-lina and South Carolina in this section.

US 21 crosses the South Carolina Line at 133 m., 7 miles northeast of Fort Mill, and continues to Chester, S. C.

TOUR 12 (US 158)

Junction with US 17—Murfreesboro—Roanoke Rapids—Warrenton—Reidsville—Winston-Salem—Mocksville, **299 m.**

Section a. JUNCTION *with* US 17 *to* ROXBORO, **181 m.**

This route parallels the Virginia-North Carolina boundary, rarely more than 10 miles south, passing through a section which was settled largely by English who came by way of Virginia. Until recently this section was tied economically and culturally to its northern neighbor. It passes from the coastal plains into the rolling farm lands of the piedmont. The economy is based chiefly on cotton, tobacco, peanuts, and corn.

US 158 veers east from US 17 at **0 m.** and penetrates a portion of the Great Dismal Swamp (*see* TOUR 1) which, at **7 m.**, presents an appearance of desolation. In places, gaunt dead cypress masts rise above thick, gray underbrush; in others the boggy surface is littered with charred logs and stumps.

At **22 m.** US 158-A by-passes Gatesville; US 158 goes through the town.

GATESVILLE, **25 m.** (27 alt., 323 pop.), is the seat of Gates County, named in 1780 for Revolutionary Gen. Horatio Gates. Here is annually held the Fisherman's Court (*3rd Mon. in Feb.*), which started when fishermen of the region came to hire slaves as laborers during fishing season. The custom of congregating on this day has remained.

Bennett's Creek (*fishing, hunting, and trapping*) borders the town on the south; freight and passenger boats once plied its waters, now used chiefly by pleasure craft.

GATES COUNTY COURTHOUSE (1836) is a stuccoed structure, one of the few public buildings in the State designed in the Gothic Revival style. Its bell was purchased in 1781. The CONFEDERATE MONUMENT, opposite the courthouse, was erected in 1915 and bears an inscription to William P. Roberts, the youngest general in the Confederate Army.

At **24 m.** US 158 forms a junction with NC 37.

Right on this road in BUCKLAND, **3 m.** is the Dr. Smith House (*visitors welcome*). The interior carved woodwork of this old columned house, built in 1775, has been sold.

At **34 m.** is the northern junction with US 13 which joins US 158 to Winton.

At **40 m.** is the Chowan (chō-wan') River.

WINTON, **43 m.** (45 alt., 834 pop.), seat of Hertford County, formed in 1759, was probably named for the Wynn family who gave the land for the courthouse; the county's name honors the Marquis of Hertford. Winton, established in 1766, soon became a port of entry. Staves and turpentine were loaded for shipment to England and the West Indies on ships made in yards along the river front. The first courthouse was set on fire in 1830 by Wright Allen, who sought thus to destroy a forged note. He was exposed, tried, and publicly hanged on the courthouse grounds. On Feb. 20, 1862, Federal gunboats shelled the town, troops were landed, and the entire town, including the courthouse, was burned. The oldest buildings now standing were built about 1870.

1. Right from Winton **3 m.** on a dirt road is TUSCARORA BEACH (*bathing and boating*), now a yacht basin. Once known as Barfields, it was also a seine fishery and earlier was known as Cotton's Ferry, where stage coaches crossed on the route from Norfolk to Wilmington and where the first court of Hertford was held.

2. US 13 leads to AHOSKIE, **9 m.** (3,579 pop.), the youngest but most progressive and fast-growing town in the Chowan area. Situated in a prosperous agricultural area, tobacco warehouses and peanut plants do a thriving business.

At **45 m.** a dirt road (R) leads to CHOWAN BEACH (*for Negroes*), known for many years as Mt. Gallant Fishery.

At **53 m.** is MURFREESBORO (2,140 pop.) (*see* TOUR 2) and the junction with US 258, which swings south at **55 m.** (*see* TOUR 2).

JACKSON, **73 m.** (131 alt., 843 pop.), seat of Northampton County, is the market town for an extremely fertile area along the Roanoke River. Cotton, corn, and peanuts are the principal crops. When the first courthouse was built in 1742 the town was known as Northampton Courthouse; it was incorporated in 1823 as Jackson, for Andrew Jackson. In 1831, during the slave insurrection led by Nat Turner in the adjoining county of Southampton, Va., North Carolina militia were mobilized at Jackson in readiness for a local slave uprising that did not materialize.

The Northampton County Courthouse (1859), with additions in recent years, has a façade of tall columns rising from a portico reached by two flights of steps, which originally were a single flight extending across the entire front. The large windows are well-proportioned, and the courtroom has some excellent original woodwork. Tradition says Cornwallis stopped at a tavern that stood on a corner diagonally opposite the courthouse. Lafayette, on his 1825 triumphal visit, dined in Jackson.

The County Library, SW. cor. of the square, the oldest public building in Jackson, was built in 1831 as the clerk's office. Later it was used as the Bank of Northampton and in 1950 was dedicated, after renovation, as the Northampton Memorial Library, in honor of the county's war dead.

The Bragg House was built in 1825 for Gov. Thomas Bragg (1855-59), also Attorney General of the Confederacy, who is buried in the family cemetery.

About 5 m. SW. of Jackson lies Occoneechee Neck, one of the largest plantation areas in the State. In this neck of land stood The Castle, the plantation home of Robin Jones, Attorney General for Lord Granville. Broad acres were owned here by his two sons, Gen. Allen Jones and Willie Jones (see HALIFAX), the affluent Pollocks and Burgwyns, and William R. Davie.

At Boone's Mill Pond, 54 m., the highway crosses a bridge over the race and dam where a mill once stood, the Site of the Battle of Boone's Mill, July 29, 1864.

At 54.5 m. a sand road (R) leads to Mowfield (private), the manor home of William D. Amis, wealthy planter, commissary of the Halifax Division in the Revolution, and the last owner of Sir Archy, termed the greatest sire of race horses in America. The manor house is typical of a style popular in Louisiana about 1800.

At 55 m. a sand road (L) leads to Verona (grounds open), 0.3 m., the plantation home of Matt W. Ransom, Confederate general, U. S. Senator (1872-95), and U. S. Minister to Mexico (1895-97), who is buried here. The manor house, built in 1857, resembles a Gulf Coast plantation home, with a high, wide porch and a long flight of outside steps.

GARYSBURG, 61 m., is at the junction with US 301 (see TOUR 3), which unites US 158 between this point and WELDON, 63 m. (see TOUR 3).

ROANOKE RAPIDS, 67 m. (169 alt., 8,156 pop.), named for the rapids of the Roanoke River, is an industrial town, founded in 1893 by John Armstrong Chaloner, a New York industrialist seeking a cotton mill site. Today, textile, paper, and fibre-board mills employ over half the industrial workers of the county. The first plants were erected at Great Falls, later known as Roanoke Rapids. Later a new mill village, Rosemary, a mile further south, sprang up so swiftly that field hands reputedly picked cotton out of the way of the carpenters.

At Roanoke Rapids is also the giant Virginia Electric and Power Co. Plant and Dam.

LITTLETON, 82 m. (389 alt., 1,173 pop.), was founded before the Revolution and named for William P. Little, whose parents built Mosby Hall. Part of Little's private tract followed what is now Mosby Ave. Lumber manufacturing and truck farming are the chief occupations. Half of the town is in Halifax and half in Warren counties.

OLD ORDINARY TAVERN, called locally the "old ornery," now housing a grade school, was erected in 1774. MOSBY HALL, or Little Manor (1774), an important early mansion, has mantel friezes with Wall-of-Troy designs, graceful interior arches, and beautifully detailed door and window facings. A lead roof was removed during the Civil War to be made into bullets.

Left from Littleton on NC 4 to AIRLIE, **8 m.**, a community of ante-bellum plantation homes, the most outstanding of which is PROSPECT HILL, built in 1825 by William Williams Thorne. Now occupied by Negroes and stripped of its interior woodwork, its chief features are its three-bay façade with triple windows, its beautifully detailed portico, its great rear loggia, whose slender columns combine functionalism and beauty, and its gracefully curved stairway and arch.

At Airlie are also the WILLIAMS-REID-MACON HOUSE, one of the finest adaptations of the Randolph-Semple House (Williamsburg, Va.) and OAKLAND, another Thorne house, whose pedimented roof represents the simplest and best in this style of architecture. Walter Clark, member of the State Supreme Court (1889-1924), Chief Justice (1902-24), and editor of the *State Records of North Carolina* was born at his home, "Airlie," which stood in Airlie.

VAUGHAN (Vaughn), **86 m.** (353 alt., 181 pop.), is a village surrounded by corn and tobacco country.

Right from Vaughan to BUCK SPRINGS (*open*), **4 m.**, home of Nathaniel Macon (1758-1837), three times Speaker of the U. S. House of Representatives (1801-07), U. S. Senator (1815-28), and North Carolina's foremost proponent of the political principles of Thomas Jefferson, after the death of Willie Jones (*see* HALIFAX). Macon County is named for him.

The house (1783), a plain structure of poplar plank, restored in 1937 by the WPA, stands in a great oak grove; it is named for a nearby spring in what was once a deer park. A neighbor of Macon's described the house as a "neat little single-storied frame house sixteen feet square, with an upstairs and a cellar furnished in the plainest style for his own dwelling, with a sufficient number of outhouses to accommodate comfortably his visitors."

At **97 m.** is the junction with NC 58 (*see* LOCAL TOUR FROM WARRENTON).

WARRENTON, **98 m.** (451 alt., 1,166 pop.), seat of Warren County, for more than half a century preceding the War between the States was known as a center of culture where men prominent in the State and nation made their homes, and where numerous private schools and academies flourished. A hotel and the 3-mile railroad connecting the town with the Seaboard Air Line R.R. at Warren Plains are municipally owned. Textile manufacturing is the chief industry.

Warrenton and Warren County were founded in 1779 and named for Gen. Joseph Warren of Massachusetts, who fell at Bunker Hill. The town was laid out in that year by William Christmas. The only building then on the site was a granary where grain was collected to finance the Revolution, though there was a settlement nearby at the junction of the Shady Grove and Halifax stage roads. A central square was set aside for the courthouse that was built in 1783. Before 1860 well-to-do plantation owners found life in Warrenton gay, with elaborate dinners and balls, horse racing, card playing, and "cocking mains" between prize birds.

Warrenton was the birthplace of Frances Boyd Calhoun, author of *Miss Minerva and William Green Hill;* and Crichton Thorne, author of *Chimney City,* which won an O. Henry Memorial Prize Award in 1931; and of William T. Polk, author and associate editor of the *Greensboro Daily News.*

EMMANUEL EPISCOPAL CHURCH, 229 N. Main St., when erected in 1824 for a parish organized three years before, was a frame structure with the inside south gallery reserved for Negroes. In 1854-55 the building was enlarged and the turreted central tower and steeple added. In this church on July 5, 1836, Horace Greeley was married to Mary Cheney, who had been teaching at one of Warrenton's private schools.

The MARY BURWELL ALLEN PARSONAGE (*private*), 306 Main St., was presented in 1952 to the Wesley Memorial Methodist Church by Mr. George F. Allen of New York. It has been variously called the Old Eaton Place, the Governor Bell Place, and the Jackson Place. The house was built in 1843 by William Eaton, Sr., who was perhaps the wealthiest owner of land and slaves on the Roanoke River. His first wife, Elizabeth, was the daughter of Nathaniel Macon. It is said he built this house as a summer home where his daughter, Ella (by his second marriage) could entertain her school friends. She later married Peter Hansborough Bell, Governor of Texas (1849-53) and U. S. Congressman from Texas (1853-57).

A charming house in the neoclassic manner, with arched doorways and leaded fanlight and side lights, it is a rectangular, two-story brick structure whose details are typical of the work of its builder, Jacob Holt, a skilled artisan who came to Warrenton from Prince Edward County, Va., in the 1840's. He, his brother Thomas, and Edward T. Rice, who specialized in brick contracting, were responsible for most of the excellent ante-bellum houses in Warren County. The boxwoods surrounding the place are particularly fine.

The MAJOR NAT GREEN HOUSE (*private*), 410 N. Main St., better known as the Tasker Polk house, is a handsome, three-story brick dwelling built in 1850. Upon the death (1862) of William H. Polk, brother of James Knox Polk, 11th U. S. President, his widow returned here to her girlhood home; Tasker Polk was her son. Later the home of William T. Polk, it is now the residence of his brother, James Knox Polk.

The PRESBYTERIAN CHURCH, 411 N. Main St., was erected of brick in 1855 along simple, classic lines for a congregation organized in 1827.

The PENDLETON PLACE (*private*), 107 Ridgeway St., the original part of which is said to date from 1779, is a handsome two-story frame house, whose portico of Ionic columns was added about 1847 when Capt. W. H. Bobbit made alterations. Lovely boxwoods and magnolias surround it. A young widow, Victoria Louise Clark Jones established here a "Select School for Young Ladies" in 1868, in which it is said she anticipated the teachings of John Dewey. Later she married Maj. Arthur Sylbert Pendleton. Her daughter, Mrs. Katherine Pendleton Arrington, the present owner of the house and President of the N. C. Art Society, has filled it with beautiful paintings and works of art.

The oldest part of the DOCTOR GLOSTER HOUSE (*private*), 209 Ridgeway St., now known as the Boyd Place, was built about 1786 by a Revolutionary surgeon. In 1857-58 it was bought by Capt. and Mrs. Thomas Crossan, who added the two-story part with its Greek Revival details, an unusual stepped-arch heading above the first-story windows and lighthouses painted on the windows.

Capt. Crossan was the first commander of the State-owned blockade runner, *Ad-Vance*. He went to England in Nov. 1862 with John White, State agent for purchase of supplies in Europe for North Carolina troops, and they bought the *Lord Clyde,* "an iron, side-wheel passenger steamer." Crossan had it outfitted and named in honor of Gov. Vance, who referred to it as "an elegant, long-legged vessel." The *Ad-Vance* ran the blockade at Wilmington until captured in Sept. 1864.

The JOHN WHITE HOUSE (*private*), 300 Halifax St., is a beautifully proportioned frame dwelling with end chimneys, built in 1850. The son of John White (*see above*), Capt. W. J. White, served as quartermaster of the 1st N. C. Cavalry Regiment in the Civil War.

The RICHARD T. ARRINGTON HOUSE (*private*), Halifax St., is a large, rectangular house, built in the early 1850's. William T. Polk described, in *Southern Accent,* his good times in this house when his great grandmother, Mrs. Susan Tannahill, lived here.

The COLEMAN-WHITE-JONES HOUSE (*private*), 306 Halifax St., built 1825-30, though remodelled in the 1840's and in 1951, has preserved its neoclassic lines, its grace, and its simplicity. The architect is said to have designed "Prospect Hill" (*above*) and "Montmorenci" (*below*).

The JUDGE JOHN HALL PLACE (*private*), 309 E. Franklin St., is a two-story frame house shaded by magnificent white oaks. Built in 1810, it has been continuously occupied by lineal descendants of the original owner. Judge Hall served as judge of superior court (1800-18), associate justice of the State Supreme Court (1818-32), and also conducted a law school.

The BRAGG HOUSE (*private*), N. Bragg St., is a two-story frame structure veneered with brick. It was erected about 1800, but subsequently remodeled, and the old part moved to a lot to the south. This was the home of Thomas Bragg, contractor and builder, and his wife, Margaret Crossland. Among their 12 children were Thomas Bragg, who became Governor of North Carolina; John Bragg, appointed a superior court judge in Alabama in 1842, and U. S. Congressman (1851-53); and Braxton Bragg (1817-76), a captain in the Mexican War, and a general in the Confederate Army. The Warrenton town spring was named Buena Vista Spring in commemoration of Bragg's participation in that engagement and Fort Bragg (*see* TOUR 5*A*) was also named in his honor.

The WILLIAM T. ALSTON HOUSE (*private*), Battle St., now called "Eaton," built about 1850, is a fine example of the Warrenton school of architecture. Restoration in 1951 included wings on each side.

The JOHN GRAHAM HIGH SCHOOL is the third building on this site, the first being the famous Warrenton Male Academy, incorporated in 1786, with the Rev. Henry Pattillo as head. From 1898 to 1918 it operated as the Graham School, a private school for young ladies and gentlemen.

LOCAL TOURS FROM WARRENTON

1. NC 59 leads south through comparatively undeveloped country. At .5 m. (R) is the JOHNSON-PLUMMER HOUSE, built about 1775 by Col. William R. Johnson, who owned a famous racetrack and a famous horse, "Boston." A Tidewater-type house on the edge of the piedmont, it has recently been brick-veneered.

. At **6 m.**, about 100 yards to the L., is the SITE OF BUTE COUNTY COURT-HOUSE. The territory between Warrenton and Louisburg, including all of what is now Warren and Franklin counties, was Bute County, formed in 1746 and named for John Stuart, Earl of Bute, first lord of the treasury under George III. So intense was the patriotism of her citizens that a current phrase in 1775 was "There are no Tories in Bute." Because of the unpopular British title, the general assembly in 1778 erased the name of the county, and the courthouse was abandoned.

In a thicket (L) at **8 m.** is the GRAVE OF GEN. JETHRO SUMNER (c. 1733-85), member of the provincial council in August 1775, who distinguished himself at the battles of Stono, McGowans Creek, and Eutaw Springs.

At **10 m.** is the junction with a sand-clay road.

Left on this road to JONES and SHOCCO SPRINGS, **1.5 m.**, where part of an old resort hotel is still standing. Built about 1835, this hotel often accommodated as many as 400 guests who came to drink the sulphur waters, attend the lavish balls, and play billiards in the game rooms. Here is the SITE OF ST. JOHN'S, built before the Revolution as the principal chapel of the Church of England in St. John's Parish. Nathaniel Macon was one of the wardens. Although the church was abandoned in 1776, an adjoining cemetery remains. Here also is MONT-MORENCI, remains of the plantation manor house of William Williams, usually called "Pretty Billy" to distinguish him from various cousins of the same name. The frame house, marked by delicate detail, was built in the early 19th century. Much of the interior may be seen in the Du Pont home, "Winterthur," now a museum, at Wilmington, Del. The spectacular, free-standing spiral stairway, superb ornamentation of the overdoors, and reeded friezes and pilasters all bear testimony to the elegance of this house.

At **11 m.** is the junction with a sand-clay road.

Right on this road, concealed in a grove of trees, is a CEMETERY (L) **0.5 m.**, containing the GRAVE OF ANNIE CARTER LEE, daughter of Gen. Robert E. Lee. Born in 1839, she died at Jones Springs at the age of 23. A granite monolith was erected over the grave by Warren County citizens in August, 1886.

At **16 m.** is the junction with a narrow dirt road.

Left on this road to an unkempt CEMETERY, **2 m.**, containing the GRAVE OF MATTHEW DICKINSON (1780-1809), of Somers, Conn., first preceptor of Franklin Academy at Louisburg (*see* TOUR *5a*). His tombstone was brought from Connecticut in 1809 by sailing ship and oxcart to this remote spot.

2.   NC 58 leads through a section of Warren County where many fine antebellum homes attest to the affluence of their plantation owners.

At **2.1 m.** a road (L) leads to ELGIN, **1 m.**, a plantation house built in 1832 for Peter Mitchel, born in Elgin, Scotland. The hall across the front opens on three columned porches. Beautiful boxwood hedges outline the house and walk.

At **13 m.** at INEZ (formerly called The Forks) is CHERRY HILL (*private*), designed by Jacob Holt and built about 1850 for Mrs. Marina Williams Alston.

Left from Inez on a road to Arcola is TUSCULUM, **3 m.**, built about 1830 by George Alston. The gallery door above the entrance is interesting.

At **14 m.** is BUXTON PLACE (*private*), built about 1850 by John Buxton Williams. This is another of the many homes of the Warrenton school designed by Jacob Holt.

At **15 m.**, road (L) leads to MOUNT PETROS, **1 m.**, built in the early 1800's by Dr. Sol Williams, whose wife was the sister of the builder of Tusculum. These two houses mark the culmination of the Morris-plan house in the State.

NORLINA, **102 m.** (438 alt., 874 pop.), is at the junction with US 1 (*see* TOUR *5*) which unites with US 158 between this point and HENDERSON, **109 m.** (*see* TOUR *5*).

At **123 m.** is a BOULDER AND TABLET TO JOHN PENN, signer of the Declaration of Independence from North Carolina, whose house is 12 miles from this marker (*see* TOURS *6 and 9*). Between Henderson and Oxford US 158 is designated the John Penn Highway.

US 158 crosses the TRADING PATH, **127 m.**, an Indian trail and traders' route from Virginia to South Carolina. Few traces of it remain.

OXFORD, **128 m.** (476 alt., 6,685 pop.) (*see* TOUR *6*), is at the junction with US 15 (*see* TOUR *6*).

BEREA, **138 m.** (200 pop.), is a farm community.

Right from Berea on an unpaved road to GOSHEN, **4 m.**, plantation of Gen. Thomas Person (1733-1800), a prominent Revolutionary leader for whom Person County and Person Hall at the University of North Carolina were named. Although he was an alleged leader of the Regulators (*see* TOUR *15B*), he escaped with a brief imprisonment when less affluent agitators were hanged. He was one of the State's leading planters, a member of all 5 Provincial Congresses, active leader of the Granville delegation during his 17 years in the general assembly, and was elected to the 1784 Continental Congress, though he did not serve. He was a charter trustee and early benefactor of the University (*see* CHAPEL HILL).

ROXBORO, 154 m. (671 alt., 4,321 pop.) (*see* TOUR 7), is at the junction with US 501 (*see* TOUR 7).

Section b. ROXBORO *to* MOCKSVILLE, 118 m., US 158

West of Roxboro US 158 traverses an area of light sandy loam which grows a high grade of bright-leaf tobacco.

LEASBURG, 12 m. (750 alt., 250 pop.), dating from 1750, is one of the oldest towns in the piedmont. An oak grove is attributed to acorns brought over from England. This was the county seat of Caswell County from 1777 to 1791. Somerville Institute, a girls' boarding school, was conducted here from 1848 until after the Civil War.

At 21 m. is the junction with NC 62.

Right on NC 62, 1 m. (L) is FOREST HOME (*private*), built in 1835 for Capt. James Poteat, father of the educator and long-time president of Wake Forest College (1905-27). It was restored in 1927 by Lawrence Stallings, co-author of *What Price Glory,* and Mrs. Stallings, the former Helen Poteat.

At 2 m. (L) is MELROSE (*private*), a quiet Classic-Revival house, built for George Williamson in 1820. The original house, built about 1770, is in the rear and is attached by a closed passage way.

At 11 m. (L) is LONGWOOD (*private*) or the Saunders House, the home of Romulus Saunders (1791-1867), Minister to Spain (1846-49), U. S. Congressman (1821-27, 1841-45), judge, and legislator. The side approach to the house is lined with century-old boxwoods. Lord Cornwallis and his staff are said to have dis mounted and held a conference under an old oak tree here. Saunders sold his house, FAIRVIEW (*private*), N. High St., in Milton, to Dr. John T. Garland in 1822. Four years later he exchanged houses with Dr. Garland in order, it is said, to entertain William H. Crawford of Georgia, candidate for president in 1824.

MILTON, 12 m. (750 alt., 317 pop.) was visited in 1728 by William Byrd, who noted there were a few settlers. The town itself, founded in 1728 and incorporated in 1796, was originally Mill Town, to which the local planters brought their grain. Its colonial records were burned by Cornwallis in his pursuit of Gen. Greene who crossed the Dan at Lewis' Ferry below Milton. It soon became the social and trade center of this tobacco- and corn-growing section when it was the terminus for tobacco brought by flatboats up the Dan River. By 1818 Archibald D. Murphey reported that "Speculation has raged there beyond my expectation. Lots on the Main Street have sold for nearly an Hundred Dollars per Foot.... A great Deal of Capital is centering in Milton and Danville [Va.]." In 1846 citizens refused to let the Richmond-Danville Railroad run through the town as it would frighten the blooded horses, lure the slaves from their labor, and bring alien influences into the smug and aristocratic little town. Before the Civil War it boasted three tobacco factories, auction warehouses, the first cotton mill in this section, silversmiths, fashion designers, cabinet-makers, one of the earliest newspapers west of Raleigh, and a male and female academy. The rerouting of the railroad, the refusal of its citizens to harness the Dan River (which was done instead at the then hamlet of Danville), and the Civil War all contributed to make Milton today a village of quiet distinction and 19th-century charm, with a few fine ante-bellum houses to remind one of its more colorful past.

In the PRESBYTERIAN CHURCH, organized in 1826, are pews built by Tom Day, a West Indian cabinet-maker, who, sensitive about his color, is said to have made the solid walnut pews free to be allowed to sit downstairs and not in the slave gallery.

The POST OFFICE, Main St. (used also as a residence), was once a branch of the N. C. State Bank. The old vault may still be seen. Across the street are the OLD YELLOW TAVERN, a pre-Revolutionary structure of yellow brick, and the HURDLE HOUSE (next door), said to have been built by a French Huguenot, Jarvis Friar, who used ruby glass in the windows around the front door.

The IRVINE HOUSE (*private*), NE. cor. Broad and High Sts., is of white clapboard, tall and steeply gabled, built in 1820 and owned 1830-1886 for Nicholas Meriwether Lewis. The magnificent boxwoods in the large formal gardens made this one of the most noted gardens in the State.

1. NC 57 leads from Milton to SEMORA, 5 m., a farming community. The RED HOUSE CHURCH, 1 m. S., was founded before 1760 by Presbyterians. In the churchyard is the GRAVE OF HUGH MCADEN (d. 1781), noted pastor, missionary, and Revolutionary patriot, who moved to Caswell for his health's sake, after serving in Duplin and New Hanover counties. His valuable papers were destroyed by Cornwallis' men, but his missionary tour of the colony, 1755-56, written as a journal, has survived and is a primary source of information for students of the period. Archibald De Bow Murphey (1777-1832), champion of public schools, canals, and roads, was born near here on Hyco Creek. His parents were in the Rev. McAden's congregation.

YANCEYVILLE, 22 m. (619 alt., 1,391 pop.), seat of Caswell County, was originally known as Caswell Court House (1791-1833). In 1833 it was established as Yanceyville to honor James Yancey, large landowner. His younger brother, Bartlett Yancey (1785-1828), served 4 years in Congress and was graduated from the University of North Carolina, despite his mother's protest that "she had never known a young man to enter that institution who was ever of any account afterwards." He usually walked the 40 miles back and forth to Chapel Hill. Later he studied law under Judge Archibald Murphey and helped create the educational fund that was the beginning of the public school system in the State.

For half a century Yanceyville was an important town and Caswell County was one of the richest in the State.

The COURTHOUSE, built in 1861, on the site of an earlier one built in 1791 which burned, was the scene of a dramatic murder in 1870, as a result of considerable Ku Klux Klan activity. The slaying of carpetbagger John W. ("Chicken") Stephens at the courthouse by members of the Klan resulted in a reign of terror and finally in the impeachment of Gov. William Holden (*see* HISTORY). When Capt. John G. Lea, former Klan leader, died in 1935, he left a sworn statement relating that "Chicken" Stephens was tried *in absentia* by a Klansmen's jury and sentenced to die for the burning of buildings and the destruction of crops. Lured to a purported conference in the courthouse, Stephens was disarmed and stabbed to death.

Martial law followed; Col. Kirk and his regiment of Tennesseans took charge. Prominent men, including Col. Lea, were arrested. However, it was never proved who killed Stephens nor even that there was a Klan in Caswell until Col. Lea's death. The Negroes, frightened by the mysterious and unpunished slaying, ceased their political activity. Klan records show that besides the Stephens case two white men and 6 Negroes were whipped, a Negro wounded, and another killed in Caswell County.

Several homes along Main Street are reminiscent of the ante-bellum prosperity.

The KERR HOUSE (*private*), a two-story Georgian townhouse was built about 1838 and was the birthplace of John H. Kerr, Superior Court Judge and U. S. Congressman from the 2nd District (1920-49).

The FLORENCE HOUSE (*private*), built about 1815 for William and Thomas Graves, is a two-story frame structure used as a part of the Yanceyville Girls' School about 1830.

DONGOLA (*private*), or the Graves House, built in 1833, is a two-story brick structure with massive coupled columns of plastered brick in classic proportion.

At 24 m., NC 86 forms a junction with US 158.

Right on NC 86 is PURLEY, 3 m. (600 alt., 50 pop.). At a nearby farm on Rattlesnake Branch the Slade Brothers, Eli and Elisha, were the first to grow bright-leaf tobacco (1852). Here a piece of gray sandy loam unsuited to other crops was planted with tobacco. It produced a leaf lighter in color, sweeter, and finer in texture, which proved highly suitable for smoking mixtures, cigarettes, and plug-tobacco wrappers.

Bright-leaf culture spread from this section, known as the Old Bright Belt, to other counties having the same type of soil. Barns used for curing are usually built of hand-hewn logs chinked with red clay and roofed with hand-riven shingles. Fireboxes, fed from the outside of the building, have metal flues that extend to the far side of the barn and back to an exit above the firebox.

During the 4 days required for curing a barn full of tobacco an attendant must keep up the fires and guard against accidents. Sometimes, the process becomes a social occasion to which neighbors are invited. In late summer they feast on watermelons and roasted corn; when nights grow colder a hot stew or other food is served and young and old gather around the fire to sing familiar hymns and ballads.

SUMMER HILL (*private*), is the HOME OF BARTLETT YANCEY, 24.3 m. (R) (*see* YANCEYVILLE *above*). The original part of the house, built for Bartlett Yancey in the early 19th century, is in the rear. It is attached by a broad hallway extending the entire length of both houses to the newer part, built about 1850 by his daughter.

The HOLDERNESS HOUSE (*private*), 27 m., built about 1835, is another fine ante-bellum home.

STAMPS QUARTER (*private*), **29 m.** (L), a tall, two-story brick house with full basement, was completed in 1790 by Samuel Moore, who acquired a quarter section (160 acres) of adjoining land. The Georgian house has simple fine 18th-century interiors with an unusually interesting stairway and candlewell. It is now being restored.

LOCUST HILL, **30 m.** (20 pop.), a village in the hills of Caswell, is named for locust trees in the vicinity. ROSE HILL (*private*) is the two-story clapboarded home of Bedford Brown, U. S. Senator (1829-40), State legislator, and opponent of secession in 1860. It was given by Col. Brown to his son, Bedford. Restored in 1953 by the latter's great-grandson, the original woodwork, contemporary wallpaper, and beautiful boxwoods have been preserved.

Here also is the HOME OF CALVIN GRAVES, Speaker of the N. C. House of Commons and Senate. He cast the deciding vote for the North Carolina Railroad in 1849 and, as a result, was defeated in the next election.

The JETHRO BROWN HOUSE (*private*), **32 m.**, was built about 1816 by Col. Jethro Brown after he had given "Rose Hill" to his son, Bedford.

REIDSVILLE, **45 m.** (*see* TOUR *8*), is at the junction with US 29 (*see* TOUR *8*).

Right on NC 65 to WENTWORTH, **53 m.** (850 alt., 100 pop.), the hill-top seat of Rockingham County, is a one-street village with a modern courthouse (1907) and jail, flanked by old-fashioned houses. Most of the county offices are located in other towns of the county. The town and county were named for Charles Watson Wentworth, Marquis of Rockingham, a leader of the faction that championed the cause of American independence in the British Parliament. Settlers were mostly English, Irish, German, and Scotch-Irish people from Virginia and other colonies to the north.

WRIGHT TAVERN (*private*), later known as the Reid Hotel and now a private residence, was built in 1812. Of dog-run construction, it has a hand-carved stairway in the run.

At **52.6 m.** is MONROETON, an agricultural village, and the junction with NC 548.

Right on NC 548 to IRON WORKS MILL, **1.5 m.**, earlier known as Troublesome Iron Works or Speedwell Furnace. This water-powered grist mill, built in 1770, still grinds corn several days a week. Both Greene and Cornwallis camped here, or in the immediate vicinity, at different times before the battle of Guilford Court House. Greene retired here after the battle and fortified the area, expecting an attack by the British general. Washington breakfasted here June 3, 1791.

Southwest of STOKESDALE, **67 m.** (949 alt.), a village named for John Stokes, a Revolutionary figure, US 158 crosses the steep foothills of the Sauratown Mountains. The bulk of Pilot Mountain looms against the hazy Blue Ridge in the distance (R).

WINSTON-SALEM, **84 m.** (*see* WINSTON-SALEM).

Points of Interest: Old Salem, Home Moravian Church, Salem College, R. J. Reynolds Tobacco Plant, Wake Forest College, and others.

Winston-Salem is at the junction with US 311 (*see* TOUR *9A*), US 421 (*see* TOUR *17B*), and US 52 (*see* TOUR *10*).

At **86 m.** US 158 passes the mill village of HANES, where cotton yarn used in making men's underwear is manufactured.

CLEMMONS, **98 m.** (765 alt., 200 pop.), most of whose residents are employed in Winston-Salem, was founded in pre-Revolutionary days by Peter Clemmons; his nephew, Edmund Clemmons, established a fund to build a secular community. Moravians of the community maintain a church and an adjoining cemetery containing small, flat gravestones.

A bridge spans the yellow Yadkin River and the adjacent bottom lands, **100 m.** Southwest of the bridge the route for 4 miles traverses WILLSHERR LODGE, country estate of S. Clay Williams, tobacco-manufacturing executive.

MOCKSVILLE, **111 m.** (814 alt., 1,909 pop.), seat of Davie County, is built around a landscaped public square with the courthouse on its southeast side. A boulder in front announces that Daniel Boone "lived and learned woodcraft in Davie County," and that his parents are buried not far away.

Davie County, named for William R. Davie (*see* HALIFAX), was first settled in the mid-18th century by English, Irish, and Scots. In 1760 a band of early settlers were harassed by Cherokee raids from the west, especially during the French and Indian Wars (1750-63).

Hinton Rowan Helper (1829-1909), born on a farm just outside Mocksville and graduated from the Mocksville Academy in 1848, was the author of *The Impending Crisis of the South* (1857), a vitriolic attack on slavery, which sought to prove, by comparative statistics, used unfairly, that slavery was responsible for the South's economic lag. The book, banned in the South, exceeded the popularity of *Uncle Tom's Cabin* in the North.

Mocksville is at the junction with US 601 and US 64 (*see* TOUR *13*).

Right from Mocksville on US 601 in the JOPPA GRAVEYARD, **1.5 m.**, are the GRAVES OF SQUIRE AND SARAH BOONE, parents of Daniel Boone. The original headstones with their 18th-century lettering and spelling remain, but have been encased in a monument. This is the site of the Joppa Presbyterian Church, built in 1792. Many soapstone tombstones indicate by their dates that there was a burial ground here before this date.

TOUR 13 *(US 64)*

Manteo—Raleigh—Hickory—Hendersonville—Franklin—Murphy—
(Ducktown, Tenn.); US 64.
Manteo—Tennessee Line, 636 m.

Section a. MANTEO *to* RALEIGH; 199 m.

This route crosses Croatan Sound and the Alligator River and passes through the flat and swampy lowlands of the tidewater and the level terrain of the coastal plain. In the eastern section, settlements are small and far apart, and the forests, rivers, and marshes abound with game and fish. Nearing the piedmont, the route passes through the tobacco belt.

US 64 officially begins, along with US 158 (*see* TOUR *15*), at the lower end of Nags Head and the eastern terminus of US 158 (*see* TOUR *15*). It leaves Manteo, **0 m.** (*see* TOUR *1A*), and continues north on Roanoke Island. At **3 m.** it turns to the left where it reaches CROATAN SOUND FERRY, **4 m.** (*free; 10 trips daily, with extra service in summer; crossing time, about 30 min.*).

Crossing Croatan Sound the ferry passes CROATAN LIGHT. Midway of the crossing there is a rear view of the sand dunes on the outer reef of Roanoke Island, the cottage lines dominated by Kill Devil Hill and the Wright Memorial; tawny Pamlico Sound appears on the south; the blue Albemarle Sound is on the north.

A $3,000,000-bridge over Croatan Sound has been approved (1954).

MANNS HARBOR, **7 m.** (*includes 3-mile ferry trip*) (5 alt., 280 pop.), a small fishing community at the western terminus of the ferry, is sometimes called Croatan, because of the legend that the Lost Colony took refuge here.

At **8.6 m.**, US 264 turns south (*see* TOUR *14*).

US 64 runs through a desolate, changing countryside of peaty swamplands, forests, and farm lands. In this region the chief occupations are fishing and lumbering. A canal parallels the road almost all of the way to EAST LAKE (150 pop.), **21.6 m.**, a small fishing community, consisting of Buffalo City (the center of lumbering operations), Twiford Neighborhood (a fishing and farming district), and Lake Neighborhood (a shipping point). During prohibition days, East Lake Rye, one of the most famous of moonshine liquors, was made in this vicinity and reputedly sold around the world.

At East Lake a ferry (*free; 8 ferries daily; crossing time, about 30 min.*) crosses a link in the Intracoastal Waterway, the Alligator River, so named for alligators found in its waters. On the R. is ATKINSONS (DURANT) ISLAND, on GREAT SHOALS. With its trees and undergrowth, the island resembles a sailboat. Clubhouses and lodges are maintained in the vicinity. The panorama of broad waters and swamp scenery, unspoiled by man, is the same that met the eye of Raleigh's men almost three and a quarter centuries ago.

The ferry docks at SANDY POINT (*includes 3-mile ferry*), 24.6 m. (*no settlement; comfort stations*) and the highway proceeds through a deep, low forest, rarely relieved by habitation.

COLUMBIA, 39.6 m. (10 alt., 1,161 pop.), seat of Tyrrell County, is on the east bank of the Scuppernong River, here a broad arm of the Albemarle Sound, 6 miles to the north. Marked contrasts exist in this old town, where the cosy compactness of the old river village, crowding the water's edge, has not entirely given way to the more expansive type of modern town layout. Columbia bustles with activity during the potato season, when the town is full of buyers and sellers; at other times there is ample leisure. Its charm is distinctive and there is a saying that when one has eaten a perch caught from under the Scuppernong River Bridge, he will not want to leave Columbia.

This section was once the home of King Blunt, a powerful Tuscarora chief who was friendly with the English. The Columbia site was once known as Shallops Landing, a trading post. As early as 1680 Capt. Thomas Miller and Col. Joshua Tarkenton came up the Scuppernong River on an exploring expedition and were so pleased with the situation that they called it Heart's Delight. In the latter part of the 17th century, settlers began to come into the district south of the Albemarle Sound, and by 1729 settlement had reached such proportions that Tyrrell County was established. In 1793 a town, Elizabeth, was laid out, and in 1800 it became the county seat. The name was changed to Columbia in 1801.

The TYRRELL COUNTY COURTHOUSE, built in 1903, succeeds a courthouse built in 1748 on Kendricks (now Mackeys) Creek (in present Washington County), and a second one built on J. Pinner's "Colonial Farm" in 1798. The site of the present building was sold to the county by Thomas Hoskins and Zebedee Hassell in 1800. Records begin in 1736 and are remarkably complete.

Tyrrell County was a part of the original land grant to one of the Lords Proprietors, Anthony Ashley Cooper, afterwards third Earl of Shaftesbury. It has the smallest population (5,048) of any county in North Carolina.

The streams and lakes near Columbia contain herring (North Carolina robin), rock, shad, bass, mullet, and other types in great quantity. Fishing is an important occupation of local inhabitants and is a major factor in the community's economy. Sport fishing is also important, the Columbia river front being a well-established and well-known starting point for sport as well as commercial fishing.

1. Right from Columbia to FORT LANDING (ALLIGATOR), 15 m., on the Little Alligator River. The site of one of the earliest settlements on the southern shore of the Albemarle Sound, its name is derived from an early fort nearby. Some old timbers, said to be remains of the fort structure, are sometimes visible off the shore at low tide. Fort Landing was formerly the western terminus of the Alligator River Ferry. The area was originally a center of Indian life, and relics are still found. Large Indian cooking kettles of earthenware and other rare articles are said to be found occasionally. There is fine fishing and hunting in the area.

On the road from Columbia to Fort Landing are several examples of a type of local architecture that is picturesque in character. The type consists of a story-and-a-half main structure of brisk vertical lines, connecting by means of a low breezeway with a low and elongated kitchen-dining room unit. The type features exceptional length of front elevation in proportion to depth, with delightful contrasts of vertical and horizontal lines.

2. Left from Columbia on NC 94 (which leads to Lake Mattamuskeet 28 miles south; see TOUR 14) is the junction with a dirt road, 6 m.; L. on this dirt road to FRYING PAN, at 12.3 m., an indentation of Alligator River whose shores trace the outline of a long-handled frying pan. In its waters, darkened by juniper trees, grows the American lotus, lovely in summer with its large cream-colored corolla (excellent fishing).

At the western edge of Columbia, US 64 crosses the Scuppernong River, a black winding stream that broadens dramatically at this point. The name is derived from *askup'-onong* (Algonquin, *at the place of the sweet bay tree*). Scuppernong grapes are native to this region, and the name seems to have been applied to the grape when wine made from it by inhabitants of the Scuppernong section had become justly famous for its excellence. Sen. Nathaniel Macon was a fancier of wine made from the "Scuppernong" grape, and when sending Thomas Jefferson a couple of bottles in 1819, he described it as "the best in America."

From the bridge the highway passes over a mile-long causeway through swampland. The road penetrates woods and farm lands where Carolina yellow jessamine and wild azalea bloom in spring, huckleberries and blackberries ripen in summer, and ageratum and purple sage blossom in the fall. In the canals along the road are American lotus and graceful cattails.

CRESWELL, 50 m. (6 alt., 425 pop.), is a small village at the edge of the Scuppernong River swamp, serving a prosperous farming community. Founded in 1874 at the junction of 5 country roads and named for John A. J. Creswell, Postmaster General at that time, the village with its white frame buildings reminds visitors of a movie-set town of the turn of the century. Creswell is at the center of an interesting and historic area known in the old days as "Scuppernong," a name that then applied to the whole region.

1. Left from Creswell on a dirt road to ST. DAVID'S EPISCOPAL CHURCH, .5 m. The middle portion of the church was built about 1803 by the Rev. Charles Pettigrew at his own expense on his plantation "Belgrade." It was known as Pettigrew's Chapel until 1858, when it was given parish organization and the new name of St. David's. Between 1851 and 1857 Parson Pettigrew's descendants and Josiah Collins, wealthy planter at nearby Lake Phelps, made extensive additions to the building, bringing it to its present size. The church is cruciform in plan, with a slave platform of backless benches in the rear. Interior furnishings are all hand carved. A handsome stained glass memorial window stands behind the pulpit.

BELGRADE (across the road from the chapel) was the home of "Parson" Pettigrew, who had previously been rector of St. Paul's in Edenton. Elected the first bishop of the Episcopal Church in North Carolina, but not consecrated, he died at Belgrade in 1807. About 1830 his remains were removed to the Pettigrew family cemetery at Bonarva, at Lake Phelps. The frame of the cottage, which has 4 large outside chimneys was first erected at Lake Phelps in 1797 but was moved to Belgrade the same year.

2. Left from Creswell on a black top road which crosses the Scuppernong River at SPRUILL'S BRIDGE, 1 m., site of a 19th-century shipping point. SOMERSET CANAL, 2 m., is the oldest of the 6 large canals connecting Lake Phelps and the Scuppernong River. Completed in 1788 by slaves brought from Africa especially for the job, the canal (6 miles long and originally 20 ft. wide and 4 ft. deep), the first in North Carolina of such size, was dug to serve both as a transportation route and as a channel for draining a huge tract of swampland between the Scuppernong River and Lake Phelps—a remarkable engineering feat for its time. The PETTIGREW (or Bonarva, or Magnolia) CANAL, 2.3 m., is a channel similar to Somerset Canal and was dug in 1814 by slave labor to drain the Pettigrew plantations of Bonarva and Magnolia. It was finished in 1814.

Right at the canal, following the dirt road on the canal bank, is MAGNOLIA PLANTATION HOUSE, 4.3 m., built for Ebenezer Pettigrew in 1844. Designed by Pettigrew himself, it is a curious and eccentric design, consisting of a two-story central structure entirely surrounded by a shed. Pettigew, proud of the fact that his design was unique, wrote a friend that he would be willing to name the house "The Oddity" if he had not already christened it "Magnolia." The house formerly had a balustrade around the flat roofed top of the central part and extravagant, Gothic-inspired gargoyle effects and battlemented features around the edge of the lower shed roof. The great tract of farmland visible from Magnolia house is the cultivated land of both Magnolia and Bonarva plantations.

3. Right at Creswell on another paved road to CHERRY, 2.5 m., a small farm village near the head of Scuppernong River. Right at Cherry to the cultivated land of "Western Farm," 4 m., the westernmost of the old Lake Phelps plantations, developed by the Collins family who lived at Somerset Place plantation. At WESTERN FARM PLANTATION HOUSE, 6 m., the route leads (L) across Western Farm and to the great opening of SHEPARD FARM, 7.5 m., and the cultivated land of Somerset Place plantation, 8.5 m. This route crosses vast flat fields consisting of thousands of acres of flat, black, elaborately drained soil, planted largely in corn, the old staple crop, although there are extensive acreages of soybeans and improved pastureland. To the south a fringe of tall cypress trees marks the shore of Lake Phelps. Approaching Somerset Place, a row of old cypress trees stands out impressively.

At SOMERSET CANAL, 9 m., the road turns (R) to PETTIGREW STATE PARK, 9.5 m. (boating and fishing). In the park SOMERSET PLACE stands on the shore of LAKE PHELPS (*stocked with fish*), a 16,600-acre natural fresh water lake, and affords a fine view of the whole lake. This fine old plantation house, built for Josiah Collins III about 1830, and 6 small buildings have been restored (gardens, orchard, yard areas and a large lawn are now being restored). In the middle of the lawn, bordered with century-old cypress, chestnut oak, and sycamore trees, is a circular planting of chestnut oaks, about 200 feet in diameter, which in the old days offered a shady retreat. Some 50 yards behind the Collins lawn is the slave cemetery of the Pettigrew plantation, Bonarva.

The house, a good example of the coastal plantation houses of its period, has a double-tiered gallery the full width of the house. Flanking the two sides of a large rear wing are other double galleries of the same style. The interior features woodwork and trim in the style of the early Greek Revival, so popular in the 1830's. The 10 fireplaces are served by 5 chimneys, which rise high above the roof to form an impressive feature of the exterior. The house is constructed of heart cypress.

In the yard numerous brick walls lead to different buildings (kitchen, dairy, smoke house, ice house, etc.) and to the sites of the slave quarters and the old "street," where the slave hospital, slave chapel, overseer's house, etc. stood.

In 1783 Josiah Collins of Edenton, an English immigrant who had made a fortune in shipping and related businesses, and two other Edenton businessmen, formed themselves into a land company to drain and develop the hitherto untouched swamplands about Lake Phelps. The Lake Company, after acquiring 125,000 acres of land, fitted out in Boston a slave ship to bring a load of slaves to dig the proposed drainage works, to clear the plantation, and to work in the projected rice fields. Upon the completion of Somerset Canal in 1787, the rice plantation was developed, and rice was grown very successfully for a number of years. However, circumstances a few years later made feasible a shift from rice to corn as the chief crop.

About 1800 Josiah Collins bought out his partners and became sole owner of the company lands and plantation. In time the greater part of the 125,000 acres was sold off, much of it to the Pettigrew family, who at the same time were developing their neighboring plantation, Bonarva, from small beginnings. In 1829 Josiah Collins III, grandson of the original owner, came to Lake Phelps and built the present mansion house and many other buildings. By 1860 Somerset Place, the center of a lavish social life, consisted of more than 2,000 acres of field land which was worked by 328 slaves.

Also in Pettigrew State Park is the SITE OF BONARVA, the old seat of the Pettigrew family, started in 1789 by the Rev. Charles Pettigrew. Bonarva was the birthplace of Confederate Gen. James Johnston Pettigrew, who figured prominently at the Battle of Gettysburg and was killed during the retreat to Virginia following. No buildings remain, the original house having burned in 1860 and the other buildings having disappeared in more recent times. Beyond Bonarva house site on a dirt road is the PETTIGREW FAMILY CEMETERY, the resting place of three generations of the Pettigrew family, including the Rev. Charles Pettigrew, first bishop-elect of the Episcopal Church in North Carolina, Ebenezer Pettigrew, and Gen. James Johnston Pettigrew. The cemetery is owned by the University of North Carolina and is administered as a part of Pettigrew State Park.

In spawning season (Feb. to May) great quantities of herring enter the canals connecting Lake Phelps with Scuppernong River. On their way up the narrow channels they are easily caught in skim nets by fishermen who stand on the banks and work the nets by means of long handles.

ROPER, 67 m. (13 alt., 793 pop.), a farm village, was formerly a busy settlement called Lee's Mill, which served the needs of the planters of Tyrrell County in colonial days.

At the close of the 17th century, Capt. Thomas Blount of Chowan, a blacksmith and ship's carpenter, settled on the eastern bank of Kendricks (now Mackeys) Creek and in 1702 built the first mill in this section. His widow married Thomas Lee, and in time both the mill and the settlement was called Lee's Mill. The mill was used continuously until 1920.

Right from Roper on a dirt road is CHESSON, 0.7 m., a hamlet on the Norfolk Southern R. R. near the SITE OF BUNCOMBE HALL, a noted colonial residence.

Joseph Buncombe, wealthy planter of south Albemarle, came from St. Kitts in the West Indies. His purchase of 1,025 acres from Edward Moseley in 1736 is the first recorded deed in Tyrrell. He built a house on Kendricks Creek, near what is known as Buncombe Landing. Legend relates that during the early days of Buncombe's residence a vessel from the West Indies was unloading at the wharf, having among her crew a youth who had once served in the Guinea slave trade. Recognizing some Guinea natives among the slaves handling cargo, he indicated to one of them a point over the stern of the vessel, and explained that a deep hole led to Guinea. One dark night the slave and several of his fellows weighted themselves, dropped into the water, and perished. The deep place in the stream is still known as the Guinea Hole.

The lands of Joseph Buncombe were bequeathed to his nephew, Edward Buncombe, who came from the West Indies about 1766 to inspect his Carolina possessions. Deciding to settle in Carolina, Edward Buncombe arranged for the construction of a large house, employing as his builder Stephen Lee of Lee's Mill. In 1768, Edward Buncombe returned to south Albemarle. Besides being a planter he engaged in shipping and owned his own schooner, the *Buncombe*. Above the entrance to his house was:

Welcome all
To Buncombe Hall.

In the hall, which had 55 rooms, all guests, rich or poor, were cordially received. The host is even supposed to have detained favorite guests by removing bridges on each side of the estate.

The Provincial Congress of 1776 appointed him colonel of the 5th Regiment of North Carolina. From Tyrrell he recruited the men of his regiment, and at Buncombe Hall he equipped and trained them at his own expense. Col. Buncombe was wounded at Germantown in 1777 and died of his wounds while on parole in Philadelphia. The hall was sold and it deteriorated until by 1878 only the naked framework of the dining room and the kitchen walls remained. There is nothing to show where the hall stood except a slight depression near the track of the railroad running over the ridge. A county in western North Carolina was named for Edward Buncombe (*see* ASHEVILLE).

PLYMOUTH, 74 m. (21 alt., 4,486 pop.), seat of Washington County, is an old port on the south bank of the Roanoke, with well-kept lawns and fine old trees whose branches arch above the streets.

Plymouth was founded in 1780 with the gift of a site by Arthur Rhodes, a former resident of Plymouth, Mass. It became a thriving shipping point, but during the Civil War was the scene of several naval battles, which by 1865 had reduced it to 11 battle-scarred buildings. Plymouth's industries include canning, lumber manufacture, and several of the best-equipped fisheries in the State.

On the courthouse lawn is the BATTLE OF PLYMOUTH MARKER, which recalls not only deeds of Confederate soldiers but also the achievement of a Union officer, Lt. William Barker Cushing. In 1864 a Confederate force under Gen. R. F. Hoke captured Plymouth after a three-day battle. The iron-clad ram *Albemarle,* which had destroyed one Federal gunboat and driven away two others, was anchored in Roanoke River. On the night of Oct. 27, 1864, the *Albemarle* was sunk by the explosion of a torpedo placed by Cushing, who escaped by swimming down the river.

GRACE EPISCOPAL CHURCH, a brick Gothic Revival structure with pointed steeple, designed by Richard Upjohn (c. 1850), surrounded by trees and flowers, is flanked on one side by the Roanoke River. Years ago 12 trees were planted in the churchyard and named for the Apostles. Lightning killed the tree named Judas without damaging any of the others. During the Civil War the church gave up its pews and gallery to make coffins for the many who had fallen in battle.

WILLIAMSTON, **95 m.** (60 alt., 4,975 pop.) (*see* TOUR *1*), is at the junction with US 17 (*see* TOUR *1*).

PRINCEVILLE, **126 m.** (58 alt., 919 pop.) (*see* TOUR *2*), is at the junction with US 258 (*see* TOUR *2*), which unites with US 64 between Princeville and TARBORO, **127 m.** (*see* TOUR *2*).

At **131 m.** (50 yds. L. of the highway) is the POWELL HOUSE or COOLMORE (*open to visitors*), a white mansion, built in 1858-61. A porch that originally extended across the front and sides has been reduced to a small entry shelter. The roof is surmounted with a lantern cupola reached by a hand-carved spiral stair. Plaster walls in the round and domed vestibule and rear entry hall, and in the circular, 4-story central hall, are hand-painted in gold with a background of faded blue. Frescoes on ceilings and cornices are covered with gold leaf. One of the two ceiling-high mirrors was cracked in April, 1865, when taken into the forest with other valuables to be hidden at the approach of Sherman's army. The Federal invaders were persuaded to spare the house by a soldier who was one of several Maryland artisans employed to erect it.

ROCKY MOUNT, **143 m.** (*see* TOUR *3*), is at the junction with US 301 (*see* TOUR *3*).

NASHVILLE, **153 m.** (180 alt., 1,302 pop.), and Nash County, of which it is the seat, were named for the Revolutionary patriot, Brig. Gen. Francis Nash (*see* TOUR *15B*). This pleasant tobacco-belt town has a wide business street which develops into a residential boulevard planted with crêpe myrtles and Norway maples. This region is favorable to diversified farming as well as to tobacco culture. The cornerstone of the brick NASH COUNTY COURT-HOUSE (1883) contains a quart of Nash County brandy.

Right from Nashville on NC 58, **3.6 m.**, and L. **1 m.** on a dirt road to ROSE HILL (*private*), a mansion built in 1792 for George Boddie on land granted to his father, Nathaniel Boddie, by Lord Granville. Its double porch is fronted by Doric columns and a circular drive winds to the entrance. The flower garden was laid out by an English landscape gardener. In 1876 the house was enlarged, and it has been subsequently remodeled and modernized, but the virginal lines have been preserved.

In SPRING HOPE, **164 m.** (261 alt., 1,275 pop.), are small brick and frame buildings lining wide, paved streets. The town—named for an older Spring Hope, a stage junction that once existed 4 miles to the south—was built on property acquired in 1887 from the Hendricks family at a price so low that grateful citizens offered the couple a trip anywhere on the Atlantic Coast Line R.R. They accepted a trip to Rocky Mount about 20 miles away.

The highway crosses the Tar River, **167 m.**, on a high steel bridge. Dorothy Perkins roses climb over trellises and cover many of the houses in this section. Many of the farms have open wells in their front yards.

ZEBULON, **178 m.** (323 alt., 1,378 pop.), a neat village with several tobacco warehouses, is at the junction with US 264 (*see* TOUR *14*).

WENDELL, **182 m.** (337 alt., 1,253 pop.), is a tobacco-marketing village with several warehouses near the highway.

At **191 m.** the highway crosses the Neuse River, narrow and muddy at this point.

RALEIGH, **199 m.** (*see* RALEIGH).

Points of Interest: State Capitol, Christ Church, Site of the Birthplace of Andrew Johnson, Joel Lane House, N. C. State College of Agriculture and Engineering, and others.

Raleigh is at the junction with US 70, 70-A (*see* TOUR *15A*), US 1 (*see* TOUR *5*), and US 15A (*see* TOUR *6*).

Section b. RALEIGH to STATESVILLE; 148 m. US 64

This section of US 64 crosses the piedmont plateau through an area of hills, watercourses, and rich bottom lands. In the region are farms and small manufacturing enterprises.

Between RALEIGH, **0 m.**, and **14 m.**, US 64 unites with US 70-A (*see* TOUR *15A*). Between **5 m.** and **8 m.** US 64 unites with US 1 (*see* TOUR *5*).

The HAW RIVER is crossed at **29 m.** In Jan., 1865, a heavy freshet swept away every bridge on the Haw. This was considered a blessing in disguise since it prevented bands of Federal raiders from crossing the river.

PITTSBORO, **33 m.** (*see* TOUR *7*), is at the junction with US 15-501 (*see* TOUR *7*).

The DEGRAFFENREID HOUSE (*private*), **36 m.**, built about 1810, was presented by Joseph John Alston to his oldest son, John Alston. Delia, a daughter of John Alston and his wife, Adeline Williams Alston, married John Baker DeGraffenreid, since which time this house has been referred to as the "DeGraffenreid House." It is one of the 6 houses presented by Joseph John Alston (Chatham Jack) to his children. Known as "40-mile Jack" because of the vast size of his plantation, Joseph John Alston, who came to Chatham County from Halifax County in 1791, was one of the largest landowners and slaveholders in this section. This dwelling, standing in a hickory grove surrounded by an ancient rail fence, has many original furnishings and portraits.

ASPEN HALL (*private*), 37 m., or the "Gideon Alston House," was the house presented by Joseph John Alston to his son, Gideon Alston, when he married Evelyn Alston, daughter of Phillip Guston Alston of Warren County. This handsome two-story frame structure has been continuously occupied by members of the Gideon Alston family since 1830. The main part of the dwelling was erected in 1830 and the rear portion of the home in 1760. This home contains many original portraits and furnishings of the Alston family, dating from the colonial period, and also rare antiques and portraits from the Gen. Thomas B. Brown family of Bladen County.

The route crosses the Rocky River, 45 m. Tobacco, wheat, sheep, poultry, and honey are important products of this region.

US 64 by-passes Siler City; US 64-A goes through the town.

SILER CITY, 50 m. (598 alt., 2,501 pop.), at the junction with US 421 (*see* TOUR *17*), is the site of one of the largest poultry-processing plants in the State, a furniture plant, and a textile and hosiery mill. The first settlement here, a stop on the stage road, was called Silers Crossroads.

West of Siler City the highway penetrates the Uharie (Uwharrie) Mountains, whose rocks are classified by geologists as among the oldest in North America. These worn hills rarely reach a height of 1,800 feet. The Deep River, as it flows through narrow valleys in the range and cascades over rocks, provides many scenic spots, as well as water power.

At RAMSEUR, 63 m. (447 alt., 1,134 pop.), an industrial village (L) hidden in the valley of the Deep River, is a cotton mill beside a stone dam. The headquarters of David Fanning, noted Tory leader, 1781-82, were located 4.5 miles southeast of here at Cox's Mill.

US 64 by-passes Franklinville; US 64-A goes through the town.

At 64 m., US 64-A crosses Sandy Creek.

About 4 m. R. on this creek is the SITE OF THE HOME OF HERMAN HUSBAND, Quaker leader in the Regulator rebellion of 1771 (*see* HISTORY). After the Battle of Alamance (*see* TOUR *15B*), Husband and other Regulators were outlawed by Gov. Tryon. Husband escaped and later settled near Pittsburgh, Pa. Some of his descendants live in this section.

FRANKLINVILLE, 65 m. (463 alt., 778 pop.), named for Gov. Jesse Franklin (1820-21), is a mill village of white cottages along a bluff that overlooks the Deep River. The founding of a gristmill here in 1801 marked the beginning of the town. In 1838 it was remodeled as a cotton mill.

FAITH ROCK, L. of the bridge spanning the river, was used by Andrew Hunter in 1781 in escaping from the Tory leader, David Fanning (*see* HILLSBORO). He rode Fanning's horse, "Bay Doe," down this steep, slippery cliff to the river below and to safety beyond.

ASHEBORO, 74 m. (*see* TOUR 9), is at the junction with US 220-311 (*see* TOUR 9).

At 78 m. is the junction with an unpaved road.

Right on this road to JOHN WESLEY STAND CHURCH, 2 m., established here in 1837. The settlers built a brush arbor on the deer stand. During the Civil War services were discontinued but when peace came the Methodists erected another arbor and finally a small building, which has been replaced by a modern structure.

At 84 m. is the junction with a dirt road.

Right on this road to the HOOVER HILL CHURCHYARD, 2 m., which contains the grave of Andrew Hoover, ancestor of Herbert Hoover, 31st President of the United States. Andrew Huber, a Quaker, came from Germany to Philadelphia in 1738 and to this neighborhood in 1774. He changed his name to Hoover and operated a plantation and gold mine nearby. Some of his descendants migrated to the Middle West; others reside in this region. Andrew's grave has a marker erected by Pres. Hoover.

At 85 m. is the junction with a dirt road.

Right on this road, 2 m. and R. .7 m., to a covered bridge over the Uharie River. This is one of the few remaining ones in the State.

The route crosses the Uharie River, 89 m. Local residents spell the name Uwharrie. The valleys were settled by German colonists who may have named it New Werra after a river in their old homeland.

LEXINGTON, 105 m. (*see* TOUR 8), is at the junction with US 70-29 (*see* TOURS 15 and 8), and with US 52 (*see* TOUR 10).

At 110 m. is REEDS CROSSROADS. On the grounds of the school is a marker memorializing the stop made here by George Washington in 1791.

At 112.5 m. a road leads (R) to the SITE OF YADKIN COLLEGE, a Methodist Protestant school, which opened in 1856, was made coeducational in 1878, and closed in 1924. The building is still standing.

At 113.5 m. US 64 crosses the Yadkin River on a 1,000-foot bridge.

MOCKSVILLE, 124 m. (*see* TOUR 12).

US 64 by-passes Statesville; US 64-A goes through the town.

STATESVILLE, 148 m. (*see* TOUR 11), is at the junction with US 21 (*see* TOUR 11), and US 70 (*see* TOUR 15B).

Section c. STATESVILLE *to* TENNESSEE LINE; 289 m. *US 64-70, 64*

Between Statesville and the Tennessee Line, US 64 crosses the foothills of the Appalachians and enters the western North Carolina mountains through a region of peaks, streams, waterfalls, and forests. The section is rich in natural resources including timber, minerals, and water power. The highway penetrates two national forests.

US 64 is joined by US 70 from Statesville to Morganton, **50 m.**

West of STATESVILLE, **0 m.**, is a region of cultivated fields interspersed with dense woodlands.

The CENTRAL PIEDMONT SOIL EROSION EXPERIMENT FARM (*open*), **10.5 m.** (L), established in 1930, is a joint project of the U. S. and N. C. Departments of Agriculture, where experiments are being conducted to determine the best methods for checking erosion.

AT **11.8 m.** is the junction with a graveled road.

Right on this road to LOOKOUT SHOALS LAKE (*fishing, boating, camping*), **5.5 m.**, one of a chain of artificial lakes formed by impounding the waters of the Catawba River for hydroelectric power.

CONOVER, **20 m.** (1,060 alt., 1,164 pop.), is a textile and furniture manufacturing town, many of whose employees live in surrounding communities.

Conover is at the junction with NC 16.

NC 16 (R) leads, almost due north, across a long concrete bridge over the Catawba River, **9 m.** To the L., at 110 yds., is LAKE HICKORY DAM (*power-house open; fishing, boating, swimming*). A walkway across the dam affords a view of LOOKOUT SHOALS LAKE (R), with a 30-mile shore line, and LAKE HICKORY (L), even larger. South of the dam (L) is POLYCARP (*picnic grounds*), employees' village of the Duke Power Co.

At MILLERSVILLE, **10 m.** (R), a small village for employees, is a small cotton spinning mill.

TAYLORSVILLE, **17 m.** (1,400 alt., 1,310 pop.), seat and market town of Alexander County, is in the foothills of the Blue Ridge Mountains. The county, formed in 1846 and named for Gov. Nathaniel Alexander (1805-07), is known among mineralogists as a sample case. Although there are no commercial mines, almost every mineral and gem found in America can be found in the county. The people of the county own and operate a railroad, the "Apple Blossom Special," between Taylorsville (incorporated in 1887) and Statesville. A mill which manufactures cloth from synthetic fibers (**2 m.** N.) employs 235 workers.

1. Left from Taylorsville is LILEDOUN, where an annual clambake is attended from all over the State; at **4 m.** is BARRETT MOUNTAIN (1,950 alt.), which gives a broad view of the surrounding countryside.

2. Right from Taylorsville along NC 90, which follows a pioneer trail along the ridge between the Catawba and Yadkin river valleys to HIDDENITE, **5 m.**

(1,140 alt., 300 pop.). Here the gem of that name was discovered about 1879 by William Earl Hidden, a scientist who had been sent to North Carolina by Thomas A. Edison to look for platinum. The transparent crystals, ranging in color from light yellow to emerald green, are found at only two other places in the world. The finest specimen of hiddenite is 2½ by ½ by ⅓ inches and is in the American Museum of Natural History. No mines have operated for years. Hiddenite was once noted as a health resort because of its sulphur springs.

STONY POINT, **9.5 m.** on NC 90, is known for the first emerald mine in the United States. After the first gem had been found in 1875 a mine, of which no traces remain, was operated for a brief period. One emerald from this mine, weighing nearly 9 ounces, is in the American Museum of Natural History.

At Conover, US 70 keeps straight west, by-passing Hickory, while US 70-A (R) leads into Hickory (*see* TOUR *19*), which is at the junction with US 321 (*see* TOUR *19*).

CONNELLY SPRINGS, **39 m.** (1,195 alt., 500 pop.), has mineral waters that once attracted summer visitors.

Right from Connelly Springs on an improved road to RUTHERFORD COLLEGE, **1 m.** (330 pop.), the second oldest town in Burke County, known first as Excelsior. Here a coeducational school of the same name was operated for many years by the Western North Carolina Methodist Conference and after 1933 leased and operated as a high school and junior college by the Burke County board of education. The forerunner of Rutherford College was the Owl Hollow Schoolhouse, opened in 1853 by Robert Abernathy in a one-room cabin. In 1869 John Rutherford gave young Abernathy funds to buy 200 acres of land to build a town, the present Rutherford College. In the 42 years of Robert Abernathy's regime the school provided free tuition to hundreds of students, many of whom became preachers. All that remains is a monument to Dr. R. L. Abernathy, founder of the institution.

VALDESE, **44 m.** (1,203 alt., 2,730 pop.), in the foothills of the Blue Ridge, was settled in 1893 by a colony of 50 families from the Cottian Alps of northern Italy. These short, dark, French-speaking Italian Protestants called themselves Waldensians for the 12-century reformer, Peter Waldo. Here they purchased a tract of 3,000 acres at $4 an acre. With the rocks taken from the hills they built their homes, school, and church. The early buildings, some of which are visible from the main street, suggest Italian farmhouses.

Under the patient toil of the settlers, hillsides worn away by erosion were covered with terraced vineyards and productive farms. Francis and John Garrou, who had left home to learn trades, returned in 1901 and set up textile mills that grew into important industries and transformed the community into a manufacturing town. Through a cooperative system Valdese established stores, dairy farms, a power plant, laundry, bakery, and butcher shop. The cooperative system has given way to private enterprise. In addition to the textile mills, there are a shoe factory, box factories, and other small plants. The Waldensian bakery distributes bread and cakes over a wide area.

In the WALDENSIAN PRESBYTERIAN CHURCH (1899), a stuccoed stone building with lancet windows and fronted with a square tower, services are conducted in French on the second Sunday in each month. The other services are in English. On the second floor of the church is a MUSEUM (*open*) containing household articles, tools, and clothing brought from Europe or made by hand in the town.

The SITE OF CAMP VANCE, **46 m.**, was used by Confederate soldiers during the Civil War.

MORGANTON, **50 m.** (1,181 alt., 8,311 pop.), seat of Burke County, is in the Catawba River Valley encircled by ranges attaining an elevation of 4,500 feet. Modern structures in the business section contrast with the century-old courthouse. Thriving industries and extensive trade create a quick-moving tempo.

For a few years after its formation from Rowan in 1777, Burke County extended to the Mississippi River. The name honors Gov. Thomas Burke (1781-82), (*see* TOUR 15A). The county seat was first called Morganborough for Gen. Daniel Morgan, a Revolutionary soldier. Previously the settlement had been called Alder Springs.

When the court square and streets were laid out, the commissioners named the latter for the principal streets of Charleston, S. C., the city to which early mountain dwellers went for their loaf sugar and Jamaica rum, and later for slaves brought from Africa.

The BURKE COUNTY COURTHOUSE (1833), now covered with cement, standing among the trees on Central Square, was built of local stone, though two members of the committee wanted to use bricks brought from South Carolina. Twin stairways lead from opposite corners of the building to the courtroom on the second floor. This hip-roof structure is surmounted with a square tower. In Feb. 1865, Gen. Stoneman's army or camp followers raided the building, threw the records into the square, and burned them. Only a "tryal docket" (1792-1804) escaped.

To the old log courthouse on this same site in 1788 was brought John Sevier (1745-1815), after he had been arrested near Jonesboro by Col. John Tipton and charged with treason against the State of North Carolina. Sevier was a leading figure in the Watauga Association (*see* TOUR 21) and was Governor of the State of Franklin, later incorporated into Tennessee. Although the State of Franklin's separation from North Carolina was caused by neglect on the part of State authorities, Sevier and his associates were vigorously condemned, and steps were taken to dissolve the insurgent State.

While the trial was in progress, Sevier's friend, James Cosby, disguised as a rustic, left Sevier's mare in front of the courthouse doorway, entered the courtroom, and as soon as he was sure that Sevier had seen the horse, interrupted the trial by demanding whether the judge wasn't "done with that man." In the ensuing confusion Sevier ran, leaped on his horse, and outdistanced pursuers. Sentiment against him subsided, and he was elected to the State assembly, was a member of the first Congress, and was elected first Governor of Tennesee (1796).

The old courthouse was the scene (1832-33) of the trial and hanging of Frankie Silver for the murder of her husband in present Yancey County (*see* TOUR 22). From 1847 to 1861 the State Supreme Court met here.

The COMMUNITY HOUSE (1935) is a white-painted brick structure in the colonial tradition with flagged walks and boxwood borders.

On the southern outskirts of the town the State owns 1,200 acres of land upon which are the STATE HOSPITAL AT MORGANTON and the NORTH CARO-LINA SCHOOL FOR THE DEAF. The hospital for mental diseases was authorized by the general assembly of 1875 and completed 11 years later and can accommodate about 2,500 patients. The School for the Deaf, authorized in 1891, includes a model farm that produces sufficient food for the more than 400 students. Academic as well as vocational subjects are taught.

Right from Morganton on NC 181 to the junction with NC 126, **1.3 m.**; L. **7 m.** on NC 105—known as the Kistler Memorial Highway in honor of Andrew M. Kistler, a proponent of good roads for the mountain section—is LAKE JAMES (*tourist camps, fishing, hunting*). This artificial reservoir, with 152 miles of mountainous shores, was created by the Duke Power Co. on the Catawba River.

At **3 m.** on NC 181 is the beginning of QUAKER MEADOWS, the site of one of the earliest settlements in this section. When Bishop August Gottlieb Spangenberg came here in 1752 in search of lands for the Moravians (*see* WINSTON-SALEM), he described the place as "fifty miles from all settlements." Local traders thought he was a Quaker because of his austere appearance. The Indians had already cleared the bottoms, which grew up in grass. Hence the name "Quaker Mead-ows." Among the first settlers (1752) at Quaker Meadows was David Vance, Revolutionary patriot, one of the founders of Buncombe County, and grandfather of Gov. Zebulon B. Vance (1862 and 1877) (*see* ASHEVILLE). After the Revolution, David Vance settled in present Buncombe County where he is buried (*see* TOUR 22).

Soon after the French and Indian War, Joseph McDowell and his cousin, "Hunting John" McDowell, came to the Catawba Valley, the former to build his home at Quaker Meadows, the latter at Pleasant Gardens. The mountain men, on their way to Kings Mountain (*see* TOUR 8), assembled at Quaker Meadows in Oct., 1780. At the McDowell home, Zebulon B. Vance was married to Miss Harriette Espy on Aug. 3, 1853.

At **8.7 m.** is the junction with the Table Rock Rd.; L. **1.6 m.** on this road to TABLE ROCK (3,918 alt.). From this point, reached by a trail, are impressive views of Chimney Mountain to the south and the sharp crest of Hawksbill and the long ridge of Gingercake Mountain to the north.

At **1 m.** is CLEARWATER BEACH, a recreation center on Steels Creek.

Beyond Clearwater Beach NC 181 begins the steep ascent of Ripshin Ridge to Loven's Hotel, **16 m.**, near Cold Spring. Visible from the hotel, under favorable atmospheric conditions at night, are the Brown Mountain Lights, a phenomenon that has puzzled scientists for 50 years. The lights, which appear behind Jonas Ridge, resemble the glow of balls of fire from a Roman candle. After reaching a maximum intensity they fade out to appear at other points. The U. S. Geological

Survey suggested that the lights might be caused by the refraction of headlights on trains and automobiles in the valley beyond. The National Geographic Society reported that the source could be from discharges of static electricity.

At Morganton US 64 leaves US 70 in a southwesterly direction. The route, at the western edge of the piedmont and beginning of the mountains, leads to Rutherfordton.

RUTHERFORDTON, 80 m. (1,096 alt., 3,146 pop.), seat of Rutherford County, is at the foot of the Blue Ridge on the edge of the piedmont plateau. Muster place of some of the Kings Mountain Men and site of early gold mines, Rutherfordton was established in 1784, town and county being named for Revolutionary Gen. Griffith Rutherford. When Bishop Asbury visited here in 1796, he recorded in his journal: "the country improves in cultivation, wickedness, stills, and mills."

Most important asset of the county is the textile industry, manufacturing a variety of products from cotton, wool, and silk. The chief crops are grain, cotton, sweet potatoes, fruits, vegetables, and melons.

Gold mines are still operated north and east of Rutherfordton. From 1790 to 1848 this was the center of the gold-mining industry of the nation, and $3,000,000 worth was minted on the spot into $1.00, $2.50, and $5.00 pieces. Christopher Bechtler, the first man in the United States to coin gold dollars (1831), had a private mint. Some of his dies are in the State Hall of History, Raleigh, and the old press on which the coins were struck is in the Museum of the American Numismatic Society in New York. Rutherford's gold fever reached its height in 1830 but subsided in the greater excitement of the California '49 rush. Mining was not resumed in Rutherford until 1931.

Rutherfordton is at the junction with US 74 (*see* TOUR *16*), which unites with US 64 between here and Bat Cave.

West of Rutherfordton the route enters the foothills of the Blue Ridge, following in general the route believed to have been taken by Hernando De Soto in 1540 on his march through the Appalachian country. Tales of hoarded gold and other precious metals brought these explorers into a region never before penetrated by white men.

At 91 m. is the eastern end of HICKORY NUT GORGE through which flows the Broad River, sometimes known as the Rocky Broad to distinguish it from the Second and French Broads. Along its banks rhododendron attains a luxuriant growth.

At the lower end of LAKE LURE, 92 m., a dam (R), housing in its base a hydroelectric plant, spans the river channel; it backs up the waters into a lake which, with its indentations, has a shore line of 27 miles. The lake, a popular resort, was impounded in 1925-26 as part of a real estate development.

LAKE LURE (village) (*hotel, golf course, bathing beach, boats and launches*), 97 m. (174 pop.).

The long mountain range towering above the lake (R) is known as RUM-
BLING BALD, because of the thunderous rumbling that sometimes ema-
nates from it. Faults exist among the rocks and landslips have exposed caves
high on the slopes.

Left from the gardened plaza in front of Lake Lure Inn a trail leads to the
BOTTOMLESS POOLS, 400 yds. (*adm. 25¢*). The path follows a rocky stream that
winds between trees and rhododendron. The pools, below the cascades, are unusually large "potholes," caused by stream erosion in one of the oldest rocks on
the face of the earth, the Henderson Granite Gneiss. Scientists can give no definite age for the pools. They may be 25,000 or 100,000 years old. It is said that
they were often the meeting place of one of the most powerful groups of the
Ku Klux Klan during Reconstruction.

The paulownia, a flowering tree sometimes called the empress tree, identified by deep lavender blooms that appear before the leaves, grows in this
vicinity. It was originally brought to western North Carolina by George
Vanderbilt (*see* ASHEVILLE), and it is believed that the seeds were scattered
by birds.

At **98 m.** the route crosses the Broad River.

CHIMNEY ROCK, **99 m.** (400 pop.), a village lying in the gorge at the
foot of the mountain, has shops featuring native hooked rugs, pottery, and
wood carving. The region abounds with scenic trails for hiking and horseback riding. Several summer camps are operated nearby. High cliffs tower
on both sides of the Broad River, which tumbles over and around huge
granite boulders.
According to the tale told by Cherokee aborigines, it was here that a clever
medicine man outwitted the Little People, those awesome gods of Chimney
Rock. On a journey through the only pass to their tobacco supply they were
stopped by strange sights. One brave warrior volunteered to fight his way
through but never returned. Thereupon the medicine man of the tribe,
invoking his magic, turned himself into a mole. He succeeded in burrowing
his way through the gap and returned, but was unable to bring any tobacco
with him. Summoning all his powers, since he believed that many of his
people were dying for want of tobacco, he swept through the gorge in the
form of a whirlwind, tearing away cliffs and hurling boulders into the valley. The boulders crushed the Little People and the way was opened. With
the procuring of tobacco, the sick were healed.
The *Raleigh Register and State Gazette* published an account (Sept. 23,
1806) of an occurrence in the gorge, as related to the Rev. George Newton,
schoolmaster of Asheville, by Patsy Reaves, "a widow woman who lives
near the Appalachian Mountain." On July 31, 1806, about 6 o'clock in the
evening Mrs. Reaves' children, startled by the appearance of figures on the
mountain, called their mother.
"...Mrs. Reaves says she went about three poles toward them and without any sensible alarm or fright, she turned toward the Chimney Mountain
and discovered a very numerous crowd of beings resembling the human
species; but could not discern any particular members of the human body,

nor distinction of sex; that they were of every size, from the tallest men down to the least infants; that there were more of the small than the full grown, and they were all clad with brilliant white raiment; that they appeared to rise off the side of the mountain, south of the said rock, and about as high; that a considerable part of the mountain's top was visible above this shining host; that they moved in a northern direction, and collected about the Chimney Rock."

Robert Siercy, who was sent for, beheld the same spectacle and added: "that two of a full size went before the general crowd about the space of 20 yards; and as they respectively came to the place, they vanished out of sight, leaving a solemn and pleasing impression on the mind, accompanied with a diminution of bodily strength."

In 1811, according to published reports, two troops of cavalry appeared to beholders, engaged in battle. This incident was described in Zeigler and Grosscup's *Heart of the Alleghanies* (1883).

The Little People and their later appearing spirits are explained as mirages. Moisture-laden atmosphere moving from the coastal plain might serve as a prism, scientists point out, refracting the light rays upon meeting the lighter atmosphere at this sharp break in topography.

The HARRIS HOUSE (*private*), built in the late 18th century, is a large frame structure, formerly a tavern and stage coach inn on the Asheville— Rutherfordton turnpike.

Left from Chimney Rock village, through a gateway where clipped hedges and bright perennial gardens soften inverted arches and rock pylons, a motor toll road (*adm.: adults, $2, children 6-12, $1*) leads across the Rocky Broad River and climbs through a mountain woodland and along ridgetops to the foot of CHIM-NEY ROCK, 3 m.

Chimney Rock is a monolith rising 225 feet from the mountain of the same name. From the parking place at the foot of the chimney, an elevator (*toll: 25¢*) leads to the summit. Along the way are platforms and balconies at vantage points. From the top of the chimney, range after range of the Blue Ridge is visible, with Lake Lure below and the foothills to the east. The stairway over the cliffs leads past the Opera Box, the Devils Head (Satan moulded in granite), and Exclamation Point. The Skyline Trail extends to the top of HICKORY NUT FALLS (400 feet high) and back along the face of the precipice by the Appian Way to the base of Chimney Rock.

At 102.8 m. is a steel bridge (L) across the Rocky Broad River. Here the stream, following a wide sandy bed, curves sharply among rocks and boulders, numerous enough to serve as stepping stones when the water is low.

Left from this bridge is a marked trail (*flashlight necessary; guide advisable*) up the mountain to a deep rock fissure, the entrance to a small, dark, damp chamber whose exit is a corkscrew drop through a pile of rocks. Here another small chamber, devoid of formations, leads into a corridor sloping steadily downward, beyond which few have explored.

To the L. of this formation is BAT CAVE, its roof formed by two massive boulders almost meeting in a peak. The entrance is 30 feet high and the cave runs back about 100 feet. In the hottest weather a current of cool air comes from this cave.

In BAT CAVE, 103 m. (1,472 alt., 175 pop.), a little village with a post office and a few stores, the route crosses the Rocky Broad River flowing through HICKORY NUT GORGE.

US 74 turns right to Asheville, via Hickory Nut Gap; US 64 swings to the left.

By easy grades the route ascends to the Hendersonville plateau, 108.3 m. This route offers the easiest ascent and least formidable barrier over the Blue Ridge, or Appalachian Divide.

In EDNEYVILLE, 110 m. (100 pop.), a delicious cider is sold during the fall. The town was named for the Rev. Samuel Edney, the first Methodist minister locating west of the Blue Ridge. Bishop Asbury recorded in his journal, Dec. 3, 1812, that he "came on through Buncombe to Samuel Edney's; I preached in the evening."

Left from Edneyville on the Sugarloaf Mountain Rd. to SUGARLOAF MOUNTAIN, 7 m. (3,967 alt.). From an observation tower here is a view of the surrounding mountains and of the three counties, Polk, Rutherford, and Henderson, which have a common corner here. The DEVIL'S SMOKE HOUSE is a cave used as a refuge, it is said, by Maj. William Mills, a British soldier wounded at the battle of Kings Mountain. Later he came with his family over the mountains via a route known as the Mills Gap Road and was the first known white settler of Henderson County. A dude ranch is located here.

The area around Edneyville and along the Blue Ridge to Dana and Hendersonville is dotted with orchards and packing houses of the State's leading apple-producing county. Fields of beans, cabbage, and peppers cover much of the county.

HENDERSONVILLE, 118 m. (2,146 alt., 6,103 pop.), the seat of Henderson County, is a well developed resort center with hotels, motels, inns, and tourist homes in town and on the highways. The town is also an agricultural and industrial center, producing textiles, hosiery, a new nylon thread, and wood products. An annual apple harvest festival is held each Sept. In the vicinity are small lakes, children's camps, and summer religious assemblies. Golf, riding, tennis, and water sports are all available.

Henderson County, created in 1838 and named for Leonard Henderson (1772-1833), Chief Justice of the N. C. Supreme Court, was the gateway to the vast territory lying beyond the Treaty line established by Gov. William Tryon in 1767 and declared by royal proclamation to belong to the Cherokee Indians. Not until after the Revolution were white settlers admitted to this region.

The area became known to Low Country people as an advantageous summer resort about 1826, when the Buncombe Turnpike was being constructed. This little group who settled estates around Flat Rock (*see*

TOUR *24*) were the vanguard of the ever-increasing stream of summer tourists to this part of North Carolina.

Hendersonville, with its 100-feet wide Main St., was established as the county seat about 1841 on a 50-acre tract given by Judge Mitchell King of Flat Rock and was incorporated in 1847.

DIXON'S SANATORIUM, 3rd Ave. and Flemington St., was begun by the Western Baptist Convention in 1858 as the Western North Carolina Female College. The great granite columns in the front of the building were cut by "Aunt Liza Corn," a noted local stone mason. Federal troops stabled their horses in the incompleted building during the Civil War. The institution, its name changed to Judson College, was opened in 1878 and continued as a coeducational school until 1898. Under contract with the U. S. Government, a number of Cherokees attended school here.

In OAKDALE CEMETERY, 6th Ave., is the TOMB OF THE SUNSHINE LADY. Before her death Mrs. Charles B. Hansell, a tubercular patient, requested that she be buried so the sun would always shine upon her. In the top of her concrete tomb are numerous lenses through which the skeleton was visible until the tomb was covered in 1939.

ST. JAMES EPISCOPAL CHURCH, E. Main St., completed in 1863, was consecrated Sept. 19, 1863.

Hendersonville is at the junction with US 25 (*see* TOUR *24*).

1. JUMPOFF MOUNTAIN, 7.5 m. out 6th Ave. W., affording wide views, is an outstanding landmark from prehistoric days which derives its name from one of the oldest known Indian legends. On its heights, at a "tankeet" or sentry lookout, a princess of the Estatoe tribe was assigned to keep the vigil by her lover, Wanteska, who was leading his band of braves from their town, Estatoe, in South Carolina, up the French Broad River to Biltmore and on to Virginia to battle the Shawanoe tribe. Her lover never returned and her remains were discovered months later at the foot of the mountain.

On its summit for 10 years stood the steel girders of the Fleetwood Hotel, surrounded by rusting radiators and corroding bathtubs, a reminder of the real estate boom of 1925-26.

2. Right from Hendersonville on Caswell St. to KANUGA LAKE (*clubhouse, annexes, cottages, water sports, and pavilion for recreational activities*), 6 m., a 400-acre summer assembly ground owned and operated by the Episcopal Church. The assembly opens about June 10.

Legend says this site was formerly an old Indian gathering place named for a prehistoric town of the Cherokee on Pigeon River—a name which means "The Coming Together of Many Peoples."

US 64 continues across the plateau and follows the French Broad River much of the way. Rich farming land alternates with woodlands. In the distance (L) are the Blue Ridge Mountains.

HORSE SHOE, 114 m. (2,083 alt., 150 pop.), is surrounded by farming country. The highway crosses Davidson River (*trout fishing*) at 136.1 m.

Right from PISGAH FOREST, **136.2 m.** (2,107 alt., 597 pop.), on improved US 276 to the entrance to PISGAH NATIONAL FOREST, **1.5 m.** At the forest entrance is the giant Ecusta Paper Corp. Plant which manufactures from flax the paper for most of the cigarettes in America. This factory and a cellophane plant are located here because of the supply of pure water from the Davidson River.

BREVARD, **139.2 m.** (2,230 alt., 3,908 pop.), seat of Transylvania County, is named for Ephraim Brevard, Revolutionary soldier and a member of the Mecklenburg Committee (*see* charlotte). In a region of mountains, forests, waterfalls, and trout streams where roads and trails are well marked, Brevard attracts many summer visitors. The town was incorporated in 1867 with 7 voters, every one of whom held office.

The high hat industry, a craft widely practiced in early Colonial days and lingering in remote spots until the Civil War, once flourished here. The town hatter made by hand wool hats, muskrat hats, and fine beaver hats. In this section any high hat is called a "beaver," or, in derision, a "bee gum." Owners of high hats once paid an annual State revenue tax of $4. A similar levy was made on those who carried gold-headed canes.

Modern Brevard's industries include the manufacture of lumber, leather, hosiery, and cotton goods. Brevard College (L), occupying a group of brick buildings, is a standard, coeducational junior college with 200 students and a faculty of 20, maintained by the Methodist Church.

Brevard is called the center of summer camps for boys and girls. Famous among these is Transylvania Music Camp, **1 m.** N. Founded and directed by James Christian Pfohl, it gives instrumental and choral training to teen-agers, offering scholarships to talented students. Frequent concerts are given, climaxed in August by the Transylvania Music Festival with a symphony orchestra and professional soloist. Both the camp and the festival are sponsored by the Brevard Music Foundation.

Left from Brevard on US 276 to the junction with an unpaved road, **4 m.**; L. **0.8 m.** on this road to MAIDENHAIR FALLS (*now private*) on Hogshead Creek.

On US 276 at **6 m.** is CONNESTEE FALLS (*adm. 25¢*), where, legend relates, many years before the coming of the white settlers a young Englishman was wounded and captured by the Cherokee. The Indians spared his life and he fell in love with the Princess Connestee who had nursed him back to health. During their courtship the two often sat by the waterfall. With the consent of Chief Wahilla, the girl's father, they were married. Later, while visiting a trading post for supplies, the white man was persuaded by friends to return to his own people. The heartbroken Indian wife threw herself over the falls, where her tragic figure may sometimes be seen in the gorge below.

During the first decade of the 19th century the land lying within this section, and in a strip about 12 miles wide, north of and paralleling the present North Carolina-South Carolina boundary, was the subject of dispute between North Carolina and Georgia, which then bordered the area, and became known as the Orphan Strip. In 1803 it was incorporated by Georgia as Walton County. This resulted in violence and bloodshed known as the Walton War. While the section was a no man's land it became the refuge of renegades and desperate characters seeking to avoid the laws of either State. Commissioners from both States met in Asheville June 15, 1807. Later, at Caesars Head, they signed an agreement that Georgia had no right to claim any territory north or west of the Blue Ridge and east or south of "the present temporary line between the whites and Indians."

CAESARS HEAD (*adm. $1*), 12 m. (3,218 alt.), is a rocky precipice that resembled Caesar, a dog belonging to the proprietor. It towers above the plains of South Carolina.

US 276 crosses the South Carolina Line 26 miles northwest of Travelers Rest.

ROSMAN, 148.3 m. (2,189 alt., 535 pop.), has developed into a small industrial town engaged in lumbering and tanning. In ante-bellum days it was, according to legend, on the Underground Railroad used by slaves escaping to the north. Rosman is at the junction of US 178, which leads S. to Pickens, S. C. Here US 64 leaves the French Broad Valley and starts the ascent of the Blue Ridge Mountains again.

At 156 m. is the junction with NC 281.

Right on NC 281 to LAKE TOXAWAY, 0.5 m. (Cherokee for "redbird"), once a fashionable summer resort built around a beautiful artificial lake. In 1916, a flood swept the dam away. NC 281 continues past 3 power lakes to NC 107 at Tuckasegee.

A concrete bridge, 156.5 m., crosses the Toxaway River (*stocked with bass and trout*). Above and below the bridge the river falls over a rugged rock formation. From here the crest of the Blue Ridge is in sight. In the foreground is Mount Toxaway (4,800 alt.).

SAPPHIRE, 162.1 m. (3,104 alt., 50 pop.), is so named for the precious stones found near here and because the sky and water seem to be an unusually intense blue. The highway winds through a region praised for its beauty by generations of travelers because of the combination of forested mountains, streams, and sky. SAPPHIRE LAKE, 165.7 m. (L), is a small body of water in a mountain setting.

At 167.5 m. is the entrance of FAIRFIELD INN (*swimming, boating; horses available*) overlooking FAIRFIELD LAKE. Back of the inn is ROCK MOUNTAIN, named for its granitine face. Long Branch Creek falls over the cliff to form the lake, which is encircled by a drive. An 18-hole golf course was being built in 1954.

CASHIERS, 170.4 m. (3,524 alt., 305 pop.), is a summer resort in the midst of impressive scenery. LAKE CASHIERS (*fishing*) is near the village. Nearby is the largest mink farm in North Carolina, where about 2,500 minks are raised for the market. Two privately owned trout-rearing farms are also nearby, on US 64 and NC 107.

Cashiers is at the junction with NC 107 leading (L) to Walhalla, S. C., and (R) to Sylva.

Left on NC 107 to HIGH HAMPTON INN AND COUNTRY CLUB (*swimming, boating, golf, tennis, riding, hiking, fishing*) 1.7 m., on land that was part of the

2,200-acre Hampton estate, planted with trees and shrubbery from many parts of the world. The old inn, built about 1850 by Gen. Wade Hampton, was destroyed by fire in 1932. Gen. Hampton, an officer in the Confederate Army, Governor of South Carolina (1876-79), and U. S. Senator, spent his summers here until his death in 1902. The inn, erected in 1933, is operated as a resort hotel; it is rustic in style, with exposed beams and the exterior covered with bark. Here also are three small lakes.

Right from High Hampton a graveled road leads to GRIMSHAWES, **5 m.**, below the imposing cliffs of Whiteside Mountain, 2,000 ft. above. This road continues through HORSE COVE (highest average annual rainfall recorded in eastern U. S.), up a winding, steep grade to Highlands.

At SUNRISE VIEW, 174.5 m. (4,150 alt.), is an overlook with sweeping views toward Terrapin, Toxaway, and the Balsam Mountains. Here is the junction with a road.

Left on this road (*toll $1 per person; open Apr. 1-Dec. 1*) to parking area, **3 m.**, on N. shoulder of WHITESIDE MOUNTAIN (4,930 alt.), whose solid rock face towers over the countryside and is one of the highest sheer precipices (1,800 feet) in eastern America. A graded trail leads 500 yds. to an observation tower on the summit.

In this section of the Nantahala National Forest (*see* NATIONAL FORESTS) hemlock and spruce grow in profusion on the mountains. During May the azaleas, which showed earlier blossoms shading from white to orange, are a flaming red. Laurel, rhododendron, and other mountain shrubs grow higher than usual among the hemlock trees. The banks of the streams are covered with moss and lacy ferns. Here and there a mountaineer's cabin breaks the wilderness.

HIGHLANDS, **182.2 m.** (3,835 alt., 515 pop.).

Season: June 1-Oct. 15.
Accommodations: Hotels, tourist courts, cottages.
Golf: Highland Golf Club, 18 holes.
Highland Club Lake: Swimming, boating, fishing.
Other Sports: Tennis, skeet, riding, hiking.

Highlands is a summer resort that attracts visitors from many parts of the country, including naturalists who come to study the diversified flora. Near the country club are several summer homes, including the former home of Bobby Jones, noted golfer.

Highlands lies on a high plateau, just north of the Georgia Line and is the highest incorporated town in North Carolina. To the northeast the Appalachians extend all the way to Canada, thus favoring the southward spread of that region's plant and animal life.

The variety of plant and animal life from the different zones makes this area an encyclopedia of the Carolina mountains. Among rare plants found in the region is the prized shortia, discovered in 1788 by the French botanist, André Michaux and rediscovered by Asa Gray a century later. It grows only in a limited region of the Carolina mountains and in Japan.

The HIGHLANDS BIOLOGICAL STATION (*open*), housed in a single-story stone building, was founded in 1927 by Dr. Clark Foreman to preserve the private collections made by the earlier residents of the town. A report by the director, Dr. E. R. Reinke, professor of biology at Vanderbilt University, led to the establishment of Weyman Memorial Laboratory in 1930. Leading southern universities lent their cooperation, as did such institutions as the Smithsonian, the American Museum of Natural History, Woods Hole Laboratory, and Charleston Museum. Designed as a regional research station in the Southern Appalachians, it serves independent investigators and graduate students.

In the station's museum there is a cross section of a 425-year-old hemlock tree. Labels on the growth rings associate historical events starting with the last voyage of Columbus in 1503. The great tree was cut when the golf course was laid out. Thomas Grant Harbison (1862-1936), botanist and horticulturist, compiled a *Check List of Ligneous Flora of the Highlands Region*. Check lists of birds and of the vascular plants of the Highlands have also been published by the station.

Opposite the museum a narrow gravel road leads to RAVENEL MEMORIAL, **0.7 m.** a favorite picnic area. Here the cliffs of Sunrise Rocks overlook Horse Cove, while Sunset Rocks overlook Highlands and The Nantahala— Great Smoky ranges to the westward.

Left from Highlands is a gravel road up SATULAH MOUNTAIN (4,560 alt.) to SLOAN GARDENS (*open daily*), **1.5 m.**, containing unusual flowers as well as common varieties.

Trails from Highlands lead to the peaks of nearby mountains, including BEAR-PEN (4,100 alt.) on the north, BLACKROCK (4,355 alt.) on the east, and FODDERSTACK (4,280 alt.) on the south.

Northwest of Highlands, past LAKE SEQUOYAH, is a series of waterfalls. The first, BRIDAL VEIL, **184 m.**, drops over the highway. At DRY FALLS (*U. S. Forest Service picnic grounds*), **184.5 m.** (L), the visitor may park his car, descend steps, and stand behind the falls, viewing the Cullasaja River through the sheet of water. LOW FALLS, **185 m.**, are visible (L) as the route descends into the Cullasaja Gorge. The highway, overlooking the river 250 feet below, was carved out of perpendicular cliffs.

Between **203.2 m.** and **204.1 m.** US 64 unites with US 23 and US 441 (*see* TOUR 23).

US 64-23-441 crosses the Little Tennessee River at **203.2 m.**

FRANKLIN, **204 m.** (2,113 alt., 1,995 pop.), seat of Macon County, is on a high ridge overlooking the beautiful valley of the Little Tennessee, which is surrounded by the peaks of the Cowee, Fishhawk, and Nantahala ranges. This was the site of the old Cherokee settlement, Nikwasi, known as Sacred Town. NIKWASI MOUND is on the bank of the Little Tennessee River (R) at the highway bridge. Although twice destroyed and rebuilt, it was occupied by the Cherokee until the land was sold in 1819. Franklin, named for

Jesse Franklin, Governor of North Carolina (1820-21), is known for the beauty of its setting and its mountain climate.

Industrial plants of the town, dependent upon the vast natural resources of the section, include a hosiery mill and textile plant, talc and mica mining and grinding, and sawmills. Well managed National Forest lands are giving a substantial yield of timber and pulpwood. Lumber companies, together with a dogwood-shuttle mill, provide a market for much of the timber.

Macon County was formed in 1828 and named for Nathaniel Macon, North Carolina statesman and Revolutionary soldier (*see* TOUR 12). For more than a century Indians and whites have mined this section for gold and precious stones. Holes in which trees bearing 300 rings are growing are believed to be mines left by the Spanish expedition of 1560 following De Soto's earlier trail. Important commercially are mica, kaolin, and asbestos. Experts estimate that the mineral resources of the region have hardly been tapped. Many precious and semiprecious stones occur, including amethyst, garnet, sapphire, beryl, aquamarine, and, on Cowee Creek, fine rubies. The section is known for its apples, cabbages, and other truck crops, though the principal agricultural income is derived from poultry raising, dairying, and livestock.

Franklin's most imposing structure, the MACON COUNTY COURTHOUSE, E. Main St., is a red brick and cast-stone building. The district ranger offices of the U. S. Forest Service are in the Federal Building.

At **208 m.** is the junction with a secondary paved road.

Right on this road (*steep ascent, many hairpin curves*) through dense forests and shrubs, cool, damp, and fragrant, to the WAYAH STATE GAME REFUGE, **2.8 m.**, a 14,000-acre wildlife area within the Nantahala National Forest. It contains deer, wild turkey, ruffed grouse, fox, gray squirrel, quail, and wildcat.

At ARROWWOOD GLADE (*picnic grounds*), **3.3 m.** (R), are trout-rearing pools.

The NANTAHALA (WAYAH) GAP CAMPGROUND (*water, cooking and sanitary facilities*) is at **9.6 m.** (*gravel road*). In Wayah (Ind. wa'-ya', *wolf*) Gap the Cherokee rallied to make a last stand against Gen. Griffith Rutherford in 1776 (*see* TOURS 22 *and* 15B). Tradition says that Daniel Boone took part in this engagement as did his brother, who was killed. After the fight the victorious whites discovered that one of the slain warriors was a woman bedecked in war paint and feathers.

The Appalachian Trail crosses here as it follows the Nantahala Range.

Right from the gap **1.2 m.** on a Forest Service road lined with flame azaleas, to WILSON LICK RANGER STATION, and up the steep course **2.8 m.** farther to the SUMMIT OF WAYAH BALD (5,336 alt.), one of the highest mountains in eastern America whose summit is reached by a motor road. From the JOHN B. BYRNE TOWER, erected in 1937 as a memorial to a former supervisor of the Nantahala National Forest, are views in all directions. The valley far below is marked with the sharp curves of the Little Tennessee River.

West of Wayah Gap on the Forest Service road is NANTAHALA (AQUONE) LAKE, **18 m.** (*fishing lodge, boat docks*), a favorite trout water. A gravel Forest Service road leads to Andrews; a black top State road leads to Nantahala and the junction with US 19, near the Nantahala Power Plant in Nantahala Gorge.

West of the junction with Wayah Rd., US 64 runs through the heavily wooded peaks that surround the Cartoogechaye Creek Valley. At WALLACE GAP, 217.1 m. (3,640 alt.), the route penetrates the crest of the Nantahala Range.

RAINBOW SPRINGS, 221.7 m., was the site of a large band sawmill and village about 1920.

In the YELLOW MOUNTAIN RIDGE is BLACK GAP, 224.2 m. (3,700 alt.). This section is sparsely settled. The few mountain cabins are of hewn logs on rough slabs nailed together.

At 226 m. is the junction with a Forest Service road.

Left on this road to DEEP GAP CAMPGROUND (*water, cooking, and sanitary facilities*), 5.5 m.

At Deep Gap is a junction with the 2,000-mile Maine-to-Georgia Appalachian Trail. This area adjoins the STANDING INDIAN STATE GAME REFUGE, of 33,000 acres, maintained under a cooperative agreement by the N.C. Department of Conservation and Development and the U. S. Forest Service as a game management area.

Right 0.5 m. on the trail (*4-foot, graded*) to STANDING INDIAN (Ind. Yunwitsulenunyi, *where the man stood*) (5,500 alt.), a bald peak called "the grandstand of the southern Appalachians." A Forest Service tower is an excellent vantage point.

Ages ago, according to Cherokee legend, on the banks of the Little Tennessee near Nikwasi (*see above*), an awful beast with widespread wings and beady eyes plunged suddenly from the sky, seized and carried away a child. Such raids, repeated elsewhere, terrorized the people who cleared the mountaintops for lookouts. The den of the marauder was finally discovered on the south slope of this peak, inaccessible even to the most dauntless hunter. In answer to supplication the Great Spirit sent thunder and lightning against the monster and destroyed it; ever after the mountaintops have remained bald. Standing Indian received its name because a warrior stationed there fled, deserting his post, when the destroying bolt flashed from the sky. For this defection he was turned to stone and still appears, a dismal figure at eternal vigil.

Dr. B. W. Wells, while believing that the "riddle of the balds" is as yet unsolved, holds the view that the Indians eliminated the original forests for camps or lookouts and that the grasses obtained so fast a hold they were able to choke out tree seedlings.

In Buck Creek Valley, 226.7 m., is (R) BUCK CREEK RANCH (*fishing, hunting*), a 1,000-acre public campground on the banks of Buck Creek.

Following the course of the Glade Branch of Buck Creek, the highway dips down and then begins a gradual ascent to GLADE GAP, 229.4 m., where it crosses the CHUNKY GAL MOUNTAINS. Unfolded to view at Shooting Creek Vista is a panorama of dark peaks and green valleys bordering the waters of the Hiwassee River.

Between Glade Gap and Elf, smaller streams flow into the waters of Shooting Creek, which parallels the highway. Corundum is found in the valley in large quantities and the creek is famous for its speckled trout. The community of SHOOTING CREEK, 234.2 m. (2,130 alt.), is on the bank of the stream of the same name.

It is said that on one occasion the people of an Indian town on the Hiwassee River, near its confluence with Shooting Creek, prayed and fasted that they might see the Nunnehi (*Immortals*). At the end of 7 days the Nunnehi came and took them under the water. There they still reside and on a warm summer day when the wind ripples the surface those who listen well can hear them talking below.

At **243.6 m.** US 64 crosses the Hiwassee River. Here is a view of Lake Chatuge, a headwaters reservoir built by the TVA. Popular for bass fishing, the lake extends into North Georgia.

HAYESVILLE, **245 m.** (1,893 alt., 356 pop.), the picturesque seat of sparsely settled Clay County stands in a maple grove overlooking the Hiwassee Valley surrounded by towering peaks including the Tusquittees, and Brasstown Bald. The county was named for Henry Clay and the town for George W. Hayes, who represented the district in the legislature. Dairying and the poultry industry are the chief means of livelihood. Eggs from this area are said to have a higher hatchability than any other eggs received by the nearest broiler market.

The mineral resources of the section (consisting of semi-precious stones, mica, rutile, corundum, kaolin, and others) are rich and varied but for the most part undeveloped. Fires Creek and Buck Creek are considered among the best trout streams to be found in southeastern America. The CHATUGE LAKE, **2.5 m.** S. of Hayesville on the Hiwassee River, is a TVA reservoir which abounds in bass, bream, and crappie and serves as a recreational area. In 1838, at the time of the Cherokee removal, Fort Embree, on a hill one mile southwest of Hayesville, was one of the collecting stockades.

The HAYESVILLE HIGH SCHOOL, a modern brick building, is a successor to Hicksville Academy, founded in 1855 by John O. Hicks. It was the oldest school in the State west of Asheville and attracted students from Georgia, Tennessee, and Alabama.

TRUETT MEMORIAL BAPTIST CHURCH, a stately edifice of Crab Orchard stone, dedicated in 1950, stands on a beautiful knoll as a memorial, by the people of Clay County and Baptists throughout the South, to George W. Truett (1867-1944). The great Baptist leader was pastor of the First Baptist Church, Dallas, Tex., 1897-1944, and president of the Baptist World Alliance. His birthplace, now restored, stands one mile northwest.

BRASSTOWN, **258.1 m.** (150 pop.), is so called through the white man's false rendering of the Indian word meaning *place of fresh green*. In the GENERAL STORE (R) is a collection of Cherokee relics.

The JOHN C. CAMPBELL FOLK SCHOOL (*visitors welcome*), on a 175-acre farm, is a nonprofit venture in rural adult education. It was organized by

Mrs. Olive Dame Campbell, in memory of her husband, director of the Southern Highland Division of the Russell Sage Foundation and author of the *Southern Highlander and His Homeland*.

The school program falls into two general phases: a course, inspired by the Danish folk schools, for young adults, to supplement public school work; and a community program involving recreational, cultural, and economic as well as educational features. Handicrafts have been developed to enable the people to create beauty as well as to supplement farm incomes. Examples of their work are on display in the CRAFT ROOM of the main building. Part of the school plant is a FOLK MUSEUM, housed in an old log cabin.

At the mouth of Peachtree Creek is a silk and nylon throwing plant.

MURPHY, 266.1 m. (1,535 alt., 2,433 pop.), at the confluence of the beautiful Hiwassee and Valley rivers, is the seat of Cherokee County and one of the oldest settlements in the extreme western section of the State. Streets of generous width center on the square. The CHEROKEE COUNTY COURTHOUSE (1926), built of local blue marble, is a two-story structure of neoclassic design, with a corner entrance in the form of a pedimented Corinthian portico. A large octagonal cupola with a clock and crowning lanterns surmounts the building. The first courthouse was burned in 1865 by local soldiers who deserted the Confederate ranks and had a Federal company in Tennessee. Most of them had cases pending against them, and the papers were in the courthouse.

When first established in 1838, as an Indian trading post, the settlement was known as Huntersville for its founder, Col. A. R. S. Hunter from Virginia, though, according to a letter to Gov. Dudley in 1837, there was a local desire for it to be named Junaluska for the great Indian chief of that name (*see* TOUR 22 *and* 22C). In 1838, when Fort Butler was set up for the Cherokee removal, Col. Hunter entertained Gen. Winfield Scott at his home. The town was renamed in honor of Archibald D. Murphey, statesman and champion of popular education. The difference in spelling is the result of a typographical error.

Murphy has several sawmills, a hosiery mill, and a throwing (yarn) mill.

Murphy is at the junction with US 19-129.

About **4 m.** NW. of Murphy, on May 6, 1865, the last battle of the Civil War east of the Mississippi was fought on Hanging Dog Creek. About 100 Confederates under Maj. Stephen Whitaker of Col. William Thomas' legion routed the same company of Federals who had burned the courthouse at Murphy.

Near KINSEY, 267.9 m. (1,609 alt., 25 pop.), talc stone is mined and ground or sawed into crayons.

At 276.1 m. is the junction with NC 294.

Right on NC 294 to SHOAL CREEK, to the junction with a marked road, **12.5 m.**; R. **4 m.** on this road to HIWASSEE DAM SITE, a TVA project begun in 1937. This dam is similar in design to the Norris Dam in Tennessee, though 35 feet higher. It is 1,265 feet long, with a spillway in the middle. It is 300 feet high and was built at a cost of $21,500,000. It creates a lake of 10 square miles, extending as far east as Murphy, makes a connecting link with the interstate navigable streams, and constitutes an aid in flood control, while developing electrical energy as a byproduct.

At **18 m.** on NC 294 is the FIELDS OF THE WOOD, the Tomlinson Church of God shrine, where may be seen a mammoth cross containing places for flags of all nations; a colossal likeness in stone of the *New Testament;* a replica of Christ's sepulchre; and the Ten Commandments, which cover a mountainside.

Near the Tennessee Line on US 64 the landscape is desolate. The vegetation was killed by sulphur fumes from the copper smelters at Copper Hill, Tenn. Though the cause was removed, vegetation has been slow to return, because the topsoil was washed away by rainfall.

Tradition relates that these copper mines were lost to the State of North Carolina because the surveyors ran out of liquor when they reached the high peak just north of the Hiwassee River. Instead of continuing the line southwest they turned almost due south to the Georgia Line, where they knew of a still.

At **289 m.**, US 64 crosses the Tennessee Line, 4 miles east of Ducktown, Tenn.

RACCOON ON THE HUNT

BRUIN AS TREE CLIMBER

MAMA OPOSSUM WITH BROOD

QUAIL HUNTING, PINEHURST (JOHN G. HEMMER)

TROUT FISHING, UPPER DAVIDSON RIVER (ASHEVILLE CHAMBER OF COMMERCE)

RHODODENDRON BLOSSOMS

SHORTIA GALACIFOLIA, FOUND ONLY IN THIS STATE

FOX HUNT, SOUTHERN PINES (EDDY'S STUDIO)

MOTH BOAT RACE, EDENTON

TYPICAL ROAD AT PINEHURST (JOHN G. HEMMER)

BRINGING IN THE GAME

CAMPING DEER HUNTERS

FORT MACON STATE PARK

FIFTH GREEN OF FAMOUS NO. 2 CHAMPIONSHIP COURSE AT PINEHURST

VISITORS WATCH THE WILD CANADA GEESE AT GADDY'S POND, NEAR ANSONVILLE

TOUR 14 *(US 264)*

Zebulon—Wilson—Greenville—Washington—Swanquarter—Engelhard—
Junction with US 64; US 264. **201 m.**

Limited accommodations after leaving Washington.

This route runs first through farm lands where bright-leaf tobacco is the
principal crop until it reaches low-lying country, where it follows the irregular outlines of the north shore of Pamlico River and Pamlico Sound.
Swamps make much of this land impractical for farming. Fishing is the
chief occupation. The region abounds with game, particularly waterfowl.

US 264 branches from the junction with US 64 at ZEBULON, **0 m.**
(*see* TOUR *13*), and is an alternate route to Mann's Harbor, where it rejoins
US 64.

The highway passes the small farming villages of MIDDLESEX, **8 m.**
(446 pop.) and BAILEY, **13 m.** (743 pop.), developed since the Norfolk
Southern R. R. was built through here in 1907.

Near Bailey is the largest stone quarry in the South. Originally opened
in 1914 to provide stone for the Cape Lookout Breakwater, it shipped 50
cars of stone per day for three years. Recently reopened, it now ships 100
cars per day.

WILSON, **25 m.** (*see* TOUR *3a*), is at the junction with US 301 (*see*
TOUR *3a*).

At **28 m.** is the junction with NC 58.

Right on this road to STANTONSBURG, **8 m.** (92 alt., 627 pop.), a thriving
village before the Revolution, when Contentnea Creek was navigable for some
miles above.

Fanny Kemble, the famous actress, breakfasted at an inn here in 1838. Her
description of the repast bears repetition:

"There were plates of unutterable-looking things, which made one feel as if
one would never swallow food again. There were some eggs, all begrimed with
smoke, and powdered with cinders; some unbaked dough, cut into little lumps,
by way of bread; and a white, hard substance, calling itself butter, which had an
infinitely nearer resemblance to tallow. The mixture presented to us by way of

tea was absolutely undrinkable; and when I begged for a glass of milk, they brought a tumbler covered with dust and dirt, full of such sour stuff that I was obliged to put it aside, after endeavoring to taste it."

At Peacock's Bridge, 1.5 m. SW of Stantonsburg on NC 55 Lt. Col. Banastre Tarleton's British dragoons engaged in a skirmish, May 4, 1781, with Col. James Gorham and his 400 militiamen from Pitt County.

Near SARATOGA, 35 m. (366 pop.), once stood Amerson's Tavern, where Prince Karl Bernhard, Duke of Saxe-Weimar-Eisenach, spent the night in 1825. He slept in an attic room of a wooden building with a brick chimney and could see through the cracks into the room beneath. He was "quite shocked that so many gentlemen had the habit of chewing tobacco in spite of the evil smell and even in the company of ladies."

FARMVILLE, 47 m. (see tour 2) is at the junction with US 258 (see tour 2).

GREENVILLE, 63 m. (55 alt., 16,724 pop.) is the seat of Pitt County, formed in 1760 and named for William Pitt. The first court met at John Hardy's house at Logtown on the south side of Tar River, marked by a tablet on a boulder (3 m. E.). Behind this, it is claimed, was the first brick road in eastern North Carolina, built by Parson Blount to enable his slaves to roll brandy barrels up the hill. In 1774 the town of Martinsboro was established on Richard Evans' land, and in 1787 it was chosen as the county seat with the name of Greenesville, later changed to Greenville. George Washington wrote in his diary that on Apr. 19, 1791, he "dined at a trifling place called Greenville."

Today, Greenville is the commercial center of the largest tobacco-growing county in the State. In the fall, when growers bring their tobacco to market, the streets are crowded with trucks, automobiles, and wagons laden with the crop.

Thomas J. Jarvis, Governor of North Carolina (1879-85), U. S. Senator, and Minister to Brazil, practiced law in Greenville. Elected lieutenant-governor in 1876, he became governor in 1879 when Gov. Vance was elected to the U. S. Senate. Thus, Gov. Jarvis served longer continuously than any governor since the Revolution. Buried at Cherry Hill Cemetery, his memory is perpetuated by the Jarvis Memorial Methodist Church.

The Courthouse (1910) is a three-story, white brick structure with Ionic porticos, corner quoins, and a clock cupola.

East Carolina College, on the east side of town, was established by the general assembly in 1907 as the East Carolina Teachers Training School. The present plant consists of approximately 130 acres of land on which are 23 buildings. Originally a girls' school, it is now a coeducational college which offers M. A. degrees.

On the south side of town are 21 Tobacco Warehouses (open in fall), with a total floor space of 3,500,000 square feet. One warehouse alone covers 11.4 acres of space. The 1953 sale amounted to $65,585,690.

Greenville was the eastern terminus of the GREENVILLE AND RALEIGH PLANK ROAD, chartered in 1850 and completed as far as Wilson in 1853, the western terminus. The road followed practically the same route as US 264. The charter required anyone using it without paying the toll to be fined $5 if white; if colored, to be given not more than 20 lashes.

Greenville is at the junction with NC 11.

Right on this road to BLOUNT HALL, 16 m., a frame two-story house with 5 dormers in front and 3 in the rear, built before 1762 by Jacob Blount, a member of the Assembly 1754-62, 1764-71, and of Provincial Congress, 1775-76. Two large rooms on the first floor have original wainscoting, though the plaster has been replaced. Jacob Blount was the father of the famous Blount brothers, prominent in Revolutionary and early State history. William, a signer of the U. S. Constitution, was appointed by Washington as Governor of the Territory Southwest of the Ohio River; Willie (pronounced Wiley) was Governor of Tenn. (1809-15); Thomas served in U. S. Congress intermittently 1793-1812; and John Gray was a merchant prince, whose lands in this and other states made him one of the largest landowners in America.

GRIMESLAND, 74.7 m. (36 alt., 414 pop.), on the south side of the Tar River, was built on part of the extensive Grimes plantation.

At 77.6 m. is the junction with old US 264.

Left on this road to the GRIMES HOUSE (*private*), 1.5 m., a two-story, clap-boarded, frame house with a single-story porch across the front and brick end chimneys. The house, erected for Dempsie Grimes I in 1793, was on one of the largest plantations of the period. Here was born Confederate Gen. Bryan Grimes (1828-80), and J. Bryan Grimes (1868-1923), who served as Secretary of State of North Carolina. Gen. Grimes, involved in a feud with three Paramore brothers, was shot from ambush on Aug. 14, 1880. William Parker was charged with the murder, but was acquitted for lack of evidence. Parker left the community but returned in 1891 and is said to have drunkenly boasted that he was the assassin. The next morning Parker's body was found hanging from the river bridge at Washington.

At CHOCOWINITY, 81 m. (*see* TOUR 1b), US 264 forms a junction with US 17 (*see* TOUR 1b), which it follows N. to WASHINGTON (*see* TOUR 1b).

East of Washington, 85 m., US 264 passes through an old agricultural country, planted mostly in tobacco and corn.

At 95.5 m. is the junction with the Camp Leach Rd.

Right on this road is a footpath, 300 yds.; L. about 30 paces on this path to the MAGIC HORSE TRACKS in a little hollow. Tradition relates that on Aug. 19, 1813, Jesse Elliott rode off to enter his horse in a Sunday race. When warned by church members against violating the Sabbath, he retorted: "I'll ride, though I ride to Hell." Here he was thrown and killed by his horse whose hoof-prints supposedly restore themselves when covered with earth.

At 96 m. is the junction with NC 92 (*see* TOUR 14A).

On the outskirts of YEATSVILLE, **104 m.** (40 pop.), is Pungo Creek, beyond which the highway passes through swampland, with the EAST DISMAL SWAMP on the L. and the HELL SWAMP on the R. The head of Broad Creek is crossed at **109 m.**, then Pantego Creek on the outskirts of PANTEGO, **111.4 m.** (6 alt., 275 pop.) (*fishing boats available here for fishing in Pantego Creek*).

Left from Pantego on NC 99 to TERRA CEIA, **5 m.** (100 pop.), a settlement of Netherlanders, who have prospered by extensive cultivation and proper drainage. One of them, Henrick Van Dorp, introduced floriculture in the area. Today about 375 acres are devoted to bulbs (*tulips, 25 acres, bloom Apr. 1-20; iris, 50 acres, and peonies 100 acres, bloom Apr. 20-May 10; gladioli, 200 acres, bloom June 1-Aug.*).

The route parallels Pantego Creek to BELHAVEN, **115 m.** (4 alt., 2,528 pop.), lying on a large bay formed by the Pungo River as it flows into Pamlico River. A 12-foot channel gives access to the Intracoastal Waterway. Lumbering, trucking, fishing, and oystering are the principal occupations. A large crabmeat canning factory is the chief industry.

LEECHVILLE, **123 m.** (200 pop.), is a village (*stores, gas; skiffs for rent*), on the banks of the Pungo River in which LM bass and stripers are caught, especially in Aug.

At **125.9 m.** is the junction with a sand road.

Left on this sand road **1.5 m.** (*bad in wet weather*) and again left, **9.5 m.** to NEW LAKE, shown on maps as Alligator Lake, a little-known lake more than three miles in diameter, hidden amid the thick forest of bays, cypresses, and myrtles, laden with Spanish moss and tropical vines, under which grow damp ferns and shrubs. Headstones in an old cemetery indicate farmers were settled here as early as 1777.

At **128.2 m.** the route crosses the Intracoastal Waterway over a canal connecting Alligator Lake and Pungo River. A drainage canal runs by the road (L).

SWANQUARTER, **145.2 m.** (10 alt., 212 pop.), seat of Hyde County, is on Swanquarter Bay, an indentation of Pamlico Sound below the Pamlico River.

Hyde County, formerly the precinct of Wickham, was formed from Bath County in 1738 and named for Edward Hyde, Governor of North Carolina (1710-12). Peat bogs abound throughout the section and salt marshes border the coast. Large oyster beds are in adjacent waters.

The HYDE COUNTY COURTHOUSE is a red brick structure built in 1850 to which two wings have been added.

The present brick PROVIDENCE CHURCH (Methodist) is on the site of an older wooden church. There was much controversy over the site for the first church. A public-spirited citizen offered space in his yard when the owner of the chosen site would not sell. In August, 1876, just after the church had been finished, a tidal wave swept over the fan-shaped bay into the village. In answer to prayers of a young ministerial student for Providential intervention to make the better site available, the church was floated across the main street to the spot first selected. Early next morning the lot owner was at the courthouse eager to give the church a deed to the property, convinced that it was holy ground. The church, then named Providence, was the only building moved by the storm. This frame structure now stands behind the brick church and is used as a Sunday School building.

East of Swanquarter the highway parallels the south shore of LAKE MATTAMUSKEET (*bass fishing*) within the U. S. Biological Survey's 50,000-acre LAKE MATTAMUSKEET WILDLIFE REFUGE. Several attempts to pump off the water from this lake, which is below sea level and on submarginal land, were not only unsuccessful but also drove away the great number of geese and swans accustomed to winter here. After the Government's purchase of this area in 1934, the pump house was converted into an administration building and many acres of grain and duck foods were planted to attract both upland game birds and waterfowl. In addition to geese, ducks, and swans, the area contains egrets, herons, terns, loons, grebes, cormorants, bitterns, eagles, ospreys, sand pipers, gulls, and quail. Two areas of approximately 5,000 acres each adjoining the lake have been set aside as public shooting grounds, operated seasonally by the North Carolina Dept. of Conservation and Development.

At **153.7 m.** is the junction with NC 94.

Left on NC 94 to a causeway (*fishing*) which bisects Lake Mattamuskeet. This causeway was constructed by a suction dredge which pulled soil from each side to form the roadbed. Concrete-bottomed culverts allow wind tides in the lake to flow east and west. This route intersects with US 64 at Columbia, 35 miles (*see* TOUR *13*).

NEW HOLLAND, **156 m.** (111 pop.), is a lake-side village built while the process of reclamation was under way on land lying below the level of the water that once covered it (*headquarters for geese hunters, hunting guides; lodge, cafe, tourist homes*).

From New Holland a dirt road runs S. along the "outfall" canal from Lake Mattamuskeet to Pamlico Sound, **8 m.** This area is being slowly developed and has a fish house at the terminus.

LAKE LANDING, **162 m.** (10 pop.), on Lake Mattamuskeet, is a hunting and fishing center. An octagonal INK BOTTLE HOUSE (*private*), two stories, with shingled walls and the chimney in the center, was erected as a dwelling before 1860.

ENGELHARD, **171 m.** (600 pop.), on Pamlico Sound is a village of many canals. Thousands of truckloads of fish, oysters, and shrimp are shipped from here annually (*a recently-built frame hotel has modern conveniences*).

From Engelhard the route runs northeast through low uninhabited swamp and forest land. Bear and deer inhabit the cranberry bogs and wild grape-vines which stretch to the west.

At **196 m.** is the junction with a marked road.

Right on this road, **1 m.**, to STUMPY POINT (4 alt., 300 pop.), an isolated fishing village lying like a half-moon around its bay (*goose and brant hunting in season*). Once the shad capital of America (as many as 3,000,000 pounds have been shipped annually), it still depends on this industry for its livelihood.

US 264 continues up the desolate wilderness of Dare County to a junction, 3 miles E. of Mann's Harbor, with US 64, **201 m.** (*see* TOUR *13*), which is joined to its eastern terminus at Nags Head (*see* TOURS *13 and 1A*).

TOUR 14A (NC 92)

Junction with US 264—Bath—Bayview—Rest Haven—Belhaven; NC 92. 24 m.

Limited accommodations at present at Bath, but there are a numer of rental cottages and boats at the 12 small river resorts adjacent to NC 92 and its offsets.

This route passes through Colonial Bath and near a number of small summer resorts.

NC 92, branching southeast from US 264 **0 m.**, 11 miles east of Washington and rejoining 264 at Belhaven, passes through a section of well-kept farms and an area of historical interest.

At **5.5 m.** is the junction with the Archbell's Point Rd.

Right on this road to the SITE OF THE HOME OF GOV. CHARLES EDEN, **2 m.**, as well as that of Gov. Robert Daniel and Secretary Tobias Knight, near the mouth of Bath Creek. On the tract, also known as the Beasley Place, is an old house in a bad state of repair. Nearby is the brick foundation of a house with a cellar and evidence of a tunnel to the Creek. This is thought to be the basement to EDEN'S PALACE.

Charles Eden was Governor of the Province from 1714 until the time of his death in 1722 (*see* EDENTON) and for a time, 1714-18, maintained his capital at Bath. It is said that the town once served as headquarters of the pirate Blackbeard (*see* "Drive Along the Banks," after TOUR *1A*), whose house and base of operations were at Plum Point, across the creek from Eden's home. Legend relates that a subterranean passage was cut from the palace to the steep bank of the creek, through which, in complicity with the pirate, Eden and his secretary, Tobias Knight, shared the pirate's plunder. Knight was tried for improper dealings with Blackbeard, and though acquitted, lost face. His accusers were unable to prove that Eden was implicated, and his defenders contend that the accusations were made by political enemies.

Blackbeard came to Bath after having taken advantage of the offer of pardon extended by Britain's king to all pirates who would surrender themselves and agree to abandon piracy. There is an interesting legend that Blackbeard paid unsuccessful court to the daughter of Gov. Eden, who was at the time engaged to another man. Incensed by his rejection, Blackbeard captured his rival, put off to sea, cut off one of his prisoner's hands, and had the young man hurled into the sea. The hand was sent in a silver casket to Miss Eden, who languished and died. Subsequently the pirate married a young girl, reputed to have been his thirteenth wife, but instead of settling down, he soon slipped into his old piratical ways, whereupon the people called upon Gov. Eden for action. The Governor failed to respond, so the appeal was taken to Gov. Spottswood of Virginia, who offered a reward of £100 for the pirate's capture. Learning that Blackbeard was in Pamlico Sound near Ocracoke Inlet, Lt. Robert Maynard of the Royal Navy came down from Hampton Roads, Va., with two small ships, sought him out and engaged him in battle, Nov. 22, 1718. Blackbeard was killed in personal combat with Maynard, who cut off the pirate's head, fastened it to the bowsprit of his ship, and sailed back to Bath where there was great rejoicing. The pirate crew was taken to Williamsburg, Va., for trial and hanging.

On the shore nearby is a new summer development known as Cool Point, with several modern cottages.

BATH, 6 m. (9 alt., 381 pop.), is the oldest town in North Carolina, the first official port of entry, and the first meeting place of the colonial assembly of the Province. This riverside town on the west bank of the peninsula formed by Bath and Back creeks, had changed little in the past century until the last decade. Now many stores and homes with modern conveniences have been built. In spite of this, the colonial atmosphere still prevails, and many of the lovely homes, old before the Revolution, still remain in a good state of repair. The home sites of many prominent settlers have recently been located by Colonial Bath, Inc., a corporation similar to that at Williamsburg, Va. This organization has recently been chartered to carry on restoration work at Bath and in the area and is now mapping plans for a pageant in 1955, commemorating the 250th anniversary of the incorporation of the town in 1705.

The old town, never large, played an important part in the early political, social, and economic life of the Province. Five governors lived at Bath: Robert Daniel, Thomas Cary, Edward Hyde, Charles Eden, and Matthew Rowan and perhaps Burrington for awhile. Gov. Samuel Ashe was born at Bath, as was his brother, Gen. John Ashe of the Revolution and his sister, Mary Ashe, who married Dr. George Moore and became the grandmother of the Hon. George Davis, Confederate Attorney General. Hon. John Baptista Ashe was Speaker of the Assembly from Bath and was the father of this famous trio. The family moved to the Cape Fear area in 1729.

Two chief justices of the colony lived here. Christopher Gale, the first chief justice (1712), lived at "Kirby Grange" near here; he was also Collector of the Port of Beaufort (see TOUR 15). Edward Moseley, after residing in Bath, moved to Edenton, when the government transferred there (see EDENTON) and later settled on the Cape Fear. Four surveyors general also lived here at one time: John Lawson; Edward Moseley (see above), Robert Palmer; and his son, also an historian, William Palmer (also Secretary to Tryon, a Naval Officer and representative from Bath County at the Hillsborough Convention). Christopher Gale, John Lawson, and Lionel Reading, a prominent planter in the area, helped to arrange for Baron De Graffenried's settlement of New Bern.

In 1709 an Anglican missionary, William Gordon, described the place: "Here is no church, although they have begun to build a town called

Bath. It consists of twelve houses, being the only town in the province. They have a small collection of books for a library, which were carried over by the Reverend Doctor Bray, and some land is laid out for a glebe; but no minister would ever stay long in the place, though several have come hither from the West Indies and other plantations in America ... in all probability it will be the centre of trade, as having the advantage of a better inlet for shipping, and surrounded with pleasant savannas, very useful for stocks of cattle."

Three decades later George Whitfield, preacher and evangelist, wrote from Bath: "I am here, hunting in the woods, these ungospelized wilds for sinners." There is a tradition that Whitfield, angered by the refusal of lodging, walked outside the town and invoked the curse of Heaven upon the place and its inhabitants. Some contend that since that time it has failed to prosper.

Bath was originally called the Town of Pamticoe (or Pamticough) on Old Town Creek. This Indian word survives in the name of the neighboring county, river, and sound. In the late 17th century an epidemic of smallpox among the Indians along the Pamlico River so reduced their number that the way was cleared for white settlers. The first of these were French Protestants from Europe, seeking religious liberty. They were followed by colonists from the upper Albemarle and from Virginia, England, and New England, who settled along the river as early as 1690.

The town was the seat of old Bath County, formed in 1696 and named for the Earl of Bath, one of the Lords Proprietors. This county, composed of the precincts of Archdale, Pampticough (Beaufort), and Wickham, extended from the Albemarle Sound to the Cape Fear River and from the Atlantic Ocean westward. In 1738 Bath County was divided, and the town became the seat of Beaufort County; in 1785 the county seat was moved to Washington. The village was a point of attack in the Tuscarora massacre of Sept. 22, 1711. For 40 years thereafter, by act of the assembly, the anniversary was observed as a day of fasting and prayer.

The TOWN MARKER (L), on Main St., is a stone monument commemorating the historical importance of the town. Bath was formally laid off in 1704 by John Lawson, surveyor general to the Crown, who with Joel Martin and Simon Alderson were its founders. When incorporated Mar. 8, 1705, at a meeting of the assembly held at the house of Capt. John Hecklefield on Little River, Bath contained 12 houses.

The MARSH HOUSE (L), Main St., was built in 1744 for Michael Cataunch. The Rev. Alexander Stewart, Rector of St. Thomas Church who married Cataunch's widow, lived there a few years. Robert Palmer bought it in 1764. He and his son, William, each of whom was surveyor general, made it their home successively for about 50 years. Jonathan Marsh, shipping master from Rhode Island, purchased it about 1810, and it remained in the family for about a hundred years. Mrs. Mary Evans, the niece of Michael Cataunch, is buried back of the house under a SOAPSTONE MARKER.

Although front porches and columns have been added and the small-paned windows have been replaced with modern sashes, the structure is well preserved. Its most curious feature is a brick end chimney, 17 feet across at the base and 4 feet thick, containing two windows that open on tile-floored closets in upper and lower stories. At the top of the house the chimney breaks into twin flues, a slanting roof covering the division. The cemented stone cellar, 8 feet deep, has a large fireplace with ovens in the side. Edna Ferber got her material for her novel *Show Boat* while staying in this house.

The BUZZARD HOTEL (L), Main St., is a remodeled dwelling built about 1740 and named for its builder. There is a stepped ivy-clad chimney.

The WILLIAMS HOUSE, SE. corner Main St., where NC 92 turns L., now called the Glebe House, is the RECTORY OF ST. THOMAS CHURCH. It is thought to have been built in 1764 as the original Glebe House, the only one ever built in North Carolina. It was later the HOME OF JOHN F. TOMPKINS, founder of the State Fair and publisher and editor of the *Farmers' Journal*. It is a weathered two-story frame structure built in 1748, shaded by arching oaks and elms, and surrounded by a hedge and an old picket fence.

ST. THOMAS EPISCOPAL CHURCH, on the R. as the highway turns L. into Bayview Rd., built in 1734, is the oldest standing church in North Carolina and one of the oldest in the United States. Certain lands were early set aside as the glebe of St. Thomas Parish. The Parish of Pamticough, for the people of Bath, was organized with a vestry in 1701 and was partly maintained from England with assistance from the Society for the Propagation of the Gospel in Foreign Parts until long after the construction of the present building. St. Thomas had the FIRST PUBLIC LIBRARY IN NORTH CAROLINA, started in 1700 by the Rev. Thomas Bray, who was founder and secretary of the society.

From the enclosing hedge a brick wall between ancient graves leads to this tiny church on a little knoll in a grassy yard. It is a simple rectangular building, without tower or apse, of common brick in Flemish bond with a slight pattern in the headers of the gabled façade. The doorway, with its arched brick pediment and hand-pegged wooden door, is the only opening in the façade. Cuspid bargeboards edge the gable rafters. Ivy has crept up the front and sides and through the window frames.

The interior of St. Thomas recalls the Tuscarora massacre when, to thwart desecration by the savages, the dead were interred beneath the straight-backed pews of the original church. These pews, elevated on wooden platforms a step above the tile floor, are still in use, the present church occupying the identical site of its predecessor. Recessed windows add to the charm of the interior. Silver candelabra on the altar, presented to the church by King George II, are still in use. The bell bears the date 1732, when it was cast in London. Known as a Queen Anne bell, it is believed to have been bought for Bath Church from the Queen's bounty money, as she left a fund for the purchase of church furniture and for charity. The silver chalice, obtained the same way, has been missing since 1905. At the right of the altar is a tablet with a long epitaph, quoted verbatim, with change of name and place, by Edna Ferber in her novel *Show Boat* (*see* ELIZABETH CITY). In 1925, Miss

Ferber visited the *James Adams Floating Palace Theater,* then anchored at Bath, "the only show boat experience I ever had." Buried beneath the church in 1765 is Mrs. Margaret Palmer, wife of the surveyor general of the lands of the Province. Under a glass case is an old family BIBLE, presented to the parish by Capt. S. A. Ashe of Raleigh. The Prayer Book and Psalms in prose and poetry are bound with the Bible.

At the south end of Main St., on Bonners Point (L), is the OLD BONNER HOUSE, a colonial structure, with many-paned windows and a doorway with side lights and transom.

An OLD SHIP'S BELL, which legend says was taken from a ship belonging to Blackbeard, hangs at the rear of the public school and is used to summon the children to classes.

After leaving Bath, NC 92 continues down the northern side of the Pamlico. Roads lead (R) at intervals to settlements of summer cottages on the banks of the River. At 8 m. a road leads (R) to PLUM POINT, where a number of summer cottages have recently been built in a new development, BREEZY SHORES.

BAYVIEW, **9 m.** (*cottages, swimming, boating, fishing*), is an older summer resort on the shore of the Pamlico River, popular for fish fries and dancing.

From Bayview, NC 92 swings north and passes, at intervals, marked roads (R) leading to small summer settlements along the beaches of the Pamlico and Pungo rivers.

At **24 m.,** NC 92 forms a junction with US 264 at Belhaven (*see* TOUR *14*).

TOUR 15A (US 70)

Durham—Raleigh—Goldsboro—New Bern—Beaufort—Atlantic; US 70. 218 m.

This route between Durham, **0 m.** (*see* DURHAM), and Core Sound traverses the hills of the industrial piedmont, the agricultural flatlands, and the recreational beaches and fishing villages of the coast. In this part of eastern North Carolina the people are as interested in the tradition of their land as in the current price of the tobacco crop.

At **5 m.** US 70-A (L) is an alternate and longer route to Raleigh.

At **8 m.** on US 70-A is the junction with NC 54, which leads (R) to Chapel Hill, **15 m.** (*see* CHAPEL HILL).

At **15 m.** (R) on US 70-A is the NANCY JONES HOUSE (*private*), a white two-story clapboarded structure built in 1805. It has a steeply pitched gable roof, exterior end chimneys, and a double-gallery entrance portico with pediment. A windmill stands behind the house.

The long undiscovered diary of Mrs. Ann (called Nancy) Jones describes a widely quoted incident. On a hot summer day in 1838, Gov. Edward B. Dudley of North Carolina (*see* WILMINGTON) and Gov. Pierce Mason Butler of South Carolina arrived at the same time, were ushered into the parlor and served tall cool mint juleps. Lany, the maid, and the houseboy ran to mix more juleps, but not quickly enough for the thirsty Governors.

Lany reentered the room as the Governor of North Carolina was saying to the Governor of South Carolina: "It's a damn long time between drinks." "Damn long!" his companion replied. When Mrs. Jones heard of the remark from the scandalized maid, she was shocked and embarrassed at the implied reflection on her hospitality.

Another version has been handed down in the family of John Motley Morehead, Minister to Sweden (1930-33), whose grandfather was Governor of North Carolina (1841-45). After futile correspondence between Governor Morehead, a Whig, and Gov. J. H. Hammond of South Carolina, a Democrat, concerning the extradition of a political offender, the two officials met with their staffs and legal advisers for a conference on the State Line, not far from Charlotte. During the discussion Governor Hammond became excited and finally announced that further refusal would result in his sending a military force into North Carolina to seize the fugitive.

"Now, sir," he shouted, crashing his fist upon the table, "what is your answer?"

"My reply, sir," answered Governor Morehead with great deliberation, "is this: It's a damn long time between drinks."

This unexpected answer had the effect of so relieving the tension that the two Governors were able to talk dispassionately and eventually to reach a settlement satisfactory to both states.

At CARY, 17 m. (496 alt., 1,446 pop.), is the western junction with US 1-64 (*see* TOURS 5 *and* 13). US 70-A unites with US 64 to Raleigh, 26 m.

At 22 m. US 70-A passes (R and L) the EXPERIMENT FARM of the State College of Agriculture and Engineering of the University of North Carolina, conducted in cooperation with the State Department of Agriculture. From the farm crimson clover was introduced into the State in 1890 and the culture of lespedeza, soybeans, and other crops has been promoted. Lespedeza was inadvertently brought to North Carolina by Union troops in hay imported from China.

At 13 m. (R) a road leads to CRABTREE CREEK STATE PARK (*fishing in streams during season, in lake from Labor Day to June 1; 2 equipped picnic areas; 39 group camping sites; tent and trailer campground; hiking; nature study with naturalist on duty June-Aug.*). The park contains 3,886 acres of heavily wooded topography with several picturesque streams. Both flora and fauna are interesting. Animals include raccoon, fox, opossum, squirrel, muskrat, rabbit, wild turkey, quail, and owl.

At 17 m. is the junction with US 15-A (*see* TOUR 6) which unites with US 70 to Raleigh, 23 m.

RALEIGH, 23 m. (*see* RALEIGH).

Points of Interest: State Capitol, Christ Church, State Art Museum, Museum of Natural History, Site of the Birthplace of Andrew Johnson, Joel Lane House, N. C. State College of Agriculture and Engineering, State Fair Arena, and others.

Raleigh is at the junction with US 1 (*see* TOUR 5), US 64 (*see* TOUR 13), and US 15-A (*see* TOUR 6).

At 26 m. (R) is the NORTH CAROLINA SCHOOL FOR NEGRO DEAF AND BLIND CHILDREN (*open on application to office*), erected in 1931, a group of 4 red brick buildings on a 200-acre tract.

GARNER, 29 m. (386 alt., 1,180 pop.).

At 30 m. is the STATE FORESTRY NURSERY, one of the three operated by the N. C. Dept. of Conservation and Development. Of the 314 acres in the tract, 25 acres are devoted to seedling production; the remainder is in forest. This nursery, established in 1926, has an annual production of about 16 million seedlings, mostly loblolly, long-leaf, short-leaf, and slash pine, but some red cedar, yellow poplar, back walnut, and black locust.

CLAYTON, 39 m. (345 alt., 2,229 pop.), is a market and industrial town (textiles, insecticides, peanut and cottonseed oil). From 1759 to 1771 the Johnston County courthouse, which was standing as late as 1809, was at Hinton's Quarter one mile south of Clayton. The town developed around and was known as Gulley's Store until 1857 when the railroad reached that point. In 1869 it was incorporated as Clayton. An earlier town known as Roxborough, located at its eastern limits, was said to have had an excellent academy, Roxborough Hall.

Following the Battle of Bentonville (Mar. 19-21, 1865) there was a skirmish in Clayton as segments of the two armies moved along. The Confederates put two brass cannon on a hill at the ELLINGTON HOUSE (*private*). As Union forces came up from Smithfield they received volley after volley from these cannon.

Clayton was the birthplace of Herman Harrell Horne (1874-1946), author, psychologist, and teacher, and Needham Y. Gulley (1855-1945), professor of law at Wake Forest College. William E. Dodd (1869-1940), ambassador to Germany (1933-37), historian, and author, was born a few miles west of Clayton just inside Wake County.

At intervals, in fields near the highway southeast of Clayton, are great, smooth granite boulders, sometimes in great heaps, with trees growing among them.

SMITHFIELD, 49 m. (*see* TOUR *3*) is at the junction with US 301 (*see* TOUR *3*).

PRINCETON, 63 m. (152 alt., 608 pop.), grew up at a trading center established at Boon Hill, the home of Joseph Boon, a member of both houses of the State legislature at different times between 1781 and 1808 and of the Constitutional Convention of 1788. Boon (d. 1813) was granted land in the area as early as 1745. The first train from Goldsboro west on the North Carolina R.R. passed through here in Oct., 1854. In 1873 the town was incorporated as Princeton. Three of the 4 paragraphs in the act were devoted to prohibiting the sale of whiskey in the village or within two miles thereof.

GOLDSBORO, 74 m. (*see* TOUR *4*), is at the junction with US 117 (*see* TOUR *4*).

At 75 m. are the REMAINS OF EARTHEN BREASTWORKS thrown up in defense of the city before the Battle of Goldsboro (1863).

LA GRANGE, 86 m. (113 alt., 1,854 pop.), a trading center with a hardware-manufacturing plant, was first known as Rantersville (or Rambertsville) and later Moseley Hall. The latter was the name of the nearby plantation of Edward Moseley (d. 1749) (*see* EDENTON) and the birthplace of William Dunn Moseley (1795-1863), first elected Governor of Florida. No traces of the plantation or hall remain.

At 99 m. is the junction with a marked, narrow dirt road.

Right on this road to the GRAVE OF RICHARD CASWELL, 0.3 m., first Governor of North Carolina under the constitution (1776-80).

At 99.4 m. is the junction with a marked road.

Left on this road to the junction with another marked road, 3.4 m. Right 1 m. on this road to DOBBS' FARM FOR NEGRO WOMEN (*open subject to regulations*), a reformatory institution of the State prison system comprising 500 acres and several buildings. The plant, opened in 1929, usually has about 275 inmates.

At **99.5 m.** (L) is the CASWELL TRAINING SCHOOL (*open subject to regulations*), a State institution for mentally defective juveniles. There are 1,250 acres of land, the larger portion of which is under cultivation.

KINSTON, **101 m.** (*see* TOUR 2), is at the junction with US 258 (*see* TOUR 2).

At **102 m.** the highway crosses the muddy Neuse River, subject to floods after excessive upstate rains.

From here the route passes through low fertile plains of the central coastal section. Fields of tobacco alternate with those of corn, cotton, potatoes, and hay.

DOVER, **112 m.** (638 pop.).

From Dover a road leads (L) to FORT BARNWELL, **9 m.** (450 pop.), a small farming village (*guide available for Fort Barnwell*) named for Col. John Barnwell, a South Carolinian appointed late in 1771 by Gov. Edward Hyde to command a force to avenge the Tuscarora massacre and to prevent further uprisings. The SITE OF FORT BARNWELL is **2 m.** N. Nearby is the marked SITE OF THE GRAVE OF GEN. WILLIAM BRYAN, commander of the Revolutionary forces at New Bern.

COVE CITY, **118 m.** (465 pop.), a farming hamlet.

US 70 passes DE GRAFFENRIED PARK (R), **134 m.**, a suburb of New Bern named for the city's founder (*see* NEW BERN).

At **135 m.** is the junction with Fort Totten Dr.

Right on the drive to the SITE OF FORT TOTTEN, **100 yds.**, a Federal defense work erected after the capture of New Bern by Union forces in 1863. Negro churches at New Bern grew from praying bands of emancipated blacks who, during and after the war, met at Fort Totten and elsewhere for services on Sunday afternoons. Negro lore tells of strange sights and sounds on dark nights— an Indian by a campfire; an aged, shrouded Negress at Reisenstein's Alley; and a white-maned horse. From the dark come hoofbeats, snorts of horses, and the tramp of soldiers marching to ghostly drumbeats and orders of long-dead commanders.

NEW BERN, **136 m.** (18 alt., 11,981 pop.) (*see* NEW BERN).

Points of Interest: Tryon's Palace, Smallwood-Ward House, Slover-Guion House, John Wright Stanly House (public library), First Presbyterian Church, and others.

New Bern is at the junction with US 17 (*see* TOUR 1, sec. b).

Leaving New Bern, US 70 crosses the Trent River over a new (1954) half-mile bridge, near which is a boatworks which serves a large part of the coast.

JAMES CITY, 137 m. (10 alt., 1,000 pop.), a Negro village, dates from the fall of New Bern in 1862. Depredations were ascribed to Negroes, and Gen. Foster, Federal commander in New Bern, ordered their segregation across the Trent. They settled on this property, which belonged to Col. James Bryan, and named the settlement for him. Col. Bryan succeeded in regaining possession of the property after the war only after prolonged litigation.

At **138 m.** is the junction with a marked road.

Right on this road to the grass-grown REMAINS OF FORT AMORY, **200 yds.** (R). Erected by Federal troops in 1862 as part of a mile-long defense works between the Trent and the Neuse, a part of its pentagonal earthen rampart and deep moat retains the original lines.

At **2 m.** is the junction with the sand-clay old Pollocksville Rd.

Right **2 m.** on this road to the REMAINS OF TRENCHES used during the Civil War.

Here are the TOMBS OF RICHARD DOBBS SPAIGHT AND RICHARD DOBBS SPAIGHT, JR., his son. The former was North Carolina's first native-born Governor (1792-95) and the latter was the last Governor elected by the general assembly (1835-36). These tombs and others of the family are on property once a part of Clermont, a 2,500-acre estate owned variously by the Spaights and Moores. Spaight, Sr. was killed by John Stanly in a duel in New Bern on Sept. 5, 1802 (*see* NEW BERN).

Madam Mary Vail Moore, whose daughter married Richard Dobbs Spaight, built a brick mansion on the Trent River at Clermont, which was burned in 1862 by Federal troops who, according to local tradition, took Spaight's skeleton from its tomb and displayed the skull atop a pole. Stories are told of Madam Moore's visits to New Bern in an elegantly equipped barge, manned by Negro oarsmen in pretentious livery.

At **7 m.** Brices Creek (*fishing boats at the bridge*) curves through thick forests. Perch and robin are abundant.

At CROATAN, **149 m.** (28 alt., 150 pop.), a FOREST FIRE TOWER (R) affords a wide view of the surrounding forest and marsh.

The SELF-KICK-IN-THE-PANTS MACHINE (*public invited; no questions asked*), set up by Tom W. Haywood in front of his filling station in July, 1937, has worn out many shoes in its service to tourists and citizens. If you feel that you deserve "a good swift kick," turn the handle; the cable will be pulled and a huge shoe laced to an iron "leg" will administer the boot.

Croatan (*see* TOUR *1A*) lies within the CROATAN NATIONAL FOREST (*see* NATIONAL FORESTS), an area of cutover timber acquired for use in the demonstration of forest conservation. The boundary contains 5 shallow spring-fed lakes, Ellis (*Forest Service campground*), Great, Long, Little, and Catfish (*see* TOUR *1, sec. b*), that overflow through seepage areas to form principal creeks. Some scientists believe that these lakes were formed by meteoric showers that struck the Carolinas thousands of years ago; others say they were low spots in the ocean floor or the result of wind action when the area first rose above the surface of the sea (*see* NATURAL SETTING).

The LAKES POCOSIN (*see* TOUR *1, sec. b*) is 40,000-acres of damp, low land under water during wet weather, extending from the lakes. Except where roads have been cut and camps built by the Forest Service, the region is inaccessible, a retreat for alligator, deer, bear, and wildcat.

At **153 m.** the highway passes deeply wooded Slocum Creek, where there is good fishing in the shadowy swamp.

HAVELOCK, **157 m.** (23 alt.), became known during prohibition days as a distributing point for C.C.C. (Craven County Corn), bootleg whiskey manufactured in the woods and swamps. Today, as a result of the Marine Air Station at Cherry Point, it is a bustling community, with super markets, drug stores, apartments, and churches.

Left from Havelock on NC 101 to CHERRY POINT, the largest U. S. Marine Corps Air Station in the world, situated on a 12,000-acre tract along Neuse River. Along the route is a large colony of civilian workers attached to the base.

Right from Havelock on a Forest Service road to ELLIS LAKE, **8 m.**, where a camp makes part of the dense forest accessible. GREAT LAKE, a mile west of Ellis Lake, abounds with fish. Bear, deer, and quantities of smaller game are in the surrounding forests. Here are stands of age-old cypress, red gum, and other virgin timber now so rare in the southern lowlands.

NEWPORT, **164.4 m.** (20 alt., 676 pop.), on the north bank of the Newport River, is an agricultural village, settled in the early 1700's by two Bell brothers, and first known as Bell's Corners. Later, Quakers from Newport, R. I., came to this section and renamed the settlement and the river. Near his home in the village is the GRAVE OF ROBERT WILLIAMS who had charge of the salt works at the mouth of Core Creek during the Revolution. The solar system of evaporation, adopted here, was not as successful as the method of boiling salt water in vats, used east of Beaufort (*see below*).

Militia were stationed west of the town during the Revolution, evidently guarding the roads to Beaufort and Swansboro. During the Civil War, the railroad bridge over the Newport River was destroyed by Confederate soldiers, which delayed the attack on Fort Macon.

In this section, bear hunting is a popular sport (*bear hunters and guides available*). On the 9-foot road leading to the town from the west, a new housing project has been blue-printed by the Cherry Point Mutual Veterans Housing Association.

At **170 m.** is the junction with NC 24.

Right on NC 24, this route parallels the north shore of Bogue Sound, about one-half mile inland, and traverses forests of maritime pine, scrub oak, and fields of corn (locally called "whiskey trees"). Numerous summer cottages (L) may be glimpsed through the trees. At **2.7 m.** road (L) leads to CAMP MOREHEAD, a summer camp for boys, 6-17.

At **4 m.** road (L) leads to HOHO VILLAGE (*bathing; fishing from 500-ft. pier; furnished homes for summer and winter rentals*), surrounded with tall pine trees and overlooking Bogue Sound.

At **6.4 m.** is GALES CREEK, a small residential community, and creek believed to be named for Sir Christopher Gales, first Chief Justice under the Lords Proprietors and first Collector of the Port of Beaufort. At **6.6 m.** road (L) to BOGUE SOUND SHORES, a residential development overlooking Bogue Sound (*cottages available in summer; small boats for rent*).

At **7.4 m.** road (L) to BROAD CREEK, a fishing community (*commercial and sport fishing both in the sound and in the ocean by way of Bogue Inlet*). At **9 m.** NC 24 crosses Broad Creek, where it empties into Bogue Sound, and continues to BOGUE, **14.5 m.**, a small community.

At **17.9 m.**, set back among the trees (R), is an OCTAGONAL HOUSE, with a cupola on top to let light into the hallways. It has 12 rooms, 4 of them square and 8 of unconventional shape. The present owner says his grandfather, in 1856, built this 8-sided house to keep the wind from whistling around the corners. The property, known as "Cedar Point," was named in the Laws of 1764 as a point of inspection for products being shipped. It has been in the same family since 1765.

At **19.9 m.** NC 24 crosses a concrete bridge, completed in 1953, and causeway over an estuary of Whiteoak River and enters Onslow County at the beginning of a second concrete bridge over Whiteoak River. At the western end is Swansboro (*see* TOUR 14).

At **170.3 m.** is the GREYHOUND RACING TRACK, where races were held every night except Sunday, June through Sept., until they were declared illegal in 1954.

The highway passes through a modern residential section, MANSFIELD PARK, with private clubs overlooking Bogue Sound and Coral Bay (*motels, gift shops, a drive-in theater, restaurants, and supper clubs*).

The old SECTION BASE property, **173 m.**, now houses the offices of the DIVISION OF COMMERCIAL FISHERIES of the N. C. Dept. of Conservation and Development, the HAMPTON MEMORIAL MARINE MUSEUM, dedicated in July, 1951, and the INSTITUTE OF FISHERIES RESEARCH of the University of North Carolina, created in 1947 to study commercial fishing with the aim of formulating long-range plans for its protection. The North Carolina State College offers a Sports Fishing Institute with a 5-day instruction course.

At **173.3 m.** is the intersection of 24th and Arendell Sts., Morehead.

Right one block on 24th St. to a modern bridge (1953) over Bogue Sound to Bogue Island. A causeway leads to ATLANTIC BEACH, **1.7 m.**, an incorporated town with a substantial summer colony and a number of year-round residents (*hotels facing the ocean, boardwalk, casino, amusement center; motels, apartments, and cottages available*). The wide beach runs in an east-west direction, causing a mild surf.

In the late 1700's and early 1800's this part of Bogue Sound, thickly covered with myrtle, cedar, and yaupon trees (many of which still survive) was used for cattle grazing. In the early 1900's a bathing pavillion, accessible only by boat, was erected, and in 1918 a hotel was built. Since the building of the first bridge in 1928, this beach area has been rapidly developed.

1. Road (R) to SALTER PATH, **11 m.**, a picturesque village isolated until recently and inhabited for generations entirely by commercial fishermen, who have a communal method of fishing and distribution of the catch. They occupy their homes through "squatter" rights, which have recently been established in court after a legal battle.

2. To the left on Fort Macon Blvd., the road passes numerous cottages, MONEY ISLAND BEACH (where according to legend pirates buried their plunder along the coastal banks), the TRIPLE ESS FISHING PIER, extending out into the ocean for 1,000 feet (*snack bar and bait and tackle shop adjacent*), to FORT MACON STATE PARK, **2.4 m.** (*picnic area, parking area, fireplaces, wooden tables, bathing beach, bath houses, refreshment stand, and short boardwalk*).

The COAST GUARD BASE, **3.4 m.** replaced the Fort Macon Life Boat Station in 1952 with additional duties of establishing lighted channel ranges to improve night operation in the harbor, of providing better aids to navigation services at less cost, and of improving off-shore search and rescue coverage.

Road winds on between sand dunes and rises gently, affording a view of Cape Lookout in the far distance. At the end of the road, **3.8 m.**, is a parking area. The beach adjoining Beaufort Inlet, or Old Topsail as it was once called, is to the right (*surf fishing but no swimming, because the current is too strong*).

FORT MACON (*open*), commanding Beaufort Inlet, is an outstanding example of the military architecture of the 19th century. Erected in 1826-34 and named for Nathaniel Macon, Speaker of the U. S. House of Representatives and U. S. Senator from Warren County, it replaced Fort Hampton, which had been located nearer to the inlet and was washed away in a severe storm in August, 1815. Restoration work was done in 1934-36 by the CCC and in 1952-53, under the direction of Mr. Milton Perry, so that this fort is one of the best preserved forts in the country. It is now operated as a State park.

The court is roughly pentagonal, with doors and windows opening on chambers constructed under the rampart of the inner fort. A deep moat, 25 feet wide, separates the inner structure from the outer defenses. Gun emplacements in both sections remain. Beneath the outer rampart are dungeons. Domed rooms, arches, supports, and vaulted stairways indicate skillful military engineering and some of the most intricate brickwork of the period. A MUSEUM of historical relics is located inside.

In April, 1861, Capt. Josiah S. Pender of Beaufort quickly took the fort from the Federals garrisoned here. Early in 1862 Maj. Gen. Ambrose E. Burnside, entering through Albemarle and Pamlico sounds, took New Bern on Mar. 13 and sent Gen. John Parke south. Gen. Parke took Morehead City Mar. 23. His main objective was Fort Macon. Guns, mortars, ammunition, and troops were sent across the sound by boat to Bogue Island and moved forward along the beach towards the Fort under cover of darkness.

Attack began at daylight Apr. 25. The fortifications at the fort had been constructed with particular reference to defending the harbor, and only a few old guns could be brought to bear on the land approach. After 12 hours of severe bombardment the fort surrendered.

MOREHEAD CITY, **174 m.** (6 alt., 5,144 pop.), on Bogue Sound, Newport River, the Intracoastal Waterway, and Calico Creek, is a resort city, a retail trade center, and the only deep-sea port north of Wilmington. Along the busy waterfront are numerous seafood restaurants and a varied fleet for all types of inshore, offshore, and Gulf Stream fishing.

Many summer residents, who prefer the facilities of the sound, have attractive cottages along Bogue Sound facing Atlantic Beach (*fishing, bathing, golfing, boating, and hunting of wildfowl and deer in the surrounding countryside in season*).

The OCEAN SHIPPING PORT TERMINAL, located at the bridgehead (R) on Bogue Sound, 3 miles from ocean shipping lanes, is accessible to large ocean-going as well as freight-carrying barges of the Intracoastal Waterway. This modern port, with spacious warehouses, rail spurs, and large docks was formally opened in 1952. The volume of exports and imports handled through this port is increasing rapidly.

The Atlantic & North Carolina R.R., nicknamed the "Old Mullet Line," because of the quantities of mullet shipped over it, bisects the main street. Morehead City is named for John Motley Morehead, Governor of North Carolina, 1841-45, who, believing that this location had the potentialities of becoming one of the great Atlantic seaports, purchased 600 acres of land in 1853 at the terminal of the recently incorporated railroad. This land, then known as Shepard's Point, was laid out as a townsite, and lots were sold off in Nov., 1857. In 1858 the railroad reached here, and the town was chartered. Four years later the town was captured by Union troops.

From Morehead City US 70 passes the MOREHEAD CITY YACHT BASIN (L), with nearby shipbuilding and repair yards, and crosses a concrete bridge and causeway. On the left is the Newport River and the Intracoastal Waterway.

On the right is PIVERS ISLAND, site of the MARINE BIOLOGICAL STATION of the U. S. Fish and Wildlife Service; SUMMER SCHOOL OF MARINE BIOLOGY, and a MUSEUM (*open to the public*).

BEAUFORT (bō'-fort) **176 m.** (10 alt., 3,212 pop.), the county seat of Carteret County and the third oldest town in North Carolina, retains the charm and flavor of an 18th-century seacoast town. Narrow streets curve between neatly whitewashed rows of spreading oaks and elms. Houses with narrow porches and no eaves front the sea, and churches with low wooden steeples, surrounded by cemeteries with weather-stained monuments, appear much as they did a century ago. The old houses, meticulously built by ship carpenters, follow a style seen by early mariners in the Bahamas. A characteristic house has a sloping roof that extends without a break to cover the front porch, with a balancing extension in the back. The two-story houses have two-tiered porches.

Facing Beaufort Inlet, this quaint old town is the center of the menhaden fishing industry, a resort town, and a retail trade center for the county. Both menhaden and food fish are caught and processed here and at Morehead. The menhaden, though not edible, is the State's most valuable fish, yielding oil for soaps, lipsticks, paints, etc. and meal for livestock feed. The fishing boats with their crow's nests or lookout stations are a distinctive trademark of the Beaufort waterfront.

Another industry unique to this area is the making of conical nets by hand. Other industries include a cannery, a metal finishing company, and a plant that processes agar-agar and fish solubles. To the east of town the Woman's College of the University of North Carolina has summer sessions in marine botany and biology and in art.

Beaufort is believed to have been settled as early as 1709 by French Huguenots, followed by English, Scots, Irish, Germans, and Swedes. Laid out into lots as early as 1713, it was, in 1722, made a port of entry entitled to a collector of customs. Chief Justice Christopher Gale was appointed collector and resided here from 1722-24. In 1723 it was incorporated and designated as the county seat of Carteret County.

In the Tuscarora War, it was not until 1713 that the local Core Indians were subdued by Col. James Moore of South Carolina at a spot not far away.

While most of the pirates rendezvoused at Ocracoke, Teach (Blackbeard) always sailed his big ship *Queen Anne's Revenge,* a vessel with 40 guns, into Beaufort Harbor and transferred to a sloop to keep rendezvous at Ocracoke (*see* TOUR 1A). On Aug. 26, 1749 Spanish privateers captured Beaufort but were driven off Aug. 28.

By 1750 Beaufort was the third ranking port in North Carolina, exceeded only by Brunswick and the combined towns of the Albemarle region. Great quantities of tar, pitch, turpentine, lumber, hides, and fish were exported, and the warehouses were filled with tea, spices, rope, furniture, and cloth from abroad. During the Revolution the harbor was white with the sails of merchantmen and privateers who brought in supplies from the French, Spanish, and Dutch West Indies. Salt was derived from a salt works 1½ miles east of Beaufort at Taylor's Creek, where salt water was boiled in large vats, leaving a residue of that indispensable commodity. Its success may be judged from the fact that in 1780 the Assembly levied a tax in kind: for every 100 pounds value of property, a peck of corn or 3 pounds of pork, except that the inhabitants of Carteret might deliver instead a gallon of salt.

From the opening of the Civil War until the fall of Fort Macon on April 25, 1862 blockade running was carried on through Beaufort Inlet. After that date the town was occupied by Union troops until the end of the war.

The first courthouse, erected in 1722, also served as the customhouse. The present (4th) CARTERET COUNTY COURTHOUSE (1907) is a red brick structure with a pedimented portico and cupola. It contains records and land grants dating from 1713. Carteret County, formed in 1722, was originally a precinct of the Great County of Bath and was named for the Lord Proprietor, Sir George Carteret.

The DR. CRAMER (SAM THOMAS) HOUSE (*private*), corner Turner and Ann Sts., served as a courthouse for many years prior to 1835, when it was moved from its original position in the street between the 4 corners. It is a tiny one-story clapboarded structure with narrow eaves and a porticoed entrance on the right.

The ODD FELLOWS BUILDING, Turner St., a two-story brick structure, was built about 1830 by masons employed at Fort Macon. Legend says that the work was done at night by torchlight.

The DAVIS HOUSE (*now an apartment house*), at the end of Front St., long a famous hostelry, has an interesting two-tiered porch of great length. Also on Front St. is a MONUMENT TO CAPT. OTWAY BURNS (1755-1850), privateer commander of the *Snap Dragon* during the War of 1812 and so picturesque a figure that biography is unable to disentangle him from legend. His daring made him the terror of British merchant ships from Greenland to Brazil. So great was the damage he inflicted that the British Government offered $50,000 for his capture, dead or alive. In 1814, when the British captured the *Snap Dragon,* he escaped capture because rheumatism had kept him ashore. After the war he built a house in Beaufort, where he resided 22 years, and operated a shipyard, where he built the *Prometheus,* the first steamboat to ply the Cape Fear River and probably the first to be built in the State.

After serving in the general assembly (1821-35), his friend Andrew Jackson appointed him keeper of Brant Island Shoal Light, "where he sank into his anecdotage, fond of his bright naval uniform, his cocked hat, good whiskey, and a good fight." A town in western North Carolina is named for him.

The THOMAS DUNCAN HOUSE (*private*), Front St., is a sturdy clapboarded structure of two stories with a lean-to, marked by upper and lower balustraded porches beneath the sloping roof on the front elevation. Originally the upstairs was for living quarters and the downstairs housed a general store, as it was adjacent to the busy shipping wharves of those days.

The ALONZO THOMAS HOUSE (*private*), corner Front and Orange Sts., has a double deck porch of the type seen in the Bahamian houses. Occupied by Union soldiers, as were many other homes in Beaufort, it has a window pane with the name and regiment of a Union soldier scratched on it.

The HAMMOCK HOUSE (*private*), at the eastern end of town, one of the oldest examples of Bahamian architecture, was used as a landmark by which ships entering the Inlet chartered their course. It is shown as such on old sailing maps.

The JULES F. DUNCAN HOME (*private*), E. Front St., extensively remodeled, was originally the old Cook house, where James Wallace Cook, Commander of the ram *Albemarle,* was born.

Legend relates that in the lovely OLD TOWN CEMETERY, Ann and Craven Sts., begun about 1724, an unidentified man was buried standing erect. Tradition says that another man who had perished at sea was buried in a drum of spirits in which his body was placed to preserve it on the return voyage. The granite tomb of Capt. Otway Burns is surmounted with a cannon taken from his privateer, the *Snap Dragon.* Also buried here is Capt. Josiah Pender, grandfather of Mrs. George C. Marshall.

From Beaufort chartered passenger boats or mail boats are available for Cape Lookout. Such boats are also available to Portsmouth and Ocracoke from Beaufort as well as from Atlantic (*see below*).

To the south of Back Sound is SHACKLEFORD BANKS, a 7-mile sand island. Here is the SITE OF DIAMOND CITY, a "lost town" of the 19th century where human skeletons have been uncovered by shifting sands. Storm and tide undermined and destroyed their homes and supposedly drove the inhabitants (600-700) to more sheltered localities. Diamond City was once the center of a great whaling industry, carried on as early as 1725.

CORE BANKS extend northeast from Shackleford Banks. On the outer point where marsh flats join the two is CAPE LOOKOUT, 12 m. Here is CAPE LOOKOUT LIGHTHOUSE (*open*), 160 feet high, distinguished by its unusual markings of alternate black and white lozenges. The tower, built in 1859, replaced one built in 1812. A fixed white light of 160,000 candlepower marks this as the most important headland south of Cape Hatteras (*see* TOUR 1A). A lightship is anchored offshore near the outlying shoals.

Off Cape Lookout are favorite fishing grounds, since the natural harbor provides quick refuge from storms. Sink nets, set at nightfall and pulled in the next morning, are used for trout and croakers. Haul nets, cast and drawn back immediately to the fishing vessel, are used for bluefish and mackerel. "Buy boats" purchase the hauls and take the fish to Beaufort or Morehead City markets.

Wild ponies roam both Shackleford and Core Banks. Originally ownerless, the ponies gradually were rounded up and branded and became private property, though they range without hindrance along the beaches. Each year the ponies are rounded up, and the new colts are branded.

Right from Beaufort on the Lennoxville Rd. through a residential section to the old LENNOXVILLE ROOKERY, a protectorate of the Audubon Society where thousands of herons and egrets used to propagate. The birds have now almost abandoned this site in favor of Phillips Island in the Newport River and Middle Marshes Island north of Shackleford banks.

At 180.5 m. is the junction with a marked road.

To the left on this road to MERRIMON, 12.7 m., a farm hamlet. On this road is the 43,000-acre experimental farm owned and directed by Miss Georgina Yeatman. It includes property formerly referred to as the Open Grounds, owned by the University of Chicago as a refuge for deer, bear, and wildcats. When all of the land is cleared, this will be North Carolina's largest farm.

US 70 crosses North River, 181.5 m., following the western shore of Core Sound, curving inland to avoid salt marshes and spanning brackish creeks.

OTWAY, 184.2 m. (350 pop.), a fishing village named for Capt. Otway Burns, is at the junction with a marked road.

Right from Otway through farm country and semitropical woodland, to STRAITS, 4.2 m. (100 pop.), a farm community named for the half-mile strip of water between the mainland and Harkers Island. STARR METHODIST CHURCH preserves the name of a minister associated with the community's most popular tradition. Legend relates that during the winter of 1813 the citizens of Straits were starving, after a crop-killing drought the previous summer. The frozen sounds prevented fishing and the Napoleonic wars and a British blockade made commerce and imports impossible. Parson Starr decided to invoke Divine assistance. "If it is predestined that there be a wreck on the Atlantic coast, please," he prayed, "let it be here!" In a few days a ship laden with flour was wrecked on Core Banks and starvation was averted.

A WPA-constructed bridge leads **1 m.** to HARKERS ISLAND (1,244 pop.) (*fishing; lodge*). Back Sound separates the island from the banks on the south and Core Sound on the east. The island is about 5 miles long and 1 mile wide. Legend says that Manteo, Indian friend of the first white settlers on Roanoke Island (*see* TOUR *1A*), was born here.

Because of their long isolation, a few older citizens have still preserved folk customs and speech characteristics of their English forebears. They say *poke* for pocket; *consentable* means to be willing; and a kiss is called a *buss*. A water dog is still the Shakespearan *kelpie. Hit* is commonly used for it; *abashed* for discredited; and *abraded* for nauseated. Molasses is referred to as *them*. Most of the inhabitants are engaged in fishing. At SHELL POINT, on the east end of the island, is a huge pile of oyster, clam, scallop, and conch shells, believed to have been put there by Indians; skeletons, earthen bowls, pipes, and arrowheads have been found here.

At **196 m.** is SMYRNA (200 pop.) and the junction with a marked road.

Right on the road to MARSHALLBERG, **3 m.,** home of the famous Core Sounder boat. Fishing, boat building, and net making are the chief industries.

US 70 passes through WILLISTON, **198.6 m.,** a clam center, DAVIS, **202 m.,** and STACEY, **205.7 m.,** small fishing villages.

At **212 m.** is SEA LEVEL COMMUNITY HOSPITAL, a modern hospital built (1953) and given to the citizens of eastern Carteret by the 4 sons of Mr. and Mrs. Maltby Taylor of Sea Level, who sought their fortunes elsewhere and succeeded beyond their fondest dreams.

At **212.4 m.** is SEA LEVEL INN, built by the Taylor brothers in 1953 for sportsmen and tourists (*dining facilities; dock*).

ATLANTIC, **216 m.** (844 pop.), at the eastern end of US 70, is a picturesque fishing town, perhaps as old as Beaufort. It was originally known as Hunting Quarters until a postoffice was established around 1885. One of its citizens, Melvin Robinson, in his *Riddle of the Lost Colony,* presents a very plausible argument contending that nearby Cedar Island was the actual site of John White's Lost Colony and that it was on Portsmouth that Amadas and Barlowe first planted the flag of Her Majesty, Queen Elizabeth I.

At Atlantic a road runs through a stretch of wilderness, around Thoroughfare Bay to a bridge which crosses a canal to CEDAR ISLAND, with villages of Lola and Roe on the eastern side. A 1200-foot fishing pier extends out into Pamlico Sound (*bait and tackle shop; snack bar*). There are many Indian shell mounds of various sizes on the marshes.

A daily mail boat, 30 passengers, leaves Atlantic 1 P.M., stops at Portsmouth, arrives at Ocracoke, 5 P.M.; return trip leaves Ocracoke 7 A.M., arrives Atlantic 11 A.M. One way fare $2 (*for Ocracoke see Tour 1A "Drive Along the Banks"*).

PORTSMOUTH, **24 m.** (18 pop.) (*accommodations limited to a few fishing camps*) is reached by a skiff which meets the Ocracoke mail boat. Located on the northern tip of Core Banks, it was once a thriving seaport, settled about 1700. A severe storm in 1765 swept away the warehouses, and the place gradually declined. Before the Civil War, it became a favorite resort of wealthy planters. Fort Granville, built in 1753, was fired by the Confederates upon the fall of Ocracoke. After World War II the Coast Guard Station was abandoned.

TOUR 15B *(US 70)*

Durham—Greensboro—Salisbury—Statesville—Morganton—Asheville;
US 70. **240 m.**

West of DURHAM, **0 m.**, US 70 winds through a gently rolling country
of woodlands and small farms.

The BENNETT MEMORIAL (L), **5 m.**, composed of two Corinthian columns
surmounted with an entablature inscribed with the word "Unity," marks the
site of the surrender of Gen. Joseph E. Johnston to Gen. W. T. Sherman. All
that remains of the old Bennett house where the negotiations took place are
the vine-covered field-stone chimney and the old well nearby.

On Apr. 26, 1865, at the third meeting of Generals Johnston and Sherman
to discuss terms of surrender, a "military convention" was signed under
which 36,817 Confederate soldiers in North Carolina and 52,453 in Georgia
and Florida laid down their arms.

The route crosses the Eno River at **6 m.** near an old Occoneechee Indian
settlement, of which no traces remain. The river is named for Eno Will,
who served as guide to John Lawson in 1708 (*see* NEW BERN).

At **10 m.** US 70 by-passes Hillsboro; US 70-A goes through the town.

At **10.6 m.** on US 70-A is the junction with the marked old Durham-
Hillsboro Rd. (dirt).

Left on this road to the DICKSON HOUSE (*private*), **0.8 m.**, standing on a hill
(R). The remodeled structure is two stories high, two small rooms wide, with
ell at rear and end chimney on the left. The exterior is covered with beaded
weatherboarding and has paneled and louvered shutters.

Here Gen. Johnston spent a week while negotiating with Sherman. Tradition
says that Johnston asked for a piece of white cloth to be used as a flag of truce.
Since the house afforded none, Alexander Dickson gave his only shirt for the
purpose.

At **12 m.** (R) is the entrance to OCCONEECHEE SPEEDWAY.

The ante-bellum estate (R), OCCONEECHEE (*private*), **12.2 m.**, remodeled
with gables and circular windows, was operated as a model farm by Gen.

Julian S. Carr until his death in 1924 (*see* DURHAM). A shaded path along the riverbank behind, known as the DARK WALK, has long been popular with romantic couples.

On the L. is the slight bulk of the Occoneechee Mountains rising some 300 feet above the countryside.

HILLSBORO, 13 m. (543 alt., 1,329 pop.), seat of Orange County, is in the fertile valley of the Eno River, just east of the low-lying Occoneechee Mountains. The Haw, Eno, and Occoneechee Indians lived here and left many relics and legends. The factories in this little industrial village contrast with weathered old houses and massive trees.

Hillsboro's manufactures include cedar chests, oil, flour, timber products, cotton, and rayon. Nearby deposits of granite, sandstone, and other minerals are a commercial asset. Much of the stone used in the Duke University buildings (*see* DURHAM) was quarried 2 miles to the north.

Almost the entire white population is descended from the Scotch-Irish, Welsh, English, and Germans who took up land in the Earl of Granville's territory. When the town was platted in 1754 by William Churton, Granville's surveyor, it was called Orange as was the county. Later it was named Corbinton for Francis Corbin (*see* EDENTON), but in 1759 it was incorporated as Childsboro for the attorney general. In 1766 Gov. Tryon named it Hillsborough in honor of the Earl of Hillsborough, kinsman of Lady Tryon and Secretary of State for the Colonies. Planters from the low country, including Governors Tryon and Martin, seeking refuge from the heat and mosquitoes, brought their families to Hillsboro, making it a gay summer capital.

As the court town and county seat it became the center of Regulator disturbances (*see* ALAMANCE BATTLEGROUND *below*). On Sept. 24, 1768, Regulators took possession of the town and for two days conducted mock courts. They plundered and burned the homes of officials, many of whom fled. After their defeat May 16, 1771, at the Battle of Alamance (*see below*), 6 of their leaders were hanged here on the Cameron Estate.

The Provincial Congress met at Hillsboro August, 1775, as did the general assemblies in 1778, 1780, 1783, and 1784. During the Revolution the town served as a concentration point. Before the Battle of Guilford Courthouse (*see* TOUR 9) Cornwallis occupied the town (Feb. 20-25, 1781) and invited all loyalists to join him. He paved the muddy main streets with great cobblestones, part of which remained until 1909.

On Sept. 13, 1781, Hillsboro was raided by a Tory band under Col. David Fanning and Col. Hector McNeill, who seized Gov. Thomas Burke and his suite and took them to Wilmington. Burke was transferred to Charleston as a prisoner and closely confined on Sullivans Island. He was paroled to James Island, where he lived in constant danger of his life. After his appeal for protection was ignored, he escaped, fled to North Carolina, and resumed his official duties.

Here in the 1788 convention anti-Federalists, led by Willie Jones (*see* TOUR 3), prevailed against the Johnston-Iredell-Davie followers to reject adoption of the Federal Constitution, delaying North Carolina's entry into the Union until November, 1789 (*see* FAYETTEVILLE).

Brig. Gen. Francis Nash (1742-77), brilliant young Hillsboro officer, left his name to a North Carolina county and town (*see* TOURS *3 and 13*) and to the capital of the State of Tennessee. A star in a pavement at Germantown marks the spot where he fell. Other noted residents were: Willie P. Mangum (1793-1861), Whig political leader, Congressman (1823-25), and U. S. Senator (1830-35, 1840-52); Dr. Edmund C. F. Strudwick (1802-79), first president of the State medical society, and J. G. de Roulhac Hamilton (1878-   ), who has written *Reconstruction in North Carolina, North Carolina Since 1860,* and numerous historical monographs, and who was the founder of the Southern Historical Collection at Chapel Hill.

Hillsboro was also the birthplace and home of John Berry (b. Aug. 18, 1788), the first native brick mason of sufficient skill to attempt an entire building of brick. Notable local structures built by him include the Presbyterian Church (1816-20), St. Matthews Episcopal Church (1825), the Methodist Church (begun in 1857), the Baptist Church (1860), the Masonic Lodge (1823), the Old Courthouse (1845), and the old jail (recently demolished). Capt. Berry also built Smith Hall (now the Playmaker's Theatre, Chapel Hill), Wait Hall (the first building at Wake Forest, destroyed by fire in 1933), and the old courthouse at Yanceyville (later destroyed by fire).

The OLD ORANGE COUNTY COURTHOUSE, SE. corner King and Churton Sts., two stories in height and constructed of hand-pressed red brick, was built in 1845 by Capt. John Berry. At the center of the low-pitched roof is a low square tower and octagonal cupola. The temple-like Doric portico is of Greek Revival design. The first of the building's predecessors burned in 1790; the second was razed and its timbers used to build the Negro Methodist church, still standing. Records date from 1752. The cupola clock was made in Birmingham, England, in 1766 and was probably presented to the town by the Earl of Hillsborough about 1769. It once reposed in the tower of St. Matthew's Church and for a time in the old market house. Its original bell was lost, the story goes, when the clock was thrown into the river by raiding Tories, and the bell was perhaps used to make cannon. An old chest contains old measuring cups and the standards of weights sent from London. This structure now houses the Board of Education.

Behind the old courthouse is the NEW COURTHOUSE, completed in 1954, a handsome Georgian building which harmonizes with the older building.

EAGLE LODGE (*private*), Churton St., a severe two-story brick building, three bays long, fronted by a 4-columned, pedimented Ionic portico, is a good example of Greek Revival design and is one of the oldest lodges in the State, receiving its charter in 1791. It was built by John Berry (1823-25) with proceeds from a lottery conducted by the lodge. The building stands on the SITE OF THE RESIDENCE OF EDMUND FANNING, which was destroyed by the Regulators. In ballads sung by the Regulators, Fanning, register of deeds of Orange County, was accused of building his fine house with ill-gotten gains.

When Fanning first to Orange came,
He looked both pale and wan;
An old patched coat upon his back,
An old mare he rode on;
Both man and mare warn't worth five pounds,
As I've been often told.
But by his civil robberies
He's laced his coat with gold.

The COLONIAL INN (*includes dining room*), across the street from the Lodge, is located on the route taken Mar. 17,1776, by Daniel Boone to Kentucky. It is a white clapboard, rambling structure, with two-tiered porches, double end-chimneys, hand-carved shutters, and stairway of virgin pine. The original part is believed to have been used as the headquarters of Cornwallis when he came to Hillsboro in the spring of 1781 in a vain effort to rally Tory support for his army, which was soon to encounter Gen. Greene at Guilford Courthouse.

The east wing of the T. E. LLOYD HOUSE (*private*), Margarets Lane, built in 1754, was the office of Gov. Tryon when he had his summer capital in Hillsboro in the 1760's. The mantle, paneling, and deep-set windows lend an atmosphere of charm to this old house, which was also used as the music room for the Nash-Kollock School (*see below*).
Miss Margaret Tryon, the governor's daughter, must have been more popular than her father, as the street in front was named for her.

The NASH HOUSE (*private*), Margarets Lane, is believed to have been erected in 1769 by Isaac Edwards, Governor Tryon's private secretary. In two sections on different floor levels, the older has flush weatherboarding 18 inches wide, large hand-hewn sills, and hand-wrought hardware. Governor Tryon may have occupied the house in 1768; it served as Governor Martin's summer residence in 1772. In 1807 it became the property of Frederick Nash, Chief Justice of the State Supreme Court (1852-58). Judge Nash was the son of Abner Nash (*see* TOUR 15 *and* NEW BERN). From his death in 1858 till 1892, his daughters and his niece conducted here for young ladies the "Select Boarding School of Misses Nash and Kollock."

The site of the early parish church, NW. corner Churton and Tryon Sts., is occupied by the CONFEDERATE MEMORIAL LIBRARY (*open 9-5 weekdays*), erected in 1934 of local stone with white trim. The façade is centered by a small Roman Doric portico. There are large chimneys at both gable ends, and the gable roof is broken by 4 small dormers. Here in 1764 the first church for St. Matthew's Parish was built. By 1784 the building was "far gone in decay," but it had been repaired for use as a "school and free meetinghouse" when the Hillsboro Convention, 1788 (which rejected the U. S. Constitution), held its sessions there. By public proclamation it was offered to the first denomination to organize and call a minister. The Presbyterians complied and it was used for both church and school until 1791 when it was destroyed to check the progress of a fire.

The PRESBYTERIAN CHURCH, Queen St. adjoining the library, was built (1816-20) from proceeds of a lottery authorized by the general assembly in 1810. The building is of Gothic Revival style with pointed-arch windows and a square tower and steeple over the central entrance. In front of the church is a monument to Archibald DeBow Murphey (1777-1832), jurist and advocate of social, economic, and educational reforms far in advance of his times.

The TOWN CEMETERY, Churton St., behind the Presbyterian Church, was set aside for a burying ground when the town was platted in 1754. Here is the original grave of William Hooper (1742-90), North Carolina signer of the Declaration of Independence, who resided in a house two doors beyond the church. When Guilford Battleground was being restored in 1891 (see TOUR 9), the committee secured permission to move Hooper's remains there and accordingly took the ashes and gravestone to the railroad station. Before the train arrived, indignant citizens, led by Josiah Turner, retrieved and replaced the stone in its original position, though Hooper's ashes were interred at the battleground.

A headstone marks the GRAVE OF WILLIAM A. GRAHAM (1804-75), U. S. Senator, Governor of North Carolina (1845-49), and Secretary of the Navy in Fillmore's Cabinet, who began the practice of law in Hillsboro after his graduation from the State university.

The NASH-HOOPER HOUSE (private), Tryon St., was built for Francis Nash in 1772 and was occupied by William Hooper (see above) in the 1780's. Later it was the home of William A. Graham (see above). It is handsomely furnished in keeping with its distinguished and venerable background.

The HOME OF THOMAS BURKE (private), Queen St. off Churton St., later known as "Hearttsease," is a one-and-a-half-story frame house with end chimneys and a two-story addition on the left. Part of the house is fronted by a porch with an extended shed roof and the gable roof is pierced by three narrow dormers. Burke was chosen Governor by the general assembly in 1781. The house was later occupied by Dennis Heartt, publisher of Hillsboro's first newspaper, the *Hillsborough Recorder* (1820). W. W. Holden, Reconstruction Governor, was Heartt's "printer's devil."

ST. MATTHEW'S EPISCOPAL CHURCH (*admittance by rector*), just off Queen St., was built (1812-15) on land given for the purpose by Judge Thomas Ruffin, because it was the spot where the lovely Ann Kirkland consented to become Mrs. Ruffin. The brick structure is of the Gothic Revival type. The entrance is through a square central tower surmounted with a tapering steeple bearing a cross. In the vestibule is a chart showing the position of graves in the churchyard. An illumined mosaic window, picturing the Savior wearing an 18th-century hat wreathed with a crown of thorns, is a memorial to Rev. Moses Ashley Curtis, rector of the church for 21 years.

BURNSIDE (*private*), separated from the churchyard by a brick wall on the edge of Cameron Park, is the stately old home of Judge Thomas Ruffin in the early 1800's. Rebecca Cameron (H. M. Le Grange), author, was born here in 1844. She died in 1936 and is buried in St. Matthew's Churchyard. She is the author of *Salted with Fire* and *A Partisan Leader in 1776*. A small frame outbuilding with stone end chimneys was JUDGE RUFFIN's LAW OFFICE. Thomas Ruffin (1787-1870) was chosen Chief Justice of the State Supreme Court by the toss of a coin, when, after the death of Chief Justice Henderson, Justice Daniel refused to choose between Ruffin and William Gaston (*see* NEW BERN), each of whom proffered the honor to the other.

The once famous park here was long ago planted with trees rare on the American continent. Many outstanding and unique specimens may still be seen here.

In the grove is the marked SITE OF THE REGULATOR HANGING on June 19, 1771. The unmarked graves of the victims—Benjamin Merrill, Capt. Messer, Robert Matear, James Pugh, and two other Regulators—are nearer the river.

AYR MOUNT (*private*), 0.9 m. out St. Mary's Rd., L. 0.3 m., also called the Kirkland Place, is a handsome two-and-a-half-story manor house of brick laid in Flemish bond. It is three bays wide, with flanking one-story, two-bay wings. It was 12 years abuilding (1788-1800) and is notable for its lateral halls, beautiful stairways, finely-detailed mantels and heart of pine paneling. The walls are two feet thick, and the floor boards, two inches thick, run the length of the spacious rooms without a break. The portrait of the original builder, William Kirkland, planter and merchant born in Ayr, Scotland, hangs over one of the mantels. It is said that the house escaped Yankee destruction during the Civil War because William Kirkland's son, sitting by the road, was asked by Yankee soldiers passing by what the place was. "I dunno," was the casual reply, "I don't go near the place myself. It's for crazy folks."

The house stands on the property on which William Few, father of William Few, Jr., the autobiographer, and of James Few, the Regulator, operated a tavern and ran a mill on the Eno River.

TYAQUIN (*private*), 1.9 m. out St. Mary's Rd., L. on this road to the junction with a side road, 1 m.; R. 1.5 m. on this road, is the site of the home of Thomas Burke (1747-83), Governor of North Carolina (1781-82). He named the estate for his family's seat in Ireland, though he had emigrated to America because of a family quarrel. Here Burke retired at the end of his term as governor. His grave, in a grove on the plantation, is marked by a heap of stones.

Right from Hillsboro on the improved Dimocks Mill Rd. to the junction with a dirt road, 2 m.; R. 0.3 m. on this road to MOOREFIELDS (*private*). This old 8-room Georgian Colonial house was built in 1752-55 for Judge Alfred Moore, Attorney General of North Carolina and early U. S. Supreme Court Justice. Hand-hewn timbers are fastened with wooden pegs and hand-wrought nails. The hinges for doors and window blinds are the handmade HL type, usually called the "Lord-help-us" hinge. The house was remodeled in 1931 but the only addition was a porch and a new roof. The original hand-carved stairway and mantels remain. On the grounds are chimneys of the slave quarters and both family and slave burying grounds, though Judge Moore was interred at Old Brunswick (*see* HISTORIC TOUR FROM WILMINGTON).

At **16 m.** US 70 turns off to the left and, avoiding all towns, is a through-route to Greensboro, 36 miles away, from this turnoff. This tour follows US 70-A to Greensboro, 39 miles from this point.

Several decaying buildings in an oak grove, **22 m.** (R), mark the SITE OF BINGHAM SCHOOL, one of the State's earliest military academies. Founded in 1793 by the Rev. William Bingham, ancestor of Robert W. Bingham, Ambassador to the Court of St. James (1932-37), the school was conducted in different localities, but occupied this site for more than 50 years. In 1889 it was removed to Asheville, where it suspended operations in 1928.

MEBANE, **23.3 m.** (678 alt., 2,068 pop.), industrial and tobacco-market town, was founded in 1854 by the Mebane, White, and Thompson families.

Flanking the highway in the heart of town are (L) the Southern Ry. tracks, and (R) the WHITE FURNITURE CO. PLANT (*open*), the oldest furniture factory in North Carolina. In 1881 the White brothers constructed a small plant for the manufacture of dogwood spindles, and soon after, they turned to the manufacture of furniture. Other manufactured products of the town include mattresses, hosiery, and lumber.

At **28 m.** is the eastern junction with NC 49.

HAW RIVER, **29 m.** (539 alt., 1,175 pop.), is a textile manufacturing town, named for its bordering stream in a region once roamed by the Sissipahaw or Saxapahaw Indians. Adam Trollinger, a German immigrant, settled here in 1747, where his son Jacob later erected a gristmill. The village became an important crossing point during the Civil War when it was known as Trollinger's Ford. Gen. Benjamin Trollinger, great-great grandson of the founder, built the first textile plant in 1844. A power dam was constructed in 1881.

Artelia Roney Duke, wife of Washington Duke, who founded the Duke tobacco interests (*see* DURHAM), is interred in the historic Haw River cemetery.

Lord Cornwallis passed the Haw River settlement en route to the Battle of Guilford Courthouse during the last days of the Revolution and camped on the Trollinger farm. When Trollinger became abusive over the raid on his mill, Cornwallis ordered him tied to a tree with a bridle bit in his mouth. The "Trollinger Tree" is still pointed out on the old farm **1.8 m.** S. of NC 49.

South of Haw River, **1 m.**, is the HOME AND FARM OF GOV. W. KERR SCOTT (1949-52). A native of this section, Scott served as State Commissioner of Agriculture from 1937 until 1948.

HAWFIELDS CHURCH, **5 m.** SE., was one of the earliest Presbyterian churches in this section, founded about 1775. The present brick church was constructed in the 1940's.

At **29.3 m.** is the junction with NC 49.

Right on NC 49, **0.2 m.,** is DIXONDALE (*private*) (L), the former home of Gov. Thomas M. Holt (1891-93). The weatherboarded house, in the style of the 1880's, has bracketed eaves and porches, elaborate iron cresting along the roof ridge, and broad verandas supported by carved wooden posts of varying design.

GRAHAM, **2 m.** on NC 49 (656 alt., 5,026 pop.), seat of Alamance County, is a textile center, connected industrially with Haw River and Burlington. It was established in 1849 and named for Gov. William A. Graham (1845-49), later Secretary of the Navy (1850-53) and organizer of Commodore Perry's expedition to Japan.

When the town was incorporated in 1851, the inhabitants passed an ordinance forbidding the building of a railroad within a mile of the courthouse; hence, the N. C. Railroad established its company shops 3 miles west at the site that became Burlington.

During the Reconstruction following the Civil War, Graham was a center of Ku Klux Klan activities, causing Gov. William Holden in 1870 to declare the county in a state of insurrection and to ask the President to suspend the writ of habeas corpus.

The ALAMANCE COUNTY COURTHOUSE, occupying the center of the common, was erected in 1923. It is a stone structure of neoclassic architecture, with columns based on the Tower of the Winds in Athens. In the basement of the building hangs an oil painting of the Battle of Alamance by C. C. and Margaret Thompson, the latter a lineal descendant of one of the leading Regulators. In front of the courthouse stands a CONFEDERATE MONUMENT, surmounted with the figure of a Southern infantryman.

The L. BANKS HOLT HOUSE (*private*), two blocks SW., is a manor house originally surrounded by a 500-acre plantation. It was decorated by Ruben Rink, famous artist of the time, and a cupola tower was constructed from which Holt, owner of the town's first mills, could watch his famous Kentucky-bred racehorses.

1. North **1 m.** on NC 87 (Main St.) stands PROVIDENCE CHURCH, on the site of one of the first meeting houses of the Congregational Christian denomination, a group founded in the late 1700's by the Rev. James O'Kelly (*see* TOUR 7). The Providence cemetery was started in the early 1700's, one of the first in central North Carolina.

2. Left from Graham, NC 54 runs through an area called Stinking Quarter, so named in early times when settlers killed buffalo here for their hides and left the carcasses to decay.

3. West of Graham on a dirt road is the SITE OF PYLE'S MASSACRE, **2 m.,** a Revolutionary skirmish in which patriot forces under Gen. "Lighthorse Harry" Lee surprised and defeated Tory troops under Col. Pyle.

BURLINGTON, **34 m.** (658 alt., 24,560 pop.), is an industrial center of the New South. The N. C. Railroad Company Shops were erected here in 1854, and the old Railroad Hotel was host to many famous visitors. The town was incorporated in 1887 when the name "Burlington" was selected.

Several of the original "company shops" and a few of the company homes still stand adjoining the railroad tracks.

The oldest industry in Burlington is a COFFIN FACTORY (*open*), one of the first in the South, established in 1884. At present the factory produces 7,000 to 10,000 caskets annually.

Burlington is the home of the internationally-known BURLINGTON MILLS CORPORATION, founded there in 1923. In addition to textiles, the city is noted for hosiery, building materials, dairy products, paper boxes, chemicals and drugs, electronic equipment, furniture, metal goods, and other industries.
It is also a tobacco-market and shopping center for the surrounding county.

R. from Burlington on NC 100 is ELON COLLEGE, 3 m. (717 alt., 1,109 pop.), the site of ELON CHRISTIAN COLLEGE, established in 1891 by the Christian Church. The college offers a 4-year liberal arts course as well as work in dentistry, medicine, religious education, and engineering. Enrollment (1953) was 705 students. A $2,500,000 building program drive to be completed in 1956 will provide for extensive additions to the college.

SW. of Burlington 5 m. on NC 62 is ALAMANCE, a mill village, the site of one of the first textile mills in North Carolina established in 1837 by Edwin Michael Holt, father of Gov. Thomas Holt. Here were manufactured "Alamance Plaids," the first colored cotton fabrics produced in the South on power looms. The village is today a hosiery manufacturing center.

At 7 m. on NC 62 is ALAMANCE BATTLEGROUND, where on May 16, 1771, a battle was fought between a group of patriots known as the Regulators and the provincial militia under the royal governor, William Tryon.
This engagement was the outgrowth of protests by large groups of farmers in the piedmont against what was claimed to be unjust taxation, ruthless methods of collection, and the imposition of illegal fees by public officers. Their petitions to the assembly in 1768 urged repeal of the tax laws and the dismissal of officials so merciless that they would sell the only cow or horse of a poor family to satisfy a tax levy and not even return the surplus due the owners. The complaints stated that beds, bedclothes, and even their wives' petticoats were being seized.
When peaceful petitions were ignored or dismissed, the issue reached a violent conclusion. Two thousand partly armed Regulators, most of whom did not expect to fight, were defeated by the Governor's troops, but not until the latter had suffered heavy casualties. Tryon set fire to the woods on the battlefield, and several hundred Regulators perished in the flames. One of the insurgent leaders was hanged on the field and 14 others were tried, 6 of whom were hanged at Hillsboro (*see above*).
The battle has been described by some as "the first battle of the American Revolution," although it had no direct connection with that war.

This is a State Historical Park, which is as yet undeveloped.

In SEDALIA, 45 m. (300 pop.), is a group of red brick buildings housing the ALICE FREEMAN PALMER MEMORIAL INSTITUTE, a junior college and high school for Negroes, with an enrollment of 250. It was begun in 1901 by Charlotte Brown, who still headed the institute in 1939.

Left from Sedalia on a marked dirt road, and then R. up the lane at the barn to the McLEAN HOUSE (*open*), 0.5 m. It was erected before 1767 by John McLean and his wife, Jane Marshall. The U-shaped structure is of poplar logs fastened together with wooden pegs and covered with clapboards. An immense chimney with a fireplace 11 feet wide occupies the west end. This house was the home of 5 generations of the McLean family and from it McLeans went out to serve in 6 wars. Col. William Washington was here in the spring of 1781, and tradition says Cornwallis plundered it.

At the COUNTY HOME, 53 m., is the junction with a paved road, marked Huffine Mill Rd.

Right on this road to the junction with another paved road, 2 m.; R. 4.4 m. on this road to the RANKIN HOUSE (*private*), at the confluence of North and South Buffalo Creeks. This weatherboarded house with stuccoed end chimney was built about 1768 by John and William Rankin on land granted them by the Earl of Granville in 1765. Both of the brothers took part in the Battle of Alamance, and William was one of those excluded from the blanket pardon offered participants by Governor Tryon. A natural stone trough is pointed out as the place where Cornwallis' horse fed while he camped here.

GREENSBORO, 55 m. (*see* GREENSBORO).

Points of Interest: Guilford Courthouse National Military Park, Woman's College, Greensboro College, Greensboro Historical Museum and Library, Masonic Temple and O. Henry Birthplace, Gov. Morehead House, Sedgefield, the Lorillard Cigarette Factory, Jefferson Standard Building, Cone Textile Mills, and others.

Greensboro is at the junction with US 29 (*see* TOUR *8*), US 220 (*see* TOUR *9*), and US 421 (*see* TOUR *17*).

US 70 joins US 29, along a 4-lane highway, from Greensboro to Salisbury, 110 m. (*see* TOUR *8 and* SALISBURY).

From Salisbury, US 70 swings left through woods and farmlands to BARBER, 121 m., a small community off to the left, known for years to railroad travelers and trainmen as "Barber's Junction," an important cross-roads on the Southern Railway.

At 123.6 m. is CLEVELAND (788 alt., 580 pop.), originally named Rowan Mill for an old grist mill located here, later named Third Creek. During the Civil War, Gen. Stoneman's raiders burned the entire town except for the Masonic Lodge, spared because the commander of the raiders was a Mason. Incorporated in 1883, the town has a hosiery mill, cotton gin, and veneering plant.

Right from Cleveland, in the cemetery of the Third Creek Presbyterian Church, 13 m., is the GRAVE OF PETER NEY, with a headstone inscribed: "In Memory of Peter Stuart Ney a native of France and soldier of the French Revolution under Napoleon Bonaparte who departed this life Nov. 15, 1846, aged 77 years."
Ney, a school teacher and fencing master who arrived in Charleston, S. C., in Jan., 1816, is believed by many to have been Michel Ney, Marshal of France. According to French history Marshal Ney was executed for treason on Dec. 7, 1815, for aiding Napoleon in the Battle of Waterloo and is buried in the Père-Lachaise cemetery in Paris.
It has been claimed that the execution and burial were feigned and that Marshal Ney escaped to America. Associates of the schoolmaster told of his intense loyalty

to Napoleon and of the documents he preserved as proof of his identity. In 1887 a group received permission to exhume the body and discovered that the skeleton did measure approximately 5 feet, 10 inches, the height of the marshal, but they failed to find a silver plate such as the marshal was believed to have worn in his head following an operation. In the *Papers of Archibald D. Murphey,* Volume I, published by the North Carolina Historical Commission, are two letters in which Murphey speaks of engaging the schoolmaster to help with historical work and of learning that Peter Stuart Ney was a Scot.

At STATESVILLE, 136 m. (*see* TOURS *11 and 13*) US 70 joins US 64 to MORGANTON, 189 m. (*see* TOUR *13*).

West of Morganton along US 70 to the low-lying ridges of the South Mountains stretched out on the left. This isolated, curious range running east and west at right angles to the Blue Ridge has long puzzled geologists.

GLEN ALPINE, 194 m. (1,206 alt., 695 pop.), is an industrial community, built around small textile and hosiery mills.

MARION, 211 m. (1,437 alt., 2,740 pop.), seat of McDowell County, is a furniture and textile manufacturing town, named for Gen. Francis Marion, Revolutionary leader known as "The Swamp Fox." The town was founded in 1843, the year after the legislature authorized the establishment of the county.

Until the courthouse was built on land given by Col. Jonathan Carson for the courthouse and town, the county court was held in the Carson House (*see below*). The first official act of the new county government was to license the sale of whiskey in the basement of this house.

On record in McDowell County, dated Nov. 10, 1795, is a copy of the will of Robert Morris (1734-1806), Philadelphia merchant and signer of the Declaration of Independence, who helped finance the American Revolution but died a bankrupt. In 1781 he founded the Bank of North America and in 1798 entered a debtor's prison in Philadelphia. At one time Morris owned 200,000 acres in western North Carolina. The city of Asheville was first named Morristown (*see* ASHEVILLE). After bequeathing his property to his wife and children, Morris closes the will with "... regret at having lost a very large Fortune Acquired by honest Industry which I had long hoped and expected to enjoy with my family during my own life, and then to distribute it amongst those of them that should outlive me. Fate has determined otherwise and we must submit to the decree which I have done with patience and fortitude."

Marion is at the junction with US 221 (*see* TOUR *21*). Between Marion and 213 m. US 221 unites with US 70.

At 213 m. is the marked SITE OF PLEASANT GARDENS. When Joseph McDowell came to the Catawba River Valley before the Revolution and settled at Quaker Meadows (*see* TOUR *13*), his cousin, John McDowell, settled here and built a two-room log cabin. He called the tract Pleasant Gardens, and he became known as "Hunting John," because of his prowess in tracking game in the wild Indian country.

"Hunting John's" son, Joseph, saw action at the Battle of Kings Mountain with his cousins, Charles and Joseph; became a colonel of the militia and a physician; and served in the house of commons (1787-88, 1791-92). He usually appended "P. G." to his signature and was called "Pleasant Gardens Joe" to distinguish him from his cousin "Quaker Meadows Joe." McDowell County was named for "Pleasant Gardens Joe."

The CARSON HOUSE, 215 m. on Buck Creek, was the home of Col. Jonathan Carson, in whose home the first county court was held. He married the widow of Col. Joseph McDowell, and she gave the name "Pleasant Gardens" to the Carson House. Thus the entire section came to be known by that name.

Their son, Samuel Price Carson, U. S. Congressman (1825-33), was a member of the N. C. Constitutional Convention of 1835, where he fought valiantly for the legal right of Catholics to hold office in the State. Over political difficulties he fatally wounded Dr. R. B. Vance in the famous Carson-Vance duel, fought just over the South Carolina line, at Saluda Gap in 1827. Carson later became Secretary of State of the Texas Republic (1836-38) and was sent as a commissioner to Washington, 1836, to intercede for the recognition of Texan independence.

At 215 m. is the junction with NC 80.

Right on NC 80 to the dam at LAKE TAHOMA (*restricted to members*), 2.5 m., a 500-acre lake that mirrors rimming mountains.

At 8.5 m. this scenic drive enters the boundaries of the Mount Mitchell Division of the Pisgah National Forest (*see* NATIONAL FORESTS). In the forest is the BLACK MOUNTAIN RANGE, for which the town of Black Mountain is named (*see below*). BUCK CREEK GAP, 12.2 m. (3,200 alt.), lies in the Blue Ridge, the major water divide of the eastern United States. At Buck Creek Gap is the junction with the Blue Ridge Parkway (*see* TOUR *19*), where there is a sweeping view of Mount Mitchell and the Black Mountain Range.

Between the junction with US 221 and Old Fort, US 70 follows the route taken by Gen. Griffith Rutherford, who led a force of patriots in 1776 during his campaign against the Cherokees, and the route taken by Maj. Patrick Ferguson on his invasion of the mountain country just prior to his debacle at Kings Mountain. The latter paid unwelcome visits at Pleasant Gardens, The Glades, and Old Fort, then Davidson's Fort.

At 220 m. is the junction with a graveled road.

Left on this road to THE GLADES, 0.4 m., built before the Revolution for Maj. William Davidson, who later moved across the Blue Ridge and helped to organize Buncombe County. In 1815 the house was enlarged by David M. Greenlee to serve as an overnight stop on the Morganton-Asheville stage.

OLD FORT, 224 m. (1,438 alt., 771 pop.), is a small manufacturing town at the foot of the Blue Ridge. This is the SITE OF DAVIDSON'S FORT, an early shelter for pioneer settlers. It was built in 1776 by the colonial militia left "to guard and range the country" while Rutherford with his "picked" army was on the expedition against the Cherokees. For over a decade this stockade was the westernmost outpost in North Carolina of the advancing whites and served as a base for exploration and settlement of the Blue Ridge. The family of Samuel Davidson fled to the fort after Davidson had been ambushed and slain by the Cherokees near Christian Creek in 1784 (*see below*).

From Old Fort, at the foot of the Blue Ridge Mountains, to Asheville, US 70 runs over the Appalachian Divide and through a scenic section that includes several summer resorts in the Black Mountain region. Before 1880 west-bound travelers started an adventurous trip from Old Fort where the railroad ended. By stagecoach they crossed the Blue Ridge to Asheville, described as "a decidedly civilized place." By a remarkable feat of engineering, railroad tracks were laid over the 12 miles between the foot of the mountains and Swannanoa gap near Ridgecrest. In crossing the backbone of the Blue Ridge the tracks run through 7 tunnels and rise 1,070 feet.

West of Old Fort, on the old US 70 to OLD FORT PICNIC GROUND, **3 m.**, in Pisgah National Forest. From here the graveled Mill Creek Rd. leads to ANDREWS GEYSER, **3 m.**, a fountain that projects its slender column of water about 75 feet into the air. The fountain was built in the 1880's and restored in 1911 by George Baker of New York as a memorial to Col. A. B. Andrews who was prominently identified with railway engineering in North Carolina.

From the early 1920's to 1954 the highway ascent of the eastern slope of the Blue Ridge twisted almost continually to follow the contours of the mountain sides. US 70's new 6-mile ascent compares in bold conception with the railroad's or the old road's ascent. Laid out in the early 1950's by R. Getty Browning, this spectacular 4-lane highway has many fills over 100 feet and one which is 180 feet deep. The entire route is located on southern slopes to minimize ice and snow hazards in the winter. There are scenic vistas at several points along the route, where large parking overlooks are provided.

At RIDGECREST, **230 m.** (2,530 alt., 300 pop.), west of the Blue Ridge crest, approximately 15,000 Southern Baptists gather during the summer for religious conferences and educational and recreational activities.

At Ridgecrest is the western portal of the Southern Ry.'s SWANNANOA TUNNEL, 1,800 feet in length. The cutting of this tunnel in 1879, at a cost of $600,000 and 120 lives, marked the completion of this line and an early use of nitroglycerine in engineering.

Cars may be parked at Ridgecrest and directions obtained for the foot trail to CATAWBA FALLS, **2.5 m.**, on the headwaters of the Catawba River. Tumbling in a continuous misty spray from 5 levels of rock, these falls are outstanding in a region noted for its streams and cascades.

BLACK MOUNTAIN, **233 m.** (2,366 alt., 1,174 pop.), is a summer tourist center in the midst of religious assembly grounds and vacation resorts. Adjoining LAKE TOMAHAWK (*boating, swimming, dancing*) is a 9-hole golf course. A small airport borders the town on the west.

At Black Mountain is the junction with NC 9.

1. Right on NC 74 to MONTREAT, 2 m. (2,400 alt., 260 pop.) (*between Sept. and July, free; between July 1 and Sept. 1, Sunday free, one hour daily free, otherwise 50¢ a day. Accommodations: 6 hotels, boarding houses, 300 private houses*).

Montreat, comprising 4,500 acres of forest, streams, and mountains, is owned and operated by the Mountain Retreat Association as assembly grounds for the Presbyterian Church in the U. S. Each year more than 20,000 people attend the July and August conferences on various branches of church work.

Fronting LAKE SUSAN (water sports) is ASSEMBLY INN, built of local granite under the supervision of the Rev. Dr. R. C. Anderson, former president of the association. The interior is of mica flint, and the floors are of varicolored marble. The Historical Foundation of the Presbyterian and Reformed Churches, located here, has a noteworthy LIBRARY of 30,000 volumes, a MUSEUM, depicting Presbyterian history, and ARCHIVES, with 4,700 volumes of minutes of church bodies. The ANDERSON AUDITORIUM, a round building of local rock, seats 4,000. MONTREAT COLLEGE (for girls), housed in a granite building, offers a standard high school and 4-year college course.

2. Left from Black Mountain to BLUE RIDGE, 3 m., southern conference center of the Student Y.M.C.A. and Y.W.C.A., a 1,600-acre mountain tract owned and operated by Blue Ridge College, Inc., a subsidiary of the Y.M.C.A. Graduate School of Nashville, Tenn. Summer sessions of the graduate school as well as interdenominational religious, social, educational, and recreational conferences are conducted here each season. During World War I, 2,500 Y.M.C.A. workers were trained at Blue Ridge.

Several small buildings surround the white, three-story main building, ROBERT E. LEE HALL, which serves as hotel and school. LAKE LAUREL provides facilities for swimming and boating.

At 231 m. is the junction with old US 70.

Right 0.7 m. on this road is the WESTERN NORTH CAROLINA TUBERCULOSIS SANATORIUM, occupying modern brick buildings, erected in 1937-38 with the aid of Federal funds.

Also right from old US 70 1.2 m. is a gravel road to LAKE EDEN (*swimming, boating*), a small resort with cottages, pavilion, and an artificial lake, and BLACK MOUNTAIN COLLEGE, an experimental coeducational institution founded in 1933 following the withdrawal from Rollins College at Winter Park, Fla., of Prof. John A. Rice. Three other professors and 15 students followed Prof. Rice to form the nucleus of the new college which is controlled by a board of fellows elected by the faculty and consisting of 6 faculty members and the chief student officer. The aims are to keep the college so small that no one person will ever have to devote full time to administrative work and, by integrating academic work with community life, to develop resourcefulness and general intellectual and emotional fitness.

Students and instructors associate on an equal basis, residing in the same building and working together in classroom, dining hall, field, and forest. There are no required courses, no fraternities or sororities, and no football team. Students are responsible for their own work and conduct. Emphasis is laid upon the plastic arts, music, and dramatics. Final examinations are given by professors from other institutions.

West of the textile village of SWANNANOA-GROVEMONT, 235 m. (2,220 alt., 1,913 pop.), the highway parallels the Swannanoa River.

For a time before the Revolution the Swannanoa Valley was regarded as a neutral hunting ground between the Cherokee and Catawba tribes. In 1776 Gen. Griffith Rutherford, during his expedition against the Cherokee, was so impressed with the beauty of the valley that he called it "Eden land." The trail is now known as the Rutherford War Trace.

At 237.2 m. is the junction with a paved road.

Right on this road to WARREN WILSON JUNIOR COLLEGE, 2 m. (coed), owned and supported by the Board of National Missions of the Presbyterian Church of the U. S. A. School fees may be worked out on the 684-acre farm.

At 238.2 m. is the junction with a narrow dirt road.

Right on this road to the home of Marsh Owens, 100 yds., where cars may be parked; R. from this point 0.2 m. on a trail to the side of JONES MOUNTAIN. Here a granite slab marks the GRAVE OF SAMUEL DAVIDSON, one of the first settlers in North Carolina west of the Blue Ridge. With his wife, child, and Negro slave, Davidson came to this section in 1784 and built a house on Christian Creek. A few weeks later, while looking for his horse, he was shot and killed by a Cherokee. His family fled for safety to the blockhouse at Old Fort (*see above*). Settlers of the Old Fort section recovered Davidson's body which they buried on a mountain side.

On the dirt road at 3 m. is the OERLIKON TOOL AND ARMS CORP. PLANT, American affiliate of the famous gun-making Oerlikon Machine and Tool Works of Zurich, Switzerland.

At 240 m. is the junction with the Blue Ridge Parkway (*see* TOUR *19*).

At 240.2 m. (R) is OTEEN (*open subject to regulations*), United States Veterans Hospital, consisting of two divisions: Oteen Division, occupying modern buildings on a 190-acre tract, and Swannanoa Division, 8 m. E., with cantonment type buildings on a 272-acre tract. The 1,000 Oteen patients are non-ambulatory tuberculosis veterans; 500 other patients are cared for at Swannanoa. Both have an active Special Service program, including radio, motion picture, and library facilities.

At 240.4 m. is the junction with the Swannanoa Rd.

Left on this road to ASHEVILLE RECREATION PARK, 1 m., an amusement center and playground operated by the city of Asheville, and (R) the ASHEVILLE MUNICIPAL GOLF COURSE (*see* ASHEVILLE), 1.2 m.

The highway enters Asheville through the BEAUCATCHER TUNNEL, cut through BEAUCATCHER MOUNTAIN.

ASHEVILLE, 245 m. (*see* ASHEVILLE).

Points of Interest: Biltmore House, Thomas Wolfe Memorial, Pack Memorial Library, Grove Park Inn, Sunset Mountain, and others.

Asheville is at the junction with US 74 (*see* TOUR *16*), US 19 (*see* TOUR *22*), US 23 (*see* TOUR *23*) and US 25 (*see* TOUR *24*).

TOUR 16 *(US 74-76)*

Junction with US 17—Lumberton—Laurinburg—Charlotte—Asheville; US 74-76, US 74. 322 m.

Section a. JUNCTION *with* US 17 *to* LAURINBURG; 107 m. US 74-76

This route runs through the low, swampy coastal plain and through the thriving piedmont where cotton and tobacco fields are broken by occasional woodlands.

US 74-76 branches west from its junction with US 17, 0 m., 5 miles west of Wilmington (*see* WILMINGTON).

Near MACO, 7 m. (49 alt.), the ghostly, ephemeral Maco Light is visible on dewy, moonless nights following warm days. Some attribute the phenomenon to phosphorescent swamp vapors. Others say it is the lantern of a flagman killed when his warning was unheeded by the engineer of an approaching train.

Between 9 m. and 14 m. US 74 crosses the northern neck of Green Swamp (*see* TOUR *18A*).

At 11 m. US 74-76 forms a junction with NC 87.

Right on this road to ACME, 0.6 m. (139 pop.), the home of the Reigel Carolina Corporation, a $25,000,000-plant which manufactures various paper products.

Near Acme, on the old Grange plantation is the GRAVE OF MAJ. GEN. ROBERT HOWE, who was commander of the American Army in the South, 1776-78.
Cornwallis, after the battle of Guilford Courthouse, passed with his army near here in April, 1781.

BOLTON, 26 m. (66 alt., 606 pop.), in a low, semi-swamp region, has several lumber mills. SAN DOMINGO is a settlement of small landholders, "almost white people," of Caucasian, Negro, and Indian blood.

At WANANISH, 30 m. (58 alt., 300 pop.), is a plant for the manufacture of tools used in the turpentine industry.

Left from Wananish NC 214 makes a 4-mile loop skirting the shore of LAKE WACCAMAW, 7 miles long and 5 miles wide, a modest summer resort (*hotels, furnished cottages, tourist homes, boats, guides; water sports*). The largest natural lake between Maine and Florida, it is an excellent white perch and bass water. Gnarled water oaks and gangling pines festooned with Spanish moss border the lake, at the eastern end of which is an INDIAN MOUND (*accessible only by boat*). An Indian legend relates that once this basin was a field of exquisite flowers, flooded by an angry god as punishment for misdeeds. Most scientists attribute the lake's origin to the infall of giant meteorites (*see* TOUR *18 and* NATURAL. SETTING).

WHITEVILLE, **43 m.** (*see* TOUR *18*), is at the junction with US 701 (*see* TOUR *18*).

CHADBOURN, **51 m.** (109 alt., 2,103 pop.), is a strawberry and tobacco marketing and shipping center. Strawberry cultivation was developed here by the "Sunny South Colony," a hardy group of Northwestern settlers.

At Chadbourn UC 76 separates from US 74 and follows a due-west course through CERRO GORDA, **6 m.** (265 pop.), to FAIR BLUFF, **12 m.** (1,056 pop.), perhaps the oldest town in Columbus County. At Fair Bluff, a picturesque town filled with live oaks and Spanish moss, the first tobacco warehouse in the county was established in 1895. At **15 m.** US 76 crosses the South Carolina Line, 16 miles from Mullins, S. C.

BOARDMAN, **63 m.** (200 pop.), an almost deserted settlement, was a busy lumber-mill town of 1,500 inhabitants before the removal of the mill in 1926.

LUMBERTON, **77 m.** (*see* TOUR *3*), is at the junction with US 301 (*see* TOUR *3*) which unites with it for 6 miles.

At **83 m.** US 74 swings (R) from US 301 and traverses the Croatan country and roughly parallels the Lumber River (Ind. *Lumbee*), formerly called Drowning Creek.

At **94 m.** US 74 forms a junction with NC 710.

Right on NC 710 to the junction with a marked road, **1 m.**; R. on this road to PEMBROKE, **2 m.** (172 alt., 1,212 pop.), center of the Croatan settlement, was named for Pembroke Jones, a railway official, when it was incorporated in 1895. Formerly it was known as Scuffletown. Hamilton McMillan, schoolmaster and local historian, who advanced the theory that the Croatans were descendants of Raleigh's Lost Colony (*see* TOUR *1A*), suggested that Scuffletown was a cor- ruption of old English Scoville Town.

In 1950 there were 920 Indians, 221 whites, and 71 Negroes in Pembroke, which is the center of the 22,553 Indians who live in Robeson County.

These Indians resent being called Croatans because it connotes an African admixture, but they have never been able to obtain tribal recognition from the Cherokee in western North Carolina (*see* TOUR *22C*). They were early given the status of "free persons of color," but were not permitted to carry firearms, a prohibition that helped to precipitate the Lowry uprising during the Reconstruc- tion period. The *Last of the Lowries,* a Paul Green play in the first series of *Carolina Folk Plays* (1922), deals with that incident.

There are few landmarks or survivals of tribal customs, and the Indians them-selves have little interest in their racial background, history, or development, nor has the field been thoroughly investigated by outside scholars. These people are readily recognized as a distinct ethnological group. Unlike the usual American Indian, their features are soft and rounded. Lips are broad, but the nose, though large, is neither broad like a Negro's nor aquiline like an Indian's. Complexions are copper to light brown; hair black, long, and straight; eyes dark. The young women are often darkly beautiful.

The PEMBROKE STATE COLLEGE (*coed*) was founded in 1887 and maintained by the State to train teachers for Indian schools. Today it has a high school department and a liberal arts college which was fully accredited by the Southern Association of Colleges and Secondary Schools in 1951. In 1953 the legislature opened the college to whites and Indians. The school occupies 16 buildings, mostly of brick, on a 35-acre campus. The faculty numbers about 20 and the student body about 135.

Straight on NC 710 to RED SPRINGS, 10 m. (204 alt., 2,245 pop.), named for a medicinal spring whose sulphur water is colored by a red pigment. Chief industrial plants are silk, rayon, and lumber mills. The population is composed of three racial groups, exemplified by separate doors at the local theater: for whites, for Robeson County Indians, and for Negroes.

The town is built on land granted to "Sailor" Hector McNeill in 1775; a large portion of it is still owned by his descendants. By 1850 this was a recognizable community known as Dora, the general assembly authorizing the change of name to Red Springs in 1885.

FLORA MACDONALD COLLEGE, a Presbyterian school for girls, started as Floral College (*see below*). In 1914 the name was changed to honor Flora MacDonald, the Scottish-American heroine who helped Bonnie Prince Charlie escape during the last Stuart uprising in Scotland (*see* FAYETTEVILLE). Although most historians maintain that none of Flora's children were buried in America, memorial services were held Apr. 28, 1937, for two children supposedly hers, whose remains were moved from an isolated spot in Montgomery County to the college campus. The college owns a collection of paintings, mostly modern American.

Flora MacDonald College confers A.B. and B.S. degrees. Seven modern brick buildings occupy a gardened campus, shaded by longleaf pines, particularly lovely when the azaleas bloom in April.

ALMA, 97 m. (182 alt., 100 pop.), is a farm community on the edge of the Sandhills where watermelons and cantaloupes are extensively grown.

MAXTON, 100 m. (195 alt., 1,924 pop.), was settled by Highland Scots whose descendants predominate in the section. A story is told that 10 men answered a train passenger's "Hello, Mac!" shouted from the car window. The weekly newspaper is called the *Scottish Chief*.

Maxton was an early trade crossing between the Cheraw district and Fayetteville. The settlement was first called Shoe Heel (Quehele in Gaelic), from the course of a small stream nearby.

In 1929 PRESBYTERIAN JUNIOR COLLEGE was opened in buildings built by the Methodists in 1908 for "Carolina College." Its present enrollment is over 200.

Right from Maxton on NC 71 (the Red Springs Rd.) to FLORAL COLLEGE COMMUNITY, **3.5 m.**, Scotch settlement and the site of Floral College, parent of Flora Macdonald College at Red Springs (*see above*). This school (1841-78), founded by John Gilchrist, was among the first nonsectarian, diploma-granting women's colleges in the South. Only one building, a two-story frame structure, now serving as a residence, remains.

LAURINBURG, **109 m.** (*see* TOURS *6 and 7*), is at the junction with US 15-501 and US 15A (*see* TOURS *6 and 7*).

Section b. LAURINBURG to CHARLOTTE; 97 m. US 74

West of Laurinburg the route leaves the Sandhills to enter gently rolling country, passing through a region believed by geologists to be a prehistoric ocean beach. The towns, well shaded by trees, many of them fine oaks and maples, stand out like oases on the plain.

OLD HUNDRED, **9 m.** (318 alt., 65 pop.), was so named because of the 100-mile post placed here when the slave-built railroad came through from Wilmington, though it should have been nearer Wilmington.

HAMLET, **17 m.** (349 alt., 5,081 pop.), is an important railroad center and trading point for peaches, small grain, corn, cotton, and some tobacco.

ROCKINGHAM, **22 m.** (*see* TOUR *5, sec. b*), is at the junction with US 1 (*see* TOUR *5, sec. b*).

At **23.6 m.** is the junction with US 220 (*see* TOUR *9*).

At **35 m.** US 74 crosses the Pee Dee River below the dam (R) that forms Blewett Falls Lake.

At WINGATE, **36 m.** (793 pop.), is WINGATE JUNIOR COLLEGE, chartered in 1897 and now sponsored by the N. C. Baptist Convention, with a student body of about 275. The EFIRD MEMORIAL LIBRARY (1948), was given by the descendants of the late J. E. Efird.

LILESVILLE, **38 m.** (478 alt., 605 pop.), is a new town in an agricultural region that was prosperous before the Revolution. Many of the most ardent Regulators (*see* TOUR *15B*) were enlisted from this section. Lumbering is an important industry.

The LILESVILLE BAPTIST CHURCH, organized in 1777, is one of the oldest Baptist congregations in the State. Here preachers Tirant (Methodist) and Durant (Baptist) debated from sunrise until dark on the question of infant baptism. The first log church was succeeded in the 1840's by a frame building with a slave shed in which the Negroes, required to accompany their masters to church, were separated from the white congregation by a low wall that permitted them to see the preacher and hear the services without being seen. The present white frame building, with a square belfry over the small vestry, was erected in 1871.

Right from the church on a dirt road to MOUNT PLEASANT, 6 m., site of the first Anson County Courthouse, a log building erected in 1755. On Apr. 28, 1768, 500 Regulators (see tour 15B) of Anson County forcibly removed the magistrates from the bench and held a public discussion of injustices in the exaction of fees and taxes. They sent Gov. Tryon a petition demanding the election of county officers by popular vote, because "no people have a right to be taxed but by the consent of themselves or their delegates." The seat of government was moved to New Town (now Wadesboro) in 1787 (see tour 10, sec. b).

The Grave of Col. Thomas Wade (1720-86), Revolutionary officer, in a grove 50 yards west of the courthouse site, is marked by a bronze tablet on Indian Execution Rock, so named because tribal executions supposedly took place here.

WADESBORO, 42 m. (see tour 10, sec. b), is at the junction with US 52 (see tour 10, sec. b).

Lee Park (swimming pool, golf course, ball park, and playground) is at 69.5 m.

MONROE, 71 m. (595 alt., 10,140 pop.), seat of Union County, was named for Pres. James Monroe. The town lies around the Courthouse Square, two of whose corner wells have been converted into ornamental drinking fountains. Great magnolias shade benches and memorials. Union County Courthouse, a two-story red brick building with arched windows and a graceful square clock tower, was erected in 1886. North and south wings were added in 1922. Marshal Foch spoke from the courthouse lawn Dec. 9, 1921, and decorated the colors of the 5th and 17th Field Artillery Regiments from Fort Bragg (see local tour from fayetteville) with the fourragère of the Croix de Guerre for conspicuous bravery with the A.E.F.

T. Walter Bickett, Governor of North Carolina (1917-21), was born and reared in Monroe. Another native son was David F. Houston, Secretary of Agriculture (1913-20) and Secretary of the Treasury (1920-21) under Woodrow Wilson. Industrial plants of the town include cotton, lumber, knitting, cottonseed-oil, and roller mills, marble works, and a creamery.

The substantial three-story red brick Town Hall was built in 1847-48 for use as the county jail. A runaway Negro slave unwittingly made possible its erection. When captured by his angry and drunken master, he was dragged the 8 miles into town with a log chain around his neck. His master, found guilty of his murder, pleaded an old English law, and escaped with paying a fine of $3,000 and $390.39 court costs with which the county built the jail.

During World War II, thousands of troops were trained here at Camp Sutton.

Left from Monroe on State 75 is WAXHAW, 12 m. (673 alt., 818 pop.), named for the Waxhaw Indians who claimed the land between the Rocky and Catawba rivers. The earliest record of the tribe is found in the diary (1709) of John Lawson, who came from Charleston, S. C., to survey territory now included in North Carolina. Lawson wrote that: "These Indians are of an extraordinary Stature, and call'd by their Neighbors Flat Heads.... In their infancy their nurses lay the Back-part of their Children's Heads on a Bag of Sand.... They use a roll, which is placed on the babe's Forehead, it being laid with its back on a flat Board, and swaddled hard down, thereon, from one end of this Engine to the other. This method makes the child's Body and limbs as straight as an arrow ... it makes the eyes stand a prodigious way asunder ... which seems very frightful; They being asked the reason ... reply'd the Indian's sight was much strengthened and quickened thereby.... He that is a good hunter never missed of being a favourite amongst the women; the prettiest girls being always bestowed upon the chieftest Sports-Men and those of grosser Mould, upon the useless Lubbers." The tribe was so reduced by the Yamasee War of 1715 that they united with the Catawba.

The GRAVE OF MAJ. JOHN FOSTER, an officer of the Revolutionary War who came from Ireland in 1765, is on the south side of Waxhaw Creek, near the site of his home.

At **14 m.** is the junction with a dirt road; L. **6 m.** on this road to the junction with another dirt road; L. **3 m.** on this road to the ANDREW JACKSON MONUMENT on the supposed site of a farmhouse in which Andrew Jackson (*see* CHARLOTTE) was born, Mar. 15, 1767. The old boundary line between North and South Carolina ran close to the house, but it was not until Jackson became a hero that the two states claimed his birthplace.

The region west of MATTHEWS, **86 m.** (716 alt., 589 pop.), is an industrial area, geologically much older than the coastal plain. There is no distinctive flora, but plants from widely scattered areas occur—yucca from the deserts and plains of the West, rhododendron from the Appalachians, and giant prickly pear from the semitropical South. Cotton growing is the principal agricultural activity.

CHARLOTTE, **97 m.** (*see* CHARLOTTE).

Points of Interest: Independence Square, First Presbyterian Church, Site of Confederate Navy Yard, Mint Museum, Martin Cannon Residence, and others.

Charlotte is at the junction with US 29 (*see* TOUR *8*), US 21 (*see* TOUR *11*), and NC 27 (*see* TOUR *7*).

Right from Charlotte on W. Trade St. into Beatties Ford Rd. At **6.2 m.** is the junction with a dirt road; L. **1.6 m.** on this road, taking two successive L. turns to the CAPPS GOLD MINE (*closed*), an old vein operated between 1937-39 by a Canadian company. Company buildings housed the miners, and a three-story processing plant extracted gold from the ore. Some veins yielded $150 a ton, though the average was less than $15 a ton. The shaft drops to a depth of 410 feet. The mine failed to yield a profit and operations were suspended.

Gold was discovered in Cabarrus County in 1799 (*see* TOUR *7*) and was mined at numerous places in this section until the California rush in 1849.

At **6.5 m.** is the SITE OF A REVOLUTIONARY SKIRMISH known as the "Battle of McIntyre's Farm," though contemporary evidence indicates that the farm belonged to the Bradley family at the time. The fighting occurred on Oct. 4, 1780. A "correspondent" (reporter) for the *Pennsylvania Packet* reported the affair as follows to his paper: "Captains Thompson and Knox, with fourteen men, attacked above 300 of a foraging party [of British from Charlotte] who were entering Mr. Bradley's plantation (eight miles from Charlotte) with near 60 waggons, and drove them back with such precipitation that, as I am well informed, many of their horses fell dead in the streets. . . ." It was exploits such as these that gave Mecklenburg County her nickname of "Hornet's Nest." A fictitious account of this engagement, entitled "The Battle of the Bees," appeared in E. P. Roe's popular novel, *The Hornet's Nest* (1886).

At **10 m.** within wall-enclosed premises is HOPEWELL PRESBYTERIAN CHURCH, known by its present name in the early 1760's. Itinerant preachers held services in this area a decade earlier. In its burying ground is the GRAVE OF JOHN McKNITT ALEXANDER, member of the Mecklenburg Committee (*see* CHARLOTTE); also, the GRAVE OF GEN. WILLIAM LEE DAVIDSON, commander of the western militia, and many other graves of Revolutionary soldiers. The present rectangular brick building, with a gallery extending around three sides, was erected in 1833 and subsequently enlarged. A two-story educational building stands in the rear. Hopewell became a wealthy congregation in the period before the Civil War. Its planter society is pictured in the historical novel *Cloud over Catawba* by Chalmers G. Davidson.

Section c. CHARLOTTE to ASHEVILLE; 116 m. US 74

This route runs from plains, across foothills, and up into rugged highlands.

Between CHARLOTTE, **0 m.**, and KINGS MOUNTAIN, **29 m.** (*see* TOUR 8) US 74 unites with US 29 (*see* TOUR 8).

At **39.7 m.** are the CLEVELAND COUNTY FAIRGROUNDS (R) where one of the largest county agricultural fairs in the State is held annually (*Sept.*).

On a wooded hillside (L) is a row of tall white columns fronting a gutted brick shell, all that remains of the hotel (burned in 1928) at CLEVELAND SPRINGS, **41 m.** Originally known as Sulphur Springs, in the 1880's this was one of North Carolina's famous watering place.

SHELBY, **43 m.** (1,000 alt., 15,508 pop.), seat of Cleveland County, is a textile manufacturing town. The business district radiates from Court Square, whose trees shade the columned courthouse.

Shelby, near the foothills of the Blue Ridge Mountains, was chartered in 1843 and named for Col. Isaac Shelby—hero of the Battle of Kings Mountain (*see* TOUR 8). Principal streets, such as Washington, LaFayette, Warren, Marion, are named for Revolutionary heroes.

Shelby was the home of O. Max Gardner, Ambassador to the Court of St. James (1947), Governor (1929-33); the Hon. Clyde R. Hoey, U. S. Senator (1946-54), Governor (1937-41); the Hon. E. Y. Webb, U. S. Federal Judge (1919-48), U. S. Congressman (1903-19); Hatcher Hughes, whose drama, *Hell Bent for Heaven,* won the Pulitzer Prize in 1924; Thomas Dixon, author of the famous novel *The Clansman* on which D. W. Griffith based his epic picture *Birth of a Nation. Heavenbound* is a musical pageant written by Violet Thomas, a Shelby Negress. John McKnight's *The Papacy* won the Mayflower Society Cup in 1952. W. J. Cash, author of *The Mind of the South,* for which he received the Mayflower Society Cup posthumously, although a South Carolinian by birth, spent the better part of his life in Shelby, where his father still resides.

Cleveland County was named for Col. Benjamin Cleveland of Kings Mountain Battle fame. Most of the early settlers came from Maryland, Pennsylvania, Virginia, and eastern Carolina between 1760 and 1820. There are more than 5,000 farms within the county raising cotton, corn, small grains, beef cattle, hogs, chickens, dairy products, and many marketable fruits. The county contains 86 manufacturing plants producing in 1950 goods valued at $92,600,000 and employing 8,000 men and women.

Left from Shelby on NC 150 to BOILING SPRINGS, 8 m. (1,145 pop.), the location of GARDNER-WEBB COLLEGE, a liberal arts junior college, first chartered as a Baptist high school in 1905. In 1928 it became Boiling Springs Junior College, and in 1942 it adopted its present name to honor the two Cleveland County families who have led in revitalizing the college. Its 12 modern buildings on a 1,200-acre campus and farm serve about 340 students.

At 61 m. the route crosses Puzzle Creek and at 61.3 m. the Second Broad River.

FOREST CITY, 63 m. (860 alt., 4,971 pop.), is a textile town, designated as "One of the Ten Best Planned and Most Beautiful Cities in the U. S." The business section is built around a large public plaza. It was once known as Burnt Chimney and was the muster ground of the Burnt Chimney Volunteers of the Confederate Army.

Forest City is at the junction with US 221 A (see TOUR 21).

SPINDALE, 68 m. (3,891 pop.), known as the "textile center of Rutherford County," was organized in 1916 and incorporated in 1923. Rayon, nylon, dress-goods cloth, thread, and hosiery mills are located here.

A portion of the SPINDALE COMMUNITY HOUSE was formerly the summer home of the Coxe family. A brick, early-Victorian building, built about 1880, it was for many years used as Spindale Inn. Before 1916 the settlement, at the junction of the Seaboard Air Line and the Southern Ry., was called Coxe's Crossing.

At RUTHERFORDTON, 70 m. (see TOUR 13), US 74 unites with US 64 to BAT CAVE, 96 m. (see TOUR 13).

From Bat Cave US 74 climbs, by a series of hairpin loops, from the gorge of the swift-flowing Broad River into the rugged highlands. Impressive mountain scenery is revealed as the road gains altitude. The pass is attained at HICKORY NUT GAP, 99.7 m. (3,000 alt.). From this point descent is made through a sharply twisting course.

ASHEVILLE, 116 m. (see ASHEVILLE).

Points of Interest: Biltmore House, Thomas Wolfe Memorial, Pack Memorial Library, Grove Park Inn, Sunset Mountain, and others.

Asheville is at the junction with US 70 (see TOUR 15), US 19-23 (see TOURS 22 and 23), and US 25 (see TOUR 24).

TOUR 17A *(US 421)*

Greensboro—Sanford—Clinton—Wilmington—Fort Fisher; US 421. **214 m.**

Between GREENSBORO, **0 m.** (*see* GREENSBORO), and Wilmington US 421 crosses North Carolina's piedmont plateau and the coastal plain. The landscape changes with the altitude: hardwood forests in the low central hills, cotton and tobacco farms on the plain, small truck farms among the pine forests of the lowlands. South of Wilmington the route runs down a peninsula between the Atlantic Ocean and the Cape Fear River to Fort Fisher.

At **2 m.** is the junction with the Alamance Church Rd.

Left on this road to the ALAMANCE PRESBYTERIAN CHURCH (1875), **4 m.**, the fourth building erected on the site. The first log church was built in 1762. In the graveyard surrounding this brick structure are the marked graves of men who fell in the Revolution and of others prominent in the early affairs of the community. Col. Arthur Forbis, wounded in the Battle of Guilford Courthouse (*see* TOUR 9), is buried here. Forbis lay on the field during the rainy night following the battle. A Tory, named Shoemaker, responded to an appeal for water by thrusting a bayonet through his leg. Next morning Forbis was found by a Miss Montgomery, who helped him upon his horse and to his home. He died about three weeks later, at the age of 34. Shoemaker was captured and hanged by a band of Whigs. Ralph Gorrell, the first white man to own land on which Greensboro was established in 1808, is buried here.

LIBERTY, **22 m.** (790 alt., 1,342 pop.), in a prairielike flat, is named for the Liberty Oak, no longer standing, under which Union officers are said to have celebrated Gen. Joseph E. Johnston's surrender in 1865 (*see* TOUR *15B*).

Left on NC 62 to SANDY CREEK BAPTIST CHURCH, **4.3 m.**, founded in 1755 by the Rev. Shubal Stearnes, a native of Boston, who joined the Baptist separatists and moved here from Virginia. The Sandy Creek Church became the center of a Baptist Association that included churches in Virginia and the two Carolinas. Stearnes is buried in the church graveyard.

SILER CITY, **34 m.** (*see* TOUR *13*) is at the junction with US 64 (*see* TOUR *13*).

At MOUNT VERNON SPRINGS, 39 m. (90 pop.), formerly called Ore Hill, mineral water is bottled and shipped. Near here is the SITE OF THE WILCOX IRON WORKS, whose furnace, still operated occasionally, was an important source of munitions during the Revolution.

Near the village of GULF, 51 m., formerly called Cummock, is the EGYPT COAL MINE, which was operated at intervals, 1855-1928. During the Civil War it supplied coal for Confederate blockade runners.

The PATTERSON HOME (*visitors welcome*), 55 m. (R), is a two-story weatherboarded house with hip roof, once the home of Charles D. McIver (1860-1906), founder of the Woman's College of the University of North Carolina (*see* GREENSBORO).

SANFORD, 59 m. (*see* TOUR 5) is at the junction with US 1 (*see* TOUR 5).

Between Sanford and JONESBORO, 62 m. (formerly a separate town, now incorporated into Sanford), is (R) the COURTHOUSE, approximately half way between the two towns. Its peculiar location was the result of a a struggle between the older town of Jonesboro and the newer town of Sanford.

Right from Jonesboro on a sand-clay road to SHALLOW WELL CHRISTIAN CHURCH, 1 m., built by a religious group that branched from the O'Kellyite sect. James O'Kelly had led a split from Southern Methodism (*see* TOUR 7) and his followers worshiped in a brush arbor near a spring. The dissenters abandoned the arbor, and about 1820 built this wooden church with elevated pulpit and mourners' corners, across the road on a pine-covered hill, and dug a shallow well for which the church was named. A cemetery occupies the site of the old arbor. A part of Sherman's army camped behind the church in 1865.

At 64 m. is PINE KNOTS (1760), home of Isaac Brooks, widely known in early days for the hospitality of its owners. A wooded tract has been set aside for the use of tourists.

SUMMERVILLE, 81 m., formerly known as Toomer, was the first seat of Harnett County (1855-58). The TIRZAH PRESBYTERIAN CHURCH was founded by Scottish settlers, many of whom are buried in the churchyard. Though the church organization has been dissolved, the building is kept in repair.

LILLINGTON, 84 m. (*see* TOUR 6), is at the junction with US 15A (*see* TOUR 6), which unites with US 421 between this point and 85 m. where US 15A branches L.

Right at Lillington on an unmarked road to BARBECUE (Presbyterian) CHURCH, 13.7 m., which, along with Long Street and Bluff (*see* LOCAL TOUR FROM FAY-ETTEVILLE *and* TOUR 6), were organized by James Campbell, missionary who came down from Pennsylvania in 1757. The present, white, clapboard, rectangular church was erected about 1895 as the third on this site. Graves of early Highland Scots are in the cemetery in the rear.

At **88 m.** is the junction with a dirt road.

Right on this road to the McKay Graveyard, **2 m.**, on the Cape Fear River, where the McKays, McCranies, and Buies, first settlers of the region, are buried. Nearby is a cemetery where slaves were interred.

BUIES CREEK, **90 m.** (435 pop.), is a town on a creek by the same name. The stream was named for the Buie family, early Scottish settlers who came to this section in 1746 after the Battle of Culloden.

Campbell College (1887), originally Buie's Creek Academy, almost concealed among the pines, grew from the one-room schoolhouse of James Archibald Campbell. Now with its impressive brick buildings, its own farm and dairy, this coeducational Baptist junior college has almost absorbed the town. Paul Green, the playwright, a former student, personally supervised the construction of the Paul Green Theater.

Until a few years ago dreams and superstitions played an important part in the life of the back-country people of this section, and conjurers were held in high respect. When a child was born the father announced the fact by firing a gun. Grown-ups finished their meals before the children were served, and children were not permitted to talk while their elders were conversing. To kill a cat brought bad luck, so dissenters were sometimes hired to dispose of the surplus felines. If mothers allowed their babies to look into a well there would be difficulty in teething.

Because of the difficulty of getting occasional labor, the farmers, until recently, banded together for corn shucking, logrolling, and hog killing, and farmers' wives regaled the workers with brandied cakes and scuppernong grape pies. For diversion there were square dances and swimming, called "goin'-in-a-washin'."

At **94 m.**, where the highway crosses the CAPE FEAR RIVER, antebellum citizens were served by a ferry. Here once stood a gallows.

ERWIN, **96 m.** (195 alt., 33,344 pop.), is a cotton-mill town.

Right from Erwin on sand-clay NC 82 to the Averasboro Battleground, **3 m.**, where on Mar. 15, 1865, Gen. William J. Hardee with 6,000 Confederate troops unsuccessfully attacked Sherman's army.

Oak Grove (*open*), the John Smith home on the battlefield, was used as a hospital by Confederate troops. The 10-room house has a chimney at each end and a large porch. Parts are held together with wooden pegs. Near the home are breastworks used during the battle. The house was directly in the line of fire, and two 6-inch balls passed entirely through the third story. In this house in 1866 neighborhood women organized one of the first Confederate memorial societies, which, on May 15, 1867, became the Smithville Memorial Association. The house once served as a station on the Raleigh-Fayetteville stage route.

The William Smith House, a frame building, standing much as it was in the 1860's, served as a Federal hospital. The Union slain, buried in the garden, were later removed to the National Cemetery at Raleigh.

CHICORA CONFEDERATE CEMETERY, enclosed by an iron railing, is the burial place for 55 soldiers killed in the Battle of Averasboro. Markers at the heads of the mounds show that from two to 11 were buried in each grave.

Right on US 421 at N. outskirts of Erwin on a dirt road to the HOME OF WILLIAM AVERA (*private*), 0.5 m., built in 1827 and a one-time show place on the Raleigh-Fayetteville stage road.

The DUSHEE SHAW HOUSE (*private*), 3 m., where the dirt road intersects with NC 55, was known as the Halfway House, since it was the midway point between Raleigh and Fayetteville. Its heart-of-pine paneling, chair rails, and barrel ceilings make this an unusual house for the period in which it was built (1806).

NC 55 leads through COATS, 6 m. At 9.2 m., a road leads 0.4 m. to BARBEE'S INN, another noted stop on the old Raleigh-Fayetteville road. Here Sam Houston, Santa Anna, and Lafayette dined. It was described by Frederick Law Olmsted in *Journeys Through the Seaboard South* (1861).

DUNN, 100 m. (*see* TOUR *3, sec. b*), is at the junction with US 301 (*see* TOUR *3, sec. b*).

CLINTON, 128 m. (*see* TOUR *18*), is at the junction with US 701 (*see* TOUR *18*).

At 168 m. is the junction with NC 210.

Right on this road to MOORES CREEK NATIONAL MILITARY PARK, 5 m. Blankets of Carolina yellow jessamine and the blue bells of clematis hang from the shrubs along the edge of the creek. The pitcherplant, trumpet, sundew, and Venus's-flytrap are among the unusual local varieties.

Here on Feb. 27, 1776, the Tory Scottish Highlanders were decisively defeated by Whigs in the Battle of Moores Creek Bridge, the first victory gained on North Carolina soil by American armies in the Revolution, a battle that determined North Carolina's stand in the long struggle for American independence and helped Southern delegates at Continental Congress to sign the Declaration of Independence.

On Feb. 19, 1776, Gen. Donald MacDonald and his Scottish troops, marching out of Cross Creek, now Fayetteville, on his way to meet Cornwallis at Wilmington, were intercepted at Moores Creek Bridge by Col. Richard Caswell and Col. Alexander Lillington with their minutemen. In the battle that followed only one Whig was killed and one wounded. The Highlanders fled, leaving 50 killed or wounded, including Donald McLeod, second in command. Their commanding officer and Allan MacDonald, husband of Flora (*see* FAYETTEVILLE), were among the 850 prisoners taken.

In this 30-acre tract are historic monuments to patriots and Scots and a marker at the bridge. The State acquired the battleground in 1898, and in 1926 the general assembly transferred the park to the Federal Government. In 1933 Moores Creek National Military Park was placed under the National Park Service.

At 183 m. US 421 unites with US 17 and US 74-76 to Wilmington.

WILMINGTON, 184 m. (*see* WILMINGTON).

Points of Interest: Customhouse, Cornwallis House, St. James Church, Bellamy Mansion, Dudley Mansion, Hilton Park, Greenfield Park, and others.

Wilmington is at the junction with US 17 (*see* TOUR *1, sec. b*), US 74-76 (*see* TOUR *16*), and US 117 (*see* TOUR *4*).

South of Wilmington on US 421 (Carolina Beach Blvd.) is CAROLINA BEACH, **199 m.**, a mainland seashore resort (*modern hotels open June 1-Sept. 1; motels, cottages, and apartments; bathing, surf casting, deep-sea fishing, and dancing*), with a year-around population of over 1,000. Development has extended some distance west from the ocean. Near the waterfront is a crowded business section and amusement area. Grounded in the sand off Carolina Beach are several battered wrecks, including the *Venus*, the *Lynx*, the *Hebe*, and the *Beauregard*, Confederate blockade runners.

Right from Carolina Beach on a road (*partly paved*) to the SITE OF THE BATTLE OF BIG SUGAR LOAF, **8 m.** Here, during the land and sea battle involving Fort Fisher, a landing party of Federal troops under Gen. Alfred H. Terry entrenched themselves and thwarted attempts of Confederate troops led by Gen. R. F. Hoke and Gen. W. W. Kirkland to reinforce the beleaguered defenders at the fort. Remnants of the entrenchments are visible. Sugar Loaf is the site of a camp of the Coree Indians, established long before white men set foot on Cape Fear soil. From this point the Coree crossed the river and made forays upon Orton and other plantations (*see* LOCAL TOUR FROM WILMINGTON).

Between Carolina Beach and Fort Fisher US 421 follows the ocean front, passing sand dunes along the beach; myrtle and turkey oaks grow with morning-glories and irises on what was once a battlefield. For two days and nights this whole area between river and ocean was swept by withering gunfire that preceded the fall of Fort Fisher, during a double attack, Dec. 24-25, 1864, and Jan. 13-15, 1865.

At **201 m.** is WILMINGTON BEACH, a small coastal resort (*surf bathing*), and at **202 m.**, KURE BEACH (*surf bathing, fishing pier, cottages, cafés*).

Right from Kure Beach on a dirt road to the ETHYL-DOW CHEMICAL PLANT (*closed*), **1 m.**, where bromines were extracted from sea water, a major feat in industrial chemistry. The water was pumped from the ocean overland to the plant for processing and then was discharged into the river to reenter the sea at a point about 16 miles from the original intake. The bromine so extracted furnished about 40% of the supply used for antiknock gasolines. The plant was constructed in 1928 and subsequently enlarged. Shortly thereafter operations were suspended, but there are prospects of the resumption of operations.

At **202.7 m.** on US 421 is the junction with a side road.

Right on this road to the SITE OF SEDGELY ABBEY, **0.2 m.**, an elaborate residence built about 1726 of coquina, a soft limestone. Near the abbey site was GANDER HALL, the colonial estate of Capt. James McIlhenny, of which nothing remains but a grove of oaks and the cellar. It was so named because in 1831, when the price of goose feathers was high, the captain decided to raise geese on a large scale. He purchased a handsome flock only to find out too late that all were ganders. Neighborhood Negroes regard the place with awe. On occasions the ruins have been searched for gold supposedly hidden there, and the belief is that, even when a search is started on a clear day, the skies begin to cloud over, wind moans through the trees, and cries and groans are heard.

At **203 m.** is FORT FISHER BEACH, on the SITE OF FORT FISHER, Confederate stronghold during the Civil War where the heaviest land-naval battle of the Civil War was fought, commemorated by a MONUMENT. The only remains of the emplacement are stretches of grass-grown breastworks, marked by a monument to northern and southern soldiers who fought in the battle (Dec. 20, 1864-Jan. 13, 1865). The Federal fleet alone, in two attacks, fired more than 2,000,000 pounds of projectiles. Cannon balls and skeletons of men have been found on the beach where the ocean has washed away the earthworks.

South of Fort Fisher on a dirt road to the ROCKS, **1.6 m.**, a dam closing the New Inlet mouth of Cape Fear River. From the Rocks (*good fishing*), a great sea-wall, there is a sweeping view of the river's mouth and of the Atlantic. To the southwest is SMITH ISLAND, at whose southern tip is Cape Fear (*see* TOUR *1, sec. b*).

TOUR 17B *(US 421)*

Greensboro—Winston-Salem—North Wilkesboro—Junction with Blue Ridge Parkway; US 421. 114 m.

West of GREENSBORO, 0 m., US 421 traverses a section of the northern piedmont along a route known as the Boone Trail, because it roughly parallels the traditional course taken by Daniel Boone from the plains to the mountains. Beyond North Wilkesboro the route ascends the Blue Ridge Mountains by an easy grade.

At 6 m. is the junction with a marked road.

Right on this road is GUILFORD COLLEGE, 1 m. (939 alt., 800 pop.), settled by Quakers in 1750 and called New Garden. The New Garden Boarding School, opened by the Friends in 1837 to avoid a school "in a mixed condition," grew into GUILFORD COLLEGE, incorporated 1889, now having an enrollment of 300. This is the oldest and most influential Quaker college in the South, though no longer "Friends' select." The shaded campus and athletic field occupy 30 of its 290 acres; its enrollment is about 500 students.

Unusual for the day in which it was founded, the school has always been co-educational. However, the first building, FOUNDERS HALL (1834-37), of hand-made brick and hand-hewn timbers, originally had three entrances: the east for boys, the west for girls, and the center for teachers and visitors. Singing was a misde-meanor in boarding school days and while music was permitted in 1887, it was not a recognized part of the curriculum until 1894. Dancing was forbidden until 1933.

During the Revolution sick and wounded soldiers were nursed by the pacifist Quakers, and British and patriot dead were buried side by side in great square graves. The school was kept open during the Civil War and the Reconstruction period, though many Quaker boys had to flee through the lines to escape con-scription at Greensboro. Baskets of food hung in the log barn behind the school farmhouse for passing Unionist, Secessionist, or bushwhacker, all alike hungry men to the Quakers.

The LIBRARY (1909) is a red brick building with classic portico and high arched windows. In its collection of 17,628 volumes is a first edition of George Fox's *Journal*. MEMORIAL (SCIENCE) HALL (1897), in memory of Mary Elizabeth Lyon, was given by her brothers, Benjamin and James B. Duke; all three were students in the 1870's.

The NEW GARDEN MEETINGHOUSE, erected in 1912 to accommodate the sessions of the North Carolina Yearly Meeting of Friends, is the college chapel. The first meetinghouse, a weatherboarded building, was erected in 1751.

Nathanael Greene was disowned by his sect for bearing arms, yet in the meetinghouse yard is the GRAVE OF WILLIAM ARMFIELD, a good Quaker who, incensed over Cornwallis' destruction of his crops, took his squirrel gun and departed ostensibly to hunt. He joined the Revolutionary forces at the courthouse and fought all day. Upon his return his family inquired about his game and he replied that "it wasn't worth bringing home."

Right from Guilford College on the Battleground Rd. to the David Hodgin farm, 2 m., containing the SITE OF THE BIRTHPLACE OF JOSEPH E. CANNON, Speaker of the House of Representatives (1901-11). While he was a Congressman from Illinois, "Uncle Joe" twice visited the place. The story is that when the old log house was pointed out as his birthplace, he remarked, "I'll be damned! Let's go." However, he later had permanent record made of his birth at New Garden.

Right from Guilford College on Friendly Rd. to the DOLLY MADISON WELL, 0.5 m., site of the birthplace of Dolly Payne Madison. John and Mary (Coles) Payne removed on certificate from Cedar Creek Monthly Meeting in Virginia to New Garden Monthly Meeting in 1765. In a house that once stood here "Dolley their Daughter was born ye 20 of ye 5 mo. 1768" The Paynes returned to Virginia in 1769.

At 2 m. on the Friendly Rd. is the SITE OF THE CALDWELL HOME AND LOG COLLEGE. Dr. David Caldwell, minister, physician, and teacher, came to North Carolina in 1765 as a Presbyterian missionary to the Alamance and Buffalo congregations (see GREENSBORO). In 1767 he opened his classical school for boys. He interceded with both Tryon and the Regulators for peaceful settlement of their difficulties. So ardent a patriot did he become that Cornwallis offered £200 for his capture, and when encamped on Caldwell's farm he ravaged it even to the precious library and family Bible. Caldwell was a member of the State constitutional convention in 1776, and in the Hillsboro Convention of 1788 he opposed ratification of the Federal Constitution mainly because it lacked a religious test. He was tendered the presidency of the University of North Carolina at its formation but declined because of his advanced age, though he subsequently taught and preached until 1820.

The LINDLEY NURSERIES, INC., 9 m. (600 acres), was begun in 1877 by J. Van Lindley to develop shrubs and trees suited to North Carolina.

At FRIENDSHIP, 10 m. is GREENSBORO-HIGH POINT AIRPORT (scheduled service by Eastern, Capital, and Piedmont Air Lines). In addition to the hangars, a low white building houses the airport offices and a station of the U. S. Weather Bureau.

KERNERSVILLE, 18 m. (1,023 alt., 2,394 pop.), a town with a few small mills, has changed little since it was settled by families of German extraction about 1770. According to tradition, about 1756 Caleb Story bought the 400-acre town site outright at the rate of a gallon of rum for 100 acres.

A marker at the Salem Street intersection on the highway indicates the SITE OF DOBSON'S TAVERN. George Washington breakfasted here June 2, 1791, according to his diary: "In company with Govr. I set out for Guilford by four o'clock—breakfasted at one Dobson's at the distance of 11 m. from Salem."

An architectural curiosity of elaborate and fantastic design is Körner's Folly (*private*), half a mile L. from US 421 on Salem St. The three-story, 22-room brick residence was built in 1880 by J. Gilmer Körner, artist and traveler. The sharp-pitched roof, covered with shingles said to have been cut from a single tree, is broken by numerous tall chimneys. The façade has recessed arches and narrow windows. Caesar Milch, a German artist, did the frescoes, using themes suggested by some of Rubens' paintings. The rooms on the lower floor have silk-paneled walls, marble floors, and profusely carved woodwork. No two doors are of the same dimensions, but all those on the first floor reach the ceiling. Narrow stairways appear in unexpected places. The third-floor music room was once used as a little theater. Mrs. Körner wrote plays performed there by local talent and Mr. Körner painted the scenery. A leaflet explains that Mr. Körner "traveled widely, painting everywhere, even upon the Rock of Gibraltar, the male bovine symbol so synonymous with the 'roll-your-own' product of a great tobacco company."

Right from Kernersville on NC 150 are several interesting houses, most notable of which is (R) the BENBOW HOUSE (*private*), **5 m.**, a two-story brick structure erected in 1823 by Charles Benbow, member of a Quaker family that came from Bladen County. The former rear of the two-story brick house faces the present road. The gabled roof of the main structure is broken by two end chimneys; at one side is a gabled one-story service wing; on the front is a broad two-story porch. The interior woodwork—a reeded mantel, the door trim, and the chair rails—evidences skillful workmanship. Behind the house is a small frame building used until a few years ago as a clubhouse by students of Oak Ridge Military Institute.

On NC 150 is OAK RIDGE, **6 m.** (885 alt., 500 pop.), seat of OAK RIDGE MILITARY INSTITUTE, occupying several brick buildings with stuccoed white columns. Founded in 1852, the school has operated without interruption except during the Civil War.

WINSTON-SALEM, 29 m. (*see* WINSTON-SALEM).

Points of Interest: Old Salem, Home Moravian Church, Salem College, Wake Forest College, R. J. Reynolds Tobacco Plant, and others.

Winston-Salem is at the junction with US 158 (*see* TOUR *12*), US 52 (*see* TOUR *10*), and US 311.

West of Winston-Salem US 421 is bordered on both sides by sugar maples and thick hedges. The avenue marks the boundary of the Reynolds estate, REYNOLDA (*private*). The mansion, in a dense grove of trees, is not visible from the highway. On the estate are a lake and the REYNOLDA GARDENS (*open to the public*), where weeping cherry trees bloom profusely in late March and early April.

The entrance to the new campus of WAKE FOREST COLLEGE (*see* WINSTON-SALEM) is 0.5 m. beyond Reynolda Post Office. Across from the Reynolda Estate (L) is GRAYLIN, the estate of the late Bowman Gray, now used as a psychiatric hospital (*not open to the public*).

Right on this road to BETHABARA (beth-ăb'-ara, Heb., *house of passage*), **2.5 m.** better known as Oldtown, as it was the first (1753) Moravian settlement in North Carolina (*see* WINSTON-SALEM). All that remains of this once-thriving communal settlement are a few houses and the old church. Two of the houses antedate the church.

BETHABARA CHURCH (*open; inquire at house across road*), built in 1788, has 2-foot-thick fieldstone walls plastered over. The one-and-a-half-story structure is built in two sections, the higher section having an octagonal tower and steeple. At the rear of the auditorium a narrow stair leads to upper rooms and the sturdy belfry with the original mellow-toned bell. Comprising the right side of the building are 4 rooms originally used as living quarters for the minister and his family. Worn stone steps wind down to a vaulted cellar.

At the NW. corner of the old village a marker indicates the SITE OF THE CABIN found by the first settlers and used by them until they could build houses of their own.

Atop a low hill behind the church in the OLDEST MORAVIAN GRAVEYARD in North Carolina are stones dated 1754. The first Moravian Easter Sunrise Service in North Carolina was held at Bethabara in 1758.

In the churchyard a huge millstone with a bronze plaque marks the SITE OF BETHABARA FORT (1756), and posts inscribed F indicate the OUTLINES OF THE STOCKADE that enclosed the principal houses of the village. The fort was a place of refuge for settlers of the region during the French and Indian War. Another marker identifies the SITE OF THE OLD TAVERN.

At **35 m.** is the junction with NC 67.

Right on NC 67 to the junction with a marked road at Oldtown School, **1.5 m.**; R. **1 m.** on this road to BETHANIA (789 alt., 100 pop.), formerly called New Town, site of the second Moravian settlement in North Carolina (1759), established by dissenters from Bethabara, but including some non-Moravian settlers.

The BETHANIA CHURCH (1807), of large, hand-made bricks, with a hooded entrance and an open-roof cupola, is similar to the Home Church in Winston-Salem. The single-manual pipe organ, built by hand in 1773 by Joseph Bullitschek, a local cabinet maker who also built organs for Bethabara and Salem, was destroyed by fire when the church burned in 1942. The walls of the church survived the fire; the church has been reconstructed.

During the time that Bullitschek was the official organist he was annoyed by Dr. Schumann, the local physician, who often went early to church to play the organ. Bullitschek finally reversed the pipes, without Schumann's knowledge. The doctor's discords so distressed him that Bullitschek was no longer disturbed.

A marker indicates the SITE OF CORNWALLIS' HEADQUARTERS where he spent a night in Bethania, Mar. 16, 1781. He destroyed much property and held the minister, Ernst, as hostage until all the best horses had been delivered to him. Bethania's small mills and stores ceased operations when Gen. George Stoneman plundered the place on Apr. 1, 1865.

At **14.8 m.** on NC 67 is the junction with a paved road; R. **0.5 m.** on this road to the junction with a sand-clay road; L. **1.5 m.** on the sand-clay road to the junction with a dirt road just before reaching Richmond Hill Church; R. **0.3 m.** on the dirt road to a lane; L. **1.2 m.** (as far as possible) on the lane;

through fields about **2 m.** to Richmond Hill (*private*), the home and school operated here from 1847 until his death in 1878 by Richmond Pearson, teacher and Chief Justice of the State Supreme Court (1858-78). The large, square, porchless brick house is decaying in grounds overgrown with brush. Of the 1,000 students who read law under his direction, Thomas Settle, David Reid, W. B. Rodman, W. P. Bynum, and R. P. Dick became justices of the State Supreme Court. Another student, James Hobson, married Sallie, Judge Pearson's third daughter; their son, Richmond Pearson Hobson, sank the *Merrimac* in Santiago Harbor, during the Spanish-American War. The judge's only son, Richmond Pearson, served as Minister to Persia and Greece (1902-9).

The route crosses the Yadkin River, **40 m.**, over a high bridge. Here a marker relates that at Shallow Ford, 5 miles south, Whigs defeated Tories in 1780 and Cornwallis' army passed that way in 1781. YADKIN VALLEY BEACH (*picnic sites*) is on the river shore at the R. of the bridge.

At **45 m.** is the junction with a side road.

Right on this road to Glennwood (*private*), **0.8 m.**, a well-preserved two-story clapboarded mansion with Greek Doric portico built in the 1830's by Tyre Glenn on an estate of 6,000 acres and continuously occupied by his descendants. The hand-made cherry doors are pegged. The brick summer kitchen has a large chimney and fireplace, and one remaining slave cabin, called the "boys' house," is now a toolroom. Several pieces of furniture, hand-made by slaves and still in use, survived raids by disbanded Union soldiers and freed slaves. The older house, in which the Glenns lived while the mansion was being built, has been remodeled.

YADKINVILLE, **112 m.** (1,050 alt., 820 pop.), seat of Yadkin County, which was formed in 1850 from Surry, was named for the river that forms its northern and eastern boundaries. The Yadkin County Courthouse (1855) has red-painted brick walls marked by stuccoed white pilasters without bases and stark white window frames. The spacious fireplaces are still in use, but the buckets for drinking water have been replaced by a more sanitary system. On the courthouse square is a Boone Trail marker.

There are a number of tobacco basket factories located in Yadkinville or in Yadkin County.

BROOKS CROSSROADS, **64 m.**, is at the junction with US 21 (*see* TOUR *11*).

At **71 m.** the highway begins to leave the flat country. Far to the north is the Yadkin Valley, and the Brushy Mountains rise to the southwest.

At **79.2 m.** US 421 skirts a ridge in the upper reaches of Hunting Creek Valley (L).

NORTH WILKESBORO, **87 m.** (1,190 alt., 4,379 pop.), largest town in the upper Yadkin Valley, was chartered in 1891 when citizens voted to separate from Wilkesboro. Industrial plants include a large tannery, lumber and furniture factories, foundries, and machine shops. It is one of the largest poultry markets in the South.

A few nearby mountain folk eke out a living by what is known in local parlance as "yarbin' it," a colloquialism for gathering and selling roots, barks, and herbs to a local firm that exports them.

North Wilkesboro is separated from Wilkesboro by the Yadkin River, whose basin is noted for its broad fertile valleys and scenic beauty.

WILKESBORO, 88 m. (1,042 alt., 1,370 pop.), seat of Wilkes County, on the south bank of the Yadkin, was settled before the Revolution and called Mulberry Fields. County and town were named for John Wilkes (1727-97), English statesman and defender of popular rights. John Wilkes Booth, Lincoln's assassin, was related to John Wilkes through his paternal grandmother.

The first log courthouse was used until 1830. The present COURTHOUSE is a Classical Revival brick and stone structure with a two-story pedimented portico and unusual roof setbacks. The first deed recorded was a grant in 1779 of 3,400 acres to Col. Benjamin Cleveland (*see below*), whose tract, Roundabout, was in a horseshoe bend of the river. "Old Roundabout" was a popular nickname for Cleveland who was widely known for his vigorous activity in the Whig cause. He led men from this region to the Battle of Kings Mountain (*see* TOUR 8), where he commanded the left flank of the Continental forces. He was a scourge to the Tories around Ramsours Mill, as well as in the New and upper Yadkin River sections. After the war he lost Roundabout to a "better title," whereupon he removed in 1785 to the Tugalo country in South Carolina. Here he became a county court judge. Possessed of little formal education, Cleveland held legal technicalities and lengthy perorations in contempt. He had attained a weight of 450 pounds and often slept serenely on the bench, content to be prodded if his snoring interrupted the business of the court. Cleveland County was named for him (*see* TOUR 16).

After the Civil War a band of army deserters and outlaws, who had been plundering Wilkes County for several months, were trapped in a house which was set afire. All of the bandits except Col. Wade, their leader, surrendered, were tried, sentenced, and shot. Tradition relates that while Wade was being sought he escaped by hiding under the waters of the Yadkin River near the bank, breathing through a reed.

The TORY OAK, NE. corner of the courthouse lawn, is a 25-foot dying remnant of the "stately oak" that served as a gibbet for 5 Tories hanged by Col. Cleveland. One of the victims was the Tory leader William Riddle, who had spared Cleveland's life under similar circumstances.

The COWLES HOUSE (*private*), a clapboarded residence with graceful portico and three dormer windows, was built in 1803 for Johnny Waugh. It was the home of Calvin J. Cowles, president of the convention that adopted the State constitution in 1868. Cowles, a Northern sympathizer, married Gov. Holden's daughter.

St. Paul's Episcopal Church, on a hill overlooking the town, is a small, quaint, weathered, brick structure erected in 1836-39.

Right on NC 268 to ADLEY CHURCH, 3.5 m. Opposite, on a high hill on the north side of the Yadkin River, is the old STOKES MANSION (*private*), a square three-story building with wide porches around three sides. This was the home of Montfort Stokes, U. S. Senator (1816-23). Elected Governor in 1830, Stokes resigned Nov. 19, 1832 to accept an appointment by President Jackson as commissioner to report on conditions in the Indian Territory.

At 8 m. is GOSHEN POST OFFICE (88 pop.), in the fertile GOSHEN VALLEY, where for generations the people have made baskets, using the simplest tools and white oak for splits. The clan spirit is strong in these families who take pride in their work though it yields a very meager living. Recently truck farming and cattle raising have furnished additional occupations for these settlers.

FERGUSON, 16 m. (175 pop.), was temporarily set back when the flood of 1916 so damaged the roadbed of the Watauga & Yadkin River R. R. that it had to be abandoned. A sawmill and lumber plant had been built at the head of the railroad constructed to transport the timber from a vast mountain area. Today, dairying and agriculture are pursued by the inhabitants.

North Wilkesboro is at the junction with NC 16-18.

Left on this road the highway runs along the broad ridge between Cub Creek (L) and Moravian Creek (R).

From the old Cub Creek Baptist Church (L), 4 m., a plain white-painted building, is visible to the north and west the towering bulk of the Blue Ridge, its many peaks, gaps, and gorges outlined against the horizon. The slopes of the Brushy Mountains to the south are checkered with peach and apple orchards.

MORAVIAN FALLS, 5 m. (1,206 alt., 500 pop.) (*hotel and picnic grounds*), received its name from the waterfalls on Moravian Creek. Here a "one-horse" editor, R. Don Laws (d. 1951) began publishing in 1895 the *Yellow Jacket*, a monthly newspaper which reached an amazing circulation figure of over 100,000 in 1940-41. Some estimates put the figure at 250,000.

1. Right from Moravian Falls on NC 18 to the junction with a dirt road. 0.1 m.; L. on this road 0.4 m. to the MORAVIAN FALLS, where a clear mountain stream flows between wooded hills and gushes over a broad expanse of steep rock. Here a group of Moravian surveyors camped in 1752.

South of Moravian Falls the route follows NC 16 through the valley of the east branch of Moravian Creek.

At 5.7 m. is the junction with a marked dirt road.

1. Right on this road to YELLOW JACKET LAKE (*swimming*), 1 m., named for the paper in Moravian Falls.

At 8 m. is the junction with a marked road.

1. Left on this road to the SUMMIT OF PORES KNOB, 4 m. (2,680 alt.). Here is a campground and a 60-foot observation tower, from which parties often view the sunrise.

At 10 m. the highway begins the ascent of the Brushies, whose slopes in spring are covered with the pale pink of myriad apple blossoms. In the fall, roadside stands offer the fruit and sweet cider.

South of KILBYS GAP, **11 m.**, a mountain pass, NC 16 enters a long narrow valley. To the L. is SUGAR LOAF MOUNTAIN, a conical mass of stone with patches of scrubby trees. NC 16 continues on to Taylorsville, **20 m.** (*see* TOUR *13*).

From North Wilkesboro US 421 heads almost due west toward the Blue Ridge Mountains.

At **96 m.** is the junction with a marked road.

Right on this road to RENDEZVOUS MOUNTAIN STATE PARK, **2.5 m.** (2,480 alt. at highest point), a 142-acre tract on a spur of the Blue Ridge between Reddies River and Lewis Fork Creek. The park (*no facilities at present*) was presented to the State in 1926 by Judge Thomas B. Finley in trust for the Daughters of the American Revolution. Here, during the Revolution, 225 men were selected and placed under the command of Col. Benjamin Cleveland, Capt. (later Gen.) William Lenoir, and 9 other captains. These men, after marching to join other patriots at Quaker Meadows in Burke County (*see* TOUR *13*), took part in the Battle of Kings Mountain (*see* TOUR *8*).

At **97 m.** is the junction with the Parsonville Rd.

Right on this road to the CLEVELAND FARMHOUSE (*unoccupied*), **1.5 m.**, a two-story, two-room-wide log house with huge stone end chimneys, built soon after 1775. This was the home of Capt. Robert Cleveland, who was wounded in the Battle of Kings Mountain, to which he had marched with his brother Benjamin (*see above*). The house, in an old apple orchard, has fallen into disrepair. Capt. Cleveland is buried with other members of his family in a fenced enclosure in an open field nearby.

The WADE HARRIS BRIDGE (*marked*), **105.5 m.**, was named for the editor (d. 1936) of the Charlotte *Observer*. The bridge is 290 feet long and 106 feet above the bottom of the gorge.

At DEEP GAP, **114 m.** (3,131 alt., 350 pop.), a pass used by Daniel Boone to cross the Blue Ridge into the wilderness beyond, US 421 forms a junction with the Blue Ridge Parkway (*see* TOUR *19*).

For a description of the continuation of US 421 through Boone, **125 m.**, and Zionville, **140 m.**, to the Tennessee Line, **141 m.**, *see* LOCAL TOUR FROM BOONE.

TOUR 18 *(US 701)*

Junction with US 301—Clinton—Whiteville—(Conway, S. C.); US 701. Junction with US 301—South Carolina Line, 111 m.

Between the junction with US 301 and the South Carolina Line, US 701 crosses generally level countryside dotted with many lakes. Rich farming lands produce tobacco, cotton, and truck crops. Nearer the South Carolina Line, berries, flowers, and garden truck are the principal crops.

US 701 branches south from its junction with US 301, 0 m. (*see* TOUR 3, *sec. b*), at a point 4 miles southwest of Smithfield.

At 12 m. is the junction with a marked road.

Left on this road to BENTONVILLE BATTLEFIELD, 7 m., where the Confederates under Gen. Joseph E. Johnston were defeated, Mar. 19-21, 1865, by Sherman's army in the last major battle of the Civil War. Federal casualties were reported as 1,517 and Confederate losses, 2,606. Approximately 10 miles of Confederate trenches, still well preserved, run across the battleground.

The BENTONVILLE BATTLE MONUMENT (1927), erected jointly by the North Carolina Historical Commission and the United Daughters of the Confederacy, stands in a triangular grassplot. On a half-acre park, over a mass grave of 41 known Confederate dead and a great number of unknown ones, is a stone pyramid, erected in 1893 by the Goldsboro Rifles.

The HARPER HOUSE, 9 m., a two-story wooden structure, with its blacksmith shop and outbuildings, was filled with Confederate wounded. Many nearby trees bear bullet holes.

NEWTON GROVE, 15 m. (374 pop.), a small farming community, is the location of the HOLY REDEEMER CATHOLIC CHURCH, and its founder Dr. John A. Monk is buried here. Here a number of parishioners resorted to violence May 31, 1953, when the Right Rev. Vincent Waters, Bishop of the Roman Catholic Diocese of Raleigh, sought to end segregation by ordering the Negro members of adjoining St. Benedict's to worship with the members of Holy Redeemer with no restrictions on seating.

At Newton Grove there is a traffic circle where US 701, NC 102, and NC 55 form a junction.

At **17 m.** is the junction with a marked road.

1. Left on this road to the BIRTHPLACE OF WILLIAM RUFUS KING, **3 m.**, U. S. Congressman from North Carolina (1811-16), Senator from Alabama for 29 years and Vice-President of the United States, 1853.

2. Right on this road to HOUSE'S MILL, **2 m.**, completed in 1812 and one of the oldest water mills in continuous operation in the State. The original mill stones, weighing 4,000 pounds, were shipped from England to Wilmington, up the Cape Fear, and overland by oxcart and mule team. The Federals captured the mill prior to the battle of Bentonville (*see above*) and had the entire output of meal hauled by House's slaves to Gen. Sherman's camp near the battle site. The HOUSE, built in 1820 for Jackie House, the original owner of the mill, is occupied by a grandson, now in his seventies.

CLINTON, **33 m.** (158 alt., 4,414 pop.), the seat of Sampson County, was founded and laid off in 1818 but was not chartered until 1852. It was named for Gen. Richard Clinton, planter, politician, and soldier, who as one of the justices of the first court held in Sampson County, June, 1784, gave 5 acres of land on which to build a courthouse, prison, and stocks for the use of the county. Clinton was the first State Senator elected from Sampson County and was re-elected for 8 of the following annual sessions of the general assembly. A marker on the courthouse square records his attainments. Also on the courthouse square is a monument to Wm. Rufus King, 13th Vice-President of the United States (*see above*).

Clinton is chiefly an agricultural town, noted mainly for its produce market, said to be the largest north of Florida. Here 12 or 13 different types of truck are sold daily at auction during the season usually beginning in May and lasting well into July. Pepper, bullnose and Italian cucumbers, squash, and sweet corn are the heaviest offerings. A poultry and egg market is operated the year around.

Hardly has the chant of the produce auctioneer ceased before it is taken up by the tobacco auctioneer. Five modern warehouses move from 10 to 12 million pounds during the season.

A meat packing plant, a daily hog-buying market, and a cattle auction market are also operated here.

The TAFT BASS HOME (*private*), Chesnutt St., built 1847-48 for A. B. Chesnutt, is probably the oldest house in town. Constructed of heart pine materials, the 8-room house has two broad halls running through both stories, hand-carved woodwork, and original floors. The grounds, covering about one-half a city block, have been restored, leaving intact the huge oak trees.

The Chesnutt's next door neighbors were Unionists during the Civil War, and when a detachment of Sherman's army came through Clinton on their way to Bentonville these neighbors secured a Federal guard to protect their home and that of their friends, the Chesnutts, which they claimed belonged to them.

Clinton is at the junction with US 421 (*see* TOUR *17*).

TYPICAL WRECK NEAR HATTERAS

NASH STREET, WILSON (WILSON CHAMBER OF COMMERCE)

CONNESTEE FALLS, NEAR BREVARD   LINVILLE FALLS (HUGH MORTON)

JUNCTION OF BLUE RIDGE PARKWAY AND GREAT SMOKIES AT MILE-HIGH OVERLOOK

CRAGGY GARDENS, NEAR ASHEVILLE

U. S. 19 BETWEEN CANTON AND LAKE JUNALUSKA

BURNSVILLE PAINTING CLASSES

MOUNT MITCHELL FROM THE BLUE RIDGE PARKWAY

MARITIME MUSEUM AT CAPE HATTERAS NATIONAL SEASHORE RECREATIONAL AREA

BREVARD MUSIC

PICNIC GROUNDS IN GREAT SMOKY MOUNTAINS NATIONAL PARK, NEAR HEINTOOGA OVERLOOK

JOHN C. CAMPBELL FOLK SCHOOL, BRASSTOWN

KERR LAKE

SMOKY MOUNTAIN BRIDGE, ASHEVILLE

CAMERON VILLAGE SHOPPING CENTER, RALEIGH

PASQUOTANK COUNTY HEALTH CENTER, ELIZABETH CITY

Right from Clinton on NC 24, in a farming section where quail and small game are plentiful, is ROSEBORO, 12 m. (137 alt., 1,241 pop.). The Culbreth family, who are said to have furnished more ministers of the gospel than any other family in the State, live here.

1. Right from Roseboro on NC 242, on Little Coharie Creek, is the SITE OF THE HOME OF GABRIEL HOLMES, 2 m., Governor of North Carolina (1821-24). At SALEMBURG, 6 m. (435 pop.), is the Duke-endowed coeducational PINELAND COLLEGE organized as a girls' school in 1912 and chartered in 1926. EDWARDS MILITARY INSTITUTE for boys was added in 1935. It offers elementary, preparatory, and junior college courses to about 300 students.

2. Left from Clinton on NC 24 is the MAJOR JAMES MOORE HOUSE (*private*), 4 m., built for Maj. Moore in 1763 and considered the oldest house in the county. A two-story house with attic and a brick cellar, it has elaborately carved mantels and paneled walls. Family records reveal that British stragglers from Cornwallis' army were confined in the cellar.

At 6 m. from Clinton, on NC 24 is the DANIEL JOYNER HOUSE (1809-11), where white women and children were quartered during the Nat Turner insurrection of Sept., 1831 (*see* TOUR 4). Behind the house is a large PECAN TREE, unofficially reported to be the oldest and largest bearing pecan tree in the State. Family tradition says that the sprout was given by Pres. James Madison to Gen. James Kenan, who planted it here.

GARLAND, 46 m. (136 alt., 539 pop.), on the South River, is a lumber-marketing center.

Between Garland and the South Carolina Line are numerous lakes and dry basins known as bays. Many geologists believe they were formed by the fall of meteors (*see* NATURAL SETTING).

WHITE LAKE, 62 m., is a resort village.

1. Left from the town is WHITE LAKE (*cafés, cottages, boating, bathhouses; fishing*), 1 m., spring-fed and surrounded by large areas of white sand broken by pines and turkey oaks. The lake is about 1.3 miles wide, and its water is unusually clear (*see* NATURAL SETTING). It was described as early as 1773 by William Bartram, the botanist, in his *Travels*. In the 1920's it was commercially developed and is now the most popular inland resort in the coastal plains.

2. Left from the village of White Lake on NC 41 is BLACK LAKE (*swimming, boating, fishing*), 6 m., about the same size as White Lake.

At 63.7 m. is the junction with NC 53.

Left on NC 55 to SINGLETARY LAKE (*park roads, boating, fishing, swimming, organized camping*), 6 m., a recreation center developed as a 1,000-acre STATE PARK and operated as the SINGLETARY LAKE GROUP CAMP within the BLADEN LAKES STATE FOREST. The group camp, operated primarily for camping by youth agencies, accommodates 100 campers. The 565-acre natural lake is surrounded by varied and interesting plant and animal life.

At 68 m. is the junction with NC 242.

Right on NC 242 to evergreen-bordered JONES LAKE STATE PARK for Negroes (*park roads, boating, fishing, hiking, camp sites, picnic shelters, refresh-*

ment stand). The lake is within the 40,000-acre Bladen Lakes Cooperative Land Use Area purchased by the Federal Government and now administered on long-term lease as Bladen Lakes State Forest.

US 701 crosses the valley of the rushing Cape Fear on a high causeway.

ELIZABETHTOWN, 69 m. (121 alt., 1,611 pop.), seat of Bladen County, on the western bank of the Cape Fear River, was settled by Scotch, English, and Irish soon after the county had been formed in 1734, and in 1773 was named for Elizabeth, the sweetheart of Isaac Jones, who gave the land for the town site. Her last name is unknown. In front of the community building is a marker commemorating the Battle of Elizabethtown.

Old plantations along the river have fallen into ruins although at present there are many prosperous farms. For several years lumbering was an important industry here. A peanut-products factory is one of the chief industrial plants.

The TORY HOLE, SITE OF THE BATTLE OF ELIZABETHTOWN, is on Broad St., near the center of town. In 1781 the region around Elizabethtown, Campbellton, and Cross Creek (now Fayetteville) was a Tory stronghold. Whigs were driven from their homes and their estates pillaged. One August night a small band of patriots, having decided to strike back, reached the banks of the Cape Fear opposite Elizabethtown, which was then held by 300 Tories under Godden and Slingsby. They waded across and launched an attack. After Godden and Slingsby had been mortally wounded the Tories retreated, some taking refuge in houses, others leaping to safety into a deep ravine, since called the Tory Hole.

At 78.3 m. is the junction with a marked road.

Left on this road 2.3 m. to the BROWN MARSH PRESBYTERIAN CHURCH (R), a weatherboarded structure with an entrance on the left side, and another on the gable end. The building has remnants of solid shutters for the windows of the 5 bays. Within are rude benches and a rear gallery. The building was erected in 1825, replacing one built in 1787. Dr. Joseph R. Wilson, father of Woodrow Wilson, occasionally preached here. In the cemetery are buried the ancestors of Anna Mathilda McNeill Whistler, mother of James Abbott McNeill Whistler, the painter.

CLARKTON, 79 m. (88 alt., 589 pop.), an agricultural village, is one of the oldest tobacco markets in the State. There was a Highland Scot settlement here as early as 1760.

WHITEVILLE, 92 m. (60 alt., 4,238 pop.), founded in 1810 and the seat of Columbus County, is in the center of a rich farming section. Originally called White's Crossing, the town was named for James B. White who gave the site for the first courthouse and jail. A MARKER on the courthouse square was erected by the local D.A.R. chapter to White, who was also the first State Senator (1809) from Columbus County. The town has 15 tobacco warehouses and a BLUE JEANS MANUFACTURING PLANT which employs 180 persons.

Woodrow Wilson and his father were guests at the old WHITE HOUSE when it was occupied by Col. W. M. Baldwin. When young Woodrow was caught climbing a tree in the White yard on the Sabbath, Presbyterian wrath is said to have broken the Sabbath calm.

Whiteville is at the junction with US 74 (*see* TOUR *16*).

In Welsh Creek Township, about 4 miles northeast of Whiteville, are several hundred so-called Free-issues, people of mixed Indian, white, and Negro blood, whose ancestors were woodsmen when turpentine was profitably produced in this region.

At **94 m.** is the junction with NC 130 (*see* TOUR *18A*).

Between **94 m.** and the South Carolina Line, US 701 crosses TRUCE LAND, set apart in June 1781 as a refuge for non-combatants during the Revolutionary War by an agreement between Col. Gainey and Gen. Francis Marion. The area was under rigid military rule. Toward the end of the war the section became a refuge for robbers and renegades.

TABOR CITY, **110 m.** (56 alt., 2,033 pop.), has recently developed into a produce market for sweet potatoes, white potatoes, strawberries, tobacco, peppers, corn, and other products.

At **111 m.** the highway crosses the South Carolina Line, 28 miles north of Conway, S. C.

TOUR 18A (*NC 130*)

Junction with US 701—Old Dock—Crusoe Island; NC 130, county road. 18 m.

NC 130 branches southeast from its junction with US 701, **0 m.** (*see* TOUR 5) 2 miles south of Whiteville, and runs through lowland swamps and pocosins.

OLD DOCK, **15 m.** (35 pop.), a waning farm village, in ante-bellum days was an important shipping point for naval stores; its name refers to wharfs that once stood along the Waccamaw River.

Left from Old Dock on a marked road through Green Swamp to CRUSOE ISLAND, **18 m.**, a community isolated for several generations. Not properly an island, this point is an elevated knoll in country consisting of meandering streams of dark water and tangled swamps where large herds of deer survive and bears often overrun the section, preying upon livestock. Almost every home has a kennel of bear hounds.

The country around the Green Swamp and Lake Waccamaw was first granted to Patrick Henry. It is said that later owners, not interested in settling the land, divided it into 640-acre tracts and used it chiefly for stakes in gambling.

One of the many explanations of the origin of Crusoe Island's inhabitants is that they are descendants of a band of pirates who fled to the back country to avoid capture after an unsuccessful raid on the river settlements. Another is that their ancestors were a tribe of coastal Indians who were forced into the swamp by the early settlers. A third, and more widely accepted version, is that the island was settled by French refugees.

This story is that in 1804, during Napoleon's rule, a number of men were sentenced to death for treason. Some of the officers in charge, including a young French surgeon, Jean Formy-Duvall, conspired to help the prisoners escape and a pseudo death report was returned by Formy-Duvall. After one of the supposedly dead men had been captured, the young surgeon, with a number of others involved, left France for Haiti. Shortly after their arrival, the island was thrown into a panic by Jean Jacques Dessalines, the Negro who expelled the French and from 1804 to 1806 reigned as emperor. Formy-

Duvall, his family, and three other French families, to escape Dessaline's cruelty, fled the island, finally reaching Smithville, now Southport. Learning of the isolated section in the Green Swamp and fearing that they might be returned to France, they moved into the interior. Still another theory is that during the Civil War many nonslaveholding whites fled here to avoid being drafted for military service. For many years there was a definite line beyond which no Negro could pass.

Most of the inhabitants are sturdy, blond, and have florid complexions. Their speech, which contains no trace of Latin, bears a close resemblance to certain northern English dialects. Particularly noticeable is the manner in which they linger on the last letter or syllable. "Th'ust a daid stick inter t'land," they say, speaking of the fertility of their soil, "an' u'd grow-awe."

TOUR 19 *(Blue Ridge Parkway)*

(Fancy Gap, Va.)—Blowing Rock—Mount Mitchell—Asheville; Blue Ridge Parkway.
Virginia Line—Asheville, 169.6 m.

Section *a*. VIRGINIA LINE *to* BLOWING ROCK, 74.5 m.

The Blue Ridge Parkway, planned as a scenic drive for the leisurely motorist, runs along the crest of the Blue Ridge and will eventually connect the Shenandoah Park in Virginia with the Great Smoky Mountains National Park in North Carolina and Tennessee. Now largely completed, it has an excellent grade, easy curves, no dangerous intersections, no commercial traffic, and it by-passes all towns. Accommodations, fuel, and refreshments, not available directly on the Parkway, can be found in a number of towns on roads intersecting the Parkway. The Parkway is open the year around except at highest altitudes, which sections are closed from Nov. until April. Along the Parkway, at intervals, are recreation areas with picnic grounds, campgrounds, trailer sites, and hiking trails.

In spring, the Blue Ridge Mountains are brilliant with flowering dogwood and with redbud at the lower elevations. In June, displays of rhododendron and mountain laurel are magnificent in the Great Smoky Mountains. Autumnal coloring reaches its peak in October.

The route leads into the heart of the CAROLINA HIGHLANDS. These Highlands suggest a giant right hand, palm up, raised half a mile above the surrounding states. The thumb forms the Great Smokies along the Tennessee border. The curving Blue Ridge forms the southern rim along the Carolina piedmont and the foothills of north Georgia. The plateau tapers off like finger tips pointing west.

This Carolina plateau is the highest part of the Appalachian Range in eastern America and is now approached by modern highways which find entrance through low passes into this verdant, sheltered table-land. Viewed from north or south, the mountain rim rises like a mile-high blue wall.

These natural boundaries have made the Carolina Highlands a distinct economic and cultural area which is focused in the city of Asheville.

A pioneer flavor survives from the century of "do for yourself or do without," before the railroads broke through the mountain wall in the 1880's. Traditional music and dances, home crafts, and outdoor activity have been revived and are again a part of mountain life.

In contrast to the strong pioneer tradition is the recent influx of settlers from various parts of America and technicians from Holland, France, Germany, Poland, Austria, and Switzerland.

With striking contrasts in scenery, climate, and racial stock (ranging from Cherokee through pioneer stock to foreign background) the Carolina Highlands are a region set apart.

The Parkway crosses the North Carolina Line at Low Gap, **0 m.**, (2,525 alt.), 15 miles southwest of Fancy Gap, Va. The route runs at first through beautiful pastoral country characterized by mountain-top meadows and gently rounding hills.

At **0.4 m.** is the intersection with NC 18.

Left on this road **1 m.** to NC 89 which leads to MOUNT AIRY, **22 m.** (*see* TOUR *10*) (*tourist accommodations*).

Right on NC 18 to SPARTA, **16 m.** (*see* TOUR *11*) (*tourist accommodations*).

At **0.7 m.** (L) is CUMBERLAND KNOB (*picnic grounds, 2.5 miles of hiking trails, refreshment stand*), one of the major Parkway developments, which covers a 1,000-acre tract. Here galax grows profusely. The leaves are processed and used in floral decorations. There are loop trails to the KNOB (2,855 alt.) and into GULLY CREEK GORGE.

FOXHUNTER'S PARADISE (*parking area*), **1.7 m.**, is one of the magnificent overlooks on the route.

At **3 m.** there is a fine display of pink azalea, which blooms in early May. By the middle of May flame azalea is in bloom at this elevation.

At **12 m.**, the Parkway crosses US 21 (*see* TOUR *11*).

Left on US 21 to ROARING GAP, **4 m.** (*tourist accommodations*) (*see* TOUR *11*).

Right on US 21 to SPARTA, **6 m.** (*tourist accommodations*) (*see* TOUR *11*).

A PIONEER LOG CABIN, at **21.7 m.**, has been restored and is maintained by the Park Service.

At **22.2 m.** is DOUGHTON PARK, formerly called "The Bluffs," which is a major Parkway recreation area (*camping and trailer grounds, picnic areas, comfort stations, gasoline, meals, and lodge*), donated by the late Robert L. Doughton, U. S. Congressman (1911-54). Here high rolling bluegrass pastures terminate in precipitous bluffs, and stands of magnificent rhododendron bloom in May and June.

At the ICE ROCKS, **25.2 m.**, the Parkway, by a remarkable feat of engineering, has been cut into the side of a tremendous rock mountain.

BASIN COVE, 27.9 m., provides a passage through a serene mountain-top pasture, which rolls gently over the crest of the Blue Ridge. Old-fashioned split-rail or zig-zag fences are on each side of the drive. From here the route enters more rugged terrain, plunging deeper into a wilderness area.

At **31 m.** the Parkway crosses NC 18.

Left on NC 18 to NORTH WILKESBORO, **24 m.** (*tourist accommodations*) (*see* TOUR *17*). This route leads through MULBERRY GAP, at **5 m.**, which is a natural pass through the Blue Ridge. Between the pass and the foot of the mountain, **10 m.**, is a steep, twisting road whose numerous, well-banked curves present broad views.

Right on NC 18 is the DOUGHTON HOME (*private*), **1 m.**, a frame farmhouse shaded by hemlock trees, the birthplace of Robert L. Doughton (*see above*). On this farm is the house in which the Siamese twins were married (*see* TOUR *17*).

LAUREL SPRINGS, **2 m.** (2,822 alt., 75 pop.), a quiet farming village, was the scene of frequent robberies and murders by bushwhackers and deserters during the Civil War.

NC 18 continues to SPARTA, **12 m.** (*tourist accommodations*) (*see* TOUR *11*).

At **45.4 m.** the Parkway intersects NC 16.

Left on NC 16 to NORTH WILKESBORO, **20 m.** (*tourist accommodations*) (*see* TOUR *17*).

Right on NC 16 to JEFFERSON, **13 m.**, and WEST JEFFERSON, **15 m.** (*tourist accommodations*) (*see* TOUR *21*).

From an overlook and parking area at **50.1 m.** is a good view of Nigger Mountain, said to receive its name from the dark hue of its foliage (*see* TOUR *21*), and its neighbor, Phoenix Mountain.

At **55.1 m.** is the CASCADES PARKING OVERLOOK, from which a steep 8-minute foot-trail leads down to the cascades of Falls Creek which tumble several hundred feet.

At DEEP GAP, **59.6 m.**, the Parkway ends temporarily at the intersection of US 421, where there is a PARKWAY INFORMATION STATION.

Left on US 421 to NORTH WILKESBORO, **22 m.** (*tourist accommodations*) (*see* TOUR *17*).

For the next 5 miles, the route temporarily follows US 421 (R) where, at **64.6 m.**, it turns left and the Blue Ridge Parkway is resumed.

US 421 leads on to BOONE, **6 m.** (*tourist accommodations and the outdoor drama,* HORN IN THE WEST) (*see* TOUR *20*).

The Parkway continues to climb through the Blue Ridge, where, at **73.5 m.** it is crossed by US 221-321 (*see* TOURS *20 and 21*).

US 221-321 leads (R) to BOONE, **7 m.** (*see above and* TOUR *20*).

From here the Parkway temporarily follows US 221 for 16 miles, though a new section through Cone Park is now under construction.

BLOWING ROCK, 74.5 m. (3,586 alt., 661 pop.).

Season: May 1-Sept. 30.
Accommodations: hotels, motels, tourist courts.
Golf: Green Park-Norwood Golf Club, 18 holes.
Annual Events: golf tournaments, June-Aug.; horse show, Aug.

Blowing Rock, one of the oldest resorts in the southern Appalachians, is the only incorporated town on the Blue Ridge Parkway, which connects the Shenandoah and Great Smoky Mountains National Parks. The village was developed in the late 1880's when stages over rough mountain roads were the only means of access, since the altitude made a railway impracticable.

In St. Mary's of the Hills, on the main street of Blowing Rock, hangs a painting by Elliott Daingerfield, the *Madonna of the Hills.* Daingerfield spent his summers at Blowing Rock for years.

In Blowing Rock is the entrance to the Moses H. Cone Memorial Park, one of the chief Parkway recreation areas. This 3,600-acre estate was given to the State by the heirs of Moses H. Cone (1857-1908), Greensboro industrialist and "Blue Denim King" (*see* greensboro). A graded road and foot trail lead to the summit of Flat Top (4,537 alt.). Cone is buried on the mountain's slope. There are bridle paths and wooded walks, including trails, around two lakes. Here are fine stands of balsam, dense forests of pine, and a deer park.

The Cone Home is used as the Parkway Craft Center of the Southern Highlands Handicraft Guild, where visitors may purchase authentic Southern Highlands crafts.

1. Right from Blowing Rock on the marked Glen Burney Trail (*hiking*) to GLEN PARK, at the head of Johns River gorge. The trail gradually descends into the gorge and parallels New Years Creek to GLENBURNEY FALLS and on to GLEN MARY FALLS (*benches, picnic tables*). The falls can be reached by motor over the Johns River Rd.

2. South of Blowing Rock US 321 penetrates a portion of the Grandfather Division of Pisgah National Forest (*see* national forests). The highway keeps high on a spur ridge for several miles.

At **2 m.** is the junction with a marked improved road.

Right on this road to the BLOWING ROCK (*parking space, refreshment stands open in summer, gift shop*), **0.7 m.,** an immense cliff (4,090 alt.) overhanging the JOHNS RIVER GORGE with its valley 2,000 to 3,000 feet below. The Blowing Rock is so called because the rocky walls of the gorge form a flume through which the northwest wind at times sweeps with such force that it returns to the sender light objects cast over the void. This current of air flowing upward prompted the Ripley cartoon about "the only place in the world where snow falls upside down." Visible from the rock down the gorge to the southwest are Hawksbill Mountain and Table Rock. To the west are Grandfather and Grandmother Mountains.

Many honeymooning couples visit Blowing Rock, long the legendary haunt of lovers. It is told that two Indian braves, fighting for the chieftain's daughter, struggled all day up and down the narrow ridge. When the stronger warrior cast his opponent over the cliff the maiden realized the defeated brave was the one she loved and she implored the God of the Winds to save him. The Wind caught up the warrior and lifted him through the air to safety. Since that day the Wind has returned any object tossed over the gorge.

Another legend relates that the Madonna of the Hills, on the morning of the summer solstice, walks out of the hills here to greet the Dawn. If her coming is attended by blue skies, fields will yield abundant crops to bring gladness to the hill country; but if clouds mask the peaks and mists roll out of the hollows to cling about her feet, barren fields, sadness, and want are in store.

At **3.3 m.** is the junction with a graveled road.

Right on this road to ROCK KNOB OBSERVATION TOWER, **2 m.**, a lookout that affords wide views.

Section b. BLOWING ROCK to ASHEVILLE, 95.1 m.

From Blowing Rock, US 221, a temporary link in the Blue Ridge Parkway, follows the general course of old Indian traces and is called the Yonahlossee Trail (from "Yanu," Cherokee: *black bear*). The drive along the crest of the Blue Ridge is nowhere below 3,500 feet in altitude. In late June rhododendron blooms so profusely that the sky seems to glow with its deep pink.

At **1.8 m.** the route crosses a stone bridge, built for horseback riders to follow trails in the Cone estate.

At **2 m.** is the first view of Grandfather Mountain, whose celebrated profile resembles an old man lying in repose. The route, passing through Pisgah National Forest, penetrates a rugged terrain with few habitations. On the left may be seen Hawksbill peak, to the left, and Table Rock on the right, both on Jonas Ridge in Burke County.

At **11 m.** is the marked entrance (L) to the RHODODENDRON GARDENS (*blooming season: azalea, May; laurel, early June; rhododendron, late June*), a 500-acre natural tract of rhododendron, wild azalea, and mountain laurel.

At BEACON HEIGHTS, **15.8 m.**, the Blue Ridge Parkway resumes and US 221 swings (R) to LINVILLE, **3 m.** (*tourist accommodations*) (*see* TOUR *21*).

Right on US 221, **1 m.**, to the Grandfather Mountain toll road, at the highest point on the Yonahlossee Trail (4,355 alt.).

Right on this road (*graded; open May to Dec.; 50¢ for adults, 25¢ for children*) is a parking place, **2 m.**, affording extensive views. The road continues **0.5 m.** to the saddle near the top of GRANDFATHER MOUNTAIN (5,939 alt.). Here is the MILE-HIGH SUSPENSION BRIDGE. Each year, since 1930 (*4th Sun. in June*), there has been a "Singing on the Mountain," on a large meadow at the base of Grandfather, drawing thousands of visitors.

In 1794 the French botanist André Michaux climbed to the top and triumphantly sang the *Marseillaise,* believing this to be the highest point in North America. Grandfather's great stone face, then as today, "was carved in rock and plumed with ferns, and in the furrows of his face, worn by the lapse of time, clung and crept the most beautiful flowers and vines."

Crowning the peak is a scattered growth of red spruce (*Picea rubra*) and Fraser fir, locally called balsam.

The panorama from Grandfather includes to the northeast Flat Top of the Blue Ridge and on clear days Pilot Mountain. Southeast are the Brushies, with the peak of Hibriten outstanding, and the long low ridge of the South Mountains. To the south the Linville River is walled in by the Linville Mountains on one side and the sharply cleft Jonas Ridge on the other. Table Rock and Hawksbill are outstanding on Jonas Ridge. Farther south is the Old Shaky Range. About southwest are the remote Blacks, whose Mount Mitchell is the highest peak east of the Mississippi.

At **16.9 m.** the Parkway passes through GRANDMOTHER GAP.

A foot trail leads **1 m.** to GRANDMOTHER MOUNTAIN (4,686 alt.).

From FLAT ROCK PARKING AREA, **19 m.**, a 10-minute walk leads to FLAT ROCK, which overlooks the beautiful Linville Valley to the east.

At **22.9 m.** is the intersection with NC 181.

Right on NC 181 to MORGANTON, **27 m.** down Jonas Ridge (*tourist accommodations*) (*see* TOUR 13).

At **27.1 m.** is a picnic and parking area, just north of Linville River (*good trout fishing*).

At **28.2 m.** US 221 again crosses the Parkway and leads (L) to LINVILLE FALLS, one of the chief Parkway attractions (*see* TOUR 21).

CHESTOA VIEW, at **31.4 m.** (*parking area and overlook*) on the crest of Humpback Mountain, affords a view of the deep gorge below, with Table Rock and Hawksbill close up.

The Parkway makes a rapid descent from Humpback Mountain to BEAR DEN OVERLOOK, **33.7 m.** (*parking area*), from which may be seen vast apple orchards.

McKINNEY'S GAP, **38.2 m.** (2,762 alt.), is one of the most famous of the Blue Ridge passes, through which pioneers pushed into the region beyond.

At GILLESPIE GAP, **41.6 m.** (2,800 alt.), a rock pyramid (L) honors the patriots or "Over the Hill Boys" who passed Sept. 29, 1780, on their way to Kings Mountain (*see* TOUR 8). Also through here came the "Swamp Fox," Gen. Francis Marion, who, with 30 picked men, was sent to dislodge the Cherokee at Etchoe Pass. As Marion and his men entered the pass, they were ambushed, and 21 of his men were killed.

The STATE MINERAL MUSEUM, designed as a repository of the 300-odd minerals of the State, is now under construction here.

At Gillespie Gap the Parkway is intersected by NC 26, which leads (R) to SPRUCE PINE, 6 m. (*see* TOUR 22); NC 26A leads (L) to LITTLE SWITZERLAND, 3 m. (*see below*).

At **44.6 m.** is (L) LITTLE SWITZERLAND (3,500 alt., 163 pop.), a 1,200-acre tract running along both sides of the Blue Ridge crest, founded in 1910 as a summer colony by Heriot Clarkson, Associate Justice of the N. C. Supreme Court (1923-1942). At the northern entrance is the SITE OF THE BIG LINN, an old tree (it fell in 1953) under which the frontiersmen on the way to Kings Mountain are said to have held council.

Much of the property is still wooded. A rustic inn and cottages, as well as a number of private homes, comprise the colony. The simplicity of this resort attracts many writers, artists, and other visitors.

From a little knoll directly behind the inn, Mount Mitchell is visible on a clear day. It is said that when it is plainly outlined, the weather will continue fine.

1. Right from the entrance to Switzerland Inn on a plainly marked road to KILMICHAEL TOWER (*open only in summer; adm. 25¢*), a 50-foot lookout on a knob with an elevation of 4,000 feet. Wooden arrows point out and identify the encircling peaks.

2. Right from Little Switzerland on the Bearwallow Gap Rd. through feldspar mining country to the McKINNEY MINES (*open*), **4 m.**

3. Right from Little Switzerland on NC 26 to the junction with an unpaved road, **3 m.**; right on this road to WILD ACRES, **5 m.**, formerly a summer hotel consisting of two large buildings at the top of the mountain. This hotel and a few cottages are all that were completed of a 1926 real estate development begun by Thomas Dixon, noted Southern author. It is now a privately owned estate used for summer conferences, especially designed to foster Christian-Jewish understanding.

4. NC 26A descends abruptly to WOODLAWN, **12 m.**, at the junction with US 221 (*see* TOUR 21).

At **44.1 m.** the Parkway enters the first of a number of tunnels. Beyond on the R. are the peaks and ridges of the Black Range.

From Little Switzerland to Buck Creek Gap there are a number of large apple orchards directly on the Parkway. They burst into bloom near the end of May.

CRABTREE MEADOWS, **50.2 m.**, is a Parkway recreational area (*picnic area, fuel, refreshments, and comfort station*), consisting of 250 acres within the Pisgah National Forest and named for the beautiful flowering crabtree which grows in profusion here.

A 40-minute trail leads to CRABTREE FALLS.

An OVERLOOK, at **52.9 m.**, affords an excellent view of the majestic Blacks. From here the entire 11-mile range from north to south may be seen. Fifteen peaks, exceeding 6,000 feet in altitude, form the greatest up-thrust of land in eastern America. Clingmans Peak (*see* TOUR 22C) may be identified by the radio tower on top and to its right is Mount Mitchell (*see below*), identifiable by a memorial tower.

At BUCK CREEK GAP, **54.7 m.** (3,346 alt.) the Parkway crosses NC 80 over a stone over-pass.

Right on NC 80 to Micaville, **14 m.**, and BURNSVILLE, **19 m.** (*tourist accommodations*) (*see* TOUR 22).

Left on NC 80 to US 70, **12 m.**, and, over a twisting road which descends swiftly, to MARION, **16 m.** (*tourist accommodations*) (*see* TOUR 15, sec. c).

An OVERLOOK, at **62.4 m.**, offers the "official" Parkway view of Mount Mitchell.

From here the Parkway ascends the highest elevations that have been opened to date.

At **68 m.** the Parkway is intersected R. by NC 128.

Right on NC 128, a modern, easy highway, to MOUNT MITCHELL, **5 m.** (6,684 alt.), the highest mountain in eastern America.

The mountain was named for Dr. Elisha Mitchell, professor at the University of North Carolina, who in 1835 measured its altitude and found it to be higher than Mount Washington, N. H., then considered the highest peak in eastern America. In 1844 Mitchell and Clingman (*see* TOUR 22, sec. c and ASHEVILLE) made measurements in the Black, the Balsam, and the Great Smoky mountains. When Gen. Clingman published a statement that he had discovered a higher peak than Mount Mitchell, Dr. Mitchell attempted to verify his own measurements by running a series of levels from the terminus of the railroad near Morganton to the Half-Way House. From this point on June 27, 1857, he started to Big Tom Wilson's in Yancey County by the route he had followed in 1844, intending to meet his son Charles. After three days had elapsed and he failed to return, his son reported the professor's disappearance and men set out to search for him. Big Tom Wilson, who had been Dr. Mitchell's guide in 1844, discovered his trail and found the body in a pool at the foot of a waterfall, since called Mitchells Falls (*see* TOUR 22). The body was taken to Asheville and there interred in the Presbyterian Churchyard, but a year later it was removed and buried at the peak of Mount Mitchell.

Early estimates place the height of the peak at 6,711 feet. A subsequent report of the U. S. Geographic Board announced the altitude as 6,684 feet. Among the peaks of almost equal height and beauty visible from the tower on the summit are Celo (6,326 feet), the Black Brothers (6,645 feet), Potato Knob (6,457 feet), and Cattail Peak (6,583 feet), accessible by trails.

MOUNT MITCHELL STATE PARK (*camping, picnicking, hiking, refreshments, dining and recreational lodge*), at the summit, covers 1,224 acres and includes a reforestation project. The program provides for the addition of recreational facilities such as trails and cottages.

The Parkway continues at a high altitude, as evidenced by the scene below and the changing vegetation, which was described by Bill Sharpe of *The State* (*see* RALEIGH) as "weather cropped and Canada-looking." Through this section are some of the largest stands of Northern Red Spruce south of Canada. Along the entire Parkway there are over 300 varieties of plants, trees, and shrubs.

The Parkway continues through the Blacks, reaching an altitude of 5,676 feet at **69.2 m.** This marks the highest point on the Parkway constructed to date. At **70.5 m.** it swings into the Great Craggy Mountains.

At PINNACLE GAP, **75.3 m.** are CRAGGY GARDENS (*parking and picnic area*), a 675-acre area famous for its massed bloom of native purple rhododendron in mid-June. To the North is a view of Craggy Pinnacle (5,892 alt.) and behind it at the right is Craggy Dome (5,845 alt.).

At **88.1 m.** the Parkway is intersected by NC 694, which leads down into ASHEVILLE via Sunset Mountain, 7 miles away (*see* ASHEVILLE *and* TOURS *15, 16, 22, 23, and 24*).

The Parkway continues at present to OTEEN, **93.3 miles,** and US 70 (*see* TOUR *15*), which leads R. 4 miles to Asheville.

For the first extension of the Parkway west of Asheville, see tour 22.

TOUR 20 *(US 321)*

Blowing Rock—Hickory—Lincolnton—Gastonia—(York, S. C.); US 321. Blowing Rock—South Carolina Line, 91 m.

Section a. BLOWING ROCK *to* CONOVER; 47 m., US 321

This route between the mountains and the piedmont foothills presents striking contrasts in spring and fall. The mountains are just beginning to stir with life in April when the gardens a short distance to the south are a riot of bloom. Early frosts turn mountain foliage to russet and gold while the plains still bask in the haze of Indian summer.

US 321 leaves BLOWING ROCK (which is 1 mile south of the Blue Ridge Parkway) at **0 m.** (*see* TOUR *19*) and penetrates a portion of the Grandfather Division of Pisgah National Forest (*see* NATIONAL FORESTS). The new highway keeps high on a spur ridge for several miles before descending into the fertile Yadkin Valley.

At **14 m.** is the junction with NC 268.

Right on this road to PATTERSON, **1 m.** (1,307 alt., 195 pop.), on the Yadkin River, at the site of a large Saura Indian village reported by an explorer in 1671.

NC 268 continues up the Yadkin River through the extensive fertile valley, known as HAPPY VALLEY.

At **1 m.** (R) is CLOVER HILL (*private*), a handsome, square, Classic Revival brick mansion built about 1840 for Col. Edmund Jones, a large planter. Col. Jones' mother was the daughter of Gen. William Lenoir, who lived at nearby Fort Defiance.

Across from Clover Hill is HOLLY LODGE (*private*), built shortly after the Civil War for Gen. Collett Levensthorpe, C.S.A., physician and author.

At LEGERWOOD, **3 m.** (25 pop.), is the PATTERSON SCHOOL, a college preparatory school founded by the will of Samuel Legerwood Patterson (d. 1908) who bequeathed his beautiful old plantation home, "Palmyra," to the Episcopal Church to be used as an industrial school for boys. The old house burned in 1922. During the summer boys earn tuition by work on the school farm. The curriculum includes handicrafts. Weekly church services are held in the more than century-old CHAPEL OF REST, the community church.

At **5 m.** (R) is FORT DEFIANCE (*visitors welcome*) on a little knoll commanding a wide view of the valley. This big old farmhouse has heavy exposed timbers, most of them whipsawed, joined with hand-made nails. The house has been weatherboarded and has a modern tin roof. Window cornices, mirrors, and other furniture were shipped from Liverpool to Charleston, S. C., thence by wagon to Happy Valley. The house also contains relics of Indian and Revolutionary days. Since Gen. William Lenoir (1751-1839), Revolutionary officer and Kings Mountain leader, built the mansion in 1788-92, it has been continuously owned and occupied by his family. The boxwood-enclosed family graveyard, which contains the GRAVE OF GEN. LENOIR, occupies the site of the early Indian fort from which the estate takes its name. Rising behind Fort Defiance is INDIAN GRAVE MOUNTAIN, where a tribe once camped, leaving graves that yielded numerous artifacts when excavated about 1900.

At **18 m.** is the junction with NC 90.

Right on NC 90 along a low shelf overhanging a narrow valley which widens at COLLETTSVILLE, **7.8 m.** (1,098 alt., 150 pop.), at the confluence of Mulberry Creek and the Johns River.

Left from Collettsville **1 m.** on a dirt road to BROWN MOUNTAIN BEACH (*cottages, dance hall; swimming, fishing*), a summer resort developed in the valley of Wilson Creek on lands scooped out by the disastrous 1916 flood.

North of Collettsville NC 90 parallels Franklin Creek. At **11.3 m.** the hills begin to close in and the route skirts sharp cliffs.

At HOPEWELL GAP, **12.4 m.**, is the junction with a dirt road. Right **3 m.** on this road to SAND MOUNTAIN (2,200 alt.), with an observation tower on its summit.

At **20 m.** is the top of WILSON RIDGE, with Grassy Knob (L) and High Knob (R). From Wilson Ridge NC 90 follows Estes Mill Creek to Wilson Creek and up that stream, through a region of waterfalls, sharp divides, and deep gaps.

EDGEMONT, **27 m.** (100 pop.), in the heart of the Grandfather Division of the Pisgah National Forest, is the center of extensive reforestation activities conducted by the U.S. Forest Service and is on the southern boundary of the DANIEL BOONE GAME REFUGE (*see* NATIONAL FORESTS).

LENOIR, **20 m.** (1,182 alt., 7,888 pop.), is a furniture-manufacturing town, and its proximity to several mountain resorts attracts many visitors. On the outskirts are lumber mills and yards. The town, named for Gen. William Lenoir, is the seat of Caldwell County, named for Joseph Caldwell, first president of the University of North Carolina (*see* CHAPEL HILL). Here is the ranger station for the Grandfather Division of Pisgah National Forest.

The LENOIR HIGH SCHOOL BAND BUILDING and the JUNIOR HIGH SCHOOL BUILDING, W. Harper Ave., are for the exclusive use of this band. The buildings and band have been written up in college textbooks including those of Columbia University. The group has made broadcasts and phonograph records, has appeared in motion pictures, and has won many prizes.

FAIRFIELD (*private*) was built in 1825 for James Harper as a 4-room dwelling of flint-like brick with 18-inch walls. Greatly enlarged later, its grounds were formerly on an estate of several hundred acres before the town had developed. In the stately parlor hang the portraits of 5 generations of Harpers through whose hands Fairfield has passed.

1. Left from Lenoir on Norwood St., past the golf course, to the junction with a marked road, 2 m.; L. 5 m. on this road (*open except during fire season; apply State forestry office*) to HIBRITEN MOUNTAIN (2,265 alt.) (*picnic ground, fireplaces*). From the observation tower are sweeping views in all directions to distant mountain chains.

2. Left from Lenoir on NC 18 is KINGS CREEK, 12 m. (300 pop.); R. from Kings Creek 1.5 m. on a dirt road to the HOLLOW SPRINGS PRIMITIVE BAPTIST CHURCH, where old-time singing has been held annually (*Aug.*) since 1895.

GRANITE FALLS, 30 m. (1,213 alt., 2,286 pop.), has textile and hosiery mills and a lumber plant.

At 35.2 m. the highway crosses the Catawba River over a bridge between two lakes (*fishing, boating, swimming*), RHODHISS (R) and OXFORD (L). Property of the Duke Power Co., these two lakes, with Lookout Shoals Lake and Lake James (*see* TOUR 13), were formed by impounding the waters of the Catawba River.

HICKORY, 39 m. (1,163 alt., 14,755 pop.), has been called Hickory Tavern, Hickory Station, and the City of Hickory. Hickory wagons have been made here since 1880, when a small wagon-manufacturing plant was established. Among the town's industrial concerns are hosiery, cotton, and knitting mills, iron foundries, and furniture factories. The SHUFORD MILLS, whose headquarters are here, comprise one of the largest groups of cordage mills in the country.

The LOG HOUSE (*open*), a two-story structure of logs weatherboarded over, is Hickory's oldest building. It was erected in 1828 and was moved from outside the city limits to its present position in 1953. It is being restored by the Catawba County Historical Society, and the location will be known as the Weidner-Robinson Memorial Park.

LENOIR-RHYNE COLLEGE, a coeducational Lutheran institution (820 students), is located on a 37-acre campus in northeast Hickory. Shade trees line the landscaped driveways and the sloping lawn. Originally called Lenoir College when organized in 1891 on the site donated by Capt. Walter W. Lenoir, the name was changed in 1923 to honor also one of its greatest benefactors, textile-manufacturer Daniel E. Rhyne.

CAROLINA PARK (*open*) has an arboretum, developed by George F. Ivey, containing foreign and domestic trees, labeled with both common and scientific names. Here also is the AMERICAN LEGION SWIMMING POOL (*open*).

Between Hickory and Conover, 47 m., US 321 unites with US 64 (*see* TOUR 13) and US 70 (*see* TOUR 15B).

Section b. CONOVER *to* SOUTH CAROLINA LINE; 44 m. US 321

This section of US 321 runs through the hills of the western piedmont plateau past old houses, scenes of Revolutionary battles, and former Indian haunts.

At CONOVER, 0 m., is the junction with NC 16 (*see* TOUR *13*). Here US 321 branches R. from US 64 (*see* TOUR *13*) and US 70 (*see* TOUR *15B*).

NEWTON, 3 m. (997 alt., 6,039 pop.), seat of Catawba County, is a textile-manufacturing town whose business section lies around the court-house square. In the southeast corner of the square is a MEMORIAL TO THE HEROES OF THE JOHNS RIVER MASSACRE in Rutherford's forced march against the Cherokee in 1776.

After Adam Sherrill had crossed the Catawba and received the first land granted in the area (1748), the region was settled, mostly by Pennsylvania Dutch. Hoke Smith, Secretary of the Interior (1893-96), Governor of Georgia and U. S. Senator was born at Catawba College, which was founded here in 1852 and later moved to Salisbury (*see* SALISBURY). A Soldiers' Re-union for veterans of all wars is held annually (*Aug.*).

1.   Right from Newton on a marked road to ST. PAUL'S CHURCH (c. 1808), 2 m., part of whose timbers came from an earlier log church in which services were said to have been held in 1759. High galleries reached by steep steps run around three sides of the interior.

2.   Right from Newton on NC 10 to the JOHN W. ROBINSON FARM (*visitors welcome*), 5 m., part of a 10,000-acre tract granted the pioneer settler, Henric Weidner, before the Revolution. Beneath a great oak on the lawn Weidner conferred with the Indians; in 1752 the Catawba painted it red as a warning to the settlers that the Cherokee were on the warpath. Here Col. Charles McDowell in 1781 mustered volunteers for the march to Kings Mountain (*see* TOUR *8*). Weidner died in 1792 and is buried in the family graveyard. Among other Revolutionary relics in the Robinson house is Weidner's will, in which he disposed of his 10 slaves and, "in order that the children might be more cheerful," devised to them two stills.

At 13.5 m. on NC 10 is the junction with a dirt road at the Bob Leatherman farm; L. 1.3 m. on this road to WESLEY CHAPEL, where an annual singing convention is held (*Oct.*) under a rustic arbor. Most of the singing is without accompaniment, and hymnbooks printed with shaped notes are used.

3.   Left from Newton on NC 10 to the junction with a graded road, 4.1 m.; L. 1.2 m. on this road to the junction with another graded road; R. 1.3 m. on this road to the junction with a dirt road; L. 1.3 m. on the dirt road to BALLS CREEK CAMPGROUND, established in 1853. Camp meetings are held here annually (*last wk. Aug.*). As many as 20,000 persons have been present at one service.

MAIDEN, 10 m. (891 alt., 1,952 pop.), is a manufacturing town. At 10.5 m. is the old BOLICK PLACE, site of the campground of Gen. Daniel Morgan and Col. William Washington, who stopped here with a train of prisoners captured at Cowpens in Jan., 1781. A marker (R), 18.5 m., indicates the SITE OF THE BATTLE OF RAMSOURS MILL (400 yds. to the R.), a Revolutionary skirmish that paved the way for the Battle of Kings Mountain. At sunrise on June 20, 1780, Francis Locke with 400 patriots surprised and routed 1,300 Tories who had been gathered at the spot by emissaries of Cornwallis, preparatory to joining the British at Camden. The Tucka-seege Rd., which crosses the bridge over Clarks Creek north of the battle-ground, was once an Indian trail.

LINCOLNTON, 19 m. (860 alt., 3,781 pop.), seat of Lincoln County and the oldest town west of the Catawba River, is dependent on cotton manufacturing. The city and county were named for Gen. Benjamin Lincoln of the Revolutionary Army.

In the region are many old plantations owned by descendants of the pioneer Germans whose names have been Anglicized. At one family reunion grandchildren present included Peter Klein, John Kline, Jacob Cline, John Small, George Little, and William Short.

After the Revolution and before the churches voiced their disapproval (1858), distilling was an important occupation here. One ordained minister owned more than 1,000 acres and conducted "a sawmill, cotton gin, tanyard, blacksmith shop, and distillery."

The county seat was at Tryon Courthouse until Lincolnton was incorporated in 1785 as the county seat. Three years later the first log courthouse was replaced by one of planks, painted a bright red. Two other courthouses preceded the present LINCOLN COUNTY COURTHOUSE (1921), a stone and concrete structure with columns across the east and west façades. Ezekiel Polk, grandfather of Pres. James K. Polk (*see* TOUR *11*), was Lincoln's first clerk of court.

James Pinckney Henderson, born near Lincolnton in 1808 and licensed to practice law here in 1829, became the first Governor of Texas (1846-47). Stephen D. Ramseur, a Confederate major general at the age of 27, who was mortally wounded at Cedar Creek, Va., is buried here.

TARLETON'S TEA TABLE, on the square, is a large boulder from which the British officer is said to have taken his meals. The INVERNESS HOTEL (1840), NE. of the square, is a three-and-a-half-story red brick inn, with interior hand-carved woodwork and a spiral stairway running up 4 flights. The exterior has end chimneys and a one-story porch in the center of its 5-bay façade. The MICHAEL HOKE HOUSE (*now apartments*), W. Chestnut St., was built in 1833. It is a clapboard house with an H-shaped plan; its pillared portico has been removed. Maj. Gen. Robert F. Hoke (1837-1912) was born here. His capture of the Federals at Plymouth (*see* TOUR *13, sec. a*) resulted in a telegram from Jefferson Davis promoting him to a major-generalship.

CONFEDERATE MEMORIAL HALL (*open hours vary*), E. Pine and N. Academy Sts., a square brick Georgian structure erected in 1813, was once the Pleasant Retreat Academy, which advertised that in 1822 "boarding, including firewood, lodging, washing, and candles can be had at the usual price of $7.50 per month." The building is used as a hall by the United Daughters of the Confederacy and contains a small library and historical relics.

The CATAWBA SPRINGS HOTEL (*private*), built in the 1820's, was until 1856 a popular inn on the stagecoach road from New Orleans to Washington. Peter Stuart Ney (*see* TOUR *15B*) was once a clerk at this hostelry, whose fine food, mineral waters, and bathhouses were famous.

The C. R. JONAS HOUSE (*private*), W. Main St., also known as the Paul Kistler or the James House, built in 1826, has brick walls two feet thick with an unusual cornice of convex-concave design encircling the house. The interior woodwork is beautifully ornamented with medallions carved in the mantels.

Lincolnton is at the junction with NC 27 (*see* TOUR 20).

Right from Lincolnton on the Tuckaseege Rd. to MAGNOLIA GROVE (*private*), 6 m., a residence built (1824) by David Smith on the site of a pre-Revolutionary inn known as Dellinger's Tavern. The tavern was used as a courthouse after the division of Tryon County into Lincoln and Rutherford in 1779, its old springhouse serving as a jail. There is a ballroom on the second floor.

At 20.8 m. is the junction with a marked, improved road.

Left on this road to LITHIA SPRINGS, 1.5 m.; here is LINCOLN LITHIA INN (*open in summer; riding, tennis, swimming*), developed in 1887 by Benjamin N. Duke and Gen. Robert F. Hoke on the latter's estate. The inn is a rambling white frame structure surrounded by broad verandas.

HIGH SHOALS, 28 m. (724 alt., 860 pop.), is a textile town on the South Fork of the Catawba River. The power dam was built in 1893 when the first cotton mill was established. Recreation grounds (*swimming, picnicking*) extend along the river and lake shore. Between 1800 and 1850 rolling mills and iron works were in operation.

At 30 m. is LONG CREEK MEMORIAL BAPTIST CHURCH, a modern brick church building (1919) on the site of one of the oldest Baptist churches in the State. The earliest gravestone in the cemetery is that of Edward Boyd, who died in 1728. The first log structure on the site was used until a lady of the congregation canvassed the region on horseback soliciting funds for a new church which was to have "glass windows."

At 32 m., US 321 forms a junction with NC 275.

Right on NC 275 to Dallas, 1 m. (784 alt., 2,454 pop.), which was the seat of Gaston County (1846-1911). Its square, weathered OLD COURTHOUSE, topped with a cupola, has been converted into a town hall.

1. Left from Dallas on NC 275 to the old HOYLE PLACE (*private*), 3 m. a two-story log house built about 1775 by Peter Hoyle. He and his wife came down from Pennsylvania and Maryland in 1747.

2. Left (north) from Dallas on a marked road is PHILADELPHIA CHURCH, 3.5 m., on the Catawba River. This Lutheran congregation was organized prior to 1767 and first called Kostner's (Costner's) Chapel. Adam Costner, who came from Germany, is buried in the churchyard beneath a slab marked 1767.

GASTONIA, 36 m. (*see* TOUR 8) is at the junction with US 29-74 (*see* TOURS *8 and 16*).

South of Gastonia US 321 crosses Catawba Creek, 37 m., and runs through a prosperous residential section into another mill district. It crosses the South Carolina Line at 44 m., 13 miles north of York, S. C.

TOUR 20A *(NC 27)*

Lincolnton—Mount Holly—Charlotte; NC 27. 32 m.

NC 27 branches southeast from US 321 in LINCOLNTON, 0 m. *(see* TOUR 20*).*

At 2 m. is the junction with a dirt road.

Left on this road to the SITE OF THE SCHENCK-WARLICK MILL, 0.5 m., first water-power cotton mill in the State. The excavation for the overshot wheel of this mill is near Old Mill Creek. It was built in 1813 by Michael Schenck, a Pennsylvania Mennonite, who came to Lincoln County in 1790. The machinery, purchased in Philadelphia, was shipped by water to Charleston, S. C., and thence by wagon to Lincoln County.

At 4.6 m. is the junction with NC 273.

Left on NC 273 to Machpelah Church, 5 m.; R. 3 m. on a dirt road to MOUNT TIRZAH *(open)*. Built in 1800 for Alexander Brevard and known also as the Brevard House, this large rectangular frame residence, surrounded by a brick wall, has an elaborate overmantel in one of the rooms and a massive chandelier in the ballroom. An iron furnace on the grounds was called Mount Tirzah Forge and later Brevard Forge.

1. From Machpelah Church a dirt road leads L. 2.7 m. to another dirt road; L. on this dirt road 1 m. to VESUVIUS FURNACE, built in 1792 for Gen. Joseph Graham. It is a large white frame house, recently altered by a two-story porch, and has gabled ends and exposed brick chimneys. It sets back from the hillside overlooking the famous Graham iron furnaces on the creek.

On NC 273 at 8.2 m. is the junction with a dirt road.

1. Left on this road 1.5 m. to INGLESIDE *(private)*, the Forney estate, built in 1817 for Maj. Daniel M. Forney, who was commissioned in the War of 1812, served as senator from Lincoln County, and U. S. Congressman. Gen. Peter Forney (1756-1834) developed profitable iron mines and furnaces on the estate. Benjamin Henry Latrobe, who designed the National Capitol, is said to have drawn the plans. Massive columns mark the front elevation. Slaves on the plantation made the bricks used in the building. The finest inlaid wood was used in the paneled drawing room. A delicate circular staircase leads from the spacious hall. Ingleside is considered one of the finest examples of classical ante-bellum architecture in North Carolina.

On the plantation stand the crumbling remains of the Log House built before the Revolution by Maj. Forney's grandfather, Jacob Forney, who came to North Carolina in 1754. Here Cornwallis and his men camped for three days until the waters of the Catawba subsided to permit their crossing in pursuit of Greene's army. They took Forney's gold and silver, butchered his animals and fowls, and confiscated his grain and wines.

2. At **9.7 m.** on NC 73 is the Morrison Estate (*private*), also called Cottage Home and the Hall. The original house was burned and replaced by the present one. Dr. Robert Hall Morrison, the first owner, was the founder of Davidson College (*see* tour 11). Three of his 5 daughters married men who became generals in the Confederate Army (*see* charlotte), one of whom was Thomas Jonathan (Stonewall) Jackson. After Jackson's death, his horse, Old Fancy or Little Sorrel, was sent to the Morrison farm for the remainder of his days. The animal's preserved body is in the Confederate Museum at Richmond, Va.

STANLEY, **14 m.** (859 alt., 1,644 pop.), an industrial town since a cotton mill was established here in 1891, is one of the oldest communities in Gaston County. Upon completion of the old Carolina Central R.R. from Charlotte in 1862, the town, then called Brevard Station, became a concentration point for Confederate soldiers from neighboring counties.

A large Talon, Inc. Plant (1954) weaves and dyes zippers.

Left from Stanley on NC 275 to the Rhyne House (*private*), **2 m.** This 11-room brick home on Hoyles Creek has been continuously occupied since 1799 by descendants of Thomas Rhyne who emigrated from Germany during the Revolution. About 1850 fire destroyed most of the woodwork but the brick walls were undamaged and the structure was restored. A cupboard remains from the original furnishings. It is 10 feet high, of solid walnut with inlays of satinwood, put together with wooden pegs. The original owner's initials and the date, 1799, are worked into the brick chimney.

NC 275 leads to LUCIA, **6 m.**; ask here for directions to Oak Grove (*private*), **2 m.** NE., built in 1782 for Col. James Johnston, a Revolutionary officer and state senator and nephew of Gov. Gabriel Johnston. Said to be the oldest brick house west of the Catawba River, it has a pair of chimneys connected by an arch and ornamented with diamond brick patterns. The house and property are owned by the Duke Power Co.

MOUNT HOLLY, **20 m.** (621 alt., 2,251 pop.), is an industrial town on a tract described in an old Armstrong grant from George II, and transferred to George Rutledge in 1754, as a parcel of land "on the So. side of the Catawba River on Kuykendall, the Dutchman's Creek." Pennsylvania Dutch were destined to play an important part in the development of this and neighboring counties. Holly trees on the creek bank suggested the town's name.

Besides textile industries, Mount Holly has a hydroelectric plant of the Duke Power Co.

The Old Hutchinson Place, W. of the Mount Holly school buildings, is the Site of the Home of Robert Alexander, soldier of the Revolution, planter, and one of the first members of the general assembly (1781-87).

On the southern edge of town is the Costner Place, called the Model

Farm by Gen. D. H. Hill (1821-89) when he came here after the Civil War. At the end of one year he renamed it Hard Scrabble and returned to Charlotte.

Left from Mount Holly on NC 273 is MOUNTAIN ISLAND, 3 m. (65 pop.), where stands the old St. Joseph's Roman Catholic Church (1842), associated with the early efforts of the bishop who later became James Cardinal Gibbons of Baltimore. In the plain frame structure are the original worn pews and clear glass windows. The Stations of the Cross are represented by simple, crudely painted pictures.

During the pastorate of Father J. P. O'Connell, James Gibbons, then 32 years of age, was made bishop and vicar apostolic of North Carolina, the State's first Roman Catholic bishop and the youngest in America at that time. In 1869 Bishop Gibbons established the Sisters of Mercy in the State, bringing nuns from Charleston, S. C., to found schools and hospitals. Among monuments to his work are Belmont Abbey and Cathedral (*see* TOUR 8).

South of Mount Holly NC 27 crosses a bridge over the Catawba River. Mills border the highway at THRIFT, 25 m. (600 pop.).

At 27 m. is the Cannon Airport, a private flying school.

At 32 m. is CHARLOTTE (*see* CHARLOTTE) and the junction with US 21 (*see* TOUR *11*), US 29 (*see* TOUR *8*), and US 74 (*see* TOUR *16*).

TOUR 21 *(US 221)*

Twin Oaks — Blowing Rock — Marion — Rutherfordton — (Spartanburg, S. C.); US 221.
Twin Oaks—South Carolina Line, **156 m.**

This route crosses wide-flung ranges, giving access to peaks, gorges, waterfalls, and interesting natural phenomena, and penetrates the busy and closely settled area of the foothills bordering the piedmont plateau.

US 221 branches southwest from its junction with US 21 (*see* TOUR *11*) in TWIN OAKS, 0 m. (2,430 alt., 75 pop.), a crossroads. Sheep from this section furnish much of the cooperatively marketed wool used in the manufacture of the hand-loomed and machine-made homespun for which western North Carolina is widely known. There is no railroad in Alleghany County and no paved highway served the region until 1920. The population, entirely rural, is evenly distributed.

At 13 m. US 221 crosses the South Fork of New River, a potential source of hydroelectric power.

JEFFERSON, 24 m. (2,900 alt., 359 pop.), seat of Ashe County, was founded in 1800 and named for Thomas Jefferson. Rows of blackheart cherry trees and weathered old buildings line the main street. The town is almost surrounded by mountains. To the west, cutting off the afternoon sun, is Paddy (4,200 alt.), named for a man who was hanged at its base. Phoenix Mountain (4,700 alt.) is to the north and Nigger Mountain (5,000 alt.) to the south.

Ashe County, named for Samuel Ashe, Governor of North Carolina (1795-98), is a mountainous plateau with a mean elevation of more than 3,000 feet.

The mountain farm lands are fertile and cultivated to the summits. Renewed interest has started in the mining industry of the county, well known for its iron and copper deposits. Drilling was started in 1953 at Ore Knob copper mine at Laurel Springs, at the copper mine in the Idlewild section, and for magnetic iron at Hilton. Exploratory work is being done in many other sections where new minerals, including gadolnite are being reported.

546

Right from Jefferson on NC 16 is CRUMPLER, 9 m. (72 pop.), in mountainous bluegrass country. Here are ALL HEALING SPRINGS and BROMIDE ARSENIC SPRINGS, once popular with tourists and health seekers.

At 25 m. is the junction with a marked road.

Left on this road to NIGGER MOUNTAIN, 4 m. (5,000 alt.), whose isolated summit affords wide views. The mountain is said to derive its name from the deep hue of the foliage.

WEST JEFFERSON, 26 m. (3,200 alt., 871 pop.), is the market and railroad (Norfolk and Western R.R.) town for this section. Located here is the largest KRAFT FOOD PLANT in the South, which annually makes more than a million pounds of cheese from 17 million pounds of milk supplied by 1900 farmers in the county. There are also livestock, bean and vegetable, and burley tobacco markets. Industries include a hosiery mill, furniture factories, and a hardwood flooring plant. Dry electrolytic components are manufactured 6 miles to the south.

The PRESBYTERIAN CHURCH, a modern structure built of biotitic granite quarried on nearby Buffalo Creek, gleams darkly with mica in the rock.

US 221 continues southward from West Jefferson through beautiful rolling country. On the right is MULATTO MOUNTAIN.

At 30 m., US 221 forms a junction with NC 194 (old US 221), which is an alternate route to Boone (19 m. by the older, winding route, in contrast to 21 m. by the new route).

US 221 skirts BALDWIN, 30 m., and continues (L) to DEEP GAP, 39 m., where it unites with the Blue Ridge Parkway (*see* TOUR *19*) and US 421 (*see* TOUR *17*).

At 44 m. the Parkway turns left (*see* TOUR *19*) and at 50 m. on US 221-421 is Boone.

BOONE (3,333 alt., 2,973 pop.) the seat of Watauga County, is located in a plateau-valley surrounded on three sides by higher mountains. Howard's Knob (4,451 alt.) to the north and Rich Mountain (5,000 alt.) to the west tower above the town which lies in the heart of the highest general elevation of the lofty Appalachian Mountains. Boone and its area are appropriately called "Roof of Eastern America." Within 5 miles 4 great river systems, Ohio (New), Tennessee (Watauga), Pee Dee (Yadkin), and Santee (Johns-Catawba) flowing north, west, east, and south have head springs. The water in the Boone valley drains into the Ohio.

Bishop August Gottlieb Spangenberg was the first known white man to visit (1752) here. Describing in his diary the view from Flat Top Mountain, he recorded he saw "hundreds of mountain peaks all around," which presented "a spectacle like ocean waves in a storm." In Watauga County alone there are 8 mountains higher than 5,000 feet (Grandfather being the highest, 5,964) and 19 others above 4,000.

The town was named (1850) for Daniel Boone. From 1760 to 1769 while making frequent hunting and exploration trips to the valleys of the New, Watauga, and Holston rivers, he used a house called DANIEL BOONE CABIN, whose site is marked by an 18-foot-high stone monument, erected in 1912, at the corner of Faculty and Newland streets. Boone is located on the famous Daniel Boone Trail and at the earliest fork of the Wilderness Road which ran from Holman's Ford on the Yadkin River in Wilkes County into Tennessee and Kentucky.

Part of this area belonged to the settlers of the Watauga who organized the Watauga Association, established the "State of Franklin," and founded Tennessee. Its pioneers fought against Col. Patrick Ferguson in the Battle of Kings Mountain.

Boone has a burley tobacco market, a branch factory of the International Resistance Corporation, and is the home of the "Watauga Sauerkraut." The Appalachian Evergreen Co. ships millions of galax leaves and other evergreens to all parts of the United States. Wilcox Drug Co., dealing in roots, herbs, bark, etc., is one of the largest of its kind in eastern America.

The area is filled with beautiful clear water streams which are stocked with trout and bass. The abundant rainfall helps grow forests which protect the wild game. The fertile valleys, picturesque hillsides, and high mountains attract many visitors.

APPALACHIAN STATE TEACHERS COLLEGE (*coed*) was established in 1899 as a private academy by two brothers, D. D. and B. B. Dougherty, and chartered as a State institution in 1903. The college now has a Junior College, Senior College, and Graduate School for teachers. The campus includes about 235 acres; however, most of the 43 buildings are located on 35 acres in the town of Boone. The property is conservatively valued at more than $10,000,000. Its yearly state appropriation for operation is more than $500,-000, an amount equivalent to the return on an endowment of $10,000,000.

The college operates under two separate state charters, one for the regular term of 9 months and one for the summer quarter of two terms. The enrollment for the regular term is about 1,400 and for the summer session, 1,784. Only two degrees are awarded, B.S. and M.A., both in teaching.

Three new buildings on the campus especially attract visitors: FINE ARTS which houses the department of public school music, ELEMENTARY DEMONSTRATION AND HEALTH which has a large gymnasium-auditorium which will seat 3,500 people and a modern SWIMMING POOL.

Kermit Hunter's *Horn in the West* (*last of June to Labor Day*), one of America's great outdoor dramas, has played in Boone since 1952. Its theme is the contribution made by the people of the piedmont and the mountain sections to the struggle for American Independence and the "American Way of Life." Daniel Boone, John Sevier, James Robertson, Gov. Tryon, Col. Tarleton, Indians, and pioneers live again in peace and war on the three stages of the DANIEL BOONE THEATRE.

Horn in the West is staged by the Carolina Playmakers of the University of North Carolina and is sponsored and produced by the Southern Appalachian Historical Association, Inc.

LOCAL TOUR FROM BOONE

US 421 and NC 194 leave Boone in a northwesterly direction and continue through RICH MOUNTAIN GAP, 4 m. (3,642 alt.), affording a
wide view of rolling grazing land.

An OLD GRIST MILL (R) with wheel intact, 5.5 m., has stood idle since
about 1920.

VILAS, 6 m. (2,850 alt., 40 pop.) is a settlement with a small cheese
factory.

At Vilas, US 421 continues (R) to SUGAR GROVE, 2 m., (2,725 alt., 350
pop.), named for the sugar maples growing here in the center of a cheese-making
section. The Sugar Grove post office was established in March, 1837, when John
Mast, first postmaster, reported revenues totaling $14 a year.

US 421, following roughly the sinuosities of Cove Creek (R), passes through
the village of AMANTHA, where the FILLMORE BINGHAM HOUSE (*private*),
built about 1860, is filled with antiques of the period. Towering above the
village is the spectacular TATER HILL MOUNTAIN.

ZIONVILLE, 9 m. (3,159 alt., 300 pop.), a mountain village, contains a Daniel
Boone Marker.

US 421 crosses the Tennessee Line at 10 m., 11 miles south of Mountain
City, Tenn.

A loop-tour may be made from here, through the rolling farm and cattle land
of Ashe County, by following NC 88 through Asheland and Creston to WAR-
RENSVILLE, 22 m. (120 pop.), where NC 194 (R) leads to JEFFERSON
(*see above*) and back down to BOONE, 70 m., from point of departure at Boone.

From Vilas, NC 194 swings right to VALLE CRUCIS, 10 m. (2,720 alt.,
150 pop.), which overlooks the Watauga River Valley where far below two
creeks form a clearly defined cross. On a slope (L) is the VALLE CRUCIS
SCHOOL for girls, outgrowth of a mission founded by the Episcopal Church
in 1842 and reorganized in 1895. The main buildings are of cement blocks,
dominated by the little CHURCH OF THE HOLY CROSS, fashioned of local gray
stone. When the mission was founded, using the Indian expression, there
was but "one smoke" in the valley. During the summer the plant is operated
as a resort hotel. The school owns about 500 acres of land and operates its
own farm, apple orchard, dairy, and hydroelectric plant. The BISHOPS HOUSE
(*vacant*) is a log house erected in 1849 for Bishop Levi S. Ives. In the MAST
CABIN (*open*), a typical pioneer log cabin erected in 1812, are three old
family looms and other antiques of the area. The present plantation house,
built about 75 years ago, is on the site of an earlier one, built in 1812.

West of Banner Elk cattle and sheep roam hillside meadows and mountainsides thick with rhododendron. This shrub serves as a thermometer on
cold days. When the temperature drops, so do the long glistening leaves,
and as the mercury falls lower, the edges begin to curl under until at zero
the entire leaf is rolled.

At **14 m.** the route begins to wind up Bowers Mountain in a series of sharp, corkscrew turns.

BANNER ELK, **18 m.** (3,700 alt., 462 pop.), is a small summer resort in the Elk River Valley surrounded by peaks 5,000 to 6,000 feet high. Banner Elk was the home of Shepherd M. Dugger (1854-1938), author of the *Balsam Groves of Grandfather Mountain* (*see* LITERATURE).

LEES-McRAE COLLEGE, a coeducational junior college accredited by the Southern Association of Colleges and Secondary Schools, has an attractive group of local-stone buildings. The college grew out of a school established in 1900 by the Rev. Edgar Tufts, a Presbyterian minister, to further education in his mission field. It is operated by the Edgar Tufts Memorial Association, under the control of the Presbyterian Church of the U. S. In summer the college buildings are operated as a resort hotel, PINNACLE INN. Its 300 students work out part of their tuition fees in the college industries, which include woodworking, ironwork, weaving, and "gallacking" (the gathering of ever-green leaves, roots, and bark). In summer they work at various tasks in connection with the operation of the inn.

Other projects of the association include GRACE HOSPITAL, founded in 1907, conspicuous among the group of buildings and serving the surrounding countryside as well as the college; and GRANDFATHER ORPHANAGE, which has it own little group of cottages and cares for some 85 mountain children. Also on the college grounds is WILDCAT LAKE (*swimming, boating, fishing*). Skiing is a winter sport.

At **23 m.** is HEATON (500 pop.), where the route crosses the ELK RIVER (*brown, brook speckled, and rainbow trout fishing*).

At **25.2 m.** is the junction with US 19E (*see* TOUR 22).

NC 194 swings left here and continues to Newland.

NEWLAND, **32 m.** (3,589 alt., 425 pop.), seat of Avery County, is the highest county seat in North Carolina. At the headwaters of the North Toe River, it was first called Old Fields of Toe, when it was a muster ground for forces to fight the Indians. Some of the Kings Mountain Boys assembled here to start their march (*see* TOUR 8).

Avery County, the 100th and last county created in North Carolina (1911), was named for Col. Waightstill Avery (1741-1821), Revolutionary patriot, and first Attorney General of North Carolina, who, when challenged to a duel by young Andrew Jackson, allowed Jackson to fire and then marched up to lecture him on his hotheadedness. Avery is one of the most mountainous of all North Carolina counties. Principal products are mica and feldspar, shrubbery, garden truck, and lumber.

From Newland the route may be reversed or continued to CROSSNORE, **36 m.**, where it forms a junction with US 221 (*see* MAIN TOUR), which can be followed in reverse back to Boone, thus completing this circuit tour.

South of Boone US 221 makes a winding climb through low mountains where rhododendron flourishes along the banks of streams.

BLOWING ROCK, 59 m. (*see* TOUR *19*) is at the junction with the Blue Ridge Parkway (*see* TOUR *19*) and US 321 (*see* TOUR *20*).

From Blowing Rock US 221 serves as a temporary link with the Blue Ridge Parkway for a 15.8-mile stretch (*see* TOUR *19*).

At BEACON HEIGHTS, 74.8 m., US 221 swings left and the Parkway resumes its course.

LINVILLE, 77.8 m. (3,623 alt., 350 pop.).

Season: June 1.-Sept. 30.
Accommodations: 3 resort hotels; furnished cottages, children's summer camps.
Golf: Linville Golf Club, 18 holes.
Annual Events: Men's Handicap Golf Tournaments, July 4 and Labor Day; Ladies' and Men's Invitation Golf Tournaments, Aug.

Linville is a cottage-colony summer resort in a 16,000-acre natural park. Rustic houses, shrub-banked, line shady roads that lead from a broad, tamarack-shaded green. In addition to the activities at the golf club and the lake, Linville River affords trout fishing.

Right from Linville on NC 181 is MONTEZUMA, 2 m. (3,797 alt., 200 pop.), where there are extensive nurseries of wholesale florists, who have beautiful displays, June to Sept.

At 77.5 m. are the LINVILLE GOLF COURSE and LAKE KAWANA (*swimming, boating*). South of the lake are extensive nurseries where, in season, packers under open sheds wrap evergreens and flowering plants for shipment. For almost a mile the road passes through a pine-bough tunnel.

At 79 m. is the TROUT-REARING STATION of the North Carolina Wildlife Service.

The route crosses the Linville River at PINEOLA, 79.5 m. (3,538 alt., 250 pop.), on the edge of the Grandfather Division of the Pisgah National Forest (*see* NATIONAL FORESTS). The Forest Service has planted spruce here on an extensive cut-over area.

The State maintains the DANIEL BOONE GAME REFUGE of 44,000 acres in the forest between Pineola and Edgemont. Deer, elk, and other game have been placed in the area, and the streams have been stocked with trout.

At CROSSNORE, 85 m. (3,546 alt., 240 pop.), is CROSSNORE SCHOOL (R), housed in 14 buildings, some of local river rock, on a 250-acre mountain tract. The school, with an enrollment of about 900, was founded in 1911 by Dr. Mary Martin Sloop. It affords educational opportunities, with emphasis on arts and crafts, to hundreds of mountain boys, girls, and adults. She and LeGette Blythe won the Mayflower Award (1953) for their volume, *Miracle in the Hills,* dealing with her life and experiences here. Dr. Eustace Sloop, husband of the founder, heads the GARRETT MEMORIAL HOSPITAL, a stone building in the school group.

US 221 is at the junction with NC 194, the Three-Mile Creek Rd.

Right on NC 194 to the junction with a dirt road, **1.5 m.**; L. **0.5 m.** on this road to the SITE OF UNCLE JAKE CARPENTER'S CABIN, marked only by a barn. From 1845 until his death in 1920 Uncle Jake recorded local deaths. His notebook includes:

"Al Wiseman age 76 Aug 9 dide 1899. He made brandy by 10000. Franky Davis age 87 dide Sept 10 1842. She fite wolves all nite at sugar camp to sav her caff threw chunks of fire the camp ware half-mil from hom she had nerve to fite wolf all nite. Margit Carpenter age 87 dide jun 5 1875 ware good womin to pore when she ware amind to be. She did not have no bed to slep on she slep on her skin to mak lik hard times. No womin has to li on her skin when she war marrid. Joe Sing age 70 dide nov 15 1890. He robed by nite made rales by day. Wm. Davis age 100.8 dide Oct 5 1841 ware old soldier in rev war an got his thi broke in las fite at Kings Montin. He ware a farmer and mad brandy and never had no dronkerds in famely. Davis Frank age 72 dide july 29 1842 ware a fin man but mad sum brandy that warnt no good. Homer Hines age 28 dide july shot hisself cos of womin and whusky. Dogs run after him. Charles McKinney age 79 dide may 10 1852 ware a farmer lived in blew ridge had 4 womin cors marrid 1 live in McKinney gap all went to fields to mak grane all went to crib for corn all went to smok hous for mete he killed 75 to 80 hogs a year and womin never had no words bout his havin so many womin. Thare ware 42 childen belong to him they all went to prechin together nothing said he made brandy all his lif never had no foes got along fin with everbody like him. Wm. Carpenter age 76 dide nov 15 1881 war fin honter kilt bar and wolves by 100 dere by 100."

At **87.2 m.** US 221 passes under the Blue Ridge Parkway.

LINVILLE FALLS, **91 m.** (3,325 alt., 130 pop.), takes its name from the spectacular falls and steep, wooded gorge of the Linville River.

Left from the village on NC 105 (Kistler Memorial Highway) is a rough stone MONUMENT TO ANDREW KISTLER of Morganton (1871-1931), **1.5 m.**, an advocate of good roads for the mountain section. Left from this marker is a parking space where Pisgah National Forest markers indicate vantage points from which to see LINVILLE FALLS and GORGE. Since its donation by John D. Rockefeller, Jr., to the National Park Service, the falls area is being developed in conjunction with the Blue Ridge Parkway.

1. A trail leads to the first cascade, UPPER FALLS, where the water rushes over a smooth 12-foot shelf of rock.

2. Another trial leads to the LOWER FALLS, where the river drops 90 feet over great boulders.

The short but boldly broken range of Jonas Ridge with its sheer precipices forms the eastern wall of the canyon. The cliffs of the Linville Mountains rim it on the west. Hawksbill (4,030 alt.) and Table Rock (3,909 alt.) are the most clearly defined peaks on Jonas Ridge, others being Chimney and Gingercake Mountains.

The rugged sides of Linville Gorge are carved out of solid rock and crowned with a forest of evergreens. Trees great and small grow out of the walls of the ravine; some lean far over the river from the crannies that give them precarious rootholds. Rhododendron grows thick among the hemlocks on the slopes. Linville Gorge is a "wild area" reservation in Pisgah National Forest.

Near Linville Falls are vantage points from which are visible the mysterious Brown Mountain Lights (see TOUR 13).

Between Linville Falls and Marion, US 221 drops downgrade. At **95.5 m.** (R), 300 yards from the highway, is LINVILLE CAVERNS (*adm., $1.00 for adults, less for children; electrically lighted*), a cavern with several side chambers, extending about a mile back into the mountain. Within are stalactites and stalagmites possessing refractory powers, a stream, and pools of clear water.

WOODLAWN **105 m.** (12 pop.), is the site of the AMERICAN THREAD Co. PLANT, built in 1953, **0.3 m.** E. of US 221.

At **110.4** is the junction with a side road.

Left on this road to the junction with a graveled road, **1.2 m.**; L. **0.5 m.** on this road to the PETE MURPHY FISH HATCHERY (*open*), with a seasonal capacity of 600,000 rainbow trout, bass, and bream.

At **112 m.** is the junction with US 70 (see TOUR 15).

MARION, **114 m.** (see TOUR 15).

From Marion US 221 continues almost due south to RUTHERFORD-TON, **141 m.** (see TOURS 13 and 16), the junction with US 64 (see TOUR 13), and US 74 (see TOUR 16).

From Rutherfordton US 221A branches (L) and unites with US 74 to Forest City, **6 m.** (see TOUR 16), where it branches (R).

At ALEXANDER MILLS, **7.5 m.** (885 pop.), sheeting, pillow tubing, and window shade cloth are produced.

US 221A passes through three continuous mill towns incorporated together as CAROLEEN-AVONDALE-HENRIETTA (3,494 pop.). The mills at Caroleen, **13 m.**, manufacture unbleached domestic. Avondale, **14 m.**, is one of the Haynes mill towns of the Cone Mills group. The mill (*open on application to supt.*) is a large brick building (L) in which chambrays and draperies are made. The mills at Henrietta, **15.5 m.**, produce print cloth and sheeting. This area, settled before the Revolution by English emigrants, was once known as High Shoals.

CLIFFSIDE, **19 m.** (1,388 pop.), is on the bank of the wide, muddy Second Broad River. The highway winds down a hill through the main part of town and passes (R) the dam and many-windowed buildings of the main HAYNES MILL (*open*), where terry cloth is made into beach wear.

At **19.5 m.** US 221A crosses Broad River and at **23 m.** crosses the South Carolina Line, 5 miles northeast of Chesnee, S. C., where it reunites with US 221.

From Rutherfordton US 221 continues south to the South Carolina Line, **156 m.**, 18 miles northeast of Spartanburg, S. C.

TOUR 22 *(US 19E-19-19A)*

(Elizabethton, Tenn.)—Elk Park—Spruce Pine—Burnsville—Asheville—Cherokee—Bryson City—Murphy—(Blairsville, Ga.); US 19E, 19, 19A, 19. Tennessee Line—Georgia Line, **198.6 m.**

Section a. TENNESSEE LINE *to* ASHEVILLE; **79.6 m.** US 19E *and* 19

This route, giving access to mountain vacation areas, crosses and recrosses the Toe River in a section of the southern Appalachians characterized by extensive forests and rushing streams. For the last 12 miles it follows the general route of the old Catawba Trail used by the Indians in the Carolinas and the tribes of the Ohio Valley.

US 19E crosses the Tennessee Line, **0. m.,** 25 miles south of Elizabethton, Tenn.

ELK PARK, **1.8 m.** (3,182 alt., 545 pop.), is a mountain town among lofty peaks. In the midst of stores and dwellings crowded about the railroad station is an old gristmill turned by a water wheel.

In this section, as elsewhere in western North Carolina, autumn brings a harvest of apples, some of which are made into apple butter. The fruit is cooked out of doors in big iron kettles. Some believe that only brown sugar and cider can give the proper flavor, though others use molasses "sweetening."

At **2.4 m.** is the junction with NC 194 (*see* TOUR *21*).

At CRANBERRY **3.3 m.** (3,202 alt., 268 pop.), is an old iron mine said to have been worked by Cherokee Indians and known to have supplied iron to the Confederacy.

South of Cranberry US 19E follows the general course of the North Toe River (Ind. Estatoe) as it grows from a small stream to a mountain river.

At MINNEAPOLIS, **6.5 m.** (3,400 alt., 700 pop.), are the largest deposits of amphibole asbestos in the State. It is shipped to plants manufacturing fireproof roofing, curtains, clothing, and insulation for furnaces and steam piping.

At **11 m.** the route crosses Roaring Creek near the point where it flows into Toe River. This tributary is associated with the men from Virginia, what is now Tennessee, and North Carolina who passed this way going to Kings Mountain. The frontiersmen, fresh from a campaign against the Indian Confederation of the Ohio, during which they had learned and adopted Indian tactics, were aroused by Col. Patrick Ferguson's threat to incite the Cherokees to destroy the mountain settlements.

Mounted woodsmen numbering about a thousand under Cols. William Campbell, Isaac Shelby, and John Sevier (*see* TOURS *8 and 21*) broke camp at Sycamore Shoals on the morning of Sept. 26, 1780, and rode into the mountains. The cavalcade ate dinner on the Grassy Bald of the Roan the next day. There two men deserted to warn Ferguson at Gilbert Town.

On reaching Gillespie Gap, near the present Little Switzerland (*see* TOUR *20*), the company divided, fearing ambuscade, because by this time the deserters could have reached Ferguson. Col. Campbell's force followed the crest of the Blue Ridge, dropped off the south side, and camped in Turkey Cove. The other detachment camped up North Cove by Honeycutt Branch. From that point they crossed the south end of Linville Mountain and took the Yellow Mountain Road down Paddie Creek to the Catawba River. The men in the Turkey Cove camp rode into the lowlands across the present site of Lake James. When the victorious woodsmen straggled back again, Ferguson was dead and his entire force slain or captured (*see* TOUR *8*).

A mica mine is operated at PLUMTREE, **14.5 m.** (2,839 alt., 300 pop.).

At INGALLS, **19 m.**, US 19E forms a junction with NC 194, leading to the Blue Ridge Parkway. Here is the HARRIS CLAY CO. PLANT, which mines kaolin and feldspar for the ceramic industry.

The valley, rimmed by Humpback and Yellow Mountains, widens into agricultural land at about **20 m.** SUNNYBROOK FARM (*tourist cabins*), **22 m.**, was homesteaded in 1778 by Samuel Bright, first white settler in the Toe River Valley. When he moved farther west his land was taken up by William Wiseman who had left London as a stowaway when a boy. In 1794, when he was gathering rare plants for the palace grounds at Versailles, the French botanist André Michaux visited Wiseman and taught the settlers how to prepare the plentiful wild ginseng for the Chinese market. A descendant of William Wiseman owns part of the original farm.

SPRUCE PINE, **26 m.** (2,517 alt., 2,280 pop.), is noted for the mining and marketing of feldspar and kaolin, almost limitless in the region. Truck loads of white rock on the roads are on the way to grinding plants where the feldspar is pulverized, then shipped to be used as a constituent of glass, in the glaze on chinaware, bathroom fixtures or other ceramics, or as an ingredient in scouring powders.

The Spruce Pine mining district is one of the few areas in the United States that ship refined primary kaolin, or china clay. In 1937 the TVA had developed methods of processing the North Carolina kaolins to the point where the finished product rivals any English kaolins and is equal to the world's best. Mica sparkles in the soil of the entire region.

Scrap mica, a byproduct of sheet and punch mica, is pulverized by a wet-grinding process and used in wallpaper, rubber, paint, decorative plaster, and axle grease. A boy's emergency use of mica in a bicycle tire in 1911 resulted in its adoption on a large scale by the manufacturers of automobile tires.

The village of Spruce Pine sprang up when the Carolina, Clinchfield & Ohio R. R. (now the Clinchfield), completed about 1908, built a station on the Toe River. When large operators were stripping the mountains of white oak, chestnut, and poplar, the town became a shipping center. Some of the timber, unsuited for lumber, has since been utilized for chemical purposes. "Wood money," small brass coins given by local buyers in payment for wood, was used for awhile and passed for full value. Ferns, mountain laurel, hemlock boughs, and millions of galax leaves are shipped from here every year. The galax is an evergreen herb with glossy round or heart-shaped leaves that turn to maroon, copper, or purplish shades in autumn. Displays of locally cut ferns can be seen (*consult Chamber of Commerce*).

The annual Mayland Fair (*Sept.*) exhibits products of Mitchell, Avery, and Yancey counties.

In Spruce Pine is the marked CAMP SITE OF THE FRONTIERSMEN (Sept. 28, 1780), where they stopped the third night of their march from Sycamore Shoals to Kings Mountain. Here is the GRAVE OF COL. ROBERT SEVIER, John Sevier's brother, who died nearby of wounds received at Kings Mountain.

Spruce Pine is at the junction with NC 26.

LOCAL TOUR FROM SPRUCE PINE

Spruce Pine—Penland—Bakersville—Roan Mountain; NC 26, 29 m.

NC 26 west from Spruce Pine follows generally an ancient trail carved out before 1800, later called the Morganton to Jonesboro road. Many North Carolinians who migrated to Tennessee, Kentucky, and the middle west before 1850 traveled this route. Thousands of turkeys, hogs, cattle, and other livestock were driven over this road to the markets of the Southeast from Kentucky and Tennessee during the pre-Civil War period. During the Civil War, it was a link in the "underground railroad" for slaves and sympathizers with the Union cause. Recent efforts have been directed toward converting it to a "Crimson Laurel Way," lined with red rhododendron to the summit of Roan Mountain. The entire route passes from smooth to extremely rugged farm country and offers outstanding views.

At 2 m. (L) are the deep pits for feldspar diggings by the MINPRO GRINDING PLANT, which was destroyed by fire in 1950.

At 3.3 m. is the junction with a paved road.

Left on this road is PENLAND, 2 m. (2,462 alt., 200 pop.). Here, on Conley Ridge, is the PENLAND SCHOOL OF HANDICRAFTS. During the summer and fall months, hundreds of students from all parts of the country and from many foreign countries take courses here in a wide variety of handicrafts under nationally known instructors. The EDWARD F. WORST CRAFT HOUSE, one of the largest log structures in the State, was named for Dr. Edward F. Worst of Chicago, a leading authority on handweaving and a member of the faculty and consultant for many years.

Adjoining the Penland School of Handicrafts and situated upon a 225-acre tract of land is the APPALACHIAN SCHOOL founded in 1912 under the auspices of the Episcopal Church. The school is a boarding school for children under 12 years of age.

BAKERSVILLE, 12 m. (2,550 alt., 428 pop.), is the seat of Mitchell County which was formed in 1861 and named for Dr. Elisha Mitchell, a scientist and professor at the University of North Carolina. Bakersville was named for the Baker family, original settlers on the site of the town. Attempts were made to establish the county seat first at Childsville, later called Calhoun, and again at Norman's Hill, now called Ledger. The court sat at Calhoun, at the Baptist Church on Bear Creek, and in the shade of a grove of trees near the present courthouse before a log courthouse was built in Bakersville in 1867. Officially, Bakersville was called Davis at the close of the Civil War, but the original name was restored by the legislature in 1868.

This section lies in territory originally claimed by the Cherokee Indians but shared as a mutual hunting ground with the Catawbas when the two tribes were not at war. By the Proclamation of 1763, white settlers were excluded from the area by the Crown as a means of pacifying the red man. This prohibition was removed by the legislature in 1778 after the State became independent of the Crown, and settlement followed rapidly. The first 4 grants were issued as early as Dec. 10, 1778. By 1795, Waightstill Avery, first attorney-general of North Carolina, and William Cathcart had secured grants covering most of the unoccupied lands in what is now Mitchell County. Since these grants were ill-defined and often overlapped earlier grants, much litigation followed later when the mineral deposits in the area became known.

From the very beginning of settlement, it was believed that valuable mineral deposits lay hidden in the area. In the early 1870's a demand for isinglass (mica) for use in heating-stove doors led to a mica-mining boom which has continued intermittently to the present. The first mines to be opened were the Sink Hole and Clarissa mines where "ancient diggings" occurred. There were evidences of early mining, believed by some to have been done by DeSoto's men; more probably they were dug by the Indians. In 1902, mining for primary kaolin for use in the manufacture of pottery began; and in 1911, the first carload of feldspar was shipped from the county. These three products, mica, primary kaolin, and feldspar, have added millions of dollars to the economy of the area.

Originally, virgin growths of poplar and other hardwoods covered the slopes. The completion of the Clinchfield R. R. in the early 1900's opened a market for logs and lumber that has continued to the present, though diminishing in importance in recent years. What was once a giant primeval forest now appears as a varying patchwork of cultivated fields and farm woodland, green in spring and summer and gorgeous in autumn colors in the fall. Agriculture, including dairying and livestock raising, has virtually supplanted lumbering as a source of income. Recently, textile manufacturing has gained a foothold and promises to be an important industry.

1. From Bakersville, a scenic highway, NC 261, leads across Pumpkin Patch Mountain and through the valley of Little Rock Creek to CARVER'S GAP. From here a U. S. Forest Service road leads to the crest of ROAN MOUNTAIN, **12 m.** Here is the site of CLOUDLAND, a 268-room framed hotel which stood here before 1900 and at which guests in large numbers were entertained. The Festival of the Rhododendron is observed at this site annually in June.

Roan Mountain is unique in that for about 6 miles it has an elevation of from 5,800 to 6,282 feet and that most of this top is relatively broad and level. Belted with fir trees on the sides and in the ravines, the grassy plateau is profusely clustered with rhododendrons, forming natural gardens of unusual proportion and beauty, which reach their peak during the last days of June. Dr. Elisha Mitchell thus described the Roan: "It is the most beautiful of all the high mountains. With the exception of a body of rocks looking into the ruins of an old castle near the southwestern extremity, the top of the Roan may be described as a vast meadow without a tree to obstruct this prospect, where a person may gallop his horse for a mile or two with Carolina at his feet on one side and Tennessee on the other, and a green ocean of mountains rising in tremendous billows immediately around him."

2. Right from Bakersville on a marked road following Cane Creek is HAWK (2,900 alt., 250 pop.), **4.1 m.** Here is ROBY BUCHANAN'S MILL where he grinds and polishes native gem stones, an art he has learned by the trial and error method without instructor. He turns out beautiful specimens of a dozen or more semi-precious stones.

At **15 m.** is "LOAFER'S GLORY," a cluster of houses near the site of a general store which was carried away by flood waters of Cane Creek in the 1901 disaster remembered locally as the "May Flood." The men of the neighborhood gathered frequently at the store to swap knives and pleasantries, and an industrious wife remarked that the place must be a "loafer's glory." The name stuck.

At **18 m.** is RED HILL (2,424 alt., 60 pop.), so named because of the reddish clay soil. Soil analysis indicates the presence of gold and manganese as well as iron.

BULADEAN, **24 m.** (2,700 alt., 450 pop.), is a village nestled in a beautiful valley under Roan Mountain which towers above it on the east. The original name was "Magnetic City," so named because of the large deposits of magnetite nearby. A forge was operated here about the turn of the century.

NC 26 crosses the Tennessee Line, **29 m.,** at IRON MOUNTAIN GAP (3,725 alt.) where the route becomes Tenn. 107, 11 miles east of Unicoi, Tenn.

At **34.5 m.** US 19E forms a junction with NC 80.

Right on NC 80 to the junction with a marked side road, **5.2 m.**; L. **0.6 m.** on this side road to KONA (corner). Here occurred the sensational murder of Charlie Silver, for which his wife, Frankie, who had reported his disappearance, was hanged in Morganton, July 12, 1832. After bone fragments had been found in the fireplace of the Silver cabin, Frankie was taken to Morganton, tried, convicted, and sentenced to death. Relatives helped her to escape in a load of hay, but she was shortly recaptured. In the confession which followed she told how, crazed with jealousy, she waited until her husband had gone to sleep before she attacked him with an ax, dismembered the body, and burned it a portion at a time in the fireplace. At the hanging a ballad was sold by peddlers which was purportedly written by Frankie.

At Kona is the CAROLINA MINERALS PLANT, the most modern feldspar plant in the world.

At **8 m.** on NC 80 in BANDANA (237 pop.) is the SITE OF THE SINK HOLE MINE. Here are indications that Spaniards, possibly under Juan Pardo, may have carried on extensive mining. Local legend has it that some of the mica taken back to Spain by these men is still in existence. Others maintain that the mines were operated by the Indians. Here in 1858 Thomas Clingman (*see* ASHEVILLE) tried unsuccessfully to locate silver. He found flattened stone picks and other evidences of Indian operations. Others have found arrowheads, stone clubs, battle-axes, and soapstone pots, indicating Indian camp sites. Mica from Sink Hole was used for windowpanes in early houses.

At MICAVILLE, **36 m.** (2,504 alt., 250 pop.), two large companies operate several mica mines and purchase feldspar from individual miners. At Micaville is the junction (L) with NC 80 which joins the Parkway at Buck Creek Gap, **14 m.** (*see* TOUR *19*).

NC 80 (R) leads through rolling farms surrounded by rugged mountains in which Mt. Celo (6,326 ft.) is predominating.

At **4.5 m.** is CELO POST OFFICE, two miles beyond which is the CELO COMMUNITY, where about 20 families, mostly Friends, have come together to bring up their children as members of a rural community. Legal title for the 1,200 acres remains with the community, which is organized as a corporation with a board of directors. Each family owns its own home and holds land under an agreement with the community.

At **8.5 m.** is the CAROLINA HEMLOCK PARK (*free camp ground, picnic tables and grills, swimming*), a recreation center with a beautiful stream and a circular drive through tall evergreen trees and rhododendron.

BURNSVILLE, **41 m.** (2,817 alt., 1,341 pop.), seat of Yancey County, is named for Capt. Otway Burns, privateer in the War of 1812 (*see* TOUR *15A*). According to an anecdote, a visitor at the unveiling of the bronze statue of Burns in the town square, remarked, "I didn't know he was an Indian!"

Yancey County, formed in 1833, was named in honor of Bartlett Yancey, U. S. Congressman, State legislator, and citizen of Caswell County (*see* TOUR *12*). Burnsville is a pleasant village partly built around a common, in which formerly stood the courthouse built in 1836. This building was replaced by a newer one built on the west side of the common. The town is built on a plateau just west and north of the Black Mountains. Yancey has the highest average elevation of any county in the State, with 15 peaks over 6,000 feet.

The NU-WRAY INN, fronting on the common, has been a landmark for more than a century, as parts of the present building were built before 1833. This inn, which has preserved the charm and atmosphere of early days, has been operated by the same family for three generations. The fame of its hickory-smoked hams is known far and wide.

The BURNSVILLE SCHOOL OF FINE ARTS, conducted as a summer term of the University of Miami, offers courses in drama, music, modern dance, and art. The school is centered around the PARKWAY PLAYHOUSE which was started by a group of local citizens.

The BURNSVILLE PAINTING CLASSES is a private summer school of art conducted by Edward S. Shorter and Frank Stanley Herring. They operate the school for 10 weeks from July into September, and 85 or more students from almost every state in the Union who are interested in painting either as a hobby or a profession attend.

DANIEL BOONE'S FORGE is operated by Daniel Boone VI, a descendant of the famous hunter and woodsman. Products of his forge, such as wrought-iron door hinges and latches, fireplace fixtures, and grills, were used in Williamsburg, Va., restoration buildings.

CAMP MT. MITCHELL, a private camp for girls, has been in operation for 25 years.

Burnsville is also the location of the GLEN RAVEN and DUPLAN PLANTS (textiles).

Left from Burnsville on NC 197 along a winding mountain road which follows the sinuosities of Cane River to PENSACOLA, a typical mountain community. At **300 yds.** a gravel road leads (L) up Cat Tail Creek to MT. HELENA ESTATES, **2 m.**, a summer colony of over 50 families from Miami, Fla., who live in attractive homes built high up on the side of the mountains.

US 19E passes small, scattered settlements along Bald Creek. Women hook rugs in summer in open sheds that line the road and exhibit their bright handiwork on clotheslines along the route.

At **48 m.** US 19E joins US 19W where it becomes US 19.

Right on US 19W to HIGGINS, **6 m.** (2,350 alt., 150 pop.), where the MARKLE HANDICRAFT SCHOOL (*open*) is operated as a community development project supervised by the Presbyterian Church.
The route follows curves of Cane River (*stocked with bass, trout, and perch*) through a valley where small mountain farms bordering the river are connected with the highway by swinging footbridges.

At **22.2 m.** US 19W crosses the Tennessee Line at SPIVEY GAP (3,200 alt.), 15 miles south of Erwin, Tenn.

At Spivey Gap is the intersection with the Appalachian Trail.

Right on the Appalachian Trail (*4-foot, cleared*) to BIG BALD MOUNTAIN, **5.8 m.** (5,516 alt.), that affords views of Mount Mitchell and Celo on the east; Little Bald and Flattop on the north, and Ogle Meadows on the south. Big Bald is sometimes called Griers Bald for David Grier, who lived a hermit here from 1802 until 1834 after having been rejected by the daughter of Col. David Vance. He became involved in disputes when settlers came and killed a man. Although Grier was acquitted on the grounds of insanity, he was later slain by one of his victim's friends, not, however, until after he had published a pamphlet explaining why he had taken the law into his own hands.

At **59 m.** is the junction with US 23.

1. Right on US 23 the highway winds through a region of towering peaks and deep valleys to SAM'S GAP (3,800 ft.) where US 23 crosses the Tennessee Line, **11 m.**, 22 miles south of Erwin, Tenn.

2. At the junction of US 19-23, NC 213 leads to MARS HILL, **2 m.** (2,300 alt., 1,404 pop.), the seat of MARS HILL COLLEGE. The college, now the oldest institution of higher learning on its original site west of the Catawba River, was founded in 1856 as the French Broad Baptist Institute and chartered as a college in 1859. When the first building was completed, built largely of hand-made brick and hand-hewn material by sons and grandsons of the original settlers of the area, a sum of about $1,200 was still due the contractors. Later a slave, named Joe, belonging to the Rev. J. W. Anderson, secretary of the board of trustees, was levied on and taken to Asheville to secure payment of the debt. Joe was soon redeemed and continued to live in the community until his death about 50 years later. In 1932 his ashes were removed from a nearby cemetery and reinterred on the campus beneath a granite MARKER TO JOE. A grandson and granddaughter of Joe are now employed in the cafeteria at the college.

Also on the campus is preserved a little schoolhouse of hewn logs, once the Frog Level school, believed to be the last of the "old field" schools in the State.

During the Civil War Confederate troops were quartered on the campus, and two of the three college buildings were burned, leaving only the original building, which was the only building occupied by the college until 1892, when the college began to emerge from the wrack and gloom of war.

At present the college occupies a 120-acre campus surrounded by scenic grandeur, on which are 17 buildings. The college, organized as a junior college in 1921, enrolls about 900 students annually.

The HAMMERLUND ELECTRONICS PLANT, constructed in 1954, is located in Mars Hill.

Turning up one of the winding roads which intersect the main highways, one is surrounded by scenes reminiscent of the times when the Southern Highlands were known as the land the twentieth century forgot. Here many of the old customs and relics of songs and speech still linger. It was from these more remote sections, where in the olden days disputes were settled without recourse to law, that the county acquired the name "Bloody Madison."

During the Civil War the county was largely in sympathy with the Union. The mountain fastnesses provided relatively safe refuge for deserters and outlaws. The upper part of the county was a center for underground activities. Capt. George W. Kirk, operating under the command of Maj. Gen. John M. Schofield of the Army of the Ohio, was the leader of these underground forces. His ruthless band, which harassed defenseless communities nearby and sometimes engaged in skirmishes with Confederate troops, was feared and hated. Factional conflicts and bitterness continued in the county after the war, a condition which was aggravated by Gov. W. W. Holden's appointing Capt. Kirk to enforce martial law in the area.

With the rapid social and economic changes, brought about by education, transportation facilities, and industry, the county is fast losing many of the characteristics which have distinguished it in the past.

At **66 m.** US 19-23 forms a junction with NC 197.

Left on NC 197 to BARNARDSVILLE, **6 m.** (2,185 alt., 500 pop.). Right **1.5 m.** from Barnardsville on the marked Craggy Gardens Highway to CAMP TOM BROWNE (L), a 19-acre summer camp for the Future Farmers of America, an organization of boys from high school agriculture classes. At **4 m.** on the Craggy Highway is DILLINGHAM (275 pop.), at the entrance gate of the Mount Mitchell Division of Pisgah National Forest (*picnic and camp sites, springs, and shelters at intervals*).

Left **2.5 m.** from Dillingham on a Forest Service road to BIG IVY CAMP-GROUND (*water, fuel, fireplaces, sanitary facilities, swimming pool*).

From STOCKSVILLE, **67.5 m.** (2,250 alt., 200 pop.), US 19-23 follows the general route of the old Catawba Trail, major tradeway between the Indians in the Carolinas and the tribes of the Ohio Valley.

Near WEAVERVILLE (*fishing, swimming*), **70.6 m.** (2,300 alt., 1,111 pop.), are sulphur, iron, sodium, and lithia springs. William Sydney Porter (O. Henry) lived here for a time.

At **72.6 m.** is the junction with the Reems Creek Rd.

Left on the Reems Creek Rd., **1 m.** is the CASHMERE CORP. PLANT, which manufactures knit garments.

At **5.5 m.** on this road, according to legend, is the BIRTHPLACE OF ZEBULON B. VANCE (*private*), (R), Governor of North Carolina (1862-65, 1877-81), and U. S. Senator (*see* ASHEVILLE). This house, built for Col. David Vance about 1786, originally was a two-story log building. About 1893 the structure was reduced to one story and sheathed with clapboards. In the VANCE (HEMPHILL) CEMETERY, across the highway, on a knoll, **300 yds.**, is the GRAVE OF DAVID VANCE I (1745-1813), Revolutionary officer and a member of the commission that ran the line between Tennessee and North Carolina in 1799. Vance liberated his slaves by terms of his will. He selected the cemetery site because: "A little knoll surrounded by mountains should be a beautiful place to start from on the Resurrection Day."

Here also is the GRAVE OF DAVID VANCE II (1792-1844), a volunteer in the War of 1812, and the unmarked GRAVE OF DR. ROBERT BRANK VANCE, son of David Vance, I, killed (1827) in a pistol duel with Samuel P. Carson, his political opponent (*see* TOUR *13*).

At **73.6 m.** is the junction with US 70-25 (*see* TOUR *24*), which unites with US 19 between this point and Asheville.

US 19 enters LAKE VIEW PARK, **75.6 m.**, a residential section bordering (R) the green shores of BEAVER LAKE (*boating, swimming*).

ASHEVILLE, 79.6 m. (*see* ASHEVILLE).

Points of Interest: Biltmore House, Pack Memorial Library, Grove Park Inn, Sunset Mountain, Thomas Wolfe Home, and others.

Asheville is at the junction with US 70 (*see* TOUR *15B*), US 25 (*see* TOUR *24*), and US 74 (*see* TOUR *16*).

Section b. ASHEVILLE *to* GEORGIA LINE; 119 m., US 19

This all-mountain route gives access to the Pisgah and Nantahala National Forests, and it runs through the Great Smoky Mountains National Park and the Nantahala Gorge.

US 19 crosses the French Broad River, **1.4 m.** on the SMOKY MOUNTAIN PARK BRIDGE.

At **3.2 m.** is the junction with narrow and winding NC 191, called the Brevard Rd.

Left on NC 191 to the APPALACHIAN FOREST EXPERIMENT STATION at Bent Creek, **6 m.** (R), one of the first experimental forests established by the U. S. Forest Service.

At **6.1 m.** is the junction with the sand-clay Bent Creek Rd.

Right **0.1 m** on the Bent Creek Rd. is the entrance to Pisgah Division of Pisgah National Forest (*see* NATIONAL FORESTS). At **3 m.** on the Bent Creek Rd. is the BENT CREEK CAMPGROUND (*open all year; water, fuel, fireplaces, sanitary equipment, and shelter*). From this point the Bent Creek Rd. is usually open in summer. At BENT CREEK GAP, **7 m.**, is the junction with the Shut-In Trail; R. on this trail to the top of FERRIN KNOB (fire lookout tower) and on to MOUNT PISGAH. At **13 m.** on the Bent Creek Rd. is the NORTH MILLS RIVER CAMPGROUND maintained by the U. S. Forest Service (*accommodations for trailers and tents, water, sanitary conveniences, swimming pool*). Left from this campground, on the North Mills River Rd., is the junction with NC 191 at **18 m.**

At **7.5 m.** on NC 191, are the low stone and brick buildings of PISGAH FOREST POTTERY (L), featuring ware with unusual glazes. All shaping, turning, decorating, and glazing is done by hand; even the cameo-decorated ware is painted freehand with porcelain paste.

At **9 m.** NC 280 joins from the left and runs with NC 191 to Mills River Bridge before turning west to Brevard.

At **14 m.** is the junction (R) with the North Mills River Rd.

On US 19 at **4 m.** is the junction with the paved and marked Johnston Blvd. (Johnston School Rd).

Right on this road (*asphalt to foot of Mountain*) to the summit of SPIVEY MOUNTAIN (3,331 alt.), **3 m.** The view from the fire tower includes the French Broad Valley and the city of Asheville.

At **5 m.** (L) is the entrance to ASHEVILLE SCHOOL, a private boys' preparatory school, occupying buildings of brick, stone, and stucco construction. It was founded in 1900 and offers a 6-year course. Many of its students come from distant states.

At 7.5 m. in the meadow beside Hominy Creek, is the traditional camp-site of Gen. Griffith Rutherford's forces on their expedition to end the Cherokee harassment of the frontier settlements in 1776. Soon afterwards the expedition's Capt. William Moore set up a "blockhouse" 0.5 m. SE. This was the beginning of the Sand Hill community, one of the earliest in the county. Graves of Capt. Moore and others, dated in the early 1800's, are on a pine knoll 0.3 m. SE. The trading path to the Middle Cherokee Settlements paralleled the S. side of US 19-23 near this camp.

The AMERICAN ENKA CORP. PLANT (*open only by invitation*) is at 8 m. (L) across a bridge over the railroad tracks. One of the largest plants in western North Carolina, Enka manufactures rayon and nylon yarns for clothing and industrial uses. About 3,000 people are employed in the modern brick plant, which commenced operations in 1929.

The company-owned ENKA VILLAGE (2,050 alt., 1,792 pop.), for key employees, has its own post office, stores, church, and club house. The plant's facilities include a dispensary and a volunteer fire department for protection of the plant and surrounding community. ENKA LAKE provides water for the manufacturing process and also is used for recreational activities.

At 10.2 m. relocated US 19-23, a 4-lane highway, follows a new route straight through to Canton and avoids Luther, at 3 miles on old US 19-23.

At 14.6 m. (L) may be seen the old TURNPIKE HOTEL (2,229 alt.), once the noonday stagecoach stop between Asheville and Waynesville. The original frame structure was built in 1866; the larger building, also frame, was added in 1880.

In CANTON, 18 m. (2,609 alt., 4,906 pop.), is (R) the CHAMPION PAPER AND FIBRE CO. PLANT (*open by permission*), one of the world's largest integrated pulp and paper mills, producing more than 700 tons of paper and paperboard daily. The company employs over 2,750 persons, owns 230,000 acres of forest land, and obtains additional pulpwood from 5,000,000 acres of independently owned woodlots.

West of Canton the 4-lane relocated highway runs south of the Southern R. R. tracks.

At CLYDE, 22 m. (2,539 alt., 598 pop.), formerly a cattle-shipping point, the highway skirts the town's southern border.

At 22.3 m. (R) may be seen the SMATHERS HOUSE (*private*). A three-story frame building, it was erected about 1795 by Vader Shook, a Pennsylvania farmer who was granted the site for his Revolutionary services. Shook entertained Bishop Francis Asbury (*see* TOUR 24) here about 1810, and the first Methodist church in Haywood County was organized here.

The third floor was equipped as a chapel or "prophet's room." A recently weatherboarded log cabin, 300 yards beyond, known as the SHOOK CABIN, was the first dwelling built by Vader Shook before he built the more pretentious one and is perhaps the oldest house in Haywood County.

LAKE JUNALUSKA METHODIST ASSEMBLY, 26 m. (2,584 alt.).

Season: June 1-Sept. 1.
Admission: Ground fee at the gates ranging from 50¢ a day to $7.50 for the season.
Accommodations: 12 hotels and boarding houses; furnished cottages for rent during the season; 50 new efficiency apartment units.

This 2,500-acre site, with its 250-acre lake, is the summer recreational and educational center of the Methodist Church, Southeastern Jurisdiction. The name honors Chief Junaluska (*see* TOUR *13*). The grounds contain over 20 miles of graded roads, of which 10 are paved, more than 225 summer homes, and 20 public buildings, including a large auditorium which seats 4,000. Swimming, boating, golf, horseback riding, and other supervised recreations are featured during the summer, as well as the educational program sponsored by the various Boards of the Methodist Church.

Right from Lake Junaluska on NC 209 to the junction with improved NC 289, **13 m.**; L. **0.7 m.** on NC 289 to the junction with improved NC 292; R. **7 m.** on NC 292 through the Fines Creek section, noted for cattle raising and fishing streams, to the junction with the Max Patch road; R. **0.5 m.** on this road to MAX PATCH (4,660 alt.), a mile-long bald. Here is unfolded a panorama of the Great Smokies and the Balsam Mountains with the deep gorge of the Pigeon River in the foreground.

A Cherokee legend connects this region with an immortal race that inhabited forests above the clouds. Once a wandering Indian maiden fell asleep and dreamed of a celestial lover who later appeared and carried her away. The tribe, believing her stolen by a neighboring tribe, set out to conquer them. Grieved by the bloodshed, the celestials permitted the maiden to summon her people to a council. When her brother raised his tomahawk to slay her husband, the brother was killed by a thunderbolt. The girl prepared to return to her people but her husband, to reconcile her, promised that all brave warriors and faithful wives should live eternally in the cloudlands after death.

NC 209 turns (R) at Lake Junaluska and is now being paved to Hot Springs, **37 m.** This scenic route, over the Newfound Mountains, leads along much of the crest or the ridges of this chain.

At **22.1 m.** is LUCK, a small mountain community along the banks of Spring Creek, which follows the highway (R) to the picturesque SPRING CREEK community, **26.5 m.** On the left are the impressive BALD MOUNTAINS in the distance. On the right is SPRING CREEK GORGE where the creek roars 700 feet below. Beyond the gorge are the long ranges of the Spring Creek Mountains.

At **37 m.** NC 209 reaches HOT SPRINGS (*see* TOUR *24*) where it joins US 25-70 (*see* TOUR *24*).

At Lake Junaluska, US 23-19A branches to the left (*see* TOUR *23*).

US 19 leads up Jonathan's Creek through Maggie Valley to Soco Gap on the boundary of the Cherokee tribal lands, and to the Great Smoky Mountains National Park.

At DELLWOOD, 31 m. (160 pop.), is the junction with NC 284 *see* TOUR 22B).

The route continues up Jonathan's Creek through beautiful MAGGIE VALLEY, a rapidly developing tourist area (*hotels, motels, cafés, craft shops*). The community is using a development plan worked out with local leaders by graduates of the Dept. of City and Regional Planning at the University of North Carolina. Houses on the grassy mountain sides are reminiscent of Switzerland. The valley lies close under PLOTT BALSAM MOUNTAIN (6,088 alt.) on the left.

Along the ascending route from Maggie Valley to Soco Gap there are State roadside picnic areas. The modern highway follows generally the route of the old Soco Gap road used as a path by Indians and pioneers as it rises from an altitude of 2,500 feet to the summit of the gap at 4,337 feet.

Along the route are blooming trees, shrubs, and plants to delight the botanist, horticulturist, photographer, or nature lover. Beginning in early spring, arbutus, serviceberry, dogwood, flame azalea, mountain laurel, and rhododendron follow in profusion through the "golden month" of October, when the maples, sourwoods, poplars, and oaks present a magnificent array of scarlet, yellow, bronze, and russet.

SOCO GAP, 36 m., at the head of Jonathan's Creek, which rises at the "old field" Cherokee Council ground at Cold Spring, is the marked boundary of the QUALLA RESERVATION of the Cherokee Indians and was the gateway to the last Cherokee stronghold in western North Carolina. In the narrow confines of the gap the Cherokees ambushed their enemies and were able for a time to repel the encroachment of the white man.

The Cherokee refer to this gap as A-ha-lu-na, meaning "ambushed," or U-ni-ha-lu-na, meaning "where they watched." At one time they are said to have ambushed a large party of invading Iroquois, slaying all but one. Following custom, they cut off the ears of this victim and released him to carry the news back to his people.

Another story concerns the great Tecumseh, Chief of the Shawnees. During the War of 1812 he and other tribes north of the Ohio were allies of the British. Tecumseh came here to enlist the aid of the Cherokee. A council was called to hear the impassioned plea of the Shawnee chief. However, the Cherokee chief, Junaluska, advised continued peace. When he realized what the outcome would be, Tecumseh is said to have made his departure by leaping over the heads of the warriors seated in a ring around the chiefs.

In March, 1865, Col. George W. Kirk with a regiment of Union troops invaded this region by way of Cataloochee (*see* TOUR 22B), burning and destroying as he went. Col. Thomas' regiment of Cherokee met Kirk at Soco and helped drive him back into Tennessee.

At Soco Gap is also the junction with a link of the Blue Ridge Parkway.

The Parkway leads into the Balsams, offering panoramic views of the Smokies, particularly at MILE HIGH OVERLOOK, from which is a view across Big Cone in the Cherokee Reservation toward the Smokies.

Right on the Parkway is BLACK CAMP GAP, 6 m. (4,492 alt.), an abandoned lumber camp. Here is a MASONIC MARKER, made of stones from almost every country in the world except Japan and Russia. Here the famous Ramp Convention, which has met annually since 1930, was held until 1952 when it was moved to Camp Hope, 15 miles SE. of Canton. Black Camp Gap is one of the few regions in America where the ramp, spelled "rampion" by Webster, is grown. Defined as "a European bellflower having an edible tuberous root used as a salad," its flavor and fragrance have been described by ramp enthusiasts as combining the best features of onion and garlic "only more so."

HEINTOOGA OVERLOOK (5,240 alt.), 11.7 m., from which is a view of the main divide of the Smokies from Clingmans Dome (L) to Mount Guyot (R). The BALSAM MOUNTAIN CAMPGROUND has camping and cooking facilities.

From Soco Gap US 19 enters the CHEROKEE RESERVATION, descending in great spiral curves, with a few scenic overlooks, into Soco Valley, a farming community now dotted with tourist camps.

At 37.2 m. is a State picnic park (*picnic tables, open air cooking places, and sanitary facilities*). At 37.3 m. are the double SOCO FALLS (R), tumbling 60 feet into a cuplike space. The moisture at the foot has produced an unusual growth of trilliums.

CHEROKEE, 48 m. (1,945 alt., 500 pop.) (*see* TOUR 22C), is at the junction with US 441 (*see* TOUR 22C).

At 52.6 m., US 19 joins US 19A (*see* TOUR 23).

ELA, 53.5 m. (1,795 alt., 200 pop.), is a tourist court village.

BRYSON CITY, 58.5 m. (1,736 alt., 1,499 pop.), is the seat of Swain County, named for Gov. David L. Swain (1832-35) (*see* ASHEVILLE). The town is in a bowlike depression formed by the Tuckasegee (Ind., *crawling terrapin*) River at the foot of Rich Mountain. At high water Fontana Reservoir (*see below*) backs up to the town. Originally called Charleston, the town was renamed for Col. Thaddeus Bryson, a local citizen. There are numerous motels for tourists. Horace Kephart, author of *Our Southern Highlanders* and authority on campcraft, is buried in Bryson City cemetery on a hill overlooking the town from the west.

At LAUADA, 64.5 m., US 19 joins NC 28, which turns (L) to Franklin, 22 m. (*see* TOUR 13) and US 23 (*see* TOUR 23).

This route passes the Horseshoe Bend of the Little Tennessee River and the Cowee Indian town-site, the chief town of the Middle Cherokees, which was destroyed during the Revolution. The council house stood on the mound 100 yds. west. William Bartram, the naturalist, who visited the town in 1776, said it was "situated on the bases of the hills on both side of the river [Little Tennessee], near to its banks, and here terminates the great vale of Cowe, exhibiting one of the most charming natural mountainous landscapes perhaps anywhere to be seen; ridges of hills rising grand and sublimely one above and beyond another, some boldly and majestically advancing into the verdant plain, their feet bathed with the silver flood of the Tanase [*sic*], while others far distant, veiled in blue mists, sublimely mounting aloft with yet greater majesty lift up their pompous crests, and overlook vast regions."

Nearby Bartram came upon "companies of young, innocent Cherokee virgins" who after having gathered strawberries, "lay reclined under the shade of floriferous and fragrant native bowers of Magnolia, Azalea, Philadelphus, perfumed Calycanthus, sweet Yellow Jessamine and cerulean Glycine frutesceus, disclosing their beauties to the fluttering breeze, and bathing their limbs in the cool fleeting streams; whilst other parties, more gay and libertine, were yet collecting strawberries, or wantonly chasing their companions, tantalising them, staining their lips and cheeks with the rich fruit." Bartram concluded that this sylvan scene was "perhaps too enticing for heavy young men long to continue idle spectators."

At **65.5 m.** US 19 crosses a high bridge over the LITTLE TENNESSEE RIVER at the head of a branch of Fontana Lake, which the highway skirts.

ALMOND BOAT PARK, **67.5 m.**, is a privately developed project on a park area leased from the State (*fishing, boats, docks, cottages, coffee shop*). From here boat trips (*daily, June 1—Sept. 15*) may be taken to FONTANA LAKE AND DAM (*a 2½ hour, 60-mile round trip; adults, $5; children, ½ fare*), to BIG ISLAND (*30-min. trip circling Big Island; $1 per person*); and to BUSHNELL BLUFFS (*1-hour trip over the submerged areas of Judson and Bushnell to the junction of the Little Tennessee and Tuckasegee Rivers; $2 per person*).

Here US 19 joins NC 28.

Right on NC 28, completed in 1954, to STECOAH, **12 m.**, a small mountain community in the Cheoah Mountains.

At **13.4 m.** NC 28 joins at Johnson Gap with a road (R) to Robbinsville, 10 miles SW.

Scenic NC 28 sweeps along the southern borders of Lake Fontana and hugs the Yellow Creek Mountains. In this region the cabins cling to the mountain sides.

Most of these people are entirely Nordic. There are few Negroes and almost no tenant farmers. Kephart says this country was settled "neither by Cavaliers nor by poor whites, but by a radically distinct ... people who are appropriately called the Roundheads of the South.... The first characteristic that these pioneers developed was an intense individualism ... the strong and even violent independence that made them forsake all the comforts of civilization and prefer the wild freedom of the border...." Their descendants have preserved to a marked degree the individualism, independence, and originality of character of their ancestors.

Although in the popular concept every mountaineer uses hillbilly dialect and handles both bullets and ballads with an Elizabethan abandon and a free frontier fervor, valley-dwelling mountaineers are not so different from lowlanders as they are from the isolated inhabitants of the coves far back in the mountains. Pungent, graphic, and expressive, the deep-cove type coins his own word if he can think of none at the moment that suits his need. Though the Scotch-Irish influence is noticeable chiefly in the sounding of the letter *r*, the English is really predominant. He speaks often in Elizabethan, Chaucerian, or pre-Chaucerian idiom; his pronoun *hit* antedates English itself, while *Ey God*, a favorite expletive, is the original of *egad* and precedes Chaucer. The highlander uses many expressions in common with the *Canterbury Tales: heap o' folks, afore, peart;* some of his *ballets* are old English folk songs.

FONTANA VILLAGE, 23 m. (1,800 alt.), a new year-around resort, located on the spot formerly known as Welch Cove, was built in 1941 as a construction village for the employees of Fontana Dam. After the dam was built, a private corporation, Government Services, Inc., leased it and converted it into a complete resort, with emphasis on recreation. It is now a tourist town, surrounded by peaks rising 3,300 feet and is two miles from Fontana Dam and Lake. The village has a 56-room lodge and 280 cottages and houses for rent. Recreation includes fishing, boating, horseback riding, pack trips, and square dances.

FONTANA DAM, a $73,000,000-project, serves as a flood barrier and power generator. The TVA dam, 480 feet high, is the highest dam in eastern America. Above the dam is the 30-mile-long FONTANA LAKE, the largest of TVA's lakes. The Appalachian Trail crosses the dam in passing southward from the Great Smokies.

NC 28 continues for 10 miles along Lake Cheoah to US 129, 33 m. (*see* TOUR 22C) near Deal's Gap and the Tennessee Line.

US 19 continues in the main through a very flat divide between the Alarkas (L) and a small ridge known as Jackson Line Mountains.

The NANTAHALA GORGE, 74.4 m., is a high light in a route presenting a succession of extraordinary views. This canyon of the Nantahala River is so deep and its sides so sheer that the Indians named it Land of the Middle Sun, believing that only the noonday sun could penetrate its depths.

One of the several Cherokee legends told of this gloomy and forbidding place is that the gorge was the haunt of the Uktena (*keen-eyed*), a huge horned serpent. The bright gem blazing from between his horns was called ulstitlu (*it is on his head*), and meant death to the family of any Indian who beheld it. However, when detached it became the ulunsuti (*transparent*), the great talisman that revealed the future to its possessor. When a wary hunter encased himself in leather, surprised the monster, killed him, and tore the great jewel from his head, the snake writhed from one side of the gorge to the other, shutting out the radiance of the sun and causing the perpetual twilight. The great jewel was said to be the rutile quartz, so rare that there was only one specimen among the eastern Cherokee in 1890.

In the gorge on the left bank of the river are caves claimed by some to have been occupied by a race that preceded the Cherokee. High up above the caves on a narrow shelf carved out of the rock is the road to Point Lookout.

At WESSER, 74.6 m. (1,714 alt., 18 pop.), between the highway and the Nantahala River (R), is the GORGE DELL CAMP PICNIC GROUND (*water, fireplaces, sanitary conveniences*). Here is also an Appalachian Trail crossing.

As the highway winds through and up the gorge the river disappears from sight and only the tops of tall trees are visible. Here and there a waterfall cascades from a high peak.

NANTAHALA, 80 m. (2,060 alt., 100 pop.), is at the junction with the Rabbit Creek Rd. (*see* TOUR *13, sec. c*). The NANTAHALA POWER PLANT of the Nantahala Power and Light Co. (Aluminum) hugs the end of a rock ridge. Its giant penstocks drop from a surge tank at the end of a rock tunnel from Nantahala Lake, several miles upstream.

At TOPTON, 84 m. (2,599 alt., 225 pop.), the highway leaves the gorge through RED MARBLE GAP and enters farming country, the basin of the Valley River bordered on the right by the Snowbird Mountains, and on the left by the Valley River Mountains of the Nantahala Range. Topton is at the junction with US 129 (*see* TOUR 22C).

ANDREWS, 93 m. (1,775 alt., 1,397 pop.), has an extract plant.

East of the town is the site of land owned by Junaluska, Cherokee Chief (*see* TOUR 22C). The first southern plant of the Berkshire Mills, reputedly the nation's largest knitters of full-fashioned hosiery, is here.
A legend tells of a silver mine from which the Indians obtained the "shiny metal" for their trinkets. At the mouth of Factory Creek, near Andrews, is a large shelving rock over the entrance to a cave, now closed by slides. Here lived an old Indian, Sontechee, who kept all white settlers away from the place. It was believed he knew where the mine was but he died without revealing the secret.

At Andrews is the junction with a Forest Service Road to Nantahala Lake and Franklin.

West of Andrews the road winds through the broader, level stretch of the KONNAHEETA VALLEY (Ind., *extra long*), old flood plains of the river that here spread to a width of about 2 miles.

On the L. at 96 m. is the ANDREWS-MURPHY AIRPORT.

The PLANT AND QUARRIES (*open*), 98 m. (R), of the Columbia Marble Co. produce a high-grade marble (Regal Blue); its predominant white shades into grayish and mottled blue with occasional streaks of pink.

In MARBLE, 99.1 m. (1,683 alt., 356 pop.), is the MUSEUM OF ARTHUR PALMER (*open*) (L). The collection includes furniture, farm implements, muskets, and cooking utensils used by the early settlers. There are also Cherokee relics, taken from mounds, and samples of minerals found in the section.

At TOMOTLA, (L), 102.1 m. (1,600 alt., 200 pop.), iron mining operations uncovered remains of an old shaft and tools believed to have been used by Spaniards some time after De Soto's expedition in 1540. Spaniards were mining and smelting in this area in 1690.

Murphy, **109 m.** (*see* TOUR *13, sec. c.*), is at the junction with US 64.

US 19 crosses the Georgia Line at **119 m.**, 11 miles north of Blairsville, Ga.

TOUR 22A (*NC 112, US 276*)

Junction with US 19-23—Mt. Pisgah—Pink Beds—Junction with US 64; NC 112, US 276. **38 m.**

This mountain route enters the Pisgah National Forest, noted for its abundant wildlife and flowering shrubs, and passes Mt. Pisgah and shimmering Looking Glass Falls.

NC 112 branches south from its junction with US 19, **0 m.** (*see* TOUR 22), at a point 9.9 miles west of Asheville. CANDLER, **1 m.** (2,108 alt., 623 pop.), on Hominy Creek, said to have been named by a group of hunters who cooked hominy upon its banks, is at the junction with the Pisgah Motor Rd., now the route.

At **4 m.** Pisgah and the Rat, twin eminences, loom above the range straight ahead. From a distance the Rat resembles a rodent with tail extended and head lowered between its front paws. When snow covers the northern slope of Pisgah, figures of a Bride and Groom stand out in heroic stature on the mountainside. A television tower was built in 1954 on this chief landmark of the plateau.

STONY FORK, **8 m.** (2,368 alt.), has a colony of summer cabins, a few permanent homes, and a sprinkling of refreshment stands.

At **9 m.** is the ENTRANCE TO THE PISGAH DIVISION OF THE PISGAH NATIONAL FOREST (*see* NATIONAL FORESTS) and (L) the STONY FORK CAMPGROUND (*water, firewood, sanitary conveniences*). South of this point the Pisgah Motor Rd. makes a steep ascent of 7 miles.
In spring the blooms of the serviceberry and the dogwood trees throw a veil of white over the new green of the forest. In May the woods are gay with azalea that varies from white to deep orange. The bloom of the laurel shades from white to delicate pink, and in June the purplish-red splotches of the rhododendron are profuse. Among flowers in the woods are columbine, bluet, wild iris, Indian pink, ladyslipper, and trillium. In autumn the deciduous trees are a riot of color against the dark blue green of the evergreens.
Although the variety and size of the trees change with the difference

in altitude, oaks predominate. Flowering native trees include the silverbell, the sourwood, and the holly. On the extreme heights the growth is generally scrubby owing to the poor quality of the soil as well as to the elevation.

Large and small game abound in the forest. The preserve is closed to hunting except in prescribed periods when shooting is permitted to reduce the game population. Trapped deer and fawns are shipped to other forests for restocking.

Apparent in the forest are bear wallows and grubbings, also deer rubs, where the bucks polish their hardening antlers. The "browse line" effect of dense deer population is noticeable at places on trees and shrubs. The forest is open to fishing for periods of a few days each, between May 15 and Aug. 31.

BUCK SPRING LODGE (*closed*), **16 m.** (L), a large structure of logs built by George W. Vanderbilt (*see* ASHEVILLE) on what was then his hunting estate, is at the junction with a dirt road.

Right on this road to the PISGAH PARKING LOT (*refreshments sold during summer*), **0.2 m.** Straight ahead from the parking lot **0.5 m.** on a foot trail over a comparatively level path through dense forest to the divide in a clearing. Left **1 m.** on the trail following a stone-stepped course through scrub oak, then bushes, finally up a stiff ascent to the TOP OF BIG PISGAH (5,721 alt.). The view includes points in North Carolina and South Carolina and sometimes Georgia, Tennessee, and Virginia.

At **17 m.** is PISGAH FOREST INN, a rustic hostelry from whose front porch the round dome of Looking Glass Rock is visible.

The FRYING PAN CAMPGROUND (*water, firewood, sanitary conveniences*), **18.5 m.** (R), is the highest campground (5,040 alt.) in the forest. A gentle trail leads **5 m.** to FRYING PAN FIRE TOWER, a lookout point giving a full sweep of the rugged peaks nearby and of the distant Blue Ridge, Smoky, Balsam, Craggy, and Black ranges.

WAGON ROAD GAP, **20.5 m.**, is at the junction with the Blue Ridge Parkway and US 276, (*see* TOUR *19*), now the route. The PINK BEDS (L), **23 m.** (3,277 alt.), are a stretch of natural garden, visible from the highway for several miles, and probably named for the wealth of mountain laurel growing here.

At **23.5 m.** is the junction with a Forest Service Rd.

Downgrade **500 yds.** from the guard station is a house of the Black Forest type, built during the George W. Vanderbilt ownership and used by foresters of the Biltmore Forest School.

Left on this road to the PINK BEDS FOREST CAMPGROUND (*water, firewood, sanitary conveniences*), **0.3 m.**

LOOKING GLASS FALLS, **29 m.** (L), is formed by the water of LOOKING GLASS CREEK tumbling 85 feet from a rocky precipice.

On the R. side of the road, across from the falls, is the junction with a trail.

Right 1 m. on this trail, following a small creek, to LOOKING GLASS ROCK (4,000 alt.), a granite monolith with a wide fan of water falling from its broad, bare top. During wet springs and in winter when the water is frozen the reflected light makes the rock glisten like a giant mirror. From the top of the rock is a panorama of peaks, valleys, and streams.

The DAVIDSON RIVER CAMPGROUND (*water, firewood, sanitary facilities, swimming pool*) is at 33 m.

Left from the Davidson River Campground on a graveled road to WHITE PINE CAMPGROUND (*water, firewood, sanitary conveniences*), 0.5 m.

At 36.5 m. the route leaves the forest to join NC 280. To the left is the giant ECUSTA PLANT of Olin Industries. Much of the cigarette paper and cellophane used by the U. S. tobacco industry is made here. The clear waters of Davidson River are taken to rinse off the refuse liquors in the process. Near the R. R. crossing is the CARR LUMBER CO. PLANT, one of the larger and older sawmill and flooring plants, which draws hardwood from the mountains.

PISGAH FOREST, 38 m. (2,107 alt., 597 pop.), is at the junction with US 64 (*see* TOUR *13, sec. c*).

TOUR 22B (*NC 284*)

Dellwood—Mt. Sterling—Davenport Gap; NC 284. 30.7 m.

Roadbed paved to Cove Creek. Route to Tenn. Line graveled and curving over two high divides. A new dual lane route down Pigeon River Gorge to Tennessee and the Midwest is now under construction. Limited accommodations.

This route entering the eastern edge of the Great Smoky Mountains National Park reveals exceptionally fine mountain views, including that from the lookout tower on Mt. Sterling. It also crosses the Cataloochee Creek section, noted for its trout fishing.

NC 284 branches north from US 19 at DELLWOOD, 0 m. (160 pop.). The road that first traversed this section was hardly more than a track though dignified by the designation of a turnpike. Bishop Asbury described crossing Cataloochee in December, 1810: "But, O the mountain, height after height, and five miles over!"

North of Dellwood for several miles the route traverses the broad flat lands of JONATHAN'S CREEK VALLEY. The stream (*trout fishing*) is named for Jonathan McPeters, one of the first white men in this section.

JONATHAN'S CREEK BRIDGE is crossed at 3.9 m. An ivy-covered mill with a water wheel is at Cove Creek, 6.5 m. To the north houses cling precariously to the sheer mountainsides that rise above the narrow, twisting road.

From COVE CREEK GAP, 12.2 m. (4,062 alt.), at the easternmost part of the GREAT SMOKY MOUNTAINS NATIONAL PARK (*see* TOUR 22) are views of Sterling Ridge, the Great Balsam Range, the main Smokies dominated by the bulk of Mt. Guyot, and Mt. Pisgah in the south. North of the gap the road broadens and winds down the northern slope of Cataloochee Divide to SAL PATCH GAP, 13.6 m. (3,473 alt.).

From MT. STERLING GAP, 22.4 m. (3,894 alt.), the rocky sides of Mt. Sterling are visible (L), rising from the surrounding forest.

Left from Mt. Sterling Gap on a foot trail mounting the slope west of the highway, to Mt. Sterling Ridge. L. on the trail to the SUMMIT OF MT. STER-

LING (5,842 alt.), **3 m.** From a 60-foot steel lookout tower is a wide view of the great wilderness area of the eastern sector of the Smokies. In the foreground, 1,000 feet below, is Cataloochee Creek.

From the gap NC 284 descends to MT. STERLING POST OFFICE, **29.3 m.** (2,950 alt., 160 pop.), where a group of buildings cluster on the banks of Big Creek.

Right from Mt. Sterling Post Office, on a level trail, is the power company's village of WATERVILLE, **1 m.** (40 pop.), on the Big Pigeon River. Here is the HYDRO-ELECTRIC PLANT (*open*) of the Carolina Power & Light Co. The waters of the Pigeon River and Cataloochee Creek are impounded by the 180-foot-high dam. A tunnel, 8 miles long, cut through the solid rock base of Mt. Sterling Ridge, carries the water to the generating plant. Built in 1928 at a cost of $13,000,000 this plant has a capacity of 145,000 hp. and supplies power for western North Carolina, eastern Tennessee, western South Carolina, and part of Georgia.

At DAVENPORT GAP, **30.7 m.,** a stone marker dated 1821 was placed by the Davenport surveying party on the North Carolina-Tennessee boundary.

At Davenport Gap is the junction with the Appalachian Trail (*4-foot, graded for horses*).

Left on the Appalachian Trail, **13.6 m.** via Mt. Cammerer fire lookout, to the summit (6,621 alt.) of MOUNT GUYOT (gee'-o, with the g hard), the second highest peak in the Smoky Mountains, discovered by S. B. Buckley, who named it for his friend, Arnold Guyot (1807-84). Guyot was born in Switzerland, came to America in 1848, and accepted the chair of geology and physical geography at Princeton. His meterological observations led to the formation of the U. S. Weather Bureau. He devoted years to the study of the Appalachian Mountains and between 1856-60 explored the Smokies and the Black Mountains. Guyot's barometric measurements of the altitudes of the peaks vary hardly 20 feet from those of the later geologic surveys, made with better equipment.

Between Mount Guyot and Clingmans Dome (*see* TOUR 22C) is a region of heath balds. These treeless areas, in the midst of spruce and hardwood at altitudes of 4,000 feet and higher, are covered with a growth of almost impenetrable rhododendron and laurel. Locally they are variously called "hells," "wooly-heads," and "slicks," the latter because from a distance the dense shrubs of almost uniform height appear to be a smooth covering.

TOUR 22C (*US 441, Tenn. 73, US 129*)

Cherokee—Newfound Gap—(Gatlinburg, Tenn.)—(Maryville, Tenn.)—
Tapoco—Robbinsville—Topton; US 441; Tenn. 73; US 129. **142 m.**

This loop route through the Great Smoky Mountains National Park
swings into Tennessee and re-enters North Carolina at the park's extreme
southwest boundary, Deal's Gap. It enters the Qualla Reservation of the
Cherokee Indians and runs for long stretches through uninhabited country.

CHEROKEE, **0 m.** (1,945 alt., 500 pop.), at the junction of US 19 and
US 441 (*see* TOUR 22) is the capital of the Eastern Band of the once-powerful
Cherokees and is located in the QUALLA RESERVATION.

This reservation comprises 50,000 acres in Swain and Jackson counties
and isolated tracts totaling 13,000 acres in Graham and Cherokee counties.
To this area came a group of Cherokee who fled from Gen. Winfield Scott's
soldiers in 1838, during the Indian removal over the "Trail of Tears," and
took refuge in the Great Smokies where they defied capture. Gen. Scott
agreed to let the fugitives remain in return for the surrender of Tsali (*see
below*) and his kinsmen who had killed a soldier in making their escape.
Purchase of this land was begun by William H. Thomas. Col. Thomas, a
mountain-born lad who was adopted by Chief Yonaguska, had become their
chief agent and had worked for years to get Congress to grant them funds
to complete buying the lands.

The Oconaluftee (Ind. *near the river*) River flows through the reservation
lands, which are mostly mountainous, though coves provide arable land.
Except the balds, the mountains are forested with hardwoods and evergreens.

This is the largest organized Indian reservation east of Wisconsin. It is
estimated that less than 15% of the 3,700 residents are full-blooded Cherokee; 31% are ¾ or more full-blooded. The lands are held in common for
the tribe under the supervision of the Office of Indian Affairs. Domestic
matters are administered by a chief, assistant chief, and a tribal council of
12, all of whom are elective. Tracts are assigned family groups who may
erect improvements in which they retain an equitable title that may be sold
to their successors. Most of the Cherokee are members of the Baptist or
Methodist churches. Nevertheless, traces of their pagan past are evidenced

by the 15 or more practicing medicine men and women and the survival of conjuring societies.

Modern brick buildings on a hill near the entrance contain the administrative offices, hospital, school, and dormitories. Approximately 1,000 Cherokee children are instructed in the central boarding school and in 5 outlying community day schools. Part of each day is devoted to training in industries and crafts. Basketry and pottery making have been well developed. Emphasis is placed on farming, dairying, and forestry. Most of the coves are reached by an extension staff offering instruction to adults in gardening, agriculture, and crafts. Great progress is now being made in agricultural pursuits.

A large athletic field occupies a level tract between the highway and the buildings. Here is held the annual Cherokee Indian Fair (*usually 1st wk. in Oct.; adm. 75¢*), a tribal gathering and exhibition of handicrafts and agricultural products. Archery and blowgun contests, primitive games, and dances are presented. One of these, the Green-Corn Dance, an ancient ceremonial celebrating the coming of the harvest, is the Indian thanksgiving. A feature of the fair is the game of Cherokee Indian ball, similar to lacrosse but much older. A purification rite formerly lasted the entire night before the game.

In and about the reservation the swarthy, impassive, solemn-visaged Indians go about their everyday pursuits. They have for the most part adopted modern attire, though the tribal dress is used on festive occasions. Many of the older women still wear voluminous gathered skirts and the red bandanna head covering and carry their children in slings on their backs.

As a result of the participation of 317 young Cherokees (of whom 18 were killed) in World War II, new ideas leading to a desire for a higher plane of living began to infiltrate the settlement. A need for additional jobs and income gave impetus to the fulfilling of a dream that had been in the minds of many Cherokee as well as their neighbors—the presentation of an outdoor drama depicting some of the history of the Cherokee people. Fostered by the Western North Carolina Associated Communities and sponsored by the Cherokee Historical Association, the Cherokee people with their white neighbors, and with the aid of Samuel Selden of the Carolina Playmakers, began in 1950 producing *Unto These Hills, A Drama of the Cherokee Indians*. Written by Kermit Hunter and produced under the direction of Harry Davis of Chapel Hill, it is presented at the MOUNTAINSIDE THEATRE (*6 nights weekly, last of June-Labor Day*).

The climax of the drama centers in the traditional story of the Indian Tsali (Old Charley). During the removal in 1838, Tsali, his wife, sons, and kinsmen, were being hurried along the "Trail of Tears" by Gen. Winfield Scott's soldiers. Tsali's feeble wife, unable to travel fast, was prodded by a soldier with his bayonet. Exasperated beyond endurance, Tsali urged his kinsmen to strike down the soldiers and escape; one soldier was killed and the others fled. Meanwhile hundreds of Indians were escaping from the stockades and from the westward march. The task of capturing the fugitives had become so difficult that Gen. Scott decided to use the Tsali incident as an opportunity for a compromise. Col. Thomas persuaded Tsali, his brother, and three sons to surrender on condition that the other fugitives be permitted to remain. The youngest son, Wasituna (Washington), was spared, because of his youth. Friendly white settlers fed and sheltered this band of a thousand who would not leave their mountain homeland. As the drama ends and the lights come on the audience sees the sequel all around, for Cherokee form most of the cast and staff of this record-breaking production.

In the MUSEUM OF THE CHEROKEE INDIAN (*open the year around; small admission fee*) is a collection of the tribe's early handicraft, artifacts, and historical material said to be the best outside of the Smithsonian. At OCONALUFTEE INDIAN VILLAGE (*open May 1-through Oct.; $1 admission*) a recreated Cherokee community of 200 years ago, modern Cherokees in traditional dress demonstrate their ancient crafts and household arts. Indian lecturers guide visitors through the village.

The OCONALUFTEE RIVER BRIDGE, 0.1 m., is at the junction with US 441. Right on US 441, now the route, the road follows the rock-laden Oconaluftee River (R). Beneath the BOUNDARY TREE (L), 1.6 m., also called the Old Line Tree, on the line dividing the Qualla Indian Boundary from the Great Smoky Mountains National Park, is a concrete pillar marked QIB. A giant poplar bears the date July 9, 1795. It was a corner of one of the grants deeded to Felix Walker of "bunkum" fame (*see* ASHEVILLE), when this was a part of Buncombe County. This tree marked the Meigs and Freeman Line, surveyed in 1819 between the Cherokee and whites.

GREAT SMOKY MOUNTAINS NATIONAL PARK, the most popular in the nation, includes the most massive mountain uplift in the East and one of the oldest land areas in the world. With an area of 508,466 acres, divided almost equally between North Carolina and Tennessee, it is one of the largest remnants of the American wilderness. The Great Smoky Mountains run the entire length of the park. The name comes from the blue haze, sometimes as dense as smoke, which almost always hangs over the mountain peaks, 16 of which are over 6,000 feet. The area is noted for its diversity of flora and fauna and contains large stands of virgin hardwood timber (*see* NATURAL SETTING).

Within the park the route continues to follow the Oconaluftee through a peaceful countryside where dwellings are far apart. Saplings, transplanted rhododendron, and shrubbery bordering the highway, as well as the absence of signboards and unsightly shacks, are evidences of the National Park Service's improvements.

At 3.8 m. is the OCONALUFTEE RANGER STATION and the PIONEER MUSEUM, where may be seen pioneer artifacts covering nearly two centuries of life in the Southern Highlands. In the meadow at the rear is a pioneer farmstead of several authentic buildings typical of the early settlers.

At **4 m.**, across the river (R), is RAVENSFORD (2,037 alt.), on Raven Fork. Here, before the park took over its lands, a lumber company maintained a village, with church, school, stores, and railroad.

Right from Ravensford on a dirt road is BIG COVE, **3 m.**, an Indian settlement that has retained more Indian atmosphere and a stronger tribal solidarity than any of the other Indian reservation towns. The Cherokee, who live in simple wooden houses, have preserved their ancient folklore, songs, and legends, and occasionally still dance the Dance of Friendship, the Beaver Dance, and the Dance of Thanksgiving for abundant crops. Here is a Log School House, built by Quakers in 1880; it has been remodeled and is now used for Cherokee children.

Near the confluence of Mingus Creek and the Oconaluftee, **4.5 m.**, stood a log house in which, local tradition says, Nancy Hanks, mother of Abraham Lincoln, lived, and in which Lincoln was born. The story, if true, would make Lincoln a North Carolinian.

At the confluence of the creek is the John Mingus House (R) sometimes called the Floyd Place, perhaps the most pretentious dwelling ever built in what is now the Park. Built in 1877 for Dr. John Mingus and his bachelor son, it has been earmarked for preservation as an historical relic of the people who occupied the land prior to the coming of the Park.

At **5.3 m.** is Couch's Creek Picnic Ground (*benches, tables, and a spring*) and at **6.9 m.** is SMOKEMONT CAMPGROUND, across the bridge and up the river, which is the only modern campground on this route this side of the Tennessee line.

SMOKEMONT, **6.9 m.** (2,188 alt., 125 pop.), was one of the Smokies' frontier communities before the coming of the Park. Trails from here lead to Thomas Ridge, Hughes Ridge, and Richland Mountain.

At Smokemont the route begins an ascent along the side of Thomas Ridge, named for Col. William Holland Thomas (*see above*). At THREE FORKS, **10 m.**, is the confluence of Kanati Fork, Kephart Prong, and Beech Flats Prong, forming the Oconaluftee River; the highway follows Beech Flats Prong.

From NEWFOUND GAP (*parking space*), **18 m.** (5,048 alt.), on the Tennessee Line, the impressive panorama includes the Balsam Mountains in the east; Mt. Le Conte (6,593 alt.) in the north; on the west Mt. Collins (6,188 alt.), and the bulk of Clingmans Dome. Near the parking area at the Gap is a stone terrace with a plaque in memory of Laura Spelman Rockefeller, whose son, John D. Rockefeller, Jr., matched dollar for dollar all donations and public funds raised to buy the land for the Park. Here Pres. Franklin D. Roosevelt dedicated the Park in 1940 "to the free people of America." At Newfound Gap is the junction with the Appalachian Trail and the Skyway.

1. The Skyway, running west from Newfound Gap to Clingmans Dome, is more than a mile high at all points, with easy grades and rounded curves, and is regarded as a masterpiece of engineering.

Left on the Skyway on the Tennessee side through a forest of balsam, hemlock, spruce, and rhododendron. At **0.3 m.** the drive crosses to North Carolina and passes around the shoulder of MT. MINGUS, **1.2 m.** (5,800 alt.). The State Line is touched again at INDIAN GAP, **1.7 m.**, which, until a road was built through Newfound Gap, had been the principal pass of the Smoky Range. Through this gap passed the Tuckaleechee and Southeastern Trail, important in war and commerce since it connected the Overhill (Tennessee) and the South Carolina settlements of the Cherokee Nation. Tradition is that De Soto and his band crossed Indian Gap in 1540. Col. William H. Thomas attempted to build a road through the gap during the Civil War but abandoned the effort. In 1864, when Gen. Robert B. Vance moved his artillery, the dismounted cannon were dragged over the bare stones of this precipitous course.

Near the head of Deep Creek, left of the gap, is the region in which, according to Cherokee legend, Ataga'Hi (Ind. *the gull place*), the Enchanted Lake, lies. A hunter coming near would know it by the sound of many wings but he would not behold the lake unless his spiritual vision were sharpened by prayer. In its purple waters bloom waterlilies and here the wounded birds and animals come to be healed.

From Indian Gap (R) is a view of The Chimneys. MT. COLLINS, **4 m.** (6,188 alt.), named by Arnold Guyot for Robert Collins, one of the first settlers on Oconaluftee, gives views on the North Carolina side.

From the FORNEY RIDGE PARKING AREA, **7.6 m.**, where Forney Ridge joins Clingmans Dome, a chain of mountains is visible in three directions with the steep final rise of Clingmans tree-clad peak to the north.

Right from this point on a paved trail to the SUMMIT OF CLINGMANS DOME (6,642 alt.), **0.3 m.**, loftiest peak in the Smoky Mountains National Park. An observation tower gives wide views in all directions. The mountain was known to the Indians as Ku wa' hi (Ind. *mulberry place*). Under this and three nearby mountains the bears were said to have their "town houses." Cherokee mythology ascribes to each kind of animal a giant progenitor. The Great White Bear was chief and doctor. The bears, believed to be really human and able to talk when they wished, met on Mulberry Place to dance and converse before going to sleep for the winter. Early white settlers called Clingmans Dome "Smoky Dome." It is named for Gen. Thomas Lanier Clingman (1812-97), Confederate general, U. S. Senator, and explorer (*see* ASHEVILLE).

2. Right from Newfound Gap on the Appalachian Trail (*4-foot, graded for horses*) to MT. KEPHART, **2.1 m.** (6,200 alt.), named in honor of Horace Kephart (*see* TOUR 22). In this region the trail traverses part of the area that was until recently the wildest, least-known section of the Smokies. At **4.1 m.** is CHARLIES BUNION (5,375 alt.), so burned during logging operations that the soil washed off. It was named because Charlie Conner, a guide, described it as about the size of "this bunion on my foot."

The cow herder of the Smokies has vanished. In the late 1920's he and his dog still patrolled the main divide and the leads, tending the herds of small Black Poll, a type of cattle which thrives on the slopes. Nipping heels, barking at heads, and running from side to side, the dog obeyed the instructions of the master's gesture or voice, needing only an occasional "pull of his years" for correction.

The herders' cabins, 5 or 6 miles apart along the ridge, were used in winter by bear hunters. The Tennesseeans stalked their bears. The Carolinians used Plott hounds, a mixture of the hound, which chased, and the Mississippi bear dog, which fought. Sometimes it took several days to drive out the bears. Division of meat was made by "selling out"; to insure impartial distribution, one man behind a tree called the name of one of the party as a piece of meat was held up, out of his sight.

At 31 m. is the junction with Tenn. 73 now the route (2 miles SW. of GATLINBURG) (1,550 alt., 1,301 pop.) where the Park Headquarters is located. Left on Tenn. 73 is MARYVILLE, TENN., **69 m.** (7,742 pop.), at the junction with US 129, now the route.

Left on US 129 is DEALS GAP, **106 m.** (1,957 alt.), on the Tennessee-North Carolina boundary and at the western extremity of the Great Smoky Mountains National Park. At Deals Gap is the junction with the Appalachian Trail.

Left on the Appalachian Trail (*4-foot, graded*) to GREGORY BALD, **6.6 m.** (4,948 alt.), with views of Parsons Bald to the west, Yellow Creek Mountains and Cheoah Bald to the south, and Rye Patch on Long Hungry Ridge to the east. The Cherokee called Gregory Bald Tsistuyi (Ind. *the rabbit place*). Here rabbits had their "town houses" and here lived their chief, the Great Rabbit, large as a deer.

Little River, rising on the Tennessee side under this range, is the locale of another Indian legend. High up in a mountain gap lived an ogress whose food was human livers. Once she destroyed an entire encampment on Little River and scattered the bones of her victims over the gap. The Indians never smiled after this. The women, however, taught their children to pray for protection. After the ogress had carried off the daughter of Chief White Feather, monster and child were found, the ogress transformed into gentleness through the prayers of the child. She returned the little girl to her father and shortly thereafter disappeared forever.

At **106.5 m.** is the junction with NC 28 (*see below*) which leads to FONTANA VILLAGE, **9 m.**, and to the DAM and LAKE, **12 m.** (*see below*).

On US 129 at **107 m.** is LAKE CHEOAH, created by the Aluminum Co. of America by damming the northward-flowing Little Tennessee River. The road follows the lake shore to the dam, **119.1 m.** A lighted concrete walkway leads (L) across the dam to the POWER PLANT (*open*).

At **109.8 m.** a bridge crosses the Little Tennessee River, which joins the Cheoah River below the dam.

TAPOCO LODGE, **110.3 m.** (1,210 alt.), is a year-around tourist hotel (*all accommodations*) owned by the Carolina Aluminum Co. The main building was built in 1930 for unmarried employees operating the Cheoah Hydroelectric Plant. Cottages are also operated by the lodge.

South of Tapoco Lodge, US 129 climbs the gorge of the Cheoah River, which falls rapidly over a rock-strewn bed and winds through wild and primitive country.

At **116.2 m.** is visible, overhead across the road, the large pipe-line that conveys water from Lake Santeetlah (Ind. *blue waters*) to Lake Cheoah as a part of the power development.

Between 119.4 m. and 129.5 m. the route follows the irregular shore line of LAKE SANTEETLAH (*small-mouthed bass and bream fishing; boats and guides available*) which has an area of 3,000 acres. Fishing camps and tourist cabins dot its shores. The tree-clad Snowbird Mountains rise from its western edge. Land west of the lake is in the Nantahala National Forest.

At 129.7 m. is the junction with a Forest Service Rd.

Right on this road to the JOYCE KILMER MEMORIAL FOREST; enter near the junction of Big and Little Santeetlah Creeks, then follow an old wagon road to a cleared parking space and picnic area, 14 m.; thence on a foot trail 0.5 m. over a mountain rise into the heart of BIG POPLAR COVE. Here is a granite boulder with a bronze plaque inscribed to Joyce Kilmer, author of the poem, *Trees*. It was dedicated on the 18th anniversary of his death, July 30, 1936.

This 3,800-acre tract, at a point where the Snowbird, Cheoah, and Unicoi Ranges converge, is in the Nantahala National Forest (*see* NATIONAL FORESTS) and is a part of a 38,000-acre area for maintenance as a primitive wilderness and wildlife sanctuary. Its virgin forest includes poplar, hemlock, and oak, one of the finest stands of its type in America. Some of the giant tulip-poplars are 125 feet high and 20 feet in circumference. Bears, deer, and wild boars are so numerous that the U.S. Forest Service allows them to be hunted annually. The boars are descended from Prussian and African wild boars that escaped from a private hunting estate established nearby in 1910.

ROBBINSVILLE, 130 m. (2,150 alt., 515 pop.), seat of Graham County, is a little mountain village at the crossroads around the stone courthouse which is nearer to the capitals of 6 other States than to its own.

A hotel, facing on this square, appears to be a one-story structure; but, being built on the side of the mountain, its first floor in front becomes the third floor in the rear. Snowbird Indians, Cherokee who live in the Snowbird Mountains, use Robbinsville as a shopping place and are often on the streets.

On a hill overlooking the village is the marked GRAVE OF CHIEF TSUNU'LA-HOSJI (JUNALUSKA) and his wife. At the Battle of Horseshoe Bend, Mar. 29, 1814, between Creeks and Federal troops, Junaluska and his Cherokees served valiantly the forces of Andrew Jackson in the Creek War. A grateful legislature made him a citizen and gave him land in the Cherokee country. A ridge west of Waynesville and a lake and the surrounding grounds are named for him (*see* TOUR 22). Junaluska died in 1858 when almost 100 years old.

Lumbering is the principal activity of this region, though fishing and hunting attract many sportsmen. A large band mill manufactures lumber. About one-sixth of the county is fenced and cultivated; the remainder is open range. Cattle, sheep, and hogs are pastured on this free range and signs warn motorists to watch out for cattle.

Southeast of Robbinsville US 129 traverses a high plateau dotted with farms. At 140 m. it passes through TULULA GAP (2,950 alt.), to POINT LOOKOUT. Here a stone lookout point offers a bird's-eye view of the Nantahala Gorge, with the river, the railroad, and the highway winding along its length far below. On the opposite wall of the gorge can be seen the mountain road known as "The Winding Stairs." High on the opposite wall of the Gorge are the surge tank and penstock of the Nantahala power house of the Nantahala Power & Light Co. Water comes through a tunnel in solid rock from Nantahala Lake.

At **142 m.** in RED MARBLE GAP (2,750 alt.) is TOPTON (2,599 alt., 225 pop.), where US 129 crosses a bridge over the Southern Ry. Topton is at the junction with US 19 (*see* TOUR 22).

TOUR 23 *(US 23-19A)*

Lake Junaluska—Waynesville—Sylva—Franklin—(Clayton, Ga.); US 23—
19A, 23.
Lake Junaluska—Georgia Line, **63 m.**

This route penetrates the heart of the Nantahala National Forest, crossing
the wooded mountain ranges of the Balsam Mountains, in a section known
for its trout streams, minerals, precious stones, wild and rugged scenery, and
beautiful waterfalls.

US 23-19A leaves US 19 at Lake Junaluska, **0 m.**, and continues in a
southwestern direction.

WAYNESVILLE, **4 m.** (2,644 alt., 5,295 pop.), named for "Mad
Anthony" Wayne, the Revolutionary general, is the seat of Haywood
County, and a vacation and health resort. The town is surrounded by the
5,000- to 6,000-foot peaks of the Balsam Mountains. Col. Robert Love
gave the land for the public square, courthouse, jail, cemetery, and several
churches. The region was settled by officers and soldiers who had received
land grants in the years following the Revolution. The county was named
for John Haywood, State Treasurer (1787-1827) (*see* RALEIGH).

The HAYWOOD COUNTY COURTHOUSE (R) is a modern stone building
erected in 1932. On the grounds is a granite boulder with a plaque memorializing the 10 Revolutionary soldiers buried in the county and another
plaque dedicated to Confederate soldiers.

On the property of the old SULPHUR SPRINGS HOTEL (1886) is a marker
claiming that this is the site where the last shot on land in the Civil War
was fired May 10, 1865, by Robert P. Conley, though histories mention
May 13 as the date and Brownsville, Tex., as the locale.

Waynesville is at the junction with US 276.

Left from Waynesville on US 276, called Pigeon Loop Rd., through rolling
country where apple orchards border the road. From DAVIS (*PIGEON*) GAP,
4 m., is a view of Mount Pisgah, about 15 miles southeast.

At WOODROW, 7 m. (20 pop.), the East and West Forks of the Pigeon River converge.

At WAGON ROAD GAP, 24 m., US 276 unites with the Pisgah Motor Rd. on the proposed Blue Ridge Parkway (*see* TOUR 22*A*).

1. Right on this road to BETHEL HIGH SCHOOL, 11 m., at the junction with the West Fork Rd. is BEECH NUT GAP. The road passes LAKE LOGAN, reservoir of the Champion Paper Co. Using the Beech Nut to Wagon Rd. Gap section of the Parkway which is to open in the summer of 1955, a loop tour may be made back to Woodrow.

Southwest of Waynesville US 19 makes a long upward climb through some of the region's largest apple orchards.

HAZELWOOD, 6 m. (1,769 pop.), separately incorporated, embraces most of the industrial plants of Waynesville: furniture, rubber, shoes, tanning, lumber, and fertilizer. The golf course and a new residential section is on the left.

The MORRISON STATE FISH HATCHERY (*open*), 12.2 m. (R), propagates trout.

At BALSAM GAP, 13 m. (3,315 alt., 308 pop.), the Southern Ry.'s station is the highest point of any standard-gage railway east of the Mississippi River. Four-unit Diesels now easily negotiate this grade, whereas the old steam-powered locomotives generally required a "pusher" locomotive. At this spot the prehistoric river, Appalachia, is supposed to have come through.

Between Balsam Gap and the Georgia Line US 19 runs within the boundaries of the NANTAHALA NATIONAL FOREST (*see* NATIONAL FORESTS) which contains much privately owned land.

Southwest of Balsam Gap the highway parallels the Tuckasegee River. At one place the railway tracks tunnel through the mountain under the road and at another the road dips down under a railway trestle. On the right is the Plott Balsam Range.

At MAPLE SPRINGS, 22 m., is a marker where the Meigs-Freeman Line, surveyed in 1802, served until 1819 as the treaty boundary between the white settlements and the Cherokee Nation.

SYLVA, 25 m. (2,047 alt., 1,382 pop.), became the seat of Jackson County in 1913. The town is named for William Sylva, a native of Denmark and an early settler who entered newspaper work here. The county was named for Pres. Andrew Jackson. Sylva is near three peaks more than 6,000 feet high. Overlooking the business section on an elevation at the head of the street is the red brick JACKSON COUNTY COURTHOUSE. Sylva has three important industrial plants: the Mead (paper) Corp., the Armour Leather Co., and the Skyline Textile Co.

About three miles E. stands the DAN BRYSON HOME, which served as the original county courthouse.

Sylva is at the junction with NC 107 (*see* TOUR 23A).

DILLSBORO, 27 m. (1,985 alt., 198 pop.), is the headquarters of mining and distributing interests. The famous JARRETT SPRINGS HOTEL (now the Jarrett House) still operates in the original building dating back in the past century.

At Dillsboro US 19A leaves US 23. US 441, from Cherokee, joins US 23 and turns L. to cross the Tuckasegee River.

Right on US 19A-441 to WILMOT, 8 m. (1,865 alt., 45 pop.). At the end of a little valley just beyond is the only view of the Smokies from this route east to Bryson City. Clingmans Dome (L) is the rounded highest mountain in the center of the group on the distant skyline.

At 9 m. US 441 leaves US 19A and leads (R) to Cherokee, 5 m. and US 19 (*see* TOURS 22 *and* 22C).

Near the site of WHITTIER, 11 m. (1,839 alt., 287 pop.), on the Tuckasegee River was the settlement, Stikayi or Stecoe. It was the first of the Tuckasegee and Oconalufti Indian towns destroyed by Col. William Moore in Nov., 1776. Moore was in command of 100 mounted men sent on special expedition by Gen. Rutherford. Rutherford with his main army had crossed the Cowees and destroyed the settlements on the Little Tennessee River in Aug. and Sept. previous. Although the Cherokee had abandoned Stecoe, the soldiers burned the town and cut the standing corn.

Stecoe is better known as the Thomas farm since it was the site chosen for his home by Col. W. H. Thomas, white leader and friend of the Eastern Band of the Cherokee, to whom they owe their existence as a tribal unit (*see* TOUR 22C).

At 13 m. US 19A rejoins US 19, 1 mile E. of Ela (*see* TOUR 22).

At Dillsboro US 23 is joined by US 441, going south.

South of Dillsboro, US 23-441 crosses the Tuckasegee River and strikes boldly across the hills toward Savannah Creek, which it ascends. Paralleling Savannah Creek, the road traverses farm country and then begins to wind and climb up the slopes of the tree-covered COWEE MOUNTAINS, rising close from the road on the R. and falling sheer to the valley on the L.

WATAUGA GAP, 38.3 m. (3,280 alt.), is in the COWEE RANGE, the water divide between the Little Tennessee and Tuckasegee Rivers.

At 45.3 m. is the junction with a dirt side road.

Right on this road to LAKE EMORY (*swimming, fishing, boating*), 0.6 m., formed by damming the Little Tennessee River for electric power.

At 47.2 m. is the eastern junction with US 64 (*see* TOUR 13C).

West of the junction the highway crosses the Little Tennessee River, which rises in Georgia and flows northward. Muskellunge, game fish seldom found south of the Great Lakes, here sometimes attain a length of 5 feet and a weight of 50 pounds.

On a rise at **47.3 m.** is an INDIAN MOUND (R) in the form of a truncated cone, the largest in North Carolina. A Cherokee house that once stood on this mound was part of the Cherokee town of Nikwasi. The Indians believed that it was the home of Nunnehi (*Immortals*), and that a perpetual fire burned within. Here a British agent held council with the Cherokee in 1730.

FRANKLIN, **48 m.** (*see* TOUR *13c*).

At **48.1 m.** US 64 turns W. continuing to San Diego (*see* TOUR *13, sec. c*).

South of Franklin US 23 parallels the course of the Little Tennessee River to the Georgia Line.

The route crosses Cartoogechaye (Ind., *the village beyond*) Creek at **50.1 m.**, so named because it empties into the Little Tennessee just beyond the old Indian village of Naguessa.

At **58 m.** on Coweeta Creek is the COWEETA HYDROLOGICAL LABORATORY, a 5,600-acre field laboratory devoted to intensive water resource management research. The study is designed to solve the problem of how to use the land and still maintain a reasonable equilibrium between deterioration processes and rehabilitation processes.

The route crosses Commissioner Creek at **62.5 m.** and reaches the Georgia Line at **63 m.**, 9 miles north of Clayton, Ga.

TOUR 23A (NC 107)

Sylva—Cullowhee—Tuckasegee—Cashiers; NC 107. **34 m.**

This route follows the gorge of the rocky and swift-flowing Tuckasegee River whose sides are lined with luxuriant forests, thick with rhododendron and azalea.

NC 107 branches south from its junction with US 19, **0 m.** in Sylva (*see* TOUR 23).

At **2.2 m.** is the junction with NC 116.

Right on NC 116 is WEBSTER, **2 m.** (2,203 alt., 142 pop.), built on an Indian mound from which relics have been taken. Webster was the county seat of Jackson County until it was replaced by Sylva in 1913. The old courthouse was torn down in 1938.

South of the junction with NC 116 is a thickly settled farming country.

At CULLOWHEE (Cherokee: Gualiyi or Callaugh-ee, *place of the spring salad*), **7 m.** (2,066 alt., 1,100 pop.) is WESTERN CAROLINA COLLEGE, founded in 1889 by Robert Lee Madison. The oldest of the three white teachers colleges in the State, it has just completed a vast building program costing approximately $3,500,000. With teacher training as its first aim, it serves the vocational needs of the area, with courses in business, home economics, forestry, and pre-professional study. Its LIBRARY and SCIENCE BUILD-ING are examples of modern functional architecture. On its campus is the old Indian mound that was opened in the latter half of the 19th century by the Valentine brothers, who removed the artifacts to their museum in Richmond, Va. Dean W. E. Bird of the College has the original account of Chief Yonaguska's trance causing him to urge all the Cherokee to renounce the use of intoxicants. This document, dictated to Col. Wm. H. Thomas by the Chief's brother, is now in the Great Smoky Mountains National Park Museum. Near the College campus, on the Speedwell road, is the old ST. DAVID'S EPISCOPAL CHURCH (no longer used for worship) and the SITE OF THE HOME OF ADAM CORN, built in 1820. Corn was an early Baptist preacher of Western North Carolina.

EAST LAPORTE, **10 m.** (2,186 alt., 200 pop.), is a pulpwood concentration point, the location of an abandoned sawmill and lumber village, the lumber industry having closed operations about 1945.

Left from East LaPorte on the dirt Caney Ford Rd. to the MILAS PARKER FARM (*visitors welcome*), **3 m.** Just off the road (L) on the farm is the JUTACULLA ROCK, whose soft sandstone is covered with mysterious tracings that have never been interpreted. Cherokee legend relates that the marks were made by a mythical giant, Tsul'kula, in leaping from his home on the mountaintop to the creek below.

At **12 m.** on NC 107 is TUCKASEGEE (2,184 alt., 55 pop.).

1. Right from Tuckasegee on an old logging trail is the SMOKE HOLE, **3.5 m.**, where passersby often warm their hands in the vapor which arises when the temperature is low. The Cherokee explain this as the smoke from the town house of the Nunnehi, immortals who dwell beneath the mountains and the rivers.

2. Left from Tuckasegee on NC 281, called the Canada Rd., is ANVIL TONGUE, **6 m.**, a great rock hanging over the Canada Prong of the Tuckasegee River. Right **0.2 m.** on a dirt road to a NATURAL ROCK BRIDGE spanning the prong and WOLF CREEK FALLS. On this prong are several power dams forming three lakes of the Nantahala Power and Light Company. NC 281 crosses the Appalachian Divide and joins US 64 near Lake Toxaway, **29 m.**

South of Tuckasegee NC 107 passes through wild country where the mountains overhang the river, houses perch on the hillsides, and bridges span the ravines in many places.

At GRASSY CREEK FALLS (R), **16.5 m.**, the creek waters spill over a cliff into the river. Here many visitors drive in warm weather to enjoy the scenery.

At **20 m.** is the power house, penstock, and surge tank of the Nantahala Power and Light Co.'s THORPE DAM. It is said to have the highest head (about 1,250 feet) of any power development east of the Mississippi. The water flows about three miles through a tunnel in the mountain rock from Lake Thorpe.

HIGH FALLS GAP (R), **20.5 m.**, is a cleared space at the top of a hill.

Right on a foot trail down the steep mountainside to a fork; L. here to another fork; L. to a point at **1.5 m.**, from which, across the ravine, are visible the HIGH FALLS OF THE TUCKASEGEE. The water plunges 60 feet in a single downpour, then is broken by a projecting ledge into twin sheets falling 25 feet.

NC 107 leads away from the Tuckasegee River ascending SHOAL CREEK. R. is the high dam of beautiful LAKE THORPE.

Southeast of GLENVILLE, **24.5 m.** (3,250 alt., 500 pop.), center of the Hamburg cabbage district, the highway skirts Lake Thorpe (*trout, bass; parking, camp space; rental boats*). The route then crosses the "long top" of the Blue Ridge or Appalachian Divide at a gap said to have a spring flowing into both the Atlantic and the Gulf of Mexico.

A swift highway descent, with a view south to WHITESIDE MOUNTAIN leads to CASHIERS, **34 m.** and the junction with US 64 (*see* TOUR *13, sec. c*).

TOUR 24 *(US 70-25, 25)*

(Newport, Tenn.)— Marshall — Asheville — Hendersonville —(Greenville, S. C.); US 70-25, 25.
Tennessee Line—South Carolina Line, **83.5 m.**

Section a. TENNESSEE LINE *to* ASHEVILLE; **50 m.** US 70-25

This route is the principal approach from the Middle West to the Asheville area of western North Carolina.

US 70-25 crosses the Tennessee-North Carolina Line, **0 m.**, 19 miles east of Newport, Tenn., and shares with the Southern Ry. the course of the picturesque French Broad River. The route was originally a trail from the settlements in what is now Tennessee to South Carolina, along which "drovers" herded their horses, cattle, pigs, and poultry to markets in South Carolina and Georgia. Some of the feeding stands along the trail later became towns or settlements.

At **0.2 m.** is the junction with a county road.

Left on this road to PAINT ROCK, **3 m.** (1,265 alt., 150 pop.), named for a sheer 100-foot cliff overlooking the French Broad River. The red stains on the surface of the rock are caused by oxidation of iron. The 1799 boundary commission, composed of Gen. Joseph McDowell, Col. David Vance, and Maj. Mussendine Mathews, surveying the North Carolina-Tennessee Line, reported that the stains resembled the figures of "some humans, wild beasts, etc." A legend says that two Indian lovers from different tribes, forbidden to marry, cast themselves from the top and stained the rock with their blood.
Near Paint Rock, in 1855, John D. Hyman, editor of the *Spectator,* and Dr. W. L. Hilliard, postmaster, both of Asheville, fought a bloodless duel after Hyman had criticized the mail service. When one round of fire with rifles was exchanged a button was clipped from Hilliard's coat.

East of the junction with the road to Paint Rock the highway twists and turns to follow the contour of the mountainsides or to find passage through gaps in the ridges. The Southern Ry. tracks along the riverbank follow the easiest course between Newport and Asheville.

HOT SPRINGS, 7 m. (1,332 alt., 721 pop.), formerly known as Warm Springs, was a famous resort until the 1920's. The curative properties of its waters, valued by the Indians and discovered by Henry Reynolds and Thomas Morgan in 1778, attracted invalids in spite of the dangerous road. Bishop Francis Asbury, writing in 1800, described some of the hazards:

"After we had crossed the Small and Great Paint Mountain, and had passed about 30 yards beyond the Paint Rock, my roan horse led by Mr. O'Haven reeled and fell over, taking the chaise with him; I was called back, when I beheld the poor beast and the carriage, bottom up, lodged and wedged against a sapling, which alone prevented them both being precipitated into the river."

Of their departure two days later the bishop wrote:

"We crossed the ferry curiously contrived with a rope and pole for half a mile along the banks of the river, to guide the boat by. And O the rocks!"

This road, long called the Old Love Road, is still in existence but little used. The Buncombe Turnpike from Saluda Gap through Asheville to Warm Springs was completed in 1828 and brought a stream of travel into western North Carolina from the south.

Zebulon Baird Vance, later (1862 and 1877) Governor of North Carolina (see ASHEVILLE), was once a clerk in the Patton Hotel, an imposing building with 13 white pillars to represent the Thirteen Original Colonies. After it burned in 1884, Col. J. H. Rumbough built the Mountain Park Hotel, destroyed by fire in the 1920's. In one of its booklets the management stated:

"Here flow the new-born crystal, untainted waters, and here, far down in the mysterious laboratories of Nature, are found the minerals which impart to these waters the life-giving virtues that bring the bloom back to the cheek, the lustre to the eye, tone to the languid pulse, strength to the jaded nerves, and vigor to the wasted frame."

The springs are on an estate once the property of Mrs. Bessie M. Safford (1858-1930), daughter of Col. Rumbough, and daughter-in-law of Andrew Johnson, 17th President of the United States.

In 1917-18 a camp for 2,700 interned German sailors and officers was operated on a part of the estate.

In the center of town is the campus of the DORLAND BELL SCHOOL FOR GIRLS, the first and last of 19 schools in Madison County, once operated by the Presbyterian Church in the U.S.A. The school, founded in 1887 by Dr. and Mrs. Luke Dorland, was later combined with the Bell School of Walnut and was known as the Dorland Bell School until it closed a few years ago.

In Hot Springs the GOODALL-SANFORD Co. began operating a textile plant in 1954.

1. Left from Hot Springs on the Appalachian Trail to RICH MOUNTAIN, 4.8 m. (3,643 alt.), where a forest fire tower gives views in all directions.

2. Right from Hot Springs on the Appalachian Trail to LOOKOUT POINT, **1.5 m.**, with a view of the French Broad River gorge (R). At GOVENFLOW GAP, **6.6 m.** (2,450 alt.), are wide mountain views.

3. Left from US 70-25 on a Forest Service road to SILVERMINE CAMPGROUND (*camping, water, fireplaces, sanitary equipment*), **0.2 m.**, maintained by the U. S. Forest Service.

South of Hot Springs the route crosses the French Broad River and begins a long mountain ascent, running for several miles through the French Broad Division of Pisgah National Forest (*see* NATIONAL FORESTS).

Good roads, automobiles, and radio and television have brought "civilization" to much of the mountain country; but in the isolated *hollers* change comes slowly and through the young people. Many highlanders still live in cabins built a hundred years ago. They plant crops, make soap, and cure ills by the same methods their ancestors used. The mountaineer kills his hogs and splits his rails when the moon is "right," and he plants some potatoes on Good Friday, even if he must dig in the mud to do so.

The older generation may have little formal education, but they have a great store of learning handed down by word of mouth. Through them are preserved many old English and Scotch ballads and dances. Even their language, quaint to lowlanders, is an Anglo-Saxon survival. Like Chaucer, the mountaineer often says *hit* for it. Like Shakespeare he calls a bag a *poke* and green garden stuff *sallet*.

At **12.8 m.** is the junction with NC 208 (*see* TOUR 24A).

Near the top of a mountain grade US 70-25 passes the village of WALNUT, **17 m.** (2,000 alt., 550 pop.). Formerly known as Jewel Hill or Duel Hill, the village was the seat of Madison County from 1851 until 1855.

MARSHALL, **28 m.** (1,650 alt., 983 pop.), named for Chief Justice John Marshall, has been since 1855 the seat of Madison County, formed in 1851 and named for James Madison. The town, built in the wooded gorge of the French Broad River, is said to be "one mile long, one street wide, and sky high." Legend says that here the first pegged shoes were made because cobblers, unable to stretch their thread to arm's length, could not make sewn soles. Many houses are on the mountain towering above the town; others seem to cling to the sides of sheer cliffs.

Since there was no other suitable place the high school was built on BLENNERHASSET ISLAND, which is sometimes flooded by high water. The island is believed to have been named for Blennerhasset Island in the Ohio River, opposite Marietta, which figured in the ill-fated ambitions of Aaron Burr.

Marshall is the shopping center for the county. Almost entirely rural, it produces more burley tobacco than any other county in the State.

South of Marshall the highway, cut from an overhanging rock, follows the east bank of the French Broad. ALEXANDER INN, of stagecoach days, stands on the east bank, north of the river bridge. At **42 m.** the route turns sharply (L) away from the river. At **44 m.** is the junction with US 19-23 (*see* TOUR 22), which unites with US 70-25 between this point and Asheville.

LAKE VIEW PARK, **45 m.**, is a residential subdivision around artificial BEAVER LAKE (R).

ASHEVILLE, **50 m.** (*see* ASHEVILLE).

Points of Interest: Biltmore House, Civic Center, Sondley Library, Grove Park Inn, Sunset Mountain, Thomas Wolfe Home, and others.

Asheville is at the junction with US 19-23 (*see* TOUR 22), US 74 (*see* TOUR *16, sec. c*), and US 70 (*see* TOUR *15*).

Section b. ASHEVILLE *to* SOUTH CAROLINA LINE; **33.5 m.** US 25

The route, following the old Buncombe Turnpike, crosses the Blue Ridge, but the grade is so gentle and the ridge so low that the crossing is barely noticeable.

From Pack Square in ASHEVILLE, **0 m.**, US 25 runs south across the Swannanoa River into the suburban village of BILTMORE, **2 m.** (*see* ASHE-VILLE).

At **6.2 m.** is the junction with a road.

Left on this road is the INTERNATIONAL RESISTANCE CO. PLANT, **1 m.**, and the ASHEVILLE-HENDERSON AIRPORT, **3.7 m.**

At SKYLAND, **7 m.**, is the junction with NC 280.

NC 280 leads to right, past the French Broad River and Forest Amphitheatre to BREVARD, **27 m.** (*see* TOUR *13C*).

Surrounding ARDEN, **9.7 m.** (2,225 alt., 300 pop.), is a region of old estates not visible from the highway.

At **10 m.** is the junction with the sand-clay Fanning Rd.

Right on this road to RUGBY GRANGE (*private*), **1.7 m.**, onetime home of George Westfeldt, Swedish diplomat, who bought the property from "Tiger Bill" Haywood of Charleston, S. C., shortly after the Civil War and named it for Rugby School in England. Solidly built of local stone with galleries on all sides, the house crowns a knoll above Cane Creek Valley.

Here the poet Sidney Lanier, a few weeks before his death in 1881, gave his last piano recital. Lanier, speaking of his host, during the last week or two of his life, said: "All my life I have searched for the father of my soul, but never have I found him until now, when I greet him in the person of George Gustav Westfeldt.

"Send him my Sunrise (his last poem) that he may know how eternally we are one in thought."

At **2.5 m.** is BUCK SHOALS (*private*), built in 1891, once home of the humorist Bill Nye. This turreted wooden house overlooks the valley of the French Broad River. While living in a cottage at Skyland, Nye made the observation: "George Vanderbilt's extensive grounds command a fine view of my place." Nye is buried in Calvary Churchyard.

At **10.4 m.** is the junction with a gravel road.

Left on this road to CHRIST SCHOOL, **1.5 m.**, an Episcopal school for boys, whose 20 granite buildings occupy a terraced, landscaped campus. Founded in 1910 by Thomas C. Wetmore, it has an enrollment of about 150 with courses from the sixth grade through high school.

STRUAN (*private*), **3.5 m.**, a white-columned mansion, is the oldest in the neighborhood. Built in 1847 by Alexander Robertson of Charleston, S. C., and named for the Robertson estate in Scotland, the house was raided by Union soldiers. The marks of their hobnailed boots are visible on the old floors, and a small sideboard door that they kicked in, looking for brandy, has never been replaced. The stairway is of graceful design. The roof of the southern veranda is made of boards curved to resemble a ship's timbers.

US 25 passes (L) CALVARY EPISCOPAL CHURCH, **11.4 m.**, consecrated in 1859, destroyed by fire in 1935, and rebuilt in 1937. During the Civil War, Federal troops were garrisoned in the church. The brick building with pointed-arch openings and a buttressed tower follows the Gothic style. In the churchyard the GRAVE OF BILL NYE is marked by a rough granite boulder.

South of FLETCHER, **12.3 m.** (2,112 alt., 800 pop.), are the rich fields of the Cane and Mud Creek Valleys. Named for the pioneer family of Fletchers, it was visited in 1800 by the Rt. Rev. Francis Asbury, first bishop of the Methodist Church in America.

HENDERSONVILLE, **21 m.** (*see* TOUR *13, sec. c*).

South of Hendersonville on US 25 is FLAT ROCK, **23.9 m.** (2,207 alt., 900 pop.), one of the oldest summer resorts in western North Carolina, "discovered" by fashionable residents of Charleston seeking a moderate summer climate. It began with the coming of Charles Baring and Judge Mitchell King, about 1828; another leader, Christopher Gustavus Memminger, joined them in 1836.

The beautiful estates developed by these three men, THE LODGE, ARGYLE, and ROCK HILL (all preserved in original condition) were the first in a little colony which, until after 1840, numbered but 20 families.

Judge King and C. G. Memminger were active leaders in the first move for building a railroad from Charleston across the Blue Ridge, by a route closely followed by the present line from Charleston, via French Broad Valley to Tennessee, and thence to Cincinnati.

When the road was eventually completed across the Blue Ridge to Hendersonville in 1879, C. G. Memminger was president of the company. In 1820 North and South Carolina, cooperating to provide for the increasing stream of traffic through Saluda Gap, issued State bonds to build its part of the Buncombe Turnpike.

St. John-in-the-Wilderness (*Episcopal*), 24.6 m. (R), was built in 1834-36 by summer residents from Charleston and Savannah under the leadership of Charles S. Baring. Rev. T. W. S. Mott, a member of Mrs. Baring's household, was appointed first rector and was for 6 years the only Episcopal clergyman in what is now the Diocese of Western North Carolina. The general plan and tower buttresses of this building of handmade yellow bricks characterize it as an odd combination of Gothic Revival reminiscent of the Early Renaissance in Italy, with round-arched windows and a square bell tower. The front gable bargeboards are decorated with a saw-tooth motif and the rear façade has a tall triple-arched window. This church replaced the small chapel of ease of the Baring family built in 1832.

In the churchyard are the Graves of the Family of Count de Choiseul, French consul at Savannah; his son Charles fought for the Confederacy and was killed in Virginia in 1862. The Grave of Christopher G. Memminger, Secretary of the Treasury of the Confederate States, is also here.

The Flat Rock is a great expanse of granite used as a landmark and old ceremonial ground of the Cherokee Indians before white men came here. It lies on both sides of US 25. Depressions, 11 in number, which were well defined until the ridge was destroyed by blasting, have been called "fire pits," said to have been used for smoke signals, to call the Red Men back to this central gathering place for ceremonials, feasts, and threats of danger.

On this outcrop of rock, lying R. of US 25, is located the Flat Rock Playhouse whose Vagabond Players conduct a year-around school of the drama, as well as a series of plays in the summer.

Among the beautiful estates in and around Flat Rock is Connemara Farm of Rock Hill (*private*) built by C. G. Memminger as his summer home in 1835-36. His family were in residence there during the Civil War, when he was the first Secretary of the Treasury of the Confederacy. After the war and the confiscation of his property in Charleston, Rock Hill provided him a retreat. The place, during war years, was often attacked by bands of renegades, and its well re-enforced basement, with thick walls of granite, provided safe shelter for women and children of the community.

The estate, restored to its original condition, is now the home of the nationally known historian, poet, and novelist, Carl Sandburg, and his family.

BONCLARKEN, 24.9 m., on HIGHLAND LAKE (*boating, fishing, swimming*), is the assembly grounds for the Associate Reformed Presbyterian Church. At varying seasons of the year other denominations hold conferences here.

At 25.7 m. the highway passes the entrance (R) to Woodfields, a building with wide, shaded piazzas, once known as Farmers Hotel, little altered since it was built in 1850.

South of Flat Rock the route crosses the Blue Ridge or Appalachian Divide and descends the Atlantic slope past Lake Summit at Tuxedo. The wooded shores of LAKE SUMMIT (*fishing, swimming, boating*) are (L) at 29.5 m.

At **33.5 m.** US 25 crosses the South Carolina Line, 30 miles north of Greenville, S. C.

US 25 follows the old Greenville Road, which, at the North Carolina-South Carolina Line, was the scene of a number of duels fought prior to the Civil War. In an encounter between Dr. Robert Brank Vance and Samuel P. Carson, 1827, the former was mortally wounded (*see* TOUR *21, sec. a*). About the year 1855 Maj. Marcus Erwin of Asheville and Judge John Baxter of Hendersonville met in a duel, the culmination of a number of newspaper articles Maj. Erwin had written on states' rights. Judge Baxter, who fired his pistol into the ground, was wounded in the hand by Maj. Erwin's bullet.

TOUR 24A *(NC 208, 212)*

Junction with US 70-25—Devils Fork Gap—Junction with US 23-19W; NC 208, 212. **35 m.**

This short route gives access to a once very remote mountain region in a country formerly characterized by moonshine and feuds.

NC 208 branches north from its junction with US 70-25, **0 m.**, 7 miles east of Hot Springs (*see* TOUR 24).

At **4 m.** is the junction with improved NC 212.

Right on NC 212 is a region known as the LAUREL SECTION OF MADISON COUNTY—sometimes called "the Land of Do Without"—whose remoteness and inaccessibility long kept the people in a primitive state. The area is divided into Shelton, Little Laurel, Big Laurel, the Spillcorn, and Foster Creek sections. The streams that give the country its distinctive character cut through wooded mountainsides where poplar, oak, gum, and haw trees tower above tangles of rhododendron, laurel, and dogwood.

The upper part is sometimes known as the "English Settlement," not because its Scotch-Irish inhabitants came from England but because many families are descended from a man named English. Many of these folk walked across the mountains through Cumberland Gap into Kentucky to join the Union Army during the Civil War.

In the mountains, 40 years ago, the making of illicit liquor, locally called "blockading," contributed to the feuds that have given this region its old name of "Bloody Madison." Men known to have given information to revenue officers were shot from ambush, and sometimes relatives of the slain would retaliate in kind. Family enmity incurred over a fist fight, rivalry in love, or even the whipping of a neighbor's dog might start a feud of long standing. While most of the families are honest, hard-working, law-abiding citizens, some in the Laurel country, as elsewhere, are inclined to terrorize the neighborhood. However, the description of primitive conditions in which most novelists delight was more appropriate to life in the mountains a half-century ago.

On NC 208 at **9 m.** is ALLANSTAND (2,000 alt.), near the Tennessee Line and close under wild Bald Mountain. Here early in the 19th century a man named Allan kept a "stand," where drovers could spend the night while driving cattle, sheep, horses, and swine from Tennessee to the South Carolina and Georgia markets.

In 1895 Frances L. Goodrich started the Allanstand Cottage Industries, since absorbed by the Southern Highland Handicraft Guild. The gift of a 40-year-old coverlet suggested to her the revival of the almost forgotten mountain arts as a means of broadening the outlook of the isolated mountain women and of bringing them an income. Older women were able to recall and teach others the secrets of the blue pot, into which go indigo, bran, madder, and lye, as well as a large amount of patience. The dyeing takes place before the wool is spun, hence the expression, "dyed in the wool." Using bark and leaves, these weavers are able to develop green, brown, yellow, orange, and black dyes. Hickory bark, with the addition of an alkali to "set the dye," gives a rich olive green.

NC 208 crosses the State Line at **10 m.**, 20 miles south of Greeneville, Tenn.

TOUR 24B *(US 176)*

Hendersonville—Saluda—Tryon—South Carolina Line; US 176. **22 m.**

The highway traverses the mountainous southwestern part of the State where the mild dry climate has made resorts popular.

US 176 branches southeast from its junction with US 25, **0 m.**, in HENDERSONVILLE (*see* TOUR *13*) and passes through farming country. EAST FLAT ROCK, **3 m.**, is the railroad station for Flat Rock (*see* TOUR *22*). At **4 m.** the route crosses the low Blue Ridge and spans Green River Gorge. A wooden aqueduct from Lake Summit to a power house runs beneath the high bridge. At **7.4 m.** is the GREEN RIVER BRIDGE, the stream almost obscured by the trees and flowers of the deep canyon.

SALUDA, **10.4 m.** (2,097 alt., 547 pop.) is built on Saluda Mountain, crossed by the steepest grade of the Southern Ry. Here is a branch of the SPARTANBURG (S. C.) BABY HOSPITAL (*open May 15-Aug. 31*), occupying a two-story frame house with accommodations for 35 infants and 18 mothers. The hospital was established in 1914 with Dr. D. Lesesne Smith as superintendent. Here are held the annual summer sessions of the Southern Pediatric Seminar, organized in 1921 by Dr. Smith to benefit the general practitioner and to provide a post-graduate course in methods of diagnosis, prevention, and treatment of children's diseases.

The MOUNTAIN HOME (*open*), **11.5 m.** (R), is a two-story frame building with large porches overlooking the Pacolet Valley. It is maintained by the Brotherhood of Railway Clerks as a summer resort for members and their families.

At **14 m.** MELROSE FALLS can be seen across the valley.

Right from Melrose on the graveled and marked old Saluda-Tryon Rd. to PEARSON'S FALLS (*adm. 25¢; shelter, ovens, tables*), **1 m.** In this 400-acre preserve are all types of flora common to the deciduous forests of eastern America. The falls, tumbling over rugged rocks, present a scene of unusual beauty. Here a wild flower sanctuary and herbarium are maintained by the Tryon Garden Club.

Southeast of Melrose US 176 crosses and recrosses the Pacolet River (*trout and bass*).

At **18.6 m.** is the junction with a side road.

Left on this road to HARMON FIELD, **0.1 m.**, Tryon's recreation center in the Pacolet Valley. The lighted field comprises a permanent horse show ring, steeplechase course, polo field, baseball and football grounds, and a well-equipped playground. The annual Horse and Hound Show and Gymkhana (*Apr.*) are sponsored by the Tryon Riding and Hunt Club. The club maintains some 500 miles of bridle paths and in season organizes "drag" and live-fox hunts.

TRYON, **21 m.** (1,085 alt., 1,985 pop.).

Transportation: Southern Ry.
Accommodations: 5 hotels, lodges, and inns.
Golf: Tryon Country Club, **1.5 m.** N. on US 176 and the Country Club Rd., 9 holes.
Annual Events: Gymkhana and Horse and Hound Show, Harmon Field (*Apr.*).

The largest town in Polk County, Tryon lies on the southern slope of the Blue Ridge close to Tryon Peak, for which the town is named. The peak retained the name of North Carolina's royal Governor, William Tryon, though the county which bore it was abolished in 1779. Tryon has an unusually mild winter climate, as it lies within the Thermal Belt, ordinarily free from frost and dew. Many fine fruits, including Tryon grapes, grow here.

The LANIER LIBRARY, 10,000 volumes in a brown-shingled building, is maintained by the Lanier Club, a women's organization founded in 1890 and named for the poet, Sidney Lanier, whose last home was near Tryon. The Little Theater Group presents plays during the winter.

GILLETTE ESTATES, once the home of William Gillette, actor and playwright, has been converted into a residential suburb. FRIENDLY HILLS (*private*), Country Club Rd., is the winter home of the writer, Margaret Culkin Banning. Other writers associated with Tryon include Anne Bosworth Greene, also an artist, and Thomas Dixon (*see* TOUR *19*).

The TOY HOUSE (*open daily, except Sun.*), on a wooded hillside on Howard St., was once the home of the Tryon Toymakers and Woodcarvers, a craft school run under the direction of the Misses Eleanor Vance and Charlotte Yale, founders of the Biltmore Industries (*see* ASHEVILLE). Today a combined workshop and salesroom makes unusual wooden toys.

The BLUE RIDGE WEAVERS, Trade St., are the Pioneer Exchange for Mountain Handicrafts, and the VALHALLA HANDWEAVERS, on US 176, display a large variety of mountain crafts, some woven on an old-fashioned loom on the place.

Left from Tryon on NC 108 in the village of LYNN, **2 m.** (500 pop.), is a frame cottage in which Sidney Lanier (1842-81), the poet, spent his last days. A MONUMENT TO LANIER was erected in the garden of the premises in 1930. Across the highway is the HOME OF DR. COLUMBUS MILLS, 18th-century county leader. It has been enlarged and operates as Mimosa Inn.

At **2.2 m.** on NC 108 is the junction with the graveled Howard Gap Rd., L. **4 m.** on this road to ROUND MOUNTAIN where in 1906 a granite shaft was erected to mark the SITE OF THE BATTLE OF ROUND MOUNTAIN (1776). Skyuka, a young Indian whom Capt. Thomas Howard befriended, warned the settlers gathered at the Old Blockhouse of an impending Indian attack. Guiding them behind Round Mountain he enabled Capt. Howard to defeat the Indians and end hostilities for the time.

At **5 m.** on NC 108 is COLUMBUS (1,145 alt., 486 pop.), seat of Polk County, a village without railway facilities, named for Dr. Columbus Mills who was a member of the general assembly that created Polk County in 1855. The handmade brick POLK COUNTY COURTHOUSE with classic portico, built in the same year, is still in use. A modern woolen mill and garment label plant are in the village.

At **21.8 m.** are the entrance gates to LAKE RANIER (*tea house; fishing, boating, swimming*), a 175-acre artificial lake bordered by 7 miles of driveway.

Right on the entrance drive to the Junction with West Shore Dr., **0.2 m.**; R. **2 m.** on West Shore Dr. to the PIEDMONT BOY SCOUTS CAMP, established in 1925.

OLD BLOCKHOUSE, **21.9 m.**, just within the North Carolina boundary, is a pre-Revolutionary structure built as an Indian trading post and later used for protection against hostile Cherokee. It is a low, one-story building with end chimneys and a long veranda.

US 176 crosses the South Carolina Line at **22 m.**, 25 miles northwest of Spartanburg, S. C.

At **12 m.** on NC 108 is the junction with the Pea Ridge Rd.; R. on this road a short distance to GREEN RIVER PLANTATION (*private*), also known as the Coxe Plantation. Built early in the 19th century for Joseph McDowell Carson from the proceeds of a private gold mine, this mansion was owned by the Carson family until it was bought in Reconstruction days by Col. Frank Coxe, pioneer builder of Asheville, for his wife, the granddaughter of the original owner. The handsome woodwork was done by Philadelphia craftsmen, the brick was brought from Charleston, and the heart of pine paneling was hewn from trees on the plantation. Union horses were stabled in the gracious drawing room during the Civil War.

Part IV

NATIONAL PARK AND FORESTS

Great Smoky Mountains National Park

Location: Western North Carolina and eastern Tennessee.

Season: Open all year; sightseeing buses operate Apr. 1-Nov. 15.

Administrative Offices: Park Superintendent, Gatlinburg, Tenn.

Admission: Free. No registration or fees for automobiles. Photographing permitted but commercial motion-picture operators requiring special settings must secure permits from Secretary of Interior.

Highway Mileage: **82 m.** of high standard roads in the park; **200 m.** of secondary roads.

Trail Mileage: **550 m.** suitable for hiking and horseback riding. Appalachian Trail traverses park. Guidebooks available from Appalachian Trail Conference, Inc., Washington, D. C.

Guide Service: Interpretive field trips and talks available.

Accommodations:
Free modern campgrounds are provided on the Tennessee side of the park at the Chimney Tops, 6 miles south of Gatlinburg, and Cades Cove, 7 miles from the Townsend entrance to the park; on the North Carolina side at Smokemont, on the transmountain highway, Balsam Mountain, 10 miles from Soco Gap on US 19 (Blue Ridge Parkway spur), and Deep Creek, 2 miles from Bryson City. Aside from these campgrounds, the only accommodations in the park are at Le Conte Lodge on the top of Mount Le Conte, accessible only by foot or horseback.

A number of hotel and tourist camp facilities are available in cities and towns near the parks, and at Knoxville, Waynesville, Bryson City, and Asheville. Inquiries regarding these accommodations should be addressed to Knoxville Tourist Bureau, Henley Street, Knoxville, Tenn.; East Tennessee Automobile Club, Knoxville, Tenn.; Chambers of Commerce of Gatlinburg, Knoxville, and Maryville, Tenn., Asheville, Waynesville, Bryson City, and Sylva, N. C.; Cherokee Association, Cherokee N. C.; and Government Services, Inc., Fontana Village, Fontana Dam, N. C.

Climate, Clothing, Equipment: Dependent on altitude; above 4,000 ft. blankets may be necessary the year around. Rainfall abundant but not excessive. April may be rainy. May bracing and pleasant. Oct. most spectacular month; rhododendron and laurel bloom in June. July and Aug. are normally the wettest months; Sept. through Nov., the driest. Horseback riders and hikers need serviceable clothing, preferably wool, to absorb perspiration and protect against chill on breezy mountaintops or after a rain. Shorts should not be used on trails. Light poncho and sweater are useful. Shoes or boots should be stout and well broken; wool socks should be worn.

Fishing: (*see* GENERAL INFORMATION).

Great Smoky Mountains National Park encloses the best surviving remnant of the forest that once extended from the Atlantic coast to the prairies of the Middle West. Its virgin tracts of hardwood and red spruce total 202,000 acres, the largest in the United States. The variety of plant life is said to be greater within the park than in any other equal area in the temperate zone. It is estimated that nearly 4,000 plant species are represented in the flora of the park, of which 1,300 different kinds of flowering plants have been identified.

Establishment of the park was authorized by an act of Congress approved May 22, 1926, after citizens of North Carolina and Tennessee had worked for many years to have the area preserved for the people. Of $11,800,878.76 spent to buy land for the park, $2,162,283.29 was raised by the State of North Carolina and $2,345,330.18 by the State of Tennessee; $5,000,000 was given by the Laura Spelman Rockefeller Memorial and $2,293,265.29 by the government.

The park area—almost 800 square miles of the wildest highlands in eastern America—lies almost equally in Tennessee and North Carolina. The axis of the reservation runs nearly east and west; its greatest length is 54 miles and greatest breadth 19 miles.

The Great Smoky Mountains, mostly included in the park, have lofty peaks, deep valleys, sharp ridges, dashing streams, and dense forests.

Fifty-three peaks in the park are more than a mile high. Clingmans Dome, the highest, has an elevation of 6,642 feet. Mount Le Conte High Top in Tennessee appears to be the highest, for its summit, 6,593 feet above sea level, rises 5,301 feet above its base. Other uplifts in the park having an altitude of more than 6,000 feet include Balsam Corner, Big Butt, Big Cataloochee, Mount Buckley, Mount Collins, Mount Guyot, Mount Hardison, Jumpoff, Mount Kephart, Mount Le Conte Cliff Top, Mount Le Conte Myrtle Point, Mount Love, Luftee Knob, Old Black, Mount Sequoyah, Thermo Knob, Tricorner Knob, and Mount Yonaguska.

From the base to the summit of the higher peaks are three life zones: the Carolinian or Upper Astral, the Alleghenian Transition, and the Canadian. Because the seasons vary with the altitude, it is possible in a short climb or ride to observe plants in different stages of growth.

There are 131 species of native trees in the park (in all of Europe the number of native tree species is 150). The highest mountains are clothed with dense forests of spruce and fir. Mountains of intermediate height are covered with hardwood, beech predominating. The open beech forests with their clean forest floors somewhat resemble the grounds of well-kept country estates. Hardwood forests at lower altitudes are in many cases almost impenetrable because of the dense undergrowth. Some mountains, covered only with a grass or heath and called "balds," offer unobstructed views in all directions. Yellow poplars attain a diameter of 9 feet.

Springs within the park feed 600 miles of cold, crystal-clear, and trout-filled streams that tumble over rocky beds and roar over falls. These branches drain into the Cataloochee, Forney, Hazel, Eagle, Panther, Abrams, and Deep creeks, and the Little Pigeon, Oconaluftee, Tuckasegee, and Little rivers, whose waters eventually find their way into the Tennessee River.

The great white rhododendron (*Rhododendron maximum*) is abundant in the area, making its best growth along streams and in the shade of the forest. This shrub occurs from the lowest elevations up to approximately 5,000 feet; its time of bloom is the latter half of June through July. On exposed ridges, at altitudes above 3,500 feet, the mountain rosebay (*Rhododendron catawbiense*) with its rose-purple flowers comes into its height of bloom during the second and third weeks of June; this is one of the most spectacular flowers in the area. A third species, *Rhododendron carolinianum*, with pink-colored blooms, has its best display on exposed cliffs at high altitudes in middle and late June. Flame azalea, a favorite with discriminating flower lovers, begins to bloom in April and may be in good bloom at higher altitudes in early July; its peak of flowering, in those places where most of these plants are concentrated, comes during the latter half of June. On Gregory Bald, on the main divide of the Smokies, and along the Heintooga Ridge road from Soco Gap are outstanding places for viewing flame azalea. Mountain laurel, called ivy by the mountaineer, reaches its maximum development in the Smokies. Arborescent laurel a foot or more in diameter and 30 feet high is not unusual. On the cool floor of the fir and spruce groves at the highest altitudes grows flora characteristic of the northern woods.

Wildlife on the slopes and peaks of the park is less abundant than in some other mountainous regions of North Carolina and Tennessee. Most of the larger animals, such as deer and black bear, once almost exterminated by hunters, are now increasing under park protection. The 54 kinds of mammals found in the park include red and gray fox, opossum, mink, spotted and striped skunk, muskrat, and raccoon.

Large birds of prey are rare. In the higher ranges are such northern species as the junco or snowbird, mountain vireo, several warblers, winter wren, raven, and certain hawks and owls. Ruffed grouse and quail or "partridge" are common and wild turkeys are seen occasionally.

The Cherokee Indians have many legends about this area, which was part of their former home. Origin of the name Great Smoky is buried in obscurity, but it was probably suggested to Indians or early settlers by "the tenuous mist, a dreamy blue haze like that of Indian summer, or deeper" that hovers almost always over the high peaks. Earliest official government use of the term is in the 1789 act of cession delimiting the boundaries of North Carolina and what is now the State of Tennessee: "... thence along the highest ridge of said mountains to the place where it is called Great Iron or Smoky Mountain." Tradition is that Hernando De Soto and his Spanish soldiers were the first white men to see the southern highlands, which they named for the Apalachee Indian tribe they had known in northwest Florida.

The Great Smoky region was the scene of early struggles between England and France for colonial dominance. However, a large part of the area has never been inhabited and very few white people lived there until about the time of the Civil War. During that conflict the ranges were an effective barrier to invasion.

Some roads within the park are part of the interstate highway system; others are being improved and will eventually be connected with these and with other attractive routes in North Carolina and Tennessee and with the Blue Ridge Parkway. Among the park roads is the Skyway, which follows the crest of the Smokies for 7 miles from Newfound Gap to Clingmans Dome. Many trails parallel or radiate from the roadways.

The Appalachian Trail, extending from Mount Katahdin, Maine, to Mount Oglethorpe, Ga., traverses the entire length of the park along its highest ridges, following in general the North Carolina-Tennessee boundary for a total distance of 70 miles. The trail gives access to numerous mountain peaks, gaps, and balds.

The park area has been largely deserted by its inhabitants, who were chiefly descendants of Scot, Irish, and English pre-Revolutionary immigrants.

The Park presents an opportunity to preserve frontier conditions of a century ago. The cultural and human interest aspects of this park are exceeded only by its scenery and natural history.

In places where the forest has not yet encroached upon them there are clearings which were the sloping little farms of the mountain pioneers. Sturdy log structures in varying stages of disintegration remain here as evidence of a way of life which has practically disappeared in eastern United States. Some of these log cabins, barns, and other buildings have been rehabilitated in their true setting. Most of them are in Cades Cove, where the park's only grist mill powered by an overshot wheel is located. Cades Cove, an isolated, oval-shaped valley surrounded by mountains, is a region of outstanding pastoral charm.

Some of the finest of various types of authentic pioneer structures can be viewed in the immediate vicinity of the Oconaluftee Ranger Station and Pioneer Museum (*open, 9* A.M.-5 P.M. *April through Oct.*) located on the cross-mountain highway about two miles north of Cherokee, N. C. On display in this museum are tools, household objects, and a variety of other hand-made items which were used by the pioneers who made their homes on lands which now comprise Great Smoky Mountains National Park.

National Forests

Season: Open all year.

Administrative Offices: Regional Forester, Southern (Eighth) Region of the Forest Service of the U. S. Dept. of Agriculture, Atlanta, Ga.

Admission: Free.

Climate, Clothing, Equipment: Climate varies with altitude (*see* GREAT SMOKY MOUNTAINS NATIONAL PARK). Antivenom kits, mosquito lotion, typhoid inoculation recommended for coastal campers.

Special Regulations: Camping: Permitted anywhere except during fire season (Apr. and May, Oct. and Nov.), when restricted to designated Forest Service campgrounds. These are improved areas set aside in the various divisions and provided with pure water, fireplaces, fuel, tables, and sanitary facilities. Campers may use own tents or trailers. Sanitary and fire regulations posted. Fire Building: Necessary fire building outside of campgrounds permitted to campers under special rules for forest fire prevention. Any dead or down timber may be used. Fishing: Permitted, unless otherwise posted, under special permit obtainable at Forest Service administrative offices, State or county license a prerequisite (*see* GENERAL INFORMATION; *see district ranger for current regulations*). Hunting: Federal and State game refuges closed; hunting permitted occasionally during open season when necessary to reduce game population of forest preserves. Hunters chosen by lot from applicants who must have State or county licenses and pay a fee for the hunt. Firearms and unleashed dogs not permitted in game refuge areas. Residence sites available in specified areas for annual rental fee, house to meet Forest Service requirements, lease renewable annually as long as regulations not violated.

Summary of Attractions: Scenery; primitive areas; nature trails; geologic, historic, and archaeologic interest; mountain climbing; hiking; picnicking; bathing; boating; fishing; hunting; camping.

The United States Forest Service has under its administration in North Carolina three National Forests and two purchase units which were established under the provisions of the Act of March 1, 1911, known as the Weeks Law, as amended by subsequent acts. The forests and purchase units, with their respective acreages are as follows (June 30, 1938):

The Nantahala National Forest was established in 1911. The present gross area within the exterior boundaries of the forest is 1,366,027 acres of which the Forest Service proposes to purchase approximately 917,861 acres; 447,150 acres are now under Government ownership or in the process of acquisition.

The Pisgah National Forest was established in 1911 and the present gross area is 1,177,303 acres of which the Forest Service expects to buy approximately 827,473 acres. A total of 475,242 acres is vested in Federal ownership or in the process of acquisition. The forest is divided into 4 ranger districts: Pisgah, Mount Mitchell, Grandfather, and French Broad, all lying in western North Carolina.

The Croatan National Forest was established in 1934 and the present gross area is 294,610 acres, 216,114 of which have been listed for possible purchase. The total acreage now in government ownership or in the process of acquisition is 152,388 acres.

The Uharie purchase unit was established in 1934 and has a present gross acreage of 560,000 acres, of which 426,900 acres have been designated for possible purchase. The total area now in Federal ownership is 43,282 acres.

The Yadkin purchase unit was established in 1911. The gross area is 194,496 acres of which 140,000 acres have been listed for possible purchase. No purchases have been made in this unit to date.

The forests were first created to protect the watersheds of navigable streams and to provide merchantable timber in perpetuity, but they have been subsequently developed also for their wildlife and forage resources and as public recreational areas. Co-ordinated plans provide for a full policy of multiple land use, with each particular area devoted to the purpose it can best serve. Every legitimate form of public use consistent with the protection and perpetuation of the timbered watersheds, streams, wildlife, and other forest resources is encouraged and promoted under Forest Service policies.

Forest resources yield financial returns through timber sales, grazing privileges, water-power licenses, the renting of land for summer home sites, and mining permits. Several CCC camps stationed within and near the forests aided materially in the development program (1932-39).

When these lands were first acquired by the Forest Service they were generally in a low state of productivity as a result of destructive methods of lumbering and devastating fires. However, improved logging methods, road and trail building, and the practice of scientific forestry in cutting and developing timber have brought about great changes. The forested areas are noticeably improved, particularly the vigorous young growth; the streams carry less mud and silt after rains, and the public has derived financial as well as recreational benefits.

Tree growth and plant vegetation in the forests range from the subtropical on the coast to the extreme northern types. The flowering season reveals a difference in development and bloom varying with altitude as well as a difference in forest or plant type. In some areas timber stands are preserved in their natural state, to retain the aspect of the original North American forests. Other areas possessing high recreational value also are left uncut.

The recreational facilities of the mountain forests have been more fully developed, while piedmont and coastal forests provide experimental grounds for the application of scientific methods in restoring denuded or burnt-over areas to timber productivity and serve as examples for private landowners in those regions.

INDEX

(Illustrations are found between page numbers in bold face type.)

611

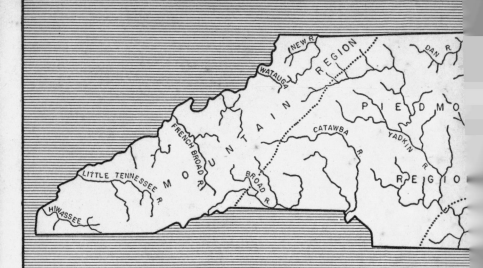